MĪMĀṀSĀ SŪTRA OF JAIMINI

MĪMĀṀSĀ SŪTRA
OF
JAIMINI

(Text with Translation in English and Notes)

By

N.V. THADANI

BHARATIYA KALA PRAKASHAN
Delhi : : (India)

Revised Edition : **2024**

Published by
BHARATIYA KALA PRAKASHAN
3421-A, IInd Floor, Narang Colony,
Tri Nagar, Delhi-110035
Ph. : 27393083
Web : www.bkpbooks.com
E-mail : sales.bkpbooks@gmail.com

MĪMĀṂSĀ SŪTRA OF JAIMINI

ISBN : 978-81-8090-171-3

Printed by :
G.S. Offset, Delhi

EDITOR'S NOTE

Mīmāṁsā means a reverent study leading to a scientific quest of Truth; and it was this search after Truth, leading to the solution of the great problem of life, that engaged the attention of the ancients in the past. The real problem of life is the attainment of happiness, and the avoidance of its opposite—misery and pain; and the ancients tried to examine it at all levels and from all points of view. They reflected for long, and realised that pleasure is but a passing episode in an endless course of pain, and permanent happiness can be attained only when there is a total extinction of pain. The author of the *Sāṅkhya*—so called because it signifies reflection— accordingly declared that the chief aim of a man's life is to secure freedom from sorrow and pain. But the great question was how to bring it about; and this meant a knowledge of the cause of pain and the means of attaining to happiness; and an inquiry into this problem gave rise to a harvest of speculations which are stored up in the different systems of Hindu Philosophy. They have their different points of view; but they are all agreed that Good is the source of happiness, and Evil of pain; and the one is called Dharma, and the other Adharma. Dharma is the law of life, and its breach is Adharma. But if this law (Dharma), the observance of which makes for a never-failing and perennial source of happiness, be really true and unerring, it cannot be laid down by mortal man, subject to all the infirmities of flesh and blood; and so it is said to emanate from an impersonal source, the Holy Vedas—the *apauruṣeya* (impersonal) revelation in the verbal form of *Brahman*.

The Veda is accordingly said to be the transcendent

authority, the sovereign voice *(nirapekṣa rava)* of the Primeval Being; and what it enjoins is Dharma, and what it prohibits is Adharma. It is believed to contain the ancient traditional knowledge of the Hindus, handed down to us from the immemorial past; but the contents and language of this mine of thought are difficult to understand. At places it is unintelligible, at others it is incongruous, and at others again it is self-contradictory and appears to be meaningless. This problem had faced a number of thinkers even in the past, and they tried to study the text carefully and to interpret it correctly. This was done in the best and most perfect manner in the *Mīmāṁsā,* which, because it formulated the principles of interpretation of the Veda, came to be regarded as the philosophy and art of interpretation. It is for this reason that it occupies, according to tradition, not only a pre-eminent place among the systems of Hindu Philosophy, but is believed to govern them all. Indeed, it is a common saying of the classical Paṇḍits that "Logic, Grammar and the like only grind the mill, but it is the *Mīmāṁsaka* (knower of *Mīmāṁsā)* alone who ordains the *Śāstras.*"[1]

Tradition tells us that there are three avenues of scholarship, —study of words *(pada),* of sentences *(vākya),* and authority in regard to interpretation *(pramāṇa),* —and they relate to Grammar, Logic and *Mīmāṁsā* respectively—the last being the most important of all. The *Mīmāṁsaka* was accordingly given the pride of place in the assemblies of great thinkers in the past, and a number of panegyrics[2] have been composed in his honour by those who knew the importance of this system.

The reason why the *Mīmāṁsā* occupies such a pre-eminent position is not far to seek. It defines Dharma or the law of life; it lays down the correct method of interpretation of the Vedas

1. Anye ghārattikās sarve, nūnam śāstra-kṛto vayam.
2. There are well-known panegyrics like *Mīmāṁsā-śāstra-yugma-śrama-vimala-manā mārgyatām mādṛśo' nyāḥ*—
   " Let one other like me be found whose mind is crystallised by his labours in the study of both parts of the *Mīmāṁsā.* "

and removes the conflict of authorities; and it gives a verdict on contentious issues and supplies maxims of universal application. This immense store of knowledge is contained in the *Sūtras* of *Jaimini,* popularly called the *Mīmāṁsā* (or *Pūrva-Mīmāṁsā) Sūtras*. Their language is simple and straightforward, though it differs a great deal from later classical *Sanskṛt,* which has undergone a number of changes with the lapse of time.

These *Sūtras* have been explained by *Sabara-svāmin,* who has been followed by a number of scholars. But, as they have all been led to believe that they refer to Vedic ceremonies and a system of ritualistic practices, they have tried to interpret the *Sūtras* in their light, with the result that the whole system has come to be regarded as dealing with ritual and the laws and practices of various sacrifices, while its more truly philosophic spirit and idea has been forgotten and lost. Indeed, what was meant to illustrate the method of interpretation of the Vedas, has been taken to be the subject-matter of the system itself; and so we have been carried very far away from the original idea of its author. Thus, when in more recent years it has come to be studied again as a part of the principal systems of Hindu Philosophy, a great Indian thinker seriously maintains that "it is unnecessary to say much about the unsatisfactory character of the *Pūrva-Mīmāṁsā* as a system of Philosophy"[1]

All the six systems of Philosophy, of which the *Mīmāṁsā* is one, are closely connected together, and present an integrated development of thought: they are consistent in themselves and with one another, so that, when all their speculations are put together, they constitute a complete whole. But this becomes clear only when the *Sūtras* are interpreted in their proper perspective, and not with a particular bias or pre-possession. Indeed, it is this predilection of critics and commentators during several centuries in the past that has led the reader astray from the simple and direct treatment of their subject-matter, and caused so much confusion about their character.

---

1. *Indian Philosophy* by Dr. S. Radhakrishnan, Vol. II, p. 428.

It is possible to interpret the text of the Sacred Books in many ways; but there are three principal methods of interpretation—the grammatical method, the logical method, and a symbolic method. Every text should be approached by means of the first method, and the sense yielded by it should be put together in a logical manner. But if that does not yield a rational or consistent meaning, a resort may be had to the third method. Indeed, it has been observed that "the names occurring in them (the Vedas) are of universal applicability, and do not have any historical reference. *Viśvāmitra* means 'the all-friendly' and not any historical character[1];" and in view of the abstract character of the Sacred Books of the Hindus, it is essential that the different systems of Philosophy and other basic texts should be properly interpreted and made available to the reader.

The Bharati Research Institute, Delhi, has been started to fulfil this long-felt need, and to help in the advancement of a proper knowledge of the Sacred Books of the Hindus. It is proposed to bring out two series at present—entitled a Library of Hindu Philosophy and Religion, and a Library of Sanskṛt Classics. The first series opens with the present volume,—a rendering of the *Mīmāṁsā*—one of the six great systems of Hindu Philosophy, the importance of which need not be re-emphasised. It is a free, but an accurate, translation of *Jaimini's Mīmāṁsā Sūtras,* made without reliance on any *Bhāṣya, Vṛtti,* or school of thought of this system. The *Sanskṛt* text has also been appended for ready reference.

The whole work is purely original, and the author of this volume, Dr. N.V. Thadani, has devoted thirty years of life to a study of the Sacred Books. His earlier work in this field—*The Mystery of the Mahābhārata*— was published in five volumes about eighteen years ago; but it met with scant recognition on account of the novelty of its approach to the Epic, which it regarded as an account of the different systems of Hindu Philosophy and Religion in story-form, and tried to explain it as such in accordance with the method of interpretation now

1. *Indian Philosophy* by Dr. S. Radhakrishnan, Vol. II, p. 392.

discovered in the *Mīmāṁsā*. Dr. Thadani has since widened his field of inquiry, and translated the *Sūtras* of all the six systems of Hindu Philosophy, and the present volume is the first to be published in this series.

The present writer must admit that, as he had been initiated into *Śāstric* studies from the orthodox point of view, when he saw Dr. Thadani's rendering of the *Sūtras* for the first time, he was filled with no small misgiving about the possibility of its yielding any satisfactory results. But when he examined the entire method of rendering them more carefully, and found how close was its fidelity to grammatical rules, he felt that it could not be rejected out of hand; and before long he saw that the whole idea was consistent throughout, and maintained a uniform level of thought. He then remembered that there were suggestions of this line of thought even among ancient scholiasts, and felt that Dr. Thadani's translation could not in reason be set aside.

Indeed, the one thing that would be patent to even the most casual reader of this work is that it contains a complete unity of thought and expression throughout. According to the *Sāstras*[1] there is a fourfold consistency of interpretation: consistency as regards inter-related systems of thought *(Śāstra-saṅgatiḥ);* consistency within the system itself *(Adhyāya saṅgatiḥ);* consistency of each topic with the rest *(pāda saṅgatiḥ);* and consistency between all sections *(Adhikaraṇa saṅgatiḥ).* The learned author has been chiefly concerned with consistency in all its aspects; and though he differs widely from the available interpretations of the various systems of thought recognised by the orthodox scholars, his work cannot fail to strike not only as grammatically correct, but also as wholly consistent in its own way.

Dr. Thadani has further amplified and illustrated his scheme of thought in an exhaustive Introduction, which too will be found to be equally consistent.

We believe that the work will bear fruit, and the devoted labours of many years will open a new vista for inquiry and

1. Introduction to Bhāṭṭa-dīpikā (N.S. Edition), p. 4.

research along new lines, and lead scholars to a fresh study of our Sacred Books, and to re-interpret them according to the method of interpretation explained by *Jaimini* in the *Mīmāṁsā*. The present volume will be followed by a rendering of the five remaining systems of Hindu Philosophy at an early date.

—S. N. Shastri

PREFACE

It is not without some hesitation that I am releasing the present work—a translation of the *Mīmāṁsā Sūtras* of *Jaimini*—the longest and, perhaps, the least understood of all the six principal systems of Hindu Philosophy, for a more regular course would have been to begin with the *Sāṅkhya,* and then go on to the other systems. But, for reasons explained in the Introduction, it has been necessary to do so, in order that the reader may be able to form an idea of the real character of the Sacred Books of the Hindus.

The present work is an attempt at a simple, but a reasonably accurate, translation of the original text. A purely literal rendering of a work, even in a modern language, would make difficult reading; and an English version of so simple a book as the *Bhagavad Gītā* has often to deviate from the original idiom to be understood. This difficulty is greatly increased in the case of the *Sūtras* of Hindu Philosophy; for they are not short, pithy, and independent utterances of great truths, as is commonly believed—but brief, exact, and clearly defined statements of great ideas, which are closely knit together and need to be properly understood. It would have been possible to translate each *Sūtra* literally and separately; but, while that may have been more exact and accurate, it would have broken up the unity of thought and continuity of expression of the work as a whole, and that was perhaps even more important. It was accordingly necessary to steer a middle course, and that has been attempted in the present work.

A correct translation of the text depends on three main factors: appropriate meanings of words used in the *Sūtras,* a just connection between the parts of a *Sūtra,* and a proper correlation between one *Sūtra* and another. But it is not always easy to satisfy these conditions, simple as they appear to be; for words in *Sanskṛt* have often a large number of meanings, out of which a proper selection has to be made; and a wrong choice can heap error on error without end. Indeed, the chief difficulty in getting at a properly connected meaning of the text would be due to this; and it is complicated by the idea, commonly held by scholars, that each *Sūtra* is complete or almost complete in itself. Nor is the language of the text always free from ambiguity, and extreme conciseness has often been gained at the expense of clarity of expression; while a total absence of punctuation within a *Sūtra* makes it difficult to disentangle its parts. But, even as the author of the *Vedānta Sūtras* tells us, it requires calmness, patience, and devotion to the task to be able to enter into the spirit of the text; and once we succeed in grasping its form and mode of expression, it is not difficult to get at the correct meaning; and the whole idea is then found to be consistent and continuous from end to end. This applies not only to the *Mīmāṁsā,* but to all systems of Philosophy composed in this form.

I should like to take this opportunity of thanking all those who have assisted me or lightened my task. I am very grateful to Dr. S. N. Shastri of Hindu College, who, at great cost of time and trouble, has gone through the entire rendering, *Sūtra* by *Sūtra,* and made some very valuable suggestions. He has also read some of the proofs and interested himself in the publication of the work. I am also very thankful to the authorities of the Sri Aurobindo Ashram at Pondicherry, for the assistance they have rendered in printing the book,— more specially the Mother, Dr. Indra Sen, and Mr. N. D. Gupta, Manager of the Press. But my deepest debt of gratitude is due to my wife who, with rare self-denial, has lightened my task, and enabled me to do my work. It was she who started me on the study of the *Mahābhārata* thirty years ago, and has throughout been a source of great comfort to me.

—N. V. Thadani

CONTENTS

ABBREVIATIONS

Adi P.	*Ādi Parva* of the *Māhābhārata*
Ait. Ar. Up.	*Aitareya Araṇyaka Upaniṣad*
AV.	*Atharva Veda*
BhG.	*Bhagavad Gītā*
Ch. Up.	*Chāndogya Upaniṣad*
Kauṣ. Up.	*Kauṣītakī Upaniṣad*
MBh.	*Mahābhārata*
MM.	*The Mystery of the Mahābhārata*
MS.	*Mimāṁsā Sūtras*
MWD.	Monier William's Sanskṛt English Dictionary
NS.	*Nyāya Sūtras*
RV.	*Ṛg Veda*
SBE.	The Sacred Books of the East
SK.	*Sānkhya Kārikā*
SS.	*Sānkhya Sūtras*
ŚBr.	*Śatapatha Brāhmaṇa*
Śānti P.	*Śānti Parva* of the *Mahābhārata*
Tait. Up.	*Taittīyak Upaniṣad*
Up.	*Upaniṣad*
VS.	*Vaiśeṣika Sūtras*
Ved. S.	*Vedānta Sūtras*
YS.	*Yoga Sūtras*

TRANSLITERATION CHART

The letters of the *Sanskṛt* alphabet are usually arranged as follows:—

Vowels a. ā; i, ī; u, ū; ṛ, ṛī;lṛ, lṛī; e, ai; o, au, Anusvāra (.); Visarga (:).

Consonants

Gutturals	*k*	kh	g	gh	ṅ
Palatals	*c*	ch	j	jh	ñ
Linguals	*ṭ*	ṭh	ḍ	ḍh	ṇ
Dentals	*t*	th	d	dh	n
Labials	*p*	ph	b	bh	m

Semi-vowels

Palatal y Lingual *r* Dental *l* Labial *v*

Sibilants

Palatal ś Lingual *ṣ* Dental *s* Aspirate *ḥ*

CHAPTER - I

THE LAW OF DHARMA

PART I

THE SUBJECT-MATTER OF THE VEDAS

Introduction

Dharma may be defined as the highest good. Its idea is not limited to sense-perception, and requires a proper teacher to explain it. It arises from action, which is the law of life. Success arises from action; and action cannot be renounced. There is action even when we do not see it; and action is eternal and universal. There is a difference between natural and deliberate action. The subject-matter of the Vedas is action.

Dharma

ॐ अथातो धर्मजिज्ञासा॥१॥

चोदनालक्षणोऽर्थो धर्मः॥२॥

तस्य निमित्तपरीष्टिः॥३॥

Let us now understand what is Dharma. It may be defined as the highest good; and so let us inquire into its cause.

How to Understand Dharma

सत्संप्रयोगे पुरुषस्येन्द्रियाणां बुद्धिजन्म तत्प्रत्यक्षमनिमित्तं विद्यमानोपलम्भनत्वात्॥४॥

औत्पत्तिकस्तु शब्दस्यार्थेन सम्बन्धस्तस्य ज्ञानमुपदेशाऽव्यतिरेकश्चार्थेऽनुपलब्धे तत्प्रमाणं, बादरायणस्यानपेक्षत्वात्॥५॥

The idea of Dharma does not arise from sense-perception,

because the latter is limited to what is present, while the idea of Dharma goes beyond the present. As it is conceived to be the highest good, its idea can best be imparted by a competent teacher, which is a valid means of acquiring knowledge, and does not require the authority of a *Bādarāyaṇa* to prove it[1].

DHARMA AND ACTION

Some people say that Dharma arises from action, and prove their point by referring to the actual facts of life; and so they believe that the idea of Dharma is not permanent.

कर्मैके तत्र दर्शनात्॥६॥

अस्थानात्॥७॥

Dharma and the Law of Life

करोतिशब्दात्॥८॥

सत्त्वान्तरे च यौगपद्यात्॥९॥

प्रकृतिविकृत्योश्च॥१०॥

वृद्धिश्च कर्तृभूम्नाऽस्य॥११॥

समं तु तत्र दर्शनम्॥१२॥

सतः परमदर्शनं विषयानागमात्॥१३॥

प्रयोगस्य परम्॥१४॥

आदित्यवद्यौगपद्यम्॥१५॥

Dharma is indeed linked up with action, for we often say that a person does his Dharma, and that implies action. Action is part of our nature, for we see that all of us are engaged in some kind of action at the same time; and we see it in *Prakṛti* or Nature in all its modifications. We also see that success in action is often the result of a number of persons acting together. At the same time we find that there are some who believe that we should be indifferent to all that is in the world. But even he who is said to be indifferent, acts. He might appear to be inactive, but is not really so; and we believe that he has not acted, because he has not succeeded in achieving his object. Indeed, we have to go beyond the commencement of an action to understand all this; for the sun may appear to be inactive, but it is acting all the time; and so are all creatures too.

Law of Action

वर्णान्तरमविकारः॥१६॥

नादवृद्धिपरा॥१७॥

There is an immutable law of action at work within all forms of life, according to which all must act. For instance, we see things growing in size, but without apparent action; yet there is sound, motion, or vibration within them unperceived.

Action is Eternal and Universal

नित्यस्तु स्याद्दर्शनस्य परार्थत्वात्॥१८॥

सर्वत्र यौगपद्यात्॥१९॥

संख्याभावात्॥२०॥

अनपेक्षत्वात्॥२१॥

प्रख्याभावाच्च योगस्य॥२२॥

लिङ्गदर्शनाच्च॥२३॥

Action is eternal, because it is meant to be performed for the sake of something else; and also because we see it all the time everywhere. The number of creatures engaged in action is so large, that it cannot be counted; and it is not necessary to refer to the same creature again, because all are acting at the same time. We say so because we know the manner in which action takes place; and if we take necessary evidence or observe the working of *Prakṛti* or Nature,[2] we shall find that it is so.

Natural and Deliberate Action

उत्पत्तौ वाऽवचनास्स्युरर्थस्यातन्निमित्तत्वात्॥२४॥

तद्भूतानां क्रियार्थेन, समाम्नायोऽर्थस्य तन्निमित्तत्वात्॥२५

लोके सन्नियमात्प्रयोगसन्निकर्षः स्यात्॥२६॥

But it may be argued that action, performed in the ordinary course of nature, is of little importance, because it does not serve any special purpose; and those who believe that all action should be of this kind, naturally argue in this way. But we see that when people have a purpose or aim in action, it is the result of deliberate intention or precise thinking.

Vedas and Action

वेदांश्चैके सन्निकर्षं पुरुषाख्याः॥२७॥

अनित्यदर्शनाच्च॥२८॥

उक्तं तु शब्दपूर्वत्वम्॥२९॥

आख्याः प्रवचनात्॥३०॥

परन्तु श्रुतिसामान्यमात्रम्॥३१॥

कृते वा विनियोगस्स्यात्कर्मणस्सम्बन्धत्॥॥३२॥

According to some, the Vedas deal with the problem of the soul as their principal subject-matter; but this is not correct, because we find that they deal with the world of Nature, which is not permanent. This has been stated to be their subject-matter; and that is how they are taught and explained; and all Vedic literature is of the same kind. As they deal with the problem of action, they tell us what actions to perform and how to perform them[3].

PART II

THE VEDAS AND THE METHOD OF THEIR INTERPRETATION

Introduction

The subject-matter of the Vedas is action. They are an exposition of Guṇas or the attributes of Nature; and refer to the laws of knowledge as well as action, which it is necessary to discover; and we can do so if we interpret the text correctly by means of the application of the rules of grammar. There is authority for this method of interpretation; but it has not been followed because of ignorance and want of application. The Vedas refer really to the laws of Nature.

Subject-matter of the Vedas

आम्नायस्य क्रियार्थत्वादानर्थक्यमतदर्थानां; तस्मादनित्यमुच्यते॥१॥

शास्त्रदृष्टविरोधच्च॥२॥

तथा फलाभावात्॥३॥

अन्यानर्थक्यात्॥४॥

अभागिप्रतिषेधच्च॥५॥

अनित्यसंयोगात्॥६॥

विधीनां त्वेकवाक्यत्वात् स्तुत्यर्थेन विधीनां स्युः॥७॥

तुल्यं च साम्प्रदायिकम्॥८॥

अप्राप्ता चानुपपत्तिः; प्रयोगे हि विरोधस्स्याच्छब्दार्थस्त्व-
प्रयोगभूतस्तस्मादुपद्येत॥९॥

The subject-matter of the Vedas is action; and they would be meaningless if we interpret them in any other light: hence they are said to be non-eternal. They are not eternal also because they give expression to conflicting opinions; because they do not yield the desired results; because no other meaning is possible; because they are the joint composition of a number of authors; and deal with things that are not eternal. Indeed, we find that they have the meaning of laws of Nature, and are meant to be a praise of these laws. This is also the traditional view; and there is no contradiction in it; and if a person is unable to understand them in this light, he should seek the assistance of a competent teacher.

An Exposition of the Guṇas

गुणवादस्तु॥१०॥

रूपात्प्रायात्॥११॥

दूरभूयस्त्वात्॥१२॥

The Vedas are really an exposition of the Guṇas or the attributes of Nature;[4] and that is so because the *Guṇas* are the most important part of Nature,—for it is chiefly in this form that Nature appears to us, when we look at it from a distance (or in a broad perspective).

Guṇas and Nature

अपराधत्कर्त्तुश्च पुत्रदर्शनम्॥१३॥

आकालिकेप्सा॥१४॥

The *Guṇas* are said to be born of Nature or *Prakṛti* in the same sense in which a child is born; for there is a natural desire to have something that will last for some time[5] (and that is why *Prakṛti* creates Guṇas and lives through them).

Knowledge

विद्याप्रशंसा॥१५॥

सर्वत्वमाधिकारिकम्॥१६॥

It is for the same reason that we praise knowledge (for it lasts); and the more complete the knowledge, the longer it lasts; and so the most perfect knowledge belongs to the Supreme.

And Action

फलस्य कर्मनिष्पत्तेस्तेषां लोकवत् परिमाणतः फलविशेषस्स्यात्॥१७॥

अन्त्ययोर्यथोक्तम्॥१८॥

विधिर्वा स्यादपूर्वत्वाद्वादमात्रं ह्यनर्थकम्॥१९॥

(We find, however, that knowledge is connected with action, for) we see that certain results follow from certain causes; and so we might say, broadly speaking, that certain special results will follow from certain special causes. But the idea of knowledge and action is the same as has been explained in the previous systems.[6] Nevertheless, there must be a law governing the two; but such a law has not yet been discovered, and a mere statement of their relation would be useless[7].

An objection

लोकवदिति चेत्॥२०॥

न पूर्वत्वात्॥२१॥

उक्तं तु वाक्यशेषत्वम्॥२२॥

विधिश्चानर्थकः क्वचित्तस्मात् स्तुतिः प्रतीयेत; तत्सामान्यादितरेषु तथात्वम्॥२३॥

प्रकरणे सम्भवन्नपकर्षो न कल्प्येत; विध्यानर्थक्यं हि तं प्रति॥२४॥
विधै च वाक्यभेदः स्यात्॥२५॥

We cannot deal with the question in a popular way, because that is already known (and it has no bearing on the idea of a law). It may, however, be argued that all that can be said in the matter has already been said, and nothing more is possible now. Further, it may be contended that it is impossible, in a number of places, to construe the text of the Vedas in the light of action; and so it is best to regard these books as consisting of hymns of praise addressed to the gods. Moreover, if there is consistency of this kind of meaning throughout, we must not drag in some other meaning; specially, as against it, a reference to a law would be inappropriate. Again, if it had been the intention of the authors of the Vedas to expound a law, the language of the text should have been different.

An Answer

हेतुर्वा स्यादर्थवत्त्वोपपत्तिभ्याम्॥२६॥
स्तुतिस्तु शब्दपूर्वत्वादचोदना च तस्य॥२७॥
अर्थे स्तुतिरन्याय्येति चेत्॥२८॥
अर्थस्तु विधिशेषत्वाद्यथा लोके॥२९॥
यदि च हेतुरवतिष्ठेत; निर्देशात्सामान्यादिति चेदव्यवस्था विधीनां स्यात्॥३०॥
तदर्थशास्त्रात्॥३१॥
वाक्यनियमात्॥३२॥
बुद्धिशास्त्रात्॥३३॥

But there is good reason for coming to conclusion that the Vedas deal with the laws of Nature, because the same can be proved, and we can get it from the text itself. The text of the Vedas does indeed support the view that it refers to the praise of the gods; but that is its first or direct meaning, without being pressed into some other sense. But even as praise it appears to be meaningless; and we might ask if it is not improper to have praise that is meaningless. While we cannot deny that the text does refer to the praise of the gods, we hold that, in the way it is commonly understood, it is so only in a secondary sense,— the primary idea being that of a law. We are, however, prepared to agree that, if the text does really refer to the laws of Nature, this conclusion should be based on well-established facts, and not on some special statements or analogies,— for that would nullify the very idea of a law. But, as a matter of fact, we get the idea of law from the text of the sacred books themselves; for we get this meaning from the very language of the text, when we apply correct grammatical rules. But he alone will understand who is learned or wise, for the language needs to be properly understood.

How to understand the Text

अविद्यमानवचनात्॥३४॥
अचेतनेऽर्थबन्धनात्॥३५॥
अर्थविप्रतिषेधत्॥३६॥
स्वाध्यायवद्वचनात्॥३७॥
अविज्ञेयात्॥३८॥
अनित्यसंयोगान्मन्त्रानर्थक्यम्॥३९॥

We cannot get the correct meaning of words from their common form; but we can do so by referring them to Nature, which is described as "a-*cetana*" or inanimate. That, however, should be done when the common meaning is contradictory; and a student of the Vedas can easily find out the real meaning of the text in this way. The reference to the laws of Nature should be made when we are unable to understand the correct meaning of the text and are confused; and (we should understand that) it would be meaningless for the Vedas to refer to something that is ephemeral.

अविशिष्टस्तु वाक्यार्थः॥४०॥
गुणार्थेन पुनः श्रुतिः॥४१॥

It may, however, be argued that the meaning of words cannot be a special one; but in this connection we might repeat that the text has a secondary meaning (which refers to the praise of the gods).

Special Mention of this Method

परिसंख्या॥४२॥

अर्थवादो वा॥४३॥

अविरुद्धं परम्॥४४॥

संप्रैषे कर्मगहनुिपलम्भः संस्कारत्वात्॥४५॥

अभिधनेऽर्थवादः॥४६॥

गुणादप्रतिषेधः स्यात्॥४७।

Indeed, there is a special mention of this method of interpreting the text; and there is an explanation of its idea too; and the principal subject-matter of the Vedas is found to be consistent when interpreted in this light. Further, if we make use of this method and understand words in their correct formation, we find that the text does not contain any censure of the actions of any one;[8] and the explanation of the meaning of words is in accordance with what is found in a dictionary. At the same time, a single thread of thought runs throughout the text, and there is no contradiction in it anywhere.

Cause of Failure to Understand

विद्यावचनमसंयोगात्॥४८॥

सतः परमविज्ञानम्॥४९॥

उक्तश्चाऽनित्यसंयोगः॥५०॥

लिङ्गोपदेशश्च तदर्थत्वात्॥५१॥

ऊहः॥५२॥

विधिशब्दाश्च॥५३॥

We do not know this explanation of the Vedas because of want of application and ignorance on the part of those who read them. But we find that they do refer to Nature, which is said to be non-eternal; and we get this meaning from the text itself; and so our conclusion is that the language of the Vedas refers to the laws of life.

PART III

THE LAW OF DHARMA AND THE VEDAS

Introduction

Dharma is founded on the word of the Vedas. It is linked up with action; but every action is not Dharma For instance, action arising from impulse is not Dharma.

Action is universal. It may be definned as a case of material contact between an object and a place; but it is universal and not local, and is without end.

All this is described in the Vedas; and we can understand it if we change the form of words used in the text.

Dharma and the Vedas

धर्मस्य शब्दमूलत्वादशब्दमनपेक्ष्यं स्यात्॥१॥

Dharma is founded on the word of the Vedas, which is the highest word.

Dharma and Action

अपि वा कर्तृसामान्यात्प्रमाणमनुमानं स्यात्॥२॥
विरोधे त्वनपेक्ष्यं स्यादसति ह्यनुमानम्॥३॥
हेतुदर्शनाच्च॥४॥

(Dharma is linked up with action, and) we find that a man is always engaged in action; and this should enable us to acquire definite knowledge in regard to the law of action. Any contradiction of the fact that there is action everywhere should be disregarded; for we know that it is impossible.

Every Action is not Dharma

शिष्टाकोपेऽविरुद्धमिति चेत्॥५॥
न शास्त्रपरिमाणत्वात्॥६॥

अपि वा कारणाग्रहणे प्रयुक्तानि प्रतीयेरन्॥७॥
तेष्वदर्शनाद्विरोधस्य समा विप्रतिपत्तिः स्यात्॥८॥
शास्त्रस्था वा तन्निमित्तत्वात्॥९॥

(But every action is not Dharma; for instance,) we cannot say that an action of the body, performed by a healthy man in the ordinary course of Nature, is Dharma; for the sacred books have their own idea of Dharma, and it is based on certain principles admitted by all to be true. There is no inconsistency or contradiction in the sacred books; and if there is any inconsistency anywhere, we should take it to be in our own ideas rather than in them. We should, therefore, accept what is contained in these books.

Action due to Impulse is not Dharma

चोदितं तु प्रतीयेताऽविरोधत्, प्रमाणेन॥१०॥
प्रयोगशास्त्रमिति चेत्॥११॥
नाऽसन्नियमात्॥१२॥
अवाक्यशेषाच्च॥१३॥
सर्वत्र च प्रयोगात्सन्निधनशास्त्राच्च॥१४॥
अनुमानव्यवस्थानात् तत्संयुक्तं प्रमाणं स्यात्॥१५॥
अपि वा सर्वधर्मः स्यात्तन्न्यायत्वाद्विधनस्य॥१६॥
दर्शनाद्विनियोगः स्यात्॥१७॥
लिङ्गाभावाच्च नित्यस्य॥१८॥

The action of a healthy body, performed spontaneously or in the ordinary course of nature, is obviously the result of impulse; and that is not the idea of Dharma as given in the sacred books; and it would be an incorrect application of the rules laid down by them to think that it is so. Their statement regarding Dharma is definite and complete, and leaves no gaps to be filled; and we can verify this for ourselves by making an experiment and a careful study of the sacred books.

If we do so, we shall find that there is only one inescapable conclusion,— that there is action everywhere, and all things are subject to it. It should, therefore, be deemed to have been proved, and regarded as a universal law of life,—for such is the nature of things, as we can see for ourselves. This is proved by the fact that we can find nothing in the world that is eternal.

Definition of Action

आख्या हि देशसंयोगात्॥१९॥
न स्याद्देशान्तरेष्विति चेत्॥२०॥
स्याद्योगाख्या हि माथुरवत्॥२१॥
कर्मधर्मो वा प्रवणवत्॥२२॥
तुल्यं तु कर्तृधर्मेण॥२३॥
प्रयोगोत्पत्त्यशास्त्रत्वाच्छब्देषु न व्यवस्था स्यात्॥२४॥
शब्दे प्रयत्ननिष्पत्तेरपराधस्य भागित्वम्॥२५॥

Action means that there is a material contact of an object with a place. This, however, does not limit the idea of action and make it local, for the same object can be in different places at different times,— just as when we say that a person belongs to *Mathurā*, we do not confine him to that place. The law of action or of the doer of the deed,—for both are the same may be illustrated by the action of a person who is devoted to something for a while; and this is not inconsistent with the law of universal action described in the sacred books. Since, however, they speak of continuous action, we have to understand the sense in which the term is used, for otherwise we might commit a mistake.

How Described in the Vedas

अन्यायश्चानेकशब्दत्वम्॥२६॥
तत्र तत्त्वमभियोगविशेषात्स्यात्॥२७॥
तदशक्तिश्चानुरूपत्वात्॥२८॥

(All this has been briefly expressed, and) it would be improper to demand that it should have been described in many words. We can, however, understand the real meaning if we make a special effort; and our inability to do so arises from the fact that we take only the form of words, and neglect their real meaning.

How to Understand the Text

एकदेशत्वाच्च विभक्तिव्यत्यये स्यात्॥२९॥
प्रयोगचोदनाभावादर्थैकत्वमविभागात्॥३०॥
अद्रव्यशब्दत्वात्॥३१॥
अन्यदर्शनाच्च॥३२॥
आकृतिस्तु क्रियार्थत्वात्॥३३॥
न क्रिया स्यादिति चेदर्थान्तरे विधनं न; द्रव्यमिति चेत्॥३४॥
तदर्थत्वात्प्रयोगस्याविभागः॥३५॥

The entire meaning of the text would be changed by changing the form of a word in a particular place; and this can be done because there are no fixed rules regarding the combination of words or their parts. But if we adopt but a single meaning, we cannot distinguish between things; and that will render the whole idea worthless. It is possible to look at the text in different ways; but the best meaning is that which refers to action. There are some, however, who believe that there is no reference to action; that there is no possibility of any other meaning than the common one; and that the words refer to one particular object only. All that we can say is that the meaning does refer to action, and there is no break in the continuity of its idea.

PART IV

THE VEDAS AND THE METHOD OF THEIR INTERPRETATION

Introduction

The sacred books, when properly interpreted, refer to action of all kinds; but more specially in connection with the *Guṇas*, which are associated with *Prakṛti*. But a name may not always express the idea of *Guṇas*.

It is not difficult to give a rational explanation of why a word should be divided into parts to give its correct meaning; but there are cases where words do not need to be altered in this way, and their common meaning remains.

We cannot lay down any hard and fast rules to get the real meaning of words; and the only test is that it should fit into the context. That is the proof of its correctness, and of the glory and greatness of the Vedas. But it must fill all gaps and be taken as a whole.

Action in the Vedas

उक्तं समाम्नायैदमर्थ्यं; तस्मात्सर्वं तदर्थं स्यात्॥१॥
अपि वा नामधेयं स्याद्यदुत्पत्तावपूर्वमविधयकत्वात्॥२॥
यस्मिन् गुणोपदेशः प्रधानतोऽभिसम्बन्धः॥३॥
तत्प्रख्यञ्चान्यशास्त्रम्॥४॥
तद्व्यपदेशं च॥५॥

It has been explained that the text of the sacred books, when properly interpreted, refers to action; and it follows from this that everything should have a bearing on that meaning. It may be that this action consists in giving a new name to an object,—something that has not been done before; but so far as the main idea of action is concerned, it should refer to the *Guṇas*, which are closely connected with *Prakṛti* or *Pradhāna*.[9] This is contained in a number of sacred books; and there is a definite statement to this effect too.

Character of a Name

नामधेये गुणश्रुतेः स्याद्विधनमिति चेत्॥६॥
तुल्यत्वात् क्रिययोर्न॥७॥
ऐकशब्द्ये परार्थवत्॥८॥
तद्गुणास्तु विधीयेरन्नविभागाद्विधनार्थे; न चेदन्येन शिष्टाः॥९॥
बर्हिराज्ययोरसंस्कारे शब्दलाभादतच्छब्दः॥१०॥
प्रोक्षणीष्वर्थसंयोगात्॥११॥
तथानिर्मन्थ्ये॥१२॥
वैश्वदेवे विकल्प इति चेत्॥१३॥
न वा प्रकरणात्प्रत्यक्षविधनाच्च; नहि प्रकरणं द्रव्यस्य॥१४॥
मिथश्चानर्थसम्बन्धः॥१५॥
परार्थत्वाद् गुणानाम्॥१६

There are some who believe that, in such a case, when a name is given to an object, the rule should be that there should be a clear mention of the *Guṇas*. But this is not possible, for a name may refer to two equal actions; and in such a case a single word would need to have another meaning too.

There are others who maintain that a word and its attributes should go together; that we should not divide it into parts to get the idea of action; and that there should not be different rules in connection with different words. But this is not always possible; for if a word and its attributes should always go together, so should a word and the object to which it refers. Again, suppose there is mention of the word *Barhis* (meaning sacrificial grass) and *ājya* (meaning clarified butter poured over the sacrificial fire) in the text, but no consecrating ceremony,—should we say that these words have no meaning? We should, of course, agree that they have their ordinary meanings if they were used in connection with vessels of holy water required for a sacrifice. The same would be true in connection with another word,—*Nirmanthya* (meaning, being stirred or churned).[10] It is true that there is no variation in the meaning of the word *Vaiśva-deva* (meaning, relating to all-gods); and that is so because of the nature of what it signifies,—something that is perceptible to the senses, and requires no discussion of the thing itself;[11] and if we were to give a different meaning to the word, it would make no sense at all. The idea of the *Guṇas*, however, is different[12].

No fixed Rules

पूर्ववन्तोऽविधनार्थास्तत्सामर्थ्यं समाम्नाये॥१७॥
गुणस्य तु विधनार्थे; तद्‌गुणाः प्रयोगे स्युरनर्थका न हि; तं प्रत्यर्थवत्ताऽस्ति॥१८॥
तच्छेषो नोपद्यते॥१९॥

As has already been observed, we cannot lay down any hard and fast rules to get the correct meaning of words; and their only test is their suitability in connection with the context. We must, however, remember that an attribute is meant to describe the characteristics of an object; and this requires that the attributes should be in their proper place, and that nothing should be meaningless; for the whole significance of the text depends on their use. This means that nothing should be left out.

Requirements of Interpretation

Now, in order to interpret a Vedic text in the light of action or the law of creation, we have to show that the whole of it,—with all its names—remains unbroken when understood in this manner; whereas it makes little sense when understood in terms of the praise of gods. It is not necessary that there should be any authority in support of this; for the authority is the manner in which we have to fix a meaning, when we are unable to find a cause, and the text makes little sense. For instance, when there is a reference to an actor, there may be a number of causes for his action, and we have to find them out; and we fix the meaning of a word in the same manner. That is the proof of the correctness of our meaning,—namely, that it fits into the text; and testifies to the glory of the Vedas, and their wealth, and shows that the matters of which they speak are eternal.

अविभागाद्विधनार्थे स्तुत्यर्थेनोपपद्येरन्॥२०॥

कारणं स्यादिति चेत्॥२१॥

आनर्थक्यादकारणं; कर्तुर्हि कारणानि; गुणार्थो हि विधीयते॥२२॥

तत्सिद्धिः॥२३॥

जातिः॥२४॥

सारूप्यात्॥२५॥

प्रशंसा॥२६॥

भूमा॥२७॥

लिङ्गसमवायात्॥२८॥

Value of this Interpretation

The value of this interpretation lies in its ability to fill all gaps of thought in case of confused, doubtful, or ambiguous expressions; but we have to understand it in the light of the meaning it yields, and conceive of it as part of a great whole

29. सन्दिग्धेषु वाक्यशेषात्।

30. अर्थाद्वा कल्पनैकदेशत्वात्।

NOTES

The figures against punctuation marks refer to the serial numbers of Sūtras in the text.

1. *Bādarāyaṇa* is the name of the celebrated author of the *Vedānta Sūtras*. The authority of a competent teacher is described as *śabda*, which means oral testimony, and is admitted to be a valid means of acquiring knowledge by all systems of philosophy.
2. The word in the text is *Liṅga*, which has a number of meanings, one of which is *Prakṛti* or Nature.
3. The *Bhāgāvad* Gītā tells us that the subject-matter of the Vedas is the three *Guṇas* or the attributes of Nature,—*Sattva*, *Rajas*, and *Tamas*,—which are said to be the cause of all action in the world. We are accordingly advised to go beyond all this, and to be "full of the soul" (BhG. II, 45; III, 5, 27-29).
   It may be of interest to point out that, while the principal subject-matter of the Vedas is Nature and its laws, that of the Epics and the *Purāṇas* is the soul or its highest expression,—God; and that is the principal difference between the *śruti* (Vedas and Vedic literature) and smṛti (post-Vedic literature, including the Epics and the *Purāṇas*).
4. *Cf*. BhG. II, 45.
5. The *Bhāgāvad Gītā* also tells us that the *Guṇas* are born of Nature or *Prakṛti*, and are the cause of all action. Indeed, all Nature appears to us in the form of these *Guṇas*, for there is nothing in the world (except, of course, the soul) that is without them (BhG. III, 5, 27-29; IV, 13; XIV, 5-20; XVII, 1-22; XVIII, 7-10, 19-44).
6. The previous systems are *Sāṅkhyas Nyāya* and *Vaiśeṣika*; and they all deal with the problem of knowledge and action. But, according to the *Mīmāṁsā*, they have not succeeded in discovering the law connecting them together.
7. The *Mīmāṁsā* sets out to discover this law, and to prove it too; and so it says that it would be useless merely to state it. It holds that we can find this law in the Vedas themselves, if we understand them aright.

As we shall see, the connecting link between knowledge and action is desire.

8. The *Mīmāṁsā* later on tells us again that one of the reasons why it is necessary to change the form of words, by dividing them into parts is that the common meaning involves a censure on the actions of gods who are otherwise esteemed and regarded as good; and it mentions *Indra* specially in this connection. As it is impossible to conceive that they could be guilty of misconduct, it is necessary, so the *Mīmāṁsā* tells us—to see if it is possible to get a different and a more suitable meaning out of the same words. And so we hit upon this method of interpretation, by means of which we divide words into the parts which compose them, and find that they bear a very different meaning, which involves no censure on any one, which has a reference to the laws of Nature, and is consistent in this sense throughout. The *Mīmāṁsā* tells us that this method applies to the text of the *smṛtis* too; and so if we apply it, we shall find that the real meaning of the great Epics and *Puāṇas* is very different from what it is commonly believed to be. For instance, we find that if we accept the common meaning of the text, a number of actions of the gods and heroes who figure in these works—*Kṛṣṇa* in particular, and even *Rāma*—are not free from censure. But if we adopt this method of interpretation, we find that the whole idea is very different; and the entire "story" is transformed into a narrative of different systems of philosophy and religion. This has been explained in the case of the *Mahābhārata* (M M. III-V), and a similar explanation of the *Rāmāyaṇa* and the *Bhāgavat* Purāṇa, which includes an account of all the principal incarnations of *Viṣṇu*, will follow in due course. As these constitute the subject-matter of a large number of *Purāṇas*, it would be found that this method of interpretation applies to the entire range of the sacred books of the Hindus; and this is what the *Mīmāṁsā* tells us.

9. *Pradhāna* refers to *Prakṛti* or Nature.

10. As these words,—*Barhis*, *ājya*, and *Nirmanthya*—appear to make little sense in their existing form and with their ordinary meanings, it is necessary to see if they can admit of some other more satisfactory meaning in some other way; and the *Mīmāṁsā* implies that we can get this by dividing them into parts or in some other manner. As we shall see later on, grass or the vegetable kingdom refers to Nature or *Prakṛti; ājya* signifies goodness; and *Nirmanthya* refers to the function of the mind.

11. *Vaiśva-deva* means "relating to all-gods"; and a god, as we shall see, refers to the great forces of Nature. Thus, all-gods would refer to the entire world of Nature, the idea of which is clear and constant. Hence, the word *Vaiśva-deva* retains its ordinary meaning throughout, and it is not necessary to change its form by dividing it into parts, to get its meaning, as we must do in the case of other words.

12. *Guṇas* are the attributes of Nature; and so they do not refer to Nature in its

entirety, but to its different forms, possessing different attributes. Although there is nothing in Nature that is free from *Guṇas*, the entire world of Nature must be regarded as different from them, for they are said to be born out of it. Hence the *Mīmāṁsā* tells us that the idea of *Guṇas* is not identical with that of Nature conceived in its entirety.

CHAPTER II

THE LAW OF ACTION

PART I

THE VEDAS AND THEIR FORM

Introduction

The idea of an action is described by means of verbs, and of an actor by means of nouns. Verbs are associated with nouns; and there are two kinds of verbs, transitive and intransitive.

Dharma requires the function of the intellect; and it is described in the Vedas in various ways.

The text of the Vedas does not consist of hymns of praise addressed to the gods, but is an examination of the laws of Dharma.

Brāhmaṇas,—hymns of praise, and laws of life and their explanation; but the essential idea of both is the same.

The Vedas are three in number,—*Rik*, *Sāma*, and *Yajus*. A fourth, *Nigada*, is sometimes added; but it should be included in the *Yajus*.

The text of the Vedas is composed in the most perfect form of language.

Verbs and Nouns

भावार्थाः कर्मशब्दास्तेभ्यः क्रिया प्रतीयेतैष ह्यर्थो विधीयते॥१॥

सर्वेषां भावोऽर्थ इति चेत्॥२॥

येषामुत्पत्तौ स्वे प्रयोगे रूपोपलब्धिस्तानि नामानि; तस्मात्तेभ्यः पराकांक्षाभूतत्वात्स्वे प्रयोगे॥३॥

येषां तूत्पत्तावर्थे स्वे प्रयोगो न विद्यते, तान्याख्यातानि; तस्मात्तेभ्यः प्रतीयेताऽऽश्रितत्वात् प्रयोगस्य॥४॥
चोदना, पुनरारम्भः॥५॥
तानि द्वैधं गुणप्रधनभूतानि॥६॥
यैर्द्रव्यं न चिकीर्ष्यते तानि प्रधनभूतानि, द्रव्यस्य गुणभूतत्वात्॥७॥
यैस्तु द्रव्यं चिकीर्ष्यते, गुणस्तत्र प्रतीयेत, तस्य द्रव्यप्रधानत्वात्॥८॥

Verbs are words which refer to action; and they have a meaning which relates to a way of thinking, feeling or conduct, all of which are associated with action. All words are not of this kind: for instance, there are nouns, which describe the form of an object; and other words depend on them, because, as soon as we use them, they give us the idea of something that is real. Verbs do not express any plan or purpose in themselves, if we utter them without reference to something else; and they can be properly understood only in association with nouns, because they depend on them. When we utter a verb, it conveys no meaning in itself; for we are compelled to direct our attention to something else, and inquire about it.

Verbs are of two kinds,—primary and secondary (or intransitive and transitive). Primary verbs are those which do not require an object for their action, because the object is unessential; while secondary verbs are those which require an object for their action, because an object is essential in their case.

Idea of Dharma

धर्ममात्रे तु कर्म स्यादनिर्वृत्तेः प्रयाजवत्॥९॥
तुल्यश्रुतित्वाद्वेतरैः सधर्मः स्यात्॥१०॥
द्रव्योपदेश इति चेत्॥११॥
न तदर्थत्वाल्लोकवत्तस्य च शेषभूतत्वात्॥१२॥

So far as Dharma is concerned, it is associated with action,—action without end, like a great sacrifice. There should be general agreement about the idea of Dharma; and the idea of the

Vedas and other works should be the same. But it is not easy to define it, because there are no fixed rules to lay down what constitutes a fit and proper object. But the difficulty itself serves a useful purpose of its own, for it calls upon us to decide what is so[1].

Text of the Vedas

स्तुतशस्त्रयोस्तु संस्कारो, याज्यावद्देवताभिधनत्वात्॥१३॥
अर्थेन त्वपकृष्येत, देवतानामचोदनार्थस्य गुणभूतत्वात्॥१४॥
वशावद्वाऽगुणार्थं स्यात्॥१५॥
न, श्रुतिसमवायित्वात्॥१६॥
व्यपदेशभेदाच्च॥१७॥
गुणश्चानर्थकः स्यात्॥१८॥
तथा याज्यापुरोरुचोः॥१९॥
वशायामर्थसमवायात्॥२०॥
यत्रेति वाऽर्थतत्त्वात् स्यात्॥२१॥

There are some who believe that there are certain texts, like *Stotra* and *śāstra* hymns,[2] which have been properly composed and about which there can be no difference of opinion,—for they are part of sacrificial texts and closely connected with the gods. But were it so, those texts which do not refer to the gods, would be deemed to be of a secondary importance; and their meaning, which is not secondary, would be rendered secondary. But this cannot be, because these texts too are an integral part of the Vedas. The difference between the two kinds of texts is due to the difference of manner in which their ideas are expressed; and there can be no question of the subsidiary character of any. It is in this light that we should understand the idea of the sacrificial texts and other formula: recited at sacrifices; and we shall find that they make a consistent whole throughout, and yield good sense in that way.

An Objection

न त्वाम्नातेषु॥२२॥

दृश्यते॥२३॥
अपि वा श्रुतिसंयोगात्प्रकरणे स्तौतिशंसती क्रियोत्पत्तिं विदध्याताम्॥२४॥
शब्दपृथक्त्वाच्च॥२५॥

But there are some who believe that this is not true of all that is taught in the sacred books, and maintain that we can see for ourselves that it is so. They also contend that there is general agreement regarding the *śruti*,[3]—namely, that it contains hymns of praise, which should be understood to refer to the offering of sacrifices; because the words used in the text (can have only that meaning, and) are quite different from anything that can be construed in any other way.

An Answer

अनर्थकं च तद्वचनम्॥२६॥
अन्यश्चार्थः प्रतीयते॥२७॥
अभिधनं च कर्मवत्॥२८॥
फलनिर्वृत्तिश्च॥२९॥
विधिमन्त्रयोरैकार्थ्यमैकशब्द्यात्॥३०॥
अपि वा प्रयोगसामर्थ्यान्मन्त्रोऽभिधनवाची स्यात्॥३१॥
तच्चोदकेषु मन्त्राख्या॥३२॥
शेषे ब्राह्मणशब्दः॥३३॥
अनाम्नातेष्वमन्त्रत्वमाम्नातेषु विभागः॥३४॥

But it is impossible to accept this, because we find that the text, construed even as hymns of praise, makes little sense; and it is admitted that there is a different meaning too,—which can properly be associated with the idea of action, and gives us complete satisfaction as to the result. With regard to the question whether hymns of praise can be the same as a law of Nature, they can have that meaning because the words are the same. Moreover, if a hymn of praise is suitable for reciting sacred formulae, it can be full of meaning too. Again, the word *Mantra* is used in giving directions (implying that it means something more than mere praise); and in the rest of the work the word *Brāhmanā* is used. There can be no doubt that the *Mantra*-part belongs to the sacred books, and this division (between the

Mantra-part and the *Brāhmaṇa*-part) is to be found in the Vedas themselves.[4]

Number of Vedas

तेषामृग्यत्रार्थवशेन पादव्यवस्था॥३५॥
गीतिषु सामाख्या॥३६॥
शेषे यजुःशब्दः॥३७॥
निगदो वा चतुर्थं स्याद्धर्मविशेषात्॥३८॥
व्यपदेशाच्च॥३९॥
यजूंषि वा तद्रूपत्वात्॥४०॥
वचनाद्धर्मविशेषः॥४१॥
अर्थाच्च॥४२॥
गुणार्थो वयपदेशः॥४३॥
सर्वेषामिति चेत्॥४४॥
न ऋग्व्यपदेशात्॥४५॥

The *Mantras* of the *Rig Veda* are always divided into certain fixed parts, for that is how we get their meaning: while the name *Sāma* is applied to verses that are meant to be sung; and *Yajus* to the rest. The *Nigada* may be regarded as the fourth, because of its special character;[5] and that is so because there is a statement to that effect. Nevertheless, the *Nigada* should be included in the *Yajus*, because it has the same form as the latter; and the peculiar character of its hymns is due to the manner of reciting them, as well as the purpose they serve. We have been told that this purpose is of a secondary character; but we cannot say the same of all,— at least of *Rig Veda*.

The Best Form of Expression

अर्थैकत्वादेकं वाक्यं; साकांक्षं चेत्, विभागे स्यात्॥४६॥
समेषु वाक्यभेदः स्यात्॥४७॥
अनुषंगो वाक्यसमाप्तिः, सर्वेषु तुल्ययोगित्वात्॥४८॥
व्यवायान्नानुषज्येत॥४९॥

In the best form of expression,—if there is a single

meaning, there should be a single statement to convey its idea; but if it is related to something else, it should be divided into parts; while in case of equal ideas, there should be separate statements. The close connection of word with word makes for perfection of statement, because all are connected together alike: only we should see that there are no gaps anywhere.

PART II

THE METHOD OF INTERPRETATION

Introduction

Different words express different ideas, and their meaning can be understood in the light of their context.

The meaning of certain words has been specially defined; while in the case of others it can be obtained by dividing them into parts. But no fixed rules can be laid down. Certain conditions must, however, be satisfied. In certain cases we can do as we like.

Words and their Meaning

शब्दान्तरे कर्मभेदः, कृतानुबन्धत्वात्॥१॥
एकस्यैवं पुनः श्रुतिरविशेषादनर्थकं हि स्यात्॥२॥
प्रकरणं तु पौर्णमास्यां, रूपावचनात्॥३॥
विशेषदर्शनाच्च सर्वेषां समेषु ह्यप्रवृत्तिः स्यात्॥४॥

Different words express different ideas of action, because we have to do different things; but if we repeat the same word without a different cause, it would be useless. (But we should be able to get the meaning from the context: for instance,) if there is a reference to the full moon, the subject-matter should indicate it even though there is no mention of its form. But if words convey different meanings in different contexts, we cannot use them in the same sense everywhere.

Special Meanings

गुणस्तु श्रुतिसंयोगात्॥५॥
चोदना वा गुणानां युगपच्छास्त्रात्, चोदिते हि तदर्थत्वात्तस्य

तस्योपदिश्येत॥६॥
व्यपदेशश्च तद्वत्॥७॥
लिङ्गदर्शनाच्च॥८॥

The special meaning of a word arises from its connection with the text of the *śruti*; and so too the idea of its attributes; and when we know the purpose for which it is used, we can settle its meaning. There is a definite statement in support of this in the sacred books; and we can see the proof of it ourselves.

Defined Meanings

पौर्णमासीवदुपांशुयाजः स्यात्॥९॥
चोदना वाऽप्रकृतत्वात्॥१०॥
गुणोपबन्धत्॥११॥
प्राये वचनाच्च॥१२॥
आघाराग्निहोत्रमरूपत्वात्॥१३॥
संज्ञोपबन्धत्॥१४॥
अप्रकृतत्वाच्च॥१५॥

(There are certain words the meaning of which has been defined: for instance,) the word *Upāṇśuyāja* refers to the full moon.[6] This is necessary in cases where the subject is not under discussion in the text. But we can get this meaning from the connection of the parts of the word itself;[6] and that is how we get the meaning in a majority of cases. (We resort to this because we get certain expressions which make little sense: for instance,) there is nothing special in the sprinkling of clarified butter over *Agni*;[7] but when we do this, we understand the whole idea clearly; and find that any other meaning would be irrelevant to the context.

Method of Division into Parts

चोचना वा शब्दार्थस्य प्रयोगभूतत्वात्तत्सन्निधेर्गुणार्थेन पुनः श्रुतिः॥१६॥
द्रव्यसंयोगाच्चोदना पशुसोमयोः प्रकरणे ह्यनर्थको द्रव्यसंयोगो न हि तस्य गुणार्थेन॥१७॥

The rule in regard to the meaning of a word through its parts arises from the fact that this division is made in conformity with a common practice, and there is plenty of sacred authority in support of it. There is the same direction in connection with the combined word *Paśu-Soma*, where we get a combination of two substances (*Paśu and Soma*); and this combination is not useless because we get its meaning by means of this division[8].

Rules cannot be laid down

अचोदकाश्च संस्काराः॥१८॥

तद्भेदात्कर्मणोऽभ्यासो द्रव्य पृथक्त्वादनर्थकं हि स्याद्भेदो द्रव्यगुणीभावात्॥१९॥

But we cannot lay down rules in connection with such formations: only we should remember that when we sub-divide a word-formation into parts, we should be very near its correct meaning; for the substance itself is made up of parts, (corresponding to which we have the parts of a word); otherwise no purpose would be served by this sub-division.

Certain Conditions should be satisfied

संस्कारस्तु न भिद्येत परार्थत्वाद्, द्रव्यस्य गुणभूतत्वात्॥२०

पृथक्त्वनिवेशात्संख्यया कर्मभेदः स्यात्॥२१॥

संज्ञा चोत्पत्तिसंयोगात्॥२२॥

गुणश्चाऽपूर्वसंयोगे, वाक्ययोः समत्वात्॥२३॥

अगुणे तु कर्मशब्दे गुणस्तत्र प्रतीयेत॥२४॥

फलश्रुतेस्तु कर्म स्यात्, फलस्य कर्मयोगित्वात्॥२५॥

अतुल्यत्वात्तु वाक्ययोर्गुणे तस्य प्रतीयेत॥२६॥

समेषु कर्मयुक्तं स्यात्॥२७॥

But if the current meaning of a word correctly conveys the idea of the attributes associated with an object, it should not be divided into parts to serve some other purpose. When we divide a word into parts, we should preserve their position as it is in the word; and if we wish to divide into parts a word connoting action, we should do so after due reflection. The clear idea of the text, obtained in this way, should be such as meets with general approval.

In case we can interpret a word in two ways, which are equally balanced, we should go in for a new combination only if there is some special merit in it. If no special purpose is served by analyzing a word connoting action, its meaning in its place in the text should be accepted. Again, if there is mention of a result, we should see that there is a reference also to its cause or action—for a result is always connected with action. If there are two ways of interpreting a word, and they appear to be of equal value,—we should select the meaning which fits in with the peculiar character of the context; and in normal cases it should be associated with action.

Special Cases

सौभरे, पुरुषश्रुतेर्निधनं, कामसंयोगः॥२८॥

सर्वस्य वोक्तकामत्वात्तस्मिन्कामश्रुतिः स्यान्निधनार्था पुनः श्रुतिः॥२९॥

(However, there are some special cases). In the hymns composed by Saubhari, in the hymn addressed to *Puruṣa*, and in the concluding passage of a *Sāman* hymn which is sung in chorus, we can do as we like.[9] In all these cases, as the author has said what he has desired, all that is necessary is that they should be pleasant to hear. The meaning of the concluding portion of a *Sāman* hymn, sung in chorus, depends on the repetition of certain notes.

PART III

THE METHOD OF INTERPRETATION: THE LAW OF ACTION

Introduction

This method of interpretation implies a deliberate plan on the part of the author. There are, however, certain works where the common meaning of words is satisfactory, and this method should not be adopted.

The popular idea of sacrifice is based on a misconception; and if we pierce through the "disguised" form of words, we shall understand what it means, and the whole idea would be found to be consistent throughout.

If we understand the text in this light, we shall find that *Agni* refers to intellect; and that will enable us to understand the whole text in terms of Dharma or the law of life.

There are some treatises which maintain that we can achieve our goal without action. But that is not the idea of the Vedas: only they have to be understood in a different light,—in the same manner as we understand the meaning of *Agni* as intellect.

Existence of a Plan

गुणस्तु क्रतुसंयोगात्कर्मान्तरं प्रयोजयेत्संयोगस्याशेषभूतत्वात्॥१॥
एकस्य तु लिङ्गभेदात् प्रयोजनार्थमुच्येतैकत्वं गुणवाक्यत्वात्॥२॥

The merit of this method of interpretation is due to its connection with an intelligent plan; and because this connection is perfect, it leads to a result very different from the apparent meaning of words. It is in this manner that we can pierce through the "disguise" of words; and so we might say that the meaning obtained by means of this method has been given to it by the author himself according to design or plan; and its unique character is due to the excellence of this mode of expression.

Importance of Intention

अवेष्टौ यज्ञसंयोगात्क्रतुप्रधनमुच्यते॥५॥
आधने सर्वशेषत्वात्॥४॥

(The idea of intention is importatant; for) in making expiation by means of sacrifice, the most important thing is intention, because it is closely connected with sacrifice.[10] (The words in text give us the idea of sacrifice), because we find that they fit into it completely, and nothing is left out when we put them in their proper place according to this plan.

A Different Meaning

अयनेषु चोदनान्तरं संज्ञोपबन्धत्॥५॥
अगुणा च कर्मचोदना॥६॥
समाप्तं च फले वाक्यम्॥७॥
विकारो वा प्रकरणात्॥८॥

लिङ्गदर्शनाच्च॥९॥
गुणात्संज्ञोपबन्धः॥१०॥
समाप्तिरविशिष्टा॥११॥
संस्कारश्चाप्रकरणेऽकर्मशब्दत्वात्॥१२॥
यावदुक्तं वा कर्मणः श्रुतिमूलत्वात्॥१३॥

In certain parts of the text, however, there is a different method of interpretation, because the current meaning of words is satisfactory, and there is a general agreement about them. In such cases the rule regarding the division of words into part does not apply; and the language of the text is complete in itself, because its result is satisfactory; and it would be a change for the worse to have a different explanation, or to believe that there is a "disguised" form of expression which needs to be seen through. We can have a proper knowledge of the text because of the excellence of its composition; and this proper knowledge is not limited to a particular object, but is of a general or universal character; and we can get it by means of the correct use of words, because no technical terms are used. In such cases we can understand the idea of an action or the meaning of a word in the same manner as we hear it (that is: in its current, common form).[1]

Popular Idea of Sacrifice

यजतिस्तु द्रव्यफलभोक्तृसंयोगादेतेषां कर्मसम्बन्धत्॥४॥

There are some who believe that the injunction in the sacred books in regard to the performance of sacrifices refers to actual sacrifices, which are to be performed with material objects, and which yield certain results, which are actually experienced. All these sacrifices are associated with certain actions, which have to be performed.

Based on a Misconception

लिङ्गदर्शनाच्च॥१५॥
विशये प्रायदर्शनात्॥१६॥
अर्थवादोपपत्तेश्च॥१७॥

संयुक्तस्त्वर्थशब्देन तदर्थः श्रुतिसंयोगात्॥१८॥

पात्नीवते तु पूर्वत्वादवच्छेदः॥१९॥

अद्रव्यत्वात्केवले कर्मशेषः स्यात्॥२०॥

But this idea arises from seeing only the "disguised" form of words used in the text;[12] and if any one should doubt this statement, he should examine the principal part of the text in this light; and then he can satisfy himself if the meaning is correct. He will find that the new meaning is all connected together through the meaning of words, and fits into the text to make a complete whole. Indeed, it may be compared to the possession of a new wife, and its difference from the old, to her being separated from her former state. If the new meaning stood in isolation, unconnected with the text, it would indeed be worthless; for then there would be some action or result which would apparently have been omitted and would need to be supplied.

Meaning of Agni

अग्निस्तु लिङ्गदर्शनात्क्रतुशब्दः प्रतीयेत॥२१॥

द्रव्यं वा स्याच्चोदनायास्तदर्थत्वात्॥२२॥

तत्संयोगात्क्रतुस्तदाख्यः स्यात्तेन धर्मविधनानि॥२३॥

When we see through this "disguise" we find that *Agni* (the god of fire) means "intelligence"[13]; and if we interpret the word according to this rule, we find that it refers to a fundamental concept of philosophy.[14] It is in this manner that we assign the meaning "intelligence" to *Agni*, as a result of which we get the idea of *Dharma* or the law of life[15].

A Different View

प्रकरणान्तरे प्रयोजनान्यत्वम्॥२४॥

फलं चाकर्मसन्निधौ॥२५॥

But different books follow different plans; and we are told that we can achieve the highest end by refraining from action[16].

The View of the Vedas

सन्निधौ त्वविभागात्फलार्थेन पुनः श्रुतिः॥२६॥
आग्नेयसूक्तहेतुत्वादभ्यासेन प्रतीयेत॥२७॥
अविभागात्तु कर्मणो द्विरुक्तेन विधीयते॥२८॥
अन्यार्थां वा पुनः श्रुतिः॥२९

But the Vedas repeatedly tell us that it is only by means of action that we can succeed in achieving results;[17] and in order to understand this properly, what has been stated in respect of *Agni*, should be extended to the other gods as well.[18] The text has two meanings, which are consistent in themselves throughout, and the reference to action in this manner is intentional. The *śruti* too repeatedly tells us that there is another or a different meaning besides the apparent one.

PART IV

THE LAW OF ACTION: NEED OF KNOWLEDGE: ACTION AND TIME

Introduction

So long as there is life, there must be action.

We can understand this if we fix the meaning of words according to the *Krama* method of reciting the text.

The sacred books also tell us that action must cease; and 1 Certain books appear to hold the view that we can achieve the highest end by tefraining from action; but this is an erroneous view. The *Mīmāṁsā* tells us later on that this view appears to find a place in the Vedas too; but the prohibition against action should be understood not in an absolute, but a relative, sense,—as a prohibition against evil or dangerous actions.

2 The *Bhagavad Gītā* too says the same things (BhG. IV, 12; XVIII,2-7).

This means that in order to understand what the gods of the Vedas reallu signify, we should divide their names into parts, as in the case of *Agni*. This is repeated in a subsequent chapter too, and we are told that the gods refer to the great forms and forces of Nature. (Cf. MM. I Chapter IX). we must understand what this really means. There are a variety of actions, but there can be only one action at a time. Action does not consist in a name; the law of one action at a time applies to all kinds of action; but it is the best action that can be performed at the time.

It is necessary to have knowledge to understand the law of Dharma; and we can understand it if we interpret the text correctly.

In certain cases, however, it is easy to understand the whole idea.

Certain actions are more important than others; but the most important thing in this connection is *Cita* or intellect, because it is its special function to decide.

All knowledge is relative, and its idea is illustrated by that of a ceremony lasting twelve days.

There is an impulse to action, and a discussion within us as to its *pros* and *cons*; and when we decide to act in in a certain manner, it means that the balance of judgement is on that side.

There is an element of time in action; and the impulse in connection with certain religious and virtuous actions is irresistible .

While each action has its own cause and a separate method of performance, a combination of a number of actions shows how all kinds of actions are mixed together in life.

The Law of Action

यावज्जीविकोऽभ्यासः कर्मधर्मः प्रकरणात्॥१॥
कर्तुर्वा श्रुतिसंयोगात्॥२॥

We find from this discussion that so long as there is life, all things must conform to the Dharma (law) of action; and the Vedic texts all agree that this is the law of the actor[19].

How to understand This

लिङ्गदर्शनाच्च कर्मधर्मे हि प्रक्रमेण नियम्येत; तत्रानर्थकमन्यत् स्यात्॥३॥

When we wish to see through the "disguise" of words relating to the Dharma or law of action, we should settle their meaning by means of the *Krama* method of reading the text;[20] and if we do anything else, the whole thing would become meaningless.

Meaning of Cessation of Action

व्यपवर्गं च दर्शयति; कालश्चेत्, कर्मभेदः स्यात्॥४॥
अनित्यत्वात्तु नैवं स्यात्॥५॥
विरोधश्चापि पूर्ववत्॥६॥
कर्तुस्तु, धर्मनियमात्, कालशास्त्रं निमित्तं स्यात्॥७॥

We are taught that action must cease, and also that if there is time, there should be variety or different kinds of actions. But because life is transient, it is not possible to have it so for ever. There is, accordingly, an apparent contradiction between these statements; but so far as the actor is concerned, it is necessary for him to act in accordance with the law of Dharma; and the direction in regard to time can only be a reason for his action[21].

Variety of Actions

नामरूपधर्मविशेषपुनरुक्तिनिन्दाऽशक्तिसमाप्तिवचनप्रायश्चि-त्ताऽन्यार्थदर्शनाच्छाखान्तरेषु कर्मभेदः स्यात्॥८॥
एकं वा संयोगरूपचोदनाख्याविशेषात्॥९॥

What is called variety of actions includes a number of things,—name, form, good actions, statement of differences, repetition of a word or sentence, censure, effort, acquisition of knowledge, command, and thought of death; and these give us an inexhaustible store of reasons for action in many different ways. Nevertheless, there can be only one action at a time.

Character of Action

न नाम्ना स्यादचोदनाभिधनत्वात्॥१०॥
सर्वेषां चैककर्म्यं स्यात्॥११॥

कृतकं चाभिधनम्॥१२॥
एकत्वेऽपि परम्॥१३॥

We cannot have action merely by calling it so or giving it a name. It requires direction or impelling force, without which there can be no action. The law of one action at a time applies to all kinds of action; and so far as giving it a name is concerned, it can easily be coined. Although we can perform only one action at a time, it is, at the time, the best action we can perform.

How to understand the Text

विद्यायां धर्मशास्त्रम्॥१४॥
आग्नेयवत्पुनर्वचनम्॥१५॥
अद्विर्वचनं वा श्रुतिसंयोगाविशेषात्॥१६॥
वाक्यासमवायात्; अर्थासन्निधेश्च॥१७॥
न चैकं प्रति शिष्यते॥१८॥
समाप्तिवच्च संप्रेक्षा॥१९॥

It is only when a person has knowledge that he can understand what is taught about Dharma or the law of life; and the idea of it can be obtained by dealing with the text in the same manner as we deal with what relates to *Agni*[22]. There are no two opinions in the matter, for all authorities are agreed; and the whole idea is expressed so briefly, that nothing can be gained by having it otherwise. It is meant to be understood not by one person, but by all; and we can have a clear and complete idea of the whole in this way.

Importance of certain Actions and of Citta

एकत्वेऽपि पराणि निन्दाशक्तिसमाप्तिवचनानि॥२०॥
प्रायश्चित्तं निमित्तेन॥२१॥
प्रक्रमाद्वा नियोगेन॥२२॥

Even though we can perform only one action at a time, certain actions, such as censure, effort, complete acquisition of knowledge, and speech are more important than others;

and the most important place is given to *Citta* (intellect), because it is the effective cause of action. That is so because (it is the function of the inteuect to decide, and) we can proceed to action only when there is an order or decision to that effect[23].

Perfection is a relative Term

समाप्तिः पूर्ववत्त्वाद्यथाज्ञाते प्रतीयेत॥२३॥
लिङ्गमविशिष्टं सर्वशेषत्वान्न हि तत्र कर्मचोदना तस्माद् द्वादशाहस्याहारव्यपदेशः स्यात्॥२४॥

When we speak of perfection, we should understand that the term is used in a relative sense,—with reference to something preceding it; and so we should understand it to mean "the best according to our knowledge." No special argument is required to prove this, because if we take a thing out of its whole, we find that we get no desire or impulse to action. (All things are, therefore, connected together,) and that is illustrated by the idea of a ceremony lasting for twelve days, to which there is a reference in the sacred books.

Process of Action

द्रव्ये चाचोदितत्वाद्विधीनामवयवस्था स्यान्निर्देशाद्व्यवतिष्ठेत; तस्मान्नित्यानुवादः स्यात्॥२५॥
विहितप्रतिषेधत् प्रक्षेऽतिरेकः स्यात्॥२६॥

If there were no impulse to action, a person would not be able to act at all, with the result that the laws of action would be proved to be untrue. But we find that there is an order from within, calling upon us to act; and, as this order is constantly repeated, there is a corresponding repetition in the text to express the idea of this law. Before we act, however, we find that there is an order to act on the one hand, and a prohibition against it on the other;[24] and when in the end we act or do not act, it means that there is a balance of judgement on that side.

Action and Time

सारस्वते विप्रतिषेधद्यदेति स्यात्॥२७॥

(Action involves a reference to Time). When there is a conflict of statements about the time of an action, we ask, in a manner of speech,—When did it take place?.

An Irresistible Impulse

उपहव्येऽप्रतिप्रसवः॥२८॥
गुणार्था वा पुनः श्रुतिः॥२९॥
प्रत्ययं चापि दर्शयति॥३०॥

In certain actions,-specially those which we regard as religious, or of a virtuous character, the impulse to action, as we have often heard, is of an irresistible character; and the explanation of it can easily be understood.

Difference and Harmony in Action

अपि वा क्रमसंयोगाद्विधिपृथक्त्वमेकस्यां व्यवतिष्ठेत॥३१॥
विरोधिना त्वसंयोगादैककर्म्ये; तत्संयोगाद्विधीनां सर्वकर्मप्रत्ययः स्यात्॥३३॥

Each action has a separate cause, and requires a separate method of performance; but, though there is lack of unity because a number of opposite forces are at work,—the connection between the laws of action gives us an idea of how all kinds of actions are linked together.

NOTES

1. This means that Dharma requires that we should use our judgement or intelligence to decide what is fit and proper according to occasion and circumstances.
2. *Stotra* is a hymn of praise which is sung; while *śāstra* is one that is recited audibly or otherwise, as distinguished from the *Stotra* that is sung.
3. *Śruti* is said to refer to sacred knowledge, which has been heard by certain holy sages, and believed to have been orally transmitted from generation to generation. The term is applied to the Vedas, as well as the *Upaniṣads* and other Vedic works. It is distinguished from *Smṛti*, which is said to refer to the whole body of sacred tradition or what is remembered by human

teachers; and, in its widest acceptance, includes the six *Vedāṅgas*, the Laws of *Manu*, the Epics of the *Rāmāyaṇa* and the *Mahābhārata*, and the *Purāṇas*,—all of which are believed to be sacred.

4. The Vedas are said to consist of two distinct parts,—(i) *Mantra*, believed to consist of hymns of praise and prayer addressed to the gods, and (2) *Brāhmaṇa*, consisting of (i) *Vidhi* or Law, and (ii) *Arthavāda*, or explanation of these laws.

   According to the *Mīmāṁsā* the real idea of the *Mantra* is the same as that of *Vidhi* or the laws of Nature or life; and it tells us that we can find out that it is so if we understand the text in the light of the method of interpretation it has described. We are told that a *Mantra* can have this meaning (as laws of Nature), because the words of the text are the same; and all that we have to do is to interpret them in a different way.

5. The *Mīmāṁsā* mentions only three Vedas,—*Rik, Sāma*, and *Yajus* —and so belongs to the period when the fourth, the Atharva, had not been composed. It may be of interest to point out that the *Bhāgāvad Glta* too mentions only three Vedas,—the same as the *Mīmāṁsā* (BhG. IX, 17).

   The *Mīmānsā* mentions *Nigada* as the fourth, but would include it in the *Yajus*. The word means "a prayer or sacrificial formula recited aloud". As it is not sung, it cannot be included in the Sāma; and, as it does not partake of the special characteristics of the *Rik*, it cannot be included in that Veda; and so only the *Yajus* remains.

6. The word *Upāṁśuyāja* consists of two parts,—*Upāṁśu* and *yāja*; and of these Upānśu is said to be a particular *Soma* oblation, while *Yāja* means "a sacrifice". Again, *Soma* refers to the Moon; and so the combined expression *Upāṁśu-yāja* means "the action of the Moon"; for a sacrifice signifies action, even as the *Bhāgāvad Gītā* tells us (BhG. Ill, 14). Hence it refers to the full moon, and that is also its meaning as defined.

7. As we shall see later on, *Agni*, which commonly means the god of Fire, refers to the Intellect, for that is how the word is said to be defined. We shall then see that "clarified butter" refers to the idea of goodness; and so "pouring clarified butter over the fire" really means associating goodness with the function of the intellect. This is necessary, because intellect, like fire, can be both creative and destructive; and it becomes creative only when it is associated with the idea of goodness. Hence in an act of sacrifice it is necessary to "pour clarified butter over the fire".

8. *Paśu* means an animal, while *Soma* means not only the moon, but also the mind; and so *Paśu-Soma* means "*(Soma)* the mind of (*Paśu*) an animal"; and the Mīmāṁsā tells us that animals have a mind. The sacred books tell us of five kinds of *Paśus* or animals,—men, horses, cows, goats, and sheep. (AV. XI. 3, 9 etc.)

9. *Saubhara* means "of Sobhari"; and the latter is the name of the author of the hymns of the *ri*g Veda, VIII, 19-22, etc. The hymn addressed to *Puruṣa* is RV. X, xc.

   The *Mīmāṁsā* tells us later on that it is necessary to divide into parts words used in the *Sāma Veda*. Here we are told that in certain hymns, which are sung in chorus, we may or may not do so, for the result is the same.

10. It is necessary to have a proper idea of Sacrifice. It is, as the *Bhāgāvad Gītā* tells us, born out of action (BhG. III, 14). It is, therefore, a kind of action which alone does not make for bondage (BhG. III, 9). It may accordingly be described as a good, intelligent, and selfless action,—meant for the benefit of all. It is in this sense that an act of Nature, like rain, is said to be a sacrifice (BhG. III, 14).

    The *Mīmāṁsā* tells us that the Vedas deal with sacrifice in this sense of the term.

11. A great deal of the language used in the *Bhāgāvad Gītā* is of this kind, and the common meaning of most words is satisfactory. It is only in the case of certain names of persons or things, that we need to apply a different method of interpretation to understand them.

12. The real idea of Sacrifice has already been explained. The common idea of Sacrifice, says the *Mīmāṁsā*, is based on a misconception, for we see only the "disguised" from of words, without understanding their meaning.

13. The *Mīmāṁsā* explains later on that seeing through the "disguise" of a word means dividing it into parts (MS. VII, iv, 16-20; IX, Hi, 7-14). This *Sūtra* therefore tells us that if we do so in the case of the word *Agni*, we shall get the idea of "intelligence". In a subsequent chapter we are again told that this is the definition of the word *Agni*.

    The word *Agni* may be divided into A,g,n,i; and of these A refers to the intellect, g and n to the senses of knowledge, and i to the mind. The meaning of the word accordingly is "(A) the intellect associated with (g,n) the senses and (i) the mind". As we shall see in the course of this work, the senses of knowledge can refer also to those of action and vice *versa*,—for one of them, the *Tongue*, is both a sense of knowledge and of action. Thus the two letters g and n,—although they refer to the senses of knowledge, would include those of action too. Hence the word *Agni* gives us a complete idea of the function of the intellect in association with the mind as well as the senses.

    There are innumerable references to *Agni* in the sacred books, from the Vedas downwards; and all of them can be interpreted in this light. For instance, we are told that there are three kinds of *Agni* or sacrificial fire: *Gārhapatya*, *āhavanīya*, and *Dakṣiṇa*; and they are commonly interpreted to mean "the householder's fire, received from his father and transmitted to his descendants"; "consecrated fire taken from the householder"s perpetual fire and prepared for receiving oblations"; and "the southern fire" respectively. But if we understand their idea correctly, we shall find that the *Gārhapatya* refers to the function of the intellect in association with the soul ("master of the house"); *āhavanīya* refers to its function in the world abroad; while *Dakṣiṇa* refers to skill in action, by means of which one can act and yet be free from the bondage of action. (Compare also MM. I, 312-338).

14. The word in the text is *dravya*, one of the meanings of which is "an elementary substance in philosophy". The *Vaiśeṣika* mentions nine such substances,tthe five great elements, Time, Space, Mind, and the Soul. The Intellect too is a *dravya* in the same sense, as, according to the *Sāṅkhya*, it is the first "substance" to arise from Nature or *Prakṛti*. The *Bhāgāvad Gītā* gives it the highest place among the eight divisions of *Prakṛti* (BhG. VII, 4).
15. If we understand *Agni* to mean "intellect", the whole idea of the text would be transformed, and what we shall get is Dharma or the law of life. It is in this manner that the *Mantras* of the Vedas can be changed from the idea of praise of gods to that of Dharma; and so they may be said to deal with the problems of life conceived in its widest significance; and this is what the *Mīmāṁsā* says too.
16. Certain books appear to hold the view that we can achieve the highest end by refraining from action; but this is an erroneous view. The *Mīmāṁsā* tells us later on that this view appears to find a place in the Vedas too; but the prohibition against action should be understood not in an absolute, but a relative, sense,—as a prohibition against evil or dangerous actions.
17. The *Bhāgāvad Gītā* too says the same thing (BhG. IV, 12; XVIII, 2-7).
18. This means that in order to understand what the gods of the Vedas really signify, we should divide their names into parts, as in the case of *Agni*. This is repeated in a subsequent chapter too, and we are told that the gods refer to the great forms and forces of Nature. (Cf. MM. I, Chapter IX).
19. The *Bhāgāvad Gītā* also tells us that no one can remain, even for a moment, without performing actions; and even the barest needs of the body cannot be supplied without some kind of action (BhG. III, 5, 8).
20. The word in the text is *Pra-krama*, which means "*Krama-pāṭha* or reading of *Krama*"; and *Krama* is a peculiar method of reading the Vedic text, according to which the reading proceeds from the first member,—word, syllable or letter—to the second; then the second is repeated and connected with the third; the third repeated and connected with the fourth; and so on. This ensures that no part of a word can possibly be omitted.

    The *Mīmāṁsā* tells us that we should regard the common form of a word as a "disguise" which hides its real meaning; and the latter can be found by reading the text according to *Krama*; and this would have the effect of dividing a word into its component syllables and letters. We can then assign suitable meanings to these and understand the real meaning of a word. The *Mīmāṁsā* contains a number of references to this method of division of words into parts, and also to *Krama*; and the idea of the two is the same.
21. The real meaning of cessation of action is that an action must come to an end at some time, and not that we must refrain from all actions; for when

one action ends, another begins. It is, however, true that all action on earth ends with death, for all life must come to an end one day. There is thus an apparent contradiction between the two statements; but the idea is clear. The *Gītā* too tells us that a person must continue to act so long as he lives (BhG. III, 5, 27-28, 33 etc.)

22. The *Mīmāṁsā* has told us that the real meaning of the word *Agni* is "intellect", and so all that relates to *Agni* has to be understood as referring to the intellect. We can get this meaning by dividing word into parts. If we do the same with regard to other words used in the sacred text, we shall be able to get a new meaning, which will have a bearing on the idea of Dharma or the law of life.
23. It is the principal function of the intellect, *Buddhi* or reason, to discriminate between different things, and arrive at a conclusion or decide.
24. This refers to a certain discussion that always goes on within us before we act. We have to consider the *pros* and *cons* of an action, and, with it, arguments for and against it; and have to decide whether to act or not to act. All this involves an exercise of our judgement or the function of the intellect; and it is for this reason that the highest place in action is given to *Citta* or the intellect.

CHAPTER III

THE LAW OF ACTION

PART I

HOW DESCRIBED IN THE VEDAS

Introduction

There can be no action without a purpose or cause; and its result is for the sake of *puruṣa* or the soul.

There can only be one action at a time; and actions may be divided into main and subsidiary ones.

We have to express all this in language, and it can be done in various ways.

Result of Action

अथातः शेषलक्षणम्॥१॥

शेषः परार्थत्वात्।२॥

द्रव्यगुणसंस्कारेषु बादरिः॥३॥

कर्माण्यपि जैमिनिः फलार्थत्वात्॥४॥

Let us consider the characteristic marks of effect or the result of action. This effect or result is meant for the sake of something else; and Badari says that it is for the purpose of acquiring some object, or wealth, or attribute, or purifying one's self. Jaimini says that it consists in action too, for that may be the result of our aim.

For the sake of the Soul

फलं च पुरुषार्थत्वात्॥५॥

पुरुषश्च कर्मार्थत्वात्॥६॥
तेषामर्थेन संबन्धः॥७॥
विहितस्तु सर्वधर्मः स्यात्, संयोगतोऽविशेषात्प्रकरणाविशेषाच्च॥८॥
अर्थलोपादकर्म स्यात्॥९॥
फलं तु सह चेष्टया; शब्दार्थोऽभावाद्विप्रयोगे स्यात्॥१०॥
द्रव्यं चोत्पत्तिसंयोगात्तदर्थमेव चोद्यते॥११॥
अर्थैकत्वे द्रव्यगुणयोरैककर्म्यान्नियमः स्यात्॥१२॥

The result, however, is for the sake of *puruṣa* or the individual soul; and the soul too is for the sake of action[1]; and all these are connected together by means of purpose. This is a universal law, applicable to all cases and in all circumstances; for if there be no purpose, there can be no action. The result of an action follows action: were it otherwise, we should be able to get the result without action; and a person is moved to action because of the effect or result he expects to produce. The purpose and qualities of a person become one in action, for that is the law of action.

One Action at a Time

एकत्वयुक्तमेकस्य श्रुतिसंयोगात्॥१३॥
सर्वेषां वा लक्षणत्वादविशिष्टं हि लक्षणम्॥१४॥
चोदिते तु परार्थत्वाद्यथाश्रुति प्रतीयेत॥१५॥

A person can engage in only one action at a time, and there is good reason for saying so. This is a characteristic of all, for it is a universal law. But all action is performed for the sake of something else, and this should be accepted, even as the sacred books tell us.

Not Applicable to Subsidiary Actions

संस्काराद्वा गुणानामव्यवस्था स्यात्॥१६॥
व्यवस्था वाऽर्थस्य श्रुतिसंयोगात्, तस्य शब्दप्रमाणत्वात्॥१७॥
आनर्थक्यात्तदङ्गेषु॥१८॥
कर्तृगुणे तु कर्मासमवायाद्वाक्यभेदः स्यात्॥१९॥

But, while this is the prescribed order of things, it does not mean that there is a fixed relation of time and place so far as subsidiary actions are concerned.[2] But there is such a relation in respect of deliberate action or action characterised by the function of the intellect; and we have the testimony of wise and trustworthy persons to prove that it is so.[3] This is proved by the fact that subordinate (or reflex) actions are without deliberate purpose or aim. But where the subordinate actions of a person cannot be integrated, there should be a separate statement about it.

Use of Language

साकांक्षं त्वेकवाक्यं स्यादसमाप्तं हि पूर्वेण।।२०।।
सन्दिग्धे तु व्यवायाद्वाक्यभेदः स्यात्।।२१।।
गुणानां च परार्थत्वादसम्बन्धः समत्वात्स्यात्।।२२।।
मिथश्चानर्थसम्बन्धत्।।२३।।
आनन्तर्यमचोदना।।२४।।
वाक्यानां च समाप्तत्वात्।।२५।।
शेषस्तु गुणसंयुक्तः साधरणः प्रतीयेत, मिथस्तेषामसम्बन्धत्।।२६।।
व्यवस्था वाऽर्थसंयोगाल्लिङ्गस्यार्थेन सम्बन्धाल्लक्षणार्था गुणश्रुतिः।।२७।।

(This leads to a consideration of how ideas should be expressed in language). When an idea is not covered by a statement already made, and it is necessary properly to describe it,—it should be possible to do so by means of a single expression. But where the matter is intricate or causes confusion, and there are other obstacles in the way, a separate statement may be necessary.

Where the subordinate parts of an action are performed for the sake of something else, they should normally be taken separately, and not closely connected with one another. Where, however, they are put together, they should be deemed to be there not because of any inherent connection with one another, but for some other purpose. Indeed, it is not a rule that they should be placed in close proximity to one another; and that is so because we desire to have as perfect a statement as possible. If, however, any part of the statement relating to the subordinate parts of an action is in excess of the requirements of the case, we should accept it in a general sense, and without any close connection with the main action. The difference between the statement and the object to be described arises from the difference in the purpose of each, because each symbol has a meaning of its own. The purpose of the text regarding the subordinate parts of an action is that the character of the idea should be properly expressed.

PART II

THE LANGUAGE OF THE VEDAS AND HOW TO UNDERSTAND IT

Introduction

The language of the *Mantras* of the Vedas does not appear to be in harmony with the objects described; but every word is not like that. It is only when the original meaning does not refer to the laws of life that we should reject it; and we shall find that the language of the Vedas, when properly understood, does refer to the laws of life.

If that be so, how do we get the common meaning bearing on the idea of sacrifice?. On the other hand, if this be the real meaning of the text, and we are also able to get another meaning, should not the latter too refer to the idea of sacrifice, for both of them are obtained from the same undivided text?.

There is a reference to the *Krama* method of reading the text, which enables us to transform a *Mantra* or a hymn of praise into *Vidhi* or the law of life. Indeed, if the Vedas have any real value, they should have a different interpretation. We are led to this conclusion by the use of certain special terms in the text. But it is necessary to have a regular system of interpretation, which indeed exists, but requires skill to use it. For instance, we can easily understand the meaning of the word

Tvashṭṛ, but not so of the number thirty. Again, there are certain words the meaning of which has been defined, and they have to be understood in that light. There is personification too: for instance, Desire is personified as a god, and associated with the *Soma* juice.

The Language of the Vedas

अर्थाभिधनसामर्थ्यान्मन्त्रेषु शेषभावः स्यात्तस्मादुत्पत्तिसम्बन्धेऽर्थेन नित्यसंयोगात्॥१॥

संस्कारकत्वादचोदितेन स्यात्॥२॥

वचनात्त्वयथार्थमैन्द्री स्यात्॥३॥

गुणाद्वाऽप्यभिधनं स्यात्सम्बन्धस्याशास्त्रहेतुत्वात्॥४॥

The *Mantras* (believed to be hymns of praise, addressed to the gods) refer to a number of objects closely connected with one another; but certain words appear to be missing, which need to be supplied, in order to understand the text. But if there are no real gaps, the original connection of words must have been based on some other meaning, about which there must have been a consensus of opinion. But if the common meaning be the real one, it should not contain anything contrary to rules of morality or what is enjoined. For instance, there is such an incongruity in the description of *Indra,*[4] and when a person breaks rules of morality, his description should correspond to his actions; (but it is not so in this case).

Need of a new Meaning

तथाह्वानमपीति चेत्॥५॥

न कालविधिश्चोदितत्वात्॥६॥

गुणाभावात्॥७॥

लिङ्गाच्च॥८॥

विधिकोपश्चोपदेश स्यात्॥९॥

तथोत्थानविसर्जने॥१०॥

सूक्तवाके च कालविधिः परार्थत्वात्॥११॥

It may be argued that (if the text of the *Mantras* has a different meaning from the apparent one,) it should be so in the case of *āhvāna* or invocation of the deity too. But this is not necessary, for it only lays down the proper time for the invocation of the deity; and there is no reference to any attributes or auxiliary acts, as can easily be proved. It is only where the meaning of a word, in its original form, appears to be incompatible with our conception of the laws of life, that we should reject it. Indeed, if we recite the hymns correctly, we shall find that they refer to the laws of Time or life.

An Objection and an Answer

उपदेशो वा याज्याशब्दो हि नाकस्मात्॥१२॥
स देवतार्थस्तत्संयोगात्॥१३॥
प्रतिपत्तिरिति चेत्स्विष्टकृद्वदुभयसंस्कारः स्यात्॥१४॥
कृत्स्नोपदेशादुभयत्र सर्ववचनम्॥१५॥
यथार्थं वा शेषभूतसंस्कारात्॥१६॥
वचनादिति चेत्॥१७॥
प्रकरणाविभागादुभे प्रति कृत्स्नशब्दः॥१८॥

It may, however, be argued that the original meaning, bearing on the idea of sacrifice, could not have come out of nowhere; and so that is the real meaning of the deities. But if that be their real meaning,—and yet there is another way of interpreting the text as well,—the latter should also convey the idea of offering a proper sacrifice; and in both cases all that is taught should remain continuous and whole, like a garland of flowers. We are justified in saying this, because both the meanings refer to the same language,—taken in its entirety and without any division.

Krama and its Significance

लिङ्गक्रमसमाख्यानात्काम्ययुक्तं समाम्नानम्॥२१॥
अधिकारे च मन्त्रविधिस्तदाख्येषु, शिष्टत्वात्॥२०॥

There is mention of the *Krama* method of reading the Vedas; and we find that it is like a "disguise" in which the narrative contains all that we seek; and the governing rule is that a *Mantra* or a hymn of praise should, in the light of these names and what has been taught, be the same as *Vidhi* or the law of life.[5]

Need of a New Meaning

तदाख्यो वा प्रकरणोपपत्तिभ्याम्॥२१॥
अनर्थकश्चोपदेशः स्यादसम्बन्धात्फलवता[१]॥२२॥
सर्वेषां चोपदिष्टत्वात्॥२३॥
लिङ्गसमाख्यानाभ्यां भक्षार्थताऽनुवाकस्य॥२४॥
तस्य रूपोपदेशाभ्यामपकर्षोऽर्थस्य, चोदितत्वात्॥२५॥
गुणाभिधनान्मन्द्रादिरेकमन्त्रः स्यात्तयोरेकार्थसंयोगात्॥२६॥

But we can say this only when we get both the meanings from the same text. But the meaning in its original form is valueless, because it does not yield any result, nor does worship or going to the sanctuary of a god give the promised fruit. This applies to the teaching of all the *Mantras*; and if this is the real meaning of the Vedas, their only purpose would appear to be to minister to eating and drinking; and so both their form and teaching would drag us down, because that is what is said to be enjoined. If, however, the Vedas have any merit of composition, the hymns,—charming as they are—should serve as a single instrument of thought, and both the meanings converge to but a single sense.

Special Terms

लिङ्गविशेषनिर्देशात्समानविधनेष्वनैन्द्राणाममन्त्रत्वम्॥२७॥
यथादेवतं वा तत्प्रकृतित्वं हि दर्शयति॥२८॥
पुनरभ्युन्नीतेषु सर्वेषामुपलक्षणं, द्विशेषत्वात्॥२९॥

There is a special mention of certain symbols or terms which convey the same idea in all circumstances. They have been used in connection with *Indra*; but, as they do not retain their special meaning, they should not have been used. A god

---

१. न ह्युपस्थानं फलवत्।

represents an aspect of Nature or *Prakṛti*; but if the word has two meanings, there is an implication that there is something in respect of the whole text which has not been properly expressed, and something needs to be taken from the one to the other side.

Need of a System

अपनयाद्वा पूर्वस्याऽनुपलक्षणम्॥३०॥
ग्रहणाद्वाऽनपायः स्यात्॥३१॥
पात्नीवते तु पूर्ववत्॥३२॥
ग्रहणाद्वाऽपनीतं स्यात्॥३३॥

At the same time it would not be possible to get the correct meaning without a system; (and the system is there, only it requires skill to use it); and if we try to "seize" the text or grab at its meaning, we shall not succeed. As has already been observed, the real meaning is like possessing a wife;[6] and if we grab at it, the whole work would be badly done and suffer from contradictions.

Instances

त्वष्टारं तूपलक्षयेत्पानात्॥३४॥
अतुल्यत्वात्तु नैवं स्यात्॥३५॥
त्रिंशच्च परार्थत्वात्॥३६॥

We can get the meaning of the word *Tvashṭṛ* (as Mind) from the reference to drinking *Soma*[7] (which means the same thing); but if the two ideas are not equal, we cannot always succeed in this way. For instance, the number thirty has a very different meaning[8].

Words with defined Meanings

वषट्कारश्च कर्त्तृवत्॥३७॥
छन्दः प्रतिषेधस्तु सर्वगामित्वात्॥३८॥
ऐन्द्राग्ने तु लिङ्गभावात्स्यात्॥३९॥
एकस्मिन्वा देवतान्तराद्विभागवत्॥४०॥

(There are certain words, the meanings of which have been defined): for instance, *Vaṣaṭ* signifies performance of action;[9] and *Chhanda* means desire, regarded as an obstacle in our path.[10] Similarly, when there is a joint reference to *Indra* and *Agni*, we should be able to distinguish between them from the character of the conclusions that are drawn; and though close to each other, we should be able to get at the idea of each one separately[11].

Desire as a God: its Character

छन्दश्च देवतावत्॥४१॥

सर्वेषु वाऽभावादेकच्छन्दसः॥४२॥

सर्वेषां वैकमंत्र्यमैतिशायनस्य भक्तिपानत्वात्सवनाधिकारो हि॥४३॥

Desire may also be personified as a god.[12] There is desire in all creatures, but one and the same desire does not exist among all. According to *Aitiśāyana*[13] the common characteristic of all desires is that they arise from attachment,—attachment to drinking;[14] and claim that they are entitled to have the Soma juice.[15].

PART III

THE LAW OF ACTION

Introduction

The claim of Desire to its fulfilment is based on reason. Desire is associated with both knowledge and action. There are primary and subsidiary causes of Desire, which can be understood by means of knowledge.

Action consists of a number of parts, each of which is associated with desire; but, as these parts progress without a break, it appears to be one.

Action is of many kinds, and all deliberate action is characterised by purpose; and in its final form it is associated with some object of Nature.

Action consists of a number of parts, and there is no action which consists of only one part; and there is always a cause or purpose for a deliberate action.

All deliberate action is characterised by reason, and is an expression of the creative power of Nature itself.

Animals alone are characterised by purpose in action; but there is reason to believe that there is purpose in the actions of the gods or the working of the great forces of Nature.

There is also a law of conflict in Nature; but in every case there is only one action at a time.

Desire and its Fulfilment

श्रुतेर्जाताधिकारः स्यात्॥१॥

वेदो वा प्रायदर्शनात्॥२॥

लिङ्गाच्च॥३॥

धर्मोपदेशाच्च न हि द्रव्येण सम्बन्धः॥४॥

त्रयीविद्याख्या च तद्विदि॥५॥

This claim on the part of Desire (that it is entitled to the object it seeks) must be based on reason. It may arise from knowledge,—chiefly from something that has been seen; or from inference; or from reference to Dharma or a law, without any connection with a particular object;[16] and the sum total of the knowledge of the three Vedas consists in understanding this[17].

Desire, Knowledge and Action

व्यतिक्रमे यथाश्रुतीति चेत्॥६॥

न सर्वस्मिन्निवेशात्॥७॥

वेदसंयोगान्न प्रकरणेन बाध्येत॥८॥

We cannot say that Desire only begins with knowledge, for it enters into everything, and its association continues to the end; but because it is associated with knowledge, it cannot be driven out by any amount of action.

Knowledge and Primary and Subsidiary Cause of Desire

गुणमुख्यव्यतिक्रमे तदर्थत्वान्मुख्येन वेदसंयोगः॥९॥
भूयस्त्वेनोभयश्रुति॥१०॥

There are primary and subsidiary causes of desire; and knowledge refers to its primary cause,—for that is the very purpose of knowledge (namely, to awaken desire). Indeed, it is by means of knowledge that we can understand both its primary and subsidiary causes.

Action and its Parts

असंयुक्तं प्रकरणादितिकर्त्तव्यतार्थित्वात्॥११॥
क्रमश्च देशसामान्यात्॥१२॥
आख्या चैवं तदर्थत्वात्॥१३॥

(Action consists of a number of parts, and) as there is a desire that each part should be properly performed, its different parts cannot be performed at the same time. There is, however, an uninterrupted progress of action, because all its parts are connected with one another by means of common properties; and it is for this reason that the whole action appears to be one.

Many kinds of Action

श्रुति-लिङ्ग-वाक्य-प्रकरण-स्थान-समाख्यानां समवाये पारदौर्बल्यमर्थविप्रकर्षात्॥१४॥

अहीनो वा प्रकरणाद् गौणः॥१५॥

असंयोगात्तु मुख्यस्य तस्मादपकृष्यते॥१६॥

द्वित्वबहुत्वयुक्तं वा चोदनात्तस्य॥१७॥

Action is of many kinds,—of the senses of knowledge (e.g. hearing), of the senses of action (e.g. speech), the mind and the intellect (e.g. inference, discussion, name);[18] and it is associated with some place. But its great weakness consists in being dragged down by a purpose or aim.[19] Nevertheless, a virtuous person is not weakened by action, however much it be.[20] Indeed, were there no purpose, we could not perform any principal or deliberate action at all; while, with a purpose, we can perform two or many more.

Nature of Purpose in Action

पक्षेणार्थकृतस्येति चेत्॥१८॥

न प्रकृतेरेकसंयोगात्॥१९॥

Purpose in action does not consist in the advancement of a particular theory or opinion alone; for it must, in any case, be associated with some object of Nature.

An Action Consists of Parts

जाघनी चैकदेशत्वात्॥२०॥
चोदना वाऽपूर्वत्वात्॥२१॥
एकदेश इति चेत्॥२२॥
न प्रकृतेरशास्त्रनिष्पत्तेः॥२३॥
सन्तर्दनं प्रकृतौ, क्रयणवदनर्थलोपात् स्यात्॥२४॥
उत्कर्षो वा ग्रहणाद्विशेषस्य॥२५॥
कर्तृतो वा विशेषस्य तन्निमित्तत्वात्॥२६॥
क्रतुतो वाऽर्थवादानुपपत्तेः स्यात्॥२७॥
संस्थाश्च कर्तृवद्धरणार्थाविशेषात्॥२८॥
उक्थ्यादिषु वाऽर्थस्य विद्यमानत्वात्॥२९॥
अविशेषात्स्तुतिर्व्यर्थेति चेत्॥३०॥
स्यादनित्यत्वात्॥३१॥

When we say that a thing is part of a whole, it means that there must at least be two things,—one coming after the other; and the impelling force of action is new (or different) in each case. It would be contrary to the laws of Nature to say that an action may consist of only one part; for all things in Nature are connected with one another, and a violation of this law would render everything meaningless, even as we cannot buy anything with only one party to the transaction. Buying a thing means at least an attraction for an object: similarly, when a person performs an action, there is always some cause for it. This rule, however, applies only to deliberate actions, characterised by a plan; but it is true of all creatures who act, because they have all, without exception, a purpose in action. It is only those things which have some useful purpose to serve that are praised; but, as it is possible to say that all things serve some useful purpose, it would be meaningless to single out any for special praise, specially when there is nothing permanent in the world.

Character of Deliberate Action

सङ्ख्यायुक्तं क्रतोः प्रकरणात् स्यात्॥३२॥
नैमित्तिकं वा कर्तृसंयोगाल्लिंगस्य तन्निमित्तत्वात्॥३३॥
पौष्णं पेषणं विकृतौ प्रतीयेताऽचोदनात्प्रकृतौ॥३४॥
तत्सर्वार्थमविशेषात्॥३५॥

All deliberate action is characterised by reason or reflection, because it is preceded by some discussion within us; and this is an expression of the creative power of Nature working in the doer of the deed; for we must admit that it is a law of Nature that there should be growth as well obstacles in the development of things; and it applies to all cases without distinction.

Animals have this Purpose

चरौ वाऽर्थोक्तं; पुरोडाशेऽर्थविप्रतिषेधत् पशौ न स्यात्॥३६
चरावपीति चेत्॥३७॥
न पक्तिनामत्वात्॥३८॥
एकस्मिन्नेकसंयोगात्॥३९॥
धर्मविप्रतिषेधच्च॥४०॥

This purpose exists in an animal; but because it does not exist in a mass of ground rice, we should not suppose that it does not exist in an animal. We cannot say that an animal too is devoid of purpose; for it cannot exist without it, because it must eat and digest food, and bear the consequence of things. But each animal is a separate entity, for such is the restriction imposed by its nature.

Purpose in the Actions of Gods or the Forces of Nature

अपि वा सद्वितीये स्याद्देवतानिमित्तत्वात्॥४१॥

लिङ्गदर्शनाच्च॥४२॥

It is possible to say that there is purpose in another entity too,—a god or a great force of Nature, because it is regarded as a cause of action; and there is reason for thinking so.

Law of Conflict

वचनात्सर्वपेषणं; तं प्रति शास्त्रवत्त्वादर्थाभावाद्धि चरावपेषणं भवति॥४३॥

It follows from this that there is a cash among things, and it is so in accordance with a law. But since there is no purpose in a pot or a saucepan, there is, of course, no conflict in it.

Law of Purpose

एकस्मिन्वाऽर्थधर्मत्वादैन्द्राग्नवदुभयोर्न स्यादचोदितत्वात्॥४४॥

हेतुमात्रमदन्तत्वम्॥४५॥

वचनं परम्॥४६॥

According to the law of purpose it is only one object that can act at a time. If there be two together, both cannot act at the same time, as it would be contrary to law; and this applies to *Indra* and *Agni* too[21]. This can be illustrated by the action of a toothless person, and is an absolute truth[22].

PART IV

THE LAW OF LIFE IN THE VEDAS: PURPOSE IN ACTION AND ACTIONLESSNESS

Introduction

This is the law of the life of Man, described in the Vedas

in a veiled manner, and we can understand it if we pierce through the "disguise" of words. But it requires deep concentration to do so; and it is in this manner that we can understand the meaning of certain words.

There is purpose in both action and actionlessness, and their idea is expressed in the text in this manner. This enables us to understand that there is a perfect law of life described in the Vedas; but it requires experience, intelligence, self surrender, and a measure of good luck to succeed.

The ordinary meaning of the text is like a woman wearing dirty clothes; but we should try to get a new meaning only when the ordinary one does not refer to a law of life. We can accept the new meaning only if the result is satisfactory, and refers to the law of Action or action performed as a Sacrifice.

The idea that desire arises from some evil or sin is a popular heresy, for it can also be part of Sacrifice; and its idea may be illustrated by the act of dying in the defence of some one.

But desire can be evil too: only the person who has it does not regard it so, for that is the very nature of desire, and that is the reason why he seeks means to attain his object.

Desire is connected with action in various ways, and success arises out of action.

We can understand the ideas of certain expressions used in the text in a special way.

Law of Man's Life, described in the Vedas in a veiled Form

निवीतमिति मनुष्यधर्मः शब्दस्य तत्प्रधनत्वात्॥१॥
अपदेशा वाऽर्थस्य विद्यमानत्वात्॥२॥
विधिस्त्वपूर्वत्वात्स्यात्॥३॥
स प्रायात्कर्मधर्मः स्यात्॥४॥
वाक्यशेषत्वात्॥५॥

तत्प्रकरणे यत्तत्संयुक्तमविप्रतिषेधत्॥६॥
तत्प्रधने वा तुल्यवत्प्रसंख्यानादितरस्य तदर्थत्वात्॥७॥
अर्थवादी वा प्रकरणात्॥८॥
विधिना चैकवाक्यत्वात्॥९॥
उपवीतं लिङ्गदर्शनात्सर्वधर्मः स्यात्॥१०॥
न वा प्रकरणात्तस्य दर्शनम्॥११॥
विधिर्वा स्यादपूर्वत्वात्॥१२॥
उदक्त्वं चापूर्वत्वात्॥१३॥
सतो वा लिङ्गदर्शनम्॥१४॥

This is the law of the life of Man, described in the Vedas in a "veiled" manner, because it is very important to use the correct expression or the right word. We know that there is this "disguise", because we can find out the correct meaning. But the new meaning should be of the nature of a law; and the largest portion of the text should refer to the law of action. We should get this result when the words required to complete the sense are supplied; and the new meaning should fit into the whole body of the text without contradiction, and remain unchanged throughout the principal part of the work,—because it is based on proper thought, after we have considered the other meaning and rejected it; and so we should be able to explain the meaning of any precept in its light. This is possible because it does refer to a law; and when we see through the "disguise", we find that all our ideas of a law are held together and purified in this way. But by reading the book as it is, we do not see anything relating to the idea of a law; whereas the new meaning should be of the nature of such a law, and it should be such as can uplift us. This is what is meant by "seeing through the disguise".

It Requires Concentration

विधिस्तु धरणेऽपूर्वत्वात्॥१५॥
दिग्विभागश्च तद्वत्सम्बन्धस्यार्थहेतुत्वात्॥१६॥
परुषि दितपूर्णघृतविदग्धं च तद्वत्॥१७॥

But the new meaning can be grasped only by means of deep concentration of thought. But because there is a reason for it, there is always something in the text to suggest what it really is; and it is in this manner that words like *Paruṣī, Dita, Pūrṇa*, *Ghṛta*, and *Vidagdha* are used in the text.[23].

Actionlessness

अकर्म क्रतुसंयुक्तं संयोगान्नित्यानुवादः स्यात्॥१८॥
विधिर्वा संयोगान्तरात्॥१९॥
अहीनवत्पुरूषस्तदर्थत्वात्॥२०॥

(It is in the same manner that we have an explanation of the idea of actionlessness); for even actionlessness has a purpose, and it is in this light that we should understand its idea[24]; and when we grasp the inner meaning of the text, we see that it gives the idea of a law; and there is no error in following this meaning.

Character of the Text

प्रकरणविशेषाद्वा तद्युक्तस्य संस्कारो द्रव्यवत्॥२१॥
व्यपदेशादपकृष्येत॥२२॥
शंयौ च सर्वपरिदानात्॥२३॥

When a person gains experience in this special treatment of the text, he will find that it contains a perfect expression of the idea of a law. Indeed, the text is so composed that an experienced person can anticipate that certain words would follow to give the required sense. But it is a fortunate one who can succeed in getting the correct meaning; and it requires complete self-surrender to do so.

Comparison between the two Meanings

प्रागपरोधन्मलवद्वाससः॥२४॥
अन्नप्रतिषेधच्च॥२५॥
अप्रकरणे तु तद्धिर्मस्ततो विशेषात्॥२६॥
अद्रव्यत्वात्तु शेषः स्यात्॥२७॥

वेदसंयोगात्॥२८॥
द्रव्यसंयोगाच्च॥२९॥

The ordinary meaning of the text may be compared to a woman wearing dirty clothes, and it is only when they are removed that we can see her purer form. This is necessary, because we refuse to accept the grosser form of what is pure and undefiled. But this idea of a law cannot be found in the principal topic of discussion, and so we have to find it in some special way. But it is only when the ordinary meaning does not refer to a concept of philosophy, that we should think of a new meaning that does so; and we can get it if we have the necessary knowledge; and we shall find that it is closely connected with these ideas of philosophy.

Test of Correctness

स्याद्वाऽस्यसंयोगवत्फलेन; सम्बन्धस्तस्मात्कर्मैतिशायनः॥३०॥
शेषाः प्रकरणेऽविशेषात्सर्वकर्मणाम्॥३१॥
होमास्तु व्यवतिष्ठेरन्नाहवनीय संयोगात्॥३२॥
शेषश्च समाख्यानात्॥३३॥

We should agree about the correctness of the new meaning only if the result achieved is satisfactory,—for that is the measure of its success; and, according to *Aitiśāyana*, it should refer to action. Indeed, there is no difference of opinion in the matter that the entire text should refer to all kinds of actions[25]. At the same time we should be able to show that the *Homa* oblation is connected with the sacred fire, *āhavanīya*[26]; and the rest of the explanation should follow from the narrative itself.

Desire and Evil

दोषात्त्विष्टिर्लौकिके स्यात् शास्त्राद्धि वैदिके न दोषः स्यात्॥३४॥
अर्थवादो वाऽनुपपातात्तस्माद्यज्ञे प्रतीयेत॥३५॥
अचोदितं च कर्मभेदात्॥३६॥
सा लिङ्गादार्त्विजे स्यात्॥३७॥
पानव्यापच्च तद्वत्॥३८॥

The idea that desire always arises from some evil or sin should be regarded as a popular heresy. The sacred books tell us that there can be no sinfulness in desire so far as it refers to knowledge. If there is no unfortunate occurrence in connection with desire, we should regard it as part of the idea of sacrifice. Such a desire does not make any distinction between action and action; and it has its own characteristics to distinguish it from other forms of desire, and is always associated with action performed as a sacrifice and at the proper time. To die in the defence of some one is an action of this kind[27].

Extent of Evil in Desire

दोषात्तु वैदिके स्यादर्थाद्धि लौकिके न दोषः स्यात्॥३९॥

तत्सर्वत्राविशेषात्॥४०॥

स्वामिनो वा तदर्थत्वात्॥४१॥

लिङ्गदर्शनाच्च॥४२॥

सर्वप्रदानं हविषस्तदर्थत्वात्॥४३॥

निरवदानात्तु शेषः स्यात्॥४४॥

उपायो वा तदर्थत्वात्॥४५॥

Desire should be deemed to arise from evil only when we are satisfied in a scientific manner that it is so, and not merely because it is said to be so in a popular form of speech; and this should be regarded as true for all times and without exception. We find that a person who has desire thinks of it in the same manner (that is, he does not regard it as an evil, so far as he himself is concerned); and that is due to the very nature of desire.[28] All gifts and oblations are made in this way; and we shall arrive at the same conclusion if we divide desires into parts and distribute them (when we shall find that the possessor of desire will have that which he regards as good for himself). That is the reason why a man seeks means to achieve his object.

Desire and Action

कृतत्वात्तु कर्मणः सकृत्स्याद्द्रव्यस्य गुणभूतत्वात्॥४६॥
शेषदर्शनाच्च॥४७॥
अप्रयोजकत्वादेकस्मात्क्रियेरञ्छेषस्य गुणभूतत्वात्॥४८॥
संस्कृतत्वाच्च॥४९॥
सर्वेभ्यो वा कारणाविशेषात् संस्कारस्य तदर्थत्वात्॥५०॥
लिङ्गदर्शनाच्च॥५१॥
एकस्माच्चेद्याथाकाम्यमविशेषात्॥५२॥

If the object of desire is unessential or secondary, we find that it is desired only once; for we see that it is so from the actual result. Even when a person does not desire to act, he must still do so, because he depends for his very existence on the result of actions; and we see that it is so from what he actually does. Thus we see that it is because of this that all creatures engage in action,—for they have the same identical motive (namely, to live); and this may be seen from their characteristics.[29] Again, if a number of persons act as a result of a common desire, their actions will be in accordance with their desire.

Special Forms of Expression

मुख्याद्वापूर्वकालत्वात्॥५३॥
भक्षाश्रवणाद्दानशब्दः परिक्रये॥५४॥
तत्संस्तवाच्च॥५५॥
भक्षार्थो वा द्रव्ये समत्वात्॥५६॥
व्यादेशाद्दानसंस्तुतिः॥५७॥

(Certain ideas have been expressed in a special manner; for instance,) priority of time gives us the idea of whåt is first or most important. If we do not hear that a person has anything for food or drink, we should take it that the word *dāna* (giving) means distribution of food; and we are familiar with that meaning of the word. Again, food is identical with a material substance, and that is how we can get its meaning. It is for this reason that the act of giving is praised, and there is a special injunction to that effect.

PART V

CHARITY, DESIRE AND SATISFACTION

Introduction

Acts of charity or *dāna* are good deeds. It is only when something is left over or saved that it can be given away as charity or gift, and it is an act of sacrifice.

A whole means the whole of what exists at a particular time, and it is divisible into parts. The same is true of all kinds of actions. Actions are different from one another; and in order to understand them, we should divide them into parts. There are some who believe that action gives satisfaction to the soul and not the mind; but we should examine this opinion carefully before accepting it.

The origin of desire is knowledge, and animate and not inanimate objects derive satisfaction from it. This idea of satisfaction is described in the sacred books in various ways.

The mind and the senses too have their share in satisfaction; and we can understand this from certain terms used in the text. But satisfaction is obtained only when a thing is transformed into something else.

Nature of Dāna

आज्याच्च सर्वसंयोगात्॥१॥

कारणाच्च॥२॥

एकस्मिन्समवत्तशब्दात्॥३॥

आज्ये च दर्शनात् स्विष्टकृदर्थवादस्य॥४॥

Acts of *dāna* or charity are good deeds in all respects; and there is good reason for thinking so. In this case the meaning is obtained by dividing the word (used for goodness) into parts;[30] and we also find that the explanation of the meaning of the expression "properly done"[31] takes us to the idea of goodness.

Conditions of Dāna

अशेषत्वात्तु नैवं स्यात्सर्वादानावशेषता॥५॥
साधरण्यान्न ध्रुवायां स्यात्॥६॥
अक्तत्वाच्च[1] जुह्वां तस्य च होमसंयोगात्॥७॥
चमसवदिति चेत्॥८॥
न चोदनाविरोधाद्धविः प्रकल्पनाच्च॥९॥

It is only when something is left over or saved that it can be given away as gift or charity; and the idea of universal gift or *dāna* cannot last (or is self-contradictory). A gift can be divided into parts like speech, and it is an intelligent act like a *Homa* sacrifice.[32] But it is not like a cake or sweetmeat;[33] for were it so, it would be incompatible with the idea of sacrifice, which requires imagination, ascertainment, selection and arrangement of things[34].

Whole and its Parts

उत्पन्नाधिकारात्सति सर्ववचनम्॥१०॥
जातिविशेषात्परम्॥११॥
अन्त्यमरेकार्थे॥१२॥
साकम्प्रस्थायये स्विष्टकृदिडञ्च तद्वत्॥१३॥
सौत्रामण्यां च ग्रहेषु॥१४॥
तद्वच्च शेषवचनम्॥१५॥

When we use the word "whole", it means in every case the whole of what is produced; and it is greater than the different things of which it is made. When we divide the whole into its parts, the last in the series can have but one purpose to serve; and the same is the case with a sacrifice or an offering properly

1. अवत्तत्वाच्चेति क्वचित्पाठः।

and intelligently made. The same is true of actions associated with *Indra* too,[35] and also of all actions referred to in the sacred books[36].

Different kinds of Actions

द्रव्यैकत्वे कर्मभेदात्प्रतिकर्म क्रियेरन्॥१६॥

अविभागाच्च शेषस्य सर्वान्प्रत्यविशष्टित्वात्॥१७॥

Actions differ although the material substances associated with them may be the same; and so all actions should be performed. In order to understand an action, we should divide it into parts till nothing is left; then, beginning with the last, go back to the first[37].

Action and Satisfaction

ऐन्द्रवायवे तु वचनात्प्रतिकर्म भक्षः स्यात्॥१८॥
सोमेऽवचनाद् भक्षो न विद्यते॥१९॥
स्याद्वाऽन्यार्थदर्शनात्॥२०॥
वचनानि त्वपूर्वत्वात्तस्माद्यथोपदेशं स्युः॥२१॥

According to some teachers, there should, in every action associated with *Indra* and *Vāyu*[38], be a measure of satisfaction; but not so in the case of action associated with *Soma*[39],-although in certain circumstances it may be so, if we see a different meaning in what they say[40]. But these teachings are new, and we should see that they do not conflict with the rules.

The Origin of Desire is Knowledge

चमसेषु समाख्यानात्संयोगस्य तन्निमित्तत्वात्॥२२॥
उद्गातृचमसमेकः श्रुतिसंयोगात्॥२३॥
सर्वे वा सर्वसंयोगात्॥२४॥
स्तोत्रकारिणां वा तत्संयोगाद्बहुश्रुः॥२५॥
सर्वे तु वेदसंयोगात्कारणादेकदेशे स्यात्॥२६॥

When we hear the name of sweetmeats or cakes, a desire arises within us, and the cause of the desire is the name itself. We may hear only one man sing the praise of the cake; or it may be all, because all are associated with it; or only the singers of its praise may desire to have it,—having been drawn to it from what they have heard. All these desires are associated with knowledge, and so should be grouped together[41].

Satisfaction

ग्रावस्तुतो भक्षो न विद्यतेऽनाम्नानात्॥२९॥
हारियोजने वा सर्वसंयोगात्॥२८॥

(There can be no satisfaction in the case of inanimate objects; and so) the sacred books do not tell us that the *Soma*-stones get any satisfaction when the *Soma*-juice is pressed out.[42] This satisfaction arises when one secures an attractive object; and so it may be said to arise from association with all objects.

How Described

चमसिनां वा सन्निधनात्॥२९॥
सर्वेषां तु विधित्वात्तदर्था चमसिश्रुतिः॥३०॥
वषट्काराच्च भक्षयेत्॥३१॥
होमाऽभिषवाभ्यां च॥३२॥
प्रत्यक्षोपदेशाच्चमसानामव्यक्तः शेषे॥३३॥
स्याद्वा कारणभावादनिर्देशश्चमसानां कर्तुस्तद्वचनत्वात्॥३४॥
चमसे चान्यदर्शनात्॥३५॥

The idea of satisfaction is expressed in terms of a cake, because we get it when we have it. The meaning of all other words, like the mention of a cake, is also in accordance with the same rules. Similarly, we should understand that the exclamation *Vaṣaṭ* refers to satisfaction in the performance of action;[43] and the same idea is expressed by *Homa* and *Soma* sacrifices.[44] The difference between cakes and other expressions is that the idea of satisfaction is obvious in the one case,—not so in the rest. But even in the case of other expressions we should understand that there is a reference to satisfaction through action, because there is good reason for doing so;

and even where there is no special mention of cakes, we should understand, from a general statement of the text, that there is a reference to the doer of the deed. In the case of a cake, we can understand the idea of satisfaction from a different point of view[45].

Satisfaction of the Senses and the Mind

एकपात्रे क्रमादध्वर्युः पूर्वो भक्षयेत्॥३६॥
होता वा मन्त्रवर्णात्॥३७॥
वचनाच्च॥३८॥
कारणानुपूर्व्याच्च॥३९॥

If we interpret the text in accordance with *Krama*, we shall find that it is the *Adhvaryu* priests[46] (the ten senses of knowledge and action) who get satisfaction through action first; or it may be the *Hotṛ* priest[47] (the mind), as we may find from the form of the *Mantras*. We get this from the meaning of the text, and for a good reason too.

Idea of Satisfaction: How Expressed

वचनादनुज्ञातभक्षणम्॥४०॥
तदुपहूत उपह्व[1] यस्वेत्यनेनानुज्ञापयेल्लिङ्गात्॥४१॥
तत्रार्थात्प्रतिवचनम्॥४२॥
तदेकपात्राणां समवायात्॥४३॥
याज्यापनयेनापनीतो भक्षः प्रवरवत्॥४४॥
यष्टुर्वा कारणागमात्॥४५॥

This satisfaction is permitted in accordance with the teachings of the sacred books. The text contains words like "invite", "invited in that place"; and if we understand the character of its language, we shall see that it is in this manner that a request is made; and it is in accordance with this meaning that these words are repeated in the text.[48] Thus there is only one meaning of the text for those who have mastered it, for they understand the intimate relation of things. But even if we

1. उपहूयस्वेति क्वचित्पाठः।

commit a mistake in grasping the idea of satisfaction, it does not mean that it is not there. Nor is it denied to the worshipper,[49] merely because there appears to be some cause.

Satisfaction Implies Transformation

प्रवृत्तत्वात्प्रवरस्यानपायः॥४६॥
फलचमसो नैमित्तिको भक्षविकारः श्रुतिसंयोगात्॥४७॥
इज्याविकारो वा संस्कारस्य तदर्थत्वात्॥४८॥
होमात्॥४९॥
चमसैश्च तुल्यकालत्वात्॥५०॥
लिङ्गदर्शनाच्च॥५१॥
अनुप्रसर्पिषु सामान्यात्॥५२॥
ब्राह्मणा वा तुल्यशब्दत्वात्॥५३॥

We can attain to perfection by means of devotion to our task, and the errors or defects of the whole family can be removed thereby. The effect of enjoyment in a cake is produced in a special manner,—namely, that its whole form is changed; and that is what the sacred books say.[50] It is in the same manner that an act of sacrifice is transformed to yield satisfaction; and this is illustrated by a *Homa* sacrifice"[51] (a good and intelligent deed). The same idea is expressed by means of cakes, but in a more obvious manner,—for this satisfaction arises as soon as we eat them. We can verify this for ourselves; and it is a matter of common observation to see people moving towards cakes; and the *Brāhmaṇas*[52] too,—for the same language is used in connection with them.

PART VI

SELF-INTEREST AND NATURAL DESIRE: HOW TO UNDERSTAND THE VEDAS

Introduction

Self-interest is inherent in man. It cannot be seen; it can only be understood.

Self-interest has two forms, which may be described as natural motive and deliberate motive; and the conflict between them may be seen in the discussion that goes on within us. But discussion has its purpose too; and it can modify natural motive as well as desire. Natural motive precedes discussion; and it is not only an intelligent, but also a good, desire that can be associated with the idea of sacrifice.

There is a common law of life applicable to all animals, because there is no essential difference between them at any time; and their similarity of behaviour is due not to similarity of motive, but of nature.

Natural desire comes first, and the idea of its purification afterwards. Lower animals are characterised by an urge in respect of primary and not secondary actions and objects; and there is little difference in their milk, which is easily affected by time.

We can understand the text of the Vedas in the same manner as we understand the laws of life relating to animals; and it should be judged in the light of the meaning it yields. For instance, if we find that there is something incongruous in a certain portion of the text, we should take it that it needs a new meaning. But certain conditions need to be satisfied before one meaning can be substituted for another.

Self-interest is inherent in Man

सर्वार्थमप्रकरणात्॥१॥

प्रकृतौ वाऽद्विरुक्तत्वात्॥२॥

तद्वर्जं तु वचनप्राप्ते॥३॥

Self-interest is not aroused by discussion. It is in the very nature of man, and does not need to be restated to be understood,—though we often speak of it.

It cannot be seen

दर्शनादिति चेत्॥४॥

न चोदनैकार्थ्यात्॥५॥

उत्पत्तिरिति चेत्॥६॥

न तुल्यत्वात्॥७॥

We cannot say that it can be seen, -for it is a rule that we can do only one thing at a time; nor can we say that we can see it arise, because it is not possible to do so, unless we mean that seeing is the same thing as understanding, because they are so similar in this case.

Natural and deliberate Interest

चोदनार्थकात्स्न्यात्तु मुख्यविप्रतिषेधत्प्रकृत्यर्थः॥८॥

प्रकरणविशेषात्तु विकृतौ विरोधि स्यात्॥९॥

नैमित्तिकं तु; प्रकृतौ तद्विकारः, संयोगविशेषात्॥१०॥

इष्ट्यर्थमग्न्याधेयं प्रकरणात्॥११॥

न वा तासां तदर्थत्वात्॥१२॥

लिङ्गदर्शनाच्च॥१३॥

(There are two forms of self-interest,—which may be described as natural motive and deliberate motive). There is an impelling force or cause in all action; but there can be a conflict between this force and the chief purpose that a man may have in view when he acts. Hence, this impelling force may be called natural motive. But because of the special importance of discussion that takes place within us, this natural motive may be an obstacle in the development of action. But discussion has its own purpose too, because it is produced by some cause, and may be said to be a modification of natural motive itself, for it is closely connected with it. Again, desire improves through discussion; and the purpose of desire, when it is associated with discussion, may be compared to putting fire in a sacrificial fireplace[53]. But discussion does not produce desire, because it is meant to serve the purpose of desire; and we can see the proof of it ourselves.

Natural Motive

तत्प्रकृत्यर्थं यथान्येऽनारभ्यवादाः॥१४॥
सर्वार्थं वाऽऽधनस्य स्वकालत्वात्॥१५॥
तासामग्निः प्रकृतितः प्रयाजवत् स्यात्॥१६॥
न वा तासां तदर्थत्वात्॥१७॥

(Natural motive precedes discussion) and may be compared to a discussion that has not yet begun. But all motive, in respect of any action, arises at its own proper time. However, of all desires, the desire to perform an intelligent action alone should, by its very nature, be regarded as preceding an act of sacrifice; but this is not true of all such desires, because of the meaning of sacrifice[54].

A Law of Life

तुल्यः सर्वेषां पशुविधिः प्रकरणाविशेषात्॥१८॥
स्थानाच्च पूर्वस्य॥१९॥
श्वस्त्वेकेषां तत्र प्राक्श्रुतिर्गुणार्थां॥२०॥
तेनोत्कृष्टस्य कालवधिरिति चेत्॥२१॥
नैकदेशत्वात्॥२२॥
अर्थेनेति चेत्॥२३॥
न श्रुतिविप्रतिषेधत्॥२४॥

The law of life that is true of the five classes of animals[55] is true of all, for the explanation in all cases is the same; and they continue to remain in their original state without change. Indeed, so far as we can understand, their attributes and objects are the same, and will be so in future too. We cannot say that they are what they are because of the effect of Time, because they are so made,—as part of a great whole. Nor can we say that their similarity of behaviour is due to similarity of motive, because it would be contrary to reason (to suppose that their motives can always be the same).

Natural Desire of an Animal

स्थानात्तु पूर्वस्य संस्कारस्य तदर्थत्वात्॥२५॥

लिङ्गदर्शनाच्च॥२६॥
अचोदना गुणार्थेन॥२७॥
दोहयोः कालभेदादसंयुक्तं शृतं स्यात्॥२८॥
प्रकरणाविभागद्वा तत्संयुक्तस्य कालशास्त्रम्॥२९॥

The first desire (of an animal is its natural desire) arising from its original state; the idea of its purification comes later,—from the object it seeks; and this can easily be proved. There is also an absence of urge in respect of subordinate objects. But there is little difference between any two kinds of milk; and that which has not been mixed with anything should be boiled, because it is affected by time. But that which is mixed with something is also affected by time, and for the same reason.

How to understand the Sacred Books

तद्वत्सवनान्तरे ग्रहाम्नानम्॥३०॥
रशना च लिङ्गदर्शनात्॥३१॥
आराच्छिष्टमसंयुक्तमितरैः सन्निधनात्॥३२॥
संयुक्तं वा तदर्थत्वाच्छेषस्य तन्निमित्तत्वात्॥३३॥
निर्देशाद् व्यवतिष्ठेत॥३४॥
अग्न्यङ्गमप्रकरणे तद्वत्॥३५॥
नैमित्तिकमतुल्यत्वादसमान विधनं स्यात्॥३६॥
प्रतिनिधिश्च तद्वत्॥३७॥

As we are able to understand the laws of life relating to animals, we can, in the same manner, understand the meaning of the sacred books; and when we do so, the whole thing appears like a new ray of light. (But we must understand them from their own point of view; because) what has been taught long ago cannot be connected together by means of present-day objects[56]. But if we are able to connect things together, we should understand them in the light of the result they yield; and that should be proved to be true by means of definite knowledge.

(Indeed, there are suggestions to guide us in the text itself: for instance,) if in a portion of a hymn addressed to *Agni*, there is something which appears to be irrelevant to the main idea, we should take it to be of this kind (that is, that it needs to be interpreted in another way). Again, if a thing is known to be produced by a certain cause, but is not described as such, we should understand that the difference lies in its mode of expression; and that is how one meaning is substituted for another.

Conditions to be Satisfied

न तद्वत् प्रयोजनैकत्वात्॥३८॥
अशास्त्रलक्षणत्वाच्च॥३९॥
नियमार्था गुणश्रुतिः॥४०॥
संस्थास्तु समानविधनाः प्रकरणाविशेषात्॥४१॥
व्यपदेशश्च तुल्यवत्॥४२॥
विकारास्तु कामसंयोगे नित्यस्य समत्वात्॥४३॥
अपि वा द्विरुक्तत्वात्प्रकृतेर्भविष्यन्तीति॥४४॥
वचनात्तु समुच्चयः॥४५॥
प्रतिषेधच्च पूर्वलिङ्गानाम्॥४६॥
गुणविशेषादेकस्य व्यपदेशः॥४७॥

But the substitute should not have the same meaning as the original word on the ground that its purpose is the same,—because that would be contrary to rules; and this restriction makes for excellence of composition of the *śruti*. But similar statements should stand together and should not be interpreted differently, because there is no difference in their explanation; and in such cases the names should be of the same kind. Indeed, the apparently different expressions are but modifications of the same thing; and have been introduced to relieve monotony, which is otherwise inevitable, because the laws of Nature, sought to be described, are eternal, and therefore the same. Even so when the same idea is differently expressed, the form of expression should be natural, not forced;

and the entire statement should make a coherent whole. This is necessary, because the symbols, understood in their traditional sense, are contradictory; but the name of each principal object has been formed in the light of its special characteristics (and so it is possible to know its exact idea).

PART VII

THE METHOD OF INTERPRETATION: NATURE, SACRIFICE AND THE SOUL

Introduction

Certain names, which appear to be unconnected with the rest of the text, refer to Nature; but we should be careful in arriving at this conclusion.

Nature is associated with the soul, without which we cannot understand the idea of action.

Certain terms used in connection with the performance of a sacrifice, refer to Nature; others refer to the function of the mind, and so on.

The result of a sacrifice accrues to the sacrificer, and so he should engage in it himself,-at least so far as its principal part is concerned; and he may employ others to do the rest. All this is described in the sacred books under different names. For instance, the ten Adhvaryu priests refer to the ten senses; and we have also the idea of detachment or disinterestedness in action. There are also other terms used in the text; and all the constituents of action are called *Ṛtvij* priests. They are sixteen in number, and the "master of the sacrifice" or the soul is the seventeenth; and all these perform all kinds of actions referred to in the sacred books.

Similarly the function of *Mitra* and *Varuṇa* is to ordain action; but we should come to this conclusion when certain other words are also used in the text. We can get the meaning of *Adhvaryu* and other words by means of this method of interpretation.

This is the method of interpretation of the Vedas, and it should be applied to other sacred books as well (50). This will enable us to understand the idea of Dharma. All this is given explicitly in the *Añgas* of the Vedas: in the remaining works not so explicitly.

Certain Words refer to Nature

प्रकरणविशेषादसंयुक्तं प्रधनस्य॥१॥

सर्वेषां वा शेषत्वस्यातत्प्रयुक्तत्वात्॥२॥

आरादपीति चेत्॥३॥

न तद्वाक्यं कि तदर्थत्वात्॥४॥

लिङ्गदर्शनाच्च॥५॥

Where certain names appear to be unconnected with the text, they should be deemed to refer to Nature (*Pradhāna*),[57] because of the special manner in which they have been explained. But all unconnected expressions are not of this kind. Nor can we apply this rule to all expressions, however removed from the context, because this mode of expression is intended to serve a special object, which can easily be proved[58].

Nature and the Soul

फलसंयोगात्तु स्वामियुक्तं प्रधनस्य॥६॥

चिकीर्षया च संयोगत्॥७॥

तथाऽभिधनेन॥८॥

तद्युक्ते तु फलश्रुतिस्तस्मात्सर्वचिकीर्षा स्यात्॥९॥

(This reference to Nature is due to the fact that) Nature is always associated with its "master" or the soul, because all action has a result, which would be meaningless otherwise.[59] This result is achieved by means of the desire to act; and that is possible only through the union of the soul with Nature,—for desire arises when they are brought into close contact with each other;[60] and the result is also achieved by means of the union of the two,—for that is the purpose of desire.

Other References to Nature

गुणाऽभिधनात्सर्वार्थमभिधनम्॥११॥

दीक्षादक्षिणं तु वचनात्प्रधनस्य॥११॥
निवृत्तिदर्शनाच्च॥१२॥
तथा यूपस्य वेदि:॥१३॥

By putting together the attributes of an object we put together its idea or meaning; and we find that the consecration for a religious sacrifice and the fee paid to the priest also refer to Nature;[61] because, like all other things in Nature, these too must come to an end. In the same manner the *Vedi* (raised piece of ground for the sacrificial altar) of *Yūpa* (a sacrificial post) also refers to Nature[62].

Reference to the Mind

देशमात्रं वाऽशिष्टेनैकवाक्यत्वात्॥१४॥
सामिधेनीस्तदन्वाहूरिति हविर्द्धानियोर्वचनात्सामिधेनीनाम्॥१५॥
देशमात्रं वा प्रत्यक्षं ह्यर्थकर्म सोमस्य॥१६॥
समाख्यानं च तद्वत्॥१७॥

Some one, incapable of being taught in connection with what has been stated above, might ask, 'What is the idea of measuring the sacrificial ground, the recitation of *Sāmidhenī* verses, and the two vessels in which the *Soma* plants are conveyed to be pressed, which, according to instruction, are associated with these verses?"[63] Measuring the ground refers to the function and purpose of the mind;[64] and the whole narrative is like that.

Sacrificer and his Servants

शास्त्रफलं प्रयोक्तरि तल्लक्षणत्वात्तस्मात् स्वयं प्रयोगे स्यात्॥१८॥
उत्सर्गे तु प्रधनत्वाच्छेषकारी प्रधनस्य तस्मादन्य: स्वयं वा स्यात्॥१९॥
अन्यो वा स्यात्परिक्रयाम्नानाद्विप्रतिषेधत्प्रत्यगात्मनि॥२०॥
तत्रार्थात्कर्तृपरिमाणं स्यादनियमोऽविशेषात्॥२१॥

The result of sacrifice, referred to in the sacred books, is obtained by the per former of the sacrifice, because he is the cause of sacrifice; and he should engage in it himself. In any case, the principal part of the sacrifice, being the most important, should be performed by him; and, as for the rest, he may do it himself, or get it done by some one else. Another person may be engaged to do the less important part of it; and the hiring out of such a person is permitted by the sacred books, specially when the sacrificer is prevented from doing it himself. Thus, the measure of the part of the sacrificer depends on the circumstances of each case; and no fixed rule can be laid down, because no special distinction can be made.

Different kinds of Actions

अपि वा श्रुतिभेदात्प्रतिनामधेयं स्युः॥२२॥
एकस्य कर्मभेदादिति चेत्॥२३॥
नोत्पत्तौ हि॥२४॥

However, the sacred books make a distinction in regard to different kinds of actions, and different names have been given to their actors. We cannot say that these different names refer to the same actor who performs these different actions, because the results are clearly different.

Adhvaryu Priests

चमसाध्वर्यवश्च तैर्व्यपदेशात्॥२५॥
उत्पत्तौ तु बहुश्रुतेः॥२६॥
दशत्वं लिङ्गदर्शनात्॥२७॥

The names of *Adhvaryu* priests have been given to them in accordance with this statement; and that has been stated in a number of sacred books. Their number should be ten, because we can verify it for ourselves[65].

Detachment

शमिता च शब्दभेदात्॥२८॥
प्रकरणाद्वोत्पत्त्यसंयोगात्॥२९॥

There should also be a *śamitṛ*[66] (detachment, which keeps the mind calm), because there is a special mention of that name.

This is clear from the subject under discussion, because we are told that we should not think of results[67].

Other Factors of Action

उपगाश्च लिङ्गदर्शनात्॥३०॥
विक्रयी त्वन्यः कर्मणोऽचोदितत्वात्॥३१॥

There is also a reference to other constituents of action,—those factors that are inclined towards their objects, as we can see for ourselves. For instance, the "seller" represents the slow movement of action, for he is the person who makes it move slowly.

Ṛtvij Priests

कर्मकार्यात्सर्वेषामृत्विक्त्वमविशेषात्॥३२॥
न वा परिसङ्ख्यानात्॥३३॥
पक्षेणेति चेत्॥३४॥
न सर्वेषामधिकारः॥३५॥
नियमस्तु दक्षिणाभिः श्रुतिसंयोगात्॥३६॥
उक्त्वा च यजमानत्वं तेषां दीक्षाविधनात्॥३७॥

All the constituents of action are called *Ṛtvij* priests, because they cannot be distinguished, and are not exclusive of one another.[68] This is not a mere theory or hypothesis, because all of them have the right to engage in an act of sacrifice; and there is a rule, about which there is general agreement, that all these "priests" should be given "gifts" when a sacrifice is performed.[69] Indeed, their different functions have been laid down, for they alone are initiated in the work[70].

Master of Sacrifice

स्वामिसप्तदशाः कर्मसामान्यात्॥३८॥

The "master" is the seventeenth to share it with them[71].

Their Actions

ते सर्वार्थाः प्रयुक्तत्वादग्नयश्च स्वकालत्वात्॥३९॥

तत्संयोगात् कर्मणो व्यवस्था स्यात्, संयोगस्यार्थवत्त्वात्॥४०॥
तस्योपदेशसमाख्यानेन निर्देशः॥४१॥
तद्वच्च लिङ्गदर्शनम्॥४२॥

All these perform all kinds of actions,—according as they are suited to them; and the idea of the "fires" is the same, because they have their proper time.[72] It is because of their combination that there is constancy in action; and that is why their combination is so important.[73] There is a reference to all this in the sacred books, and a detailed description of it in the form of a narrative; and we can see it for ourselves in that form.

Mitra and Varuṇa

प्रैषानुवचनं मैत्रावरुणस्योपदेशात्॥४३॥
पुरोऽनुवाक्याधिकारो वा प्रैषसन्निधनात्॥४४॥
प्रातरनुवाके च होतृदर्शनात्॥४५॥

According to the teachings of the sacred books, the function of the two gods, *Mitra* and *Varuṇa*,[74] is to ordain action, and to lay down instructions in connection with its performance. But this conclusion can be drawn only when certain words are repeated in the text, and the word *Praisha* (meaning "direction") occurs in close proximity; and there is also a reference to the Hotṛ (the mind) in the hymns to be recited in the morning[75].

Meaning of Adhvaryu

चमसांश्चमसाधवर्यवः समाख्यानात्॥४६॥
अधवर्युर्वा तन्न्यायत्वात्॥४७॥
चमसे चान्यदर्शनात्॥४८॥
अशक्तौ ते प्रतीयेरन्॥४९॥

The *Adhvaryu* priests get their share of sweetmeats (satisfaction), because it is so stated in the text; and the meaning of the word can be obtained by applying the method of interpretation.[76] We can do so when we understand the other meaning of the word Chamasa[77]; and also grasp the idea (of Adhvaryu) in a state weakness[78].

Result of Interpretation

वेदोपदेशात्पूर्ववद्वेदान्यत्वे यथोपदेशं स्युः॥५०॥

तद्गुणाद्वा स्वधर्मः स्यादधिकारसामर्थ्यात्सहाङ्गैरव्यक्तः शेषे॥५१॥

This is the method of interpreting the Vedas, and it should be applied to other sacred books as well.[79] This will enable us to get a proper idea of Dharma.[80] The authority for this is given explicitly in the *Añgas* of the Vedas, because the meaning there is clear; while it is not so explicit in the remaining works[81].

PART VIII

THE PROBLEM OF ACTION: THE METHOD OF INTERPRETATION

Introduction

The task of the "master" or the soul is to acquire some-thing. The impressions of previous actions impel the soul to act; and the other faculties engage in action because of the the soul. The urge to action depends on the nature of the soul; and, as all souls are not equal, their actions are different; *Tapas* or meditation too is a cause of this difference; but all other faculties depend for their action on the soul. Desire too is associated with the soul.

The *Mantras* also refer to the soul; and we should understand them in their proper light.

Actions may be referred to the different organs of the body in which the soul abides We should interpret the text in the light of action, the idea of which is described in different ways; but the fruit of action always belongs to the soul.

Action implies improvement as well as change, but not the creation of a new substance; and this is stated in the Vedas.

As action implies change, the form of words in the text

has to be changed in order to get their real meaning; but this change should be made only when we are unable of get a suitable meaning otherwise.

There is an element of Time in action, and it too implies change; but its idea is dealt with elsewhere.

We should not divide into parts words which are not in close proximity to one another.

Task of the Soul

स्वामिकर्मपरिक्रयः कर्मणस्तदर्थत्वात्॥१॥

वचनादितरेषां स्यात्॥२॥

The task of the "master of action"[82] (the soul) is to acquire something,—for that is the object of his action. The acquisition of something can be the task of others (other faculties of man) only if it is so expressly mentioned in the text.

Impressions of Previous Actions

संस्कारास्तु पुरुषसामर्थ्ये यथावेदं कर्मवद्व्यतिष्ठेरन्॥३॥

याजमानास्तु तत्प्रधनत्वात्कर्मवत्॥४॥

व्यपदेशाच्च॥५॥

गुणत्वेन तस्य निर्देशः॥६॥

There are impressions of acts, done in a previous state of existence, on the powers or faculties of *purusha* or the individual soul, which, so far as we are aware, compel it to engage in action.[83] But all the faculties, associated with the "master of the sacrifice"[84] (the soul), engage in action, because of the importance of the soul. All this is quite well known; and we know it from the fact that they all depend on the soul[85].

Action and Nature of the Soul

चोदनां प्रति भावाच्च॥७॥

अतुल्यत्वादसमानविधनाः स्युः॥८॥

तपश्च फलसिद्धित्वाल्लोकवत्॥९॥

वाक्यशेषश्च तद्वत्॥१०॥
वचनादितरेषां स्यात्॥११॥
गुणत्वाच्च वेदेन न व्यवस्था स्यात्॥१२॥

The impelling urge to action depends on the nature of the soul; and, as all souls are not equal,[86] their methods of performing actions are different. *Tapas* or meditation is also a cause of this difference, as we find from the achievement of results in ordinary life. But the general idea in regard to the other faculties has already been explained; and because they all depend on the soul, the latter cannot be restricted to any one of them[87].

Desire and the Soul

तथा कामोऽर्थसंयोगात्॥१३॥
व्यपदेशादितरेषां स्यात्॥१४॥

Desire too is associated with the soul,[88] because of its connection with the object to be achieved. It can be associated with the other faculties only when so expressly mentioned[89].

Mantras and the Soul

मन्त्राश्चाऽकर्मकरणास्तद्वत्॥१५॥
विप्रयोगे च दर्शनात्॥१६॥

The *Mantras* too, when they do not refer to the performance of action, are like that (that is, they refer to the soul). They are associated with the inspired and wise ones in this way, as we may see for ourselves.

How to Understand Them

द्व्याम्नातेषूभौ द्व्याम्नानस्याऽर्थवत्त्वात्॥१७॥

ज्ञाते च वाचनं; न ह्यविद्वान् विहितोऽस्ति॥१८॥

A *Mantra*, occurring in two places in two different sacred books, is true in respect of both, because it is full of meaning; and we should recite *Mantras* in such a manner that we understand them. An unlearned person is verily not intended for the task.

Actions and Adhvaryu Priests

याजमाने समाख्यानात्कर्माणि याजमानं स्युः॥१९॥
अध्वर्युर्वा तदर्थो हि; न्यायपूर्वं समाख्यानम्॥२०॥

We find from an account of the text, that actions are referred to what belongs to the sacrificer;[90] and they should indeed be referred to that. That is the idea of the *Adhvaryu* priests (the senses), and the whole statement of the text follows an organised plan.

How to interpret the Text

विप्रतिषेधे करणः; समवायविशेषादितरमन्यस्तेषां, यतो विशेषः स्यात्॥२१॥
प्रैषेषु च पराधिकारात्॥२२॥
अधवर्युस्तु दर्शनात्॥२३॥
गौणो वा कर्मसामान्यात्॥२४॥

In case of conflict of statements, we should interpret the text in terms of action, because that is how the principal ideas have been put together. With regard to the rest, such meaning as is suitable, may be assigned. The idea of action is expressed in terms of orders issued by some one in authority. The *Adhvaryu* priests also refer to action, as may be seen; but they are subordinate to some one else because action is shared by others (other faculties) too[91].

Fruit of Action, and meant for Whom

ऋत्विज्फलं करणेष्वर्थवत्त्वात्॥२५॥
स्वामिनो वा तदर्थत्वात्॥२६॥
लिङ्गदर्शनाच्च॥२७॥
कर्मार्थं तु फलं; तेषां स्वामिनं प्रत्यर्थवत्त्वात्॥२८॥
व्यपदेशाच्च॥२९॥

When we understand the significance of this, we shall see that the action of the *Ṛtvij* priests (faculties of man other than his soul) makes for the fruit or result of action. But the fruit really belongs to the "master" or the soul, because it is meant for it. This can easily be proved, because the object of all action is its result or fruit, which, in every case, belongs to the "master" or the soul; and we know that it is so.

Action and Improvement

द्रव्यसंस्कारः प्रकरणाऽविशेषात् सर्वकर्मणाम्॥३०॥
निर्देशात्तु विकृतापूर्वस्याऽनधिकारः॥३१॥
विरोधे च श्रुति[1] र्विशेषादव्यक्तः शेषे[2]॥३२॥
अपनयस्त्वेकदेशस्य विद्यमानसंयोगात्॥३३॥

All action, without exception, is meant for improvement or a better order of things. But while action implies change, it does not mean the creation of a new substance. This is expressly stated in certain special texts of the Vedas; while with regard to the rest, the idea is not so explicit. If, however, there is an error of interpretation in regard to a portion of the text, it can easily be discovered by means of close study.

Change of Form of Words

विकृतौ सर्वार्थः शेषः प्रकृतिवत्॥३४॥
मुख्यार्थो वाऽङ्गस्याचोदितत्वात्॥३५॥
सन्निधनविशेषादसम्भवे तदङ्गानाम्॥३६॥
आधनेऽपि तथेति चेत्॥३७॥
नाऽप्रकरणत्वादङ्गस्यातन्निमित्तत्वात्॥३८॥
तत्काले वा[3] लिङ्गदर्शनात्॥३९॥
सर्वेषां वाऽविशेषात्॥४०॥
न्यायोक्ते लिङ्गदर्शनम्॥४१॥

---

१. विरोधादिति वृतौ पाठः।
२. वृतौः शेष इति च।
३. वेति वृतौ नास्ति।

All things are subject to change, and so they are like Nature or *Prakṛti* in this respect; (and that is one of the reasons why the form of certain words referring to these objects is changed). But in interpreting the text we should first of all get the principal meaning of a word, without reference to its parts; and it is only when there is a special cause,—that is, when we get an inconsistent or impossible meaning that we should resort to its division into parts.

When we divide a word into parts, its whole sense is altered; for the parts have no connection with the text, and the reason for having them is that they alter the sense. We can see the proof of this at once, for this is true; of all cases without exception; and we can verify it if we but pronounce the words correctly.

Action and Time

मांसं तु सवनीयानां चोदनाविशेषात्॥४२॥

There is an element of Time in connection with the performance of all action; but there is a Special rule in connection with it[92].

Restrictions

भक्तिरसन्निधवन्याय्येति चेत्॥४३॥

स्यात्प्रकृतिलिङ्गद्वैराजवत्॥४४॥

It is, however, possible to say that it would not be correct to divide into parts words which are not in close proximity to one another; for instance, if we wish to know the real meaning of the word *Virāj* in its rudimentary form, we should know the context in which it is used[93].

NOTES

1. The soul is said to be the enjoyer or experiencer of the result of action, and so it is the soul that is said to feel pleasure and pain (BhG. XIII, 21-22). In that case the soul must be deemed to be an actor too.
   The point of view of the *Sāṅkhyas* is somewhat different. While it agrees that all result is meant for the sake of *puruṣa* or the soul,-the highest result

is that which makes for the purification of the soul, and so makes it free. The *Bhāgāvad Gītā* also tells us that all action is meant for the purification of the soul (BhG. V, 11). The *Sāṅkhya*, however, believes that it can be attained by means of knowledge.

2. The *Mīmāṁsā* has divided actions into two kinds,—main and subsidiary, or deliberate and reflex. The law of one action at a time applies only to deliberate actions, because subsidiary or reflex actions can go on at the same time. There is a fixed relation of time and place in respect of deliberate, and not subsidiary, actions.
3. The word in the text is *śabda*, which means oral testimony of wise and trustworthy persons. We know from their statement that there is a fixed relation of time and place in respect of deliberate actions. We have no other means of finding this, and have no reason to doubt their statement.
4. We have already been told that there are certain descriptions in the text of the Vedas which appear to reflect on persons otherwise held in high esteem; and that leads us to believe that there is likely to be some other meaning of the text (Cf. I, ii, 45).
5. The idea of *Krama* has already been explained (Cf. II iv. 3, n.).
6. *Cf.* II, iii, 19.
7. *Tvashṭṛ* is said to be a god,—"the heavenly builder and creator of living beings". He is also said to be a maker of divine implements-specially of *Indra's* thunderbolt.

   The *Mīmāṁsā* tells us that he refers to the mind, because of the reference to his drinking *Soma*, which also means the mind. This means that *Tvaṣṭṛ* is conceived to be the supreme Mind which creates all things. The special attribute of the Mind is Desire; and the *Upaniṣads* tell us that creation takes place through the desire of the Supreme (RV. X, cxxix, 3-4; Ch. Up. VI, ii, 3; Tait. Up. II3 vi). *Indra*"s thunderbolt would accordingly refer to the function of the mind.
8. The number thirty is a multiple of 3 and 10; and the one refers to the mind and the other to the senses of knowledge and action, as the *Mīmāṁsā* tells us later on. Hence, it refers to the function of the mind in association with the senses. We cannot get the meaning of this number in the same simple way as that of *Tvāṣṭṛ*, for it requires a different approach.
9. *Vaṣaṭ* is an exclamation uttered by the *Hotṛ* priest at the end of the sacrificial verse, on hearing which the *Adhvaryu* priest casts the oblation offered to the deity into the fire.

   As we shall see, the Hotr priest refers to the mind, and the Adhvaryu to the senses; while fire, as the *Mīmāṁsā* has told us, refers to the function of the intellect. We are now told that *Vaṣaṭ* signifies the performance of action: that is to say, it is an indication by the mind *(Hotṛ)* to the senses *(Adhvaryu)* that a particular action may be done in accordance with the direction of the intellect.

10. The word *Chanda* has a number of meanings, one of which is desire, which, as the *Gītā* tells us, may be an obstacle in our path (BhG. III, 37-43).
11. *Agni*, as we have been told, refers to the intellect; while Indra, the Upanishads tell us, refers to the self-conscious soul; and the two may, for practical purposes, be identified. But we can also distinguish between them, as the *Mīmāṁsā* tells us.
12. This means that there are certain desires which are both intelligent and good, and so are personified as gods; for all desires are not an obstacle in the path of our progress. The *Bhāgāvad Gītā* also tells us that Kṛṣṇa or God himself is Desire, unopposed to Dharma, in all creatures (BhG. VII,); that is to say, whenever a person has a desire which is characterised by Dharma (good and intelligent desire, meant for the benefit of all), he should regard it as the voice of God within him.
    Desire is personified as a god in the sacred books in the form of *Kāma-deva*,—"the god of Desire" or "Desire regarded as a god";
    and he is also spoken of as the god of love, because that is the highest and purest form of desire; and so *Kāma-deva* is said to be the name of *Viṣṇu*, the supreme Creator, himself.
13. *Aitiśāyana* means a descendant of Itiṣa, about whom very little is known. But his opinion is cited in the *Mīmāṁsā* in more than one place.
14. Drinking means drinking wine, which refers to the mind, for *Soma* means wine as well as the moon or the mind. The *Mīmāṁsā* tells us that Desire is a characteristic of the Mind, for it arises from attachment to the function of the mind (drinking wine).
15. *Soma* or the *Soma* plant refers to the mind, and its "juice" to desire, which is "pressed" out of it. Desire also refers to a desirable object, or the object of desire; and it is in this sense that it is used here in the text.
    According to *Aitiśāyana* it is a common characteristic of desire that all those who have it believe that they are entitled to have it fulfilled,—that is, to possess the object of their desire.
16. It is not possible to have a real desire unless we also believe, however erroneously, that it can be satisfied, and we can achieve the object we seek. That is how desire is followed by action, which would be impossible otherwise.
17. The Vedas, as the *Mīmāṁsā* has told us, deal with the three Guṇas or attributes of Nature, which are said to embrace all forms of life in the universe, including Man,—all except his soul. But, as the *Mīmāṁsā* tells us later on, we cannot understand the nature of the soul except with reference to the other faculties of man,—his intellect, mind, and the senses; and, as all these are subject to the *Guṇas*, we might say that all that we can imagine, including the character and functions of the soul,—in so far as we can understand them-comes under the purview of the *Guṇas*, and so constitutes the subject-matter of the Vedas.

But, as the *Mīmāṁsā* tells us, the Vedas deal with the problem in the light of Dharma or a moral law of life, which is also its own subject-matter; and Dharma is based on action characterised by knowledge or discrimination. The *Mīmāṁsā* has told us that the other systems have dealt with the problem of knowledge and action, but not discovered its law; and its own problem is to discover it. Now what integrates the two is Desire which, as the *Mīmāṁsā* tells us, begins as knowledge and ends as action, and is reborn as knowledge again. Thus, if we wish to understand the law of knowledge and action, we should understand the law of Desire; and if we do so, we can understand the essence of what is contained in the three Vedas.

18. The function of the mind is twofold,—*Nāma* and *Rūpa*—giving a name and calling up an image; while the function of the intellect is discussion, decision, or drawing an inference.
19. The highest form of action is said to be that which is disinterested or devoid of any special purpose or aim; and so having a purpose is sometimes regarded as a weakness or defect in action.
20. At the same time we cannot act without purpose; and so the *Mīmāṁsā* makes it clear that good actions or the actions of virtuous men do not involve any taint. These actions are a sacrifice,—good, intelligent and meant for the benefit of all; and so, as the *Bhāgāvad Gītā* tells us, we can perform such actions and yet be free from any taint (BhG. III, 9, 13; IV, 19-23, 32; V, 7-12, etc.).
21. There are a number of hymns in the Vedas addressed jointly to *Indra* and *Agni*; but that does not mean that they can act jointly.
22. Toothlessness can illustrate the idea of one action at a time; for when a toothless person puts food into his mouth, he can only swallow it. We cannot say in his case that the teeth act on the food or the food on the teeth; and as it is he himself that is acting on it, we see clearly that there can be only one action at a time.
23. It would be diffcult to explain the meaning of these words without reference to the context.
24. The *Bhāgāvad Gītā* tells us that he is a wise man who sees in-action (actionlessness) in action, and action in actionlessness; and so performs all kinds of actions (BhG. IV, 18). Thus there is no essential difference between the two; and so, if there is purpose in action, there must be one in actionlessness too. The *Mīmāṁsā* explains later on that the idea of actionlessness must be understood in a relative and not an absolute sense,—and with reference to time. That is, that there comes a time when a person cannot act; and that is the time of death,—for it is only then that he can really give up action.
25. The *Mīmāṁsā* tells us that this is the subject-matter of the *rig* Veda: it deals with the problem of action conceived in the widest sense of the term, and without any limitations.

26. *Homa* is an act of making an oblation to the gods by pouring clarified butter into the fire. We have seen that fire refers to intelligence; and, as we shall see, clarified butter refers to the idea of goodness. *Homa* is, therefore, an act of adding goodness to intelligence in an action; and it is this that makes it an act of sacrifice.
    We have explained that of the three kinds of sacrificial fires, *āhavanīya* refers to intelligent action performed in the world; and as such action must be for the benefit of others too, *āhavanīya* is closely associated with *Homa*.
27. This is the idea of desire that is not opposed to Dharma, referred to in the *Bhāgāvad Gītā* (BhG. VII, 11).
28. It is the nature of desire that the possessor of it does not regard it as evil,—at least so far as he himself is concerned.
29. We have the same idea in the *Bhāgāvad Gītā* (BhG. III, 8).
30. The word used in the text is *ājya* which, as has already been observed, signifies goodness. This *Sūtra* tells us that we can get this meaning by dividing the word into parts; and we are told later on that we should divide it into two parts.
    The word *ājya* would accordingly have to be reduced to aja, for it means "relating to *aja*"; and *aja* may be divided into *aja*; and we have to understand its idea by giving suitable meanings to these letters.
    The letter "a" has a number of meanings; but the most suitable here would be "not" and "like"; and, similarly, the most suitable meanings of "*ja*" would be "poison" and "enjoyment". *Aja* would, accordingly, mean "not poison" or "like enjoyment"; and, with reference to desire, imply that desire is not evil, and may be deemed to be even enjoyable. Hence it signifies goodness as an essential element of desire.
    Ajya also means "clarified butter" poured over the sacrificial fire: and, as the *Mīmāṁsā* has told us that fire or *Agni* means intelligence, "the pouring of *ājya* (clarified butter) over *Agni*" would mean adding goodness to intelligence in an act of sacrifice.
31. The word in the text is *Sviṣṭa-kṛt*, which means "properly done"; and it is also a name of *Agni*. As the latterrefers to the intellect, the idea is that an action intelligently done alone can be properly done; and it leads to the idea of goodness too.
32. The idea of *Homa* as a good and intelligent action has already been explained.
33. Giving *dāna* or making a real offering of charity is not like giving away sweetmeat or a cake. It is an act of sacrifice. The *Bhāgāvad Gītā* tells us of the different ways in which dāna can be made; and the best gift is that which is made to a proper man, in a proper place, and at the proper time, and is given because it is the right thing to do (BhG. XVII, 20-22).
34. The word in the text is *Kalpanā*, which means "imagining, ascertaining, selecting, putting in proper place".

35. *Indra*, as the Upaniṣads tell us, refers to *Prājñātman* or the self-conscious soul.
36. All actions may be divided into parts, and the last in the series can serve but one purpose.
37. As the idea of the division of a word into its parts corresponds to that of an action, we have, in a number of cases, to put together the meanings of the parts of a word in the manner explained in this *Sūtra*: that is, begin with the last letter, and go back, step by step, to the first. There are a number of such cases in the MM. I-V.
38. *Indra* refers to the soul, and *Vāyu*, commonly believed to be Air, to its vital breath; and the two are closely allied.
39. *Soma* refers to the Mind, as has already been explained.
    The point of these two *Sūtras* is that there are some who believe that, while action gives satisfaction to the soul and its vital breath, it does not give satisfaction to the mind. The author of the *Mīmāṁsā*, however, does not agree with this view; for he tells us later on that not only the mind, but the senses too get their share of satisfaction.
40. But he is careful to add that, although these teachers hold certain views, it is possible to read some other meaning too in what they say; and, in that case, we may find that the mind has its share of satisfaction in action too.
41. The origin of desire is knowledge, which arises when the senses (ears) come into contact with an object (or when we hear the praise of a cake). The *Bhāgāvad Gītā* also tells us that when a man thinks of the objects of the senses, he forms attachment for them, and that gives rise to desire (BhG. II, 62); and again we are told that the senses are drawn towards their objects (BhG. Ill, 34), which gives rise to the function of the mind and its attribute,—desire.
42. *Soma* refers to the mind; and *Soma-stones* would refer to the objects of nature, by means of which desire is generated or "pressed out". Desire is, accordingly, expressed in terms of *Soma-juice*.
43. The idea of *Vaṣaṭ* has already been explained. It refers to the performance of action; and the *Mīmāṁsā* tells us that the fact that we are directed to perform an action implies that there is satisfaction in it.
    The expression for "satisfaction" in the text means literally "eating and drinking".
44. *Homa* refers to a good and intelligent act; and both goodness and intelligence are of the essence of the idea of sacrifice.
    Soma refers to the mind; and so *Soma*-sacrifice refers to the proper function of the mind.
    The *Mīmāṁsā* tells us that there is satsifaction in doing a good and intelligent act (*Homa*), and also in a proper function of the mind (Soma-sacrifice).
45. The idea of satisfaction in a cake is obvious, for we get it when we eat it. It is not quite so obvious in the other instances, and we have to make an

effort to understand it. There can be no action without satisfaction of some kind; nor can there be any without a doer of the deed: and this is what the *Mīmāṁsā* tells us.

46. It is said that there are four *Ṛtvij* priests who take part in a sacrifice instituted by a *Yajamāna* or a sacrifices, who pays for it. They are *Brāhmaṇa*, *Udgātṛ*, *Hotr*, and *Adhvaryu* of these the *Mīmāṁsā* defines *Brāhmaṇa* to mean the intellect and tells us that the *Adhvaryus* are ten in number, and so would refer to the ten senses of knowledge and action. Of the remaining two, the *Mīmāṁsā* tells us that we can get their meaning by dividing the words into parts; and then we shall see that they refer to *ahankara* (or the I-as-an-actor) and the mind respectively. Thus the four *ritvij* priests refer to the four faculties of man,—his intellect, the I-as-an-actor, mind, and the senses; and this will enable us to understand that the *Yajamāna* or the sacrificer, for whose sake these "priests" engage in action, is really the soul.

It is said that each of these *ri*tvij priests is assisted by three more; and if we understand the meaning of their names, we shall find that they refer to the same faculties of man. For instance, a *Brāhmaṇa* or intellect is assisted by three others, who refer to *ahaṃkāra* (the I-as-an-actor), mind, and the senses respectively; *Udgātṛ* is assisted by those who refer to the intellect. mind, and the senses; and so on. The idea obviously is that, in any intelligent action, all the four faculties of man have their part to play: only the principal role, at a particular time, may belong to any one of them.

47. As *Adhvaryu* refers to the senses, the *Hotṛ* refers to the mind. The idea of satisfaction is described in the *Sūtras* in terms of eating food.

48. The terms "invited", "invite" mean an invitation to eat or to share in the performance of an action and derive satisfaction from it.

49. The worshipper, as has been pointed out, refers to the soul, for whose sake all the faculties of man take part in action. Were there no soul, there would be no action. But the soul is not "actionless" as some would believe; for it has its place in action, and "pays" for it,—even as the *Yajamāna* bears the cost of the sacrifice. As the *Bhāgāvad Gītā* tells us, the soul is an enjoyer or experiencer of action; and so it has a principal share in satisfaction.

50. A cake gives pleasure when it is eaten; but, when it is eaten, its entire form is changed. This may be said to be a law of joy or satisfaction. In order to give pleasure, satisfaction or joy, a thing must transform itself, and cease to be what it is.

51. To do this is an act of sacrifice; and so sacrifice implies a transformation of a person or thing that engages in, or is offered as, a sacrifice. The *Mīmāṁsā* tells us that this is illustrated by a Homa sacrifice, in which an offering is made by casting clarified butter into the fire. But the latter is totally changed when cast into the fire; and this would illustrate the point.

The idea of Sacrifice, as a means of this transformation, is exemplified in the story of *Sikhaṇḍin* in the *Mahābhārata*, where we are told that a person, born as a woman, was transformed into a man by its means. The real idea, however, is that the form of Nature or *Prakṛti* (represented as a woman) can be transformed into that of *Puruṣa* or God (represented as a man) by means of the idea of Sacrifice (MM. IV, 153-155).

52. The *Mīmāṁsā* defines a *Brāhmaṇa* as one characterised by intelligence,—or a particularly intelligent person. Even intelligent persons like to take eat sweetmeats or cakes; and so the latter can easily symbolise the idea of pleasure or satisfaction obtained through action.

53. When desire is associated with discussion,—that is, when our motive of action is under discussion within us, the object is that the desire should be purified or rendered fit for action performed as a sacrifice.

54. Sacrifice requires that an action should not only be intelligent but also good. Intelligence, however, is a necessary pre-requisite of action performed as a sacrifice; and so an intelligent desire precedes such action. But, as it is only a desire that is also good that can make an act of sacrifice, it is not all intelligent desires that can be associated with sacrifice.

55. The word used in the text is *Paśu*, which refers to five classes of animals,-men, cows, horses, goats and sheep (p. 21. n.). But the law of life that is true of these animals, is true of all, says the *Mīmāṁsā*

56. The Vedas were composed long ago, and they need to be interpreted in the light of the ideas of their own times. This is as true today as it was in the days of *Jaiminī* when he wrote the *Mīmāṁsā*. But even in his days the original idea of the Vedas appears to have been almost lost.

57. The word used in the text is *Pradhāna*, which refers to Nature or *Prakṛti*.

58. The special object is to explain the character of action, which is so closely connected with Nature; and this is made clear in the following *Sūtras*.

59. We cannot understand the character of action, so closely associated with Nature, without reference to the soul. We can grasp its idea only in the light of our own actions, or the experience of those who live; and, as we cannot have an idea of life without that of the soul, we cannot understand the character of action without it. Hence the necessity of associating Nature with the soul.

    The word for the soul in the text is *Svāmin*, which means "master, lord", and is also the name of *Viṣṇu* or *Shiva*. The "master" of Nature is the soul or God.

60. The *Bhāgāvad Gītā* says the same (BhG. II, 62; III, 34, etc.).

61. This means that the forces of Nature can be associated with the idea of Sacrifice; that is to say, we can believe that they act in accordance with a law, which is characterised by both goodness and intelligence, and is applicable to all alike. It is this that gives us the idea of God; and we might say that Nature itself is transformed into God by means of the idea of sacrifice. This is exemplified in the story of *Sikhaṇḍin* in the *Mahābhārata*, to which reference has already been made.

62. All this is meant to illustrate the idea of sacrifice in Nature; that is to say, the raised ground, altar, sacrificial post, etc.., are all intended to represent

the working of the great forces of Nature in accordance with a moral and intelligent law.

63. *Sāmidhenī* verses are recited while the sacrificial fire is kindled, and so would refer to the function of the intellect, for that is the idea of fire in the sacred books.
As the *Soma* plant refers to the objects of Nature, the two "vessels" which convey it to be pressed, would obviously refer to the two kinds of senses,—of knowledge and action,—which come into contact with these objects.

64. The word used in the text is *Soma*, which refers to the mind, as has already been explained.

65. *Adhvaryu priests* refer to the senses of knowledge and action, which are ten in number.

66. *Samitṛ* means "one who keeps his mind calm"; and it refers therefore to detachment or disinterestedness in action. There are a number of references to this in the *Bhāgāvad Gītā* (BhG. II, 56-58 etc.).

67. The *Bhāgāvad Gītā* also tells us that we are entitled to act, but not to claim the fruit or result of action (BhG. II, 47).

68. The *Ṛtvij* priests, as has already been pointed out, refer to the four faculties of man,-his intellect, *ahañkāra* or the I-as-an-actor, mind, and the senses. As the *Mīmāṁsā* explains later on, all these are closely connected with one another, and it is not always easy to distinguish between them. For instance, the intellect and the mind may, in certain circumstances, be identified. On the other hand, the mind is sometimes regarded as an organ of sense.

69. Although these faculties are connected with one another, they yet have their special functions to perform; and the "gift" or "fee" paid to them indicates that their work has been properly done. The *Mīmāṁsā* has explained that a "gift" signifies satisfaction in the performance of action.

70. All these faculties have their special functions, and the work of the senses cannot be done by the mind, and so on; nor can the function of one sense organ be performed by another. Thus each is specially initiated to do its own work.

71. There are four principal *Ṛtvij* priests, and each of them is assisted by three more,-making a total of sixteen; and their idea has already been explained. The "master" or *Svāmin* is the soul; and he is the institutor of the sacrifice; and all these "priests" work for him, and are paid their "fee".

72. As has already been explained, "fire" refers to intellect or intelligent action; and the three fires,*Gārhapatya*, *Ahavanīya*, and *Dakṣiṇa*-refer to the three ways in which an intelligent action can be performed: to preserve one"s self or the family; to work for others in the world; and so to act that one is not tainted by the evil effects of action (See II. iii. 21. n.).

73. The importance of the combination of all these faculties is described in terms of the three assistants of each one of the principal *Ṛtvij* priests. The idea is that, even if we assign the principal role to the intellect, *ahañkāra*, mind, or an organ of sense,-the remaining three must also be there before

an action can take place. That is why each of the *Ṛtvij* priests has three assistants to help him.

74. The original form of the word *Mitra is Mitra*; and Mit is is derived from Mi, meaning "to measure, to judge", which is a function of the intellect; while Tra is the same as Tri, meaning "three", which, as the *Mīmāṁsā* tells us, refers to the mind. *Mitra or Mit-tra*, accordingly, signifies the function of the intellect and the mind; and the two, as the Mīmāṁsā tells us, may even be identified.

Varuṇa is described as the lord of waters which, as the *Mīmāṁsā* tells us, refer to Nature. He represents, therefore, the idea of Nature or Prakṛti as the supreme creator of life (*Cf.* MM. I, 392-397).

Now, if we believe in Nature as the chief creator of life, the logical conclusion is that we must renounce all actions if we wish to be happy and free. The idea of renunciation of action is accordingly associated with *Varuṇa*; and this is said to be his "noose", from which it is difficult to escape.

But *Varuṇa* and *Mitra* are often invoked together; and when that is done, they ordain action, for so the *Mīmāṁsā* tells us. As *Mitra* refers to the function of the intellect and the mind, it means that if we look at Nature in an intelligent manner, we realise that we cannot refrain from all actions; for to do so would be to put an end to one's life.

Varuṇa accordingly does not represent an uncompromising attitude towards action, and so is friendly to other gods, who represent different points of view. The attitude of total renunciation of action s represented by *Vṛtra*, the Serpentdeity, who stops all flow of waters or the working of the great forces of Nature, and so must be "slain" (*Cf.* MM. I, 304-310).

75. But even *Varuṇa* and *Mitra* do not represent the idea of action without end: they do so under certain conditions, which are represented in a particular manner in the Vedas. According to their idea, we can act only when all life is before us (or we are in the morning of our life), and our mind is fresh and vigorous; and so there should be a reference to the *Hotṛ* priest, who refers to the mind, in the hymns recited in the morning. When, however, the evening of life approaches (or we are at the point of death), all actions must cease; and so the idea of the renunciation of action has its point too.

The idea of *Vedānta*, on the other hand, is that after death there is life again, and even God himself is born from age to age; and so there is no end whatever to action.

76. We are told that there are ten Adhvaryu *priests*; and, as the number ten refers to the ten senses of knowledge and action, this enables us to understand that the *Adhvaryu* priests refer to these senses.

Again the word *Adhvaryu* means "one who institutes an *Adhvara*", which is said to be the name of a *Soma* sacrifice. The word *Adhvara* is *A-dhvara*; and the latter is derived from the root Dhvr; and we have to get its meaning from "a" and "*Dhvṛ*"; and the latter is composed of *Dh, u, r*; so that the whole word depends on the meaning of these four letters. Of these "a" is a particle of negation; "*dh*" refers to the mind; "u" to the senses of knowledge; and "*r*" to the senses of action; and so the whole meaning is "(a) not (dh) the mind; but (u) the senses of knowledge and (ṛ) the senses of action".

As the senses, however, cannot be dissociated from the mind, Adhvara is said to be a name of a Soma sacrifice or a function of the mind.

77. *Camasa* is said to be a vessel used for drinking *Soma*. It also means sweetmeat, which symbolises satisfaction. We are required to take the latter meaning.

78. When we are in a state of weakness, our senses refuse to function, and we get no satisfaction in action. This enables us to understand the part of the senses in satisfaction; and this corresponds to the *Adhvaryu* priests getting their share of sweetmeats.

79. The word Veda is mentioned in the text twice; and, as it refers to Vedas as well as a book of sacred knoweldge, it has been taken in both these senses. It is in this sense that both the *Rāmāyaṇa* and the *Mahābhārata* are spoken of as Vedas. The *Mīmāṁsā* tells us later on that this method of interpretation is applicable to *śruti* as well as the *smṛti*. Indeed, it applies to the great Epics and the *Purāṇas* as well as the *Upaniṣads* and other sacred works.

80. This method of interpretation enables us to understand that the Vedas deal with the problem of Dharma or the law of action in the world, conceived in its widest significance, and characterised by both goodness and intelligence.

81. There are six *Vedāñgas* (*Añgas* or sub-divisions of the Vedas). They are regarded as auxiliary to, and a part of, the Vedas, and are composed in *Sūtra* form. The *Mīmāṁsā* tells us that we can understand their idea directly and explicitly from their text; while in the case of other works we have to resort to this method of interpretation.

82. The word in the text is *Svāmin* which, as has already been explained, refers to the soul.

83. All this is clearly described in the *Bhagāvad Gītā* (VI, 37-45); and there are references to it in the Upaniṣads too. It is a cardinal point of Hindu belief, and explains the law of human action in terms of continuity of life without end.

84. The word in the text is *Yajamāna*, which means "master or institutor of the sacrifice"; and that, as has already been observed, refers to the soul.

85. The dependence of the other faculties on the soul is rendered in the Upaniṣads in terms of the story of the "quarrel" of the *Pranas* or the organs of man,-each striving for supremacy. In the end they are satisfied that they all depend on the vital breath, the vehicle of the soul (Ait-Ar. Up. II, i, 4,5; Kauś. Up. II, 14).

86. As all souls do not begin their journey of life at the same time, they may be said to be at different stages, and so are not equal. The *Mīmāṁsā* has told

us that the impressions of previous actions impel the soul to action; and if we assume that the soul begins its journey through life at some time, we will also assume that the story of its actions begins at that time; and then the chain of action can go on without end. This gives us a rational explanation of inequalities between man and man; and that is the idea of inequality between souls. But this theory postulates that we must agree to begin the story of life somewhere.

87. This means that all the faculties of man have their fixed abode in the body,—all except the soul. It is obvious that the senses have their fixed place; and the ancients fixed the mind in the lower, and the intellect in the upper, part of the head. But the soul was conceived to be free to move among all these faculties; and they function when it is associated with them. Thus, when the soul associates itself with the eye, the latter sees; when it associates itself with the ear, the latter hears; when it associates itself with the lower part of the head, corresponding to the brow, there is thought; and when it associates itself with the upper part of the head, there is judgement or decision.

88. As the soul is conceived to be an actor, desire must necessarily be associated with it. It may be of interest to observe that both Nyāya and *Vaiśeṣika* associate desire with the soul (NS. Ill, ii, 39; VS. I, i, 5-6).

89. Desire is said to be a special attribute of the mind. But that only means that when the soul associates itself with the mind-centre, a man has desire; even as when the soul associates itself with the eye, a man sees.

90. The "sacrificer" is the soul; and what belongs to him are the different organs of the body in which the soul abides. This is made clear in the following *Sūtra*, where we are told that the reference is to the *Adhvaryu* priests or the organs of the senses.

91. It is not the senses alone that take part in action. The other faculties,-the mind, *ahaṅkāra*, and the. intellect have a share in it too; and the senses are subordinate to them.

92. This has been explained in Chapter IV, iii.

93. *Virāj* is sometimes described as a male and sometimes as a female power; and we can understand its true character only if we know the context in which it is used.

CHAPTER - IV

ACTION, MOTIVE AND THE SOUL

PART I

THE METHOD OF INTERPRETATION

Introduction

Let us inquire into the laws of action with reference to the soul, and understand the nature of motive in action.

The cause of action is the desire to obtain some satisfaction; and, as this desire serves the purpose of the soul, the soul is concerned in each action; for the result belongs to the soul, and without it there can be no action. But this applies to animate and not inanimate objects, which serve the purpose of living creatures and impel them to action; for it is a self-evident truth that the soul cannot engage in action by itself.

It is necessary to understand the nature of purpose in action. A person who is in a state of uncertainty or divided opinion, cannot act; and so there must be a definite purpose before he can act. Desire means that there is such purpose; and it implies dependence as well as attachment.

There is diversity of purpose and action: nevertheless, all things meet and mingle in the world; and this is symbolised by the formation of curd out of milk as well as by Nature or *Prakṛti*.

A principal word in the text has a special significance.

Action and purpose as well as all things are dependent on

one another; but we can see the working of this law more clearly in animals than in inanimate objects.

If a substance is produced in a particular place, it means that there is a certain connection between the two.

The difference in the performance of the same action is due to the skill of the doer of the deed. But certain courses of action have a special cause, and require special direction. This, however, does not apply to cases where the principal cause of action is well known.

If the principal cause of action is not clear, the explanation should be contained in the language of the text itself, without the division of words into parts. But the common meaning of certain words like *Jauhava* and *Anuyāja* makes little sense, and they need to be understood in a different way.

Action and the Soul

अथातः क्रत्वर्थपुरुषार्थजोर्जिज्ञासा॥१॥

Let us inquire into the law of action with reference to *purusha* or the individual soul, and understand the nature of motive or the cause of action.

Cause of Action

यस्मिन्प्रीतिः पुरुषस्य तस्य लिप्सा, ऽर्थलक्षणाऽविभक्तत्वात्॥२॥

A man always desires to obtain some satisfaction or pleasure: that is the object of his life; and the motive or cause of action is the same (that is, to obtain some satisfaction or pleasure).

Desire

तदुत्सर्गे कर्माणि[1] पुरुषार्थाय; शास्त्रस्यानतिशङ्क्यत्वान्न च द्रव्यं चिकीर्ष्यते; तेनार्थेनाभिसम्बन्धत् क्रियायां पुरुषश्रुतिः॥३॥

अविशेषात्तु शास्त्रस्य यथाश्रुति फलानि स्युः॥४॥

अपि वा कारणाऽग्रहणे तदर्थमर्थस्याऽनभिसम्बन्धात्॥५॥

1. कर्मणीति वृत्तौ पाठः।

Desire is the root of action, for an action can be performed only when there is some desire to urge it on; and it is performed for the sake of the soul: the sacred books say so too. That an action is meant to serve the purpose of the soul is evident from the fact that an inanimate object can have no desire of its own. Hence purpose or desire is the basis of all action, and that is how it is connected with it; and the sacred books tell us that the *purusha* or the individual soul is concerned in each action. Thus, as there is no difference of opinion in the matter, the result of action should belong to the soul, as has been stated in the *śruti*. But even if we do not understand the exact cause of action, we cannot deny that it is meant to serve the purpose of the soul,—for the purpose is always there; for otherwise there can be no connection between purpose and action, and so no action at all.

This is True of all Living Creatures

तथा च लोकभूतेषु॥६॥
द्रव्याणि त्वविशेषेणाऽऽनर्थक्यात् प्रदीयरेन्॥७॥
स्वेन त्वर्थेन सम्बन्धे द्रव्याणां पृथगर्थत्वात्तसमाद्यथाश्रुति स्युः॥८॥
चोद्यन्ते चार्थकर्मसु[1]॥९॥
लिङ्गदर्शनाच्च॥१०॥
तत्रैकत्वमयज्ञाङ्गमर्थस्य गुणभूतत्वात्॥११॥
एकश्रुतित्वाच्च॥१२॥
प्रतीयत इति चेत्॥१३॥
नाऽशब्दं तत्प्रमाणत्वात्पूर्ववत्॥१४॥
शब्दवत्तूपलभ्यते तदागमे हि दृश्यते तस्य ज्ञानं[2] हि यथाऽन्येषाम्॥१५॥
तद्वच्च लिङ्गदर्शनम्॥१६॥
तथा च लिङ्गम्॥१७॥

This is true of all living creatures in the world, but it does not apply to inanimate objects, which can only be given away,

---

1. चार्थकथास्विति वृत्तौ पाठभेदः।
2. तं यथेति वृत्तौ पाठः।

because they cannot act by themselves. Inanimate objects are associated with living creatures because they serve their purpose; and so their use is different from that of the latter; and we should accept what the sacred books tell us in this connection. They impel the living to different kinds of actions, which are characterised by purpose; and all this can easily be proved, for the soul cannot engage in any action by itself, and must be associated with something else as an auxiliary, to be able to do so. That something is desire, which is like a string, connecting the soul with its object; and all the sacred books are agreed that it is so.

This does not require any further proof, for it is a self-evident truth, and requires no words to establish it. Indeed, we understand it as soon as we read and grasp the language of the Vedas,—the knowledge of which can be acquired in the same way as that of other things. It is in this manner that the whole thing can be proved, and indeed is proved.

The Nature of Purpose

आश्रयिष्वविशेषेण भावोऽर्थः प्रतीयेत॥१८॥
चोदनायां त्वनारम्भो विभक्तत्वान्न ह्यन्येन[1] विधीयते॥१९॥
स्याद्वा द्रव्यचिकीर्षायां भावोऽर्थे च ॥२०॥
अर्थे[2] समवैषम्यमतो द्रव्यकर्मणाम्॥२१॥
एकनिष्पत्तेः सर्व समं स्यात्।२२॥
[3]संसर्गरसनिष्पत्तेरामिक्षा वा प्रधनं स्यात्॥२३॥

It is necessary to understand the nature of purpose of all objects, without exception, that are connected with one's self. We find that when a person is directed to act, but does not do so, it is because he is in a state of uncertainty or divided opinion, and does not know what to do; (and this means that there must be a definite purpose before a man can act). Desire means that

---

1. ह्यनेनेति वृत्तौ पाठः।
2. याद्धिीति वृत्तौ पाठः। क्वचिदन्यत्र यादद्वीति पाठः।
3. अर्थेनेति वृत्तौ पाठः।

there is such a purpose, which is associated with some object, and implies dependence arising from attachment.[1] It is for this reason that there is diversity of purpose in connection with the actions of a person; and what is true of one, is true of all. But it is also a law that all things must meet and mingle in the world, and this is symbolised by the formation of curd out of milk, as well as by Nature or *Prakṛti*[2].

How Described

मुख्यशब्दा[1] भिसंस्तवाच्च॥२४॥
पदकर्माप्रयोजकं नयनस्य परार्थत्वात्॥२५॥

The principal word in the text has a special significance, without which the word itself would not serve any useful purpose[3].

Action, Purpose and Objects

अर्थाभिधनकर्म च भविष्यता संयोगस्य तन्निमित्तत्वात्तदर्थो हि विधीयते॥२५॥
पशावनालम्भाल्लोहितशकृतोरकर्मत्वम्॥२७॥

It is a law of Nature that purpose and action should be linked together, and both associated with the objects of life; for it is ordained that all things should depend on one another. But it is in animals more than in inanimate objects that we see a clear evidence of this law, for there is no action of blood and excrement in the case of the latter.

Law of Production

एकदेशद्रव्यश्चोत्पत्तौ विद्यमानसंयोगात्॥२८॥
निर्देशात्तस्यान्यदर्थादिति चेत्॥२९॥
न शेषसन्निधनात्॥३०॥
कर्म कार्यात्॥३१॥
लिङ्गदर्शनाच्च॥३२॥

---

1. शब्दसंस्तवेति वृत्तौ पाठः।

If a substance is produced in a particular place, it means that there is a certain connection between them. We cannot say that the two are only in close proximity to each other and there is some other cause of the origin of the thing, because there are a number of things in close proximity to that place but are not produced there. This can be proved to be true by working it out.

Cause of Difference in Action

अभिधारणे विप्रकर्षादनुयाजवत् पात्रभेदः स्यात्॥३३॥

न वा पात्रत्वादपात्रत्वं त्वेकदेशत्वात्॥३४॥

हेतुत्वाच्च सहप्रयोगस्य॥३५॥

अभावदर्शनाच्च॥३६॥

सति सव्यवचनम्॥३७॥

न तस्येति चेत्॥३८॥

स्यात्तस्य मुख्यत्वात्॥३९॥

समानयनं तु मुख्यं स्याल्लिङ्गदर्शनात्॥४०॥

(The difference in the performance of an action between man and man is due to the skill of the doer of the deed, specially where the task presents some difficulty: for instance,) in a sacrifice, the act of sprinkling clarified butter from a distance requires some skill, and so there is a difference between person and person in this respect; but if the sprinkling is done from the same place, there can be no question of want of skill, because all can do it. It follows from this that each course of action has its own cause, and there is no exception to this: only it requires a proper direction to pursue a particular course. A particular course, however, may not always be necessary where the principal cause of action is well known: only in that case it should be proved that the principal cause can bring about the required result.

How Described

वचने हि हेत्वसामर्थ्यम्[1]।।४१।।
तत्रोत्पत्तिरविभक्ता स्यात्।।४२।।
तत्र जौहवमनुयाजप्रतिषेधर्थम्।।४३।।
औपंभृतं तथेति चेत्।।४४।।
स्याज्जुहूप्रतिषेधन्नित्यानुवादः।।४५।।
तदष्टसङ्ख्यं श्रवणात्।।४६।।
अनुग्रहाच्च जौहवस्य।।४७।।
द्वयोस्तु हेतुसामर्थ्यं श्रवणं च समानयने।।४८।।

(All this is described in the sacred books). But if the principal cause of action is not clear, the explanation should be found in the language of the text itself; and in this case there should be no division of words into parts. But there are certain words like *Jauhava* and *Anuyāja*,[4] which do not appear to make sense. It may be argued that the text refers to a sacrifice, and so these words do make sense. This may be a convenient way of avoiding a difficulty, for if we do not accept the meaning of the word *Juhū*, it would be necessary to explain what it really means. But the Vedas tell us that the number of *Jauhavas* (sacrificial ladles) is eight (and we should be able to explain this too). This follows logically if we accept the ordinary meaning of the word; but its secondary meaning[5] is more suitable, because it is more in harmony with the entire text.

PART II

ACTION, PURPOSE AND SACRIFICE: THE METHOD OF INTERPRETATION

Introduction

We must choose the meaning of a word that suits the context best, as in the case of the word *Svaru*.

---

1. सामर्थ्ये इति न्यायमालायां पाठः।

Acting means drawing something near to one's self. Action requires the use of a limb of the body, and different limbs perform different actions; and this is signified by the word *Upaveṣa*. The words *Juhoti* and *Haraṇa* have similar meanings.

We cannot accept the common meanings of words; and must have new ones as in the case of *ājya*, or make a selection, as in the case of *Sam-yavana*.

The meaning of certain terms is specially defined: for instance, *Mitra* and *Varuṇa* signify renunciation of action when the work of life is done.

There is purpose in action, and its idea is illustrated by the *Soma* sacrifice.

Action with a purpose arises because of a close connection between the actor and the objects of life.

All purpose has its value; but the final purpose of action is purification.

There is no fixed time or place for action; but all purpose is governed by a law, according to which the purpose of action is not so much the attainment of material objects, as perfection or purification.

Sacrifice means the association together of action, a proper person and a deity; and the same idea is expressed by the word *Juhoti*.

Dana or *charity* is connected with theidea of renunciation.

It is a law that when one action ends, another begins.

It is action that creates, and so is linked up with a purpose.

How to Understand the Text

स्वरूत्वनेकनिष्पत्तिः स्वकर्मशब्दत्वात्॥१॥

जात्यन्तराच्च शङ्कते॥२॥

तदेकदेशा वा स्वरुत्वस्य तन्निमित्तत्वात्॥३॥
शकलश्रुतेश्च[1]॥४॥
प्रतियूपं च दर्शनात्॥५॥

(It is in this manner that we have to understand the meaning of the text). For instance, the word *Svaru* is not limited to a single meaning to complete its sense, and has a number of meanings in connection with its own actions. We can find out its correct meaning from the different ways in which it is used in the text; and there it must be taken as a part of the whole context, and referred to its cause. One of the meanings of the word is "a piece of wood"; and it is also associated with a sacrificial post, as may be seen[6].

Action and its Differentiation

आदाने करोति[2] शब्दः॥६॥
शाखायां तत्प्रधनत्वात्॥७॥
शाखायां तत्प्रधनत्वादुपवेषेण विभागः स्या[3]द्वैषम्यात्॥८॥
श्रुत्यपायाच्च॥९॥

When we say that a person does something, what is meant by doing is that he has drawn something near to himself. The most important part of action is the function of a limb of the body: he has drawn something near to himself, and, in order to be effective, it (action) must be apportioned among the different limbs of the body; and it is this that makes for diversity of action. This (idea of action) is signified by the word *Upaveṣa*; and we get it when we depart from its more common meaning[7].

Meaning of Juhoti and Haraṇa

हरणे[4] जुहोतिर्योगसामान्याद्द्रव्याणां चार्थशेषत्वात्॥१०॥
प्रतिपत्तिर्वा शब्दस्य तत्प्रधनत्वात्॥११॥

---

1. चशब्दरहितः पाठो वृत्तौ।
2. कर्मशब्द इति वृत्तौ पाठ3.
3. वैषम्यं तदिति न्यायमालायां पाठः।
4. तु इति न्यायमालायां अधिकः पाठः।

There are other words like *Juhoti* and *Haraṇa*, which too have to be understood in their supplementary sense;[8] and that is how we get the real meaning of the text.

Common Meaning is not the Real Meaning

अर्थेऽपीति चेत्॥१२॥

न तस्यानधिकारादर्थस्य च कृतत्वात्॥१३॥

उत्पत्त्यसंयोगात्प्रणीतानामाज्यवद्विभागः स्यात्॥१४॥

संयवनार्थानां या[1] प्रतिपत्तिरितरासां तत्प्रधनत्वात्॥१५॥

We cannot say that the common meaning of a word is its real meaning, because it does not give us a proper connection between things, and so we get no meaning at all; and, as we do not get any satisfactory result, we have to think of another method of interpretation, as in the case of the word *ājya*.[9] In some cases we have to choose the meaning that suits the context best: for instance, there are some who explain the word *Samyavana* in one way, and some in another;[10] and we have to choose the best.

Mitra and Varuṇa

प्रासनवन्मैत्रावरुणस्य[2] दण्डप्रदानं कृतार्थत्वात्॥१६॥

(The meaning of certain expressions has been defined in a special way; for instance,) when the rod of authority is handed over to what belongs to *Mitra* and *Varuṇa* (or the priests of that name), it represents the idea of one who has done his life's work, and sits in a great posture of devotion[11].

Purpose and Action

अर्थकर्म वा कर्तृसंयोगात्स्रग्वत्॥१७॥

कर्मयुक्ते च दर्शनात्॥१८॥

उत्पत्तौ येन संयुक्तं तदर्थ तच्छ्रुतिहेतुत्वात्तस्यार्थान्तरगमने शेषत्वात्

---

1. 'वा' इति न्यायमालायां पाठः।
2. वरुणायेति न्यायमालायां पाठः।

प्रतिपत्तिः स्यात्॥१९॥

सौमिके च कृतार्थत्वात्॥२०॥

(There can be no action without a purpose); and when a person engages in action, his action and purpose are linked together like flowers in a garland, each following each in order. We can see this for ourselves when a person engages in action. Purpose is born with a man, according to the teachings of the Vedas; and he goes on from one action to another, because after achieving one purpose he goes on to another. This is illustrated by the *Soma* sacrifice in which we are shown how purpose is achieved.

Action and Purification

अर्थकर्म वाऽभिधनसंयोगात्॥२१॥

प्रतिपत्तिर्वा तन्यायत्वाद्देशार्थाऽवभृथश्रुतिः॥२२॥

It is because a person is brought into contact with the objects of life, that a desire arises within him, and it is followed by action with a purpose. It is in this manner that action takes place, and all purposes have their place; (but they make for bondage too, and so) the Vedas speak of purification (by means of which a person can act and yet be free from taint)[12].

Object of Action

कर्तृदेशकालानामचोदनं प्रयोगे नित्यसमवायात्॥२३॥

नियमार्था वा पुनः[1] श्रुतिः॥२४॥

तथा द्रव्येषु; गुणश्रुतिरुत्पत्तिसंयोगात्॥२५॥

संस्कारे च तत्प्रधनत्वात्॥२६॥

यजति, चोदनाद्रव्यदेवताक्रियं, समुदाये कृतार्थतवात्॥२७॥

तदुक्ते श्रवणाज्जुहोतिरासेचनाधिकः स्यात्॥२८॥

ददातिरुत्सर्गपूर्वकः[2] परस्वत्वेन सम्बन्धः॥२९॥

There is no fixed rule in regard to the relation between

1. पुनश्शब्दरहितः पाठो न्यायमालायाम्।
2. इदं सूत्रं भाष्ये न्यायमालायां च नास्ति।

the actor, place and time; but they are always associated together in any plan of things. But the *śruti* says that all purposes are governed by a law. That is indeed true,—but in so far as it relates to the attainment of material objects. But that, according to the *śruti*, is a secondary object of action, because it only gives rise to action and is not its end; while the highest end of action is purification.[13] (This leads us to the idea of Sacrifice; and) Sacrifice, according to prescribed rule, means the association of a proper person with the great forces of Nature and action; and we get this in the light of the accomplishment of all things.[14] The same idea is expressed by means of *Juhoti*, with the addition of sprinkling water.[15] *Dāna* or an act of charity or gift is clearly connected with the idea of renunciation, because it implies an admission that some one else has a prior claim to the possession of what is given away as a gift.

Action is without End, and it Creates

विधेः कर्मापवर्गित्वादर्थान्तरे विधिप्रदेशः स्यात्॥३०॥
अपि वोत्पत्तिसंयोगादर्थसम्बन्धेऽविशिष्टानां प्रयोगैकत्वहेतुः स्यात्॥३१॥

(There is no end to action, because) it is a law that when a person has done one deed, he must have another object to pursue. Again, it is action that creates; and it is for this reason that it is linked up with a purpose. This is true of all things without exception; and, so far as the commencement of an action is concerned,—the cause in every case is the same[15].

PART III

ACTION AND PURIFICATION: THE METHOD OF INTERPRETATION

Introduction

The highest end of action is purification; but this applies to deliberate, and not accidental, action.

The idea of the purification of material objects is part of the idea of sacrifice.

The Vedas enjoin action, and not their fruit; but we need to understand their language correctly to grasp their idea. This may be illustrated by the idea of Heaven.

Purpose, action and result are connected together like the limbs of the body; and that is the subject-matter of the Aṅgas, "limbs" or parts of the *Mantras* of the Vedas.

The result of an action is achieved more by skill than Time; but if we have done our best and yet fail, we can attribute the failure to Time. The decay of the body may be caused by Time; but, apart from this, the result of an action is due to the character of the impelling force.

Action and Purification

द्रव्यसंस्कारकर्मसु परार्थत्वात्फलश्रुतिरर्थवादः स्यात्॥१॥
उत्पत्तेश्चातत्प्रधनत्वात्॥२॥
फलं[1] तु तत्प्रधनायाम्॥३॥
नैमित्तिके विकारत्वात्क्रतुप्रधनमन्यत्स्यात्॥४॥
एकस्य तूभयत्वे संयोगपृथक्त्वम्॥५॥
शेष इति चेत्॥६॥
नार्थपृथक्त्वात्॥७॥

The highest aim of action is not only to purify the actor, but also the material objects used in connection with it; and if we study the Vedas properly, we shall find, as a result, that this is the explanation of their real meaning.

But action does not begin with the object of purification, although that is its end, and the most important one. This, however, does not apply to occasional or accidental action, which arises in a very different way; and it may or may not contain the idea of purification. We cannot say that this is true of all kinds of actions, because the purpose of deliberate and accidental actions is different.

1. इदं सूत्रं वृत्तौ नास्ति।

Purification and Sacrifice

द्रव्याणां तु क्रियार्थानां संस्कारः क्रतुधर्म[1]त्वात्॥८॥

पृथक्त्वाद्व्यवतिष्ठेत॥९॥

The idea of the purification of the material objects used in connection with a sacrifice is part of the idea of sacrifice itself; for, if we separate the two, the very idea of sacrifice would become meaningless[16].

Vedas and Action: Their Language

चोदनायां फलाश्रुतेः; कर्ममात्रं विधीयेत; न ह्यशब्दं प्रतीयते॥१०॥

अपि वाऽऽम्नानसामर्थ्याच्चोदनार्थेन गम्ये[2]तार्थानामर्थवत्त्वेन वचनानि प्रतीयन्तेऽर्थतोप्य[3]समर्थानामान्त्यें[4] प्यसम्बन्धस्तास्माच्छत्येकदेश[5]स्सः॥११॥

वाक्यार्थश्च गुणार्थवत्॥१२॥

तत्सर्वार्थमनादेशात्॥१३॥

एकं वा चोदनैकत्वात्॥१४॥

स स्वर्गः स्यात्सर्वान्प्रत्यविशिष्टत्वात्॥१५॥

प्रत्ययाच्च॥१६॥

The Vedas enjoin action, but not its fruit; and what is not given in them should not be accepted.[17] The language of the text is appropriate, and we should understand that there can be no effect without purpose. But if the language does not appear to make sense, we should take it that even words in close proximity to one another have not been properly connected together. The *śruti* is really part of a great whole (and all parts of it should be connected together). Words have their meaning, even as qualities convey their own idea; and that is the best meaning which cannot be substituted by any other. A word

1. धर्मः स्यादिति न्यायमालायां पाठः।
2. गम्यते अर्थानां ह्यर्थेति न्यायमालायां पाठः।
   वचनानि प्रतीयन्तेऽर्थतोप्य
3. अपिपदं वृत्तौ नास्ति।
4. न्तर्येण समिति वृत्तौ पाठः।
5. स इत्येतद्रहितः पाठो न्यायमालायाम्।

can have but one real meaning, because it can refer to but one impelling force. (This can be illustrated by means of the idea of) Heaven, as being that which is desired by all without exception: it is also a matter of faith.

Limbs of the Body and Aṅgas of the Vedas

क्रतौ फलार्थवादमङ्गवत्कार्ष्णाजिनिः॥१७॥
फलमात्रेयो निर्देशादश्रुतौ ह्यनुमानं स्यात्॥१८॥
अङ्गेषु स्तुतिः परार्थत्वात्॥१९॥
काम्ये कर्मणि नित्यः स्वर्गो, यथा यज्ञाङ्गे क्रत्वर्थः॥२०॥
वीते च कारणे नियमात्॥२१॥
कामो वा तत्संयोगेन चोद्यते॥२२॥
अङ्गे गुणत्वात्॥२३॥
वीते च[1] नियमसतदर्थम्॥२४॥
सार्वकाम्यमङ्गकामैः प्रकरणात्॥२५॥
फलोपदेशो वा प्रधनशब्दसंयोगात्॥२६॥
तत्र सर्वेऽविशेषात्॥२७॥

Purpose, action, and result are all connected together like the limbs of the body: so says *Kārṣṇājini*. *Atreya* says that there can be no action without result; and if the result is not known, it should be inferred. Thus the praise mentioned in the *aṅgas* (limbs or parts) of the *Mantras* of the Vedas is not mere praise, and is meant for a different and a higher purpose.[18] This refers also to the idea of Heaven, for there is an idea of Heaven in all good actions, even as there is an intelligent purpose in each part of sacrifice. This is how purpose is fulfilled in accordance with the law of life; and it is in accordance with the same law that there is an urge of desire. It is this that is to be found in the aṅgas or sub divisions of the *Mantras* of the Vedas, because the whole idea is so excellent. This law, however, includes the fulfilment of desire, because it is meant to be so; and the aṅgas deal with the objects of desire, as is clear from the explanation of

---

3. चशब्दरहितः पाठो वृत्तौ।

the text; and the reference to the result of action is to be found in the principal word, in all cases without exception.

Result, Skill and Time

योगसिद्धिर्वाऽर्थस्योत्पत्त्यसंयोगात्[1] ॥२८॥
समवाये चोदनासंयोगस्यार्थवत्त्वात्॥२९॥
कालश्रुतौ काल इति चेत्॥३०॥
नासमवायात्प्रयोजनेन[2] ॥३१॥
उभयार्थमिति चेत्॥३२॥
न शब्दैकत्वात्॥३३॥
प्रकरणादिति चेत्॥३४॥
नोत्पत्तिसंयोगात्॥३५॥
अनुत्पत्तौ तु कालः स्यात्प्रयोजनेन सम्बन्धत्॥३६॥

This result is brought about by skill in action,[19] and is not connected with the origin of purpose (or desire); and there is always an impelling force which brings about the union of action with result, and the connection between them is important. We cannot say that the *śruti* refers to Time as the cause of result, for Time is not the cause; for a result does not occur merely because of the passage of time, but requires intention and the means of achieving it. Nor can we say that Time has this double meaning,[20]—because it has but one; and we cannot explain it in that way, because its original meaning is different.[21] But if there is intention and effort, and yet failure to achieve the result, we may attribute this failure to Time.

Idea of Time in the Text

उत्पत्तिकालविशये कालः स्याद्वाक्यस्य तत्प्रधनत्वात्॥३७॥
फलसंयोगस्त्वचोदिते, न स्यादशेषभूतत्वात्॥३८॥

Again if, in our study of the text, there is a doubt about the time of an occurrence, we should conclude that there is a reference to Time only if there is a special mention of it. If

---

१. संयोगित्वादिति न्यायमालायां पाठः।

there is an impelling force, making for a certain result, we should not bring in Time, because it cannot accomplish everything.

Time is the Cause of Decay

अङ्गानां तूपघातसंयोगे निमित्तार्थः॥३९॥

प्रधनेनाभिसंयोगादङ्गानां मुख्यकालत्वम्॥४०॥

अपवृत्ते तु चोदना तत्सामान्यात्स्वकाले स्यात्॥४१॥

An injury to the limbs of the body is the result of some definite cause; but they are all connected with Nature, and so bring out the importance of Time.[22] But where there is no question of this action of Time, all things happen at their own proper time in accordance with the universal character of the impelling force.

PART IV

THE KINDS OF ACTION: THE METHOD OF INTERPRETATION

Introduction

Efforts may be divided into primary and secondary; and between the two are efforts which may be described as neutral. The idea of neutral effort has a special significance, and refers to a state of equanimity in action. There is no contradiction in this, and the point is that an effort which refers to fruit is inferior to that which does not.

All important results are produced by a cause; and this is expressed by means of the word *Jyeṣṭha*.

We should be able to understand the exact idea of effort, because the meaning of these terms is fixed; so is that of a number of others: for instance, *Vaiśvānara*; the number six; oblation offered to the deceased ancestors; rope tied round an animal; the sacrificial posts; ransom; bondage; redemption; and sacrifices performed on the days of the new and the full moon.

A sacrifice or a great good action consists of parts, which may be described as major and minor.

All this is described in the sacred books; and qualities and causes of things are personified and given separate names, which are intended to explain certain effects. This is how we get an account of *Jyotishṭoma*, which refers to rays of light, and is based on scientific knowledge.

Classification of Efforts

प्रकरणशब्दसामान्याच्चोदनानामनङ्गत्वम्॥१॥

अपि वाऽङ्गमनिज्याः स्युस्ततोविशिष्टत्वात्॥२॥

मध्यस्थं यस्य तन्मध्ये॥३॥

सर्वासां वा समत्वाच्चोदनातः स्यान्न हि तस्य प्रकरणं देशार्थमुच्यते मध्ये॥४॥

प्रकरणाविभागे च विप्रतिषिद्धं ह्युभयम्॥५॥

अपि वा कालमात्रं स्याददर्शनाद्विशेषस्य॥६॥

फलवद्वोक्तहेतुत्वादितरस्य प्रधनं स्यात्॥७॥

(The text of the Vedas is so composed that) the same sounds (words, syllables, or letters) have the same meaning; and that tells us that certain efforts should be regarded as primary; while others, not connected with a sacrifice or a great and good action, as secondary; because that is how they have been differentiated. Efforts which are between these two, shoul be regarded as neutral. This is the normal division of efforts,— because that is the character of their impelling force—and it requires no explanation. The effort that is said to occupy a middlemost place has, however, a special meaning[23] .

It may be argued that the word *Madhya*, used in the text, has two meanings,—"middlemost" and "neutral", which are contradictory; and so it is not possible to conceive of a netural effort; or there may be a reference to time, because there can be nothing special in the meaning of the word[24] .

Nevertheless, when we are considering the two kinds of effort, that which is associated with result or fruit should be regarded as inferior to that which is not; and the latter is the most important one[25].

Result is produced by a Cause

दधिग्रहो नैमित्तिकः श्रुतिसंयोगात्॥८॥
नित्यश्च ज्येष्ठशब्द[1]त्वात्॥९॥
सार्वरूप्याच्च॥१०॥

It requires no great excercise of intelligence to understand that result is produced by means of a cause, just as curd is out of milk. All important results are of this kind; and that is signified by the use of the word *Jyeṣṭha*[26] in the text; and that is so because all such efforts are well-arranged.

Meaning of Effort is fixed

नित्यो वा स्यादर्थवादस्तयोः कमण्यसम्बन्धाद्भङ्गित्वाच्चान्तरायस्य॥११॥

We should be able to understand the exact idea of effort, because the explanation of its two meanings (with and without desire for fruit) is fixed. It is only when there is no reference to action, or a roundabout mode of expression, that a difficulty can arise.

Other Words with fixed Meanings: Vaiśvānara

वैश्वानरश्च नित्यः स्यान्नित्यैः समानसङ्ख्यत्वात्॥१२॥
पक्षे वोत्पन्नसंयोगात्॥१३॥

(There are also a number of other words used in the text whose meaning is fixed: for instance,) the meaning of the word *Vaiśvānara* is fixed, because the action which sums up its meaning is fixed; and its idea is connected with what is produced thereby[27].

No. Six

षट्चितिः पूर्वव[2]त्स्यात्॥१४॥
ताभिश्च तुल्यसंख्यानात्॥१५॥

---

1. ज्येष्ठाशब्दादिति न्यायमालायां पाठः।
2. पूर्वत्वादिति न्यायमालायां पाठः।

अर्थवादोपपत्तेश्च॥१६॥

एकचितिर्वा स्यादपवृक्ते हि चोद्यते निमित्तेन॥१७॥

विप्रतिषेधत्ताभिः समानसङ्ख्य[1]त्वम्।१८॥

The number six should be understood to refer to the thinking mind, from what has already been stated; and we shall find that it is so if we follow the same method of calculation; for the explanation of the meaning of this number arises from the correctness of this calculation.[28] But the mind should be regarded as a single entity, because it always acts as such;[29] and if we understand by what objects it is kept in check, we shall find that the reckoning is correct[30].

Oblation to deceased Ancestors

पितृयज्ञः स्वकालत्वानङ्गं स्यात्॥१९॥

तुल्यवच्च[2] प्रसंख्यानात्।२०॥

विप्रति[3]षिद्धे च दर्शनात्॥२१॥

The oblation offered to the deceased ancestors should, because of the appropriateness of time, be referred to the mind;[31] and if we reflect on it, we shall find that it is so, even though it may be denied on the ground of what is seen[32].

The Rope

पश्वङ्गं रशना स्यात्तदागमे विधनात्॥२२॥

The Rope represents what belongs to the animal, when it is born in the world according to the law of creation[33].

Yūpa or sacrificial Post

यूपाङ्ग वा तत्संस्कारात्॥२३॥

अर्थवादश्च तदर्थवत्॥२४॥

स्वरुश्चाप्येकदेशत्वात्॥२५॥

निष्क्रयश्च तदङ्गवत्॥२६॥

---

1. सङ्ख्यमिति न्यायमालायां पाठः।
2. वकारस्तु न्यायमालायां नास्ति।
3. विशब्दरहितः पाठो न्या॰ मा॰।

Yūpa or the sacrificial post (to which the animal is tied) represents the idea of purification[34] (by means of which it can make itself free); and the explanation of the meaning of these words is like that. The same applies even to the word *Svaru*, which is part of the same conception.[35] The idea of giving a "ransom" to redeem one's self, is of the same kind[36].

Ransom

पश्वङ्गं वा[1]र्थकर्मत्वात्॥२७॥
भक्त्या निष्क्रयवादः स्यात्॥२८॥

What belongs to an animal (or what he brings with himself at birth) should be considered with reference to acts done deliberately or with a purpose[37] .

The explanation of "ransom" should be deemed to be "devotion"[38].

New and Full moon Sacrifices

दर्शपूर्णमासयोरिज्याः प्रधनानयविशेषात्॥२९॥

Again, all sacrifices performed on the days of the new moon and the full moon are equally important, because there is no distinction between them[39].

Parts of a Sacrifice

अपि वाङ्गानि कानिचिद्येष्वङ्गत्वेन संस्तुतिः सामा[2]न्यादभिसंस्तवः॥३०॥
तथा चान्यार्थदर्शनम्॥३१॥
अवशिष्टं तु कारणं प्रधनेषु गुणस्य विद्यमानत्वात्॥३२॥
नानुक्तेऽन्यार्थदर्शनं परार्थत्वात्॥३३॥
पृथक्त्वे त्वभिधनयोर्निवेशः श्रुतितो व्यपदेशाच्च तत्पुनर्मुख्यलक्षणं यत्फलवत्त्वं तत्सन्निधवसंयुक्तं तदङ्गं स्याद्भागित्वात् कारणस्या-श्रुते[3]श्चा-न्यसम्बन्धः॥३४॥

A Sacrifice (or a great good action) consists of a number of parts, some of which are highly praised; but the praise is shared also by the other parts; and that is so because they have

---

1. वास्यार्थत्वादिति न्यायमालायां पाठः।
2. सामान्योभिसम्बन्ध इति न्यायमालायां पाठः।

another meaning too. But it is the same cause that makes for the performance of the more as well as the less important parts of a sacrifice; and unless there is a definite statement to that effect, we should agree that there is no other meaning, because the highest importance attaches to the ordinary one. When, however, we separate the parts of a sacrifice (into major and minor ones), it is because there is a good reason for it; and that is what is enjoined by the sacred books as well. The principal part, however, is that which brings about the main result; while that which, though present, does not, should be regarded as subsidiary; for we cannot think of anything else.

How Described in the Vedas

गुणाश्च नामसंयुक्ता विधीयन्ते; नाङ्गेषूपपद्यन्ते॥३५॥
तुल्या च कारणश्रुतिरन्यैरङ्गा[1]भिसम्बन्धः॥३६॥
उत्पत्तावभिसम्बन्धस्तस्मादङ्गोपदेशः स्यात्॥३७॥
तथा चान्यार्थदर्शनम्॥३८॥

(The Vedas deal with all this) and the qualities or attributes of objects are personified and given separate names, and not included in the parts of a sacrifice. The text relating to the causes of things is of the same kind; and the connection between them,—close like the relation of one limb of the body to another is described by means of other names. These names are intended to explain how certain effects are produced; and the meaning given to the parts of a word is intended to serve the same purpose. That is how we can understand the text of the Vedas.

Jyotiṣṭoma

ज्योतिष्टोमे तुल्यान्यविशिष्टं हि कारणम्॥३९॥
गुणानां तूत्पत्तिवाक्येन सम्बन्धत्कारणश्रुतिस्तस्मात्सोमः प्रधनं स्यात्॥४०॥
तथा चान्यार्थदर्शनम्॥४१॥

Similarly in *Jyotiṣṭoma*[40] all parts are equal, because their cause is the same; and the *śruti* relating to the cause is based on the knowledge of these divisions. It is on account of this that *Soma* should be regarded as the most important;[41] and we can understand the rest of the text in the same manner.

NOTES

1. *Cf*. BhG. II, 62.
2. We see the working of this law in the world of Nature itself, where all things meet and mingle with one another.
3. These *Sūtras* tell us how the preceding idea is described in the text. It is done by means of the principal word, which has a special significance attaching to it.
4. The word *Jauhava* means "relating to *Juhū*, or a sacrificial ladle"; and *Anu-yāja* means "a secondary or final sacrifice". Both these meanings do not appear to make sense; and so it is necessary to find out if they can bear some other meaning. This can be done by dividing the words into parts.
5. The second meaning of the word *Juhū* can be obtained by dividing it into parts; and that gives us J, u, h, ū,-meaning "(J) the senses of action, and (u) the senses of knowledge, and (*h*, "water," symbolic of Nature) *Prakṛti*, (*ū*) woven together"; and the idea is that we should look at Nature in the light of our senses, and see what it can tell us.

   There is a reference to the number eight; and that obviously would refer to the eight divisions of *Prakṛti*, mentioned in the *Bhāgāvad Gītā* and other sacred books,-intellect, *ahaṅkāra* (I-as-an-actor), mind, and the five great "elements" (BhG. VII, 4). The point is that if we look at Nature in the light of our senses, we find that it is divisible into eight parts; and so the text refers to eight "sacrificial ladles".

   We can understand the meaning of *Anuyāja* in the same manner.
6. The word *Svaru* has a number of meanings,—"a large piece of wood, stake, sacrificial post, sacrifice, sunshine, thunderbolt, etc.". The *Mīmāṁsā* says that we must select the meaning that suits the context best; and this rule applies to all words which have more than one meaning. The *Mīmāṁsā* illustrates this by giving two meanings of the word, indicating that we must select the more suitable one.
7. The common meaning of the word *Upaveṣ* is "a stick of green wood used for stirring the sacrificial fire". But this would not appear to make much sense. On the other hand, if we derive the word from *Upaviṣ*, which means "to be active or effective", we can understand that it signifies "effectiveness", referred to in the *Mīmāṁsā*. We shall then understand that its more common meaning, associated with "stirring the fire", refers to making action effective too.

   The idea of "a stick of green wood used for stirring the sacrificial fire" is explained in the *Mīmāṁsā* as representing one who dies in the midst of a great good action, even as a stick of green wood is burnt or charred in the process of stirring the fire; and this is another idea of "effectiveness".
8. The word *Juhoti*, as we shall see at the end of this part of the chapter gives us the idea of purification in action; and it" in this sense that we have to take it. Its more common meaning, as referring to certain sacrificial ceremonies, would not be satisfactory.

The word *Haraṇa* has a number of meanings,—"carrying holding removing, dividing; a hand; arm"; and of these, the last two being the instrument of action, would give us the best idea.

9. We have explained that the real meaning of the word *ājya* is "goodness".
10. The word *Sam-yavana* means "mixing, mingling", as well as "with *Yavana*",—a word which has a number of meanings; and we have to select that which suits the context best
11. The idea of *Mitra* and *Varuṇa* has already been explained. When invoked together, they refer to action during life, and renunciation at the end of it. The "rod of authority" represents the idea of a just point of view; and the meaning is that when a person has done his life"s work, he is justified in renouncing action and sitting down in a posture of meditation. This is the real idea of Siddhārtnha *(Siddha-artha)* or one who has satisfied all his objects;-and so Buddhism, founded by *Siddhārtha*, is a creed of renunciation at the end of one"s life. It may be said to be perfection in the path of death.
12. This is emphasised by the *Bhāgāvad Gītā* a number of times (*Cf.* BhG. Ill, 9, 31; IV, 14-15. 19-23; V, 11, etc.).
13. *Cf.* BhG. V, 11.
14. The words in the text are *Dravya* and *Devatā*. Dravya has a number of meanings, including "a fit and proper person", and that is what has been taken here; while *Devatā* or a god, as has already been explained, refers to a great force of Nature.

    The idea is that an action can be called a sacrifice only when a fit and proper person, who is both good and intelligent, takes part in it, and the great forces of Nature assist; and then alone can we accomplish our object or achieve success.

    The *Bhāgāvad Gītā* tells us that "rain arises from sacrifice" (BhG. Ill, 14); and that would illustrate the role of the great forces of Nature in what is called an act of sacrifice.

    Juhoti is a technical term for certain sacrificial ceremonies; and water refers to Nature or *Prakṛti*; and the reference to the latter emphasises the role of the great forces of Nature in an act of "sacrifice". It is this that is signified by the word *Juhoti*.
15. This cause is purpose.
16. The *Mīmāṁsā* has told us that, in order to give satisfaction or joy, a thing must transform itself; and joy is of the essence of the idea of sacrifice, for it is meant to minister to the well-being of all. Similarly, the material objects used in a sacrifice are transformed or purified; and that is the reason why they are regarded as sacred. Indeed, the ancient idea is that Nature itself is transformed into the idea of God by means of sacrifice: that is to say, when we believe that Nature acts in accordance with a law that is both good and intelligent, and makes for the well-being of all, we have transformed Nature itself into God, for that is the real idea of God. This, as has already been observed, is illustrated in the story of *Sikhaṇḍin* in the *Mahābhārata*.

17. The *Bhāgāvad Gītā* also tells us that we are entitled to act, but not to claim the fruit of action (BhG. II, 47).
18. The aṅgas of the *Mantras* of the Vedas deal with the problem of purpose, action, and result, which are said to be connected together like "aṅgas" or limbs of the body; and that is the reason why these parts of the *Mantras* or hymns are called "*aṅgas*". The praise mentioned in them is meant to describe all this.
19. *Cf.* BhG. IV, 12
20. The double meaning of Time would refer to the idea of its own passage and the means of achieving result.
21. The *Mīmāṁsā* tells us that the idea of Time is limited to its own passage, and we should not imagine that it can, by itself, secure results. But, if after putting forth our best effort we still fail to achieve our end, we may attribute the cause of failure to Time. The idea of Time is thus linked up with failure and death, as that is its ancient conception; and it is for this reason, as the *Mīmāṁsā* tells us later on, that Time cannot .e represented as a god.
22. This *Sūtra* brings out more clearly the ancient conception of Time as the cause of natural decay of the body. Time may be said to be a great natural force that changes things for the worse; and so is the cause of deterioration, death and decay. So far as success in life is concerned, we must attribute it to effort, not Time.
23. A neutral effort is obviously one that is devoid of any special object to be achieved; and so it may be said to be a disinterested effort; and that, as the *Bhāgāvad Gītā* tells us, is of the essence of the idea of sacrifice, enabling us to act and yet be free from the taint or bondage of action.
24. This is an objection to the statement made in the previous *Sūtra*, on the ground that it is not possible to conceive of a *purely* disinterested effort. There can be no action without purpose; and a purpose implies interest and not its absence. Hence, there can be no neutral or disinterested effort, and we cannot agree to a special meaning of the term *Madhya*, as signifying disinterestedness. The answer to this is given in the next *Sūtra*.
25. This is an answer to the objection in the previous *Sūtras*. When we speak of disinterestedness, we mean that it is an effort which is not actuated by any personal motive or desire for personal achievement. The result would accrue to all, including the doer of the deed, but no more than the rest; and it is this that is signified by the idea of "partaking of the remnants of a sacrifice" referred to in the *Bhāgāvad Gītā* (BhG. III, 13).
26. *Jyeshtha* means "best, most excellent".
27. *Vaiśvānara* means "belonging to all men"; it is also a name of *Agni*, which, as we have seen, refers to the intellect. It is this intellect that belongs to all men, and constitutes the definition of man as a rational animal; and so the meaning of the word *Vaiśvānara* is fixed, as signifying intellect.

28. We have this calculation in the topics of the *Sāṅkhya* system, where the mind takes its place above all that is included in the number five, the five great "elements" and their respective properties, and the five senses of knowledge and five of action. The number six belongs, therefore, to the mind. We can calculate in the same manner in connection with the eight divisions of Prakṛti, referred to in the *Bhāgāvad Gītā*,-Earth, Water, Fire, Air, Ether, Mind, *Ahaṅkāra*, and the Intellect (BHG. VII, 4)
29. The author is careful to add that, though the number six refers to the mind, the latter is not divisible into parts. It should be regarded as a single entity, because it always acts as such.
30. The mind is kept in check by the five "elements" from below, and *ahaṅkāra* and the intellect from above; and so it is the sixth from the bottom. Hence the number six refers to the mind.
31. The *Bhāgāvad Gītā* tells us of the time when the departed one, passing way from the earth, goes to the abode of the Moon, and returns after dwelling there for some time. As the Moon refers to the mind, the *Mīmāṁsā* tells us that the oblation offered to the deceased should be deemed to refer to the mind (*Cf.* BhG. VIII, 25).
    The idea of the ancients was that the soul, after death, dwells in the region best suited to its character. If, during its sojourn on earth, it was absorbed in the life of the senses, it dwelt in the region of the "elements",—to which the senses correspond: that is, it became a ghost. But if it was at the mind-stage of its growth, it passed on to the region of the Moon; and it was there that most souls dwelt. If, on the other hand, it was at the stage of the intellect, it passed to the region of the Sun; and if it had attained to the character of the pure soul, it was merged into the Eternal.
    As the deceased ones are believed to be at the mind-stage of their evolution, the soul is said to abide in the region of the Moon; and so the oblation offered to them is deemed to refer to the mind.
32. But no one has seen where exactly the soul goes after death; and so it is possible for a person to deny the statement previously made. But if we reflect on it, we shall understand that this is a very rational way of looking at the whole problem. If the soul must dwell somewhere after death, its best abode is that to which it is suited in character.
33. The *Mīmāṁsā* has told us that the soul carries with itself the impressions of previous actions, even after death; and when it is reborn, it acts in accordance with these impressions. This is also stated in the *Bhāgāvad Gītā* (BhG. VI, 40-45). This *Sūtra* tells us that it is customary to tie a rope round an animal, and then to bind it to a sacrificial post. But all this is symbolic; and the rope represents the idea of the bond of previous actions, and serves to indicate the link between the past, present, and future of life. As previous actions "bind" us to future ones, the animal, with the rope, is bound to a sacrificial post which, as we shall see, represents the idea of action.
34. The idea of *Yūpa* and *Svaru*, both of which are said to be sacrificial posts,

is explained in a subsequent chapter (XI, iii, 3-10); and there we are told that *Yūpa* refers to sacrifice or action of the intellect, meant for the benefit of all. It is in this manner that a person can "purify" or make himself free from the bondage of action,—that is, by acting intelligently and for the benefit of all.

35. *Svaru*, as explained later on, refers to action meant to secure a limited object; and so it is distinguished from *Yūpa*.

36. The idea of a "ransom" is explained in a subsequent *Sūtra*, as meaning "devotion" or an act of self-surrender. We can "redeem" ourselves by means of perfect devotion or complete self-surrender.

37. The "bondage" (represented by a rope), arising from previous actions, is the result of acts done deliberately, and not reflex actions.

38. This is the explanation of the word "ransom".

39. As the Moon refers to the mind, the new moon would refer to the first awakening of the mind,—that is, in the form of desire; while the full moon would refer to the full working of the mind,—that is, when it is engaged in action. The *Mīmāṁsā* explains all this later on.

    The point of this *Sūtra* is that, as the mind is associated both with desire and action, both are equally important; and that is signified by the importance attaching to the sacrifices performed on the days of the new and the full moon.

40. *Jyotiṣṭoma* is said to be the name of a Soma ceremony; but the word is made up of *Jyotiṣṭoma*, which means "(*stoma*) mass or multitude of (*jyotis*) light." Thus it means literally "mass or rays of light".

    This *Sūtra* tells us that *Jyotiṣṭoma* consists of a number of equal parts; and it is said that it consisted originally of three, and later of four, five, and seven sub-divisions. If, therefore, *Jyotiṣṭoma* refers really to the rays of light, these should be the divisions of the rays of light. The sacred books give us the names of these divisions of *Jyotiṣṭoma*; and the *Mīmāṁsā* tells us later on that we can understand their meaning by dividing them into parts. It would be found, on examination, that their idea corresponds closely to the seven rays of light, of which modern science tell us (See Appendix II).

41. *Soma*, as has already been observed., refers to the mind; and, if *Jyotiṣṭoma* refers to the rays of light, *Soma* or the mind too should refer to the same. Now the ancient books tell us that the energy of the mind or the moon is electric, for it is said to create the clouds charged with lightning (MBh. *Vana* P. III, iii, 6-7); and so we may conclude that the most important among the rays of light is the electric or the electromagnetic ray.

CHAPTER-V

KRAMA AND THE METHOD OF INTERPRETATION

PART-I

Introduction

The text of the Vedas should be interpreted in accordance with the *Krama* method of its recitation, and we should assume that there is an intelligent plan underlying the whole, when we shall get the correct meaning of the entire text.

It is, however, not necessary to interpret every portion of the text in this manner, for the whole of it is not composed in this way. We should do so only when it does not make sense otherwise.

The meaning of the principal word can be understood by means of *Krama*, and of others by reference to the principal word; and we should adhere to the order of words in the text.

When we pronounce a word according to *Krama*, the word itself should remain intact; and if we have to break up the form of a word in accordance with *Krama*, it should be done immediately, when it would give us the required meaning.

The *Krama* method of reading the text is not intended to regulate time. But the reason for changing the form of a word is that the text does not appear to be coherent otherwise. But the form of casual or entirely new expressions, never used before, should not be changed.

Certain expressions have a special meaning attaching to them: for instance, the idea of the Sun, *Agni*, and the intellect is the same; and the Soma-juice refers to the mind.

The Krama Method

श्रुतिलक्षणमानुपूर्व्यं त[1]त्प्रमाणत्वात्॥१॥
अर्थाच्च॥२॥
अनियमोऽन्यत्र॥३॥
क्रमेण वा नियम्येत, क्रत्वेकत्वे तद्गुणत्वात्॥४॥
अशाब्द[2] इति चेत्स्याद्वाक्य शब्द त्वात्॥५॥
अर्थकृते[3] चाऽनुमानं स्यात्क्रत्वेकत्वे; परार्थत्वात्स्वेन त्वर्थेन सम्बन्धस्त-
स्मात्स्वशब्दमुच्यते॥६॥
तथा चान्यार्थदर्शनम्॥७॥
प्रवृत्त्या तुल्यकालानां गुणानां तदुपक्रमात्॥८॥

The language of the *śruti* is such that each part follows the other in an orderly succession,—and that is the measure of its correctness; for that is how we get its meaning, whereas otherwise the whole thing would be irregular. But the meaning should be settled by means of the *Krama* method of reciting the text; and we should assume that it constitutes an intelligent whole, for such indeed is its character. It is possible that some one, considering the manner in which the sounds of words are produced in accordance with this method,—might say that it is not sonorous. But in trying to get at the meaning, we should believe that the text is characterised by an integrated intelligent design; and that would give us a great meaning of a great idea, and convince us that that is the real meaning of words; and so the original word is suitable and has been properly used. It is in this manner that we can understand the meaning of the rest of the text; and by means of the application of this rule we shall find that there is unity of time as well as general agreement about the attributes of things.

---

1. तत्प्रधनत्वेति न्यायमालायां पाठः।
2. अशाब्दमिति वृत्तिकृत्पाठः।
3. कृते वान्विति न्यायमालायां पाठः।

Application of this Method

सर्वमिति चेत्॥९॥

नाकृतत्वात्॥१०॥

क्रत्वन्तरवदिति चेत्॥११॥

नासमवायात्॥१२॥

स्थानाच्चोत्पत्तिसंयोगात्॥१३॥

We cannot say that this should be so in every case, for the whole text is not composed in this manner; nor can we say that the plan is full of defects,—because it is coherent in every part. But this method should be used only when there is occasion for it, and when we need to produce a certain result[1].

Illustration

मुख्यक्रमेण वाङ्गाना[1] तदर्थत्वात्॥१४॥

प्रकृतौ तु स्वशब्दत्वाद्यथाक्रमं प्रतीयेत॥१५॥

मन्त्रतस्तु विरोधे स्यात्प्रयोगरूपसामर्थ्यात्तस्मादुत्पत्तिदेशः सः॥१६॥

The meaning of the principal word used in the text can be understood by means of *Krama,* and of others by reference to the principal word, and fitting them into its idea. For instance, we can find out the meaning of the word *Prakṛti* by pronouncing it correctly according to *Krama.*[2] But in case of apparent contradiction or incongruity, we should follow the order of the *Mantras,* because the words are suitable and in their proper place; and it is this that gives us the proper result.

Requirement of Krama

तद्वचनाद्विकृतौ यथाप्रधनं स्यात्॥१७॥

विप्रतिपत्तौ वा प्रकृत्यन्वयाद्यथाप्रकृति॥१८॥

विकृतिः प्रकृतिधर्मत्वात्तत्काला स्याद्यथाशिष्टम्॥१९॥

अपि वा क्रमकालसंयुक्ता सद्यः क्रियेत तत्र विधेरनुमानात्प्रकृतिधर्मलोपः स्यात्॥२०॥

When we pronounce a word according to *Krama,* the word

1. वाङ्गेति न्यायमालायां पाठः।

itself should remain intact, even though it is changed. In case of contradiction, the natural form of a word should be retained: for instance, the word *Prakṛti* should remain unchanged as *Prakṛti*[3].

When, however, it is necessary to make a change in the form of a word, the change should be made immediately, because that is what the natural form of a word requires; and when we follow the rules laid down in connection with *Krama,* we shall understand this method of interpretation; and then the original form of a word will break up to give the required meaning.

Krama does not refer to Time

कालोत्कर्ष इति चेत्॥२१॥
न तत्सम्बन्धत्॥२२॥
अङ्गानां मुख्यकालत्वाद्यथोक्तम् उत्कर्षे स्यात्॥२३॥
तदादि वाऽभिसम्बन्धत्तदन्तमपकर्षे स्यात्॥२४॥
प्रवृत्त्या कृतकालानाम्॥२५॥
शब्दविप्रतिषेधच्च॥२६॥

The *Krama* method of reciting the text does not regulate time required to pronounce a word, but is connected with the method of interpretation. Indeed, if it were meant to regulate time, certain parts of a word would be more important than others; for instance, the part of a word at the beginning would be emphasised, and that at the end dropped; for that is what happens when people act with reference to time; and that is how the tone of voice is regulated.

Reason for changing the Form of a Word

असंयोगात्तु वैकृतं तदेव प्रतिकृष्येत॥२७॥
प्रासङ्गिकं च नोत्कर्षेदसंयोगात्॥२८॥
तथाऽपूर्वम्॥२९॥

The only reason for making a change in the form of a word is that the text does not appear to be coherent otherwise.

But this does not apply to casual or occasional expressions, which should not be broken apart in any case. Nor should this apply to entirely new words, never used before.

Special Meanings

सान्तपनीया तूत्कर्षेदग्निहोत्रं सवनवद्वैगुणमात्॥३०॥
अव्यवायाच्च ॥३१॥
असम्बन्धत्तु नोत्कर्षेतु ॥३२॥
प्रापणाच्च निमित्तस्य॥३३॥
सम्बन्धत्सवनोत्कर्षः॥३४॥
षोडशी चोक्थ्यसंयोगात्॥३५॥

(There are certain expressions or ideas which have been explained in a special manner: for instance,) where the idea of a sacrifice offered to the Sun does not make sense, we should take it that it means a sacrifice offered to *Agni* (or the intellect). That is like pressing out the *Soma-juice* from something that is defective otherwise.[4] We get this meaning because the idea of the two (Sun and *Agni)* cannot be separated. But we should be careful to see that we do not draw out meanings which are not connected; and we should be able to give a satisfactory reason for our explanation. It is because of proper explanation that the idea of pressing out the *Soma-juice* becomes important; and it is said to consist of sixteen parts and is praised on that account[5].

PART II

KRAMA AND THE METHOD OF INTERPRETATION (*CONTINUED*)

If there are a number of principal words in a sentence, they should all be regarded as synonyms. There are certain words which express their own ideas completely; but even they need to be divided into parts when read in accordance with *Krama*, though there should be no change in their contents. There is good reason for following the *Krama* method; but the meaning of words is not obtained by merely adding up their parts.

The division of things, like the division of animals into their species, is not a mechanical process; and even so the importance of a *Mantra* is due to the character of its meaning.

Certain ideas have been described in a special manner: for instance, grain and the cup for holding it; and among all kinds of grain, rice is regarded as the best. All this is associated with the idea of sacrifice.

In dividing a word into parts, we may take the most im-portant part first or last as suits us best; and when the plan of the most important part has been fixed, the rest can fit into the scheme. This applies also to compounds

Synonyms

सन्निपाते प्रधनानामेकैकस्य गुणानां सर्वकर्म स्यात्॥१॥

सर्वेषां वैकजातीयं कृतानुपूर्व्य[1]त्वात्॥२॥

कारणादभ्यावृत्तिः॥३॥

If there are a number of principal words in a sentence, they should be regarded as synonyms; and all kinds of actions, associated with them, should be referred to them alike. This is necessary if ideas are to be expressed in an orderly manner; and that is the reason why these names are repeated in the text.

Application of Krama

मुष्टिकपालावदानाञ्जनाभ्यञ्जनवपनपावनेषु चैकेन॥१॥

सर्वाणि[2] त्वेककार्यत्वादेषां तद्गुणत्वात्॥५॥

संयुक्ते तु प्रक्रमात्त[3]दङ्गं स्यादितरस्य तदर्थत्वात्॥६॥

There are certain words used in the text which express their own ideas completely: for instance, words meaning fist, cup, cutting into pieces, applying an ointment, shaving, or an

---

1. पूर्वस्येति न्या. मा. पाठः।
2. सर्वाणि वैकेति वृत्तिकृत्पाठः।
3. त्तदन्तमिति वृत्तौ पाठः।

act of purification. These words are all satisfactory, because they express their own ideas completely; but even these words need to be divided into parts when read in accordance with *Krama;* and so too all other words, and for the same reason.

Pronunciation and Meaning

वचनात्तु परिव्याणनतमञ्जनादिः स्यात्॥७॥
कारणाद्वा[1]ऽनवसर्गः स्याद्यथा पात्रवृद्धिः॥८॥
न वा शब्दकृतत्वान्न्यायमात्रमितरदर्थात्पात्रविवृद्धिः[2]॥९॥

So far as pronunciation is concerned,-whether a word be at the beginning or the end—it should remain unchanged: for instance, the word *añjana,* at the beginning, should be *añjana,* and *Parivyāṇa,* at the end, as *Parivyāṇa.* There is, as in the case of the success of a worthy person, good reason for not following one's own inclination (in the matter of interpretation of the text); and we must remember that the form of a word into which it goes back[6] (in order to give the correct meaning) is not obtained merely by addine up its parts. The prosperity of a worthy person arises from a different cause (and so also success in gettine at the correct meaning)[7].

Need of Knowledge

पशुगणे तस्य तस्यापवर्जयेत् पश्वेकत्वात्॥१०॥
दैवतैर्वैककर्म्यात्॥११॥
मन्त्रस्य चार्थवत्त्वात्॥१२॥

This division of words into parts is not a mechanical process: for instance,) when we divide animals into their species, we have to deal with them separately, because of their different characteristics But this has to be done in accordance with their natural attributes[8], because a number of actions are common to all. Even so the value of a *Mantra* or a Vedic hymn arises from the character of its meaning.

---

1. द्वावसर्ग इति वृत्तौ पाठः।
2. प्रवृद्धिरिति वृत्तौ पाठः।

Special Cases

नानाबीजे[1] एकमुलूखलं विभवात्॥१३॥
विवृद्धिर्वा नियमानुपूर्व्यस्य तदर्थत्वात्॥१४॥
एकं वा तण्डुलभावाद्धन्तेस्तदर्थत्वात्॥१५॥
विकारे त्वनुयाजानां पात्रभेदोऽर्थभेदात् स्यात्॥१६॥

(Certain ideas have been described in a special manner: for instance,) we are told that while there are a number of different kinds of grain, there is only one mortar-shaped cup for holding *Soma;* and that is so because of its power; for it is in accordance with a law that all that which makes for growth should minister to *Soma*[9]. But in all kinds of grain rice, because of its special character, is given a unique place; for, when pounded, it is offered to *Soma*. But different kinds o food, provided in the final sacrifice, represent different ideas, according to their use.

Method of Division into Parts

प्रकृतेः पूर्वोक्तत्वादपूर्वमन्ते स्यान्न ह्यचोदितस्य शेषाम्नानम्॥१७॥
मुख्यानन्तर्यमात्रेयस्तेन तुल्यश्रुतित्वादशब्दत्वात्प्राकृतानां व्यवायः स्यात्॥१८॥
अन्ते तु बादरायणस्तेषां प्रधनशब्दत्वात्॥१९॥
तथा चान्यार्थदर्शनम्॥२०॥
कृतदेशात्तु पूर्वेषां स देशः स्यात्; तेनप्रत्यक्षसंयोगान्न्यायमात्रमितरत्॥२१॥
प्राकृताच्च पुरस्ताद्यत्॥२२॥
सन्निपातश्चेद्यथोक्तमन्ते स्यात्॥२३॥

In analysing the natural form of a word, the first part should be uttered first; and that which comes later, after that; and we should not mention that the last, which is uttered slowly According to *Atreya,* the principal part (of a sentence) should be the most important, and should come first, and it is by means of it that we should understand the meaning of the rest—whether uttered or implied; and it is in the same manner that we should

---

1. बीजेष्विति न्या. मा. पाठः।

understand the meaning of a word when its natural form is changed. But *Bādarāyaṇa* says that the most important part should come in the end. However, it is in these ways that we can understand the meaning of the rest of the text[10]. When the place of the most important word (or its part) has been fixed, we can fix the place of all other words (or their parts) by its means; and when the first connection has been established, the rest is but a matter of fitting into the scheme. It is in this manner that we should divide the natural or original form of a word into parts. In the case of a compound, what should come in the end has already been explained[11].

PART III

THE METHOD OF INTERPRETATION —THE LAW OF ACTION

Introduction

Growth, progress or progress or prosperity is the result of variuos kinds of action, which again are made up of parts; and if we cont them up, we can trace its development from its very source.

Special meanings have been assigned to certain words: for instance, the difference between *Dyu* and *Pṛthivi* corresponds to that between a desire and its fulfilment; and this is also the difference between two Vedic metres, —*Uṣṇik* and *Kakubha*. Again, the ceremony lasting twelve days is intended to express the idea of a large, expanding action, —the end of which corresponds to the final syllable of a word. The place of the last two parts of an object should be at the end; and this is contained in *Gāyatrī, Bṛhati,* and *Anuṣup* metres.

There can be no action without a direction by the intellect, for it is the function of the intellect to decide.

The idea of desire and disinterestedness in action is represented by means of the use of certain bricks in the building of the sacrificial altar.

The object of all action is the achievement of more and more perfection.

The real meaning of *Agni* is intellect; and we can understand the text correctly in its light, because there is a definite design in this mode of expression, and the whole idea is consistent throughout.

Certain letters and words have a special meaning: for instance, the letter *Ya* refers to the intellect; and *atha* means "inexhaustibleness". This is how we can understand the idea of a law of life in the hymns of the Vedas.

Progress and composite Action

विवृद्धिः कर्मभेदात्पृषदाज्यवत्तस्य तस्योपदिश्येत॥१॥
अपि वा सर्वसङ्ख्यत्वाद्विकारः प्रतीयेत॥२॥
स्वस्थानात्तु विवृध्येरन्कृतानुपूर्व्यत्वात्॥३॥

Growth, progress, or prosperity is the result of expanding action or action of various kinds, which may be called composite action or an action made up of a number of parts, and compared to the use of clarified butter in a sacrifice; for we can point out the different parts of such action. If we sum up all the parts of such action, we can know the form into which it is finally changed, for there is a regular order of succession in such action, and we can trace its development from its very source.

Special Explanation

समिध्यमानवतीं समिद्धवतीं चान्तरेण धय्याः स्युर्द्यावापृथिव्योरन्तराले समर्हणात्॥४॥
तच्छब्दो वा॥५॥
उष्णिक्ककुभोरन्ते दर्शनात्॥६॥
स्तोम विवृद्धै वहिष्पवमाने पुरस्तात्पर्यासादागन्तवः स्युस्तथा हि दृष्टं द्वादशाहे॥७॥
पर्यास इति चाऽन्ताख्या॥८॥

अन्ते वा तदुक्तम्॥९॥
वचनात्तु द्वादशाहे॥१०॥
अतद्विकारश्च॥११॥
तद्विकारेऽप्यपूर्वत्वात्॥१२॥
अन्ते तूत्तरयोर्दध्यात्॥१३॥
अपि वा गायत्रीबृहत्यनुष्टुप्सु वचनात्॥१४॥

(Special meanings have been given to certain words used in the text: for instance,) the difference between the two gods *Dyu* and *Pṛthivī* corresponds to the difference between the desire for an object and the fulfilment of that desire;[13] and there is an oral or traditional authority in support of this view.[12] That is also the difference between the Vedic metres, *Uṣṇik* and *Kakubha*. Again, the ceremony lasting for twelve days is intended to give us an idea of what should be included in an object, the mass of which is increasing,—namely, that we should include in it all that can be included before we come to the end of its conception; and the end of such a thing corresponds to the final syllable of a word or the last word of a compound,—for that is how it is expressed or uttered at the end. It is this that has been expressed in terms of a sacrifice lasting twelve days, as we have been taught. There is nothing extravagant in this conception, except perhaps that it is new. Again, the place of the last two parts of a large object is at the end of an expression; and [1] that is specially so in *Gāyatri, Bṛhatī,* and *Anuṣup* metres, as we have been taught.

Action and Intellect

ग्रहेष्टकगौपानुवाक्यं सवनचितिशेषः स्यात्॥१५॥
क्रत्वग्निशेषो वा चोदितत्वादचोदनानपूर्वस्य[1]॥१६॥
अन्ते स्युरव्यवायात्॥१७॥
लिङ्गदर्शनाच्च॥१८॥

When a person lays hold of what is desirable, or recites what ought to be recited, it means that an order to that effect

1. चोदना तु पूर्वस्य-इति क्षेमराजीये। चोदना नु पूर्वस्य-इत्यानन्दाश्रमीये।

has emanated from his intellect. (This is determination to act, and) determination is the result of the function of the intellect,—arising from what has been directed by it. There can be no determination without such direction or impelling force, as has been stated before; and it should be deemed to be a characteristic of the intellect, because the two cannot be separated, as can easily be proved.

Disinterestedness and Interest in Action: how Described

मध्यमायां तु वचनाद् ब्राह्मणवत्यः॥१९॥
प्राग्लोकम्पृणायास्तस्याः सम्पूरणार्थत्वात्॥२०॥

In building the sacrificial altar certain bricks, called *Brāhmaṇavatī*, are placed in the middle, because they represent the idea of "what is in the middle"[14] (neutrality or disinterestedness); while, as opposed to them, are placed other bricks, called *Lokampṛṇā*, which represent the idea of eating to one's satisfaction[15] (or action with a desire).

Object of Action is Perfection

संस्कृते कर्म संस्काराणां तदर्थत्वात्॥२१॥
अनन्तरं व्रतं तद्भूतत्वात्॥२२॥
पूर्वं च लिङ्गदर्शनात्॥२३॥
अर्थवादो वाऽर्थस्य विद्यमानत्वात्॥२४॥
न्यायविप्रतिषेधच्च॥२५॥

The object of action is the achievement of more and more perfection; and the proper performance of action is for the sake of this perfection. It is this that makes the mode of our life continuous or whole, as can easily be proved, because this is the real explanation of the meaning of action; and anything else would be a negation of the right mode of life itself.

Méaning of Agni

सञ्चिते त्वग्नि चिद्युक्तं प्रापणान्निमित्तस्य॥२६॥
क्रत्वन्ते वा प्रयोगवचनाभावात्॥२७॥
अग्नेः कर्मत्वनिर्देशात्॥२८॥

परेणाऽऽवेदनाद्दीक्षितः स्यात्, सर्वैर्दीक्षाभिसम्बन्धत्॥२९॥
इष्ट्यन्तेवा तदर्था ह्यविशेषार्थसम्बन्धत्॥३०॥
समाख्यानं च तद्वत्॥३१॥
अङ्गवत्क्रतूनामानुपूर्व्यम्॥३२॥
न वाऽसम्बन्धत्॥३३॥
काम्यत्वाच्च॥३४॥
आनर्थक्यान्नेति चेत्॥३५॥
स्याद्विद्यार्थत्वाद्यथा परेषु सर्वस्वारात्॥३६॥

The god *Agni* represents the idea of the intellect, which we constantly use, and which enables us to explain the causes of things; and this should be the meaning of *Agni* in the text unless there is an express statement to the contrary. This is the real activity of *Agni* (the function of the intellect), of which there is a special mention in the text; and this would enable us to understand the real idea of that god, expressed in terms of a respectful mode of address. This will initiate us in the art of interpreting the text, and enable us to see the close connection between its parts. We can succeed in our task if we so desire, for these meanings are uniformly consistent throughout; and the whole text is of this kind.

In this way we can understand that there is a definite design and a sequence of ideas in the text,—all closely connected with one another like the limbs of the body. This would obviously be impossible without a close connection between parts; and so we conclude that this connection is intentional.

We cannot say that there is no such connection on the ground that the whole text is meaningless. It is, however, possible that we may not be able to make any sense out of it at the beginning,—just as when we hear a number of sounds, all mixed together, from a distance, we cannot make them out at once.

Special Meanings

य एतेनेत्यग्निष्टोमः प्रकरणात्॥३७॥

लिङ्गाच्च॥३८॥
अथान्येनेति संस्थानां सन्निधनात्॥३९॥
तत्प्रकृतेर्वाऽऽपत्तिविहारौ हि न तुल्येषूपपद्येते॥४०॥
प्रशंसा च विहरणाभावात्॥४१॥

When we get the letter *Ya* in the text, we should understand that it refers to *Agni* or the intellect, for that is its special explanation. It is so because it is a word used to fix the meaning of another.

The word *atha* means "inexhaustibleness", for that is what has been laid down; and that is its idea in its natural form. Indeed, there should be no change in words of this kind; and in such cases the beauty of the text consists in the absence of making any change.

Idea of Vidhi or Law

विधिप्रत्ययाद्वा न ह्येकस्मात् प्रशंसा स्यात्॥४२॥
एकस्तोमो वा क्रतुसंयोगात्॥४३॥
सर्वेषां वा चोदना विशेषात्प्रशंसा स्तोमानाम्॥४४॥

But the idea of *Vidhi* or Law is obtained by means of the division of words into parts, for the beauty of the text does not consist in one mode of expression alone; and the idea of Law has intentionally been explained in this manner in a hymn of praise.[16] All hymns, however, are beautiful in their own way; and there are special rules in connection with their interpretation[17].

PART IV

KRAMA AND THE METHOD OF INTERPRETATION: MIND, INTELLECT, AND THE SOUL

Introduction

We should read the text properly according to *Krama* and analyse words according to correct grammatical rules, when we shall get their real meaning.

There are some who would include the mind in the intellect; but it is possible to regard it as a separate entity too.

The mind is associated with the Moon in the text of the Vedas and other sacred books; and this should enable us to understand the laws of life.

But the full moon also refers to a fixed point of time, implying that the mind can be properly controlled. On the other hand, possession signifies impropriety of conduct, for there is no fixed time for it. The connection between the mind and the Moon is based on reason.

The same words should have the same meaning throughout.

Food does not minister directly to the intellect; but goodness is associated with both the intellect and the soul.

The idea of Change arises from Nature as well as Time.

Things that are essentially good and associated with both the intellect and the mind, are not subject to change; while those that are associated with only the mind, are; and this corresponds to the changes of the moon, from the new to the full moon.

Krama and the Meaning of the Text

क्रमकोपोऽर्थशब्दाभ्यां श्रुतिविशेषादर्थपरत्वाच्च॥१॥

अवदानाभिघारणाऽऽसादनेष्वानुपूवर्यं प्रवृत्त्या स्यात्॥२॥

यथाप्रदानं वा तदर्थत्वात्॥३॥

लिङ्गदर्शनाच्च॥४॥

वचनादिष्टिपूर्वत्वम्॥५॥

The failure of *Krama* (to give the required result) arises from (defective) meaning and expression,—that is, when we hear a word in a peculiar manner, and give a strange meaning to it.

When, however, we divide words into parts, extend them

over to other words or parts, or take them as they are, we should do so in order, and in accordance with correct grammatical rules; and then we shall get the real meaning of the text, as can easily be proved. But we are[18] told by learned teachers that, in applying these rules, we should give precedence to the opinion of grammarians who are considered to be authoritative.

Mind and the Intellect

सोमश्चैकेषामग्न्याधेयस्यर्तुनक्षत्राऽतिक्रमवचनात् तदर्थे[1]नानर्थकं हि स्यात्॥६॥

तदर्थवचनाच्च नाविशेषात्तदर्थत्वं॥५॥

अयक्ष्यमाणस्य च पवमानहविषां कालविधना[2]दानन्तर्याद्विशङ्का स्यात्॥८॥

इष्टिरयक्ष्यमाणस्य तादर्थ्ये[3] सोमपूर्वत्वम्॥९॥

उत्कर्षाद् ब्राह्मणस्य सोमः स्यात्॥१०॥

According to the opinion of some authorities, the mind should be taken to have no special purpose of its own, because it can be included in the intellect; and it is the function of the latter to acquire certain (or definite) knowledge, which can transcend time and the stars.[19] This is the opinion of some, but is not held uniformly by all.

If a person does not wish to act, he will hesitate, if required to do so immediately, even though it be a great act of sacrifice,—which his intellect bid him do; and this desire not to act is an expression of the mind, as has already been pointed out.[19] (At the same time) the mind arises from the abundant flow or function of the intellect[20].

Mind and the Moon

पौर्णमासी वा श्रुतिसंयोगात्॥११॥

सर्वस्य चैककर्मत्वात्॥१२॥

---

1. तदन्तेन इति आनन्दाश्रमपाठः।
2. निर्देशा इति पाठभेदः।
3. तादर्थ्ये न सोमेति क्षेमराजीयः पाठभेदः।

स्याद्वा विधिस्तदर्थेन॥१३॥
प्रकरणात्तु कालः स्यात्॥१४॥
स्वकाले स्यादविप्रतिषेधत्॥१५॥
अपनयो वाऽऽधनस्य सर्वकालत्वात्॥१६॥
पौर्णमास्यूधर्वं सोमाद्ब्राह्मणस्य वचनात्॥१७॥

The mind is associated with the full moon in connection with the text of the Vedas; and this is true of all texts, because their object is the same;[21] and this should enable us to understand the laws of life. But there is also a special idea associated with the full moon, where it refers to a fixed point of time; and there can be no two opinions that the full moon appears at its appointed time.[22] On the other hand, appropriating things to one's self signifies impropriety of conduct, for it can be done at all times.[23] But when *Soma* or the mind refers to the full moon in the upper regions, we should understand that it is in accordance with the teachings of the intellect[24].

Meaning of Symbols

एकं वा शब्दसामर्थ्यात्प्राक् कृत्स्नविंधनम्॥१८॥

The same notes (letters, syllables etc.) should have the same meaning throughout, and it should be fixed before arranging the whole idea.

Need of Knowledge

पुरोडाशस्त्वनिर्देशे तद्युक्ते देवताभावात्॥१९॥
आज्यमपीति चेत्॥२०॥
न मिश्रदेवतात्वादैन्द्राग्नवत्॥२१॥

But it is necessary to have knowledge of the laws of life to be able to understand the text: for instance, food does not minister directly to the intellect; and so) there is no special mention of the offering of the the rice-cake to *Agni* (intellect). It is, however, associated with it in a general way, because it is a great force of Nature. But we cannot say that there need be no special mention of the association of goodness (represented by clarified butter) with the intellect *(Agni),* because goodness is inseparable from both the intellect and the soul[25].

Change and Time

विकृते प्रकृतिकालत्वात्सद्यस्कालोत्तरा विकृतिस्तयोः प्रत्यक्ष-शिष्टत्वात्॥२२॥

द्वैयहकाल्ये तु यथान्यायम्॥२३॥

वचनाद्वैककाल्यं स्यात्॥२४॥

सान्नाय्याग्नीषोमीयविकारादूर्ध्वं सोमात्प्रकृतिवत्॥२५॥

तथा सोमविकारा दर्शपूर्णमासाभ्याम्॥२६॥

Similarly, we get the idea of Change from Nature or *Prakṛti,* which is subject to Time, and it takes place from moment to moment; and this fact of the interaction of Change and Time becomes apparent from what we see of things that remain (after others have disappeared); and we can see this even in a period of two days, according to a universal rule.[26] According to this, Time and Change occur simultaneously.

Anything that is essentially good (mixed with clarified butter), and associated with both the intellect and the mind *(Agni* and *Soma)* is above change. But all that arises from the mind is like *Prakṛti,* —(subject to change);[27] and this corresponds to the changes of the moon from the new to the full moon[28].

NOTES

1. This means that we should resort to this method when the text does not make sense otherwise.
2. According to the *Krama* method of reading the text, we proceed from the first member, —word, syllable, or letter—to the second; then the second is repeated and connected with the third; then the third is repeated and connected with the fourth; and so on. Thus if we pronounce the word *Prakṛti* according to *Krama,* we shall have to say *Pra-kṛ, kṛ-ti;* and that will break up the whole word into *Pra-kṛ-—ti,* when its meaning would be "*(ti,* an older form of *iti)* that is to say *(kṛ,* 'to act") action *(pra)* going forward". It signifies, therefore, that action is going forward, or that *Prakṛti* is the cause of all action.
3. In case of a difficulty, we should retain the word *Prakṛti* as a whole word,

and follow its dictionary meaning. This word is used a number of times in these *Sūtras,* and it should not be divided into parts to get its meaning.

4. As has already been explained, *Soma* refers to the mind, and *Soma-juice* to the function of the mind, or desire, its special attribute. Pressing out the *Soma-juice* means, therefore, doing something desirable, or attaining to one"s desire. The meaning of the *Sūtra* accordingly is that, if we explain the idea of the Sun as *Agni* or the intellect, we shall succeed in getting the correct meaning, or the object of our desire.

5 *Soma*-juice refers to desire which is an attribute of the mind; and it is said to consist of sixteen parts: that is, the mind, with its ten senses and five objects of the senses (sound, touch, form, taste, and smell, –the five attributes of the five great "elements"), –making a total of sixteen. The idea is that desire *(Soma-juice)* is "pressed out", obtained or satisfied, by means of the function of the mind in association with the senses and their objects.

6. This is obtained by dividing a word into parts,-for that is what a word goes back into, when divided. The word in the text is *Nyāya* which has a number of meanings, including "original type; that into which a thing goes back".

7. In *Sanskṛt* words, syllables, and letters have all a number of meanings; and this method of interpretation requires both knowledge and skill, for the meanings selected should be appropriate.

8. The word in the text is *Daivata* (from *Devatā)* which as has already been explained, refers to a force of Nature.

9. *Soma* refers to the mind; and the "mortar-shaped cup" would refer to the form of the brain where, according to the ancients, tha mind is located; for they believed that it was centred in the fore-head which can be imagined to have a "mortar-shape".

   The Upaniṣads contain a number of references to the associatation of food with the mind; and the subtlest portion of food is said to becaome the mind (Chh.Up.VI, v. i).

10. Whether the most important part of a word, when divided into parts! should be taken first or last, depends on the circumstances of each case. For instance if we divideTheword Viṣṇu into its parts, *V, i, sh,ṇ, u*—we may begin with the letter *V* or the letter *u,* and then go on to the other end. According to *Bādarāy ṇa,* if the ideaconveyed by the letter *V* is the most important, it should come last, so that we should begin with the letter *u. Atreya,* on the other hand, holds tie opposite view But there is not much difference between the two for the essence of the meaning remains unchanged. Both the methodsrhave been followed in *The Mystery of the Mahābhārata,* though the felt has been preferred. The same is the case with words used in thj *Rāmāyaṇa* and the *Bhāgavat Purāṇa.*

11. Whether the most important part of a word should come first on last has already been explained; and the same rule applies to compounds.
12. *Dyu* and *Pṛthivi* are commonly believed to refer to Heaven and Earth respectively; but they really refer to the senses of knowledge and of action (MM. I, 358-361). The *Mīmāṁsā* describes the same idea in terms of desire and its fulfilment, or knowledge and action.
    The text refers to certain verses relating to "desire for kindling the fire" and to the "fire as kindled"; and that is the difference between desire and its fulfilment.
13. The text uses the word *śabda,* which means oral or traditional authority or evidence, as a means of acquiring knowledge.
14. *Brāhmaṇavatī* is said to be the name of a particular "brick" used in building the sacrificial altar; and the word for a "brick" is *"ishṭakā",* which is derived from *"ishṭa",* one of the meanings of which is "desired". A "brick" used in building a sacrificial altar, is, accordingly, symbolic of the idea of desire, which constitutes the basis of action, – represented by this sacrifice. The *Brāhmaṇavatī* bricks are placed in the middle, because they represent what is in the middle, – namely, the idea of neutrality or disinterestedness in action, as has already been explained.
15 *Lokam-pṛṇā* means "penetrating everywhere"; and so *Lokam-pṛṇa* "bricks" represent a more common idea of action with desire, which is seen everywhere.
16 We have already been told that if we divide words into parts to get their real meaning, the idea of *Mantras* or hymns of praise would be transformed into *Vidhi* or the law of life.
17 These rules of interpretation have already been laid down. The meanings of certain words, like *Agni,* have been specially defined, and we should understand them in that light. In certain cases we may accept the common meaning of a word if it makes sense; but if it does not, we should divide it into parts, and understand it in the light of the meaning of these parts, – and see that it has a bearing on the idca of action.
18 The words used in the text are *Soma* and *Agni,* which refer to the mind and the intellect respectively. This is their meaning throughout.
19 This means that the mind cannot always be included in the intellect; for were it otherwise, a man should always act at the bidding of his intellect, even though he may not wish to act; and desire, ashas already been pointed out, is a special attribute of the mind.
20 At the same time the mind and the intellect are closely allied.Indeed, the *Sāṅkhya* tells us that out of the intellect arises *ahaṇkāra* or the I-as-an-actor, and out of the latter the mind. The *Mīmāṁsā* means the same thing when it says that the mind arises out of the abundance of the intellect.
    The word for the mind in the text is *Soma,* and for the intellect *Brāhmaṇa.*
21 There are a number of references to the association of the mind and the

Moon in the Vedas and other sacred books (*Cf.* RV. X, xc, 13; ŚBr. VIII, i, 2, 7-8). If we understand this, we can understand the laws of life, and integrate the idea of the forces of Nature with the working of the human mind.

22 The appearance of the full moon at the appointed time means that the Moon is subject to a law; and, as it refers to the mind, it implies that the mind too can be properly regulated and made subject to a law. The appearance of the full moon is accordingly symbolic of the proper control of the mind when it is engaged in action.

23 As fixity of time signifies control, its opposite implies irregularity or impropriety of conduct or lack of self control. This is represented by the acquisition of wealth, because it can be acquired at any time.

24 The *Mīmāṁsā* tells -us that the association of the mind with the Moon is based on reason; that is to say, they have common charac teristics, and so the Moon is said to be a symbolf of the mind. It is believed that the Moon is connected in a special manner with the birth of life on earth: and its effect on the waters, which refer to Nature or *Prakṛti,* is well known. This may be said to be symbolic of desire, which is a special characteristic of the mind. Then the energy of the Moon is said to be electric, and so is that of the mind. the mind refers to the Moon, so does intellect to the Sun; and there is a common link between their ideas too (*Cf.* MM. I, 48, n. 1).

25 The word used in the text is *Indra* who, as has already been explained, refers to the self-conscious soul *(Prajñātman).*

26. A period of two days should be understood to illustrate this idea of change in Nature.

27 The special attribute of the mind is desire, which changes from moment to moment. But when this desire is characterised by both goodness and intelligence, it does not change in the same manner.

28. The idea of the changeability of the human mind is represented by the changes of the moon from the new to the full moon. The new moon refers to desire, and the full moon to the action of the mind under the direction of the intellect; and so the changes from the new to the full moon represent the process of development from desire to action. Then, when the mind acts, its desire is satisfied, and it is one with the intellect; and corresponding to this the full moon and the setting sun appear to be alike,—and the Sun refers to the intellect, as has already been explained. And so we are told that *Agni* and *Soma* may be identified.

CHAPTER - VI

THE PROBLEM OF ACTION

PART I

Introduction

Action implies a close connection between objects. All persons are entitled to act; but the manner of action of each is different.

The actor may be described as a man; but the term "man" refers to the whole human species, and so a woman is an actor too. But if the term "man" expressly refers to the male, it should be taken to be so.

There are some who believe that a woman cannot own property; but she can do so; only she is second to man; but what belongs specially to her is the power to bless and to remain chaste.

The four castes represent the same idea of subordination and inter-connection of things.

When it is said that the *śūdra* cannot act, the reference is to the efficient cause of action; and the meaning of the word is a different one.

When the Vedas say that the *śūdra* cannot act, we should understand the sense in which they say so. We should also understand the sense in which they say that the three castes can acquire wealth.

We must not, however, forget to consider the function of the soul, which cannot in any case be omitted.

Not only has the word *śūdra* another meaning, but also some other words like *Saudhanvana* and *Niṣāda;* and they need to be properly understood.

Definition of Action

द्रव्याणां कर्मसंयोगे गुणत्वेनाऽभिसम्बन्धः॥१॥

असाधकं तु तादर्थ्यात्॥२॥

प्रत्यर्थं चाऽभिसंयोगात् कर्मतो ह्यभिसम्बन्धस्तस्मात्कर्मोपदेशः स्यात्॥३॥

When an action is performed, the different objects associated with it are closely connected with one another, because they are subordinate to one another. It is in this manner that even an inefficient person can play his part in action. We find, in every case, that there is action only if there is such a close connection; and we might say that this closeness of connection itself is a form of action.

All are entitled to Act

फलार्थत्वात्कर्मणः शास्त्रं सर्वाधिकारं स्यात्॥४॥

कर्तुवा श्रुतिसंयोगाद्विधिः कात्स्न्येंन गम्यते॥५॥

As an action is performed for the sake of its result, all persons should be regarded as entitled to act, as the sacred books tell us.[1] But they also tell us that the manner of action of each is different, and should be understood in the light of action taken as a whole.

The Actor in terms of Man and Woman

लिङ्गविशेषनिर्देशात्पुंयुक्तमैतिशायनः॥६॥

तदुक्तित्वाच्च दोषश्रुतिरविज्ञाते॥७॥

जातिं तु बादरायणोऽविशेषात्; तस्मात् स्त्र्यपि प्रतीयेत; जात्यर्थस्या-
ऽविशिष्टत्वात्॥८॥

अ. विभक्त्येति चेन्न॥९॥

चोदितत्वाद्यथाश्रुति॥१०॥

According to *Aitiśāyana,* an actor should be described as a man (or a word in the masculine gender), because that is the best way of doing so. We should accept his view; but, if in spite of this, we misinterpret or find fault with the text, the error would lie in our own lack of knowledge. *Bādarāyaṇa* says that the reference to "man" is to the species or the human race (as opposed to an individual), and so the term is used without any special distinction of sex. For that reason even a woman should be regarded as an actor, because so far as the species is concerned, there is no distinction (between man and woman); and we cannot admit that there is any.[2] But if the term "man" is distinctly said to refer to the male, we should take it to be so in accordance with what the sacred books have said.

Woman and Wealth

द्रव्यवत्त्वात्तु पुंसां स्याद्द्रव्यसंयुक्तं क्रयविक्रयाभ्यामद्रव्यत्वं स्त्रीणां द्रव्यैः समानयोगित्वात्॥१०॥

तथा चाऽन्यार्थदर्शनम्॥११॥

तादर्थ्यात्कर्मतादर्थ्यम्॥१२॥

फलोत्साहाऽविशेषात्[1]॥१३॥

अर्थेन च समवेतत्वात्॥१४॥

क्रमस्य धर्ममात्रत्वम्॥१५॥

स्ववत्तामपि दर्शयति॥१६॥

स्ववतोस्तु वचनादैककर्म्यं स्यात्॥१७॥

लिङ्गदर्शनाच्च॥१८॥

क्रीतत्वात्तु भक्त्या स्वामित्वमुच्यते॥१९॥

फलार्थित्वात्तु स्वामित्वेनाऽभिसम्बन्धः॥२०॥

फलवत्तां च दर्शयति॥२१॥

द्व्याधनं च द्वियज्ञवत्॥२२॥

गुणस्य तु विधनत्वात्पत्न्या द्वितीयाशब्दः स्यात्॥२३॥

तस्या यावदुक्तमाशीर्ब्रह्मचर्यमतुल्यत्वात्॥२४॥

There are some who believe that, so far as the possession of wealth is concerned, the reference should be to men as such, because they alone can have wealth. They state that women cannot have wealth, because they can be bought and sold, and

1. भाष्ये अविशेषात्तु इति पाठः।

so are like property or wealth themselves. They also give another reason in support of their contention, – namely, that all action is meant for the sake of some one else, – and so woman should be intended for the sake of man. But we find that, so far as effort to secure a certain result is concerned, there is no distinction between a man and a woman; and this is proved by the fact that the two are united together to secure a common end (an offspring). So far as the purchase of a woman is concerned, it is only a matter of custom; for we can see for ourselves that women do possess wealth; and if a woman can do so, it follows that she can also act; and this can easily be proved. But even if a woman is "bought", she can still own property through some one else (or through devotion to her man). Indeed, she is closely connected with the ownership of property, because we see that both man and woman seek the fruit of action jointly; and we see that it accrues to both.

It is for this reason that the union of the two is said to be like a sacrifice of both. But, as in an action we have a principal and a subordinate part, the word "second" should refer to the wife, for she is not the equal of man; but what belongs specially to her is the power to bless and to remain chaste.

The Four Castes

चातुर्वर्ण्यमविशेषात्॥२५॥

निर्देशाद्वा त्रयाणां स्यादग्न्याधेये ह्यसम्बन्धः, क्रतुषु ब्राह्मणश्रुति-रित्यात्रेयः॥२६॥

निमित्तार्थे च बादरिस्तस्मात् सर्वाधिकारः[1] स्यात्॥२७॥

अपि वाऽन्यार्थदर्शनाद्यथाश्रुति प्रतीयेत॥२८॥

निर्देशात्तु पक्षे स्यात्॥२९॥

वैगुण्यान्नेति चेत्॥३०॥

न काम्यत्वात्॥३१॥

संस्कारे च तत्प्रधनत्वात्॥३२॥

---

१. सर्वाधिकारमित्यानन्दाश्रमपाठः।

अपि वा वेदनिर्देशादपशूद्राणां प्रतीयेत॥३३॥
गुणार्थि[1]त्वान्नेति चेत्॥३४॥
संस्कारस्य तदर्थत्वाद्विद्यायां पुरुषश्रुतिः॥३५॥
विद्यानिर्देशान्नेति चेत्॥३६॥
अवैद्यत्वादभावः कर्मणि स्यात्॥३७॥
तथा चान्यार्थदर्शनम्॥३८॥

The four castes represent the same idea of subordination and inter-connection of things in every case. According to *Atreya,* it is only the (first) three castes that have a right to act, because there is a special reference to that effect in the sacred books, – for the fourth caste cannot be included in anything that is connected with the intellect;[3] while the *śruti* says that the *Brāhmaṇa* is associated with all things connected with the intellect.[4] *Bādari* says that it is only in the sense of an efficient cause that action is limited to the first three castes[5] and because of this every one should be entitled to act.

However, as there is some other meaning attaching to the text, it should (at first) be taken as it is.[6] But the description should have a bearing on the matter under discussion: and we cannot say that it is not so, – on the ground of imperfect knowledge of the text. In any case, we cannot construe it as we like; and when we understand the correct formation of words, we shall find that we get the real meaning from the words themselves, – for that is the beauty of this form of composition[7].

However, if the Veda says so, we must agree that the *right* to act belongs to all with the exception of the *śūdra*. It is possible to say that we cannot accept this, – on the ground that we need to know all the parts of action, and the *śūdra* cannot be excluded. But the *śruti* deals with *purusha* or the soul, and so refers to the problem of knowledge; and we have to understand the correct use of words in the light of this meaning. It is possible

---

१. णर्थत्वेति वृत्तौ। पठः। गुणर्थेनेति च जीवानन्दपाठः।

to disagree with this explanation, on the ground that there is (always) a special reference to knowledge, where necessary. That is indeed so, because if there is no knowledge, there can be no action; and it is in this manner that we get the other meanings of the text[8].

Wealth and its Use

त्रयाणां द्रव्यसम्पन्नः कर्मणो द्रव्यसिद्धित्वात्॥३९॥
अनित्यत्वात्तु नैवं स्यादर्थाद्धि द्रव्यसंयोगः॥४०॥
अङ्गहीनश्च तद्धिर्मा॥४१॥
उत्पत्तौ नित्यसंयोगात्॥४२॥
अत्र्यार्षेयस्य हानं स्यात्॥४३॥

The three castes can acquire wealth because it is acquired through action.[9] But because life itself is transitory, we cannot go on acquiring wealth for ever; and wealth is acquired only for its use. This can be illustrated by means of what a person does when he has lost a limb;[10] and we find this in everything that takes place, because there is an unfailing connection between wealth and its use. (All this has been explained in the Vedas;) but he who does not believe in this idea of the three Vedas of sacred descent (or composed by the *riṣis),* can never be convinced, and must be given up (as an impossible man).

Function of the Soul

वचनाद्रथकारस्याधने सर्वशेषत्वात्॥४४॥
न्यायो वा कर्मसंयोगाच्छूद्रस्य प्रतिषिद्धित्वात्॥४५॥
अकर्मत्वात्तु नैवं स्यात्॥४६॥
आनर्थक्यं च संयोगात्॥४७॥

In this consideration we have kept out "the master of the body" or the soul, whose function, according to what has been taught, is to employ the different faculties of man. It is only in the fitness of things that we should think of the soul or "the master of the body", because of its association with action; where as it is possible to omit the *śūdra.*[11] But if there is nc action, it is not necessary to think of anything at all: only, in that case, there will be no purpose in anything; and all are agreed on this point.

Special Meanings

गुणार्थमिति चेत्॥४८॥
उक्तमनिमित्तत्वम्॥४९॥
सौधन्वनास्तु हीनत्वानमन्त्रवर्णात् प्रतीयेरन्॥५०॥
स्थपतिर्निषादः स्याच्छब्दसामर्थ्यात्॥५१॥
लिङ्गदर्शनाच्च॥५२॥

We can agree that the term *śūdra* has a subsidiary meaning; and that it is not an instrumental cause of action. As language is an imperfect medium of expression, (we have to use certain terms to express our ideas; and so) the word *Saudhanvana* may be said to refer to the *śūdra.*[12] Similarly *Niṣāda* should be understood to mean *Stha-pati*[13] for the meaning of the two words is the same: and we can understand its idea by piercing through its "disguise[14].

PART II

THE LAW OF ACTION AND INACTION

Introduction

A law is a statement of general truth; and what is said to be true of one man may be deemed to be true of all; and it is this that we should find in the sacred books. All this is described in the Vedas in accordance with certain rules; and we can fix upon the meaning by reading the text in accordance with *Krama*.

It is necessary to have knowledge of science to be able to understand the idea of action, which is related to Time; and that will enable us to have knowledge of the soul.

The sacred books enjoin action, but do not promise their fruit.

They also contain prohibition against action; but that does not mean inaction: it only means prohibition against action that ought not to be done by a good man.

All these things were taught a long time ago, and we have forgotten them; but it is not difficult to understand them, and we can do so by means of proper study. But we should understand all these things in the light of human effort; and this will enable us to know what are duties of a *Brāhmaṇa*.

Idea of Law: from Particular to General

पुरुषार्थैकसिद्धित्वात्तस्य तस्याधिकारः स्यात्॥१॥

अपि वोत्पत्तिसंयोगाद्यथा स्यात् सर्व[1]दर्शनं तथाभावोऽविभागे स्यात्॥२॥

प्रयोगे पुरुषश्रुतेर्यथाकामी प्रयोगे स्यात्॥३॥

प्रत्यर्थं श्रुतिभाव इति चेत्॥४॥

तादर्थ्ये न गुणार्थताऽनुक्तेऽर्थान्तर-त्वात्कर्तुः प्रधनभूतत्वात्॥५॥

[5]अ. चोदनैकत्वात्[2]।

अपि वा कामसंयोगे सम्बन्धत् प्रयोगायोपदिश्येत प्रत्यर्थं हि विधिश्रुतिर्विषाणावत्॥६॥

If we prove the object of the pursuit of the soul[15] in one case, it means that we have proved it in all cases. Whatever is true of one creature in accordance with the law of its nature or birth, must be true of all without distinction; and so, when in the text there is a reference to the soul in any affair, it means that any one who likes may take part in such an affair. It is not necessary to find out the intention of the text in every case; because if we say that "a man" has the sense of "any man", it is because we do not assign any special attributes to a man; and any other meaning would be improper, because what is important is the idea of the doer of the deed, and not a particular person. Indeed, a single direction in the text should enable us to understand this[16]; and, if we succeed in doing so, we should be able to indicate the plan of the whole from the connection of its parts. Similarly, we should take it that, if the text is an exposition of the laws of life, it should be the best of its kind (or composed in the most perfect form).

---

1. गुणार्थैनेति पाठान्तरम्।
2. अन्यस्यादिति चेदित्येवं नञं विहायापि पाठो जै. न्या. मा.।

Fixed Rules

अन्य[1]स्यापीति चेत्॥७॥
अन्यार्थेनाभिसम्बन्धः॥८॥
फलकामो निमित्तमिति चेत्॥९॥
न नित्यत्वात्॥१०॥
कर्म तथेति चेत्॥११॥
न समवायात्॥१२॥
प्रक्रमात्तु नियम्येतारम्भस्य क्रियानिमित्त[2]त्वात्॥१३॥
फलर्थित्वाद्वाऽनियमो यथानुपक्रान्ते॥१४॥
नियमो वा तन्निमित्तत्वात्कर्तुस्तत्कारणं स्यात्॥१५॥

We cannot say that this is but one of the many ways of understanding the text, because if we have a different meaning, we find that there is no close connection between its different parts. Nor can we say that the cause of this interpretation is the desire to get a particular explanation, because the rules of interpretation are fixed; whereas actions are not fixed, –for we see that they are of different kinds and often clash with one another.[17] But we should fix upon the meaning of the text by reading it according to *Krama,* because the text has been composed in that manner; and if the new meaning could arise merely because of our desire to understand the text in a particular way, there would be no fixed rules in regard to the method of interpretation, just as there can be no fixed rules in connection with a thing that does not exist. As, however, there is a fixed rule by means of which the text can effectively be interpreted, it should be regarded as the governing principle in respect of all that concerns the doer of the deed[18].

Knowledge, Action and its Fruit

लोके कर्मणि वेदवत्ततोऽधिपुरुषज्ञानम्॥१६॥
अपराधेऽपि च तैः शास्त्रम्॥१७॥
अशास्त्रात्तूपसम्प्राप्तिः शास्त्रं स्यान्न प्रकल्पकं तस्मादर्थेन गम्येताप्राप्ते

---

1. अन्यस्य स्यादिति चेत्--इति आ. पाठः।
2. नियम्येति आ. पाठः।

वा शास्त्रमर्थवत्॥१८॥
देवता[१]श्रये च। १८अ.॥

In all action, having a bearing on time, we should have knowledge of science; and that will enable us to acquire knowledge of *puruṣa* or the soul. We are directed to perform such actions even if we make mistakes.[19] But the sacred books do not tell us that we can obtain the fruit of actions for ourselves; and it is an error to suppose that there is any such direction in them.[20] Hence, the fruit of action should not be deemed to consist in wealth; and even if we are unable to achieve any result, the direction to act has its own value; whereas, so far as the result is concerned, it depends on the will of the gods[21].

Action and Inaction

प्रतिषेधेश्वकर्मत्वात्क्रिया स्यात्प्रतिषिद्धनां विभक्तत्वादकर्मणाम्॥१९॥

(Prohibition against action is not inaction). When there is a prohibition, this non-activity should be taken to be a form of activity in respect of things prohibited, because there are many forms of inaction[22].

शास्त्राणां त्वर्थवत्त्वेन पुरुषार्थो विधीयते; तयोरसमवायित्वात्तादर्थ्ये विध्यतिक्रमः॥२०॥
तस्मिंस्तु शिष्यमाणानि जननेन प्रवर्तेरन्॥२१॥
अपि वा वेदतुल्यत्वादुपायेन प्रवर्तेरन्॥२२॥
अभ्यासोऽकर्मशेषत्वात् पुरुषार्थो विधीयते॥२३॥
एतस्मिन्नसंभवन्नर्थात्॥२४॥
न कालेभ्य उपदिश्यन्ते॥२५॥

Character of the Vedas and their Idea of Inaction

The directions of the sacred books are full of purpose, and they need to be understood in the light of the object of *puruṣa* or the soul; but if we are unable to understand the

१. इदं सूत्रमधिकं वृत्तिग्रन्थ पठयते, भाष्यग्रन्थे वातिकग्रन्थ न्यायमालायां च न दृश्यते।

intimate connection between the two (sacred books and the soul), it would be a violation of rules to force the meaning into something else. But what is taught in them requires the work of a life-time to understand. Moreover, all the Vedas are equally important, and we should seek such means of understanding them as would lead to success; and, in order to do so, we should make a repeated study of them; and understand the idea of inaction referred to in them, in a secondary sense, – that is, only when it is meant to serve the purpose of *puruṣa* or the soul (or is good for a man).[23] This is a self evident truth and requires no argument to prove it; but it seems that we cannot say so, because these things were taught long ago (and need to be restated to be understood)[24].

Idea of Time

दर्शनात्काललिङ्गानां कालविधनम्॥२६॥
तेषामौत्पत्तिकत्वादागमेन प्रवर्त्तेत॥२७॥
तथा हि लिङ्गदर्शनम्॥२८॥
तथान्तःक्रतु युक्तानि॥२९॥
आचाराद्गृह्यमाणेषु तथा स्यात् पुरुषार्थत्वात्॥३०॥
ब्राह्मणस्य तु सोमविद्याप्रजमृणवाक्येन संयोगात्॥३१॥

(But it is not an impossible task: for instance,) if in the text we find a description of the character istics of Time, we should take it that it is a statement regarding Time. Things like this relate to eternal truths or the origin of things, and can be understood only by means of proper study; and that would enable us to know the proper reason for this explanation, as well as the inner design of the composition of the text. Again, when we try to understand things relating to tradition or immemorial custom, we should do so in the light of the purpose of the *puruṣa* or the soul (or human effort); and so we shall find that there is general agreement in regard to the duties of a *Brāhmaṇa* (or an intelligent person), – namely, that he should act in the light of the proper function of the mind, acquire knowledge, and have offspring[25].

PART III

ENERGY AND ACTION : THE LANGUAGE OF THE VEDAS

Introduction

Energy means activity which pervades each part of an organism. We can divide energy into parts, but not action, which is a unit, and is characterised by a purpose; and its success is due to the power of predominant thought that prompts effort.

All actions are interdependent, and cannot be separated from one another or the language that describes them. Hence, there is an intimate connection between an object and its name.

This is the basis of the language of the Vedas. Their text is authoritative, and no unauthorised additions should be made.

We can understand its meaning from the words themselves. The meaning of some has specially been explained; while of others we must understand from the context or the effect they produce. Where there is a doubt about an occurrence, we can understand it from its description, for there is nothing that cannot be described in words.

There is no error or impropriety in the language of the Vedas; and so a substitute expression can be used only if it has the same meaning as the original one. But it is not easy to find an exact substitute; and so it is possible that, in such cases, the language is not perfect.

The chief difficulty in connection with the text is that it is not easy to understand. But if we find that the description of an object is inconsistent, we should attach more importance to the object than the description; and if there is an inconsistency between an object and its use, we should attach more importance to its use. But there should be a method in our work, and we should be able to connect the parts with the whole.

When, however, there are a number of meanings, we should take those which are apposite.

Energy is Activity

सर्वशक्तौ प्रवृत्तिः स्यात्तथाभूतोपदेशात्॥१॥
अपि वाऽप्येकदेश स्यात्प्रधने ह्यर्थनिवृत्तिर्गुणमात्रमितरत्तदर्थत्वात्॥२॥
तदकर्मणि च दोषस्तस्मात्ततो विशेषः स्यात्प्रधनेनाऽभिसम्बन्धत्॥३॥

In all forms of energy there should be activity; and this is true of all things that exist. This activity is to be found in every single part of the whole organism, though its purpose is fulfilled by the principal part,—the remaining parts being subsidiary to the latter and ministering to its ends. If the principal part does not function, the whole organism suffers from its evil effects; while, on the other hand, if it functions properly, the whole attains to a degree of excellence, because of its close connection with the principal part.

Action, Purpose and Result

कर्माऽभेदं तु जैमिनिः प्रयोगवचनैकत्वात् सर्वेषामुपदेशः स्यात्॥४॥
अर्थस्य वयपवर्गित्वादेकस्यापि प्रयोगे स्याद्यथा क्रत्वन्तरेषु॥५॥
विध्यपराधे च दर्शनात्समाप्तेः॥६॥
प्रायश्चित्तविधनाच्च॥७॥
काम्येषु चैवमर्थित्वात्॥८॥
असंयोगात्तु नैवं स्याद्विधेः शब्दप्रमाणत्वात्॥९॥
अकर्मणि चाप्रत्यवायात्॥१०॥

Jaimini says that while we may divide energy into a number of parts, we cannot divide action in the same manner; and a single statement in connection with the commencement of an action should serve to explain the character of the whole. But, as the purpose of each action is different, there must be a mention of at least one purpose at the commencement of such action, just as we find in the case of other plans. (This would enable us to have a proper idea of action;) and this is proved by the fact that we find that we are able to accomplish our purpose even though we might have committed mistakes in regard to the manner of performing an action. This is due to the power of predominant thought (that prompts us); and its effect can specially be seen in actions which are to our liking,—because of the state of our desire. (But this success is also due to close application,) and if we do not apply ourselves closely to our task, we cannot succeed in this way; and there is oral authority[26] to that effect in connection with the manner of doing things. (This is borne out by the fact that) we find that when we deliberately abstain from an action, we do not feel any disappointment.

Action and Language

क्रियाणामाश्रितत्वाद्द्रव्यान्तरे विभागः स्यात्।

अपि वाऽव्यतिरेकाद्रूपशब्दाविभागाच्च गोत्ववदैककर्म्यं स्यान्नमधेयं च सत्त्ववत्॥१२॥

All actions are inter-dependent, and one action has share in another. Actions cannot be separated from one another, nor from the form of words which express their idea. Hence there should be unity between the idea of an action and the name given to it, just as in the case of the character of the cow (and its name);[27] for the name should be full of life (or expressive of the object described).

Language of the Vedas

श्रुति प्रमाणत्वाच्छिष्टाभावेऽनागमोऽन्यस्याऽशिष्टत्वात्॥१३॥

क्वचिद्विधनाच्च॥१४॥

आगमो वा चोदनार्थाविशेषात्॥१५॥

नियमार्थः क्वचिद्विधिः॥१६॥

तन्नित्यं तच्चिकीर्षा हि॥१७॥

(This is the character of the language of the Vedas). The text of the *śruti* is authoritative; and unless we are specially instructed to do so, we should not make any additions of our own to it, because it would be contrary to the laws of learning. Indeed, there is no need to make any additions, because the statement of all the required particulars is found in the same place in the text. But an addition may be made if its meaning is uniform with the rest of the text. The rule in regard to making an addition is based on the meaning we obtain, —in whatever it is done; for it is necessary that we should get a proper meaning, and that indeed is also our desire.

How to Obtain a Meaning

न देवताग्निशब्दक्रियमन्यार्थसंयोगात्॥१८॥

देवतायां च तदर्थत्वात्॥१९॥

प्रतिषिद्धं चाविशेषेण हि तच्छ्रुतिः॥२०॥

तथा स्वामिनः फलसमवायात् फलस्य कमयोगित्वात्॥२१॥

बहूनां तु[1] प्रवृत्तावन्यमागमयेदवैगुण्यात्॥२२॥

स स्वामी स्यात्संयोगात्॥२३॥

कर्मकरो वा क्रीतत्वात्॥२४॥

तस्मिंश्च फलदर्शनात्॥२५॥

स तद्धर्मा स्यात्त[2]त्कर्मसंयोगात्॥२६॥

सामान्यं तच्चिकीर्षा हि॥२७॥

(The meaning of a word is contained in the word itself: for instance,) the meaning of the word *Agni* as a god[28] (or a great natural power) is not derived from the meaning of some other word; and it means a god because that is its own meaning. But there are some who deny this on the ground that the text does not define the meaning of the word. Even so the text does not define the meaning of the word *svāmin;* but we understand its meaning (as soul, master or lord) from the result arising from its use, and the result arises from its connection with action.[29] If a word has a number of meanings, we have to take that which is the least imperfect; and it is in this manner that we get the meaning of ' the word *svāmin* from the context. The

1. त्वित्यस्य स्थाने चेति पाठो वृत्तिग्रन्थे, प्रवृत्तेऽन्य0-इति पाठभेदः।
2. क्वचित् तदिति न दृश्यते।

same is the case with the word *karma-kāra* (a workman, servant), because of the reference to his being hired or paid a wage. Thus we get the meaning of a word from the result of its use; and so the character of a person is connected with his actions, and even the desire to do a certain deed indicates the same.

Power of Language

निर्देशात्तु विकल्पे यत्प्रवृत्तम्॥२८॥

अशब्दमिति चेत्॥२९॥

नाऽनङ्गत्वात्॥३०॥

संस्काराश्च[1] खादिरे कर्तव्याः॥३०अ.॥

If there is a doubt about what has happened, we can find it out from its description. We cannot say that there are things that cannot be described in words, because it is all within the power of the mind to describe them;[30] and it is the mind that enables us to make a correct use of words.

Language of the Vedas

वचनाच्चाऽन्याय्यमभावे तत्सामान्येन प्रतिनिधिरभावादितरस्य॥३१॥

न प्रतिनिधै समत्वात्॥३२॥

स्याच्छ्रुतिलक्षणे नित्यत्वात्॥३३॥

न तदीप्सा हि॥३४॥

मुख्याधिगमे मुख्यमागमो हि तदभावात्॥३५॥

We are told on authority that there is no error or impropriety in the use of words in the text of the Vedas; and so a substitute or alternate expression should be used only if it has the same meaning as the original word, because anything else would convey a very different sense. It may not, however, be possible to find an exact substitute, with an identical meaning,

---

1. इदं सूत्रं भाष्ये सूत्रत्वेन नोक्तम्।
जै. न्या. वृत्तिग्रन्थे त्वस्ति।

specially where the text deals with fundamental ideas or the eternal character of things. It is possible that in such cases even the original language is not perfect, because perfection can never be achieved, and we are always wanting to achieve it; and that is the reason why the more we study the text, the greater is the knowledge we acquire.

The chief Difficulty and how to overcome it

प्रवृत्तेऽपीति चेत्॥३६॥

नानर्थकत्वात्॥३७॥

द्रव्यसंस्कारविरोधे द्रव्यं तदर्थत्वात्॥३८॥

अर्थद्रव्यविरोधेऽर्थो द्रव्याभावे तदुत्पत्तेर्द्रव्याणामर्थशेषत्वात्॥३९॥

विधिरप्येकदेशे स्यात्॥४०॥

अपि वाऽर्थस्य शक्यत्वादेकदेशेन निर्वर्तेतार्थानामविभक्तत्वाद्गुणमात्र-मितरत्तदर्थत्वात्॥४१॥

It is not correct to say that this would be so in any case, however great our devotion to the task; (for the chief difficulty is not that the language is not perfect, but that) the text does not make any sense at all. (But there is a way out,) and if we find that the description of an object is inconsistent, we should attach more importance to the object than to its description, because the object is the primary thing, and the description is for the sake of the object. Again, if we find that there is an inconsistency between an object and its use, we should attach more importance to its use. In case there is no reference to an object, we should see what arises out of it as a result, because what remains of objects is their use. There should thus be a method of doing things in connection with each part of the entire text; and, as it is possible to get a rational meaning in this way, we should be able to explain each part of the whole. When, however, there are a number of meanings, we should take those which are most apposite,—for that is the measure of their excellence; and the rest of the text is intended to contribute to that excellence.

PART IV

THE METHOD OF INTERPRETATION

Introdution

It is necessary to make a selection of our meaning; but if there is a special mention of a particular meaning or a particular cause, we should accept that in preference to anything else, even if some other meaning also makes sense. But there can be only one predominant thought, which must produce its own effect or result. The main and subordinate parts of the text are closely connected together, for other wise the whole thing would become meaningless.

There are, however, certain terms or expressions which have a special meaning: for instance, "burning to ashes" means "burning everything"; "inexhaustibleness" refers to this world; *tad* means sacrifice of all kinds; the idea of renewing the sacrificial fire and "cooked rice" is the same; the "offering of five cups" is a substitute for something else; there is an idea behind the invocation of the deity of a substance without the worshipper; "conquest of the world" means harmony of thought, feeling and action; the austerities of a father mean that he wants to benefit his son; the idea of Time arises from something that makes its appearance, or the word "immeasurable", or the birth of a son.

The meaning of the word *sva* or soul cannot be expressed in words; we can understand the idea of Time because of its connection with some characteristic of the soul; and we can understand the idea of both Time and the soul because of the purposefulness of Time.

It is necessary to arrange things in an orderly manner; and it is this that gives us the idea of Time.

Importance of special Meanings

शेषाद्द्व्यवदाननाशे स्यात्तदर्थत्वात्॥१॥
निर्देशाद्वाऽन्यदागमयेत्॥२॥
अपि वा शुषभाजां स्याद्विशिष्टकारणात्॥३॥

निर्देशाच्छेषभक्षोऽन्यैः प्रधनवत्॥४॥
सर्वैर्वा समवायात्स्यात्॥५॥
निर्देशस्य गुणार्थत्वम्॥६॥
प्रधने श्रुतिलक्षणम्॥७॥
अश्व[1]वदिति चेत्॥८॥
न चोदनाविरोधत्॥९॥
अर्थसमवायात्प्रायश्चित्तमेकदेशेऽपि॥१०॥
न त्वशेषे वैगुण्यात्तदर्थं हि॥११॥
स्याद्वा प्राप्तनिमित्तत्वादतद्धर्मो नित्यसंयोगान्न हि तस्य गुणार्थत्वे-नानित्यत्वात्॥१२॥

When in our interpretation of the text we come to two meanings which are equally significant, we should select that which has a bearing on the result, because that is the purpose it has to serve. But if there is a special reference to some other meaning, it should be preferred; because, if there is mention of a special cause, result is but a poor support to uphold a different one. When there is special mention of a particular cause, it should be regarded as most important, and the result should be "absorbed" or explained away in some other way. But whatever the explanation, the meaning of the whole should be closely knitted together,—with an intimate relation of each part to the other. However, the cause that has been specially mentioned, has an excellence of its own; and it is only in matters of great importance that there is a detailed description of things in the *śruti*.

No other explanation can make as good sense as the special meaning given in the text, because there can be no conflict with it anywhere. At the same time, as the [31], whole meaning is closely inter-connected, the predominant thought of the text can be found only in one place (and two explanations cannot be equally satisfactory). But the prominent thought cannot exist without result,—for, were it so, it would be an unskilful way of handling it. Indeed, it is there for the purpose of producing a

1. अर्थवदिति पाठो न्या. मा.।

result. This should be so, and this is actually found to be the case; and anything else would be unthinkable. As all parts of the text are closely connected together, the meaning based on result cannot be regarded as subsidiary; and it would be a very unusual thing to think that it is.

Main and Subordinate Parts

गुणानां च परार्थत्वाद्वचनाद् व्यपाश्रयः स्यात्॥१३॥
वचनाद्विकल्प इति चेन्न निमि त्तार्थेन संभवात्॥१३अ.॥
भेदार्थमिति चेत्॥१४॥
नाशेषभूतत्वात्॥१५॥
अनर्थकश्च सर्वनाशे स्यात्॥१६॥

So far as the subordinate parts of the text are concerned, since they are meant to serve the purpose of some higher object, they need to be supported by some statement in the text. Nor need the statement create a doubt as to the exact idea of these parts, because there is always a reason for them;[32] and their meaning cannot be different in different places, because it is obtained from the entire body of the text. Indeed, if they were to lose their meaning, the whole text would be broken up.

Special Explanation of certain Terms

क्षामे तु सर्वदाहे स्यादेकदेशस्याऽवर्जनीयत्वात्॥१७॥
दर्शनाद्वैकदेशे स्यात्॥१८॥
अन्येन वैतच्छास्त्राद्धि कारण प्राप्तिः॥१९॥
तद्धिविः शब्दान्नेति चेत्॥२०॥
स्यादिज्यागामी हविः शब्दस्तल्लिंगसंयोगात्॥२१॥
यथाश्रुतीति चेत्॥२२॥
न तल्लक्षणत्वादुपपातो हि कारणम्॥२३॥
होमाभिषवभक्षणं च तद्वत्॥२४॥
उभाभ्यां वा न हि तयोर्धर्मशास्त्रम्॥२५॥
पुनराधेयमोदनवत्॥२६॥
द्रव्योत्पत्तेश्चोभयोः स्यात्॥२७॥
पञ्चशरावस्तु द्रव्यश्रुतेः प्रतिनिधिः स्यात्॥२८॥

चोदना वा द्रव्यदेवताविधिरवाच्ये हि॥२९॥
स प्रत्यामनत्स्थानात्॥३०॥
अङ्गविधिर्वा निमित्तसंयोगात्॥३१॥
विश्वजिद[1]प्रवृत्ते भावः कर्मणि स्यात्॥३२॥
निष्क्रयवादाच्च॥३३॥
वत्ससंयोगे व्रतचोदना स्यात्॥३४॥

(There are certain expressions used in the text which have been explained in a special manner: for instance,) when we speak of "burning to ashes", the meaning is the same as "the burning of everything", because we can put one for the other in the same place; and that is how we should understand the meaning of words used in the same place.

When the word *anya* is used, meaning "inexhaustibleness" we should understand that it means *etad* or "this world"; and the reason for this is to be found in the sacred books themselves.

Similarly, the word *tad* means *havis* or sacrifice, and we cannot say that their meanings are different, for the word *havis* should be deemed to refer to sacrifice because of its connection with the word *tad.*[33] It is not necessary that all this should be contained in the *śruti,* for this is the very definition of the word; and so offering sacrifices to the god, religious bath, and even acts of eating and drinking are said to be like *tad* (or sacrifice). When a word has been specially defined, its meaning should be obtained in two ways,—the word itself and its definition; and no *Dharma-śāstra* or code of laws is required further to explain it.

Again, the idea of "renewing the sacrificial fire" is the same as that of "cooked rice" (for they both refer to food conceived in terms of sacrifice); and so the meaning of both the expressions arises from the mention of the object associated with them.

There is a mention of "an offering of five cups" in the *śruti;* and it should really be a substitute for something else[34] .

१. 'जित्त्वपृवृत्तेः' इति पाठभेदः।

There is also a rule in regard to "the deity of an object"; but there is no express mention of "the worshipper" in every case.[35] But the worshipper would wish to be present at the sacrifice because of the opportunity it would give him. Indeed, we might say that each limb of the body is a worshipper or sacrificer, because it can be the instrumental cause of action.

If a person desires to conquer the world, he should put himself in such a state of thinking and feeling as would enable him to engage in action; and this idea is expressed in terms of "payment of a wage or price"[36].

When a father is devoted to his son, and wishes to do something for him, there is an impelling urge within him to submit even to austerities for his sake[37].

The Idea of Time: How Expressed

कालो वोत्पन्नसंयोगाद्यथोक्त[1]स्य॥३५॥
अर्थापरिमाणाच्च॥३६॥
वत्सस्तु श्रुतिसंयोगात् तदङ्गं स्यात्॥३७॥
कालस्तु स्यादचोदनात्॥३८॥
अनर्थकश्च कर्मसंयोगे॥३९॥

The idea of Time arises from something that makes its appearance; and we can get it from what has already been mentioned.[38] We can also get it from the meaning of the word immeasurable.[39] Again, when there is mention of the birth of a son in the *śruti,* it should be understood to refer to a sub-division of Time. It should be regarded as pointing to Time, without reference to any other direction or rule; for the idea of the birth of a son would be found to be meaningless if we associate it with action instead.

Soul and Time

अवचनाच्च स्वशब्दस्य॥४०॥
कालश्चेत्सन्नयत्पक्षे तल्लिङ्गसंयोगात्॥४१॥
कालार्थत्वाद्वोभयोः प्रतीयेत॥४२॥

---

1. यथोक्तस्येति क्वचित्पुस्तके नास्ति।

The meaning of the word *sva* or soul cannot be expressed in words.[40] But if Time enables us to associate ourselves with anything, it is because of its connection with some characteristic of the soul;[41] and because Time has some purpose to serve (in the order of the universe), we can understand the idea of both Time and the soul[42].

The Law of Time

प्रस्तरे शाखाश्रयणवत्।।४३।।

कालविधिर्वोभयोर्विद्यमानत्वात्।।४४।।

अतत्संस्कारार्थत्वाच्च।।४५।।

तस्माच्च विप्रयोगे स्यात्।।४६।।

उपवेषश्च पक्षे स्यात्।।४७।।

When ideas and objects are scattered about, their arrangement in some scientific manner is a source of comfort, —like an asylum; and the idea of the law of Time arises from the existence of both (things and their orderly arrangement). We cannot understand the idea of Time from anything else, however perfect it be; and if we pursue any other course to understand what is Time, we shall find that, far from coming anywhere near it, we are farther removed from its idea; for we can succeed only if we look at it from a particular point of view[43].

PART V

THE METHOD OF INTERPRETATION

(*CONTINUED*)

Introduction

As when we discover an error in a course of action, we adopt some other way to remove the defect, we must do the same in connection with the text of the sacred books. In some cases we may have to repeat the same process, while in others we have to find out where the weakness lies; and we should be satisfied only if a thing is found to be both intelligent and good.

There are certain directions enabling us to understand the meaning of the text: for instance, we know the idea of boiled milk and of sacrifice offered silently.

According to *Asmarthya,* we should take the meanings of words as they are, without making any change; and treat as exceptions those which have been defined in a special way; and this will enable us to understand the meaning of a number of words. This requires devotion to the task, but is amply rewarded by the results achieved.

In this manner we can understand the nature of action, its relation to time and desire, and how it can be purified of taint by means of control of the mind.

We need to understand the text of the Vedas in the light of all this; and should, where necessary, change the form of words to get their real meaning. The two meanings may create difficulties in some cases, but they can be overcome. In some cases they can be reconciled; while in others we must accept the second meaning, obtained by changing the form of words, as being the better of the two: only we must remember that the whole idea must remain consistent throughout.

An Alternative Method of Action and Interpretation

अभ्युदये कालापराधदिज्याचोदना स्याद्यथा पञ्चशरावे॥१॥
अपनयो वा विद्यमानत्वात्॥२॥
तद्रूपत्वाच्च शब्दानाम्॥३॥
आतञ्चनाभ्यासस्य च दर्शनात्॥४॥
अपूर्वत्वाद्विधनं स्यात्॥५॥
पयोदोषात्पञ्चशरावेऽदुष्टं हीतरत्॥६॥
सान्नाय्येऽपि तथेति चेत्॥७॥
न तस्यादुष्टत्वादविशिष्टं हि कारणम्॥८॥

If, at the commencement of an action, we find that we have committed a mistake in regard to occasion or time, we wish to invoke the gods and make an offering to them, like the sacrifice of the five cups (or five senses);[44] and this is done in order to remove the error when it has been discovered. We are able to discover our error in connection with the text in the same manner, because such is the form of words used in it. We can discover our error in making curd by repeating the process, and gaining experience; for this is the manner of discovering error when we are new to our task. In case of deficiency of strength, we may find fault with the function of the five senses (five cups), although they might be faultless. We cannot say that this is possible in all cases, —even of good actions, which require exercise of the intellect,[45] because such actions would be without fault, and their cause would be general, and not a particular one[46].

Special Meanings

लक्षणार्था शृतश्रुतिः॥९॥
उपांशुया[1]ऽवचनाद्यथा प्रकृति वा॥१०॥
अपनयो वा प्रवृत्त्या यथेतरेषाम्॥११॥
निरुप्ते स्यात्तत्संयोगात्॥१२॥
प्रवृत्ते प्राणान्निमित्तस्य॥१३॥
लक्षणमात्रमितरत्॥१४॥
तथा चान्यार्थदर्शनम्॥१५॥

(Certain words have been specially defined: for instance,) the expression "boiled milk" or "cooked rice" is for the sake of accurate description.[47] In the case of prayer uttered silently, —because no words are spoken, —the natural form of words should remain unchanged.[48] In such cases if we follow our own predilections, we are likely to commit mistakes, as it happens in a number of other cases; and we shall fritter away our energy without achieving any result, —which can only be done by understanding the real meaning of things. (This is most important of all;) with regard to the rest, it is all a matter of description or illustration; and we can understand the rest of the meaning of the text in this manner.

१. "याजेष्ट इति पाठेभेदः"।

Opinion of Scholars

अनिरुप्तेऽभ्युदिते प्राकृतीभ्यो निर्वपेदित्याश्मरथ्यस्तण्डुलभूतेष्वपनयात्॥१६॥
व्यूर्ध्वभाग्भ्यस्त्वालेखनस्तत्कारित्वाद्देवतापनयस्य॥१७॥
विनिरुप्ते न मुष्टीनामपनयस्तद्गुणत्वात्॥१८॥
अपाकृंतेन हि संयोगस्तत्स्थानीयत्वात्॥१९॥
अभावाच्चेतरस्य स्यात्॥२०॥
सान्नय्यसंयोगात्सन्नयतः स्यात्॥२१॥
औषधसंयोगाद्वोभयोः॥२२॥
वैगुण्यान्नेति चेत्॥२३॥
नातत्संस्कारत्वात्॥२४॥

Asmarthya says that we should normally take words in their natural or original form before they have been distributed into something else; and that will give us their correct idea. There are, however, certain words which have to be treated as exceptions, such as *taṇḍula*[49] (meaning "rice").

Alekhana says that the word *ūrdhava* (meaning "raised above") is the opposite of *bhāj* ("possession") (that is, it means non-possession); and it is because of this that it has been personified into a deity[50].

The word *mushit* (a fist) may similarly be included in some other idea; but it does not belong to the class of exceptions; and that is due to the quality of the word. Indeed, we can get its correct meaning by taking it away from its own place, and putting it somewhere else; (for this is the best way of dealing with it) and anything else would make the whole thing meaningless[51].

The real meaning of the word *sāmnāyya* should be obtained from its connection with the word *samnaya*[52] while that of the word *aushadha* ("consisting of medicinal herbs") from its connection with both.[53] We cannot deny this connection on the ground that medicinal herbs are not always effective, because their failure is due to some other cause.

Certain Other Expressions

साम्युत्थाने विश्वजित्क्रीते विभागसंयोगात्॥२५॥
प्रवृत्ते वा प्रापणान्निमित्तस्य॥२६॥
आदेशार्थेतरा श्रुतिः॥२७॥
दीक्षापरिमाणे यथाकाम्यविशेषात्॥२८॥
द्वादशाहस्तु लिङ्गात्स्यात्॥२९॥
पौर्णमास्यामनियमोऽविशेषात्॥३०॥
आनन्तर्यात्तु चैत्री स्यात्॥३१॥
माघी वैकाष्टकाश्रुतेः॥३२॥
अन्या अपीति चेत्॥३३॥
न भक्तित्वादेषा हि लोके॥३४॥
दीक्षापराधे चानुग्रहात्॥३५॥
उत्थाने चानुप्ररोहात्॥३६॥
अस्यां च सर्वलिङ्गानि॥३७॥

Rising up to depart too quickly, and making an all-inclusive bargain, express the idea of separation and union respectively .

If a thing has occurred and we can establish that it has occurred, it means that we know what is called its efficient cause .

If we understand the *śruti* in any other way, it would give us a substituted form of meaning and not the real one. A person can succeed in. obtaining the desired result by dedicating himself to the study of the text; and then he would know the difference between the two meanings.

It is in this manner that, by means of inference, we can understand the idea of sacrifice lasting twelve days.[54] But there is an uncertainty in regard to the idea of the full moon, because there is no difference between one full moon and another[55] (and so an explanation becomes necessary.

If there is only a simple reference to the full moon, and nothing follows immediately after the statement has been made, it should refer to the full moon of the month of *Caitra.*[56] But the word *ekāshṭakā* in the *śruti* refers to the full moon in the month of *Māgha*[57].

We cannot say that there is another *ekāshṭakā* too, for there is no other *ekāshṭakā;* and it is only for the sake of convenience of understanding by the people that it has been divided into two.[58] Indeed, we think of another : *ekāshṭakā,* —and that too by mistake—when we are exclusively occupied with a certain idea, and think of it as something that confers benefits;[59] for we get this idea of it according as it appears to us; but all its characteristics are in this one form.

Sacrifice Purifies

दीक्षाकालस्य शिष्टत्वादतिक्रमे नियतानामनुत्कर्षः प्राप्तकालत्वात्॥३८॥
उत्कर्षो वा दीक्षितत्वादविशिष्टं हि कारणम्॥३९॥
तत्र प्रतिहोमो न विद्यते यथा पूर्वेषाम्॥४०॥
कालप्राधन्याच्च॥४१॥
प्रतिषिद्धच्चोर्ध्वमवभृथादिष्टेः॥४२॥

As there is an appointed time for dedication to a task, to neglect it would detract from the idea of duty in regard to what ought to be done at the proper time. On the other hand, the common cause of action is the desire to rise to something higher, when we are prepared for the task. There is in this nothing against the acts of making oblations to the gods, as the ancients used to do; for actions take place when the time is ripe for them. But by controlling desire, we elevate ourselves, because the desire is removed or purified thereby[60].

Function of the Intellect and the Mind

प्रतिहोमश्चेत्सायमग्निहोत्रप्रभृतीनि हूयेरन्॥४३॥
प्रातस्तु षोडशिनि॥४४॥
प्रायश्चित्तमधिकारे सर्वत्र दोषसामान्यात्॥४५॥

If there is anything against *Homa, Agni-hotra* offerings

should be made every evening;[61] but every morning we should make use of that which consists of sixteen parts;[62] but it should always be under the authority of predominant thought (or the intellect) because evil is so common.

The Text and its Interpretation

प्रकरणे वा शब्दहेतुत्वात्॥४६॥
अतद्विकाराच्च॥४७॥
व्यापन्नस्याप्सु गतौ यदभोज्यमार्याणां तत्प्रतीयेत॥४८॥
विभागश्रुतेः प्रायश्चित्तं यौगपद्ये न विद्यते॥४९॥
स्याद्वा प्रापतनिमित्तत्वात्कालमात्रमेकम्॥५०॥
तत्र विप्रतिषेधद्विकल्पः स्यात्॥५१॥
प्रयोगान्तरे वोभयानुग्रहः स्यात्॥५२॥
न चैकसंयोगात्॥५३॥
पौर्वापर्ये पूर्वदौर्बल्यं प्रकृतिवत्॥५४॥
यद्युद्गाता जघन्यः स्यात्पुनर्यज्ञे सर्ववेदसंदद्याद्यथेतरस्मिन्॥५५॥
अहर्गणे यस्मिन्नपच्छेदस्तदावर्त्तेत कर्मपृथक्त्वात्॥५६॥

There is a corresponding "evil" or difficulty in the text, and it arises from the use of words; but it disappears when their form is changed. When, however, a word is substituted by another, it loses its value, like food thrown into water, unfit to be eaten by a wise man.[63] There would, in such a case, be simultaneous alternative readings, and it would be impossible to grasp the main idea. This is only to be expected, because there can only be one instrumental cause of a thing, and it can be expressed by only one word at a time. But where there is a conflict of statements, there is likely to be a difference of opinion (or doubt) as to the exact idea of the text. In some places, however, the idea may improve with two readings; but that will not be (commonly) so, because things are united together into a single whole.

If two things are related as prior and posterior, the former is the weaker of the two; and such is the case with the natural form of a word.[64] But if, on second thought, we find it necessary to change the form of words, the entire Veda should again hold together in the same manner as in the other case;[65] for if a work is continuous, –however extensive it be, there can be no break in it unless it is intended to be so[66].

PART VI

THE METHOD OF INTERPRETATION : THE PROBLEM OF ACTION

Introduction

We can accept the meaning of words in their natural form only if it is the very best; out it should not be derived from some detached or casual remark, except in very special cases. It should not be obtained by breaking up the unity of idea of the text or by mixing up words; and the best result is obtained by dividing words into parts as in the case of *Bṛhat* and *Rathantara-Sāman* hymns of the Vedas. But we should be careful to see that the whole text is connected together and has an unbroken unity of thought.

When we get two meanings of a word, we must make up our minds as to which of the two we should accept; and we may find that the one we do has little connection with the ordinary meaning of the word.

In this way we shall find that all human faculties are capable of performing action; but it is the special privilege of the intellect to direct it; and so the highest place belongs to the intellect. It is, however possible to say that all of them are equal with reference to the soul, because they are equally dependent on it; nevertheless the function of the one, – say the mind, cannot be performed by the others, –the intellect, the senses, or their objects.

Pleasure or enjoyment has power to impel us to action; and so we see that purpose and action are closely intertwined.

There may be a doubt as to whether an action like speech etc., which may be a natural or reflex action, is impelled by purpose or not; and in such cases we should accept the opinion of trustworthy persons. The simplest way of finding out the character of action is to observe the behaviour of a person in a state of distress or agitation.

It is necessary to refer to all kinds of actions in order to understand their connection with purpose or aim; and this would include sacrifice, which is an exalted kind of action, and free from any element of special interest or aim.

How to Interpret the Text

सन्निपातेऽवैगुण्यात्प्रकृतिवत्तुल्यकल्या यजेरन्॥१॥

वचनाद्वा शिरोवत्स्यात्॥२॥

न वाऽनारभ्यवादत्वात्॥३॥

स्याद्वा यज्ञार्थत्वादौदुम्बरीवत्॥४॥

न तत्प्रधनत्वात्॥५॥

औदुम्बर्याः परार्थत्वात्कपालवत्॥६॥

अन्येनापीति चेत्॥७॥

नैकत्वात्तस्य चानधिकाराच्छब्दस्य चाविभक्तत्वात्॥८॥

सन्निपातात्तु निमित्तविघातं[1] स्यात् बृहद्रथन्तरवद्विभक्त शिष्टत्वाद्वसिष्ठ-निर्वर्त्ये॥९॥

अपि वा कृत्स्नसंयोगादविघातः प्रतीयेत स्वामित्वेनाभिसंबन्धः[2]॥१०॥

साम्नोः कर्मवृद्धियै[3] कदेशेन संयोगो; गुणत्वेनाभिसंबन्धस्तस्मात्तत्र विघातः स्यात्॥११॥

When we get a number of words in the text, we should accept their meaning in their natural form only if it is suitable, because the text is without any defect. Indeed, the meaning we get should be the best; but it should not be obtained from some detached or casual remark, though it may be so in certain cases, just as we may get the idea of sacrifice from a reference to a branch of the sacred Fig-tree.[67] The reference may not be a

---

1. घाताद्वहति वृत्तिग्रन्थे पाठान्तरम्।
2. "संबन्धत्"-सूत्रमिदं संबन्धस्स्यात् आ॰ पाठे।
3. कर्मवदेकेति क्षे॰ पाठः।

prominent one; but the idea of sacrifice arises from the pereminence of it, as in the case of the word *kapāla*[68].

We cannot say that it is possible to get the same idea by means of something else, because it is necessary to maintain unity of thought, whereas there would be an absence of proper relation in the case of casual expressions; and so it would not be possible to work the meaning into a harmonious whole. Indeed, if we mix up words, we fail to understand the real idea of the text; and the correct meaning can be obtained by dividing words into regular parts, as in the case *Bṛhat* and *Rathantara-Sāman* hymns.[69] Even so the whole text should be connected together, and there should be no impediments in the way, —because that is the test of our mastery of the text. In the two *Sāmans, —Bṛhat* and *Rathantara—* the result of this method can be extended from end to end. Each part of the whole is connected with and dependent on the other; but in order to understand this it is necessary to divide words into their parts.

Need of Selection

वचनात्तु द्विसंयोगस्तस्मादेकस्य पाणित्वम्[1]॥१२॥

अर्थाभावात्तु नैवं स्यात्॥१३॥

अर्थानां च विभक्तत्वान्न तच्छ्रुतेन संबन्धः॥१४॥

पाणेः प्रत्यङ्गभावादसंबन्धः प्रतीयेत॥१५॥

We get two meanings of a word in this way, and must make up our mind as to which of the two we should have; but this should not be so merely because of the absence of sense in the other meaning.[70] Indeed, when we get our meanings by dividing words into regular parts, we shall find that they have no connection with those that are ordinarily taught or heard. For instance, if we interpret the word *Pāṇi* as mere hand, — as a minor limb of the body—we shall not get any essential idea of the text.[71]

---

1. वत्-क्षे. पाठः।

Function of Human Faculties

सत्राणि सर्ववर्णानामिविशेषात्॥१६॥

लिङ्गदर्शनाच्च॥१७॥

ब्राह्मणानां वेतरयोरार्त्विज्याभावात्॥१८॥

वचनादिति चेत्॥१९॥

न स्वामित्वं हि विधीयते॥२०॥

गार्हपते वा स्यान्नामाविप्रतिषेधत्॥२१॥

न वा कल्पविरोधत्॥२२॥

स्वामित्वादितरेषामहीने लिङ्गदर्शनम्॥२३॥

वासिष्ठानां वा ब्रह्मत्वनियमात्॥२४॥

सर्वेषां वा प्रतिप्रसवात्॥२५॥

वैश्वामित्रस्य हौत्रनियमाद्भृगुशुनकवसिष्ठानामनधिकारः॥२६॥

All human faculties[72] are capable of performing meritorious deeds, because there is no distinction between them in this respect; and this can be proved. But such deeds are the special privilege of the intellect, because the other two (the mind and the senses) cannot direct action.[73] There is no statement in the sacred books to the effect that they can; and all that has been laid down refers to the character of the soul[74] which is also described as "a master of the house" without any derogation of the name,[75] or conflict with the manner in which action takes place. Indeed, we can see the proof of the strength of all the rest by reason of the character of the soul;[76] and that will enable us to understand that the intellect is necessarily the best.[77] Or we might say that all of them are equal if we refer them to their original state (or dependence on the soul).[78] (But even this is not possible, for) it is a rule that when the mind performs its own function, the same cannot be done by the intellect or the senses[79].

Pleasure and Purpose in Action

विहारस्य प्रभुत्वादनग्नीनामपि स्यात्॥२७॥

सारस्वते च दर्शनात्॥२८॥

प्रायश्चित्तविधनाच्च॥२९॥
साग्नीनां वेष्टिपूर्वत्वात्॥३०॥
स्वार्थेन च प्रयुक्तत्वात्॥३१॥
सन्निवापं च दर्शयति॥३२॥

The power of pleasure is so great that even those who are not intelligent (or those who wish to renounce action)[80] have to engage in action; and we can easily see this in the case of one who seeks pleasure. All this arises from the power of predominant thought (which impels a man to action); and in the case of intelligent persons (or those who do not wish to renounce action), action arises from the innate condition of their desire. This is so because all are impelled to action by means of purpose or aim; and we can see for ourselves that purpose and action are closely intertwined.

Doubtful Cases

जुह्वादीनामप्रयुक्तत्वात्संदेहे यथा कामी प्रतीयते॥३३॥
अपि वाऽन्यानि पात्राणि साधरणानि कुर्वीरन्विप्रतिषेधच्छास्त्रकृतत्वात्॥३४॥

There may, however, be a doubt as to whether an action like speech etc. is impelled by purpose or not; and in such cases we may take it as we like.[81] But, whenever there is a difference of opinion in regard to the idea of the sacred books, we should, even in such cases, accept the conclusion of trustworthy persons who agree.

A Suggestion

प्रायश्चित्तमापदि स्यात्॥३५॥
पुरुषकल्पेन वा विकृतौ कर्तृनियमः स्याद्यज्ञस्य तद्गुणत्वादभावादितरान्प्रत्येकस्मिन्नधिकारः स्यात्॥३६॥
लिङ्गाच्चेज्याविशेषवत्॥३७॥
न वा संयोगपृथक्त्वाद् गुणस्येज्याप्रधनत्वादसंयुक्ता हि चोदना॥३८॥
इज्यायां तद्गुणत्वाद्विशेषेण नियम्येत॥३९॥

(One of the simplest ways of finding out the character of such action is to) observe the dominant thought of a person in a state of danger or distress; for we can understand the real character of a man's actions when he is in a state of agitation. As acts of sacrifice are free from agitation, we have to examine other kinds of actions; —for it is necessary to refer to all kinds of actions to understand this.

We have, for instance, the idea of a real (or excellent) sacrifice. It is not correct to say that acts of sacrifice are altogether different from other kinds of actions; nor do they have a different relation to those regarded as subsidiary. But the idea of sacrifice is necessarily an exalted one; and so the impelling force that makes for it is not the same as in other cases. Indeed, we might say that, as sacrifice has this character, the idea of purpose or special interest should altogether be eliminated from it.

PART VII

THE PROBLEM OF ACTION : THE METHOD OF INTERPRETATION

Introduction

The idea of giving in charity: giving away one's self means giving away everything; a person can give away only what he has; neither the earth nor the *śūdra* can be given away. It is only what belongs to a person that should be accepted as a gift by a priest.

One action follows another, and one aim is succeeded by another.

We cannot say that what remains after an action is its result, for the result is uncertain, and may be different from what is intended.

An examination of an action spread over a number of days

shows that one action follows another; and this is expressed by the number 112 or *Prakṛti*; and both imply change as well as increase.

Prakṛti may be described in a number of ways: as something that confers benefits, or as something that is beyond all measure or limitations.

It is natural for a person to narrate action, – of some other person or of past times; and this is what the sacred books contain; and we can get this meaning by dividing words into parts, when it will be found to have a bearing on the laws of life. We can translate the text in this light by this means.

For instance, if some one is stated to have lived for a thousand years, it cannot possibly refer to a human being. It can refer only to a law of life, which would, of course, include man; and so there is no incongruity in the reference to a man living for a thousand years, – for the reference is really to a law of life. Indeed, the term man refers to the whole human race; and so we might say that the whole includes each individual too.

According to *Lāvukāyana* if there is a difference of opinion about the meaning of a word, it should be divided into parts.

But there are certain terms the meaning of which has been defined: for instance, a full year refers to *Prakṛti,* and so also a large number of days.

Idea of Charity or Gift

स्वदाने सर्वमविशेषात्॥१॥
यस्य वा प्रभुः स्यादितरस्याऽशक्यत्वात्॥२॥
न भूमिः स्यात्सर्वान्प्रत्यविशिष्टत्वात्॥३॥
अकार्यत्वाच्च ततः पुनर्विशेषः स्यात्॥४॥
नित्यत्वाच्चानित्यैर्नास्ति संबन्धः॥५॥
शूद्रश्च धर्मशास्त्रत्वात्॥६॥
दक्षिणाकाले यत्स्वं तत्प्रतीयेत तद्दानसंयोगात्॥७॥

If a person gives away his own self, it means that he gives away everything without exception. A person can give away only what he has, and anything else would be impossible. Nor can the earth be given away, because it belongs to all without distinction. It would be improper to give away the earth; and so, if a person does so, he should retract, and give away something else which is his own in a special way. Again, what is permanent can have no connection with what is impermanent; and the *śūdra* too cannot be given away according to sacred law[82] *(Dharma-śāstra)*. Then, when a person makes a gift to a priest, the latter should accept only that which belongs to the person, —for there is agreement of opinion that that is the real meaning of a gift.

One Action Follows Another

अशेषत्वात्तदन्तः स्यात्कर्मणो द्रव्यसिद्धित्वात्॥८॥
अपि वा शेषकर्म स्यात्क्रतोः प्रत्यक्षशिष्टस्वात्॥९॥
तथा चान्यार्थदर्शनम्॥१०॥
अशेषं तु समञ्जसमादाने[1] शेषकर्म स्यात्॥११॥
नादानस्यानित्यत्वात्॥१२॥
दीक्षासु विनिर्देशादक्रत्वर्थेन संयोगस्तस्मादविरोधः स्यात्॥१३॥
अहर्गणे च तद्धर्मः स्यात्सर्वेषामविशेषात्॥१४॥
द्वादशशतं वा प्रकृतिवत्॥१५॥
अतद्गुणत्वात्तु नैवं स्यात्॥१६॥
लिङ्गदर्शनाच्च॥१७॥
विकारः सन्नुभयतोऽविशेषात्॥१८॥
अधिकं वा प्रतिप्रसवात्॥१९॥

When nothing is left, it means that there is an end to a thing; and that is how an action is completed by means of certain things.[83] Even so, after one action has been completed, another remains to be done; and that is clearly inherent in the plan or design of action. We can understand in this manner how one aim follows another.

---

1. साऽऽवानेनेति भाष्ये पाठः।

It may be argued that nothing is left after a deed is done, and what remains is its result or effect, and the manner of our taking it. But this is not correct, because of the uncertainty of our getting the result. It often happens that in a series of undertakings, – because of our determination to achieve our end – we do something which we had not intended or desired; and this too shows that there is no conflict (with the previous statement that one action follows another). Indeed, if we examine action spread over a series of days, we shali find that this is the law of action, applicable to all cases without exception[84].

The number 112 or 1200 is like *Prakṛit* itself[85] (or it represents the idea of the action of *Prakṛti);* but it would not be so if the latter had some other characteristics; and this can easily be proved. Indeed, there is change implied in both (this number and *Prakṛti)* without any distinction; and they can be made more numerous by repeated procreation (or multiplication)[86].

Idea of Prakṛti: How Expressed

अनुग्रहाच्च पादवत्॥२०॥
अपरिमिते शिष्टस्य[1] सङ्ख्याप्रतिषेधस्तच्छ्रुतित्वात्॥२१॥
कल्पान्तरं वा तुल्यवत्प्रसङ्ख्यानात्॥२२॥
अनियमोऽविशेषात्॥२३॥
अधिकं वा स्याद्बह्वर्थत्वादितरैः सन्निधनात्॥२४॥
अर्थवादश्च तदर्थव[2]त्॥२५॥

(The idea of *Prakṛti* arises) also from that of conferring benefits, like a ray of light from a heavenly body.[87] All that remains (of *Prakṛti)* is so measureless that it is impossible to reckon it, – because the state of our intellect is so limited; and any other expression for it should be of the same kind, so far as enumeration is concerned.[88] Equally so, it is not subject to any limitations; and can be even more than this, by means of the

1. अत्र सूत्रे शिष्टस्येति पदं नास्ति वृत्तिग्रन्थे।
2. तद्वदिति आ० पाठः।

many uses that can be assigned to it, —because of the different ways in which it exists. This is how its meaning is explained.

Narrative Form of the Vedic Text

परकृतिपुराकल्पं च मनुष्यधर्मः स्यादर्थाय ह्यनुकीर्तनम्॥२६॥
तद्युक्ते च प्रतिषेधत्॥२७॥
निर्देशाद्वा तद्धर्मः स्यात्पञ्चावत्तवत्॥२८॥
विधै तु वेदसंयोगादुपदेशः स्यात्॥२९॥
अर्थवादो वा विधिशेषत्वात्तस्मान्नित्यानुवादः स्यात्॥३०॥

It is natural for a man to give an account of another person or of former times. Indeed, the act of narration should serve some useful purpose too; and this purpose is to be found in the sacred books in spite of apparent contradictions. Its character (or nature) can be seen from the details given in the text (if we divide words into parts), just as we may divide a thing into five (or some definite) parts; and, as it is connected with the Vedas, its teaching should refer to the laws of life *(Vidhi);* and the explanation of the meaning should be such that the conclusion has a bearing on these laws; and it should be possible to translate it in their terms.

An Illustration

सहस्रसंवत्सरं तदायुषामसंभवान्मनुष्येषु॥३१॥
उपचारोन्यार्थदर्शनम्॥३१अ.॥
अपि वा तदधिकारान्मनुष्यधर्मः स्यात्॥३२॥
नासामर्थ्यात्॥३३॥
सम्बन्धदर्शनात्॥३४॥
स कुल्यः[2] स्यादिति कार्ष्णाजिनिरेकस्मिन्नसंभवात्॥३५॥
अपि वा कृत्स्नसंयोगादेकस्यैव प्रयोगः स्यात्॥३६॥

When there is mention of a thousand years as being the duration of the life of some one, it can refer only to things the life of which can last so long, because it is impossible to refer it to a man. It is a figurative expression, and we can see that it has some other meaning.[89] Nevertheless, because of the reference to the laws of life, there should also be a reference to the law of man (as a part of the law of life); and there is no incongruity in this idea, because there is a latent connection between the law of man and the law of life. *Kārṣṇājini*[90] says that when we speak of the law of man, we speak of the law of the human race, because it would be improper to speak of it as such if it referred only to an individual. But if it refers to the whole race it means that it refers to each individual too.

Method of Interpretation

विप्रतिषेधत्तु गुण्यन्यतरः स्यादिति लावुकायनः॥३७॥

संवत्सरो वा विचालित्वात्॥३८॥

सा प्रकृतिः[1] स्यादाधिकारात्॥३९॥

अहानि वाऽभिसङ्ख्यात्वात्॥४०॥

According to *Lāvukāyana*[91] if there be a conflict of opinion in regard to the meaning of the text, one way of reading it should be such that we divide words into parts.

If there is mention of a full year, we cannot understand its meaning, because it passes on; and so it should be deemed to refer to *Prakṛti,* because of the special reference (made to it in this connection); and that is also the idea of a large number of days[92].

PART VIII

THE CHARACTER OF SACRIFICE: THE METHOD OF INTERPRETATION

Introduction

Sacrifice is an intelligent action, but begins initially with desire; and this is true of all action deliberately performed. It may be said that *Japa* or silent repetition of a name has no connection with the intellect; yet it is an act of sacrifice. *Homa* is an intelligent action, and is also associated with desire; but

१. वृत्तिग्रन्थे इदं सूत्रमधिकिम्।

both *Japa* and *Homa* are like an oblation offered to the deceased ancestors.

Certain actions are not performed at the bidding of the intellect; but an action performed without expectation of result is an act of pure sacrifice. The *upanaya* ceremony of initiating a boy into knowledge is also of this kind (*n*), for action systematically performed gives rise to knowledge.

A proper performance of action as a sacrifice requires the co-operation of both husband and wife. We can refrain from action only at the end of our life, when all our tasks are done; and this is in accordance with the law of life.

A sacrifice is action meant for the benefit of all; and in such a case a person should not seek any special benefit even for his son. But the birth of a son symbolises the fulfilment of desire, and so one should have a son; and a person should pray to his deceased ancestors for the birth of a son.

If a person desires to become great, he must exercise his intellect, for the desire itself is inseparable from his intelligence.

Things associated with the gods are described in the sacred books in certain special ways,—*e.g.*, the first half of the year, a day in the bright fortnight of the lunar month, or an auspicious day,—for we can remember them best in that form; but the entire action should be completed on that day; and other days should be associated with the deceased ancestors.

Certain words have certain specified meanings: for instance, "begging" or "buying" implies some deficiency. Certain other words like eating, calling, etc. have also a fixed meaning.

In the case of animals, however, there is no fixity of meaning, because we cannot assign any fixed attributes to them; and so the meaning of a word like *chhāga* (goat, etc.) has to be understood from its use in the text. Nor can the meanings of such words be derived from their roots or basic forms.

The general rule, however, is that the same word should have the same meaning throughout: the word *chhāga* may accordingly mean "action".

A fundamental word cannot be obtained from some other word; and when its form is changed, it becomes an entirely different word, with no connection with its original form. This change has no connection with the attributes of an animal, the idea of which should be obtained by means of its own character and the meaning of the principal word used in the text.

Nature of Sacrifice

इष्टिपूर्वत्वादक्रतुशेषो होमः संस्कृतेष्वग्निषु स्यादपूर्वोऽप्याधनस्य सर्वशेषत्वात्॥१॥

इष्टित्वेन तु संस्तवश्चतुर्होतृनसंस्कृतेषु दर्शयति॥२॥

उपदेशस्त्वपूर्वत्वात्॥३॥

सर्वेषामविशेषात्॥४॥

अप वा क्रत्वभावादनाहिताग्नेरशेषभूतनिर्देशः॥५॥

जपो वाऽनग्निसंयोगात्॥६॥

इष्टित्वेन संस्तुते होमः स्यादनारभ्याग्निसंयोगादितरेषामवाच्यत्वात्॥७॥

उमयोः पितृयज्ञवत्॥८॥

निर्देशो वाऽनाहिताग्नेरनारभ्याग्निसंयोगात्॥९॥

पितृयज्ञे संयुक्तस्य पुनर्वचनम्॥१०॥

उपनयन्नाधीत होमसंयोगात्॥११॥

स्थपति[1]वल्लौकिके वा विद्याकर्मानुपूर्वत्वात्॥१२॥

आधनं च भार्यासंयुक्तम्॥१३॥

Homa[93] is a pure intelligent action, which begins originally with desire, and becomes free from desire in the end; and even though the act be quite new or incomplete, it is still an intelligent act (or an act of sacrifice). All actions begin with desire; and it is an imperfect action in which the four *Hotṛ* priests are found

---

1. स्थपतौष्टिवल्लौ–आ. पाठः।

to take part;[94] and the teaching in regard to an act of sacrifice does not refer to action as it is in its earliest state[95].

This is true of all action without distinction; and an action without desire cannot be regarded as a deliberate act, performed, at the bidding of the intellect. (It can only be a reflex or accidental action,) whereas we are dealing with a description of what is not accidental.

But *Japa* (or silent repetition of a sacred name) is without any connection with the intellect and yet it is an act of sacrifice[96].

So far as *Homa* is concerned, it is an action which is associated with desire; and that which, at its commencement, is not connected with the intellect, refers to something else, and not *Homa*[97].

But the idea of both *Japa* and *Homa* is like an oblation offered to the deceased ancestors[98].

But there is a special mention of certain actions which are not affected by the intellect, because they have not been commenced at its bidding; and so far as acts of oblation made to deceased ancestors are concerned, they are (pure acts of sacrifice) as has already been stated.[99] The *upanaya* ceremony of initiating a boy in spiritual knowledge is of the kind of a *Homa* sacrifice[100], and should be brought about; for knowledge arises systematically from the performance of action[101]; and it builds up life like an architect, to use a popular form of speech. But in order that an act of sacrifice should be properly performed, it is necessary that the husband should associate himself with his wife.

Cessation of Action

अकर्म चोर्ध्वमाधनात्तत्समवायो हि कर्मभिः।।१४।।
अकर्म च दारक्रियाधनोत्तरः काले।।१४अ.।।

श्राद्धवदिति चेत्॥१५॥
न श्रुतिविप्रतिषेधत्॥१६॥
अर्था[1]दन्यदेवेति चेत्॥१६.॥

The cessation of action comes at a later stage, after the family fire has been lighted (and all tasks are done); for the intimate life of the family continues by means of action. Indeed, the cessation of action means the breaking up of all that we do or hold, and so it should come at a later time[102]. It does not require any degree of faith to believe this, for all this is in accordance with the law of life, and anything else would be contrary to the teaching of the *śruti*.

Sacrifice and a Son

सर्वार्थत्वाच्च[2] पुत्रार्थो न प्रयोजयेत्॥१७॥
सोमपानात्तु प्रापणं द्वितीयस्य तस्मादुपयच्छेत्॥१८॥
पितृयज्ञे तु दश्र्नात्प्र[3]गाधनात्प्रतीयेत॥१९॥

When a thing is meant to be for the benefit of all,[103] a person should not contrive to secure any special advantage out of it even for his son. But when desire is satisfied,[104] a son is born; and so one should have a son.[105] Hence, if a man understand the law of life, he should pray to his deceased ancestors and make an offering to them[106] before the union of the sexes.

Intelligence and Desire for Greatness

स्थपतीष्टिः प्रयाजवदग्न्याधेयं प्रयोजयेत्तादर्थ्याच्चापवृज्येत॥२०॥
अपि वा लौकिकेऽग्नौ स्यादाधनस्यासर्वशेषत्वात्॥२१॥
अवकीर्णि[4]पशुश्च तद्वदाधनस्याप्राप्तकालत्वात्॥२२॥

If a person desires to become great, he must exercise his

---

1. इदं सूत्रमधिकं वृत्तिग्रन्थे।
2. त्वादपुत्रेति वृत्तिग्रन्थे पाठान्तरम्।
3. दर्शनात्प्रतीति वृत्तिग्रन्थे पाठान्तरम्।
4. कीर्णी इति पाठान्तरं वृत्तिग्रन्थे।

intelligence, as is necessary in the case of a great sacrifice,[107] and his desire would be fulfilled because he has that intention.[108] This desire would, in common parlance, be spoken of as part of intelligence, as it cannot be separated from it[109]; and a person who controls his vital energy, because the proper time for union has not arrived, is like that (is intelligent).

Description of What Belongs to the Gods

उदगयनपूर्वपक्षाहः पुण्याहेषु दैवानि स्मृतिरूपान्यार्थदर्शनात्॥२३॥
अहनि च कर्मसाकल्यम्॥२४॥
इतरेषु तु पित्र्याणि॥२५॥

Things belonging to the gods are associated with the first half of the year,—from winter to summer, during the progress of the sun in the northern path,—a day in the bright fortnight of the lunar month, and an auspicious day; and that is so because we can understand and remember them best in this form, and also because it conveys some other meaning.[110] But the entire action should be completed on that day; while on other days action associated with the deceased ancestors should be done[111].

Words with Fixed Meanings

याच्ञाक्रयणमविद्यमाने लोकवत्॥२६॥
नियतं वार्थवत्त्वात्स्यात्॥२७॥
तथा भक्षप्रैषाच्छादन संज्ञप्तहोमद्वेषम्॥२८॥
अनर्थकं त्वनित्यं स्यात्॥२९॥

When there is a reference to "begging" (an entreaty) and "buying" in the sacred books, they should be understood to imply some deficiency, —something that is not present,—just as we say in common speech[112]; and this should always be so, because that is the meaning of these words. In the same manner there are other words,—eating, calling, covering (or concealing), making an oblation after slaying a sacrificial animal, and enmity,—which have a fixed meaning;[113] for a meaning that is not constant is of little use.

Actions of Animals

पशुचोदनायामयिनमोऽविशेषात्॥३०॥
छागो वा मन्त्रवर्णात्॥३१॥
न चोदनाविरोधत्॥३२॥
आर्षेयवदिति चेत्॥३३॥
न तत्र ह्यचोदितत्वात्॥३४॥

(All this has a bearing on the actions of men, who are governed by reason). In regard to the impelling force of animals, there can be no fixed rule, because we cannot assign any such fixity to them;[114] and so the meaning of the word *chhāga* has to be obtained from the description of the *Mantra* or the hymn,[115] even though this may appear to be contrary to rules. Nor can we say that words relating to animals should be such as can be derived from their basic or uninflected forms, like the word *ārshya* (from *riṣi,* meaning "a sage"), for that too would be contrary to rules[116].

A General Rule

नियमो वैकार्थ्यं ह्यर्थभेदाद्भेदः पृथक्त्वेनाभिधनात्॥३४॥
अनियमो वार्थान्तरत्वादन्यत्वं व्यतिरेकशब्दभेदाभ्याम्॥३५॥
न वा प्रर्यागसमवायित्वात्॥३७॥
रूपा[1]लिङ्गाच्च॥३८॥
छागेन कर्माख्या रूपलिङ्गाभ्याम्॥३९॥

The general rule, however, is that the same word should have ,the same meaning throughout; for if a single name is given a number of meanings, it means that its very idea has been modified. But it may be argued that there is no such rule; and that the meaning of a word is different, because the thing itself is different; and so when a word has two different meanings, we have really to distinguish between two different things, the idea of which is best expressed by two different words. But this is not necessary, because we can get the correct meaning of a word from its intimate connection with the

१. इदं सूत्रं वृत्तिग्रन्थ्ने नास्ति।

context; and this can be proved from the form of the words used in the text. This would tell us that the meaning of the word *chāga* is "action"; and it can be understood from the form of the word and the evidence at our disposal.

Character of Change of Form of a Word

रूपान्यत्वान्न जातिशब्दः स्यात्॥४१॥
विकारो[1] नौत्पत्तिकत्वात्॥४१॥
स नैमित्तिकः पशोर्गुणस्याचोदितत्वात्॥४२॥
जातेर्वा तत्प्रायवचनार्थवत्त्वाभ्याम्॥४३॥

A fundamental word cannot be obtained from another or a different form of the same word[117]; and the change of form of a word has nothing to do with its original idea. This change is made in accordance with a definite cause, but is not effected by a consideration of the attributes of an animal, the idea of which should be obtained by means of its true character, described by means of the principal word and its meaning.

NOTES

1. This has already been referred to by the *Mīmāṁsā* (Cf. BhG.11,47).
2. This *Sūtra* does not occur in some texts.
3. The four castes refer to (i) intellect, (2) *ahaṅkāra* and mind, (3) the senses, and (4) the objects of the senses (See Appendix III).
   Atreya is a descendant of *Atri,* a great *riṣi* and author of a number of Vedic hymns.
   As the fourth caste or *śūdra* refers to the objects of the senses, it cannot obviously engage in any action which refers to the intellect.
4. A *Brāhmaṇa* refers to the intellect, for that is the meaning of the word.
5. *Bādari* is the name of a philosopher. He says that the *śūdra* (objects of Nature) cannot act in the sense of being an efficient cause of action: they can only be the material cause of action.
6. If the text says that the *śūdra* cannot act, we should accept it: only we should understand the sense in which the words are used. If we do so, we shall find that what is stated in the text is correct; for the material objects of Nature cannot be the efficient cause of action; and so the *śūdra,* who refers to these objects, cannot be said to act in the same sense as the intellect or the mind,

---

१. विकार दति चेदिति चेत्पदं संयाज्य तदन्तं पृथक् सूत्रं वृत्तिग्रन्थे।

7. If we interpret these names correctly, we shall find that we get the real meaning from the words themselves (See Appendix III).
8. The whole idea may be explained as follows:
   If the Veda says that the *śūdra* cannot act, we should agree, because the *śūdra* refers to the objects of Nature which cannot act by themselves. But it can be argued that if we wish to understand all the parts of an action, the objects of Nature cannot be excluded, because they are the material cause of action.
   This is true; but we have to understand the context in which the first statement has been made in the Veda; and we find that the reference is to the problem of the soul, and of knowledge, not action. The Veda is not dealing with the question of action as such: it is dealing with the problem of knowledge which, however, may, in a certain sense, be regarded as a form of action; and it is in accordance with this that it says that the *śūdra* is not entitled to act; for the objects of Nature cannot, in any case, acquire knowledge,—whatever we might say about their part in action.
   But it is possible to disagree with this explanation on the ground that there is no special reference to knowledge in this part of the text; whereas it is always there whenever it is required. Hence the reference to action cannot mean a reference to knowledge.
   The answer to this is that this is not a correct point of view, because knowledge and action are closely allied, and there can be no action without knowledge: hence if there is a reference to action, it should be construed to include a reference to knowledge too.
   It is in this manner that we can understand this as well as all other meanings of the text.
9. Wealth is acquired by means of the function of the intellect, mind, and the senses, – represented by the three "castes". The fourth "caste" or the objects of the senses cannot acquire wealth,because they are wealth themselves. The same argument has been used in connection with a woman; but where a woman refers to Nature or *Prakṛti,* – as she does in the sacred books – we can understand what the real meaning is: an object of Nature cannot acquire wealth.
10. When a person loses his limb, it ceases to be of use to him, and so he does not regard it as his "wealth".
11. We can omit the *śūdra* from a consideration of action, because he refers to the objects of Nature, which cannot be regarded as an efficient cause of action. But we cannot, in any case, omit the soul, because it is by means of it alone that the other organs of the body act.
12. *Saudhanvana* means "the son of *Su-dhanvan* or one with an excellent bow". But *Su-dhanvan* is said to be the son of an outcaste *Vaiśya* by a woman of the same class; and so he must belong to a "caste" lower than the *Vaiśya,* – and that is the *śūdra*. *Saudhanvana,* the son *Sudhanvan,* is

accordingly said to refer to the *śūdra*. The idea of "having an excellent bow" is not without a significance of its own.

The *śūdra* or an object of Nature is a cause of action in the same sense in which a bow may be said to be so. It cannot act or discharge an arrow by itself; and so it may be said to be a material and not an efficient cause of action. The idea of a *śūdra* is the same.

13. The word *Niṣāda* is said to refer to a wild *non-āryan* tribe, described as hunters, fishermen, etc., and also to an outcaste. But the *Mīmānsā* says that it has the same meaning as *Sthapati,* which means "a king, chief; a *Vaiśya* or even a person of a lower caste who has celebrated the *Go-sava* sacrifice after being chosen king; an architect; charioteer; etc." *Go-sava* is the name of an *Ekaha* ceremony, which is said to last one day only; it also refers to a *Soma* sacrifice, or the function of the mind.

Sthapati is accordingly one who has been elevated from a lower to a higher state by means of sacrifice or a proper function of the mind; and the *Mīmānsā* tells us that this is the real meaning of *Niṣāda.*

14. It also tells us that we can understand this meaning of *Niṣāda* by piercing through the "disguised" form of the word; that is to say,

by dividing it into parts, and understanding the meaning of each part. The word *Niṣāda* may, accordingly, be divided into *N, i, ṣ, ā da,* when its meaning would be "(y) the senses ot knowledge *(i)* associated with *(sh)* the mind, and (a) leading to *(ā)* sacrifice". *Niṣāda,* accordingly, is one who begins at the stage of the senses, goes on to the stage of the mind, and ends in the idea of sacrifice; and this is in exact keeping with the meaning of the word as a *Vaiśya* (senses) who becomes king (mind), and performs a *Go-sava* sacrifice.

There are a number of references to this word in the *Mahābhārata,* where too it has the same meaning.

15 The word in the text is *puruṣa,* which generally refers to the soul in the *Mīmāṁṣā* as well as the *Sāṅkhya.* But it is possible to interpret it as "a man", at least in the present case.

16. This *Sūtra* does not occur in certain texts.

17. The argument may be summed up as follows:

There are definite rules of interpretation; and if we do not follow them and pursue a different course, we find that the text does not make any coherent sense.

We cannot follow a new method of interpretation merely because we desire to get a particular meaning, for the rules of interpretation are fixed, and we cannot have any new method we like.

On the other hand there are innumerable actions, and if we were to follow our own inclination in regard to the method of interpretation, there would be an equally large number of methods of interpretation; and as there are no fixed rules in regard to actions, there would be no fixed rules in connection with these methods of interpretation too. But, as the rules of interpretation are fixed, while actions are not, it follows that there is a design in the whole method.

We can understand this if we read the text according to *Krama*.

18. The whole idea has to be understood in the light of action and the doer of the deed.
19. The *Bhāgāvad Gītā* says so too (BhG. XVIII, 48).
20. Cf. BhG. II, 47.
21. The *Bhāgāvad Gītā* mentions five causes of action, the last of which is *Daiva* or what belongs to the gods (BhG. XVIII, 13-14).
    This *Sūtra* does not occur in some texts.
22. The *Bhāgāvad Gītā* tells us that he who sees inaction in action, and action in inaction is a wise man; and the *Mīmāṁsā* means the same thing when it says that inaction is a form of action in connection with prohibited things. That is to say, when we .refrain from doing something that has been prohibited, we are really engaged in a kind of action.
23. Absence of action serves the purpose of the soul at the last stage of a man's existence, when he has done his life"s work, and is at the point of death. This has already been explained.
24. This tells us that even in the days of *Jaimini*, when he wrote the *Mīmāṁsā*, people had forgotten the real idea of the Vedas, which had been composed long before his time.
25. The *Bhāgāvad Gītā* tell us of the natural duties of a *Brāhmaṇa* who, as has already been explained, refers to an intelligent person (BhG. XVIII, 42) According to manu (VI,35) and Taittirīya saṁhitā(VI,iii,Io,5) a *Brāhmaṇa* has three obiligation ,—to the Rishis, to the gods, and to his deceased ancestors.To the first is his study of the vedas, to the second worship and sacrifice; and to the last the procreation of a son. The idea of the Mīmāṁsā would appear to be the same.
26. The word in the text is *śabda,* –the testimony of wise and trust worthy persons in acquiring definite knowledge. Its chief basis is said to be personal experience of such persons.
27. The point of this is that when we utter the word *go,* meaning a cow, we understand that it means a cow, and it gives us also an idea of the character of the cow.
    The word *go* may be divided into *ga, u,* –the meaning being "*(go)* the senses of knowledge, associated with (u) the senses of knowledge"; and, as this name is said to have been given with a special design, we may conclude that the ancients believed that the cow was endowed with specially keen sense-organs. Further, as the idea of the senses corresponds to that of magnetic energy or special properties of attraction, it also means that they believed that the cow or its milk had such properties. It is in this way that a name expresses the character of an object.

28. *Agni* means intellect, as has already been explained; and intellect is the highest "division" or form of Nature. Hence, as a god represents a great power of Nature, and intellect is such a power, *Agni* is described as a god. Again, the *Mīmāṁsā* tells us that the meaning of the word is contained in the word itself, – that is, we can obtain it from the context in which it is used or its division into parts (*Cf.* p. 26, n.).
29. Thus we can understand the meaning of the word *svāmin,* asreferring to the soul, from its use in the text and the result that is obtained.
30. The mind has two characteristics, – *nāma* and *rūpa* – name and form: that is, when we give a name to an object or cast up its image, it is the mind that is functioning. Hence there can be no description beyond the powers of the mind, or of language, for the mind expresses itself in its form.
31. This *Sūtra* does not occur in certain texts. The word for the mind is *khādira,* which refers to the moon, – a symbol of the mind.
32. This *Sūtra* does not occur in certain texts.
33. The *Bhāgāvad Gītā* tells us that there are three names of *Brahma,* – *Om, Tad and Sat;* and of these *Tad* is specially associated with the idea of sacrifice (BhG. XVII, 25). The literal meaning of the word (ta, *d)* is "(d) sacrifice, associated with (to) the senses of action".
34. The "five cups" are obviously substitutes for the five organs of sense, by means of which we can act. As we can drink out of a cup, so we may be said to perform a function by means of these organs.
35. The idea of a "worshipper" is defined in the following *Sūtras* as a limb or member of the body. As it is possible to conceive of the great forces of Nature (and that is the idea of a deity) acting without reference to man, the presence of a "worshipper" is not essential.
36. There is an alternative reading, which means that "If we do not succeed in the conquest of everything, the failure should be attributed to our manner of action". The idea of "payment of a wage" is that we have to pay for our success, – which can be achieved by means of action (*Cf.* BhG. IV, 12).
37. A reference to the austerities of a father should be interpreted to mean that he wants to do something for the benefit of his son, because of his love for him.
38. We get the idea of Time when something new makes its appearance. There is also a reference to Time in an earlier chapter.
39. When we get the word immeasurable in the text, it generally refers to Time; or we might say that Time cannot be measured, for it is without a beginning or end. But we can understand something of it as it passes, and sub-divide it too; and so the idea of the birth of son in the text is that it refers to a sub-division of Time.
40. It is not possible to describe the soul as it is; and we can only understand it in terms of the character of some other faculties, – intellect, *ahaṅkāra,* mind, or the senses. That is to say, we can describe it as supreme

intelligence and the essence of rationality in man; or say that it is an actor; or that it is characterised by desire; or that it is an instrument of knowledge as well as action There is no other way of describing the soul; and its special characteristic is that all other faculties function because of it.

41. These are the characteristics of the soul; and it is by means of them alone that we can get an idea of Time, or associate ourselves with anything in the world.

42. It is by means of our intellect that we can get a proper idea of Time; and as the intellect and the soul may, for practical purposes, be identified, it enables us to understand the character of the soul as well.

It may be of interest to point out that the ancient divisions of Time into *Yuga, Manvantara,* and *Kalpa* all refer to the exercise of our mental faculties. For instance, the word *Yuga* is derived from" *yuj,* one of the meanings of which is "to fix or concentrate the mind". The word, *Manvantara* is derived from *Manu,* which is the same as *manas* or the mind; while one of the meanings of the word *Kalpa* is "research, investigation". Indeed, the word *Kāla* for Time is itself derived from *kal,* which means "to perceive, consider". Hence we might say that the idea of Time involves a process of thought or a function of the intellect or the mind.

43. It is only an orderly arrangement of things, —events occurrring in proper succession, that can give us an idea of Time. The appearance of a new thing, or the birth of a son, is meant to express this idea of an orderly arrangement of things in the world; and that is why it represents the idea of Time, as the *Mīmāṁsā* tells us.

44. We have already explained that the five "cups" refer to the five organs of sense, The gods refer to the great forces of Nature; and "invoking" them would mean understanding the character of these forces.

The point of this *Sūtra* is that when we discover a mistake, we wish to take stock of things again, retrace our steps, and begin afresh, so that we might succeed in our next attempt. We have to do the same thing in the case of the sacred text, when we find ourselves at fault.

45. The word in the text is *sāmnāyya,* which means "any substance mixed with clarified butter and offered as a burnt offering". We have explained that "clarified butter" refers to goodness; while anything partaking of the character of *Agni* or fire refers to the intellect. Hence the meaning here.

46. The cause of a good and intelligent action is a general and not a particular one, because it partakes of the character of a law.

47. Boiled milk or cooked food is but a detailed description of food, which, as the *Mīmāṁsā* has told us, refers to Nature or *Prakṛti*. There are a number of similar references in the Upaniṣads.

48. There are three ways of reading the sacred text: singing aloud, silent repetition, and normal reading. In the case of the first we are told that the form of words should be changed, because that is what we do when we

sing; and in the case of the second the *Mīmāṁsā* tells us that the natural form of words should remain unchanged; while in the case of the third we may do what is necessary in each case.

49. Rice, as the *Mīmāṁsā* has told us, is the best form of grain, and so refers to *Prakṛti* or Nature in a special way. This is a special case even according to *Asmarthya,,* where the common meaning of a word is not satisfactory, and a different interpretation is required.

50. Non-possession of the material objects of life is something that is "raised above": that is, it is a high ideal, and so is personified as a god.

51. The word *muṣṭi* has a number of meanings, including a fist (the hand closed to grasp something). It accordingly refers to the idea of possession; and, as the hand is an instrument of action, it implies action performed for the sake of possession. The *Mīmāṁsā* tells us that we can get its correct meaning by replacing it by the word possession, to which there is also a reference in a previous *śutra*.

52. As has already been explained, *sāmnāyya* refers to a good and intelligent action; while *sam-naya* means "bringing together". As the meaning of the one is to be derived from the other, it means that the idea of a good and intelligent action *(sāmnāyya")* is obtained from bringing things together *(sam-naya):* that is to say, bringing things together is a good and intelligent act.

53. *Aushadha* means "consisting of herbs", and is derived from *oshadhi,* "a medicinal plant or herb". It is said that the meaning of *aushadha* or "what relates to medicinal plants",—that is, their healing power—should be obtained from a good and intelligent act as well as puttings things together: that is to say, medicinal herbs get their healing power when things are put together intelligently and for a good cause.

54. Sacrifice means a great good action performed selflessly, intelligently and in accordance with a law; while a period of twelve days is symbolic of intelligence and length and continuity of time; for the number twelve refers to the intellect, as the ten to the ten senses, and eleven to the mind. This is how we can understand its idea by means of inference: for if the number ten refers to the ten senses, leven must refer to the mind, and twelve to *Buddhi* or the intellect.

55. As has already been explained, the moon refers to the mind; and so the new moon signifies its awakening as desire, and the full moon its fulfilment in action. But as there are different kinds and conditions of action, a simple reference to the full moon cannot explain all, because one full moon is so like another, while actions are different.

56. Hence one kind of reference to the full moon refers to a particular full moon,—of the month of *Caitra,* the beginning of the Hindu year,—and so points to action at the commencement of our career, an action that must go on for some length of time.

57. Another reference to the full moon, where the word *ekāshtakā* occurs (and it refers to Nature or *Prakṛti* with its eight divisions) – leads us to conclude that it refers to action at the end of our life, when it is necessary to renounce it, – even as the month of *Māgha* comes at the end of the Hindu year, for it is the last of the winter months.

 Ekāṣṭakā is said to be the eighth day after the full moon, and so it refers to the number eight. As a woman refers to Nature or *Prakṛti* – and it is a noun in the feminine gender – it may be said to refer to *Prakṛti* too. This is further supported by the reference to night, specially of the dark fortnight of the moon, – for that too refers to *Prakṛti*. We may therefore, conclude that *ekāṣṭakā* refers to Nature or *Prakṛti;* and this is borne out by what follows. *Prakṛti* is said to have eight divisions, as the *Bhāgāvad Gītā* tells us (BhG. VII, 4).

58. *Ekdṣṭakd* or *Prakṛti* is only onej and it is only for the sake of convenience of understanding its idea that we are told that there are two forms of it, – one making for life and the other making for death. There is a reference to two kinds of *Prakṛti* in the *Bhāgāvad Gītā* too (BhG. VII, 5); but later on we are told of only one (BhG. XIII, 20-24; XIV, 3-5).

59. The *Prakṛti* that confers benefits is the same as the higher *Prakṛti,* referred to in the *Bhāgāvad Gītā,* which is said to be the "life of all creatures, and sustains the universe" (BhG. VII, 5). It is this idea of *Prakṛti* that is closely associated with that of God, for it can easily be transformed into the latter by means of the idea of Sacrifice. This has already been explained.

60. As has already been explained, the gods refer to the great and beneficent forces of Nature; and making oblations to them means that we admit that these forces have a part to play in action. The idea of human action, performed as a duty, or as a sacrifice, is thus in complete harmony with the part that the great forces of Nature play in it; and this is exemplified by the fact that actions take place when the time is ripe for them. At the same time it is necessary to control our desires, for desires are removed or purified in this manner (*Cf.* BhG. III, 37-43; V, 7-12; etc.).

61. *Homa* is an act of making an oblation to the gods by casting clarified butter into the fire. As gods refer to the forces of Nature, clarified butter to goodness, and fire to the intellect, – it means a good and intelligent action associated with the great powers of Nature: that is to say, we believe that the latter are characterised by both goodness and intelligence, and regulate our life accordingly.

 Agnihotra is an oblation to *Agni;* and there are two kinds of *Agnihotra,* – *nitya* or obligatory, and *kāmya* or optional. As *Agni* refers to the intellect, it means an intelligent action, whether it be obligatory or optional. The point of this *Sūtra* is that even if we do not believe in the forces of Nature as being characterised by goodness and intelligence, our own actions, whether obligatory or optional, should be.

The reference to "evening" is also significant, as it is the end of the day, and so implies that, however we begin such actions, the end at least should be characterised by intelligence.

62. But the beginning (morning), though characterised by desire (an attribute of the mind, which consists of sixteen parts), should be governed by the highest thought or thought of death, for we should be afraid of evil which is so common.

The morning refers to the beginning; that which consists of 16 parts is the mind; and *Prāya-citta,* the word used in the text, means "predominant thought, or thought of death."

63. When one meaning is substituted by another, the original meaning becomes useless. However, when we are dissatisfied with the original meaning, there can be a number of alternative ways of handling the text; and we have to choose the best, for even two cannot be alike, though, in some cases, it may be an advantage to have them.

64. This means the same thing as saying that second thoughts are best. Similarly, if in the case of words we find it necessary to change their form, it would be found that, as between their original form and the changed one, the latter, being the last, is the better of the two.

65. The *Sūtra* in its original form may be rendered as follows:–

55. "If, at the repeated acts of prayer and praise, the *Udgātṛ* priest comes last, the entire Veda should hold together, as in the other case."

The *Udgātṛ* priest is said to chant or sing aloud the hymns of the *Sāma Veda;* and, according to the *Mīmāṁsā,* singing aloud is an indication that the form of words should be changed. The idea of *Udgātṛ* priest coming last would accordingly be that we find; on later thought, that it is necessary to change the form of words in order to understand their meaning; and the *Mīmāṁsā* tells us that this is specially necessary in the case of the *Sāma Veda,* which deals with the problem of living creatures; and that is the reason why its hymns are intended to be sung.

The meaning of the *Sūtra* would now be as follows:

"If we find repeatedly (at the repeated acts of prayer and praise) that, on second thought, the form of words should be changed (the *Udgātṛ* priest comes last), the entire Veda should hold together, as in the other case."

The *Mīmāṁsā* warns us that if we find it necessary to change the form of words we should take care to see that the meaning of the text remains continuous and consistent in its light throughout, and that this consistency is not less than it is in its original form.

66. The *Sūtra* in its original form may be rendered as follows:

"In a particular series of days of sacrifice there can be a break only if there is a break in action."

We have explained that sacrifice refers to a good and intelligent action; and the idea of a series of days would be that it is both cȯn-tinous and extensive. The point is that in the case of such an action there can be no break unless it is so intended; even so there should be no break in the meaning of the Veda when we interpret it in the light of action, conceived as a sacrifice, by changing the form of words.

67. The Fig-tree has always been regarded as sacred, as being symbolic of *Prakṛti* or Nature itself (*Cf*. BhG. XV, 1-4); and, as Nature is governed by a law which may be conceived in terms of sacrifice, the Fig-tree or a branch of it may be regarded as a symbol of that sacrifice.

68. "*Kapāla* means "the alms-bowl of a beggar", and so symbolises a life of renunciation, which may be regarded as a form of sacrifice. A reference to a single word like *kapāla* can give us this idea; and so also a reference to a branch of the sacred Fig-tree. But these are exceptions to the rule.

69 The word *Sāman* has a number of meanings in *Sanskṛt*. Here it refers to a particular kind of sacred text or verse called a *Sāman,* which is intended to be chanted or sung. There are four kinds of verses mentioned in the *rig Veda* (RV. X. xc, 9)—*Rich, Yajus, Chandas* and *Sāman;* and *Bṛhat* and *Rathantara* are two *Sāman* verses which are intended to be chanted. This *Sūtra* tells us that the words in these verses need to be divided into parts to enable us to understand their meaning; and the next *Sūtra* says that the principle involved in this method of interpretation can be extended in these verses from one end to the other.

70. The principle of interpretation is that when we reject one meaning and accept another, it should not be merely because the first meaning does not make sense. It is equally necessary that the other meaning should make good sense.

71. The hand is an instrument of action; and it is necessary to understand the word *Pāṇi* to refer to action, when we shall get a proper meaning of the text.

72. The word in the text is *Varṇa,* which is commonly believed to refer to the "castes". But we have seen that it really refers to the different faculties of man and the objects of Nature. We have also seen in what sense we have to understand the idea when it is said that only the first three"castes"can act: for it refers to the three faculties of man,—his intellect, mind, and the senses.

73. The word for intellect in the text is *Brāhmaṇa* which, as we have seen, refers to the intellect, as the *Kṣatriya* to *ahaṅkāra* and the mind, and the *Vaiśya* to the senses.

Another word in this *Sūtra* is *Ārtvijya,* which means "the office of a *ritvij* priest"; and as his office is to direct a sacrifice, it has been rendered as "directing action", for that is the idea of sacrifice.

74. The word in the text is *Svāmin* (lord, master) which, as has already been explained, refers to the soul.

75. The soul is also described as "a master of the house"; and the *Mīmāṁsā*

tells us that there is no real conflict between the two names, which have been distinguished in a later chapter.

76. All these faculties derive their strength from their association with the soul, for they cannot act without it.

77. When we understand how all these faculties function in association with the soul, we shall realise that the intellect is the highest of all, –for its special characteristic is decision, without which no action can take place. The word in the text is *Brāhmaṇa,* which, as has already been explained, refers to the intellect.

78 Since all the faculties of man depend for their function on the soul, and cannot act without it, it may be argued that they are alike. But even that is not tenable.

79. The text of this *Sūtra* may be rendered as follows:—
26. "As according to rule, *Viṣvamitra* performs the function of the *Hotṛ* priest, *Bhṛgu, Ṣunaka* and *Vasiṣ–ha* do not lay any claim to it."
We have explained that the *Hotṛ* priest refers to the mind; and so should *Viśvāmitra,* because he is said to perform his functions.
We have explained that *Mitra* refers to the intellect associated with action; and so *Viśvāmitra* would mean *"(Mitra)* intellect *(Viśvā)* in its universal or comprehensive form;" and this, as we now gather from this *Sūtra,* is closely allied to the mind. Indeed, the.*Mīmāṁsā* tells us that the mind and the intellect can be identified, and this is represented by the identity between *Soma* and *Agni,* who refer to the mind and intellect respectively. But *Soma* also refers to the full moon, which means the full development of the mind from desire into action. Hence *Viśvāmitra* gives us a comprehensive idea of the intellect, where the latter is the fully developed mind engaged in action. In other words, when the mind is fully engaged in action it is like the intellect; and this is the same thing as saying that when the intellect is engaged in action, it is the same thing as a fully developed mind. The *Mahābhārata* accordingly tells us that when the intellect desires anything, it is called the mind *(Sānti P.* XII, cxciv, 20).
Thus we might say that *Viśvāmitra* gives us the idea of the identity between the intellect and the mind, when the two are engaged in action. He figures in a number of places in a large number of sacred books, and it would be found that he refers to this idea throughout.
Vasiṣṭha literally means *Vasu-iṣa (Va, su, iṣṭha)* – *"(iṣṭha)* the highest or the best *(su)* born of *(va)* Nature or *Prakṛti";* and so refers to the intellect, as the first or highest "born" of Nature. He too figures largely in the sacred books, and retains this meaning throughout.
We are told of the rivalry between *Viśvāmitra* and *Vasiṣṭha;* and the cause lies in their different points of view in connection with the idea of the intellect: for *Viśvāmitra* represents the idea of the intellect in the closest association with mind and action; while *Vasiṣṭha,* "born of *Prakṛti*", be-

lieves that *Prakṛti* is the supreme creator of life, and so the highest goal can be attained only by means of renunciation of action; and this is the conclusion of the intellect as represented by him. Hence, as it is not easy to reconcile their conflicting points of view, their rivalry continues.

Bhṛgu – means "*(u, g)* the senses of knowledge and (r) the sense of action, associated with *(bh)* Nature."

Sunaka – s, *u, na, ka* – means "(s, *u, nd)* the senses of knowledge associated with *(ka)* Nature."

The difference between *Bhrgu* and *Sunaka* is that, while the one refers to both the senses of knowledge and action, the other refers to the senses of knowledge only.

Again all the three – *Vasiṣṭha, Bhrgu,* and *Śunaka* – refer to their association with Nature.

Thus, we see that *Viśvāmitra* refers to the mind fully engaged in action; while *Vasiṣṭha* to the intellect, and *Bhṛgu* and *Sunaka* to the senses.

80. The word in the text is *Anagni,* meaning "without fire" or without intelligence. There is a reference in the *Bhāgāvad Gītā* to one "who is without fire and without action" (BhG. VI, 1); and the idea apparently is that it is only a foolish person who thinks of giving up action during his life. Both the renderings have been given here.

81. Certain actions, like speech, can be deliberate as well natural or reflex; and we can take them as we like according to the circumstances of each case. But we should follow the opinion of trustworthy persons – There they agree – whenever there is a conflict of opinion

82. The *śūdra* cannot be given away as a gift, because he refers to the objects of the senses or Nature itself. This has already been explained.

83. An action may be said to come to an end when the things there associated with it come to an end.

84. This is a universal law of life, – that one action follows another without a break; and it can be proved in a number of ways.

85. The text has *Dvā-daśa-śatam* which can mean 112 or 1200; and both numbers refer; to Nature or *Prakṛti*.

The following *Sūtras* tell us that these numbers represent the idea of change or evolution of *Prakṛti;* and we have to see how that can be proved. The word for "change" in the text is *vikāra,* which has a number of meanings, including "a production or derivation from *Prakṛti";* and it is in this sense that it needs to be understood here: that is to say, it refers to the evolution of life from *Prakṛti*.

This is described in some detail in the *Sāṅkhya,* which tells us that when *Prakṛti* begins its course, the first to arise from it is *Mahat* or the intellect, from which arises *Ahaṅkāra* or the I-as-an-actor; and the latter gives rise to the five attributes of the five great "elements"; then we have the Mind, the five great elements, and the ten senses of knowledge and action (SS. I, 61, 71-72).

Thus, we see that it is possible to divide this process into two parts, – intellect, *ahaṅkāra,* and the five attributes of the "elements" on the one hand, and the mind together with the great "elements" and the senses on the other; and the former consists of seven parts, and the latter of 16, – the multiple of which is 112, giving us a complete idea of the evolution of *Prakṛti.*

It is possible to deal with number 1200 in a similar way. The *Sāṅkhya* tells us that the action of *Prakṛti* may be compared to the passage of Time (III,60), and the same idea is repeated in the *Mīmāṁsā.* Now the ancients divided Time into *Yugas, Manvantaras,* and *Kalpasi* and the *Yugas* are said to be four in number; while the duration ot all the four constitutes a *Manvantara;* and a thousand *Yugas* make a *Kalpa.* The basis of all this is a *Yuga.*

Now the four *Yugas* are *Satya, Tretā, Dvāpara,* and *Kali;* and their duration is said to be 1,728,000, 1,296,000, 864,000, and 432,000 years of men respectively. It will be found on examination that all these figures are multiples of the number 1200, which may, accordingly be said to refer to Time or to *Prakṛti.* Indeed, the number 1200 is itself based on the idea of the number 12, which is the real number representing the idea of Time or of *Prakṛti.*

Thus we see how the numbers 112 or 1200 refer to the idea of the evolution of Nature or *Prakṛti.*

86. We have seen from the idea of numbers, as explained here, how the idea of multiplication and creation is the same.

87. This corresponds to what the *Bhāgāvad Gītā* calls the higher form of *Prakāti,* which is said to be the life of all creatures and to sustain the universe (BhG. VII, 5).

 The idea of *"Kāma-dhuk* or the "Cow of Plenty", which is said to confer benefits, would be of this kind.

88. Any description of *Prakṛti* would refer to it as measureless etc. (Cf. BhG. XV, 1-3, where the "eternal *Aśvattha"* refers to Nature or *Prakṛti).*

89. This *Sūtra* does not occur in cerain texts. It is said that *Rāma* ruled in *Ayodhyā* for ten thousand years; and we have to understand the idea in a similar way; for he too represents a great system of thought which prevailed for a long time. The *Mahābhārata* tells us that the terms hundred, thousand, hundred thousand refer to an infinite or an indefinitely large number *(Adi P.* I, ccxix, 8).

90. This is a name of a philosopher.

91. *Lāvukāyana* or *Lābukāyana* is the name of a philosopher.

92. We have already explained that the idea of Time is closely con-nected with that of Nature or *Prakṛti,* as both refer to change, which is action conceived in its widest significance.

93. *Homa* is an act of making oblations to the gods by casting clarified butter into the fire. We have explained that fire or *Agni* refers to intelligence, and clarified butter to goodness of desire. *Homa* is accordingly a good and intelligent action, or an act of sacrifice.
The word for "intelligence" in the text is *Agni* which, as the *Mīmāṁsā* has told us, refers to the intellect.

94. A sacrifice, as the *Mimānsā* will tell us presently, is an act meant for the benefit of all, including the doer of the deed himself, but no more than the rest; and no one can derive any special advantage out of it.
But we find in general that human actions are imperfect, becausethey are characterised by desire, –aiming to obtain a particular result; and in such actions the mind plays a most important part; and the mind, as has already been explained, is represented by the *Hotṛ* priest.
We have seen that there are four *ritvij* priests, –one of whom is the *Hotṛ;* and each of them is assisted by three more, who again refer to the three remaining faculties of man: the idea being that, though a particular faculty may have the most important role in an action, the remaining three have also their place. The three assistants of the *Hotṛ* priest are accordingly the intellect, *ahaṅkāra* and the senses; and this *Sūtra* tells us that the action in which they take part is an imperfect one, because it is dominated by desire, the special attribute of the mind.

95. An intelligent action is not an act of sacrifice at its commencement. It is only when, like *Homa,* it becomes free from desire, that it can be regarded as an act of sacrifice.

96. No intelligence is required in merely repeating a sacred name; and so Japa is not characterised by intelligence: even so it is not characterised by desire, which awakens when the intellect functions and is transformed into the mind by means of desire. Hence *Japa* is a pure act of sacrifice from the very beginning (*Cf*. BhG. X, 25).

97. *Japa* is not like *Homa,* which is characterised by desire at the beginning, and becomes free from it in the end; and so it is only at the end that it can be like *Japa*.

98. But both *Japa* and *Homa* are acts of sacrifice, –free from desire; and so they are like an oblation offered to deceased ancestors, from whom we cannot, in reason, expect any return. Hence an offering made to the deceased ancestors is an act of pure sacrifice, free from desire for fruit.

99. It has already been explained that an offering made to deceased ancestors represents the idea of a pure sacrifice, because we cannot, in reason, expect any result out of it.

100. *Upanaya* or initiating a boy in spiritual knowledge is like *Homa* in so far that it begins with a particular desire, but becomes free from it in the end. To give knowledge is a form of desire; but when it is given, there is an end to it; and so to give knowledge is an act of sacrifice like *Homa*.

101. The *Bhāgāvad Gītā* tells us that all action is made more complete in knowledge (BhG. IV, 33).
102. This *Sūtra* does not occur in certain texts: it only clarifies the idea of the preceding one. A person can renounce all action only at the end of his life, when he has done all his life"s work.
It is this that is exemplified in the life of *Buddha*, whose real name is *Siddhārtha (Siddha-artha)* or "one all whose objects have been attained or satisfied". When a person comes to a stage of life when all his desires are satisfied, he can think of renouncing actions. But, as this stage arrives only at the end of one"s life, the creed of *Buddha*, with its emphasis on renunciation, may_be said to be one of perfection in the path of death.
103. A real act of sacrifice is meant to be for the benefit of all (*Cf.* BhG. V, 25).
104. The expression in the text is "drinking *Soma"*; and, as *Soma* refers to the mind or its attribute, desire, "drinking *Soma"* means satisfying one"s desire, – even as one may do by drinking wine, which is another meaning of the word.
105. The birth of a son is accordingly symbolic of the satisfaction of desire; and this is how we should understand its idea in the sacred books. Indeed, the desire to have a son can often be very great,perhaps the greatest of all, as it symbolises the idea of the preservation of the race; and so the birth of a son can appropriately represent the idea of satisfaction of desire.
106. The offering made to deceased ancestors represents the idea of pure sacrifice; and the desire to have a son should be of the same kind, – a pure sacrifice, and the son born should live and do his work for the benefit of all.
107. An act of sacrifice requires intelligence; and the greater the act, the greater the intelligence. It needs intelligence to rise to greatness in life.
108. A desire can be fulfilled only when a person has the desire or the intention.
109. When a person has a desire—to rise to greatness, the desire itself is a proof of his intelligence. It is only an intelligent man who can desire to become great.
110. The gods refer to the great powers of Nature which sustain life; and the first half of the year, etc. are symbolic of this idea. That is to say, the gods are associated with bright, beautiful, and beneficent things in Nature.
The *Bhāgāvad Gītā* contains a reference to something similar (BhG. VIII, 23-26), and the same idea occurs in the *Upaniṣads* too.
111. The deceased ones are said to abide in the region of the Moon, from where they are said to return to be reborn on earth after sometime. They are those who depart from the earth during the progress of the sun in the other half of the year, etc.; and so the latter refers to them, as the *Bhāgāvad Gītā* tells us (BhG. VIII, 25-26).
112. When we beg or buy anything, it means that we want something; so that there is some deficiency to be made good.

113. It is not possible to explain the meanings of these words without reference to the context.
114. Animals, other than human beings, are not governed by reason; and so the meanings of word's referring to them are not fixed. Fixity is a mark of reason or the intellect.
115. The word *chāga* may mean a goat or a sign of the Zodiac (Aries), or something else according to the context. It may also have to be divided into parts to be understood.
116. It would be contrary to rules to have fixity of ideas in connection with what are called lower animals, because their own behaviour is not fixed or governed by known rules.
117. When we change the form of a word, what we do is to divide it into parts, which are, as a rule, letters. This cannot give us a fundamental word. This method of interpretation requires that each letter should be treated like a word itself; and so the word in its changed form has nothing in common with the original word.

CHAPTER - VII

THE METHOD OF INTERPRETATION

PART I

The meaning of the entire text should be in accordance with the teachings of the *śruti*. This will convince us of its correctness; and we shall find the description to be so accurate that the ideas and objects appear to be like living beings.

If, however, the common meaning be the real meaning of the text, it should make sense, and the actions of persons should be consistent with their character; but it is not so.

This method of interpretation applies to both the *śruti* and the *smṛti*.

Where a word has a number of meanings, it is necessary to make a selection; and it is this principle that has been applied in this method of interpretation, as may be seen from the meanings of certain words. The new meaning transforms the whole idea of the text, and the words retain their meaning throughout. There are, however, certain words the meanings of which have been specially defined.

The Method of Interpretation

श्रुतिप्रमाणत्वाच्छेषाणां मुख[1]भेदे यथाधिकारं भावः स्यात्॥१॥
उत्पत्त्यर्थाविभागाद्वा सत्त्ववदैकधर्म्यं स्यात्॥२॥
चोदना शेषभावाद्वा ताद्वा तद्भेदाद्व्यवतिष्ठेरन्नुत्पत्तेर्गुणभूतत्वात्॥३॥
सत्त्वे लक्षणसंयोगात्सार्वत्रिकं प्रतीयेत॥४॥

---

1. मुख्यभेदे इति पाठान्तरं वृत्तिग्रन्थे

When the meaning of the principal word has been explained in accordance with the authority of the *śruti,* the meaning of the rest of the text should also be explained in accordance with the same authority. It will then be found that the text, unseparated from its original meaning, comes to possess its true essence, and retains the same character throughout. We shall thus find, from the conclusions arrived at and the truth disclosed, that the direction we have followed is the correct one, as it will partake of the characteristics of the original words. Indeed, the description is so accurate, that the ideas and objects appear in every case to be like living beings[1].

An Objection

अविभागात्तु नैवं स्यात्॥५॥

द्व्यर्थत्वं च विप्रतिषिद्धम्॥६॥

It may be argued that this is not possible, because the meanings cannot be divided in such a manner as to give us this result; and so it is not possible to agree that there can be two different meanings in this way.

An Answer

उत्पत्तौ विध्यभावाद्वा चोदनायां प्रवृत्तिः स्यात्ततश्च कर्मभेदः स्यात्॥७॥

यदि वाऽप्यभिधनवत्सामान्यात् सर्वधर्मः[1] स्यात्॥८॥

अर्थस्य त्वविभक्तत्वात्तथा स्यादभिधनेषु पूर्ववत्त्वात्प्रयोगस्य; कर्मणः शब्दभाव्यत्वाद्विभागाच्छेषाणामप्रवृत्तिः स्यात्॥९॥

But if this contention were correct, and if the meaning of the text has no bearing on the laws of life, it follows that what the text teaches should be true, and all that we are told should take place, so that if we act in conformity with it, our actions should blossom forth and produce the promised results. If the names are real names, and if this is the normal form of the text, we should be able to grasp the essential characteristics of all

1. सर्वविसिद्धिः स्यादिति वृत्तिग्रन्थे पाठान्तरम्।

things. If, however, we must take the meanings as they are, and cannot divide words into parts, it is possible to say that the names are the names of objects; but the text also refers to their actions, which do not appear to be consistent with their character. Hence we cannot apply the same rule to the rest of the text (and say that the names refer to living beings).

Method Applicable to both Śruti and Smṛti

स्मृतिरिति चेत्[1]॥१०॥

न पूर्ववत्त्वात्॥११॥

It may be argued that this method may apply to the *smṛti,* but not to the *śruti*. But this is not possible, because the *smṛti* is nothing but conclusions drawn from what precedes it *(śruti)*[2].

Need of Selection

अर्थस्य शब्दभाव्यत्वात्प्रकरणनिबन्धनाच्छब्दादेवान्यत्र भावः स्यात्॥१२॥

समाने पूर्ववत्त्वादुत्पन्नाधिकारः स्यात्॥१३॥

श्येनस्येति चेत्॥१४॥

नासन्निधनात्॥१५॥

अपि वा यद्यपूर्वत्वादितरदधिकार्थे ज्यौतिष्टोमिकाद्विधेस्तद्वाचकं समानं स्यात्॥१६॥

पञ्चसञ्चरेष्वर्थवादातिदेशः सन्निधनात्॥१७॥

सर्वस्य वैक[2]शब्द्यात्॥१८॥

लिङ्गदर्शनाच्च॥१९॥

The words used in the text have a number of meanings; and it is only because we restrict ourselves to a particular explanation that (a difficulty arises, and) we get a different meaning. (It is a common rule of interpretation that) if a word has similar meanings, we should accept that which has already been referred to in the text. But this does not apply to the word

---

1. अग्रिमसूत्रस्थं नञ्पदमत्रैव सूत्रान्त्ये वृत्तिग्रन्थे पठ्यते।
2. स्य चैकेति वृत्तिग्रन्थे पाठान्तरम्।

śyena,[3] because it does not make sense. Again, if a word is quite new, and has more than one meaning, the term "similar" should apply only to such meanings as have a bearing on a law of Nature,—as, for instance, that which is derived from *Jyotiṣtoma*[4] If, however, there is a reference to "five motions" in the text, it is easy to explain its meaning[5]; and we get it by substituting one expression for another; and this substitution can be made throughout the text, because it is one and the same idea that is expressed, which can be understood when we see through this "disguise".

Oneness of Meaning

विहिताम्नानान्नेति चेत्॥२०॥

नेतरार्थत्वात्॥२१॥

एककपालैन्द्राग्नौ च तद्वत्॥२२॥

There are some who maintain that it is not possible to have the same meaning throughout, because the sense is fixed by the context in each case. But this cannot be accepted; for if we take the meanings as they are, we find that they are unsuitable, and we are compelled to reject them; and it is in this manner that we find that there is but one assemblage of ideas in connection with *Indra* and *Agni*[6].

Words with Fixed Meanings

एककपालानां वैश्वदेविकः प्रकृतिराग्रयणे सर्वहोमापरिवृत्तिदर्शनादवभृथे च सकृद् द्व्यवदानस्य वचनात्॥२३॥

There are certain words which have only one meaning: for instance *Viśvadevas* (all-gods) refers to Nature or *Prakṛti;* and the ā*grāyana* sacrifice should be understood to include all sacrifices. There is also a reference to *avabṛtha* sacrifice, and it is only once that the word has to be divided into parts; and that too in accordance with an express direction[7].

1. एकार्थे इति वृत्तिग्रन्थे पाठान्तरम्।

PART II

THE METHOD OF INTERPRETATION (*CONTINUED*)

Introdution

The name *Sāman* refers to active life. Action is associated with desire, and is divisible into parts, corresponding to which the words used in the text are also divisible into parts.

We must not make any alteration in the language of the Vedas; and we should also accept the meanings of words bearing on the idea of action, without change of form. When we change the form of a word, the meaning may appear to be unusual; but we will not err, because there are certain technical terms to guide us. Words, the origin of which can be traced, are the best. If words had but a single meaning, there would be no need to have this multiplicity of forms; but, as we are unable to make any sense of the text, we are obliged to think of some other meaning. There can be no objection to this, because the language of the text is not altered, and it is only a question of its proper use.

Meaning of Saman

साम्नोऽभिधनशब्देन प्रवृत्तिः स्याद्यथाशिष्टम्॥१॥
शब्दैस्त्वर्थविधित्वादर्थान्तरेऽप्रवृत्तिः स्यात्पृथग्भावात्क्रियाया ह्यभिसम्बन्धः॥२॥

The word *Sāman,* correctly understood, means active life[8], as has been taught; and it is only when we understand its correct use that we shall be able to get a meaning bearing on the laws of life. But if we interpret it in some other way, we shall find no reference to active life. If, on the other hand, we take it in its correct sense, we shall find that there is a close connection with the idea of life.

Action: How Described

स्वार्थे वा स्यात्प्रयोजनं क्रियायास्तदङ्गभावेनोपदिश्येरन्॥४॥
शब्दमात्रमिति चेत्॥४॥

नोत्पत्तिकत्वात्॥५॥
शास्त्रं चैवमनर्थकं स्यात्॥६॥
स्वरस्येति चेत्॥७॥
नार्थाभावाच्छ्रुतेरसम्बन्धः॥८॥
स्वरस्तूत्पत्तिषु स्यान्मात्रावर्णाविभक्तत्वात्॥९॥
लिङ्गदर्शनाच्च॥१०॥

We can see our motive of action in our own aim. Action consists of parts, and should be understood by means of them; (and this would explain why words need to be divided into parts, —for that is how they express the idea of the parts of an action). We cannot say that words are mere sounds (and cannot do this), because we see that they produce certain results; and if words were mere sounds, the sacred books would be useless. We cannot say that their value lies in the tone of their recitation; for if there were no proper meaning, they could not have any value. The tone of recitation does indeed produce certain effects; and that is how the value of the outward form of the text is measured when the words are not divided into parts; and we can see the proof of this for ourselves.

he Text must not be Changed

अश्रुतेस्तु विकारस्योत्तरासु यथाश्रुति॥११॥
शब्दानां चासामञ्जस्यम्॥१२॥

Any deviation from the natural form of the text would mean that it does not belong to the Veda. This is particularly enjoined in the second part of the *Sāma Saṁhitā,* where we should take the *śruti* as it is; (for if we make any change, we shall find) that the words do not yield a proper meaning.

Words Denoting Action should not be Changed

अपि तु कमशब्दः स्याद्भावोऽर्थः प्रसिद्धिग्रहणत्वाद्विकारो ह्यविशिष्टोऽन्यैः॥१३॥
अद्रव्यं चापि दृश्यते॥१४॥

If there is a word denoting action, its meaning can be obtained in its usual form without making any change. In such a case a change would not be for the best; (and we should adhere to its original form even if) the object concerned should appear in an unfavourable light.

Special Cases

तस्य च क्रिया ग्रहणार्था नानार्थेषु विरूपित्वादर्थो ह्यासामलौकिको विधनात्॥१५॥

तस्मिन्संज्ञाविशेषाः स्युर्विकारपृथक्त्वात्॥१६॥

When a word has a number of meanings, we should accept that which refers to action. When there are different meanings, – the correct meaning, because of its change of form (in accordance with the method of interpretation), – might appear to be an uncommon one. There are, however, certain technical terms in the text (to enable us to understand it), for otherwise there can be a number of variations of meaning.

Words and their Origin

योनिशस्याश्च तुल्यवदितराभिर्विधीयन्ते॥१७॥

अयोनौ चापि दृश्यतेऽतथायोनिः॥१८॥

Words whose origin can be traced are the best; and the meaning of other words can be traced by means of them. But there are also a number of words whose origin cannot be traced. We can understand their meaning, but not in the same manner as that of others.

Need of a New Interpretation

ऐकार्थ्ये[1] नास्ति वैरूप्यमिति चेत्॥१९॥

स्यादर्थान्तरेष्वनिष्पत्तेर्यथालोके[2]॥२०॥

शब्दानाञ्च सामञ्जस्यम्॥२१॥

---

1. एकार्थे इति वृत्तिग्रन्थे पाठान्तरम्।
1. यथा पाके इति वृत्तिग्रन्थे पाठान्तरम्।

It is possible to say that if there were but a single meaning of words, there would be no need to have this multiplicity of forms. But it is only because we are unable to get any sense out of the text, that we have to think of some other meaning, even as is common among the people. (The new meaning given to words is not foreign to the text,) and it is only a question of making a proper use of its language.

PART III

THE METHOD OF INTERPRETATION (CONTINUED)

Introduction

The real meaning of a word is often very different from its common one; and we can understand its idea by dividing it into parts or referring it to its origin or root.

The meaning of certain words has been specially defined: for instance, *viśva-jīt* (all-conquering) means *sarva-pṛṣṭha* (or universal action); and *Jyotiṣṭoma* is action,—with special reference to mind-energy or electric energy. If we do not interpret the text in this manner, the whole of it would become meaningless.

It is in the same manner that we get the meaning of *Soma,* and can understand the idea of the purification of the sacrificer through it.

There is a law in connection with the division of words into parts; and if we follow it, we can get a proper meaning of the word *puroḍāśa* which, in its original form, makes little sense. But we should not divide words into parts if we get a properly balanced meaning of the text otherwise. On the other hand it should be followed in the case of a word like *nirmanthya* (to be churned) which makes little sense in its existing form.

It is not possible to accept the ordinary meanings of words like *Soma* (moon) or *uttara-vedī* (northern altar of the sacred fire), because they do not make any sense as they are.

The explanation of the meaning of a word can be obtained in three ways: by means of its special definition, or its common meaning, or division into parts. The common meaning of the word *uttara-vedī* is not suitable; but where two meanings are equally balanced, as in the case of the word *gati,* we can take that which we consider appropriate.

The meanings of certain words like *svara-sāma, eka-kapāla,* and *āmikṣa* can be obtained by piercing through their "disguised" forms; but we can do so when we have the entire text before us.

The meaning of certain words is obtained from the function they perform. Thus action may be said to be like a sacrificial post; and so the word *yūpa* (sacrificial post) refers to action. This is a deliberate mode of expression and is not accidental.

In case of doubt, we may follow the common meaning of a word, if it serves our purpose; but it may not be its Vedic meaning, which can usually be obtained by dividing words into parts; and in the light of this the word *pṛṣṭha* would mean "action", and no other meaning would suit the text.

How to Understand the Text

उक्तं क्रियाभिधनं तच्छ्रुतावन्यत्र विधिप्रदेशः स्यात्॥१॥
अपूर्वे वापि भागित्वात्॥२॥
नाम्नस्त्वौत्पत्तिकत्वात्॥३॥
प्रत्यक्षाद्गुणसंयोगात्क्रियाभिधनं स्यात्तदभावेऽप्रसिद्धं स्यात्॥४॥
अपि वा सर्वत्र कर्मणि गुणार्थैषा श्रुतिः स्यात्॥५॥

A word that in ordinary speech is the name of an action, may mean something very different when used in the Vedic text; but, even if it is quite new, we can understand its meaning by dividing it into parts. The meaning of a word may also be obtained by referring it to its origin;[9] and the idea of action can be obtained by combining together the different parts of a word; for in the absence of this, it cannot be proved. With regard to a great action, involving the function of the mind,[10] the correct meaning is always associated with the parts of words; and we should take it that that is the correct way of understanding the *śruti*.

Words with Defined Meanings

विश्वजिति सर्वपृष्ठे तत्पूर्वकत्वाज्ज्यौतिष्टोमिकानि पृष्ठान्यस्ति च पृष्ठशब्दः॥६॥

षडहाद्वा तत्र हि चोदनाः॥७॥

लिङ्गाच्च[1]॥८॥

उत्पन्नाधिकारो ज्योतिष्टोमः॥९॥

द्वयोर्विधिरिति चेत्॥१०॥

न व्यर्थत्वात्सर्वशब्दस्य॥११॥

(The meaning of certain words has been specially defined: for instance,) the word *viśva-jīt* has, from the very beginning, the same meaning as *sarva-pṛṣṭha*[11] Indeed, all that relates to *Jyotiṣṭoma* is the same as *pṛṣṭha*[12] for that is the meaning of the word *pṛṣṭha:* or the meaning may be obtained from the idea of a *Soma* festival, lasting six days[13]; and all this can seen by piercing through the "disguise" of words.[14] Indeed, the word *Jyotiṣṭoma* is entitled to be associated with the word *pṛṣṭha;* and we cannot say that there are separate rules in regard to the two words; for if we do so and interpret the text accordingly, the whole language would become meaningless.

Meaning of Soma

तथावभृथः सोमात्॥१२॥

प्रकृतेरिति चेत्॥१३॥

न भक्तित्वात्॥१४॥

लिङ्गदर्शनाच्च॥१५॥

It is in this manner that we can understand the idea of the purification of the sacrificer through *Soma*[15] (or the function of the mind). We cannot say that we get the meaning of the

---

2. लिङ्गदर्शनाच्चेति पाठान्तरं वृत्तिग्रन्थे।

word from its original or uninflected form, for we get it by means of its division into parts; and we can understand it by seeing through its "disguise"[16].

Rule regarding Division of Words into Parts

द्रव्यादेश तद्द्रव्यः श्रुतिसंयोगात् पुरोडाशस्त्वनादेशे तत्प्रकृतित्वात्॥१५॥
गुणविधिस्तु न गृह्णीयात्समत्वात्॥१७॥
निर्मन्थ्यादिषु चैवम्॥१८॥

(There is a rule in connection with the division of words into parts). We find that when we describe the ingredients of a substance, we get a proper idea of the substance itself; and it is this that has been done in connection with the words used in the *śruti*. (They need to be divided into parts in order to give us an idea of what they contain,) like the word *puroḍāśa,* which tells us nothing in its original form.[17] But this rule in regard to the division of words into parts should not be followed where there is already a properly balanced explanation of the text; where-as it should be applied in the case of words like *nirmanthya*[18], etc., which make little sense as they are.

Reason for Rejecting Common Meanings

प्रणयनन्तु सौमिकमवाच्यं हीतरत्॥१९॥
उत्तरवेदिप्रतिषेधश्च तद्वत्॥२०॥
प्राकृतं वाऽनामत्वात्॥२१॥

(It is not possible to accept the ordinary meaning of certain words: for instance,) we have to reject the meaning of the word *Soma* as the moon or wine, because it would be highly improper to bring forward a vessel containing the one or the other.[19] Similarly, we are unable to accept the meaning of the word *uttara-vedi*[20] (as the northern altar for the sacrificial fire), because it contains little substance in its original form.

Three ways of Explanation

परिसङ्ख्यार्थं श्रवणं गुणार्थमर्थवादो वा॥२२॥
प्रथमोत्तमयोः प्रणयनमुत्तरवेदिप्रतिषेधत्॥२३॥

मधयमयोर्वा गत्यर्थवादात्॥२४॥
औत्तरवेदिकोऽनारभ्यवादप्रतिषेधः॥२५॥
स्वरसामैककपालामिक्षं च लिङ्गदर्शनात्॥२६॥
चोदनासामान्याद्वा[1]॥२७॥
कर्मजे कर्म यूपवत्॥२८॥
रूपं वाऽशेषभूतत्वात्॥२९॥

The explanation of the the meaning of a word can be obtained by associating it with some special meaning; by taking the common meaning which we have heard; and by dividing it into parts. As we find it difficult to accept the common meaning of *uttara-vedī,* we have to reject the second method, and make use of the first and last. When, however, there are two equally balanced meanings, we should take that which suits the context best, as in the case of the word *gati*. The difficulty in accepting the common meaning of *uttara-vedi* is that it does not fit into the context, for there is no reference to an altar; and to interpret it as "the northern altar made for the sacrificial fire" would be to make use of an argument that has not yet commenced.

The meaning of certain words like *svara-sāma, eka-kapāla,* and *āmikṣa* can be obtained by piercing through their "disguise"; but we can understand them when we have the entire text before us, for then we get a direction about what should be done.

(The meaning of certain words is obtained from the function they perform: for instance,) in a thing that is produced from action, action may be said to be like a *yūpa* or a sacrificial post;[21] and this is a deliberate and not an accidental mode of expression.

Cases of Doubt

विशये लौकिकः स्यात्सर्वार्थत्वात्॥३०॥
न वैदिकमर्थनिर्देशात्॥३१॥

---

1. इदं सूत्रं वृत्तिग्रन्थे नास्ति

तथोत्पत्तिरितरेषां समत्वात्॥३२॥
संस्कृतं स्यात्तच्छब्दत्वात्॥३३॥
भक्त्या वाऽयज्ञशेषत्वाद्गुणानामभिधनत्वात्[1]॥३४॥
कर्मणः पृष्ठशब्दः स्यात्तथाभूतोपदेशात्॥३५॥
अभिधनोपदेशाद्वा विप्रतिषेधद् द्रव्येषु पृष्ठशब्दः स्यात्॥३६॥

In case of doubt we should follow the common meaning of a word if it serves our purpose; but it may not be the real Vedic meaning, —and for reasons that have already been explained. It is in this manner that we get other meanings of the text, because they appear to be on the same level with the real ones; but we can get a proper meaning if we interpret words in the manner explained. When we find that what remains of the meaning of a word has no bearing on the idea of a sacrifice, we should get its real meaning by dividing it into parts, and treating each part as if it were a name by itself. According to this the word *pṛṣṭha* would mean "action", even as we have been taught, and also because no other meaning would suit the context[22].

PART IV

THE METHOD OF INTERPRETATION (*CONTINUED*)

Introduction

There is good reason for following this method of interpretation. The common meaning of a word arises from retaining its existing form; but if we pronounce words correctly, we shall know their real meaning, which will be obtained by dividing them into parts. There is nothing irregular in this, and it enables us to know the exact meaning of the text.

The meaning of a word should be determined by means of its division into parts. Roots should not be divided into parts;

1. धनादिति वृत्तिग्रन्थे पाठान्तरम्।

and roots and parts of words should not be mixed together in the same word.

The secret of this method of interpretation consists in dividing words into their parts; and this is the meaning of "seeing through the disguise". The common meaning of a word is its meaning without this "disguise" or division into parts. In case of doubt or difficulty there are suggestions in the text to guide us.

It is necessary to have knowledge to be able to understand the text; and there is a reference to it in a special way.

The design of composition is such that each part is closely connected with the other, and there is no lack of words to complete the sense.

A "disguise" is a collection of qualities, from which we have to draw our own conclusions; and we can understand these qualities by means of inference. "Seeing through the disguise" consists in our ability to show how things are connected with one another. But this method of division of words into parts applies only to the principal or the most important words.

Method of Interpretation

इतिकर्तव्यताविधेर्यजतेः पूर्ववत्त्वम्॥१॥

This is the reason for following this method of interpretation. Its result is in conformity with the previous statements of the text; and it is worthy of all honour and praise.

Common and Real Meaning

स लौकिकः स्याद्दृष्टप्रवृत्तित्वात्॥१॥
वचनात्तु ततोऽन्यत्वम्॥२॥
लिङ्गेन निवा यम्येत लिङ्गस्य[1] तद्गुणत्वात्।३॥
अपिवाऽन्यायपूर्वत्वाद्यत्र नित्यानुवादवचनानि स्युः॥५॥
मिथो विप्रतिषेधच्च गुणानां यथार्थकल्पना स्यात्॥६॥

---

1. लिङ्गस्येति पदं वृत्तिग्रन्थे नास्ति।

What is called the common meaning of the text, current among the people, arises from our allowing its obvious form to continue. But if we pronounce the words correctly, we shall find before long that the real meaning is different. That meaning is determined by means of the very words of the text, – words that serve to fix the meaning of other words too; and it arises from the parts into which they can be divided. It is not possible to draw an irregular or irrelevant conclusion in this way, because there is always a confirmation or explanatory translation of the real meaning in what follows. The different parts of a word hold each other in mutual check, with the result that we can know the exact meaning of the text even as it was conceived in the author's mind.

An Illustration

भागित्वात्तु नियम्येत गुणानामभिधनत्वासम्बन्धदभिधनवद्यथा धेनुः किशोरेण।

The meaning of a word should be determined by means of its division into parts which, when put together, are so closely connected that they are like a single name, and can easily be pronounced like the word *go* (a cow) uttered by a boy.

Roots

उत्पत्तीनां समत्वाद्वा यथाधिकारं भावः स्यात्॥८॥

उत्पत्तिशेषवचनं च विप्रतिषिद्धिमेकस्मिन्॥९॥

With regard to the roots of words, since that is their norm, their meaning should be determined according to their position in the text; and a root and subsidiary parts of a word are not permitted in one and the same expression[23].

Meaning of "Disguise"

विधयन्तो वा प्रकृतिवच्चोदनायां प्रवर्त्तेत[1] तथा हि लिङ्गदर्शनम्॥१०॥

The secret of this method of interpretation lies in reducing

1. प्रवर्तते इति वृत्तिग्रन्थे पाठान्तरम्।

words to their rudimentary form, by dividing them into parts; and this should be done in all cases where this method is applied. This is indeed the meaning of "seeing through the disguise".

The Common Meaning

लिङ्गहेतु[1]त्वादलिङ्गे लौकिकं स्यात्॥१२॥

When a word is under a "disguise", but we take it as if it had none, that should be regarded as its common or popular sense.

Suggestions for Guidance

लिङ्गस्य पूर्ववत्त्वाच्चोदनाशब्दसामान्यादेकेनापि निरूप्येत, यथा स्थालीपुलाकेन॥१२॥

In case the words in the text are evenly balanced, and yet we believe that they are under a "disguise" which needs to be pierced, we shall find that there is at least one word to point the way,—just as we can understand the idea of the contents of a whole plate from a single grain.

Need of Knowledge: How Expressed

द्वादशाहिकमहर्गणे तत्प्रकृतित्वादैकाहिकमधिकागमात्तदाख्यं स्यादेकाहवत्॥१३॥

लिङ्गाच्च॥१४॥

When in a series of days we say something that relates to the twelfth day,—that, in its original idea, would refer to only one day, the twelfth. But if we mean something more than this, it would require special knowledge to express it; and that is done in terms of the reference to a particular day; and there is good reason for doing so[24].

Design of Composition

न वा क्रत्वभिधनादधिकानामशब्दत्वम्॥१५॥

---

2. लिङ्गस्य हेत्विति वृत्तिग्रन्थे पाठान्तरम्।

The design of composition is such that each part of the text is closely connected with the other, and there is no lack of words for making additional points.

Character of "Disguise"

लिङ्गं सङ्घातधर्मः स्यात्तदर्थापत्तेर्द्रव्यत्॥१६॥
न वार्थध[1]र्मत्वात् सङ्घातस्य गुणत्वात्॥१७॥
अर्थापत्तेर्द्रव्येषु धर्मलाभः स्यात्॥१८॥
प्रवृत्त्या नियतस्य लिङ्गदर्शनम्॥१९॥
विहारदर्शनं[2] विशिष्टस्यानारभ्यवादानां प्रकृत्यर्थत्वात्॥२०॥

The "disguise" of a word should be regarded as a collection of qualities, from which we have to draw our own inferences; and if we succeed, the result is worth while, —like the idea of a proper person or thing. This, however, cannot be obtained from the meaning of words as they are, but only from the parts of the "collection" spoken of as a "disguise". We can understand the qualities of these objects by means of the process of inference; and "seeing through the disguise" consists in our ability to show how things are connected with or dependent on one another. We must, however, take notes of the fact that the distribution or division of words into parts refers only to the principal words; and so far as detached statements are concerned, the meaning of words should be obtained from their common or popular sense.

NOTES

1. This would explain why the characters in the Epics and the *Purāṇas*, which are really ideas of philosophy personified, appear to be like living beings. As the *Mīmāṁsā* tells us, this method of composition, and so of interpretation, is common to both the *śruti* and the *smṛti*, or the *Vedas* and post-Vedic literature, and the latter includes the Epics and the *Purāṇas*.
2. This shows that this method of interpretation applies to both Vedic and post-Vedic literature. It has been applied to the *Mahābhārata*, and is found

---

1. धर्मः स्यात्सेति वृत्तिग्रन्थे पाठान्तरम्।
2. दर्शनं चेति चकारधिको वृत्तिग्रन्थे।

to be equally applicable to the *Rāmāyaṇa* and the *Bhāgavat Purāṇa;* and so it follows that it would apply to all sacred books.

3. The word *śyena* commonly means a "hawk or falcon" which is said to have brought down the *Soma-juice* to man. The *Mīmāṁsā* tells us that we cannot accept this or any other meaning given in the dictionary, because it does not make sense, and so we have to divide the word into parts (*Cf.* MM. I, 376).

4. *Jyotiṣṭoma,* said to be a *Soma* ceremony, refers really to the rays of light (See Appendix II). The *Mīmāṁsā* tells us that "similar" meanings, which we are asked to accept, should refer to the laws of life, – for that is the essential idea of the text.

5. "Five motions"would obviously refer to the function of the five senses, – especially those of action, for motion and action are closely allied.

6. We have already explained that *Indra* really refers to the self conscious soul *(Prajṃātmari)* and *Agni* to the intellect; and this is the meaning they retain throughout the range of sacred books.

7. As has already been explained, a god refers to the great powers of Nature; and so *Viśve-devas* or all-gods would refer to all the powers of Nature, – that is, the whole of Nature itself.

   Agrayana is said to be the first *Soma*-libation at the *Agnishtoma* sacrifice. As *Soma* refers to the mind and *Agni* to intellect, while sacrifice is action, – *āgrāyana,* being associated with both, would refer to the functions of both the mind and the intellect. As the attribute of the mind is desire, which is characterised by an element of goodness, – and always so where the doer of the deed himself is concerned – we have here the association of goodness and intelligence, which is of the essence of the idea of sacrifice. Hence *āgrāyaṇa* includes all kinds of sacrifice.

   Avabṛtha means "the purification or ablution of the sacrificer and sacrificial vesselsafter a sacrifice"; it also means "a supplementary sacrifice". The *Mīmāṁsā* tells us that it generally retains this meaning; and it is only once that its meaning is different, and it has to be divided into parts to be understood.

8. The *Mīmāṁsā* tells us elsewhere (X, v, 58) that we have an account of all that relates to living creatures in the *Sāma Veda;* and here we are told that the meaning of word *Sāman* itself has been defined as "active life" or a life of action, which only living creatures are capable of.

   The word *Sāman* is said to refer to a particular kind of hymns, which are intended to be sung by the *Udgātṛ* priest; and we have explained that the latter refers to *ahaṅkāra* or the I-as-an-actor, whose special function is action.

   The *Mīmāṁsā* tells us that we should understand the text of all *Sāman* hymns in the light of the idea of action; but if we do not do so, we shall not find any reference to the laws of life in the text.

It may be of interest to observe that the Vedas are all characterised by a plan. The *Mīmāṁsā* tells us that the subject-matter of the *Ṛg Veda* is action, conceived in its widest significance, and embracing all forms of it without exception (IX, ii, 4-5), – so that it would include Nature as well as animal life. The *Sāma Veda,* on the other hand, deals with the problem of animal life; and so we are told that whatever is in the *Sāma Veda* is also in the *Ṛg Veda* (X, v, 58-61); but obviously not *vice-versa,* for the *Ṛg Veda* deals with all that is in the world of Nature too.

The *Yajur Veda,* even as its name indicates, refers to action in terms of sacrifice; and so it would limit itself to the actions of man, in so far as living creatures are concerned. But it would also deal with the action of the great forces of Nature in terms of the idea of sacrifice.

The *Atharva Veda* would appear to be a later composition, as there is no mention of it in the *Mīmāṁsā* or even the *Bhāgāvad Gītā.* Its author is said to be *Atharvan,* who is believed to be the first to institute the worship of *Agni* and offer *Soma.* As *Agni* refers to the intellect and *Soma* to the mind, the *Atharva Veda* may be said to deal with these, and so limit itself to the actions of man.

Thus the *Ṛg Veda* includes everything, – the living and the nonliving; the *Sāma Veda* deals with the problem of the living; *Yajur* with the actions of man and Nature as a sacrifice; and *Atharva* with the actions of man alone.

9. The o*ri*gin would refer to the root etc., from which a word is derived.
10. The word in the text is *satra,* which means a great *Soma* sacrifice; and *Soma,* as we have seen, refers to the mind, and sacrifice to action.
11. *Viśva-jīt* means "all-conquering"; while *Pṛṣṭha,* as the *Mīmāṁsā* explains at the end of this part, means "action". The idea obviously is that a person can conquer or succeed in everything by means of action (Cf. BhG. IV, 12).
12. We have explained that *Jyotiṣṭoma,* which is said to be a name of a *Soma* ceremony, really means "a mass or rays of light"; and now we are told that its idea is the same as that of *Pṛṣṭha* or "action" that is to say, it is really the action of light. The seven divisions of *Jyotiṣṭoma* would accordingly refer to the seven divisions of light, arising from its action.
13. *Soma,* as has already been explained, refers to, the mind; and so does the number six, – for the mind is the sixth after the five senses; and the *Mīmāṁsā* explains it in this manner too. We are told that the meaning of *Jyotiṣṭoma* can be obtained by referring to the idea of a *Soma* festival, – that is, the display of the mind or its energy, which is said to be electric. *Jyotiṣṭoma* may thus be said to be a grand display of electric energy (See Appendix II).
14. We are told that we can get the correct meaning of these words by piercing through their "disguise"; and this, as the *Mīmāṁsā* has explained, is done by dividing them into parts, and assigning meanings to these parts. This

may also be done by tracing them to their roots. So far as the word *Jyotiṣ ṭoma* is concerned, we may divide it into *jyotis* and *stoma,* when the meaning would be " *(stoma)* mass of *(jyotis)* light"; while the word *Pṛṣṭha,* which usually means "height, top", may be referred to its root, *pṛ,* meaning "to be busy or active".

This word is generally believed to be made up of *pra-stha,* meaning "standing forth prominently"; but the *Mīmāṁsā* tells us that we should pierce through its "disguise"; and in that we are not allowed to change *"pr"* into *"pra";* and so the real form of the word is *pr-stha* and not *pra-stha;* and its correct meaning, *"(stha)* standing in association with *(pṛ,* 'to be active") action." This agrees with the meaning of the word as it is given at the end of this part (VII, iii, 35-36).

15. *Soma* refers to the mind; and sacrificer is actor or doer of the deed. The *Mīmāṁsā* tells us that if we understand the text aright, we shall also understand how a person is "purified" when he uses his mind properly and acts. The *Bhāgāvad Gītā* tells us how actions can purify the soul (BhG. V, 11).

16. The *Mīmāṁsā* tells us that we get the real meaning of the word *Soma* by dividing it into parts, –*sa, u, ma*–when the meaning would be *"(sa)* the mind associated with *(u, ma)* the senses." This is the meaning of "seeing through the disguise of a word".

17. The common meaning of the word *puroḍāśa* or *puroḍāś* is "a mass of ground rice rounded into a kind of cake (usually divided into pieces, placed on receptacles, and offered as an oblation in fire). The *Mīmāṁsā* tells us that it makes little sense as such, and we can get its real meaning by dividing the word into parts.

The word is really *puras-ḍāśa,* which may be divided into *p, u, ra, s, d, āśa,* –when its meaning would be *("āśa)* obtaining *(ḍ) Prakṛti,* associated with *(s)* the mind, *(ra)* the senses of action, (ṇ) the senses of knowledge, and *(p)* the objects of the senses". The word accordingly gives us the idea of *Prakṛti,* associated with the mind, the senses and their objects; and that is its real meaning.

It will be found on examination that its meaning as "a mass of ground rice, etc." is subsidiary to its idea as *Prakṛti;* for rice, as the best kind of grain, which it is said to be, would represent Nature or the whole vegetable kingdom, even as the *Mīmāṁsā* tells us; and its division into parts would correspond to the divisions of *Prakṛti* into intellect, *ahaṅkāra,* mind, etc., as has already been explained. There is also a reference to fire, which would refer to the intellect.

18. The word *nirmanthya* means "to be churned", but it makes little sense as such. But if we divide it into *nir-manthya,* and derive *manthya* from *maniha* or *man, tha,* –meaning *"(tha)* an auspicious prayer, associated with *(man,* 'to think, understand") thought or understanding" –the idea of "churning" is transformed into that of "thinking, observing, understand-

ing"; and so we can understand the real idea of the story of the "Churning of the Ocean" or *Prakṛti*.

19. *Soma* refers to the mind,and the vessel which contains it is the brain.
20. The word *uttara-vedī* does not make sense in its common meaning as the northern altar for the sacrificial fire, specially, as the *Mīmāṁsā* tells us, there is no reference to any altar whatever. But the word *uttara* also means "higher, superior", and *vedī* "knowledge, science"; and if we interpret it as "higher knowledge", we shall find that it makes good sense.
21. The word *yūpa* is defined to mean "action"; and this is what the *Mīmāṁsā* tells us in a subsequent chapter too, where it is said to refer to action meant for the benefit of all (XI, iii, 2-7). This would explain why the "animal" (man) has to be tied to a *yūpa* or a sacrificial post if it wishes to be happy and free.
22. We have already explained that the real meaning of the word *pṛṣṭha* is action.
23. It follows from this that roots cannot be divided into parts. At the same time we cannot have roots and subdivision of the remaining part of a word in the same expression. For instance, if we derive the meaning of the word *Pṛṣṭha* from its root *"pṛ,* we cannot divide the remaining portion *shtha* (or *ṣṭha)* into parts. Similarly, we cannot divide the word *Kṛṣṇa* into *Kṛ, ṣ, ṇa,* – for that would be a root *(kṛ)* and a division of the remaining portion of the word into parts.

    The meaning of the word *Kṛṣṇa* has accordingly to be obtained from all the letters composing the name, – *Kṛ, ṣ, ṇa* – when it would be *"(K) Prakṛti, (r,* 'to reach, obtain") associated with *(ṣ)* the mind and *(ṇa)* the intellect". That is to say, when we believe that *Prakṛti* or Nature is governed by a law that is both good and intelligent, we get the idea of God, that is *Kṛṣṇa;* and it will be found that this is the highest conception of God that a man can understand, *andKṛṣṇa,* as the highest "incarnation" of *Viṣṇu,* retains this character throughout the range of sacred literature.

    In this connection we have explained that the idea of goodness is inherent in desire, which is the special attribute of the mind; and so the association of the mind with the intellect *(ṣ-ṇ)* in *Kṛṣṇa* gives us the idea of an intimate connection between goodness and intelligence. We get the same in the name *Viṣṇu, – V, i, ṣ-ṇ, u.*
24. The number twelve, as has already been explained, refers to Time as well as Nature. It also refers to the intellect, as the first manifest form of *Prakṛti* or Nature: for we have the ten senses, with the mind as the eleventh, and intellect as the twelfth. As the special attribute of the intellect is decision or definite knowledge, the idea of knowledge is expressed in terms of the duration or happenings of the twelfth day.

CHAPTER - VIII

THE METHOD OF INTERPRETATION: THE LAW OF ACTION

PART I

Introduction

Let us consider certain words that are said to haye a "disguise". The word *Soma* is such a word; and it has not been properly understood because it has been taken as a whole word, and not divided into parts. The word *sruc* is another; and we cannot accept its common meaning, because it would render the whole idea incomplete.

Desirable things have been associated with the new and the full moon.

Animals too have desires; and the only difference between them and men is that the latter have desires relating to religious devotion.

The number eleven refers to the function of the mind, expressed in two ways,—attraction and repulsion. There is the idea of action too; but in the case of animals it is expressed in terms of *yūpa* or the sacrificial post, but without reference to desire.

The idea of the number twelve is important.

The idea of a piece of pasture land, as also of things that have a body or material form, is expressed in terms of "this, that".

Where action cannot be described properly, it is compared with its ideal form. Even active life or the life of an active man is represented in the same manner; and this has been done to keep knowledge a secret.

Activity arises, from association with desire and the *Guṇas* (or attributes of things); and we can escape from the evil effects of actions by distinguishing between different kinds of actions; and so one activity is changed into another.

A single action cannot be divided into parts; but there is an option before it is undertaken. An option is determined by means of singleness of aim; but a person may not be able to exercise it. This gives rise to different aims; but in case of difference of opinion, the matter has to be decided by reference to the intellect, which alone can make for action.

We can understand the idea of the gods of the Vedas by dividing their names into parts; and they represent Nature which is truly imperishable.

Nature is represented by means of herbs or the vegetable kingdom, as that is its most obvious form. It is also represented by means of a cloud (containing water); and it is in this manner that we can understand the meaning of the text.

When water is sweetened, every part of it is transformed; and it represents the idea of the transformation of Nature; and Nature is indeed unborn.

Certain Disguised" Names

अथ विशेषलक्षणम्॥१॥

यस्य लिङ्गमर्थसंयोगादभिधनवत्॥२॥

Let us consider certain specific symbols or names used in the text, and which, with the meaning they have in their "disguised" form, appear to be like names.

Soma

प्र[1]वृत्तित्वादिष्टेः सोमे प्रवृत्तिः स्यात्॥३॥

लिङ्गदर्शनाच्च॥४॥

कृत्स्नविधनाद्वाऽपूर्वत्वम्॥५॥

(The word *Soma* is of this kind, for we are told that) there should be appearance of activity in *Soma*, because of the

1. वृत्तत्वेति वृत्तिग्रन्थे पाठान्तरम्।

appearance of desire[1]; and we can understand the idea if we see through the "disguise" of the word[2]. It has not been properly understood, because the word has been taken as a whole (and not divided into parts).

Sruc

स्रुगभिघारणाभावस्य च नित्यानुवादात्॥६॥
विधिरिति चेत्॥७॥
न वाक्यशेषत्वात्॥८॥
शङ्कते चानुपोषणात्॥९॥

The text contains the word *sruc* (the common meaning of which is "a wooden ladle for pouring clarified butter on the sacrificial fire"). But this is followed by certain words by way of explanatory repetition, from which we find that no ladle could have been meant. We cannot say that the word does mean a ladle, on the ground that it occurs in a formula which cannot be changed; because if it were so, it would require a number of other words to complete the sense (and they are not to be found in the text). We hesitate to accept this conclusion because we do not apply ourselves to the task of finding out the real meaning of the text[3].

Desire and the Moon

दर्शनमैष्टिकानां स्यात्॥१०॥
इष्टिषु दर्शपूर्णमासयोः प्रवृत्तिः स्यात्॥११॥

We should understand that there are desirable things in the world; and we find (from the text) that desires are associated with the new and the full moon[4].

Animals and Desires

पशौ च लिङ्गदर्शनात्॥१२॥
दैक्षस्य चेतरेषु॥१३॥

We can see from certain characteristic signs that animals too have desires; and the difference between them and men is that the latter have desires relating to religious devotion or consecration.

No. 11

ऐकादशिनेषु सौत्यस्य द्वैर[1]शन्यस्य दर्शनात्॥१४॥
तत्प्रवृत्तिर्गणेषु स्यात्प्रतिपशु यूपदर्शनात्॥१५॥
अव्यक्तासु तु सोमस्य॥१६॥

There is in things associated with the number eleven[5] (mind or desire) something that is related to the pressing out of the *Soma-juice*[6]; and that can be understood in two ways from the sight of what is seen.[7] it is the idea of this activity that is to be found in the parts of words[8]. With regard to animals, the same idea is to be found in the sight of *yūpa* or the sacrificial post.[9] But the essence of the idea of *Soma* is not obvious (in the word itself)[10].

No. 12

गणेषु द्वादशस्य॥१७॥

Among numbers the idea of the number twelve[11] is specially important.

This, That

गव्यस्य च[2] तदादिषु॥१८॥
निकायिनां च पूर्वस्योत्तरेषु प्रवृत्तिः स्यात्॥१९॥

The idea of a piece of pasture land (or a place of residence) is expressed by means of "this, that, etc."; and these expressions would also apply to other things that have a body or material form.

Action and the Ideal

कर्मणस्त्वप्रवृत्तित्वात्फलनियमकर्तृसमुदायस्या- न्वयस्तद्बन्धनत्वात्॥२०॥
प्रवृत्तौ[3] चापि तादर्थ्यात्॥२१॥
अश्रुतित्वाच्च॥२२॥

So far as action is concerned, where it cannot properly be described by means of the application of this rule (that is, in proper terms), we can get the totality of its result, as well as its necessity, together with the idea of the doer of the deed, by

1. शन्यदर्शेति पाठान्तरं वृत्तिग्रन्थे।
2. स्य चैतदेति पाठान्तरं वृत्तिग्रन्थे।
3. त्तावपि इति पाठान्तरं वृत्तिग्रन्थे।

means of comparison with its ideal, because that is how the whole idea has been knitted together. The idea of activity can be represented in the same manner too, because it refers to action[12]; and this has been done so that it may not easily be understood[13].

Means of Freedom

गुणकामेष्वाश्रितत्वात्प्रवृत्तिः स्यात्॥२३॥
निवृत्तिर्वा कर्मभेदात्॥२४॥
अपि वाऽतद्विकारत्वात्क्रत्वर्थत्वात्प्रवृत्तिः स्यात्॥२५॥

Activity arises from association with desires and *Guṇas* or the attributes of things;[14] but we can escape from the evil effects of action by distinguishing between different kinds of action,[15] for activity can also arise from another state of change, namely, the purpose the intellect has in view[16].

Action and Option

एककर्मणि विकल्पोऽविभागो हि चोदनैकत्वात्॥२६॥
लिङ्गसाधरण्याद्विकल्पः स्यात्॥२७॥

A single action cannot be divided, because it has a single direction or urge; but there is an option before it is undertaken. This option arises as a result of conclusions drawn from things with opposite properties[17].

Determination of Option

ऐकार्थ्याद्वा नियम्येत पूर्ववत्त्वाद्विकारो हि॥२८॥
अश्रुति[1]त्वान्नेति चेत्॥२९॥
स्याल्लिङ्गभावात्॥३०॥
तथा चान्यार्थदर्शनम्॥३१॥
विप्रतिपत्तौ हविषा नियम्येत कर्मणस्तदुपा[2]स्यत्वात्॥३२॥
तेन च कर्मसंयोगात्॥३३॥

An option is determined by means of singleness of aim, and it marks a change from an existing state. It is possible that a person may not be able to exercise his option, because he

1. अ तत्वेति पाठान्तरं वृत्तिग्रन्थे।
2. पाख्यत्वेति पाठान्तरं वृत्तिग्रन्थे।

may have indistinct ideas about things, for it depends on the nature of the conclusions he is able to arrive at. We can see in this manner that a person may have different aims. But where there is divergence of opinion, the matter has to be decided by reference to the intellect,[18] because that is how all action is performed; and it is by means of the intellect that all things connected with action are produced.

The Idea of the Gods

गुणत्वेन देवताश्रुतिः॥३४॥
हिरण्यमाज्यधर्मस्तेजस्त्वात्॥३५॥
धर्मानुग्रहाच्च॥३६॥

We can understand the idea of the gods of the Vedas by dividing their names into parts[19]. (They represent Nature, which consists of) imperishable matter[20], and is uncreated or unborn; and that is so because of the essence of its vital power[21]; and we can arrive at this conclusion by making a study of its character.

Nature: How Described

औषधं वा विशदत्वात्॥३७॥
चरुशब्दाच्च॥३८॥
तस्मिंश्च श्रपणश्रुतेः॥३९॥

Nature is said to consist of herbs (or the vegetable kingdom) because that is its most obvious or manifest form[22]. We can also understand it from the use of the word *caru*[23] (a cloud) in the text; and it is in this manner that we can get a properly developed (or mature) meaning of the *śruti*.

Sweetened Water

मधूदके द्रव्यसामान्यात्पयोविकारः स्यात्॥४०॥

When water is sweetened, all its ingredients share the property of its sweetness (or what it contains), as a result of which its own character is transformed[24].

Nature is Unborn

आज्यं वा वर्णसामान्यात्॥४१॥
धर्मानुग्रहाच्च॥४२॥

पूर्वस्य चा[1]विशिष्टत्वात्॥४३॥

When we look at Nature as it is in its entirety, we cannot resist the conclusion that it is unborn, if we accept its essential attributes; and that is in conformity with the statement previously made[25].

PART II

ACTION AND THE MIND: THE METHOD OF INTERPRETATION

Introduction

In all actions, of whatever kind, the mind comes first, because of its attribute, desire; and this is represented by the exclamation *vaṣaṭ*, and also the invitation to eat and drink. The acts of buying, marrying, etc. are of the same kind; but they should all be performed as a sacrifice; and that is why those words are so important.

An animal is associated with *puroḍāśa* or Nature; and the idea of sacrifice in connection with Nature should be understood from the "sacrifice" of animals, the offering of substances mixed with clarified butter, and the sight of an intelligent person.

Nature is represented in terms of curd and water, or animals; but it is generally conceived to be a fluid substance, and is represented by curd, milk, and water.

A perfect function of the mind or the intellect is the result of unity of action; and it is easy to understand this idea of perfection by means of that of sacrifice.

The number thirteen represents the idea of perfection or completion of things; while the number fifteen signifies a sudden end to all action.

These expressions signify perfection of different kinds; but that alone is real perfection which attains its end through sacrifice; and it is easy to understand its idea in the text.

---

3. चकाररहितः पाठो वृत्तिग्रन्थे।

Importance of the Mind : How Described

वाजिने सोमपूर्वत्वं सौत्रामण्यां च ग्रहेषु ताच्छब्द्यात्॥१॥
अनुवषट्काराच्च॥२॥
समुपहूय भक्षणाच्च॥३॥
क्रयणश्रपणपुरोरुगुपयामग्रहणासादनवासोपनहनञ्च तद्वत्॥४॥
हविषा वा नियम्येत तद्विकारत्वात्॥५॥
प्रशंसा सोमशब्दः॥६॥
वचनानीतराणि॥७॥
व्यपदेशश्च तद्वत्॥८॥

In all acts of emulation the mind *(Soma)* comes first; so also in all acts of sacrifice associated with the soul (in honour of *Indra);* and that is so because of the nature of desire (or what relates to *Soma* or the mind)[26]; and this is represented in the text by means of the exclamation[27] *"vaṣaṭ"*, as well as by the invitation to eat and to drink. The acts of buying, approaching, shining in front, marrying, holding, laying down, and binding together,—are all of that kind. But each of these actions should be regulated by sacrifice, because it is a form of sacrifice. But the mind *(Soma)* is praised most[28] because of its part in action, though there is praise for others too; and that is how we understand each principal name in the Vedas.

Nature and Animals

पशुपुरोडाशस्य लिङ्गदर्शनम्॥९॥
पशुः पुरोडाशविकारः स्याद्देवतासामान्यात्॥१०॥
प्रोक्षणाच्च॥११॥
पर्यग्निकरणाच्च॥१२॥
सान्नाय्यं वा तत्प्रभवत्वात्॥१३॥
तस्य च पात्रदर्शनात्॥१४॥

We can now understand the reason for the association of a animals with Nature (or *puroḍāśd*)[29]. Indeed, an animal should be regarded as a modification of the ides of Nature; and that is so because of the universal conception of the great forces of Nature, which are personified as gods.[30] (The idea of sacrifice associated with Nature can be understood) from the consecration of animals effected by sprinkling holy water on them, as well as from the ceremony of carrying fire round the sacrificial animal[31]. The idea of offering a substance mixed with clarified butter as a burnt offering is derived from the same source;[32] and we get the same idea from the sight of a capable or competent person[33].

Nature and a Fluid Substance

दध्नः स्यान्मूर्तिसामान्यात्॥१५॥
पयो वा कालसामान्यात्॥१६॥
पश्वानन्तर्यात्[1]॥१७॥
द्रवत्वं चाविशिष्टम्॥१८॥
आमिक्षोभयभाव्यत्वादुभयविकारः स्यात्॥१९॥
एकं वा चोदनैकत्वात्॥२०॥
दधिसङ्घातसामान्यात्॥२१॥
पयो वा तत्प्रधनत्वाल्लोकवद्दध्नस्तदर्थत्वात्॥२२॥
धर्मानुग्रहाच्च॥२३॥
सद्योभावं[1] च दर्शयति॥२३अ.॥

Nature should be regarded as being of the form of curd or coagulated milk, because that is said to be its common appearance.[34] Or it is like water or a liquid substance, if we take into consideration the totality of Time.[35] But it may be described in terms of an animal, if we consider it in terms of ournext of kin, or of life nearest allied to our own.[36] Nature, however, is generally conceived to be in a fluid state, and is represented by curd,—which is the product of both curd and milk. Or we may regard milk and curd to be the same, because they are made by the same power.[37] On the other hand *dadhi* (or thick curd) arises from general hardening (and so represents the process of hardening in Nature); while water, because of the importance of curd, is, as we might say in popular language, for the sake of the curd.[38] All this is in accordance with the law of Nature, as we can see every day.

Mind, Intellect, and Unity of Action

सत्रमहीनश्च द्वादशाहस्तस्योभयथा प्रवृत्तिरैककर्म्यात्॥२४॥

When we see a perfect function of the mind *(Soma)* or a

1. यच्चेति पाठान्तरं वृत्तिग्रन्थे।

clear function of the intellect (a sacrifice lasting twelve days),[39] we find that it arises from unity of action.

Sacrifice and Nature

अपि वा यजति श्रुतेरहीनभूतप्रवत्तिः स्यात्प्रकृत्या तुल्यशब्दत्वात्॥२५॥

When we hear the expression "he sacrifices", we may take it that the perfect being who is said to sacrifice, is *Pravṛtti*, which is synonymous with *Prakṛti* or Nature[40].

Perfection of the Mind: How Described

द्विरात्रादीनामैकादशरात्रादहीनत्वं यजतिचोदनात्॥२६॥

If we take a certain period of time, say two days or nights, we shall find that we get the idea of wholeness or perfection from the sacrifice or proper function of the mind;[41] and that is signified by the direction that a person should make a sacrifice.

No. 13

त्रयो[1]दशरात्रादिषु सत्रभूतस्तेष्वासनोपायि चोदनात्॥२७॥
लिङ्गाच्च॥२८॥

On the thirteenth days or nights the sacrifice is completed, because there is, on these nights, a direction in regard to a certain posture, which signifies the attainment of objects; and so we may reasonably infer (that this number represents the idea of the completion of things[42]).

No. 15

अन्यतरतोऽतिरात्रत्वात्पञ्चदशरात्रस्याहीनत्वं; कुण्डपायिनामयनस्य च; तद्भूतेष्वहीनत्व[2]स्य दर्शनात्॥२९॥

Again, when an action is suddenly concluded, its idea of perfection is represented by the fifteenth day or night. There is also a mention of the path of those who drink water out of pitchers. These expressions give us an idea of wholeness or perfection[43].

---

1. इदं सूत्रमधिकं वृत्तिग्रन्थे पठयते।
२. इदं सूत्रं वृत्तिग्रन्थे नास्ति।

Perfection through Sacrifice

अहीनवचनाच्च॥३०॥
सत्रे[1] वोपायिचोदनात्॥३१॥
सत्रलिङ्गं च दर्शयति॥३२॥

These expressions convey the idea of a certain kind of wholeness or perfection, because that is the meaning of these words. But real perfection is that which attains its end through sacrifice,[44] because that is the teaching of the sacred books; and it is easy to understand this symbol or mode of expression of the idea of sacrifice.

PART III

INTELLIGENT ACTION AND SACRIFICE: THE METHOD OF INTERPRETATION

Introduction

In a series of intelligent actions, the last is likely to be the best. We should always act intelligently: acts of sacrifice are always guided by reason: so too are all other actions,-even habits.

In the formation of habit the innate disposition of a man is very important. Habits grow through a series of actions, but not actions limited to a single day.

The *Gāyatrī* verses and certain other hymns deal with this problem of disposition. But they have to be interpreted by means of the method of division of words into parts. There are, however a number of words which have to be interpreted in a different way. But we must not mix up words or omit any sentence. We have to depend on our intelligence in interpreting the text in this manner: only the meaning should be obtained from the words themselves and it should be confirmed as we proceed with the text.

Even in the *Ṛg Veda* we get the correct meaning of words by dividing them into parts; and this is to be found everywhere. Nor does it conflict with our taking words complete as they

---

१. सत्रे चोपेयीति पाठान्तरं वृत्तिग्रन्थे।

are, for the meanings obtained in the two ways are often the same. But it would be better to divide words into parts; and we can always check up whether our meaning is correct or not.

The Last Action is the Best

हविर्गणे परमुत्तरस्य देशसामान्यात्॥१॥

देवतया वा नियम्येत शब्दवत्त्वादितरस्याश्रुतित्वात्॥२॥

If a person performs a series of good and intelligent actions (or acts of sacrifice), the last is likely to be the best, if they are all performed in the same place. Such an act should be deemed to be regulated by the deity[45],—as a matter of language or mode of expression, because that is what is commonly heard.

Importance of Reason

गणचोदनायां यस्य लिङ्गं तदावृत्तिः प्रतीयेताग्नेयवत्॥३॥

When there are a number of directions or forces impelling us to action, we should follow that for which we can give a good reason, as indeed we do in the case of an intelligent act[46].

Place of Reason in Habit

नानाहानि वा सङ्घातत्वात्प्रवृत्तिलिङ्गे, न चोदनात्॥४॥

तथा चान्यार्थदर्शनम्॥५॥

कालाभ्यासेऽपि बादरिः कर्मभेदात्॥६॥

तदावृत्तिं तु जैमिनिरह्नामप्रत्यक्षसङ्ख्यत्वात्॥७॥

तस्मात्व[1]डहाभ्यासः।७अ.

संस्थागणेषु तदभ्यासः प्रतीयेत, कृतलक्षणग्रहणात्॥८॥

There are many kinds of good and intelligent actions (or acts of sacrifice) which yet are characterised by conflict; but when actually performed, we find that they too are guided by reason, and not impulse; and we find that it is so in all other things that we see. *Bādari*[47] says that it is even so in the case of habits of long standing, because they too are a kind of action. *Jaimini*[48] says that a habit arises from the connection of

---

1. इदं सूत्रमधिकं वृत्तिग्रन्थे।

imperceptible but intelligent actions performed every day; and that is why we speak of a habit of six days.[49] Habit can be recognised in a multitude of forms; and we can do so when we understand the effect of actions done.

Part of Disposition

अधिकाराद्वा प्रकृतिस्तद्विशिष्टा स्यादभिधनस्य तन्निमित्तत्वात्॥९॥
गणादुपचयस्तत्प्रकृतित्वात्॥१०॥
एकाहाद्वा तेषां समत्वात्स्यात्॥११॥

In this formation of habit the innate nature or disposition of a man should be deemed to be the most important, because it is the cause of bringing things together into close connection. Habit begins with disposition, and grows through a series of actions. But where such a series is limited to a single day, the action should be regarded as a normal one, (and not the result of habit).

Described in the Vedas

गायत्रीषु प्राकृतीनामवच्छेदः; प्रवृ[1]त्त्यधि-कारात्सङ्ख्यात्वादग्निष्टो-मवदव्यतिरेकात्तदाख्यत्वम्॥१२॥
तन्नि[2]त्यवच्च पृथक्सतीषु तद्वचनम्॥१३॥
न विंशतौ दशेति चेत्॥१४॥
एकसंख्यमेव स्यात्॥१५॥

In the *Gāyatrī* verses there is a particular mention of what relates to the disposition of men. When, however, we consider the power of nature or disposition, we find that there is no real distinction between it and an intelligent action[50] performed over a length of time; and we should readily state that it is so. This idea of the power of disposition occurs also in a number of other metres, which are widely apart from the *Gāyatrī;* and the same language is used in them too. This, however, does not occur frequently,—not even in two out of twenty metres, if we reckon them in that way.

---

1. प्रकृत्य इति पाठभेदः।
2. तन्नीत्यत्र तदिति पदरहितः पाठो वृत्तिग्रन्थे।

How to Interpret the Text

गुणाद्वा द्रव्यशब्दः स्यादसर्वविषयत्वात्॥१६॥
गोत्ववच्च समन्वयः॥१७॥
संख्यायाश्च शब्दतत्त्वात्॥१८॥
इतरस्याश्रुतत्वाच्च॥१९॥
द्रव्यान्तरेऽनिवेशादुक्थ्य[1]लोपैर्विशिष्टं स्यात्॥२०॥
अशास्त्रलक्षणत्वा[2]च्च॥२१॥
उत्पत्ति नामधेयत्वाद्; भक्त्या पृथक्सतीषु स्यात्[3]॥२२॥
वचनमिति चेत्॥२३॥
यावदुक्तम्॥२४॥
अपूर्वे च विकल्पः स्याद्यदि सङ्ख्याविधनम्॥२५॥

But the language of the text is such that a word relating to an object should be understood by means of the parts of which it is composed, for otherwise we cannot cover the entire range of its idea; and the regular succession of the parts of a word should be as in the case of the word *go* (cow),—just as we utter it.[51] There are, however, a number of words which have to be explained in a way different from that in which they are pronounced. There are cases where we can get the best meaning if we do not mix up one word with another or omit a sentence.[52] But this method, of interpretation is not derived from anything defined in the sacred books (and we have to use our own intelligence in the matter). (In any case) the meaning of a name should be obtained from the name itself; and we should find the same idea in a number of different metres in succession. This has already been stated and is nothing new; (but it is necessary that we should get this confirmation, because) there can easily be a doubt in regard to a new expression, specially when there is a conflict of opinion in connection with the meaning of a name.

Interpretation of Ṛg Veda

ऋग्गुणत्वान्नेति चेत्।२६॥
तथा पूर्ववति स्यात्॥२७॥

---

1. लोंपे वीति वृत्तिग्रन्थे पाठान्तरम्।
2. त्वादिति चरहितः पाठो वृत्तिर्गंथे।
3. स्यादिति पदरहितं पाठान्तरं वृत्तिग्रन्थे।

गुणावेशश्च सर्वत्र॥२८॥
निष्पन्नग्रहणान्नेति[1] चेत्॥२९॥
तथेहापि स्यात्॥३०॥
यदि वाऽविशये नियमः प्रकृत्युपबन्ध[2]च्छब्देष्वपि प्रसिद्धः स्यात्॥३१॥
दृष्टः प्रयोग इति चेत्॥३२॥
तथा शरेष्वपि॥३३॥
भक्त्येति चेत्॥३४॥
तथेतरस्मिन्॥३५॥
अर्थस्य चासमाप्तत्वान्न तासामेकदेशे स्यात्॥३६॥

Even in the words used in the hymns of the *Ṛg Veda* we can get their correct meaning by dividing them into parts in the manner already stated; and this is to be found everywhere. But this does not mean that we cannot take words as a whole without dividing them into parts; for we can do so even in this system of interpretation. But if we wish to be quite certain whether the meaning of a word taken as a whole is correct, we should see that the meaning of the parts gives us the meaning of the whole, because there is a close connection between the parts of a word and the word as a whole. There is thus an obvious connection between the two ways of interpreting the meaning of words,—for the word taken as a whole is connected with the parts into which it can be divided. But we should prefer the meaning obtained by means of the division of words into parts, and it should be done in the rest of the text. In any case, if the correct meaning is not completely obtained, we shall find that there is no coherence in the verses in the very passage of the text[53].

PART IV

THE METHOD OF INTERPRETATION

Introduction

The word *darvi-homa* is the name of a sacrifice; so also *vastu-homa*.

The reasons for dividing a word into parts is that the

1. ग्रहान्नेतीति पाठान्तरं वृत्तिग्रन्थे।
2. बन्धनाच्छरेष्वपीति वृत्तिग्रन्थे पाठान्तरम्।

different ingredients of an object can be specified. It is in this manner that we get the meaning of the words *Agni, haviṣ,* and *Soma*. On the other hand we do not get the meaning of the word *svāhā* in the same manner, and it is different from *vaṣaṭ*. The word *svāhā* invokes a blessing on action, and implies that after one work is done another should begin; and we get this from the first part of the word, which is better than the second.It is in this manner that we get a reference to a law of life, and pierce through the "disguise" of words. But this is not the only method of interpretation.

If, however, we divide words into parts, and find that the meaning of one fits into that of the following two, we should take it that it is correct; and then we can arrange our ideas of action by means of inference.

We find that there is a reference to medicinal herbs as well as to sacrifice; and their ideas can cohere only if we understand the text aright and with reference to a law of life.

Meaning of Certain Words

दर्विहोमो यज्ञाभिधनं होमसंयोगात्॥१॥
स लौकिकानां स्यात्कर्त्तेस्तदाख्यत्वात्॥२॥
सर्वेषां वा दर्शनाद्वास्तुहोमे॥३॥
जुहोतिचोदनानां वा तत्संयोगात्॥४॥

Darvi-homa (or an oblation made with a ladle) is the name of a sacrifice, because of its connection with the word *Homa*.[54] That is the meaning of the word current among the people, because the person who engages in this action is said to perform a sacrifice. But when the word *vastu-homa* (the house of sacrifice) occurs in the text, it should be understood to mean a sacrifice (or a good and intelligent action) performed by all persons; and the directions in regard to a sacrifice arise from this connection.

Reasons for Dividing a Word into Parts

द्रव्योपदेशाद्वा गुणाभिधनं स्यात्॥५॥
न लौकिकानामाचारग्रहणत्वाच्छब्दवतां चान्यार्थविधनात्॥६॥

दर्शनाच्चान्यपात्रस्य॥७॥
तथाग्निहविषो:॥८॥
उक्तश्चार्थेऽसम्बन्ध:॥९॥
तस्मिन्सोम: प्रवर्त्तेताव्यक्तत्वात्॥१०॥

The reason for dividing a word into parts is that the different ingredients of a substance can be specified. We assign meanings to the parts of a word, not because it is the practice of common men, but because those who understand the use of words can get a different (or a better) meaning in that way; and we have this from the experience (or teaching) of many competent persons (working on the text). It is in this manner that we get the meaning of the words *Agni* and *haviṣ*[55] and their real meaning has no connection with what is commonly spoken about them. It is in this way that we should be able to get the real meaning of the word *Soma,*[56] which is not apparent at the surface.

Svāhā and Vaṣaṭ

न वा स्वाहाकारेण संयोगाद् वषट्कारस्य च, निर्देशात्तन्त्रेन, विप्रतिषेधत्॥११॥
शब्दान्तरत्वात्॥१२॥
लिङ्गदर्शनाच्च॥१३॥
उत्तरार्थस्तु, स्वाहाकारो, यथा साप्तदश्यं, तत्राविप्रतिषिद्ध पुन: प्रवृत्तिर्लिङ्गदर्शनात्पशुवत्॥१४॥
अनुत्तरार्थो वाऽर्थवत्त्वादानर्थक्याद्धि प्रा[1]थम्यस्योपरोध: स्यात्॥१५॥

On the other hand by uttering the word *svāhā* we do not get the same meaning that we do when we utter the word *vaṣaṭ*; and that is due to the fact that there is no connection between them, and there is also a special mention of the meanings in this system of interpretation, from which we find that there is a fundamental difference between their ideas. That is so because of the difference in their meanings; and we can understand it when we know the reason for their use[57].

As the word *svāhā* invokes a blessing, it can be uttered only after the deed is done; and so it is used for a higher purpose, even as we find in the case of the number seventeen.[58] But this does not mean that since the deed is done, nothing else should follow.[59] When we understand the reason for this, we find that it is true of all animals (that after finishing one, they begin another action). It is this purpose that is served by the word *svāhā,* because that is its object (in invoking a blessing); and were it otherwise, we should find something to obstruct us in the original form of the word itself.

How to Understand the Meaning of Svāhā

न प्रकृतावपीति चेत्॥१६॥
उक्तं समवाये पारदौर्बल्यम्॥१७॥
तच्चोदना वेष्टेः प्रवृत्तित्वाद्विधिः स्यात्॥१८॥
शब्दसामर्थ्याच्च॥१९॥
लिङ्गदर्शनाच्च॥२०॥
तत्राभावस्य हेतुत्वाद्गुणार्थे स्याददर्शनम्॥२१॥

There are some who believe that this idea of *svāhā* is not contained even in the original form of the word. But it has been said that in an assemblage of things the following member of a series is inferior to the preceding one; and this has a reference to our effort to understand the meaning of words: only when we apply this rule we should see that the meaning refers to a law of life. That is so because the words used are suitable; and we can see through their "disguise" in this manner.[60] If, however, there is no real reference to a law, we shall not find it in the meaning of the parts of a word.

Different Ways of Interpretation

विधिरिति चेत्॥२२॥
न वाक्यशेषत्वाद्गुणार्थे च समाधनं नानात्वेनोपपद्यते॥२३॥
येषां वाऽपरयोर्होमस्तेषां स्यादविरोधत्॥२४॥
लिङ्गाद्वा शेषहोमयोः॥२४अ.॥

Nevertheless we cannot say that this is the only method of interpreting the text, because there are cases where certain parts of a sentence are missing and have to be supplied: again, when we divide words into parts to get their meaning, we can arrange these parts in various ways. But if we divide a word into parts, and find that the meaning of one fits into that of the

1. प्राकृतस्यो इति वृत्तिग्रन्थे पाठान्तरम्।

following two, we should take it that we have found its correct meaning; and then we shall be able to get the idea of a perfectly good and intelligent action *(Homa* sacrifice) because of its consistency throughout; and then we can get the idea of two more good and intelligent actions by means of inference in this way[61].

Medicinal Herbs

तत्रोषधनि चोद्यन्ते, तानि स्थानेन गम्येरन्॥२५॥
लिङ्गाद्वा शेषहोमयोः॥२६॥
सन्निपाते विरोधिनामप्रवृत्तिः प्रतीयेत, विधयुत्पत्तिव्यवस्थानादर्थस्या-
परिणेयत्वाद् वचनादतिदेशः स्यात्॥२७॥

We find that there is a reference to medicinal herbs, and they are invited (or invoked) on certain occasions; and it is necessary that they should be understood in their proper role[62]; We find by means of inference that the text refers to two acts of sacrifice (*Homa*)[63], but there is an opposition between them (or their ideas do not cohere), with the result that we are unable to make any progress with the text. We find that our failure to understand the idea from the sentence used in the text persists; and it is in such cases that there is a reference to a law of life, which can be substituted for the other (or ordinary) meaning[64].

NOTES

1. If we know that *Soma* means the mind, we can understand that,as the attribute of the mind is desire, wherever there is desire, there must be an activity or function of the mind: or we might say that the mind becomes active by means of desire; and so there is activity in *Soma* (mind) because of the appearance of desire.
2. As the *Mīmāṁsā* has explained, in order to pierce through the "disguise" of a word, we need to divide it into parts. The word *Soma* has accordingly to be divided into *sa, u, ma*—when its meaning would be "*(sa)* the mind associated with *(u, ma)* the senses of knowledge". But, as we have two letters for the senses of knowledge, and the idea of the senses of knowledge and action is closely intertwined, and the Tongue is both a sense of knowledge and action,we can take it that there is a reference to the senses of action too.
3. Similarly, the word *sruc*—*sru, c*—would mean *(sru* 'to rouse,stir") to stir *(c)* the mind". *Sruc* means, therefore, "stirring the mind"; and that is why it is said to be "a ladle for pouring clarified butter on the sacrificial fire,"—for "clarified butter" refers to goodness as an attribute of desire or the mind; and *Sruc* is something that stirs the mind or produces desire.

4. As has already been explained, the Moon refers to the mind, which has desire for its attribute. We have also pointed out that the new moon refers to desire, and the full moon to its completion in action; and so desires are associated with the new and the full moon.
5. The number eleven refers to the mind, as being the eleventh after the ten senses, or the five "elements" and their five properties, to which the ten senses are closely allied. As desire is a special attribute of the mind and inseparable from it, this number can refer to desire as well.
6. *Soma* refers to the mind, and its "juice" is obviously desere Thus we mightr say that the mind is related to desisre (or a things associated ith the number eleven—the mind—is related to the pressing out of the *Soma-juice*—or desire).
7. Desire expresses itself in two ways,—attraction and repulsion (*Cf.* BhG. III, 34).
8. It is this idea of the different activities of the mind that is expressed in the different parts of words; and so, in order to understand these activities, we have to divide words into parts. This is the logic of this method of interpretation.
9. *Yūpa* or a sacrificial poast, as has already been explained, refers to action meant for the benefit of all. But there are a number of these sacrificial poasts in a great sacrifice, indicating that there are a number of different kinds of such actions that a person has to perform. The actions are expressed in terms of sacrificial posts.
10. We have to divide the word *Soma* into parts to understand its meaning: it is not clear otherwise.
11. We have explained that the number twelve refers to Time , *Prakṛti,* as well as intellect.
12. If, for instance, the author is unable properly to descibe the functions of the mind in a particular case, he may compare it with the Moon, which is a symbol of the mind, and so may be referred to the its ideal. Similarly, the character of *Prakṛti* may be referred to the Ocean or to waters in general; and there are a number of such instances in the sacred books.
13. The *Mimāṁsā* tells us that the Vedas contain an account of the knowledge of the anccients, Some of which is secret knowledge, and is not meant to be easily understood.
14. The *Bhagvad Gītā* tells us that all action arises from the three *Guṇas (Sattva, Rajas and Tamas),* which are said to arise form Nature or *Prkṛti* (BhG. III, 5, 27, 29 etc.) It is these that make for the bond of life,—*Sattva* for knowledge and joy, *Rajas* for action, and *Tamas* for heedlessness and sleep (BhG. XIV, 5-20). All things in the world, faith , food, penance, alms and sacrifice, as well as renunciation, knowledge, acton, actor, intellectr, fortitude and joy—partake of the character of *Guṇas* or the attributes of Nature (Bhg. XVII, 2-22; XVIII, 2-0-39). Indeed, there is no earth or among the gods in heaven that is free from the three *Guṇas,* born of *Prakṛti:* so says the *Gītā* (BgG. XVIII, 40).

   We have been told that the appearance of desire means the activity of the mind (MS. VIII, i 3); and now this *Sūtra* tells us that it is desire that makes for all activity. This means that the mind is associated with all action.

15. According to the *Sāṅkhya* we can escape from action itself by means of discrimination, when we realise that the soul is different from all that is in Nature. This, however, is not what the *Mīmānsā* says. It only tells us that we can avoid the evil effects of actions by distinguishing between dofferent kinds of actions, and doing only good and intelligent deeds. We have the same idea in the *Bhāgvada Gītā,* whivh tells us that we cannot obtain freedom from action by refusing to perform actions or by means of renunciation (BhG. III, 4-5); but a person can attain to the highest goal by performing actions without any attachment (BhG. III, 19). It is also necessary to distinguish between action, inaction, and improper action (BhG. IV, 17-18).
16. We have been told that activity arises from association with desires and the *Guṇas;* but it is also due to the function of the intellect, which enables us to distinguish between defferent kinds of actons, and so to acoid their evil effects.
17. This refers to a consideration of the *pros* and *cons* of things.
18. Intellect plays a most important part in action, for it has to decide to act; and without its decision no action can take place.
19. This is how the idea of the principal gods of the Vedas has been explained in MM. I, Chapter IX.
20. The word in the text is *Hiraṇya* , which has a number of meanings, including "imperishable matter". which would appear to be the most suitable here. There are a number of references to *Hiraṇya* and *Hiraṇya-garbha* (the Golden Egg) in the sacred books; and they have all a reference to Nature.
21. The *Bhagavad Gītā* also tells us that not only *Puruṣa* (God), but *Prakṛti* too is without a beignning; that is, it is unborn (BhG. XIII, 20).
22. There are a number of references to plants, medicinal herbs, forest life, and deffernt kinds of grain,—all of which have a bearing on the edea of Nature or *Prakṛti.* We have seen that the sacred Fig-tree refers to it; and all references to forest life in the sacred books ate really references to the ideas associated with Nature.

    It may be of interest to observe that *Karṇa* in the *Mahābhārata and Kumbh-karṇa* in the *Rāmāyaṇa* represent the philosophy of Nature or *Prakṛti.* The word *Karṇa* has a number of meanings, one of which is "furnished with chaff (as grain)". It refers, therefore, to grain as the seed of the vegetable kingdom, fit for cultivation; and the idea of these two characters can be understood in this light throughout the two Epics.
23. A cloud is a receptacle of water, which represents Nature (MS. VIII, ii, 16).
24. Sweetened water represents the idea of the transformation of *Prakṛti* into something that is sweet, or as embodying the idea of God. This can be done by means of the idea of Sacrifice, which can sweeten *Prakṛti,* and link it up with God. It is this idea that is expressed in terms of the transformation of *Sikhaṇḍin* from a woman (*Prakṛti*) into a man *(Puruṣa or God)* in the story of the *Mahābhārata.*

25. There is a previous statements that *Prakṛti* is unborn (*Sūt.* 35)
26. As has already been explained, *Soma* refers to the mind, and *Indra* to the self-conscious soul *(Prajñātman).*
The *Mīmāṁsā* tells us that the mind comes first in all actions, of whatever kind, including those associated with the soul; and that is due to the fact that all action is preceded by desire, which is an attribute of the mind.
27. *Vaṣaṭ* is an exclamation uttered by the *Hotṛ* priest at the end of the sacrificial verse, on hearnig which the *Adhvaryu* priest casts the oblation offered to the deity into the fire.
We have explained that the *Hotṛ* priest refers to the mind, and the *Adhvaryu* to the senses; and so this exclamation signifies that the mind *directs* the senses to act.
28. This would explain why a whole book of the *rig Veda* (IX) is devoted to the "praise" of *Soma:* it is intended to explain the character and functions of the mind.
29. We have explained that *puroḍāśa* really refers to Nature. The *Mīmāsā* tells us that the reference to animals in the sacred books is really a reference to Nature and its powers, because that is how we get the idea of their personification as gods.
There are a number of such references to animals in the sacred books, and they need to be interpreted in this light. For instance, we have a reference to a host of monkeys and bears in the *Rāmāyaṇa,* and they constitute the great army of *Rāma,* the hero of the Epic. It would be impossible to understand the idea of the Epic as a Veda or a book of knowledge, as it is described to be, in its existing form; but if we understand the real meaning of names, in accordance with the method explained in the *Mīmāṁsā,* we shall find that it is really a narrative of different systems of philosophy. We shall then find that *Rāma,* who is also spoken of as *Candra* or the Moon, refers to the mind; while the ten-headed *Rākṣasa, Rāvaṇa,* represents the ten senses of knowledge and action; and the conflict between them corresponds to that between the mind and the senses, and the systems of thought based on their character. *Sītā,* in this "story," refers to the idea of Sacrifice in Nature; and both *Rāma* and *Rāvaṇa* lay claim to her; but, for obvious reasons, it is *Rāma* alone who can succeed; In this conflict of ideas both seek the assistance of Nature, *Rāma* of monkeys and bears, and *Rāvaṇa* of his brother *Kumbhakarṇa,* who represents the vegetable kingdom as symbolic of Nature. The whole story has been composed in this form, and will be explained in this light in its proper place.
30. The gods represent the great forces of Nature which, in their turn, are represented by animals; and so the gods are represented in the form of animals too, as human beings and others.
31. Nature is governed by the law of Sacrifice: that is to say, it is characterised by goodness, intelligence, etc.; and this idea of the law of Sacrifice is described in terms of the "sacrifice" of animals,—for they represent Nature. As fire refers to intelligence, carrying the fire round an animal would imply that we agree that animals have intelligence.
32 Clarified butter refers to goodness, while fire or "burnt offering" to intelligence; and the two together give us the idea of sacrifice.

33. The sight of a capable or competent person shows that there is both goodness and intelligence in Nature; for a man, being an animal, is part of Nature too.
34. Curd is said to represent Nature; and that is its idea in the story of the *Bhāgavat Purāṇa,* where *Kṛṣṇa* is described as being very fond of both butter and curd. As *Kṛṣṇa* is God, this would represent the affection of God for Nature, or of *Puruṣa* for *Prakṛti*. The same idea is expressed in terms of the love of *Kṛṣṇa* and the *Gopīs,* as well as of the sixteen thousand "wives" of the Deity. As a woman refers to Nature, they all represent different forms and forces of Nature, which are drawn towards God. All this will be explained in its proper place.
35. This means that if we take into consideration long periods of time, *Prakṛti* or Nature appears to be not like curd, but like water; so Nature is described in terms of Waters both at the beginning and end of life. This will explain all references to Waters in the sacred books, and their association with God: for instance, *Viṣṇu* is said to lie on the waters at the commencement of life, and so on.

    The different forms in which water appears would also refer to Nature: for instance, we have been told that the cloud does so. Similarly, rivers, seas, ocean, etc. all refer to Nature or *Prakṛti*.
36. This would explain the reference to monkeys and bears in the story of the *Rāmāyaṇa*. They represent Nature, as being nearest allied to man.
37. It is the same power of Nature that produces milk in the cow, and curd out of milk.
38. We cannot have curd unless there be water in milk; and so water may be said to be there for the sake of curd. But it has another significance too. We have been told that the original form of Nature corresponds to that of water, but in course of time it hardens into that of curd; and this may be said to be the relation between water and curd.

    It may be of interest to point out that the ancients believed that whatever is in the organic cell is also in Nature *(Yathā piṇḍe tathā Brahmāṇḍe);* and the organic cell is like curd or a jelly-like substance. Thus when there is a mention of water in the sacred books, we should take it that it refers to Nature in its pristine form; whereas a reference to curd gives us the idea of Nature in its later or maturer state.
39. We have explained that *Soma* refers to the mind, and the number twelve to the intellect; and so a sacrifice lasting twelve days would refer to the action of the intellect.
40. *Pravṛtti* means activity or active life; and the idea of *Prakṛti* is the same. The point of this *Sūtra* is that when there is a reference to sacrifice in the sacred books, we should take it that it normally refers to Nature or *Prakṛti:* that is. Nature is characterised by the law of Sacrifice, or acts in accordance with it. This has already been explained.
41. The reference in the text is to the eleventh night; and the number eleven,—as has already been explainedrefers to the mind.

    This *Sūtra* tells us that there is a direction that a person should make a sacrifice on the eleventh night; and that means that his mind should always function in a spirit of sacrifice.

42. The *Mīmāṁsā* tells us that the number thirteen represents the idea of the completion of things, or the attainment of objects. This would explain the reference to the thirteen years of the exile of the *Pāṇḍavas* in the story of the *Mahābhārata*. Of these the first twelve were to be spent in the forest, and the last in a place where they could not be discovered. We have seen that a forest refers to Nature, and the number twelve to the intellect; so that they were required to examine the whole problem of Nature in the light of the intellect. Then, as after the intellect there is the unmanifest soul, they had to remain unknown during the thirteenth year; and, as this completes the whole inquiry after truth, the number thirteen represents this idea of completeness there too. All this has already been explained (MM. IV, 351, *seq.)*
43. When a person suddenly decides to give up all things, retire into a forest, and lead a simple life,—drinking water out of a pitcher,—it is something good, and may be said to be a kind of perfection; but it is a limited kind of perfection.
44. Real perfection is attained by means of sacrifice or good, intelligent, selfless and self-controlled action. It is on this kind of action that the *Bhāgāvad Gītā* lays emphasis throughout (*Cf.* BhG. VI,i-32, etc.).
45. The best actions are commonly spoken of as the actions of the gods. Eut the *Bhāgāvad Gītā* tells us that there is an element of divine power in all actions (BhG. XVIII, 13-14).
46. The word in the text is *Agni,* which refers to the intellect.
47. *Bādari* is the name of a philosopher.
48. *Jaimini* is the celebrated author of the *Mīmāṁsā Sūtras*.
49. This *Sūtra* (7a) does not occur in certain texts.
50. The word in the text is *Agniṣṭoma,* which means "mass or praise of *Agni* ". As *Agni* refers to the intellect, it has been rendered as "intelligent action." It may also be understood as "a function of the intellect."
51. The word *go* can be divided into *ga, u*-according to the rules of *Sanskṛt* grammar. This *Sūtra* tells us how to divide words into their parts: we should utter a word as it is commonly spoken, and then divide it into the syllables or letters which compose it, in accordance with the rules of grammar.
52. The author has already explained that there are three ways of finding out the meaning of words: we may take their ordinary meaning; or their meaning may have been specially defined; or we may divide them into parts in the manner explained.
53. This would serve as a check, warning us that we should begin again. This is found to be correct from experience.
54. *Homa* is an act of making an oblation to the gods by casting clarified butter into the fire. As clarified butter refers to goodness, and fire to the intellect, it means a good and intelligent action, or an act of sacrifice.
55. If we divide *Agni* into parts, we get *A,g,n,i,*—and the meaning is *"(a)* intellect associated with *(g,n)* the senses and (z) the mind".

    The word *haviṣ* or *havis* may be divided into *ha,vi,s,* when the meaning would be *"(ha)* intellect *(vi)* distinguished from *(sh* or *s)* the mind". The emphasis in this word is on the intellect as distinguished from the mind; and so it means "a burnt offering, or anything offered as an oblation with fire"; and we have explained that fire refers to the intellect.

56. We have already explained that the meaning of *Soma* can be obtained by dividing it into *sa, u, ma,* when we shall get the idea of "*(sa)* the mind associated with *(u, ma)* the senses".

57. The reason for this is explained in the following *Sūtras*. We have explained that *vaṣaṭ* signifies that the mind is satisfied that a particular action should be done, and it directs the senses to do it. *Svāhā,* on the other hand, invokes a blessing on action, and asks for more and more action, each following each. There is thus a fundamental difference between them: the one indicates that only necessary action should be done, while the other upholds the idea of action without end,—provided, of course, it is performed as a sacrifice, and is a "blessed" action.

58. The number seventeen refers to the soul. There are four *ritvij* priests, each of whom has three assistants, making a total of sixteen; and after them is the *Yajamāna,* sacrificer, or the soul, as the seventeenth. The highest purpose of action is that it is performed for the sake of the soul (*Cf.* BhG. V, 11); and it is also that it should be "blessed", and done again and again. The number seventeen can also refer to the intellect, as the mind is represented by the number sixteen (ten senses, five attributes of the "elements", with the mind as the sixteenth),— and so the intellect can be represented by the number seventeen; and we have seen that the intellect and the soul may, for practical purposes, be identified.

59. The word *svāhā* implies that one action should follow another; and we find that all animals are governed by this law. They cannot abstain from action even for a moment (*Cf.* BhG. III, 5).

60. These *Sūtras* tell us that if we divide the word *svāhā* into parts, the first would be the most important, and we can get its meaning from it. The word may accordingly be divided into *Sva, ā, hā,* meaning "*(sva)* the soul, (*ā*) leading to or associated with *(hā,* 'an exclamation of satisfaction") satisfaction". Hence, it expresses the satisfaction of the soul with action, with the result that it can continue to act. This reference to the soul would explain the idea of the number seventeen in a previous *Sūtra* (14).

61. This *Sūtra* does not occur in certain texts.

62. As plants or the vegetable kingdom refer to Nature, medicinal herbs would refer to the healing powers of Nature. Thus they enable us to understand the idea of the essence of goodness in Nature, and so are associated with the idea of its sacrifice.

63. The two acts of sacrifice would obviously refer to the idea of sacrifice associated with Nature and man. Medicinal herbs refer to the essence of "sacrifice" in Nature, and their use by man to his own ends.

64. This *Sūtra* explains the circumstances in which we are obliged to think of a different method of interpreting the text, which would enable us to understand it in the light of a law of life.

We find that medicinal plants are invoked, and there is a reference to two acts of sacrifice; but all this does not appear to make any sense, with the result that we are unable to make any progress with the text. This compels thought, and we are obliged to think of some other method of interpretation to enable us to understand all this.

The whole idea has already been explained.

CHAPTER - IX

SACRIFICE AND THE INTELLECT : THE METHOD OF INTERPRETATION

PART- I

Introduction

The most important thing is Sacrifice, because it sanctifies; and so is associated with Dharma. Purification and sacrifice are synonymous terms, and their relation corresponds to the fruit of action and the deity who grants it; and it is not necessary to divide words into parts to understand this.

Sacrifice is associated with the idea of a god; and we may also compare the idea of its importance with that of a guest.

When we give a particular name to an object, there is usually a good reason for it,—that is, because it has certain qualities; and this can be done when the word is quite new.

When names are arranged in this manner, they can cover the entire range of the subject-matter of Dharma; and their meaning is fixed. There are also certain instructions in connection with them; and when a name is repeated, the repetition is for the sake of further explanation.

When the intellect is associated with desire, it is like the full function of the mind; but it can perform only one act at a time.

The relation of the intellect to the other faculties is like that of the husband to his wife; and this enables us to understand the idea of dedication. However, a person can perform only one action at a time.

If the *Mantras* of the Vedas have a rational meaning, we must find out a way of interpreting them in that light; and when we do so, we shall find that the whole idea is transformed into that of a law of life. But it does not lead to the conclusion that we must renounce action, for the meaning is different and of a higher character.

Certain ideas have been personified: for instance, *Sarasvatī* has been described as a woman; and the result is that an object gets a special distinction from being described in that way, and all this can be done by using a single correct word.

There are, however, certain instructions given in the text which should be strictly adhered to,—specially in connection with *Sāman* hymns; while with regard to the rest, we can use our intelligence.

With regard to hymns that are not to be sung aloud, the instructions are that they should be understood without any change; and it is only in the case of those that are to be sung aloud that we are required to change the form of words or divide them into parts; and that is indicated by their having to be sung aloud.

Sacrifice and Purification

यज्ञकर्म प्रधानं; तद्धि चोदनाभूतं; तस्य द्रव्येषु संस्कारस्तत्प्रयुक्त-
स्तदर्थत्वात्॥१॥
संस्कारे युज्यमानानां; तादर्थ्यात्तत्प्रयुक्तं स्यात्॥२॥
तेन त्वर्थेन यज्ञस्य संयोगाद्धर्मसंन्धस्तस्माद्यज्ञप्रयुक्तं स्यात्संस्कारस्य
तदर्थत्वात्॥३॥
फलदेवतयोश्च॥४॥
न चोदनातो हि तादृगुण्यम्॥५॥

An act of sacrifice is the chief thing, and it is obligatory.

Its scanctifying effect exists in all things, and it is performed for the sake of that effect. An act of sacrifice makes for the purification of a proper person, and it should be performed for the sake of that purification. Sacrifice is associated with Dhārma (the law of *ri*ghteousness) because its object is purification, and it is linked up with purification; and that is the reason why sacrifice should be performed. Indeed, purification and sacrifice are synonymous terms. The relation between purification and sacrifice corresponds to that between the fruit and the deity who grants the fruit[1].

(These ideas are easy to understand and have been directly expressed; and) we do not need to divide words into parts to know their meaning.

Sacrifice and a God: Sacrifice and a Guest

देवता वा प्रयोजयेदतिथिवद्भोजनस्य तदर्थत्वात्॥६॥

आर्थ[1]पत्याच्च॥७॥

ततश्च तेन सम्बन्धः॥८॥

अपि वा शब्दपूर्वत्वाद्यज्ञकर्मप्रधानं स्याद् गुणत्वे देवताश्रुतिः॥९॥

अतिथौ तत्प्रधानत्वमभावः कर्मणि स्यात्तस्य प्रीतिप्रधनत्वात्॥१०॥

In all our actions we should aim at acting like a god;[2] and that should be our object, even as the object of food is to satisfy hunger. It is in this way that we can have a complete idea of the meaning of sacrifice; and it is for this reason that sacrifice is associated with the idea of a god. But, as has already been stated, an act of sacrifice is the best in itself, and that is its primary conception; while its association with the idea of a god arises in a secondary manner. We get this idea of importance in that of a "guest,[3] but not in every action; for the satisfaction in connection with a guest arises from his own importance.

Reason for a Name

द्रव्यसङ्ख्याहेतुसमुदायं वा श्रुतिसंयोगात्॥११॥

---

1. अर्थपेतेति पाठान्तरं वृत्तिग्रन्थे।

अर्थकारिते च द्रव्येण न व्यवस्था स्यात्॥१२॥
अर्थो वा स्यात्प्रयोजनमितरेषामचोदनात्तस्य[1] च गुणभूतत्वात्॥१३॥
अपूर्वत्वाद्व्यवस्था स्यात्॥१४॥

When we give a particular name to an object, it is because there is usually a good reason for it; and when the meaning has been fixed, there should be no variation from it, so far as the object is concerned. The name given to an object is intended to serve some purpose, though there are several names for which no particular reason can be assigned. But (very often) the reason why an object is given a particular name is that it possesses certain qualities; and its meaning can be fixed if it is quite new[4].

Names and the Idea of Dharma

तत्प्रयुक्तत्वे च धर्मस्य सर्वविषयत्वम्॥१५॥
तद्युक्तस्येति चेत्॥१६॥
नाश्रुतित्वात्॥१७॥
अधिकारादिति चेत्॥१८॥
तुल्येषु नाधिकारः स्यादचोदितश्च सम्बन्धः; पृथक् सतां यज्ञार्थेनाभिसम्बन्ध स्तस्माद्यज्ञप्रयोजनम्॥१९॥

When names are arranged in this manner, they can cover the entire range of the subject-matter of *Dharma*. This does not apply only to such words as have been specially adapted for the purpose, as that is likely to cause confusion. Nor is it due to the subject-matter of the text or the authority of learned men, because they are used in the same sense in different places, and this cannot be ordered by force. There is a reason for the meaning of these words: for instance, good people, though widely apart, are drawn together by means of objects of sacrifice; and that is why sacrifices are performed. (Even so words of the same kind, though widely apart, have the same meaning because of a common bond between them).

1. तस्य गुणेतिशब्दरहितं पाठान्तरं वृत्तिग्रन्थे।

The Meaning is Fixed

देशबद्धमुपांशुत्वं तेषां स्याच्छ्रुतिनिर्देशात्त[1]स्य च तत्र भावात्॥२०॥
यज्ञस्य वा तत्संयोगात्॥२१॥

The meaning of these words is fixed; and if we utter them in a low tone, it is because of the instructions of the śruti, which are due to the character of the ideas sought to be expressed.[5] It is in this manner that we get the real meaning of *yajña* or sacrifice.

Idea of Repetition

अनुवादश्च तदर्थवत्॥२२॥
प्रणीतादि तथेति चेत्॥२३॥
न यज्ञस्याश्रुतित्वात्॥२४॥
तद्देशानां वा सङ्घातस्याचोदितत्वात्॥२५॥

When a name is translated or repeated in some other form, the repetition is for the sake of explanation, and is intended to convey the same idea. This is not so merely because we have been taught that it is so, because there is no mention of the word *yajña* or sacrifice in the text (and so the idea is inherent in the words themselves). These words are found in the same place, and are closely allied; and this cannot be secured by complusion or force.

Law of the Intellect

अग्निधर्मः प्रतीष्टकं सङ्घातात्पौर्णमासीवत्॥२६॥
अग्नेर्वा स्याद्द्रव्यैकत्वादितरासां तदर्थत्वात्॥२७॥
चोदनासमुदायात्तु पौर्णमास्यां तथात्वं स्यात्॥२८॥

The Dharma of *Agni* (or the law of the intellect) with reference to an object of desire, —when the latter is intense—is that it is like the full moon (or the full function of the mind).[6] But the intellect (*Agni*) can function in association with only one object at a time; and the other faculties, subordinate to it, act only to serve its purpose. It is because the intellect comes

1. निर्देशेति पाठान्तरं वृत्तिग्रन्थे।

under the influence of desire, that its state becomes like that of the full function of the mind[7] (full moon).

Relation of Intellect and Other Faculties

पत्नीसंजायान्तत्वं सर्वेषामविशेषात्॥२९॥
लिङ्गाद्वा प्रागुत्तमात्॥३०॥
अनुवादो वा दीक्षा यथा नक्तं संस्थापनस्य॥३१॥
स्याद्वाऽनारभ्य विधानादन्ते लिङ्गविरोधात्॥३२॥
अभ्यासः सामिधेनीनां प्राथम्यात्स्थानधर्मः स्यात्॥३३॥

(The relation of the intellect and other faculties may be compared to that of a husband and wife). A wife may offer sacrifice together with her husband; but she comes after him, and that is true in all cases without exception. We arrive at this conclusion by means of inference, because all things are directed towards the best;[8] otherwise the explanation of the idea or an act of dedication would be as difficult as the erection of a building at night. There may be an error because of improper arrangement of words or their parts, or inconsistency of our inference; but the repeated experience of those who have studied the functions of the intellect[9] should,—because of their superiority—be regarded as the law of life.

First Things First

इष्ट्यावृतौ प्रयाजदावर्त्तेताऽऽरम्भणीया॥३४॥
सकृद्वाऽऽरम्भसंयोगादेक‘; पुनरारम्भो यावज्जीवप्रयोगात्॥३५॥

When we are surrounded by a number of desires, we should, as in the case of a preliminary sacrifice, attend to those which are necessary;, for a man can do only one thing at a time, even though he may attempt to do a number of them simultaneously. So long as he lives, he has to begin every time afresh whenever he wishes to perform an action, because that is the law.

How to Interpret the Text

अर्थाभिधानसंयोगान्मन्त्रेषु शेषभावः स्यात्तत्राचोदितमप्राप्तं चोदिताभि-
धनात्॥३६॥

ततश्[1]चावचनं तेषामितरार्थं प्रयुज्यते॥३७॥
गुणशब्दस्तथेति चेत्॥३८॥
न समवायात्॥३९॥
चोदिते तु परार्थत्वाद्विधिवद्विकारः स्यात्॥४०॥
विकारस्तत्प्रधाने स्यात्॥४१॥
असंयोगात्तदर्थेषु तद्विशिष्टं प्रतीयेत॥४२॥
कमभावादेवमिति चेत्॥४३॥
न परार्थत्वात्॥४४॥

If we believe that some (rational) meaning has been put in the language of the *Mantras* or hymns of the Vedas, we shall have to agree that it is something that has been left out and not included in their ordinary meaning. But if we do not search for it, we shall not find it, because it has been fixed in the names themselves; and since that is so, there is no further mention of it. There is thus a different and a more suitable meaning of these hymns. We cannot, however, say that the exact qualities of an object have been expressed in these words in this manner, because they can be obtained only by means of a closer, inner connection. But when we understand the real meaning of the text, we shall find that, because it has a different and a higher meaning, the whole idea is transformed into that of a law of life; and this transformation takes place in the most essential part of the text. The new meaning would be found to have no connection with any other meaning, and would be acknowledged to be the best. But this is not based on the conclusion that we should renounce all actions, because there is a different and a higher meaning of the text.

Personification

लिङ्गविशेषनिर्देशात्समानविधानेष्वप्राप्ता; सारस्वती स्त्रीत्वात्॥४५॥
पश्वभिधानाद्वा; तद्धि चोदनाभूतं; पुंविषयं; पुनः पशुत्वम्॥४६॥
विशेषो वा तदर्थनिर्देशात्॥४७॥
पशुत्वं चैक[2]शब्द्यात्॥४८॥

1. वृत्तिग्रन्थे इदं सूत्रं नास्ति।
2. एकशब्दादिति पाठान्तरम्।

यथोक्तं वा सन्निधानात्॥४९॥
आम्नातादन्यदधिकारे, वचनाद्विकारः स्यात्॥५०॥
द्वैधं वा तुल्यहेतुत्वात्सामान्याद्विकल्पः स्यात्॥५१॥

There is mention of certain special forms that can be given to things: for instance, what relates to *Sarasvatī* has been given the garb of a woman, because it is not possible to find the same exact details of description in any other statement of particulars regarding her (*Sarasvatī*).[10] That is the purpose served by describing an object as an animal. That is what we are enjoined to do; that is why we have the category of a man; and that is what is repeated again and again in the sacred books. Indeed, an object gets a special distinction from being described in this way; and it can be done by using but a single correct word.[11] All this that has been stated has been done by putting things together, and representing them correctly. In case, however, there is a different explanation (or authority) in the sacred books themselves, this statement should be modified; for if there are two equally satisfactory ways of interpreting the text, there is likely to be a doubt about it (and so the direction given in the text should be preferred).

How to Interpret the Sāman Hymns

उपदेशाच्च साम्नः॥५२॥
नियमो वा श्रुतिविशेषादितरत्साप्तदश्यवत्॥५३॥
अप्रगाणाच्छब्दान्यत्वे तथाभूतोपदेशः स्यात्॥५४॥
यत्स्थाने वा तद्गीतिः स्यात्पदान्यत्वप्रधानत्वात्॥५५॥
गानसंयोगाच्च॥५६॥
वचनमिति चेत्॥५७॥
न तत्प्रधानत्वात्॥५८।

The meaning of the *Sāman* hymns should be in accordance with this teaching; for there is a fixed rule in regard to the interpretation of these hymns, based on a special reference in the *śruti*;[12] while with regard to the rest, we can use our intelligence. With regard to the hymns that are not to be sung aloud, the teaching is that they should be understood in their orginal form, as they are.[13] It is only that part of the *śruti* which has to be sung aloud, that has to be given its proper place; and it has a different position because of its special importance, which is indicated by means of its connection with singing aloud. The fact that these hymns have to be sung aloud is not due merely to an injunction to that effect; it is so because of their special importance[14]

PART II

THE METHOD OF INTERPRETATION

Introduction

According to some all *Mantras* are intended to be sung, as that is the best way of remembering them; but this is an erroneous view.

The law of life is action; and so it is best described in terms of action; and action, in its widest connotation, is the subject-matter of the Ṛg Veda. But we can get this only if we interpret the text properly; and we can succeed if we divide words into parts, and practise the art in accordance with the rules of grammar. We should bear in mind that there is unity of idea underlying the whole text; and we must not omit any part of it. In case of doubt we should consult competent teachers; though there are sometimes differences of opinion among them. However, this method of interpretation involves a complete substitution of one meaning for another, with a new natural order of connection between words, which would itself be a test of its correctness. According to *Jaimini* it would be stupid to ask for more.

The cause of this form of composition is that the properties of objects, which are closely connected with one another, should be properly described; and so if there are any examples, they too should be in the same form. This is possible because the words are quite new; and there is no similarity between the original and the new meaning. But it is only when we are unable to get a proper meaning from the original form of the text, that we should adopt this method.

If the words or their parts are badly arranged, we cannot get the correct meaning; and this is how we can test this method. But this does not apply to great phenomena, which take place in accordance with a law, such as the new and the full moon, which are described as gods.

These phenomena do not give us the idea of Time, which cannot be personified as a god.

All Hymns are not to be Sung

सामानि मन्त्रमेके स्मृत्युपदेशाभ्याम्॥१॥

तदुक्तदोषम्॥२॥

According to some all *Mantras* or hymns are *Sāmans*,—that is, intended to be sung aloud—on the ground that that is the best way to remember them, and we are enjoined to do so; but this is an erroneous view.

Action, and its Idea in the Ṛg Veda

कर्म वा विधलक्षणम्॥३॥

तदृग्द्रवयं वचनात्पाकयज्ञवत्॥४॥

तत्राविप्रतिषिद्धो द्रव्यान्तरे व्यक्ति रेकः प्रदेशश्च॥५॥

(The law of life is action; and so) Action is an accurate description of the law of life. It is expressly mentioned that action is the subject-matter of the *Ṛg Veda*,—action conceived as a sacrifice, like the sacrifice of cooking food;[15] and there is no restriction in regard to the comparison and contrast of the idea of action in connection with any object.

How to Understand This

शब्दार्थत्वात्तु नैवं स्यात्॥६॥

परार्थत्वाच्च शब्दानाम्॥७॥

असम्बन्ध कर्मणा शब्दयोः पृथगर्थत्वात्॥८॥

संस्कारश्च प्रकरणेऽग्निवत्स्यात् प्रयुक्तत्वात्॥९॥

अकार्यत्वाच्च शब्दानामप्रयोगः प्रतीयेत॥१०॥
आश्रि[1]तत्वाच्च॥११॥
प्रयुज्यत इति चेत्॥१२॥
ग्रहणार्थं प्रतीयेत॥१३॥
तृचे स्याच्छ्रुतिनिर्देशात्॥१४॥
शब्दार्थत्वाद्विकारस्य॥१५॥
दर्शयति च॥१६॥

But we cannot get this by means of the ordinary meaning of words; and we can get their real meaning if we realise that they have been used in some other sense. If we take the words of the text as as they are and give them their common meaning, we find that there is no reference to action even in two of them, taken one by one; and in such a case we should understand that their correct formation, in connection with the text and its explanation, is the same as in the case of the word *Agni*.[16] (But we have to be careful in our task) and unless the words (in their new meaning) produce the desired effect, we should not admit their connection with one another; and this condition is an integral part of this method. It is, however, possible to say that this is what we do and yet do not succeed. In any case, if we wish to interpret the text correctly, we should accept only such meanings as have a bearing on the idea of action;[17] and according to the directions of the *śruti*, the reference to action should be found in a *tṛcha* or a strophe consisting of three verses. If, on the other hand, we accept the usual meaning of words, we shall find that the whole idea is changed for the worse, as we can see for ourselves.

Method of Interpretation and Test of its Correctness

वाक्यानां तु विभक्तत्वात्प्रतिशब्दं समाप्तिः स्यात्संस्कारस्य तदर्थत्वात्॥१७॥
तथा चान्यार्थदर्शनम्॥१८॥
अनवानोपदेशश्च तद्वत्॥१९॥
अभ्यासेनेतराः श्रुतिः॥२०॥

1. अश्रुतत्वाच्चेति क्वचित् पाठः।

तदभ्यासः समासः स्यात्॥२१॥

लिङ्गदर्शनाच्च॥२२॥

नैमित्तिकं तूत्तरात्वमानन्तर्यात्प्रतीयेत॥२३॥

ऐकार्थ्याच्च तदभ्यासः॥२४॥

प्रागाथिकं तु॥२५॥

स्वे च॥२६॥

प्रगाथे च॥२७॥

लिङ्गदर्शनाव्यतिरेकाच्च॥२८॥

When we divide a word into parts, each sound (syllable or letter) should be complete in itself; and that is the meaning of the correct formation of words. It is in this manner that we can find a different meaning of the text, and its entire teaching would remain unbroken in this way. We can get the real meaning of the whole *śruti* by means of repeated practice, relating to the composition of words; and we can see through their "disguise" in this manner. This excellence of meaning is produced by means of a definite cause;[18] and we should accept the meaning of parts of words in immediate succession to one another;[19] and we can resort to this practice because there is unity of idea underlying the whole text. This applies specially to certain verses derived from the *Pragātha* stanzas of the *Ṛg Veda*,[20] and also the *Pragātha* stanzas themselves. But in our effort to see through the "disguise" we must not omit or exclude anything.

Authority of Teachers

अर्थैकत्वाद्विकल्पः स्यात्॥२९॥

अर्थैकत्वाद्विकल्पः स्यादृक्सामयोस्तदर्थत्वात्॥३०॥

वचनाद्विनियोगः स्यात्॥३१॥

समप्रदेशे विकारस्तदपेक्षः स्याच्छास्त्रकृतत्वात्॥३२॥

वर्णे तु बादरिर्यथाद्रव्यं द्रव्यव्यतिरेकात्॥३३॥

स्तोभस्यैके द्रव्यान्तरे निवृत्तिमृग्वत्॥३४॥

सर्वातिदेशस्तु सामान्याल्लोकवद्विकारः स्यात्॥३५॥

अन्वयं चापि दर्शयति॥३६॥

निवृत्तिर्वाऽर्थलोपात्॥३७॥

अन्वयो वार्थवादः स्यात्॥३८॥

अधिकं च विवर्णं च जैमिनिः स्तोभशब्दत्वात्॥३९॥

If the text had only one meaning, we should doubt its value, both in respect of the *Ṛg Veda* and *Sāma Veda*; for we have been taught by competent teachers that there should be correlation or continuity of thought in the Vedas. If, therefore, we find that the text can be interpreted equally well in two ways,—the change of form of words should be made with due regard to the injunction of these teachers, who know how it has been composed.

But *Bādari* says that when there is a reference to the character of objects, we should understand their names as they are, because each object has a separate existence of its own. On the other hand some others say that, even as in the case of the hymns of the *Ṛg Veda*, there is no conflict between the properties of objects (and their names). But in this method of interpretation,—since the fundamental notions are so different —there should be a complete substitution of one meaning for another; and the change of form should be complete, as people would say. We shall then find that there is a new natural order or connection of words in the text; but if we are uanble to get a proper meaning, this order too will cease to exist. Indeed, this natural order itself would give us the explanation of the meaning of the text; and *Jaimini* says bluntly that it would be stupid to demand more.

Object of this Form of Composition

धर्मस्यार्थकृतत्वाद्, द्रव्यगुणविकारव्यतिक्रमप्रतिषेधे, चोदनानुबन्धः, समवायात्॥४०॥

तदुत्पत्तेस्तु निवृत्तिस्तत्कृतत्वात् स्यात्॥४१॥

आवेश्येरन् वाऽर्थवत्त्वात्संकारस्य तदर्थत्वात्॥४२॥

आख्या चैवं तदावेशाद्विकृतौ स्यादपूर्वत्वात्॥४३॥

परार्थे न त्वर्थसामान्यं संस्कारस्य तदर्थत्वाद्॥४४॥

क्रियेरन् वाऽर्थनिवृत्तेः॥४५॥

एकार्थत्वादविभागः स्यात्॥४६॥

निर्देशाद्वा व्यवतिष्ठेरन्॥४७॥

As the text has been composed for a special purpose, namely, to describe the laws of life,—and it is free from all extravagance— the cause that has made for this form of composition is the idea that the properties of objects should be correctly described, for they are closely connected with one another; and it requires that if there are any examples to be cited, they too should be in the same form. We should be able to get all this from the meaning so obtained, because that is the purpose of this formation of words. Thus, when a name is used in this form of composition, it would undergo a change, because it is quite new.[21] Indeed, there is no similarity between the original and subsequent meaning of a word, because that is the very purpose of this form of composition, which is based on the correct formation or use of words. But it is only when we are unable to get a proper meaning, that words should be construed in this manner; and if we are satisfied with the one meaning as it is, there should be no division of words into parts; and their meaning should be determined on the basis of their description.

Test of Correctness

अपाकृते तद्विकाराद्विरोधाद्व्यवतिष्ठेरन्॥४८॥

उभयसाम्नि चैवमेकार्थापत्तेः॥४९॥

स्वार्थत्वाद्वा व्यवस्था स्यात्प्रकृतिवत्॥५०॥

If, however, the words (or their parts) are badly arranged, the change would be for the worse, and there would be no consistency of ideas, with the result that the correct meaning cannot be determined. In this manner we can find out the correct meaning of any two *Sāman* hymns by means of oneness of inference drawn from circumstances, and feel convinced in regard to the true meaning of words in the same manner as in connection with their orginal form[22].

Special Cases

पार्वणहोमयोस्त्वप्रवृत्तिः; समुदायार्थसंयोगात्तदभीज्या हि॥५१॥

कालस्येति चेत्॥५२॥

नाप्रकरणत्वात्॥५३॥

मन्त्रवर्णाच्च॥५४॥

तदभावेऽग्निवदिति चेत॥५५॥

नाधिकारिकत्वात्॥५६॥

उभयोरविशेषात्॥५७॥

यदभीज्या वा तद्विषयौ॥५८॥

प्रयाजेऽपीति चेत्॥५९॥

नाचोदितत्वात्॥६०॥

But this rule does not apply to two actions (or sacrifices) performed in accordance with a law, which take place at different times, such as the new and the full moon. These phenomena (or actions) are personified as gods and honoured as such; and that is how they are connected with the meaning of the text. We cannot say that this is intended to give us the idea of Time,[23] and so Time should be personified in the same manner (that is, as a god), because that is not the principal topic of the text; and we get this from the description of the text itself. Nor can we say that, if it is not possible (to agree that the new and the full moon refer to Time),—the idea of Time should be like that of *Agni*[24]—because (that too does not fit into the text, and) we have to see what constitutes the principal topic of the text and what does not. Indeed, there is uniformity of representation in regard to the idea of both Time and *Agni* throughout the text; for what is worshipped as a god is their different spheres of activity.[25] We cannot even say that we should honour Time as a god at least at the beginning of things (preliminary sacrifice), because we cannot conceive of it at that stage[26] (or it cannot be acted upon by anything).

PART III

THE METHOD OF INTERPRETATION (*CONTINUED*)

Introduction

When a word is divided into parts, we may begin from the beginning or the end as may be convenient: only we must remember that there is a cause for all things.

According to some there should be no change in the form of words used in the text. But a change should be made where necessary, and for reasons already explained.

A "disguise" means that we need to have a proper meaning of the text; and there are rules in regard to the manner of seeing through it,—both as to whether words should be divided into parts or not.

If the meaning of words taken as a whole is incompatible with the character of the text, we should be able to find an alternative meaning; for, if the parts of a word are the same, it would be wrong to construe it in only one way.

If an expression is quite new, its form should not be changed, unless there are express directions to that effect in the text.

If the meaning of a word has not been defined in a special way, we cannot define it ourselves; but if we are unable to get a proper meaning, we can divide a word into parts; but the word cannot come to possess any new properties by reason of this division.

A name is formed when we utter a particular word and give it a particular meaning; but certain words express the idea of a single action, and no change should be made in their form. This, however, does not apply to a word like *tvac*.

The form of the word *medha-pati* should not be changed, for its meaning has been defined.

In this method of interpretation we get two series of words, —the original one and that formed by means of division into parts; and we should see that they correspond each to each in an exact order.

The word *svāmī* has a special meaning; and so also *Devatā*; and they retain their meanings throughout.

Words which express the idea of a single action should remain unchanged in form.

The form of the names of a large number of gods should be changed; and their ideas should be connected with one another.

Method of Interpretation

प्रकृतौ यथोत्पत्ति वचनमर्था[1]नांतथोत्तरस्यां; ततौ[2] तत्प्रकृतित्वादर्थे चाकार्यत्वात्॥१॥

लिङ्गदर्शनाच्च॥२॥

जातिर्नैमित्तिकं यथास्थानम्॥२॥

लिङ्[3]गदर्शनाच्च॥३अ.॥

विकारमेकेऽनार्षत्वात्॥४॥

लिङ्गदर्शनाच्च॥५॥

विकारो वा तदुक्ते हेतुः॥६॥

When a word is reduced to its rudimentary form (or divided into parts),—so far as its meaning is concerned—its first part is like a subsequent part. In the whole mass of the parts of a word, the meaning is due to its rudimentary form, and is not affected by the manner of construing it; and we can understand this if we see through its "disguise"[27].

The true state of a thing is produced by means of some definite cause, according to its place; and we can understand this if we see through the "disguise" of words.[28] According to some, however, there should be no change in the form of words, as it is unauthorised; but they say so because they look only to the symbols used in the text (and not to their meaning). On the other hand a change should be made where necessary, and for reasons already explained.

---

1. र्थानामुत्तेति पाठः।
2. तताविति नास्ति क्वचित्।
3. इदं सूत्रं वृत्तिग्रन्थेधिकं दृश्यते।

Purpose of "Disguise" and the Need for Piercing through It

लिङ्गं मन्त्रचिकीर्षार्थम्॥७॥

नियमो वोभयभागित्वात्॥८॥

लौकिके दोष[1]संयोगादपवृक्ते हि चोद्यते; निमित्तेन प्रकृतौ स्यादभागित्वात्॥९॥

अन्यायस्त्व विकारेण, दुष्ट[2]प्रतिघातित्वादविशेषाच्च तेनास्य॥१०॥

विकारो वा तदर्थत्वात्॥११॥

अपि त्वन्याय[3]सम्बन्धात्प्रकृतिवत्परेष्वपि यथार्थं स्यात्॥१२॥

यथार्थं त्वन्या[4]यस्याचोदितत्वात्॥१३॥

छन्दसि तु यथादृष्टम्॥१४॥

अंन्याय[5]स्याचोदितत्वात्॥१४अ॥

A "disguise" is for the purpose of desiring to bring out the real meaning of the *Mantras* or the hymns of the Vedas; and there are rules in connection with the method of seeing through it, both in respect of words taken as a whole and divided into parts.[29] If we find that the common meaning of a word, current among the people, is defective, (we should take it that it is incomplete, and so) understand it in the light of its completer or more highly evolved form. Indeed, in such a case there should be good reason for allowing a word to remain in its orginal form. without dividing it into parts; for it would be improper not to make a change in order to remove a defect, specially when there is no difference between the two forms of a word; and a change is made in order to remove the defect. But when the defect has been removed, the meaning of words in the latter form should be as suitable as in the original one. Indeed, when we get the true meaning of the text, we find that it is free from defect; and we see an illustration of this in our own desires, because we understand what is proper when we are free from the influence of what is improper[30].

---

1. सप्रसंगादिति वृत्तिग्रन्थे पाठान्तरम्।
2. अदृष्टेति वृत्तिग्रन्थे पाठान्तरम्।
3. न्यायसेति वृत्तिगन्थे पाठान्तरम्।
4. र्थं चान्यायस्येति वृत्तिग्रन्थे पाठान्तरम्।
5. इदं सूत्रं वृत्तिगन्थेधिकं दृश्यते।

Need of an Alternative Meaning

विप्रतिपत्तौ विकल्पः स्यात्तत्समत्वाद् गुणे त्वन्यायकल्पनैकदेशत्वात्।
प्रकरणविशेषाच्च॥१६॥
उत्कर्षो[1] वा द्वियज्ञवत्॥१६अ.॥
अर्थाभावात्तु नैवं स्याद्, गुणमात्रमितरत्॥१७॥
द्यावोस्तथेति चेत्॥१८॥
नोत्पत्तिशब्दत्वात्॥१९॥
अपूर्वे त्वविकारोऽप्रदेशात्प्रतीयेत॥२०॥
विकृतौ चापि तद्वचनात्॥२१॥
अध्रिगुः[2] सवनीयेषु तद्वत्समानविधानाश्चेत्॥२२॥
प्रतिनिधौ चाविकारात्॥२३॥

If we find that (in case we accept the meaning of the text as it is) certain erroneous ideas arise and they are incompatible with the character of the text, we should be able to find an alternative meaning; because if the parts of a word are the same, it would be wrong to construe it in only one way; and we come to this conclusion because we are able to get a better explanation; and its excellence is like a double sacrifice.[31] But we should do this (find an alternative meaning by means of dividing words into parts) only when there is no suitable meaning, and anything else fails to satisfy us. (All expressions, however, are not like that); for instance, *Dyāva-Pṛthivī* is not an expression of this kind, because we can get its meaning from the origin of the sounds which compose it[32].

If an expression is quite new, its form should not be changed;[33] and it is not necessary to point to any precedent or rule in such a case. But if we change the form of such an expression, it should be done in accordance with some express direction in the text; and, if the rules are the same, the idea of *adhṛgu*,—in what relates to a *Soma* sacrifice—should be obtained in the same manner.[34] In this case the meaning is to be found in a substitute expression, because no change of form is necessary.

1. इदं सूत्रं वृत्तिग्रन्थेधिकं दृश्यते।
2. अध्रिगाविति न्यायमालायां पाठान्तरम्।

Method of Division of Words into Parts

अनाम्नानादशब्दत्वमभावाच्चेतरस्य स्यात्॥२४॥
तादर्थ्याद्वा तदाख्यं स्यात्संस्कारैरविशिष्टत्वात्॥२५॥
उक्तं च तत्त्वमस्य॥२६॥
संसर्गिषु चार्थस्यास्थित परिमाणत्वात्॥२७॥
लिङ्गदर्शनाच्च॥२८॥

If the meaning of a word has not been handed down (or explained) by the sacred books themselves, we cannot hit upon the correct explanation ourselves; but if we are unable to get a proper meaning, we should resort to this method of interpretation (by means of division of words into parts). A name is intended to convey an idea; and if its meaning is obtained from the name itself, we should retain its existing form; for it cannot come to possess any special properties by reason of its new formation (or division into parts). The essence of this has already been explained; for when we take words as a whole, with their parts joined together, the meaning that we get is not of a lasting value,—whereas we understand them better by piercing through their "disguise".

Formation of a Name

एकधेत्येकसंयोगादभ्यासेनाभिधानं स्यादसर्वविषयत्वात्॥२९॥
अविकारो वा बहूनामेककर्मवत्॥३०॥
सकृत्त्वं[1] चैकधयं स्यादेकत्वात्त्वचोऽनभिप्रेतं तत्प्रकृतित्वात्परेष्वभ्यासेनैवं[2] विवृद्धावभिधानं स्यात्॥३१॥

(This is how a name is formed). We utter a particular word once, and give it a particular meaning; and then repeat the same: when we do this, it should be construed to be a name, with a limited connotation (or range of activity). But there are a number of words the form of which is not changed, just as there is no change when there is only one action to describe. But the term "once" (referred to in the previous *Sūtra*) means

1. त्वं वैकेति. न्या. मा. पाठान्तरम्।
2. सेन विव्रिति. न्या. मा. पाठान्तरम्।

"acting suddenly or at once"; and it follows from this that this rule cannot apply to the word *tvach* ("skin"). In such a case we have to go down to the rudimentary form of a word in the manner explained, proceed from one part to the other, and add them together, till in the fully lengthened form we get the name (and its meaning)[35].

Meaning of Medha-pati

मेधपतित्वं स्वामिदेवतस्य समवायात्सर्वत्र च प्रयुक्तत्वात्तस्यान्याय-निगदत्वात्सर्वत्रैवाविकारः स्यात्॥३२॥

The expression *medha-pati* (or lord of sacrifice) is always used in the sense of one who has mastered the great forces of Nature (and sc is described as the lord of the gods).[36] This is the inherent connection between the two expressions (*medha-pati* and "lord of the gods"); and so if we find that this expression has been used, but we do not understand its meaning, we should not make any change in its form (but accept its idea as explained[37]).

Application of this Method

अपि वा द्विसमवायोऽर्थान्यत्वे यथासङ्ख्यं प्रयोगः स्यात्॥३३॥

When we apply this method of interpretation, we get two series or assemblages of words (the original one, and that formed by means of division into parts); and we should see that the second corresponds to the first in an exact order,—the first word of the first series to the first word of the second series, and so on.

Svāmī

स्वामिनो वैकशब्द्यादुत्कर्षो देवतायां स्यात्; पत्न्यां द्वितीयशब्दः स्यात्॥३४॥

देवता तु तदाशीष्ट्वात्सम्प्राप्तत्वास्वामिन्यनर्थिका स्यात्॥३५॥

उत्सर्गाच्च भक्त्या तस्मिन्पतित्वं स्यात्॥३६॥

उत्कृ[1]ष्येतैकसंयुक्तौ द्विदेवते संभवात्॥३७॥

1. इदं सूत्रमधिकं न्यायमालायाम्।

एकस्तु समवायात्तस्य तल्लक्षणत्वात्॥३८॥
संसर्गित्वाच्च तस्मात्तेन विकल्पः स्यात्॥३९॥

(There are certain words which have special meanings: for instance,) whenever the word *svāmī* (or master) is used in the text, its higher meaning is associated with the idea of a god (or the great forces of Nature)[38]; while with regard to the idea of a "wife" some other word (and not *svāmī*) is used. It might, at first sight, appear to be incongruous (or meaningless) to associate the idea of a "master of a sacrifice" with that of a god; because if he offers a sacrifice, it would be because he wants to gain some object; whereas if he is called a "master" it should mean that he has already obtained everything. But if we divide the word into parts in accordance with the general rule, we shall find that the idea of a master is contained in the word (*svāmīn*) itself[39]. But if the word is associated with two gods, it is only once that it needs to be drawn out of its original form, and divided into parts; for the word has only one meaning throughout the text; and that is so because of its permanent connection with its parts and the meaning given to it. And thus, since this connection is known, the form of the word can be changed in its light.

Words expressing the Idea of a Single Action

एकत्वेऽपि न गुणाऽपायात्॥४०॥

Nevertheless, when a word expresses the idea of a single action, it should not be divided into parts, because it would lose its meaning thereby.

How to obtain the Meaning of Gods

नियमो बहुदेवते विकारः स्यात्॥४१॥
विकल्पो वा प्रकृतिवत्॥४२॥
अर्थान्तरे विकारः स्याद्देवतापृथक्त्वादेकाभिसमवायात्स्यात्॥४३॥

The rule in regard to the case of a large number of gods is that there should be a change in the form of their names; that is they should be reduced to their rudimentary form[40] (by means of division into parts). But (even in their case) it is only when we are unable to get a proper meaning, that this should be done; and even though the gods express their own separate or individual ideas, there should be a close and constant connection between them[41].

PART IV

THE METHOD OF INTERPRETATION : THE LAW OF ACTION

There is a special meaning attaching to the number 26, which cannot be understood by means of addition or by dividing the word into parts.

It is necessary to use our intelligence to understand the idea of numbers: for we have to take them together as well as separately, like the ribs of an animal; or we may compare them to the relation between husband and wife; or between the institutor of a sacrifice and the priests employed by him to assist.

We should accept what the sacred books say about these numbers; but the idea of their total is important; and so also of the ribs of an animal.

It is said that the horse has 34 ribs. But this number refers not to ribs of a horse, but to Nature or *Prakṛti*, which is said to have thirty-four parts. This is supported by the sacred books, though we are permitted to make small changes in the details of this idea.

We can obtain the meaning of certain words like *śyena*, *śalā, Kaśyapa, Kavasha*, and *sreka-parṇa* from their reference to the context and the manner in which they have been formed. We can find out the meaning of adhrigu from the purpose for which it is used. But we cannot understand a main idea from a casual expression. The meaning of *dhāraṇa* should be of the best; and if the text refers to the idea of action, we should select that meaning of a word which has a bearing on action.

A thing should not be said to exist before its time has arrived.

When we see food being prepared on the fire, we should take it that it is meant to be eaten.

If a thing is not suitable for teaching, it would be found to be in a form which no one can understand; and except for this we should be able to understand the real meaning of all words.

If it is necessary to give up this method of interpretation, we should do so,—but only in conformity with rules : otherwise we should apply it without reserve.

It is necessary to control desires; and this should specially be done in a state of prosperity; and it is necessary to control them even in eating and drinking.

This method of interpretation means a new approach to the Vedas, and throws a new light on their value; but we can understand this only if we admit the necessity of action, without which all our attempts would be futile.

We should understand that the word *ājya* is a substitute for something else.

So far as action is concerned, it is a law that if we suspend one, we must begin another. The idea of the renunciation of action is expressed in terms of forest trees; but that should come at the end of life. On the other hand the idea of sacrifice is represented in terms of a god.

No. 26

षड्विंशतिरभयासेन पशुगणे; तत्प्रकृतित्वाद्गुणस्य; प्रविभक्तत्वादविकारे हि; तासामकात्स्न्येंनाभिसम्बन्धे; विकारात्र समासः स्यादसंयोगाच्च सर्वाभिः॥१॥
अभ्योसेऽपि तथेति चेत्॥२॥
न गुणादर्थकृतत्वाच्च॥३॥
समासेऽपि तथेति चेत्॥४॥
नासम्भवात्॥५॥
स्वाभिश्च वचनं; प्रकृतौ तथेह स्यात्॥६॥

When we say twenty-six, we get to this number by means of addition, as in the case of twenty-six animals. (But, so far as the text is concerned, this does not satisfy us). Yet, if we take the basic form of the word, we find that it is not a fit case for division into parts; and if we actually divide it, we find that it should not have been altered. Now, if we do not take these numbers in their totality, we find that they admit of a connection; but there is no connection if we change the form of the word, or take them in their totality[42]. We cannot get the real idea of this number by means of addition, nor yet by dividing the word into parts; and we see that it is so when we understand its proper meaning. We do not have this problem in the case of all compounds (or combinations); and the direction in this case is that the meaning should be obtained by means of all the numbers[43]; and so far as reducing a word to its rudimentary form is concerned, it should be resorted to in the manner explained.

Use of Intelligence

वङ्क्रीणान्तु प्रधानत्वात्समासेनाभिधानं स्यात्; प्राधन्यमध्रिगोस्तदर्थत्वात्।
तासां च कृत्स्नवचनात्॥८॥
अपि त्वसन्निपातित्वात्पत्नीवदाम्नातेनाभिधानं स्यात्॥९॥
विकारस्तु पदेशत्वाद्यजमानवत्॥१०॥
अपूर्वत्वात्तथा पत्न्याम्॥११॥

(It is necessary to use our intelligence in order to understand the idea of these numbers: for instance,) the ribs of an animal are very important to its life, and function collectively; and they cannot be separated without injury to the animal. This is how (in order to understand the idea of these numbers) we have to use our judgement; and that is the real purpose of the intellect.[44] The rule in such cases is that we must take all numbers together; but, as they cannot be combined, their association together is like that of the state of a wife[45], as has been taught in the sacred books. In such a case, if we may appeal to a precedent, the change of meaning would correspond to the idea of a person who institutes a sacrifice, but employs a priest to perform it[46]; but if there is no precedent, their association should correspond to that of a wife[47].

Importance of Explanation given in the Sacred Books

आम्नातस्त्वविकारात्सङ्ख्यासु सर्वगामित्वात्॥१२॥

सङ्ख्या त्वेवं प्रधानं स्याद्वङ्क्रयः पुनः प्रधानम्॥१३॥

अभ्यासो वाऽविकारात् स्यात्॥१४॥

अना[1]म्नातवचनमवचनेन हि वङ्क्रीणां स्यान्निर्देशः॥१५॥

पशुस्त्वेवं प्रधानं स्यादभ्यासस्य तन्निमित्तत्वात् तस्मात्समासशब्दः स्यात्॥१६॥

What is taught in the sacred books in connection with the idea of numbers should be accepted without any change, because that is their all-pervading character; but the total is as important as the ribs of an animal; and even if the numbers are added together, there should be no change in their idea[48].

If there is no special explanation of a name in the sacred books, we should never say that there is; and if the ribs of an animal mean anything special, there should be a special mention of it in the sacred books. Thus the word *paśu* (an animal) is important; and if it is added to or combined with some other word, it is because of that importance[49].

No. 34

अश्वस्य चतुस्त्रिंशत्तस्य वचनाद्वैशेषिकम्॥१७॥

तत्प्रतिषिध्य प्रकृतिर्नियुज्यते सा चतुस्त्रिंशद्वाच्यत्वात्॥१८॥

ऋग्वा स्यादाम्नातत्वादविकल्पश्च न्यायः॥१९॥

तस्यां तु वचनादैरेवत्पदविकारः स्यात्॥२०॥

सर्वप्रतिषेधो वाऽसंयोगात्पदेन स्यात्॥२१॥

वनिष्ठुसन्निधानादुरूकेण वपाभिधानम्॥२२॥

प्रशसा[2]ऽस्यभिधानम्॥२३॥

बाहुप्रशंसा वा॥२४॥

It is said that the horse has thirty-four ribs; and, as there

1. इदं सूत्रं वृत्तिग्रन्थे नास्ति, भाष्यकृन्मते न्या. मा. चास्ति।
2. प्रशंसात् वृत्तिग्रन्थे पाठान्तरम्।

is a special reference to this number, it has a special significance. The reference to the number thirty-four cannot be to the ribs of a horse; and if we reject this meaning, we should put Nature or *Prakṛti* in its place, because it has thirty-four parts, as has expressly been stated in the sacred books[50]. There are verses in the *Ṛg Veda* in support of this explanation; and so it is only right that it should be accepted without hesitation or doubt. But there is authority for making a change in parts of this idea, even as we do in the case of water or food.[51] But the whole idea would be negatived if there were no connection between the parts of this number.[52] (It is, however, permissible to make a little change in detail, without affecting the main idea: for instance,) a liberal-hearted person, if he has the owl for a neighbour, may be described as a "mower of grass"; or we may substitute the word sword for a hatchet or knife, to express the glory of the arm of the person who uses it.

Special Terms

श्येन-शला-कश्यप-कवयोषो[1]रुस्त्रकपर्णेष्वाकृति- वचनं प्रसिद्ध सन्निधनात्॥२५॥

का[2]त्स्न्यं वा स्यात्तथाभावात्॥२६॥

अध्रिगोश्च तदर्थत्वात्॥२७॥

प्रासङ्गिके प्रायश्चित्तं न विद्यते; परार्थत्वात्तदर्थो हि विधीयते॥२८॥

धारणे च परार्थत्वात्॥२९॥

क्रियार्थत्वादितरेषु कर्म स्यात्॥३०॥

न तूत्पन्ने यस्यचोदनाऽप्राप्तकालत्वात्॥३१॥

प्रदान[3]दर्शनं श्रपणे तद्धर्मभोजनार्थत्वात्संसर्गाच्च मधूदकवत्।३२॥

संस्कारप्रतिषेधश्च तद्वत्॥३३॥

तत्प्रतिषेधे च तथाभूतस्य वर्जनात्॥३४॥

अधर्मत्वमप्रदानात्प्रणीतार्थे; विधानादतुल्यत्वादसंसर्गः॥३५॥

---

1. वषस्त्रेकेति न्या. मा. पाठान्तरम्।
2. उत्तरसूत्रेण सहैकमेव सूत्रमिदं वृत्तिग्रन्थे।
3. वृत्तिग्रन्थे प्रधानेत्यपपाठो दृश्यते।
   नार्थत्वात्संसर्गाच्च मधूदकवत्।

परो नित्याऽनुवादः स्यात्॥३६॥
विहितप्रतिषेधो वा॥३७॥
वर्जने गुणभावित्वात्तदुक्तप्रतिषेधत्स्यात्कारणत्केवलाशनम्॥३८॥
व्रतधर्माच्च लेपवत्॥३९॥

The meaning of certain words like *śyena*, *śalā*, *Kaśyapa*, *kavasha*, and *sreka-parṇa*, which have a well-known form, should be obtained in accordance with a definite juxtaposition or association of ideas; and these words should be taken in the manner in which they have been formed[53].

In order to get the real meaning of the word *adhṛgu*, we should find out the purpose for which it is used[54].

We cannot understand the principal idea from a casual expression; but where an expression is meant to serve some higher purpose, its meaning in connection with the latter should be accepted. In the case of the word *dhāraṇa*, we should take it to refer to a higher purpose[55]; and if the text refers to the idea of aiming at action, the meaning of other words should have a bearing on action.

A thing should not be said to have appeared (or to exist) if we are told that its time has not arrived.

When we see a gift of food being prepared on the fire, we are confirmed in our belief that it is meant to be eaten; and so it may be compared to honey and water.

Thus, where the correct formation of words is not possible (or we are unable to divide words into parts), we may have language of this kind; and the use of it arises from inability to divide words into parts.

If a thing is not suitable for writing or teaching, it should be deemed to be something that is contrary to the law of life (Dharma); and in such a case we shall find that there is no proper connection between the different parts of the text; and the whole arrangement of words would be irregular. Except for this, there should always be some explanatory reference or translation of meaning somewhere in the text, to indicate what the real meaning is; for the prohibition of knowledge would not be proper in such cases.

If it is necessary to give up this method of interpretation, —even where it is possible to apply it, for we can divide words into parts—we should give it up where its application is expressly prohibited. Otherwise, on principle, we should apply it without reserve, as freely as if we had to go across and get at the thing (correct meaning). This rigid practice in connection with the application or otherwise of this method of interpretation follows a certain law, as in the case of food[56].

Control of Desires: How Described

रसप्रतिषेधो वा पुरुषधर्मत्वात्॥४०॥

अभ्युदये दोहापनयः स्वधर्मा स्यात्प्रवृत्तत्वात्॥४१॥
शृतोपदेशाच्च॥४२॥
अपनयो वार्थान्तरे विधानाच्च रुपयोवत्॥४३॥
लक्षणार्था[1] शृतश्रुतिः॥४४॥

(Desires are of many kinds, and) we are required to restrain them, because that is the law of a man's life. This restraint should specially be exercised in a state of prosperity, because there is then a natural tendency to indulgence. Indeed, we have to exer cise restraint even in the case of eating cooked food or boiled milk; and this is expressed by means of the word *apanaya* (which means "taking away"), and its idea should be understood in the light of the statement of particulars in the text, where it is said to be like a pot of milk (for carrying it away); while the expression "boiled milk" is for the sake of illustration[57].

Result of this Method of Interpretation

श्रयणानां त्वपूर्वत्वात्प्रदानार्थे विधानं स्यात्॥४५॥
गुणो वा श्रयणार्थत्वात्॥४६॥
अनिर्देशाच्च॥४७॥

---

1. इदं सूत्रं वृत्तिग्रन्थ नास्ति, भाष्ये त्वस्ति।

श्रुतेश्च तत्प्रधानत्वात्॥४८॥
अर्थवादश्च तदर्थवत्॥४९॥
संस्कार प्रति भावाच्च तस्मादन्यप्रधानम्॥५०॥
पर्यग्निकृतानामुत्सर्गे तादर्थ्यमुपधानवत्॥५१॥
शेषप्रतिषेधो वाऽर्थाभावादिडान्तवत्॥५२॥
पूर्ववत्त्वाच्च शब्दस्य संस्थापयतीति चाप्रवृत्ते नोपनद्यते॥५३॥

This method of interpretation means a new approach to the Vedas; and whenever we have recourse to it, we should accept the new meaning only when it has something worthwhile to teach; and the division of words into parts is intended for that purpose; and we need to resort to it when there is nothing else to guide us. Indeed, the value of the *śruti* arises from the chief importance of this method; and the explanation of the meaning of the text is intended to serve this purpose (or to give us something of real value). We make use of the correct formation of words (by means of their division into parts), in order to get sense out of the text; and when we do so, we get other things of importance out of it too. For instance, there is an expression which means "encircled with *Agni* or fire", but it makes little sense in that form; whereas if we apply the general rule of interpretation, we find that it has a meaning full of excellent sense[58]. If, however, we are unable to get a proper meaning by means of this method, we shall find that we do not get any meaning at all; or if we do, the result would be self-contradictory, as in the case of the word *iḍānta*, which has no meaning at all.[59] Indeed, as each word is connected with the one that precedes it, we cannot say that it is complete in itself; and we actually find that it is not so.

Belief in Action

प्रवृत्ते[1]र्यज्ञहेतुत्वात्प्रतिषेधे संस्काराणामकर्म स्यात्तत्कारितत्वाद्यथा प्रयाजप्रतिषेधे ग्रहणमाज्यस्य॥५४॥
क्रिया वा स्यादवच्छेदादकर्म सर्वहानं स्यात्॥५५॥

---

1. इदं सूत्रं वृत्तिग्रन्थ नास्ति।

(But we can understand the real meaning of the text only if we admit the necessity of action; for) action is the basis of all sacrifice[60]; and if we deny the necessity of action, we might just as well give up all attempts at finding out the real meaning of the text by means of the proper formation of words (or their division into parts). If we do so (deny the necessity of action), it would be as futile to try to understand the text as to undertake a subsequent sacrifice (or a sacrifice with clarified butter) without performing a previous one.[61] Action is the distinguishing attribute of all things; and if we deny action, it would mean the end (or destruction) of everything.

Ājya

आज्यसंस्था प्रतिनिधिः स्याद् द्रव्योत्सर्गात्॥५६॥
समाप्तिवचनात्॥५७॥

When we get the word *ājya* in the text, we should understand that it is a substitute for something else; and we shall know what that is when we cast away the "substance" (that it commonly means); and understand it completely[62].

Action and its Renunciation

चोदना वा कर्मोत्सर्गादन्यैः स्यादविशिष्टत्वात्॥५८॥
अनिज्यां च वनस्पतेः; प्रसिद्धाऽन्तेन दर्शयति॥५९॥
संस्था तद्देवतात्वात् स्यात्॥६०॥

With regard to action, the rule is that when one action is suspended, we have to resort to another, for there is no essential difference between them. So far as the idea of the negation of action (or sacrifice) is concerned, it is expressed in terms of forest trees; but its proper place is at the end.[63] On the other hand, the form of anything associated with the idea of sacrifice corresponds to the state of a god (godhead)[64].

NOTES

1. This means that the fruit or result of an action performed as a sacrifice is the purification of the doer of the deed. There are a number of references to this idea in the *Bhāgāvad Gītā*. All action makes for bondage, except

that performed as a sacrifice; and those who partake of the remnants of sacrifice are freed from sin (BhG. III, 9, 13). There are many kinds of sacrifices; but the best is the sacrifice (or proper use) of knowledge,—for all action is made complete in knowledge (BhG. IV, 24-33); and it is by means of knowledge that a person can cross over all evil, for there is nothing in the world which can purify like knowledge (BhG. IV, 36-38).

2. The gods represent the great forces of Nature working according to the law of sacrifice,—that is, intelligently and for the well-being of all; while the opposite idea of Nature,—that it makes for sorrow, evil and death, is represented by the "demons" or *Asuras*; and the conflict between the two, as described in the sacred books, is the conflict between these two points of view, and the systems of thought based on them.
   Acting like a god would therefore signify action as a sacrifice or perfect action like that of a great good force of Nature, like the sun, moon, etc.
3. A reference to a guest in the sacred books is sometimes meant to illustrate the idea of sacrifice; for it is obligatory to be kind and considerate to a guest; and that is the basis of action conceived as a sacrifice.
4. A number of words used in the sacred books are quite new.
5 We have explained that there are three ways of reading the *Vedas*, —singing aloud, silent recitation or recitation in low tone, and normal reading. Of these the first indicates that the form of words should be changed, for that is what we do in singing; the second, the opposite of this, indicates that there should be no change; while in the third, we can do as we think appropriate.
6. *Agni* refers to the intellect, and the full moon to the full function of the mind when it is engaged in action. This *Sūtra* tells us that when the intellect desires anything intensely, it becomes just like the mind when it acts. We get the same idea in the *Mahābhārata*, where we are told that when the intellect desires anything, it is called the mind (*Sānti* P. XII, cxciv, 20).
7. This is the same thing as saying that when the intellect desires anything, it is called the mind.
8. The reference to husband and wife in the text signifies the relation subsisting between the intellect and the other faculties of man,—his mind and the senses; and is meant to illustrate their idea. It must not, therefore, be taken in its literal sense, as referring to the actual relationship of husband and wife. Indeed, we have been told that man includes a woman too; and the precedence given to the "husband" does not necessarily belong to a man unless he is really the best.
9. The word in the text is *sāmidhenī*, meaning "a verse recited when the sacrificial fire is kindled". As fire refers to the intellect, the "kindling of fire" would refer to the function of the intellect.

10. *Sarasvatī* is said to be the name of a river; and, as water symbolises Nature, and so does a woman, she is represented as a woman. Indeed, this is the idea of all goddesses in sacred literature: they represent *Prakṛti* and are described as women. The gods too refer to Nature, but with special reference to the law of sacrifice, with which the goddesses are only indirectly concerned.
11. To personify an idea or to represent it as an animal or a man is the simplest and the briefest way of describing it. It is perhaps also the best.
12. The special reference in the *śrūti* would indicate that these hymns have to be sung aloud, implying that the form of words used in them has to be changed.
13. We have already explained that the recitation of hymns in a low tone,—befng the opposite of singing—signifies that the form of words has not to be changed, and we should take them as they are.
14. The *Mīmāṁsā* tells us that the *Sāma* Veda deals with the problem of all living creatures; and, as some of this would be secret knowledge, the words used are under a "disguise", and we need to change their form to understand their real meaning. That is the important reason why this method has been adopted.
15. A sacrifice is a good and intelligent action; and eating cooked food is such a good and intelligent action on the part of man; and so it is symbolic of the idea of sacrifice. On the other hand giving up cooked food, and living on the produce of the forest is symbolic of renunciation of action; and this has already been explained.
16. We have explained that we can get the meaning of the word Agni as intellect, associated with the mind and the senses, by dividing it into parts.
17. The text has the word *grahaṇa*, which means "the hand"; and it is an instrument of action.
18. We are able to get this meaning because of the correct formation of words or the application of rules of grammar in connection with their compounding. But a subsequent *Sūtra* tells us that the cause of this form of composition is that the properties of objects, which are closely connected with one another, should be properly understood (Sūt. 40); and that is done by means of the meaning of each part of a word.
19. This may be illustrated by means of a name,—say *Kṛṣṇa*. We can divide it into K, ṛ, ṣ, ṇa, and have to take the meaning of each letter one after the other. So too with regard to other names. (*Cf.* p. 185, n.).
20. *Pragātha* is the name of a stanza. The eighth *Maṇḍala* of the *Ṛg Veda* contains a number of these stanzas.
21. The *Mīmāṁsā* tells us quite clearly that a number of names used in the text have been newly coined for this purpose. Indeed, it would be impossible to have this form of composition without it.

22. The hymns of the *Sāma Veda* have been specially mentioned because it is necessary to change the form of words used in them. This, as has already been explained, is indicated by their having to be sung.

23. The new and the full moon do not express the idea of Time. As has already been explained, the moon refers to the mind; and so the new moon is the birth or the earliest function of the mind as desire; while the full moon represents its association with action.

24. *Agni* refers to the intellect; and the perception of Time, as has already been explained, is purely intellectual. Hence, it may be argued that Time should be represented in the same manner as *Agni*,—that is, as a god.

25. The *Mīmāṁsā* explains that Time cannot be represented as a god, because a god represents the great forces of Nature acting in accordance with the law of sacrifice,—that is, as creating and sustaining life. But Time cannot always be understood in this light,—for it is often believed to be a great destructive force: hence it cannot be represented as a god.

It may be of interest to observe that the *Bhāgāvad Gītā* describes *Kṛṣṇa* (God) as revealing himself to Arjuṇa in the form of Time; but the latter is unable to bear the sight (BhG. XI, 15-46).

Time, in the sacred books, is often represented as a Serpent; and the word *Kāla* means Time as well as a poisonous serpent. This is the idea of *Kālīya*, the serpent, subjugated by *Kṛṣṇa* in the story of the Bhāgavat *Purāṇa*; and it would be explained in its proper place. The association of Time with the idea of a serpent has also a special significance of its own, and is not merely due to the fact that some serpents are deadly, and so is Time believed to be. The ancients believed that Time is part of the energy of the Sun,—a radiation, which has the form of a wave, and could best be represented as a Serpent-wave, or a Serpent. This has been explained at some length elsewhere (MM. I, 107-118).

It may be of interest to observe that *Vṛtra*, who is described in the Vedas as a serpent, conforms to the same idea (*Cf.* MM. I, 304-3,10).

26. It may be argued that Time should be represented as a god at least at the beginning of things,—when life is created; for then at least it cannot be regarded as destructive. The answer to this is that at that stage we cannot conceive of Time at all; and so it cannot be personified in any form,—even as a god. But when life begins, Time begins to act upon things, and cannot be acted upon by anything itself.

27. When we divide a word into parts to understand its real meaning, it makes no difference whether we begin with the first letter or syllable and proceed, step by step, to the last,—or begin with the last and go back, step by

step, to the first; for all these are symbols, with definite meanings; and when they are brought together in a word or name, it means that certain ideas or substances are connected together in a certain way. For instance, we may divide the word *Kṛṣṇa* into K, ṛ, ṣ, ṇa; and it would make little difference to the idea whether we begin with and end with ṇa, or vice *versa*. In some cases, however, there is a definite advantage in beginning from the one or the other end; but, on the whole, there is little substantial change in the idea. In the case of *Kṛṣṇa* it would clarify the idea if we begin with K, for it gives us the idea of Nature; so that we get the idea of God, beginning with Nature and ending in the supreme Intellect; and that is what *Kṛṣṇa* really signifies.

28. This *Sūtra* does not occur in some texts. The point of this is that when we see through this "disguise" of words, we understand not only the real idea of a thing, but also its cause.

29. A "disguise" does not refer only to the division of words into parts. The meaning of certain words has been specially defined, and they have to be taken as they are, and are not to be divided into parts: yet they too are under a "disguise", which is "pierced" when we take them as defined.

30. This *Sūtra* does not occur in some texts; but it clarifies the idea of the preceding one. We understand a thing as being free from defect only when we refer it to our own desires: that is, when we like a thing without any reservation, it appears to us to be so. Similarly, the new meaning would appear to be free from defect when we like it.

31. This *Sūtra* does not occur in some texts. The point is that, if the original meaning appears to be good enough, but the new one is better, we should accept the latter, for it is doubly good, or a double sacrifice. We have already explained that a sacrifice is a good and intelligent act.

32. *Dyu* and *Pṛthivī*., commonly spoken of as *Dyāva-Pṛthivī*, are said to refer to Heaven and Earth. But their meaning can be understood from the "sounds" or letters which compose their names, when it would be found to refer to the senses of knowledge and action (See MM. I, 358-36i).

33. The "new" expression does not refer to newly coined words, made to express new ideas, to which the *Mīmāṁsā* has referred a number of times. The "new" expressions in the present *Sūtra* refer to words used only once and not repeated again.

34. *Adhrigu* is the name of a formula concluding with an invocation of *Agni*. As *Agni* refers to the intellect, and *Soma* to the mind, "the idea of *adhrigu* in what relates to a Soma sacrifice" means the use of the intellect in connection with the function of the mind; and we have seen how closely allied the two can be. The next *Sūtra* tells us that we should not divide the

word *adhrigu* to get its real meaning, but substitute one expression for another,—the function of the intellect for adhrigu, and"the mind for *Soma*, when we shall understand what it means.

35. We have been told that the form of certain words should not be changed; but this rule does not apply to the word *tvach*, which means ordinarily "skin". If that does not make sense, we are asked to divide it into parts in the manner explained.

36. The "lord of sacrifice" is really the soul; and it is for this reason that is called the "lord of the gods", for the soul alone can master the great forces of Nature, to which the gods refer. Indeed, even as the *Sāṅkhya* tells us, Nature itself acts for the sake of the soul, and so is subordinate to it.

37. We are required to accept the meaning of the word *medha-pati* or "the lord of sacrifice" in the manner explained, that is, as the soul.

38. The word *svāmī* or "master" also refers to the soul; and so it is associated with the idea of the gods in the same manner as *medha-pati*, and for the same reason.

39. The *Mīmāṁsā* tells us that we can get the meaning of "master" or soul from the word *svāmīn* (or *svāmī*) itself, if we divide it into parts. There are a number of ways of this division; and we can derive the word from *sva*, which means "the soul". It may also be derived from *sva* and in,—when the meaning would be "master of property". Thus we find that both the meanings,—master as well as soul, are contained in the word itself.

40. This is how the idea of the principal gods of the Vedas has been explained in another place (MM. I, Chapter IX).

41. The gods of the Vedas represent the great forces of Nature; but while these forces can be separated, there is also a close inherent connection between them. The same, says the *Mīmāṁsā*, should be the case with the gods.

42. The *Mīmāṁsā* tells us that if we take the number twenty-six as a whole number, it would not convey any idea to us. Nor can we understand anything if we count one, two, three, etc., and go up to twenty-six; nor yet if we divide the word used in the text into its parts.

43. We have to adopt some other method of finding out the real meaning of this number; but it is necessary that, when we fix upon the meaning, it should include all the numbers, from one to twenty-six.

44. The importance of this number may be compared to the ribs of an animal,—and it is said that the ox has twenty-six ribs. These ribs function collectively, and cannot be separated; and we have to use our intellect to understand the idea of the number twenty-six in the same manner.

45. As these numbers cannot be combined, we might compare them to the

status of a wife, who is associated with her husband, and vet has a personality of her own.

The number twenty-six refers to the idea of God in relation to all that is contained in Nature as well as the soul. The *Sāṅkhya* tells us of its twenty-four topics,—(1) unmanifest *Prakṛti*, (2-4) intellect, *ahaṅkāra*, and the mind; (5-14) the five great "elements" and their respective properties; and (15-24) the ten, senses of knowledge and action. The *puruṣa* or the individual soul, it says, is the twenty-fifth (SS. I, 61). Above all this is the idea of the Supreme *Puruṣa* or God, and that is represented by the number twenty-six.

46. The number 26 refers to several categories that go to make up the idea of Nature, soul, and God. We can thus take them together as well as separately; and they may be said to assist one another. If, therefore, there is a precedent for the comparison, we may refer them to the idea of the institutor of a sacrifice, who engages a priest to assist him.

47. But if there is no such precedent, we may compare them to a husband and wife.

The *Mīmāṁsā* tells us that the idea of the number twenty-six has been represented in various ways: in terms of the ribs of an animal, of the relation between husband and wife, and between the institutor of a sacrifice and the priests who assist him.

We have already explained that the relation between husband and wife corresponds to that between *Puruṣa* and *Prakṛti* (or God and Nature)" and the "institutor of the sacrifice" is the soul, and the "priests" he employs are the different faculties of man,—his intellect, *ahaṅkāra*, mind, and the senses. The number twenty-six refers to all these.

48. The total—twenty-six—is important, because it refers to God, soul, and all that is included in Nature or *Prakṛti*; and when we understand what it signifies, it would make no change in the idea if we add its parts together. These, as has already been explained, are the senses, the "elements" and their properties, mind, *ahaṅkāra* and the intellect, together with the idea of the unmanifest *Prakṛti*, soul, and God.

49. When the word *paśu*, meaning "an animal" occurs in connection with the idea of "ribs", we should take it that they refer to the ribs of an animal; not otherwise. For instance, when it is said that an ox has 26 ribs, we should take it that an animal is meant; but if there is only a general mention of these ribs, we should take it that they have some other meaning.

50. We have explained that the number twenty-four refers to Nature or *Prakrit*, as consisting of (1) the Unmanifest, (2-4) intellect, *ahaṅkāra* and the mind; (5-14) the five great "elements" and their respective properties; and (15-24) the ten senses of knowledge and, action. If to these we add the ten

functions of the ten senses, we get the number thirty-four, as completing still more fully the idea of Nature or *Prakṛti*.

The addition of the ten functions of the ten senses is by no means arbitrary, for we have a reference to the ribs of a horse which, as the *Upaniṣads* and the *Mīmāṁsā* both tell us (X, iii, 65-68) refers to the senses; and so in dealing with the idea of this number we have to take into special consideration the significance attaching to the horse, who is said to have thirty-four ribs.

51. But the *Mīmāṁsā* tells us that we can make a change in the details of this idea, even as we do in the case of water or food. Their essence remains the same; and any change we make can refer only to details.

Now the sacred books tell us that there are thirty-three gods, and their creator is *Prajāpati*, the thirty-fourth; and all this should refer to Nature or *Prakṛti*, for that is the general significance of the number thirty-four; and we have seen that the gods refer to the great forms and forces of Nature. It would therefore be of interest to consider how this number is made up. The sacred books tell us that this number is made up of twelve *Adityas*, eleven *Rudras*, eight *Vasus*, with *Dyāvā-Pṛthivī* or the two Aśvins making a total of thirty-three. These should accordingly refer to the thirty-three manifest forms of Nature.

Now an *Āditya* is the name of the sun; and the twelve *Ādityas* are said to refer to the sun in the twelve months of the year. But the sun is also a symbol of the intellect, as we have seen in the case of *Agni*; and so the twelve *Ādityas* would refer to the function of the intellect, as including itself, *ahaṅkāra* or the I-as-an-actor, and the elements- and their properties.

With regard to the eleven *Rudras*, we have seen that the number eleven refers to the function of the mind, as including itself and the ten senses. The name *Rudra* also refers to the mind, for it is a name of *Śiva*, who refers to it.

The word *Vasu—Va, su* means literally "(*su*) born of (*va*) Nature"; and so the eight *Vasus* refer to the eight divisions of *Prakṛti*, —intellect, *ahaṅkāra*, mind, and the five great "elements"—mentioned in the *Bhāgāvad* Gītā (BhG. VII, 4). There is a reference to the eight *Vasus* in the story of the *Mahābhārata*, and there too their idea is the same.

We have observed that *Dyāvā-Pṛthivī* refers to the senses of knowledge and action, and so do the two Aśvins, or horses, as they are called.

Thus we see that the number thirty-three refers to the manifest forms of Nature; and whatever variations there are do not affect the main idea. The thirty-fourth, *Prajāpati*, may be said to be the creator of all this; but his idea does not correspond to that of a moral creator of the universe. That is developed later in the ideas of *Śiva* and *Viṣṇu*; and *Śiva* means the good, and *Viṣṇu* is the supporter of life.

52. We have explained that the different entities included in this number are all connected with one another. Indeed, the "elements" and their properties, and the senses and their functions can all be integrated; while with regard to the rest, the intellect is said to be the first manifest form of *Prakṛti*, and all the rest arise out it in order: *ahaṅkāra* from the intellect, the mind from *ahaṅkāra*, and so on.
53. We can get the real meaning of these words in accordance with this method of interpretation: they have either to be divided into parts, or have a specially defined meaning. According to this s"*yena* would refer to Nature, which fills us with desire; *salā* is an argument relating to the functions of the ten senses; *Kaśyapa* symbolises a withdrawal of the senses from their objects; *kavaṣa* signifies protection from the evil effects of desire; and *śrekaparṇa* the relation of the universe to one creator.
54. *Adhrigu* refers to the intellect, as has already been explained.
55. The word *dhāraṇa* has a number of meanings,—holding, preserving, restraining, immovable concentration of the mind". The last, being the highest, should be accepted. In the case of other words, the meaning bearing on action should be preferred.
56. There can be rigid rules in connection with eating food,—what should or should not be eaten. Even so there are rules in comnention with this method of interpretation, as to when it should or should not be applied.
57. The word *apanaya* means "taking away; bad policy"; and its use implies that certain desires should be "taken away" or shunned; and so it is like a pot for "carrying away" milk, which is an object of desire. It is in this manner that the idea of restraint is illustrated.
58. As *Agni* refers to intelligence, "encircled with *Agni*" means full intelligence; and that makes excellent sense.
59. There is no word like iḍānta in the dictionary.
60. *Cf.* BhG. III, 14.
61. Unless we understand the law of action, we cannot understand the Vedas, even as we cannot undertake a subsequent sacrifice (or action) without a preceding one.

    The word in the text is *ājya*, which commonly means "clarified butter poured over the sacrificial fire"; but, as has already been explained, it really signifies goodness. The point then would be that we cannot do a good deed unless we know how to act.
62. We have already explained that the meaning of the word *ājya* has to be derived from *aja—a-ja—*when it would mean "(*a*) not (*ja*) poison" or "(a) like (*ja*) enjoyment". It accordingly refers to action that is not evil, and may even give joy.
63. The idea of renunciation of action is represented in terms of life in the

forest; and there are innumerable references to it in the sacred books. But this is the last stage of our life, says the *Mīmāṁsā*, when alone renunciation has a meaning.

63. We have already explained that the idea of sacrifice is associated with that of a god. Indeed, that is the literal meaning of the word *Deva,—da,i,va—* "(da) sacrifice (*j*) associated with (*va*) Nature": or Nature governed by the law of sacrifice.

CHAPTER - X

THE METHOD OF INTERPRETATION : DESIRE, PURPOSE AND ACTION

PART I

Introduction

The special characteristic of this explanation is that it enables us to understand the working of the laws of Nature and the great forces associated with them,—which are otherwise unintelligible.

Desire is an inseparable attribute of the mind; and once it begins, it goes on without end, expressing itself in newer and newer forms, and beginning its course each time afresh. It is a precursor to action; and may be compared to a preliminary sacrifice.

All action is meant to secure some purpose, and it involves an exercise of the intellect. But this applies to animate and not inanimate objects.

All this is given in the sacred books, and we can understand it if we interpret them aright. We shall then find that they refer to the law of action, and that the idea of a preliminary sacrifice fits into that of desire.

In this manner we can explain the idea of *ājya* as well as *prayāja*. The word *paśu* is self-explanatory; but we have to change the form of the word *kapāla* to understand its meaning.

So far as the planets are concerned, each name has its own special meaning, and they refer to the great forces of

Nature. But if we divide these words into parts, we should make use of our knowledge to understand their idea.

When we find that the meaning of the text is self-contradictory, we should understand that it is possible to get its correct idea by changing the form of words; but it is necessary to have knowledge to be able to do so, for different words have to be treated in different ways. We do not give any meaning we like to a word, and have often a good reason for doing so.

Each action is meant to secure an object, for which necessary means have to be provided. There must also be a sequence of cause and effect; and it is in this manner that we get the meaning of an obscure word by reducing it to its rudimentary form.

Special Characteristic of this Explanation

विधेः प्रकरणान्तरेऽतिदेशात्सर्वकर्म स्यात्॥१॥
अपि वाऽभिधानसंस्कारद्रव्यमर्थे क्रियते तादर्थ्यात्॥२॥
तेषामप्रत्यक्षशिष्टत्वात॥३॥

The special characteristic of this explanation is that when we substitute one meaning for another, we come to know the working of the laws of Nature, and the association together of the great elemental substances of which it consists; for all this has been taught in an indirect manner.

Desire and Mind: A Precursor to Action

इष्टिराम्भसंयोगादङ्गभतान्निवर्तेतारम्भस्य प्रधानसंयोगात्॥४।
प्रधानाच्चान्यसंयुक्तात्सर्वारम्भन्निवर्तेतानङ्गत्वात्॥५॥
तस्यां तु स्यात्प्रयाजवत्॥६॥
न वाऽङ्गभूतत्वात्॥७॥
एकवाक्यत्वाच्च॥८॥

Desire is an attribute of the mind, and is associated with it from the beginning; and when once it begins its course, it goes on, expressing itself in newer and newer forms. It is very important to understand this; for such is the nature of the mind that, when desire seeks a new object, it begins its course every time afresh. (Desire is a precursor to action, and) may be compared to a preliminary sacrifice[1],—though the latter may not have the same connection with the mind[2]; and there is unanimity of opinion on the point.

Object of Action

कर्म च द्रव्यसंयोगार्थमर्थाभावान्निवर्तेत; तादर्थ्यं श्रुतिसंयोगात्॥९॥

स्थाणौ तु देशमात्रत्वादनिवृत्तिः प्रतीयेत॥१०॥

All action is meant to secure some object, and there can be no action without some purpose or aim; and the latter arises because of its connection with the intellect.[3] But this does not apply to inanimate objects like a pillar or a stump of a tree, which is fixed in one place.

The Sacred Books, and how to Understand Them

अपि वा शेषभूतत्वात्संस्कारः प्रतीयेत॥११॥

समाख्यानं च तद्वत्॥१२॥

मन्त्रवर्णश्च तद्वत्॥१३॥

प्रयाजे च तन्न्यायत्वात्॥१४॥

लिङ्गदर्शनाच्च॥१५॥

तथाऽऽज्यभागाग्निरपीति चेत्॥१६॥

व्यपदेशाद्देवतान्तरम्॥१७॥

समत्वाच्च॥१८॥

(All this is described in the sacred books, and we can understand it if we interpret them a*r*ight). But it is only when something is obscure or is left unexplained, that we should change the form of words in order to understand their meaning; and we shall find that the names are like that, because the outward form of the *Mantras* (or hymns) is like that; and so the idea of *prayāja* (a preliminary sacrifice) would fit into the narrative, when we see through the "disguised" form of the word[4].

It is possible to hold that we should be able to get the

meaning of the word *ājya*, and its connection with *Agni* in the same manner;[5] and that should give us its connection with some force of Nature (deity)[6], because of the similarity of action between the two.

Paśu

पशावपीति चेत्॥१९॥
न वद्भूतवचनात्॥२०॥
लिङ्गदर्शनाच्च॥२१॥

This, however, does not apply to the word *paśu*, for its meaning is obtained from the word itself; though we can get it by piercing through its "disguise" as well[7].

Kapāla

गुणो वा स्यात्कपालवद्गुणभूत विकाराच्च॥२२॥
अपि वा शेषभूतत्वात्तत्संस्कारः प्रतीयेत; स्वाहाकारवदङ्गानामर्थ-संयागात्॥२३॥
व्यृद्धवचनं च विप्रतिपत्तौ तद्वर्थत्वात्॥२४॥
गुणेपीति चेत्॥२५॥
नासंहानात्कपालवत्॥२६॥

But in the case of the word *kapāla*, it is necessary to change its form and divide it into parts[8]; for its meaning is obscure, and leaves something to be explained; and if we divide it into parts, we shall get a proper meaning in the same manner as we do in the case of the word *svāhā*.[9] That is the object of an imperfect or obscure word, for it makes the sense self-contradictory. We cannot say that the defect persists even after a word has been divided into parts; for we find that it disappears, as in the case of the word *kapāla*.

Planets

ग्रहाणां च सम्प्रतिपत्तौ तद्वचनं तदर्थत्वात्॥२७॥
ग्रहाभावे तद्वचनम्॥२८॥
देवतायाश्च हेतुत्वे प्रसिद्धं तेन दर्शयति॥२९॥
अविरुद्धोपपत्तिरर्थापत्तेः; श्रुतवद् गुणभूतविकारः स्यात्॥३०॥

So far as the planets are concerned, each particular name has a particular meaning, so that we can understand their ideas properly[10]. Where, however, the name of a planet is not mentioned, there is always some other word, with a special meaning, to convey its idea; and, as it refers to a great force of Nature (deity), the whole idea is properly arranged in this way. There is no inconsistency between the idea of a planet and a great force of Nature (deity), because we are able to infer that a planet is really such a force; and if, in this case, we change the form of a word and divide it into parts, we should make use of our knowledge to get its meaning.

When to Change the Form of a Word

स द्व्यर्थः स्यादुभयोः श्रुतिभूतत्वाद्विप्रतिपत्तौ; तादर्थ्याद्विकारत्व मुक्तं; तस्यार्थवादत्वम्॥३१॥
विप्रतिपत्तौ तासामाख्याविकारः स्यात्॥३२॥
अभ्यासो वा प्रयाजवदेकदेशाऽन्यदेवत्यः॥३३॥
चरुर्हविर्विकारः स्यादिज्यासंयोगात्॥३४॥
प्रसिद्धग्रहणत्वाच्च॥३५॥
ओदनो वाऽन्नसंयोगात्॥३६॥
न द्व्यर्थत्वात्॥३७॥
कपालविकारो वा विशयेऽर्थोपपत्तिभ्याम्॥३८॥
गुणमुख्यविशेषाच्च॥३९॥
तच्छ्रुतौ चान्यहविष्ट्वात्॥४०॥
लिङ्गदर्शनाच्च॥४१॥
ओदनो वा प्रयुक्तत्वात्॥४२॥
अपूर्वव्यपदेशाच्च॥४३॥
तथा च लिङ्गदर्शनम्॥४४॥

When we find that the text is self-contradictory, we should understand that there is a second meaning too; and that is the reason for the change of form of words, for it enables us to explain the real meaning of the text. Indeed, where the text is self-contradictory, the form of names should be changed.

In certain cases, however, we may have to add something to find out the real meaning of an expression, as, for instance, in the case of the word *prayāja*,[11]—for each part of a word may refer to a different force of Nature. Similarly, the word *caru* should be regarded as a variation of *havis*, because of its connection with sacrifice;[12] and we shall find that it is so when we arrange it properly and understand it aright. Similarly, the word *odana* is a variation of *anna*, because it is connected with it;[13] but in this case there are no two meanings of the words[14].

But in the case of the word *kapāla* a doubt arises within us as to the propriety of its meaning, and we consider it necessary to change its form[15]; and that, because of the special characteristics of its principal part, is true of *caru* too; but we can understand it because of its being regarded as another havis or burnt offering, and also by seeing through its "disguise"[16].

On the other hand the meaning of the word *odana* ("boiled rice") is suitable in itself[17]; but the form of even this word may have to be changed if it is used in connection with some extraordinary statement; and it is in this manner that we see through the "disguise" of words.

Cases of "Disguise"

स कपाले प्रकृत्या स्यादन्यस्य चाश्रुतित्वत्॥४५॥
एकस्मिन्वा विप्रतिषेधात्॥४६॥

We see that the word *kapāla* has this "disguise" when we consider its meaning in its original form; while in the case of other words this arises from our inability to understand them; and in some cases it may also arise from contradiction[18].

Reason for a Meaning

न वाऽर्थान्तरसंयोगादपूपे; पाकसंयुक्तं धरणार्थं चरौ भवति; तत्रार्थात्पात्रलाभः स्यादनियमोऽविशेषात्॥४७॥
चरौ वा लिङ्गदर्शनात्॥४८॥

तस्मिन्पेषणमनर्थलोपात्स्यात्॥४९॥
अक्रिया वा अपूपहेतुत्वात्॥५०॥

But even though a word may have another meaning, (it cannot be anything we choose to call it: for instance,) we cannot say that *kapāla* means "a cake of flour". (There must be a reason for giving a a certain meaning to a word: for instance,) the word charu means "a pot or vessel," because it is connected with "drinking", and a vessel or pot can hold a liquid; and in the absence of this distinction we would always be uncertain about its idea[19]. But in the case of the word *caru*,we can get its real meaning by piercing through its "disguise"; and if we break it up into parts, we shall do away with all that is meaningless in its original form; because so long as we associate it with the idea of eating (a cake of flour), we cannot get the idea of action out of it[20].

Action, Object, and Means

पिण्डार्थत्वाच्च संयवनम्॥५१॥
संवपनं च तादर्थ्यात्॥५२॥
सन्तापनमधः श्रपणात्॥५३॥
उपधानं च तादर्थ्यात्॥५४॥

(Each action is meant to secrte some object, for which necessary means must be provided: for instance,) if we wish to make a round mass of things, we must mix them together, and in order to min them together and in order to mix them together, we must "throw"or "pour" them into one another. Even so, if we eish to cook anything, we need to provide fire underneath, and a cover or lid on top.

Sequence of Cause and Effect

पृथुश्लक्ष्णे चाऽनपूपत्वात्॥५५॥
अभ्यूहश्चोपरिपाकार्थत्वात्॥५६॥
तथा च ज्वलनम्॥५७॥
व्युद्धृत्याऽऽसादनं च प्रकृतावश्रुतित्वात्॥५८॥

(Further, there must be a sequence or cause and effect:

for instance,) we cannot get the idea of what is very large or very small from a cake of flour, because the argument has nothing to do with the desire for eating. Similarly we cannot get the idea of shining or blazing out of it. Thus, when the meaning of a word is indistinct or obscure, we can get its real idea by reducing it to its rudimentary form.

PART II

THE METHOD OF INTERPRETATION : LIFE AND ACTION

Introduction

It is necessary to understand the meaning of words in the light of their context; but in certain cases the ordinary meaning is unsuitable, and we have to find out a better one.

Action consists of parts, corresponding to which words too have been divided into parts to express their idea.

Articles of food express the idea of pleasure or satisfaction; but even these words may have to be divided into parts if necessary.

Certain words cannot be divided into parts; the meaning of some has been defined; while others have to be divided into parts to be understood.

Those who are devoted to spiritual knowledge cannot be accused of misconduct; and if we understand the language of the text properly, we shall find that they have acted properly all the time. But words should be divided into parts only when their common meaning is not satisfactory.

Certain ideas are associated with certain objects; and it is necessary to know them in order to understand the real meaning of the text.

We should not act under the urge of desire; but the desires of those who make sacrifices should be satisfied.

All action is performed by the living: the action associated with the dead refers to their funeral rites.

Health is necessary to life, and the idea can easily be understood; but in certain cases it may be necessary to divide words into parts to get it.

Actions meant for the sake of Dharma should always be performed. If we are obliged to omit any, they should be secondary, and not principal actions. If, however, we omit a small portion of such actions, we should not be troubled about it.

There can be no extinction of action, because some part of it will always remain; and thought is closely allied to action. This is easy to understand; and in this case it is not necessary to reduce words to their rudimentary form to understand their meaning.

But in the case of certain words relating to fundamental objects, it is necessary to divide them into parts to understand their meaning. In certain other cases, however, we may have to adopt a different course.

We sometimes find that the latter part of a statement contradicts an earlier one. This is intentional, and is meant to indicate that we have to divide words into parts to understand their meaning.

Meaning Depends on the Context

कृष्णलेष्वर्थलोपादपाकः स्यात्॥१॥
स्याद्वा प्रत्यक्षशिष्टत्वात्प्रदानवत्॥२॥
उपस्तरणभिघारणयोरमृतार्थत्वादकर्म स्यात्॥३॥
क्रियेत वाऽर्थवादत्वात्तयोः संसर्ग हेतुत्वात्॥४॥
अकर्म वा चतुर्भिराप्तिवचनात्सह पूर्णं; पुनश्चतुरवत्तम्॥५॥

(We can understand the meaning of words only in the light of their context: for instance,) the word *kṛṣṇala* (meaning "a small piece of gold", does not appear to make sense, and) seems to indicate immaturity of expression; but it can have this meaning if it is clearly stated that it is used in connection with a donation or a gift.

If the words *upastaraṇa* and *abhighāraṇa* have any permanent value, their common meanings as "spreading over" and "besprinkling" cannot be of any use; and we have to find meanings of a more permanent value in order to explain them, for otherwise there would be confusion.

The word *catur* (meaning "the number four"), which appears to serve no special purpose, signifies "completeness" when understood in its exact sense; and it is for this reason that we get the word *catura* again and again (for it is the same as *catur*, but means "clever, skilful")[21].

Parts of an Action, and of a Word

क्रिया वा मुख्यावदानपरिमाणात्; सामान्यात्तद्गुणत्वम्॥६॥
तेषां चैकावदानत्वात्॥७॥
आप्तिः संख्या समानत्वात्॥८॥
सतोस्त्वाप्तिवचनं व्यर्थम्॥९॥
विल्पकस्त्वेकावदानत्वात्॥१०॥
सर्वविकारे त्वभ्यासानर्थक्यं; हविषो हीतरस्य स्यादपि वा स्विष्टकृतः स्यादितरस्यान्यायत्वात्॥११॥
अकर्मा वा संसर्गार्थनिवृत्तित्वात्, तस्मादाप्तिसमर्थत्वम्॥१२॥

Action is measured in terms of its principal achievement, but it consists of a number of parts into which it can be divided; and they all contribute to that achievement. We get the idea of numbers, because in every case they represent the parts of a principal action. Similarly, it is equally impossible to get a single word to express the idea of all the parts of such action; and it would be necessary to combine together a number of words to express the idea of but a single achievement. In any case it would be impossible to describe all the changes an action undergoes by adding together words in this manner. It may be possible to do so in the case of certain kinds of actions which relate to the idea of a sacrifice or an intelligent action; but it would be impossible to do so with regard to the rest. Indeed, the thing will not work if the meaning of each part does not blend with that of the other; (and so it is necessary to get a proper meaning of words).

Articles of Food and Drink

भक्षाणां तु प्रीत्यर्थत्वादकर्म स्यात्॥१३॥
स्याद्वा निर्धानदर्शनात्॥१४॥

So far as articles of food and drink are concerned, they signify pleasure or satisfaction; and the idea is so clear, that it would serve no useful purpose to change the form of these words to understand their meaning. But even they may have to be changed if there is no reference to a receptacle (or recipient) of food.

An Illustration

वचनं त्वाज्यभक्षस्य प्रकृतौ स्यादभागित्वात्॥१५॥
वचनं वा हिरण्यस्य प्रदानवदाज्यस्य गुणभूत्वात्॥१६॥

Thus the word *ājya-bhakṣa* (meaning, "eating or drinking clarified butter") should be taken in its original form,—as a whole expression,—because it should not be divided into parts.[22] On the other hand the meaning of the word *hiraṇya*[23] ("gold") is like the making of an offering in the fire (an intelligent action); while that of the word *ājya*[24] is obtained by dividing it into parts.

Need of Proper Understanding

एकधोपहारे सहत्वं ब्रह्मभक्षाणां, प्रकृतौ विहितत्वात्॥१७॥
सर्वत्वं च तेषामधिकारात्स्यात्।१८॥
पुरुषापनयो वा तेषामवाच्यत्वात्॥१९॥
पुरुषापनयो वा तेषामवाच्यत्वात्॥२०॥
एकार्थत्वादविभागः स्यात्॥२१॥

(It is necessary properly to understand the language of the text to know the exact idea: for instance,) those who are devoted to spiritual knowledge are for ever engaged in acts of sacrifice; and their ability to have that knowledge is tested by their acts, because sacrifice is a part of their very nature or character. Such persons should be able to attain to all that they desire as a matter of right; and it would be a calumny to say that they are guilty of misconduct in anything that they do. If, however, they are accused of misconduct, it would be found, on a proper examination of the language of the text, that they have acted suitably to the occasion.[25] (It may be necessary to divide words into parts to understand all this;) but if the words give us a single satisfactory meaning, they should not be divided into parts.

Special Terms: Dadāti

ऋत्विग्दानं धर्ममात्रार्थं स्याद्ददातिसामर्थ्यात्॥२२

(Certain ideas are expressed in a certain way, and it is necessary to understand them to know the real meaning of the text: for instance,) the gift given to the *Ṛtvij* priests has a meaning corresponding to the actions of each;[26] and we get it from the proper idea of the word *dadāti* (meaning "he gives").

Dakṣiṇā: A Purchase: Produce of Forest: Remnants of Food

परिक्रयार्थं वा कर्मसंयोगाल्लोकवत्॥२३।
दक्षिणायुक्तवचनाच्च॥२४॥
न[1] चाऽन्येनाऽऽनम्येत परिक्रयात्, कर्मणः परार्थत्वात्॥२५॥
परिक्रीतवचनाच्च॥२६॥
सनिवन्ये च भृति वचनात्॥२७॥
नैष्कर्तृकेण संस्तवात्॥२८॥
शेषभक्षाश्च तद्वत्॥२९॥
संस्कारो वा द्रव्यस्य परार्थत्वात्॥३०॥
शेषे च समत्वात्॥३१॥
स्वामिनि च दर्शनात्तत्सामान्यादितरेषां तथात्वम्॥३२॥
तथा[2] चान्यार्थदर्शनम्॥३३॥

Again, a gift implies a certain sense of satisfaction or enjoyment,—because that is the object of action, as we find among the people. It is *dakṣiṇā*, because of its appropriateness;[27] and it should not be held in low esteem because it ministers to satisfaction or enjoyment, —for all action is

1. इदं सूत्रं वृत्तिकृन्मते नास्ति।
2. न्यायमालायां इदमधिकं सूत्रम्।

performed with the object of obtaining something. It is this idea that is expressed in terms of purchasing or paying for a thing; while the acquisition of something that grows naturally in a forest is called food that has merely to be fetched; for it is obtained without doing any work, and that is the reason why it is praised.[28] The remnants of food may also be regarded in the same light[29].

Other Meanings of Remnants—(The idea of remnants may also be taken in a different way). If an object is intended for some important use, it may be described in ornate terms; but all remnants are alike. A learned man or a spiritual teacher may come to the conclusion that all things are alike; and so we may, from this, form a general notion that all things should be regarded as alike (and so they may be described in terms of remnants of food).[30] It is in this manner that we find a different meaning in the language of the text.

Honour of Ṛtvij Priests: their "Wage."

वरणमृत्विजामानमनार्थत्वात्सत्रे न स्यात्स्वकर्मत्वात्॥३४॥

परिक्रयश्च तादर्थ्यात्॥३५॥

Similarly, the honour paid to the *Ṛtvij* priests in a great *Soma* sacrifice is not for the purpose of saluting them, but is meant to express the idea of our own actions; and the payment of a "wage" is intended to show that it is in connection with *Soma* that they do so[31].

Prohibition against Action: How Described

प्रतिषेधश्च कमवत्॥३६॥

स्याद्वाप्रसर्पिकस्य धर्ममात्रत्वात्॥३७॥

The idea of prohibition against action is like that of action too; and it is expressed in terms of proceeding, as a matter of duty, to that part of the sacrificial enclosure where the fire has been extinguished[32].

Dakṣiṇā

न दक्षिण ष्टाब्दात्तस्मान्नितयानुवादः स्यात्।।३८।।

The word *dakṣiṇā* does not refer to prohibition in any case[33]; and so is constantly repeated by means of a number of synonyms.

Desire, Action and a Gift

उदवसानीयाः सत्रधर्मा स्यात्तदङ्गत्वात्तत्र दानं धर्ममात्रं स्यात्।।३९।।

There is a characteristic mark of the mind (desire) in the concluding part of an action, because the mind enters into every part of it. In the circumstances, the offer of a gift (which represents the idea of satisfaction in action) should be regarded as a matter of duty[34].

These Meanings are Defined

न त्वेतत्प्रकृतित्वाद्विभक्तचोदितत्वात्।।४०।।

तेषां तु वचनाद्द्वियज्ञवत्सहप्रयोगः स्यात्।।४१।।

We do not get these meanings by reducing words to their rudimentary form, but by means of a distinct injunction to that effect. We get them from the text itself, through the usual form of words; and there is no ambiguity or doubt, even as there is none when we speak of a double sacrifice[35].

How to Obtain the Meaning of Ṛtvij Priests

तत्रान्यानृत्विजो वृणीरन्।।४२।।

एकैकशस्त्वविप्रतिषेधात्प्रकृतेश्चैकसंयोगात्।।४३।।

In these circumstances different *Ṛtvij* priests should be selected for the grant of these "gifts"; and the meaning of each of them can, without exception, be obtained by reducing their names to their rudimentary form; and we shall find that there is only one system of connecting the parts of words with one another[36].

Dāna

कामेष्टौ च दानशब्दात्।।४४।।

वचनं वा सत्रत्वात्॥४५॥
द्वेष्ये[1] वा चोदनाद्दक्षिणापनयात्॥४६॥

When we get the word *dāna* (a gift), we should understand that it really means the attainment of an object of desire, or satisfaction or enjoyment arising out of it; and it is used in connection with the function of the mind[37] (*Soma*). There is no such satisfaction in the case of an evil deed (or the act of an enemy); and so we are told that it would be bad policy to give *dakṣiṇā*[38] (or a sacrificial fee) to an enemy.

Bone-Sacrifice

अस्थियज्ञोऽविप्रतिषेधादितरेषां स्याद्विप्रतिषेधदस्थ्नाम्॥४७॥
यावदुक्तमुपयोगः स्यात्॥४८॥

(The bone-sacrifice refers to death); and while it is necessary to perform it, it should be performed (not by the *Ṛtvij* priests, but) by others,—for they are not permitted to take part in it[39]; and all that which has been said in this connection should be regarded as appropriate.

Japa

यदि तु वचनात्तेषां जपसंस्कारमर्थलुप्तं; सेष्टि तदर्थत्वात्॥४९॥

We find from the statement of the sacred books that the consecration (or sacrifice) of *japa* (or silent repetition of a sacred name) signifies action without any (selfish) aim; and the desire for it is intended to indicate that (selflessness of action)[40].

Action with a Purpose

क्रत्वर्थं तु क्रियते गुणभूतत्वात्॥५०॥
काम्यानि तु न विद्यन्ते कामाज्ञानाद्यथेतरस्यानुच्यमानानि॥५१॥
ईहार्थाश्चाभावात्सूक्तवाकवत्॥५२॥
स्युर्वाऽर्थवादत्वात्॥५३॥

But we are also required to perform other actions,—

1. द्वेष्ये चाचोदेति न्या. मा. पाठान्तरम्।

characterised by a purpose or aim— though they would be regarded as being of a secondary importance. But actions which are prompted by personal gain,—where we do not know the exact nature of our desire —should be regarded as unsuitable, and should not be done. Where, however, there is no motive of personal gain, the object of action becomes as sweet and melodious as a well-recited hymn; and such actions should always be performed, as being worthy of all praise.

Action and Urge of Desire

नेच्छाभिधानात्तदभावादितरस्मिन्॥५४॥
स्युर्वा होतृकामाः॥५५॥
न तदाशीष्ट्वात्॥५६॥

We should not act under the urge of desire; and if we are able to eliminate it in some cases, we shall succeed in others too. But the desires of those who act in a spirit of sacrifice should be satisfied; but these desires should not be limited to blessing some particular object only[41].

Action of the Living and the Dead

सर्वस्वारस्य दिष्टगतौ, समापनं न विद्यते, कर्मणो जीवसंयोगात्॥५४॥
स्याद्वोभयोः प्रत्यक्षशिष्टत्वात्॥५५॥
गते गर्मास्थियज्ञवत्॥५६॥

All action is associated with living creatures; and no action, however small, which involves the function of the mind,[41] can be performed by the dead. It is, however, possible to think of action in connection with both the living and the dead, if there is a clear reference to that effect. But when a person dies, the action associated with him refers to his funeral rites[41].

Life and Death

जीवत्यवचनमायुराशिषस्तदर्थत्वात्॥६०॥
वचनं वा भागित्वात्प्राग्यथोक्तात्॥६१॥

If a person is alive, it should be presumed that he wishes

to keep in health; and it is not necessary to make a special mention of it, because life is meant for health (or health is essential to life). But there may be a special mention of it too; and its idea will be obtained by means of a division of words into parts in the manner already explained.

Obligatory Actions

क्रिया स्याद्धर्ममात्राणाम्॥६२॥

गुणलोपे तु[1] मुख्यस्य॥६३॥

We should always perform actions which are meant purely for the sake of Dharma (duty or righteousness). If, however, we are obliged to omit some, they should be secondary and not principal actions.

Omission of Small Things

मुष्टिलोपात्तु सङ्ख्यालोपस्तद्गुणत्वात्स्यात्॥६४॥

But if we omit a small portion of such actions, we should not think of it, for calculation depends on the quantity to be calculated (or it would be necessary to think of it if a large portion were involved).

No Extinction of Action

न निर्वापशेषत्वात्॥६५॥

सङ्ख्या तु चोनां प्रति सामान्यात्तद्विकारः; संयोगाच्च परं मुष्टेः॥६६॥

न चोदनाभिसम्बन्धात्प्रकृतौ संस्कारयोगात्॥६७॥

There can be no extinction of action, because some part of it will always remain; and if we understand this relationship, we shall find that calculation is only a modified form of quantity (or thinking is proportionate to the amount of work), for the two are equal: only the amount or quantity comes first, and thinking or calculation afterwards. If we understand this rule, it is not necessary to reduce words to their rudimentary form to understand their correct meaning.

---

1. पे च मुख्येति न्यायमालापाठः।

Meaning of Words Relating to Dravyas or Fundamental Substances

औत्पत्तिके तु द्रव्यतो विकारः स्यादकार्यत्वात्॥६८॥
नैमित्तिके तु कार्यत्वात्प्रकृतेः स्यात्तदापत्तेः॥६९॥

विप्रतिषेधे तद्वचनात्प्राकृतगुणलोपः स्यात्तेन[1] कर्मसंयोगात्॥७०॥

But in the case of words relating to the original properties of things, it is necessary to divide them into parts, according to the nature of the substance (*dravya*)[44] concerned, because they are original substances, and not produced from something else, like effect from a cause. But in the case of words which refer to occasional things, produced by some cause—since they are an effect (and not the cause), their meaning may be obtained by means of division into parts, if that is how they have been framed. In this case, however, if we find that the meaning so obtained is contradictory, we should give up the attempt to divide them into parts, and take them as they are, because that is how they have been formed to refer to action.

Idea of Contradictory Statements

परेषां प्रतिषेधः स्यात्॥७१॥
[2]प्रतिषेधाच्च॥७२॥
अर्थाभावे संस्कारत्वं स्यात्॥७३॥
अर्थेन च; विपर्यासे तादर्थ्यात्तत्वमेव स्यात्॥७४॥

We sometimes find that a subsequent part of a statement contradicts an earlier one. That is indeed intentional; for, when there is an absence of sense, it is an indication that we should understand the correct use of words (that is, by means of division into parts). We follow this method, with its change of form of words,—because the text makes sense in this manner; and so we conclude that it is intended that the real meaning should be found in that way.

1. त्तेन च केति न्या. मा. पाठः।
2. विप्रेति वृत्तिकृत्पाठः।

PART III

THE METHOD OF INTERPRETATION

Introduction

We can get only the main idea by changing the form of a word; while subsidiary ones are obtained from words that lie in close proximity. There is no difficulty in understanding the real meaning of the text in this way.

Words have been newly coined to fit into this scheme, and each succeeding idea is connected with the preceding one.A single word can describe a composite action in this manner. But all words cannot be treated in the same way and the meaning of certain words, like *hiraṇya* is the same, whether we divide them into parts or accept their common idea. This method of interpretation is based on the substitution of one form of a word for another. It becomes necessary to resort to it because we cannot get a rational meaning of the text otherwise: for instance, it is only in this way that we can get a proper meaning of the number six when it is used in a certain context. But it requires deep study and repeated practice, as may be seen from an illustration.

The meaning of the principal word enables us to understand the rest; and this may be illustrated too. The meaning may sometimes be obtained by means of effect produced by a certain cause. In the case of *dravyas* or fundamental substances referred to in systems of philosophy, their idea is obtained by dividing words into parts . All words are directly or indirectly connected with the principal word.

The meaning of certain words has been defined; of others can be obtained by dividing them into parts; but the two are often connected with each other. This change of one form of a word for another is like an exchange; but it is a strictly equal one; and the whole idea can be illustrated. The test of the correctness of this method consists in the result it can produce, as we may see from certain illustrations.

Importance of the Principal Word

विकृतौ शब्दवत्त्वात्प्रधानस्य; गुणानामधिकोत्पत्तिः सन्निधानात्॥१॥
प्रकृतिवत्त्वस्य चानुपरोधः॥२॥
चोदनाप्रभुत्वाच्च॥३॥

When the form of a word is changed,—such is the character of the language used—that it can express only the main idea; while with regard to subsidiary ones, they are expressed by means of other words in close proximity. When a word is changed to its rudimentary form, there is no difficulty in the way of understanding its real meaning; and that is due to the fact that we get a kind of power over the meaning of words in this way.

Newly Coined Words

प्रधानं त्वङ्गसंयुक्तं; तथाभूतमपूर्वं स्यात्तस्य विधयुपलक्षणात्सर्वो हि पूर्ववान्विधिरविशेषात्प्रवर्तितः॥४॥
न चाङ्गविधिरनङ्गे स्यात्॥५॥

The meaning of the principal word is connected with its parts; and so it should be deemed to have been newly coined for the purpose.[45] If we follow this method, we shall find that every succeeding idea is connected with what precedes it; and we accept it because of its uniform application throughout. Indeed, if it is correct that words should be divided into parts to get their meaning, we cannot use any other method which does not divide them into parts.

A Single Word can describe a Composite Action

कर्मणश्चैकशब्द्यात् सन्निधाने विधेराख्या संयोगो; गुणेन तद्विकारः स्याच्छब्दस्य विधिगामित्वाद्गुणस्य चोपदेश्यत्वात्॥६॥
अकार्यत्वाच्च नाम्नः॥७॥
तुल्या च प्रभुता गुणे॥८॥

If the idea of an action can be described by putting down

a single word,—it would need to be subjected to this method (that is, divided into parts), when we shall get its real meaning in the manner explained. This has to be done because the original name,—as it is—is ineffective otherwise; whereas the parts have the power to give us a meaning equally like the word itself.

Can all Words be Treated Alike?

सर्वमेवं प्रधानमिति चेत्॥९॥
तथाभूतेन संयोगाद्यथार्थविधयः स्युः॥१०॥
विधित्वं चाविशिष्टं[1] वैकृतैः कर्मणा योगात्तस्मात्सर्वं प्रधानार्थम्॥११॥
समत्वाच्च तदुत्पत्तेः संस्कारैरधिकारः स्यात्॥१२॥

It is possible to say that all words should be regarded as principal words in this manner (that is, they should be divided into parts to be understood). But if that were so, all methods or rules of interpretation should give us the same true meaning of the text; so that there would be but one uniform method of interpretation, and those who believe in reducing words to their rudimentary form would be able to change all of them. This method would then apply to all words denoting action; and all other words would correspond to the form of the principal word. Thus when all words can be treated uniformly, and we are able to get the required result,—that would be our authority for holding this to be the correct way of using words[46].

Hiraṇyagarbha

हिरण्यगर्भः पूर्वस्य मंत्रलिङ्गात्॥१३॥
प्रकृत्यनुपरोधाच्च॥१४॥
उत्तरस्य वा मंत्रार्थित्वात्॥१५॥

The word *Hiraṇyagarbha*[47] is of the aforesaid kind, as is evident from the hymns of the Vedas; and that is so because it does not conflict with its rudimentary form; and we shall find that its latter meaning is in harmony with the meaning of the hymns.

---

1. विशिष्टमेवं प्राकृतानां वैक्रिति न्यायमालापाठः।

Substitution of One Form for Another

विधयतिदेशात्तच्छ्रुतौ विकारः स्याद्गुणानामुपदेश्यत्वात्॥१६॥
पूर्वस्मिंश्चामन्त्रदर्शनात्॥१७॥
संस्कारे तु क्रियांतरं तस्य विधायकत्वात्॥१८॥
प्रकृत्यनुपरोधाच्च॥१९॥

This method of interpretation is based on the substitution of one form of a word for another; and that may be described as its transformation or change; and the meaning of its parts is in accordance with what is taught or authorised[48]. Indeed, we accept the traditional meaning of words because we do not know the real import of the Vedic hymns. But when we "purify" words or use them correctly, we find, as a result, that they convey a very different idea (or refer to a very different business); and there is no difficulty in reducing them to their rudimentary form.

Need of a New Interpretation

विधेस्तु तत्र भावात्सन्देहे यस्य शब्दस्तदर्थं स्यात्॥२०॥
संस्कारसामर्थ्याद् गुणसंयोगाच्च॥२१॥
विप्रतिषेधात्क्रिया प्रकरणे स्यात्॥२२॥

The rule in regard to this method of interpretation is that, if we have a doubt in regard to the meaning of a word, whatever other meaning we give it should be in conformity with the nature of the word; and that is possible because of the suitability of the new (or correct) form of words, and the connection of their parts with one another. We have to resort to this method because the statements in the text are conflicting; and that calls for an explanation (and we are able to get it in this way).

An Instance

षड्भिर्दीक्षयतीति; तासां मन्त्रविकारः श्रुतिसंयोगात्॥२३॥

For instance, it has been said that a person consecrates himself for the purpose of a *Soma* sacrifice by means of six things. (As we are unable to understand this,) we find it necessary to make out the idea of these things; and we can do so by using our intellect[49].

Need of Study

अभ्यासात्तु प्रधानस्य॥२४॥
आवृत्त्या मन्त्रकर्म स्यात्॥२५॥
अपि वा प्रतिमन्त्रत्वात्प्राकृतानामहानिः स्यादन्यायश्च कृतेऽभ्यासः॥२६॥
पौर्वापर्यञ्चाभ्यासे नोपद्यते नैमित्तिकत्वात्॥२७॥
तत्पृथकत्वं च दर्शयति॥२८॥
न चाविशेषाद्व्यपदेशः स्यात्॥२९॥

It is by means of repeated study or practice that we can get the meaning of the principal word in this way; and we can get the result (or the real meaning) of the hymns by thinking over the same point again and again. But the composition of the sacred text is such that those who believe in the method of reducing words to their rudimentary form cannot fail to get the correct meaning; and in their case even constant practice is not necessary. A succession of ideas cannot be produced by means of constant practice, for they are produced by some other cause; and so we have to adopt some other way of understanding the text. Thus, it is not possible to have a uniform method of interpretation applicable to all cases.

An Illustration

अग्न्याधेयस्य नैमित्तिके गुणविकारे दक्षिणादानमधिकं स्याद् वाक्यसंयोगात्॥३०॥
शिष्टत्वाच्चेतरासां यथास्थानम्॥३१॥
विकारस्त्वप्रकरणे हि काम्यानि॥३१॥
शङ्कते च निवृत्तेरुभयत्वं हि श्रूयते॥३२॥
वासो वत्सञ्च सामान्यात्॥३४॥
अर्थापत्तेस्तद्धर्मः स्यान्निमित्ताख्याभिसंयोगात्॥३५॥

(This may be illustrated by means of an example:) It is said that there is a special cause for kindling the sacred fire; but if a change is made in its subsidiary parts, an additional fee should be paid (to the priest)[50]; for that is how the statement is connected together. If we understand how all this is arranged, (that is, if we understand the correct meaning of this), the rest will be in its proper place.

We find that a change is necessary (and it has to be made in the principal words); for it is only in what does not refer to the main subject that we have the option to do as we like. When,however, a person is in doubt as to whether he should give up (omit) a particular course or not, both the options[51] may be open to him. Thus the words *vāsa* and *vatsa*, though apparently different, may express the same idea. We can understand their character by means of inference, when we shall find that the reason for these names lies in the close connection of their parts[52].

Special Meanings

दाने पाकोऽर्थलक्षणः॥३६॥
पाकस्य चान्नकारितत्त्वात्॥३७॥
तथाभिधारणस्य॥३८॥
द्रव्य[1]विधिसन्निधौ सङ्ख्या तेषां गुणत्वात्स्यात्॥३९॥
समत्वात्तु गुणानामेकस्य श्रुतिसंयोगात्॥४०॥

If we wish to know the real meaning of the word *dāna* (gift), we should understand it through the effect (or result) it can produce[53].

The real meaning of the word pāka (cooking) is obtained from what is done to anna or food[54].

We can get the meaning of the word *abhighāraṇa* (sprinkling clarified butter on the fire) in the same manner[55]

The rule in regard to *dravyas* (fundamental substances like the "elements", etc.) is that the meaning of the names should be obtained by means of their division into parts:[56] If, however, the parts of names appear to be alike, we should get the meaning of the principal substance by using our intelligence.

Relation of Principal Word to Other Words

1. द्रव्यविधीति सूत्रमारभ्य लिङ्गदर्शनाच्चेत्येनतेमकमधिकरणं न्यायमालानुसाराद् भवति।

यस्य वा सन्निधाने स्याद्वाक्यतो ह्यभिसम्बन्धः॥४१॥
असंयुक्तास्तु तुल्यवदितराभिर्विधीयन्ते; तस्मात्सर्वाधिकारः स्यात्॥४२॥
असंयोगाद्विधिश्रुतावेकजाताधिकारः स्याच्छ्रुत्योकापात्क्रतोः॥४३॥
शब्दार्थश्चापि लोकवत्॥४४॥
सा पशूनामुत्पत्तितो विभागात्॥४५॥
अनियमोऽविशेषात्॥४६॥

When a word is placed in juxtaposition to the principal word, its meaning should conform to the statement of the text. But there may be some words which are not connected with the principal word, but have been spread over, and are connected with the rest of the text: we should assume that they too are in their proper place. With regard to other words, which do not appear to conform to this rule,—they too are in their proper place, and do not contradict the rest of the text. Their meaning is easy to understand, even like that of the common people; and their place in the text corresponds to the idea of animals, which have their different characteristics. But there is no restriction in regard to the use of the term (animal), because of uniformity[57] (among all).

Meaning of "Go" and "Dāna"

भागित्वाद्वा गवां स्यात्॥४७॥
प्रत्ययात्॥४८॥
लिङ्गदर्शनाच्च॥४९॥
तत्र दानं विभागेन प्रदानानां पृथक्त्वात्॥५०॥

But the real meaning of the word "*go*" (cow) should be obtained by means of its division into parts;[58] and we feel convinced that that is the correct way of getting it; and that is what is meant by seeing through its "disguise". Similarly, the word *dāna* should also be understood by means of its division into parts,[59] when it would be found to convey a different idea from that of a "gift".

Character of Change of Form of a Word

परिक्रयाच्च लोकवत्॥५१॥
विभागं चापि दर्शयति॥५२॥
समं स्यादश्रुतित्वात्॥५३॥
अपि वा कर्मवैषम्यात्॥५४॥

We change one meaning for another in the same manner as is popularly done when we purchase an article; and we can see for ourselves that it is so when we divide words into parts. The meaning of words should, however, be the same throughout, for otherwise we cannot understand them; and that should be so even though they refer to different actions.

The Test of Correctness

अतुल्याः स्यु परिक्रये विषमाख्या; विधिश्रुतौ परिक्रयान्न कर्मण्युपपद्यते; दर्शनाद्विशेषस्य तथाभ्युदये॥५५॥

When, however, we buy or exchange one thing for another, we know that the two things are not absolutely equal, and they have different names. (On the other hand) the rule in regard to the interpretation of the Vedic text is not based strictly on the model of buying or exchange (for in this case, though one form is exchanged for another, the terms are equal and the names are the same): only it is necessary to use our intelligence, for they are special terms, and our criterion of correctness is the result that is achieved.

An Illustration : Dhenu

तस्य धेनुरिति गवां प्रकृतौविभक्तं चोदितत्वात्तत्सामान्यात्तद्विकारः स्याद्यथेष्टिर्गुणशब्देन॥५६॥
सर्वस्य वा; क्रतुसंयोगादेकत्वं दक्षिणार्थस्य; गुणानां कार्यैकत्वादर्थे विकृतौ श्रुतिभूतं स्यात्त[1]या समवायाद्धि कर्मभिः॥५७॥

An example of this is the word *dhenu* (meaning "a cow").

1. त्तस्मात्सेति न्या. मा. संमतः पाठः।

The meaning of the word *go* (a cow) is the same; and if we reduce the words to their rudimentary form, we shall find that they are similar too. We can make this change (divide *dhenu* into parts) in the same manner as we divide the word *iṣṭi* into parts.[60] All such words are like that; and in the same manner the word *dakṣiṇā* fits into the plan of the text, and means only one thing ("skill in action").[61] When we divide words into parts, we should use our intelligence in the process of making a change, so as to produce unity of result; and it is in this manner that we get a connection between the different meanings of a word in the light of the idea of different actions signified by it[62].

Test of Correctness

चोदनानामनाश्रयाल्लिङ्गेन नियमः स्यात्॥५८॥

एका[1]पञ्चेति धेनुवत्॥५९॥

त्रिवत्सश्च॥६०॥

तथा[2]लिङ्गदर्शनम्॥६१॥

These rules of interpretation do not depend on authority so much as on what they can establish or prove. In the light of this the number five is like (means the same thing as) a *dhenu*;[63] and the number three means the same thing as *vatsa*[64] and it is in this manner that we can see through their "disguise".

How to find out the Meaning

एके तु श्रुतिभूतत्वात्सङ्ख्यया गवां लिङ्गविशेषेण॥६२॥

If in a particular case, —say of the word "*go*"—we assume that it has been intelligently used, and reflect on it, we shall find that we can understand its real meaning by means of certain special symbols used in the text[65].

---

2. एकां पेति न्या. मा. संमतः पाठः।
3. तथा चेति चशब्दोधिकः न्या. मा. मते पाठः।

An Objection Answered

प्रकाशौ च[1] तथेति चेत्॥६३॥
अपि त्ववयवार्थत्वाद्विभक्तप्रकृतित्वाद्गुणेदन्ताविकारः स्यात्॥६३॥

It is possible to argue that there are two equally satisfactory ways of explaining the same word. But were it so, there should be no change in the meaning of a part of a statement (or logical argument) (in its common form and) when a word is reduced to its rudimentary form.

Difference between Horse and Cow

धेनुवच्चाश्वदक्षिणा; स ब्रह्मण इति; पुरुषापनयो यथा हिरण्यस्य॥६५॥
एके तु कर्तृसंयोगात्स्त्रग्वत्तस्य लिङ्गविशेषेण॥६६॥
अपिवा तदधिकाराद्धिरण्यवद्विकारः स्यात्॥६७॥
तथा च सोमचमसः॥६८॥

The *dakṣiṇā* of the horse is like that of the cow; and it belongs to the *Brāhmaṇa*.[66] The mistake committed by people in grasping this is the same as in the case of the word *hiraṇya*. But the difference between the idea of a horse and a cow is that the former is associated with an actor, because it can turn or wind about (more freely than a cow).[67] It is by means of this special symbol that we can obtain the meaning of the word. But this method of interpretation also makes a special claim, according to which, if we change the form of the word *aśva* (meaning a horse), we shall get its real meaning in the same manner as in the case of the word *hiraṇya*.[68] In the same way we can get the meaning of *Soma-chamasa*[69] (a cup for drinking *Soma*).

Words for Animals

सर्वविकारो वा क्रत्वर्थे पशूनां[2] प्रतिषेधात्॥६९।

In this scheme of interpretation we have to change the form of all words denoting animals, if we cannot admit that they can be animals[70].

---

1. चशब्दोधिको वृत्तिकृन्मते।
2. र्थे प्रतिषेधात्पशूनामिति न्यायमालाकृत्संमतः पाठः।

Need for a Change of Form

ब्रह्मदानेऽविशिष्टमिति चेत्॥७०॥

उत्सर्गस्य क्रत्वर्थत्वात्प्रतिषिद्धस्य कर्मत्वान्न[1] च गौणः प्रयोजनमर्थः स दक्षिणानां स्यात्॥७१॥

यदि तु ब्रह्मस्तदूनं तद्विकारः स्यात्॥७२॥

सर्वं वा पुरुषापनयात्तासां क्रतुप्रधानत्वात्॥७३॥

It is possible to hold that there is nothing special in the giving of a gift to a *Brāhmaṇa*. But, if the gift is to be made in connection with an act of sacrifice, it should not be in connection with a prohibited act. (Since, however, it is to be made in connection with the latter too,) that is the reason why the meaning of the word *dakṣiṇā* has to be obtained by means of division into parts.[71] Thus, when there is this kind of defect in the character of a *Brāhmaṇa*, it becomes necessary to make a change in the form of a word. That is so because we get a meaning bearing on the misdeeds of men, whereas the idea of *dakṣiṇā* (or sacrificial fee) is always associated with excellence of design or plan.

Dakṣiṇā and Adhvaryu Priest

यजुर्युक्तऽध्वर्योर्दक्षिणा विकारः स्यात्॥७४॥

अपि वा श्रुतिभूतत्वात्सर्वासां तस्य भागो नियम्यते॥७५॥

Thus, when there is a mention of the *Adhvaryu* priest in connection with a sacrifice, the form of the word *dakṣiṇā* should always be changed.[72] Indeed, as all kinds of *dakṣiṇā* are produced by the intellect, the share of the *Adhvaryu* is of a restricted kind[73].

PART IV

THE METHOD OF INTERPRETATION

Introduction

The meaning of seeing through the "disguise" of a word

1. प्रस्यात्रेति न्यायमालासंमतः पाठः।

is that we should reduce it to its rudimentary form, connect the parts together, and understand its real meaning. We can understand the meaning of all the *Prajāpatis* in this manner: only we must not import our own ideas in the matter, for there is a unity of idea underlying the "disguised" form of words.

In certain *Sāman* hymns it is not necessary to change the form of words to understand their meaning; in a number of others, however, it is.

In the *Pavamāna* hymns sung at the *Jyotiṣṭoma* sacrifice, it is necessary to change the form of words: we are also permitted to make a change at our discretion. The words used are quite new, and the method of interpretation depends on the nature of the text; and the only test is that we should be able to understand the text properly.

When we divide a word into parts, the word itself should remain intact; but there should be no change in its form if it makes good sense otherwise.

The word *budh* needs to be understood in a special manner. If it is stated that there should be no change in the form of the name of a god, no change should be made.

We have to use our intelligence in interpreting the text, specially if there is a conflict of opinion. Certain ideas have been expressed by means of similes and metaphors; and the "purification" or correct form of a word really means that it is being expressed more exactly than before,—that is, by means of division into parts.

In the hymns of the *Ṛg Veda*[1] beginning with the word *Manotā*, the form of words should not be changed. We can understand the meaning of words in different ways; and in certain cases from the effect they produce.

We should be able to get the idea of a god from a strophe

consisting of three verses. Planets too are a kind of gods; and in some cases the form of their words should not be changed But we need to use our intelligence to understand their idea.

All things exist for the sake of others, except the soul, which exists for the sake of its own self. This is expressed by means of the invocation of the gods, who represent the great powers of Nature; and we can understand their idea from the fundamental substances themselves.

The idea of *dadhi* (curd) is important, and we can understand it if we divide the word into parts: so too in the case of the word *ājya* (clarified butter).

Where the form of a word is changed, there is an implication that it has not been clearly expressed in its original form. But this may not be so; and we may change its form because it has been stated that we should do so.

Criterion of Correctness

प्रकृतिलिङ्गासंयोगात्कर्मसंस्कारं विकृतावधिकं स्यात्॥१॥

चोदनालिङ्गसंयोगे तद्विकारः प्रतीयेत प्रकृतिसन्निधनात्॥२॥

सर्वत्र तु ग्रहाम्नातमधिकं स्यात्प्रकृतिवत्॥३॥

अधिकश्चैकवाक्यत्वात्॥४॥

लिङ्गदर्शनाच्च॥५॥

If the symbols[74] used in the rudimentary form of a word are not properly connected together,—far from getting a proper idea of action,— we shall get confused more and more. The rule in regard to the connection of these symbols is that the change made in the form of a word should correspond exactly to its rudimentary form[75]; and in every case we should be able to understand more and more of what is taught in the sacred books by means of this rudimentary form. There is unanimity of opinion on this point; and this is the meaning of seeing through the "disguise".

An Instance: Prajāpatis

प्राजापत्येषु चाम्नानात्॥६॥
आमने लिङ्गदर्शनात्॥७॥
उपगेशु शरवत्स्यात्प्रकृति लिङ्गसंयोगात्॥८॥
आनर्थक्यात्त्वधिकं स्यात्॥९॥
संस्कारे चान्यसंयोगात्॥१०॥
प्रयाजवदिति[1] चेन्नार्थान्यत्वात्॥११-१२॥

This is true in respect of what relates to the *Prajāpatis* (lords of creatures), as we find from what is handed down in the sacred books; and we can understand their meaning if we see through their "disguised" form.[76] If we are able to fix upon their correct meaning, we shall find that it is like arrows that have hit their mark,—for such is the connection of the symbols used in the rudimentary form of these words. If, on the other hand, we are unable to do so, the whole idea would become redundant; and then we shall have to get at the correct meaning by means of some other connection. We cannot say that the idea of *Prajāpatis* corresponds to that of a pre-sacrifice (or desire), because they have a different meaning[77].

The Test of Correctness

आच्छादने त्वैकार्थ्यात्प्राकृतस्य विकारः स्यात्॥१३॥
अधिकं वाऽन्यार्थत्वात्॥१४॥
समुच्चयं[2] च दर्शयति॥१५॥

There is a unity of idea underlying the "disguised" form of words, and we can understand them if we change their original or common form. But if we resort to some other way of interpreting them, the whole idea would become redundant. If, on the other hand, we grasp them correctly, we can understand the whole idea.

---

1. दिति चेतित्यन्तमंके तत उत्तरमेकमिति सूत्रद्वयमिति न्या. मा. मते।
2. इदं सूत्रं वृत्तिकृन्मते नास्ति। भाष्ये न्यायमालाकृन्मते चास्ति।

Scope and Limitations of this Method

सामस्वर्थान्तरश्रुतेरविकारः प्रतीयेत॥१५॥
अर्थे त्वश्रूयमाणे शेषत्वात्प्राकृतस्य विकारः स्यात्॥१६॥
सर्वेषामविशेषात्॥१८॥
एकस्यां वा श्रुतिसामर्थ्यात्प्रकृतेश्चाविकारात्॥१९॥

In the *Sāman* hymns, because of the different (or special) circumstances of the sacred text, no alteration in the language is allowed.[78] But if in these hymns we are unable to understand the meaning, and something is left out (or obscure), we should make a change in the common form of words; and that will enable us to understand the meaning of all words without exception. In the case of one set of these hymns, however, we can get a proper meaning from the text as it is; and it is not necessary to make any change in the common form of words.

A General Rule

स्तोमविवृद्धौ त्वधिकं स्यादविवृद्धौ द्रव्यविकारः स्यादितरस्याश्रुतित्वात्॥२०॥

There is a general rule in connection with the interpretation of these hymns. Where the words are long and give pleasure in their utterance, we can get an excellent meaning out of them as they are. Where, however, this is not the case, the form of words expressing the idea of fundamental substances (*dravyas*) should be changed. With regard to the rest, we should make a change only when we do not understand the meaning.

Special Cases: Pavamāna Hymns

पावमाने स्यातां तस्मिन्नावापोद्वापदर्शनात्॥२१॥
वचनानि त्वपूर्वत्वात्॥२२॥
विधिशब्दस्य मन्त्रत्वे भावः स्यात्तेन चोदना॥२३॥

शेषाणां वा चोदनैकत्वात्तस्मात् सर्वत्र श्रूयते॥२४॥
तथोत्तरस्यां ततौ तत्प्रकृतित्वात्॥२५॥

(There are, however, some special cases.) In the *Pavamāna* hymns, sung at the *Jyotiṣṭoma* sacrifice, it is necessary to change the form of words; and we are also permitted to insert an additional word or to remove one according to our judgement.[79] The words in this text are quite new, and the method of interpretation depends on the nature of the text,—for that is the rule. But so far as the result is concerned, there is only one rule,—namely, that we should understand the text properly; for that is the reason why we hear of (or read) these books everywhere; and the same names occur in the whole mass of later works, because we can get their real meaning from their rudimentary forms[80].

Application of this Method

प्राकृतस्य गुणश्रुतौ सगुणेनाभिधानं स्यात्॥२६॥
अविकारो वाऽर्थशब्दानपायात् स्याद् द्रव्यत्॥२७॥
आरम्भा[1]समवायाद्वा चोदितेनाभिधानं स्यादर्थस्य श्रुतिसमवायित्वादवचने च गुणशासनमनर्थकं स्यात्॥२८॥
द्रव्येष्वारम्भगामित्वादर्थे विकारः[2] सामर्थ्यात्॥२९॥

When we wish to understand the meaning of a word by dividing it into parts, we should see that the word itself remains intact, and all its parts are put together. But we should not make any change in its form if it makes good sense as it is. Similarly, if a word does not make any sense from the very beginning, we should deal with it as we have been enjoined to do (that is, divide it into parts). But if, in spite of this, it conveys no intelligent idea, the rule regarding its division into parts would be valueless. Again, when objects fit into one another from the very beginning, there should be no change in the form of words, because they and their meaning agree.

1. तथारेति न्या. मा. संमतः पाठः।
2. कारे सति वृत्तिकृत्सम्मतः पाठः।

Special Cases

वृध[1]न्वान्यवमानवद्विशेषनिर्देशात्॥३०॥
मन्त्रविशेषनिर्देशान्न देवताविकारः स्यात्॥३१॥
विधिनिगमभेदात्प्रकृतौ तत्प्रकृतित्वाद्विकृतावपिभेदः स्यात्॥३२॥
यथोक्तं वा विप्रतिपत्तेर्न चोदना॥३३॥
स्विष्टकृद्देवतान्यत्वे तच्छब्दत्वान्निवर्त्तेत॥३४॥
संयोगे वाऽर्थापत्तेरभिधानस्य कर्मजत्वात्॥३५॥
सगुणस्य गुणलोपे निगमेषु गुणा[2]स्थाने यावदुक्तं स्यात्॥३६॥
सर्वस्य वक्कर्म्यात्॥३७॥
स्विष्टकृदावापिकोऽनुयाजे स्यात्; प्रयोजनवदङ्गानामर्थसंयोगात्॥३८॥

(Certain expressions have to be understood in a special way: for instance,) a word containing the root *budh*[81] has to be understood in a special manner, like words in the *Pavamāna* hymns, because there is a special instruction to that effect. Again, when we are specially told that there should be no change in the form of the name of a god, no change should be made. If, however, we adopt a different method in regard to such a word occurring in a certain passage of the Vedas, and reduce it to its rudimentary form, it would not make any sense.

In case of conflict of opinion (we have to exercise our intelligences, for,) as has already been stated, there can be no rules to guide us in such a matter. But if there is a conflict of opinion in regard to the meaning of the name of a god, the character of whose actions we know,—specially as in the case of *Agni*,—we should reject all other forms of the name, and interpret it as we know it.[82] If, however, there is agreement of opinion, arising as a result of inference drawn from circumstances,—we should fix the meaning of the name in the light of actions performed by that god.

Where it is possible to divide a name into parts, but its meaning has specially been defined, without reference to these

---

1. बुधेति न्यायमालाकृतः भाष्यकृतः शास्त्रदीपिकाकृतश्च सम्मतः पाठः।
2. गुणस्थाने इति पदं वृत्तिकृन्मते एवाधिकम्।

parts,—what has already been stated should be done (that is, we should not divide it into parts, but accept the meaning as defined); and this should be done specially where such words refer to a single action. If there is a reference to a supplementary action (or sacrifice), it should come at the end of the previous action; for there it can serve a useful purpose, and we can get a connected meaning by dividing it into parts.

Use of Similes

सअन्वाहेति च शस्त्रवत् कर्म स्याच्चोदनान्तरात्॥३९॥

(Certain ideas are expressed by means of similes: for instance,) when a word has been pronounced, it cannot be recalled: so too is an action; and it may be compared to the action of a sword. That is another rule in this connection.

Purpose of "Purification" of Words

संस्कारो वा चोदितस्य शब्दस्य वचनार्थत्वात्॥४०॥

अव्राच्य[1]त्वान्नेति चेत्॥४०अ.

The "purification" or correct formation of words is for the purpose of enabling us to understand the meaning of such statements. It is possible to say that this is not a case of "purification" at all, for what is done is to express more clearly (or properly) what is not clear otherwise,—and that is done by means of the meaning of parts.

Certain Hymns of Ṛg Veda

स्याद् गुणार्थत्वात्॥४१॥

मनोतायां तु वचनादविकारः स्यात्॥४२॥

पृष्ठार्थेऽन्यद्रथन्तरात्तद्योनिपूर्वत्वात्॥४३॥

स्वयोनौ वा सर्वाख्यत्वात्॥४४॥

यूपवदिति चेत्॥४५॥

---

1. इदं सूत्रमधिकं वृत्तिकृन्मते।
   स्यादृचां प्रविभक्तत्वात्।

न कर्मसंयोगात्॥४६॥
कार्यत्वादुत्तरयोर्यथाप्रकृति॥४७॥

(In any case, certain expressions have to be interpreted in a particular manner: for instance,) in the hymns of the *Ṛg Veda*, beginning with the word *Manotā*, there should be no change in the form of words, because there is a special direction to that effect. Again, if there is a word, the meaning of which is important, but different from what, on mature consideration has already been appoved by our intellect[83], we should not accept it, unless it has occurred in a previous context too, and has been understood by means of the method of division into parts. Indeed, from all that has been stated in the text, we should be able to get at the source of what we want somewhere. We may not be able to say that the whole idea is as clear as that of the word *yūpa*[84] (a sacrificial post), because it can be understood from its connection with action. But where there are two possible ways of looking at a thing, we can understand its idea from the effect it produces as surely as we can by reducing a word to its rudimentary form.

Idea of a God and the Planets

समानदेवते वा तृचस्याविभागात्॥४८॥
ग्रहाणां देवतान्यत्वे स्तुतशस्त्रयोः कर्मत्वादविकारः स्यात्॥४९॥
उभयपानात्पृषदाज्ये दधनोप्युपलक्षणं निगमेषु पातव्यस्योपलक्ष[1]णत्वात्॥५०॥

Similarly, we should be able to get the idea of a god from a strophe consisting of three verses, without dividing the word into parts. The planets are another type of gods,[85] and there are *stotra* and *śāstra* hymns,—to be sung and recited—in their praise. They refer to action; and there should be no change in the form of these words. But we have to use our intelligence to understand their idea,—just as in the case of curdled butter we know that there is curd in it, and it is the result of the union or

1. क्षणादिति न्या. मा. मते पाठः।

mixing together of two things,—curd and butter. Even so if we examine the text carefully, and consider the statement of what has taken place, we shall know the implications of it, although there is no specific mention of anything.

Object of Action: How Represented: Soul and the Gods

न वा परार्थत्वाद्यज्ञपतिवत्॥५१॥
स्याद्वा आवाहनस्य तादर्थ्यात्॥५२॥
न वा संस्कारशब्दत्वात्॥५३॥
स्याद्वा द्रव्याभिधानात्॥५४॥

Certain things exist for their own sake, and not for the sake of something else; and their idea is represented by the soul or "the master of the sacrifice".[86] But certain other things exist for the sake of others; and their idea is expressed by means of invocation of the gods.[87] But we cannot understand all this from the "purification" of words or their division into parts, but rather from the names of the *dravyas* or the fundamental substances themselves.

Dadhi

दध्नस्तु गुणभूतत्वादाज्यपानिगमाः स्युर्गुणत्वं श्रुतेराज्यप्रधानत्वात्॥५५॥
दधि वा स्यात्प्रधानमाज्ये प्रथमान्त्यसंयोगात्॥५६॥
अपि वाऽऽज्यप्रधानत्वाद्गुणार्थे व्यपदेशे भक्त्या संस्कारशब्दः स्यात्॥५७॥

There are passages in the Vedas where *dadhi*[88] (curd) has been described as a protector of *ājya* (clarified butter); and we can understand the idea if we divide the word into parts. It is only reasonable that we should do so, because the idea of *ājya* is important. The idea of *dadhi* is important too, because it is connected with *ājya* both at the beginning and the end. But the idea of *ājya* is also important; and there is a statement to the effect that the meaning of the word should be obtained by means of division into parts[89]; and that is what is meant by "purification" or correct formation of a word.

Reason for Division of a Word into Parts

अपि वाऽऽख्याविकारात्वात्तेन स्यादुपलक्षणम्॥५८॥
न वा स्याद्गुणशास्त्रत्वात्॥५९॥

When the form of a word is changed, there is an implication that its idea has not been clearly expressed in its original or common form. But it may not be so; and we may divide it into parts because there is a direction to the effect that we should do so.

PART V
THE METHOD OF INTERPRETATION

Introduction

When we divide a word into parts, some parts which have the same meaning may be dropped. We may begin with the first part and go on successively to the last; or, when so directed, begin with the last, and go back to the first. This is illustrated in a set of strophes consisting of three verses, where there is a description of what a man desires to do at mid-day.

The rule in regard to the expression of new ideas is that there should be a "disguise"; but when we see through it, the meaning should be clear, and there should be no doubt about it. The meaning of principal words is obtained by means of division into parts; of their synonyms without it; while with regard to the rest, we should change their form if their meaning does not appeal to reason. But it is necessary to have knowledge to be able to understand the meaning of some synonyms; while in some cases we may have to "negotiate" their meaning, though not in the case of the best synonyms.

Apart from certain "improvements", the text of the *Ṛg Veda* is the same as that of the *Sāma Veda*; and the repetition of certain parts is meant to complete our chain of reflection. In certain hymns this repetition is made by means of words which need to be divided into parts, but not in others; and in any case we must judge the whole thing by the results achieved.

The number sixteen refers to the mind, but not to its complete action, which can be understood only when the mind functions in association with the intellect. That is expressed by the number three; and that is how we distinguish between the two numbers. But the word *tra* ("three") does not always refer to the mind; it does so only in certain cases.

The number four signifies complete or full development.

We have an account of all that relates to living creatures in the *Sāma Veda*; but in its absence we may refer to the *Ṛg Veda*, which contains it too. It is important to understand the meaning of the principal words; and that will enable us to understand the rest.

If we know what *Indra* and *Vāyu* mean, we shall understand that they are inseparable, though they have their own special characteristics; and, as their connection is important, it is expressed by means of the word *agra*, which means "chief, foremost". The importance of their connection is proved by the fact that when they leave the body, it decays; when they abide in it, it cannot.

If we examine the function of the mind, as represented by the number three, we shall find that it is like that of the intellect; but the latter is more important, because it can create order out of disorder by means of reasoning or proof, provided there is unity of action.

The idea of the number three and eleven is the same, and they can be substituted for each other; and this enables us to understand the idea of the number thirty-three, which is a multiple of the two.

All desires undergo a change through lapse of time; and so do words, expressing this idea, a change of form.

Omission of Certain Parts of Words

आनुपूर्व्यवतामेकदेशग्रहणेष्वागमवदन्त्यलोपः स्यात्॥१॥
लिङ्गदर्शनाच्च॥२॥
विकल्पो वा समत्वात्॥३॥

When a number of things are mentioned in succession and we have to make a choice in a particular place, those that come last are rejected, as in the case of a meaningless letter or syllable. That has to be done when we see through the "disguise" of an expression; because otherwise there would be a doubt in regard to its correct idea where more than one part has the same meaning in succession[90].

Rule of Composition and Interpretation

क्रमादुपसर्जनोऽन्ते स्यात्॥४॥
लिङ्गमविशिष्टं सङ्ख्याया हि तद्वचनम्॥५॥
आदितो वा प्रवृत्तिः स्यादारम्भस्य तदादित्वाद्वचनादन्त्यविधिः स्यात्॥६॥

There is a rule sanctioned by tradition that the subordinate part of a word should come at its end; and the proof of this calculation lies in the meaning we are able to obtain. When we explain the meaning of a word by means of its division into parts, we should commence with the first part first, because that is how it begins. If, however, we begin with the last part first, we should do so when there is a direction to that effect.

An Instance

एकत्रिके तृचादिषु माध्यंदिन[1]छन्दसां श्रुतिभूतत्वात्॥७॥
आदितो वा तन्न्यायत्वादितरस्यानुमानिकत्वात्॥८॥
यथानिवेशञ्च प्रकृतिवत्वसंख्यामात्रविकारत्वात्॥९॥
त्रिकस्तृचे धुर्ये स्यात्॥१०॥
एकस्यां वा स्तोमस्यावृत्तिधर्मत्वात्॥११॥

---

1. न्दिने छन्देति न्या. मा. संमतः पाठः।

(An instance of this is to be found in) a set of strophes consisting of three verses, where there is a description of what a person desires to do at mid-day,— and it is a perfectly reasonable desire. To begin with, we get this from the propriety of the manner of life at midday; and, as for the rest, we understand the idea from inference: for instance, we desire to halt or encamp at mid-day; and the idea of this can be obtained by reducing words to their rudimentary form, at the very beginning of the verse-triad. In one place there is a reference to the letting of a dwelling place, for that is the right thing to do at the time.

Rule regarding New Ideas

चोदनासु त्वपूर्वत्वाल्लिङ्गेन धर्मनियमः स्यात्॥१२॥

प्राप्तिस्तु रात्रिशब्दसम्बन्धात्॥१३॥

अपूर्वासु तु संख्यासु विकल्पः स्यात्सर्वासामर्थवत्त्वात्॥१४॥

There is, among the rules we have, a fixed rule in regard to the peculiar characteristics of things,—namely, that where there is a new idea to express, it should be done by means of a "disguise"; and when we see through this "disguise", the meaning should be as clear as that of the word *rātri*[91] ("night"). But when altogether new names are used, there is likely to be a doubt as to their correct meaning,—because they must all have a proper meaning to convey.

Synonyms and Other Words

स्तोमविवृद्धौ प्राकृतानामभ्यासेन सङ्ख्यापूरणमविकारात्सङ्ख्यायां गुणशब्दत्वादन्यस्य चाश्रुतित्वात्॥१५॥

When there are a number of additional names or synonyms used in their common form, we should be able to get their meaning without making any change in that form. With regard to the principal names, which have these synonyms, we should get their meaning by means of their parts. With regard to the rest, we should change their form only if they are obscure (or their meaning does not appeal to reason).

Need of Knowledge

आगमेन वाऽभ्यासस्याश्रुतित्वात्॥१७॥
सङ्ख्यायाश्च पृथक्त्व निवेशात्॥१८॥
उक्ताविकाराच्च॥१९॥
अश्रुतित्वादिति चेत्॥२०॥
स्यादर्थचोदितानां परिमाणशास्त्रम्॥२१॥
आवापवचनं वा[1]भ्यासे नोपपद्यते॥२२॥
साम्ना चोत्पत्तिसामर्थ्यात्॥२३॥
धुर्येष्वपीति चेत्॥२४॥
नावृत्तिधर्मत्वात्॥२५॥

In case we are unable to understand the meaning of synonyms, we should acquire more knowledge, when we shall be able to understand them. We shall then find that these names have an individuality of their own, because of certain arrangement of ideas expressed by them,—which are objective or refer to the outside world; and we can get their meaning without making any change in their utterance. It is possible to hold that we should do all this only if the meaning is obscure (or opposed to reason),—for meaning is the measuring rod of all rules of interpretation. But in the case of synonyms we do not have the same orderly arrangement as in the original names; and we have to "negotiate" their meaning in order to conform to the latter. This, however, is not necessary in the case of the best synonyms, which contain the idea of the original names in themselves.

Text of Ṛg Veda and Sāma Veda

बहिष्पवमाने तु ऋगागमः सामैकत्वात्॥२६॥
अभ्यासेन तु सङ्ख्यापूरणं; सामिधेनीष्वभ्यासप्रकृतित्वात्॥२७॥
अविशेषान्नेति चेत्॥२८॥
स्यात्तद्धर्मत्वात् प्रकृतिवदभ्यस्येताऽऽसङ्ख्यापूरणात्॥२९॥
यावदुक्तं वा कृतपरिमाणत्वात्॥३०॥

1. नं चेति न्या. मा. संमतः पाठः।

अधिकानाञ्च दर्शनात्॥३१॥
कर्म[1]स्वपीति चेत्॥३२॥
न चोदितत्वात्॥३३॥

Apart from certain "improvements", the text of the *Ṛg Veda*, as fixed by tradition, should be the same as that of the *Sāma Veda*; and the idea of repetition is to complete our reasoning or chain of reflection. In the *Sāmidhenī* verses, (which are recited when the sacrificial fire is kindled, and so refer to the commencement of intelligent action), this repetition is made by means of words which have to be divided into parts to be understood. This, however, may not be true of all; but the peculiar character of these verses is such that they have a number of words which have to be reduced to their rudimentary form in order to complete their chain of thought. However, as has already been stated, the method of interpretation is to be judged by the measure of the result that is achieved,—even as in all other things we judge as we see. We cannot say that this applies to action too, because there is a rule which enjoins otherwise[92].

The Idea of Numbers: No. 16

षोडशिनो वैकृतत्वं तत्र कृत्स्नविधानात्॥३४॥
प्रकृतौ चाऽभावदर्शनात्॥३५॥
अयज्ञवचनाच्च॥३६॥
प्रकृतौ वा शिष्टत्वात्॥३७॥
प्रकृतिदर्शनाच्च॥३८॥
आम्ना[2]नं परिसङ्ख्यार्थम्॥३९॥
उक्तमभावदर्शनम्॥४०॥
गुणादयज्ञत्वम्॥४१॥
तस्याग्रयणाद्ग्रहणम्॥४२॥
उक्थ्याच्च वचनात्॥४३॥

(It is necessary to understand the idea of certain numbers

1. न कर्मेति न्या. मा. पाठः।
2. म्नातं पेति न्या. मा. संमतः पाठः।

in this connection: for instance,) we can understand the idea of that which consists of sixteen parts by means of a certain change; and that, in this case, refers to a statement of all these parts.[93] We have to do this, because the rudimentary form of the word makes no sense; and it does not refer to the idea of a sacrifice (or action)[94], where we can reduce a word to its rudimentary form only if we are specially directed to do so; and we can understand this if we reduce (such an expression) to its rudimentary form. This number occurs in the sacred books, and we study them in order to reason about or reflect on things exhaustively; and it has already been stated that they do not make much sense. When, however, we say that this number does not refer to action, what is meant is that it refers to its subordinate part;[95] for we can understand the idea of sacrifice (or action) only when the mind functions in association with the intellect;[96] and that is why it is expressly mentioned that such actions are worthy of praise.

No. 3

तृतीयसवने वचनात्स्यात्॥४२॥
अनभ्यासे पराक्छब्दस्य तादर्थ्यात्॥४३॥
उक्थ्यविच्छेदवचनाच्च[1]॥४६॥
आग्रयणाद्वा पराक्छब्दस्य देशवाचित्वात्पुनराधेयवत्॥४७॥
विच्छेदः स्तोमसामान्यात्॥४८॥

It has expressly been mentioned that the number three refers to *Soma*[97] (or the mind); and unless there is a reference to some expected result, it should be deemed to refer to that (*Soma* or the mind); and it has been praised for a variety of reasons. As the function of the mind is closely connected with that of the intellect, the mind may be identified with the intellect, when it is concentrated on a particular point or place[98] (and it is this that is represented by the number three). We have to make a distinction between the idea of the two numbers (three and sixteen), because they have common properties,[99] —(and that is how it is made).

1. चनत्वादिति चशब्दशून्यः पाठो न्या. मा. संमतः।

Other uses of the word *Tra* (three)

उक्थ्याऽग्निष्टोमसंयोगादस्तुतशस्त्रः स्यात्सति हि संस्थान्यत्वम्॥४९॥

सस्तुतशस्त्रो वा तदङ्गत्वात्॥५०॥

लिङ्गदर्शनाच्चं॥५१॥

वचनात्संस्थान्यत्वम्॥४२॥

अभावादतिरात्रेषु गृह्यते॥५३॥

अन्वयो वाऽनारभ्य विधानात्॥५४॥

The number three (idea of the mind) is praised in the sacred books because of its connection with *Agniṣṭoma* (or the function of the intellect);[100] but this does not mean that whenever the syllable *tra* (meaning "three") occurs, it conveys the same idea: for instance, we have it in the word *śastra* (*śas-tra*),[101] and in this case the idea of "*tra*" is very different. But even the word *śastra* is worthy of praise because of its association with "*tra*"; and we can understand what it means when we see through its "disguise"[102].

The difference between the two forms of *"tra"*[103] is due to the different statements made in the text. The syllable "*tra*" also occurs in the word *ati-rātra*;[104] but there it does not refer to these meanings of "*tra*"; though there may be a connection between them, which can be understood with reference to a statement which has not yet been made[105].

No. 4

चतुर्थे चतुर्थेऽहन्यहीनस्य गृह्यते; इत्यभ्यासेन प्रतीयेत भोजनवत्॥५५॥

अपि वा सङ्ख्यावत्त्वान्नाहीनेषु गृह्यते; पक्षवदेकस्मिन्सङ्ख्यार्थ-भावात्॥५६॥

भोजने चः तत्सङ्ख्यं स्यात्॥५७॥

(The number four signifies completeness or full development; and so) we are told that on the fourth day we should take hold of the whole or the most perfect thing. We can verify this by examining the development of things, and see how results take shape,—as in the case of eating food.[106] But if we count this number (as one, two, three, four,) we cannot find the idea of completeness or wholeness in it; and that is so because this meaning of the number is to be found in a special way;[107] and then we should be able to count (the four stages of development) too, as in the case of eating food[108].

Subject-Matter of Sāma Veda and Ṛg Veda

जगत्साम्नि; सामाभावादृक्तः; साम तदाख्यं स्यात्॥५८॥
उभयसाम्नि; नैमित्तिकं विकल्पेन समत्वात्स्यात्॥५९॥
मुख्येन वा नियम्यते॥६०॥
निमित्त विघाताद्वा क्रतुयुक्तस्य कर्म स्यात्॥६१॥

We have an account of all that relates to living creatures in the *Sāma Veda* or *Sāman* hymns; but in its absence, we may refer to the *Ṛg Veda*; and that is the reason why the *Sāma Veda* is regarded as important.[109] Whatever is in the *Ṛg Veda* is also in the *Sāma Veda*. If, however, there is something of special importance, it may occur in a different form; but it must have the same meaning, which is regulated by the principal word. When we remove the cause of difficulty in the way (that is, understand the meaning of the principal word), we shall be able to understand the whole idea of action in an intelligent manner.

Indra and Vāyu

ऐन्द्रावायवस्याग्रवचनादादितः प्रतिकर्षः स्यात्॥६२॥
अपि वा धर्मविशेषात्तद्धर्माणां स्वस्थाने प्रतिकरणादग्रत्वमुच्यते॥६३॥
धारासंयोगाच्च॥६४॥
कामसंयोगे तु वचनादादितः प्रतिकर्षः स्यात्॥६५॥
तद्देशानां वाऽग्रसंयोगात्तद्युक्ते[1] कामशास्त्रं स्यान्नित्यसंयोगात्॥६६॥

If we understand from the beginning what *Indra* and *Vāyu* really mean, we shall know that they are inseparable.[110] But because of their different characteristics, there is a difference

1. द्युक्तं केति न्या. मा. सम्मतः पाठः।

in their actions too;[111] and it is for this reason that each has his own place and distinguishing qualities. But they are connected together at the highest point;[112] and are, in any case, combined together, because of association with desire.[113] As there is an inherent connection between the parts of what they represent, it should enable us to understand the nature of desire, because it is connected with both[114].

Their Connection is Expressed by the word Agra

परेषु[1] चाग्रशब्दः पूर्ववत् स्यात् तदादिषु॥६७॥

प्रतिकर्षो वा नित्या[2]र्थेनाग्रस्य तदसंयोगात्॥६८॥

प्रतिकर्षञ्च दर्शयति॥६९॥

पुरस्तादैन्द्रवाय[3]वादग्रस्य कृतदेशत्वात्॥७०॥

तुल्यधर्मत्वाच्च॥७१॥

तथा च लिङ्गदर्शनम्॥७२॥

सादनं चापि शेषत्वात्॥७३॥

लिङ्गदर्शनाच्च॥७४॥

परेषु[4] चाग्रशब्दः पूर्ववत् स्यात्तदादिषु॥६७॥

प्रदानं चापि सादनवत्॥७५॥

न वा प्रधानत्वाच्छेषत्वात्सादनं तथा॥७६॥

The connection between the two—*Indra* and *Vāyu*—is of the highest importance, and lasts from beginning to end; and that is expressed by the word *agra* (which means 'chief"). But even if we believe that the bond between them is not of the highest (or it is without the connection of the word *agra*), we must admit that they are connected together by means of a common invariable object (viz., life); and we can see this

1. चशब्दो नास्ति न्या. मा. मते।
2. षु चाग्रेति नया. मा. पाठः।
3. त्याग्रस्येति क्वचित्पाठः।
4. यवस्याग्रति न्या. मा. पाठः।

connection for ourselves.[115] Indeed, the connection between *Indra* and *Vāyu* exists from the very beginning, (and is really expressed by the word *agra*) because of the position accorded to the latter; and that is due to the fact that their essential character is the same, as can easily be proved; for we see that there is decay of the body when they leave it behind. We can understand their meaning when we see through the "disguised" form of these words[116] (*Indra* and *Vāyu*).

The act of sustenance (of the body) is similar to that of its decay (it is due to the association of *Indra* and *Vāyu*); for so long as they abide in the body in their preeminence, it cannot decay[117].

Mind and the Intellect

त्र्यनीकायां न्यायोक्तेष्वाम्नानं गुणार्थं स्यात्॥७७॥

अपि वाऽहर्गणेष्वग्निवत्समा[1]नं विधानं स्यात्॥७८॥

द्वादशाहस्य व्यूढसमढत्वं पृष्ठतव्समानविधानं स्यात्॥७९॥

व्यूढो वा लिङ्गदर्शनात्समूढ विकारः स्यात्[2]॥८०॥

कामसंयोगात्॥८१॥

तस्योभयथा प्रवृत्तिरैककर्म्यात्॥८२॥

In connection with the character of the mind, as represented by the number three,— when something is to be properly expressed in the sacred books, its meaning should be obtained by means of division into parts.[118] Indeed, if we consider the character of its functions over any calculated period of time, we shall find that it is like the intellect[119]. But the function of the intellect should be regarded as a higher one, as it can create order out of disorder (or what is disarranged); and that is done when proper proof is seen, and we attain the object of our desire. But in both cases (whether it is the mind or the intellect that functions), it is necessary that there should be unity of action[120].

---

1. मानवीति न्या. मा. सम्मतः पाठः।
2. न्यायमालायां स्यादिति नास्ति।

No. 3 and No. 11

एकादशि[1]नीवत् त्र्यनीका प्रवृत्तिः स्यात्॥८३॥
स्वस्थानविवृद्धिर्वाऽह्लामप्रत्यक्षसङ्ख्यत्वात्॥८४॥

The idea of the mind, as represented by the number three, and as consisting of the number eleven, is the same, and they can be substituted for each other;[121] and this is how we should amplify the idea of the number of these days, when it is not clear otherwise.

No. 33

पृष्ठ्यावृत्तौ चाग्रयणस्य दर्शनात् त्रयस्त्रिंशे परिवृत्तौ पुनरैन्द्रवायवः स्यात्॥८५॥
वचनात्परिवृत्तिरैकादशिनेषु॥८६॥
लिङ्गदर्शनाच्च॥८७॥

If we are able to rise to a height of thought, we can, by understanding the function of the mind in association with the intellect, see that all that is contained in the number thirty-three is but a substitute for what belongs to *Indra* and *Vāyu*[122] (or the soul and its vital breath). We are taught that we can understand all this if we substitute what can be substituted for the numbers representing eleven; and we can know what this means if we see through their "disguise".[123]

Special Terms

छन्दोव्यतिक्रमाद् व्यूढे; भक्षपवमानपरिधिकपालमन्त्राणां यथोत्पत्ति-वचनमूहवत्स्यात्॥८८॥

All desire undergoes a change with lapse of time; and so words which express this idea also undergo a change of form. Such are words like *bhaksha* (food), *pavamāna* (flow of mind), *paridhi* (enclosure, etc.), and *kapāla* (an alms-bowl); and their form should be changed according to the effect produced by them[124].

1. शिवनवत्र्यपनीका परिवृत्तिरिति न्या. मा. पाठभेदः।

PART VI

THE METHOD OF INTERPRETATION : INTELLECT AND MIND : SACRIFICE AND SATISFACTION

Introduction

There are different ways of reciting the sacred text, each of which has a bearing on the idea of sacrifice.

Intellectual perception alons is real knowledge; and it is by its means that we can measure Time, which is divisible into parts.

Similarly, there is a conciseness of expression in the idea of numbers,—*e.g.* the number eleven; and it can be divided into parts like the duration of Time; but the division should be such as can appeal to common sense, and follow a well defined pattern.

We cannot expand the number three in the same way; and its meaning has been defined: so is that of the word *pṛshṭha*.

The different *Sāman* hymns constitute a single whole, and can be understood by dividing words into parts; but this need not be done in all cases,—specially of words which refer to action.

It is not necessary to divide the word *tri* into parts, for its meaning has been defined; and we can understand the meaning of the word stoma by means of inference in connection with the word *Tri* (meaning 'three').

In the case of *Bṛhat-sāman* and *Rathantara-sāman* hymns, we can get their meaning by dividing words into parts.

Pleasure or enjoyment in association with physical objects arises because of the action of the mind and the intellect; but an interval of time is necessary for its recurrence.

Enjoyment is not meant for students: all their life should be a sacrifice. Their time of enjoyment will come when they enter the next stage,—that of the householder's life. There are good reasons for making these divisions of life; but they are chiefly a matter of convenience, for life is a whole, yet divisible into parts.

One tenth expresses the idea of division; and the number ten of multiplication.

Similarly, one animal can express the idea of the character of many.

The meaning of a number of words in the text can be obtained by reducing them to their rudimentary form, as in the case of *Ṛtvij* priests, and the institutor of the sacrifice.

But the idea of "the master of the sacrifice" is not the same as that of "the master of the house".

In the case of a number of synonyms there is a special mention of the manner in which their meaning can be obtained; but they must not be contradictory.

The function of the intellect can be like that of the mind.

Sacrifice makes for purification of action; while *dakṣiṇā* or "sacrificial fee" expresses the idea of skill.

The idea of the division of time is like that of curdled butter,—together and yet apart.

All the faculties of a man get their share of satisfaction in performing action; and we can understand this by dividing words into parts. When we get a detailed description of an object in this way, it should convince us that we have hit upon the correct meaning. The whole process is intellectual, and enables us to think in a continuous chain.

There are, however, different ways of interpreting ideas: for instance, the function of the mind can be expressed in terms of wearing clothes, though it may necessitate a change of words to their rudimentary form.

Different ways of Recitation and their Idea

एकर्चस्थानानि यज्ञे स्युः स्वाधयायवत्॥१॥

तृचे वा लिङ्गदर्शनात्॥२॥

स्वर्दृशं प्रति वीक्षणं कालमात्रं परार्थत्वात्॥३॥

पृष्ठ्यस्य युगपद्विधेरेकाहवद्द्विसामत्वम्॥४॥
विभक्ते वाऽसमस्त विधानात् तद्विभागेऽप्रतिषिद्धम्॥५॥

There are different ways of reciting the sacred text, and each verse has its own bearing on the idea of sacrifice (or good and intelligent action); and where a strophe consisting of three verses is concerned, we have to get the meaning by piercing through the "disguise" of words[125].

Knowledge and Perception of Time—Intellectual perception alone is real knowfedge; and it is only by its means that we can measure Time,[126] which exists for the sake of something else,[127] When we rise to a height of thought, and understand the many-sided application of the laws of life, we can understand the nature of Time.[128] We can also see that it can be divided into two parts, and represented in terms of the duration of a day.[129] There is no contradiction in this, because Time itself is divisible into parts, and we do not think of it as a whole.

Idea of Numbers

समासस्त्वेकादशिनेषु तत्प्रकृतित्वात्॥६॥
विहारप्रतिषेधाच्च॥७॥
श्रुतितो वा लोकवद्विभागः स्यात्॥८॥
विहारप्रकृतित्वाच्च॥९॥
यावच्छक्यं तावद्विहारस्यानुग्रहीतव्यं; विशये च तदासत्तेः॥१०॥

Similarly, there is a conciseness of expression in referring to numbers, as consisting, for instance, of eleven parts, because they conform to the same pattern as the duration of time (that is, can be divided into parts in the same manner). We have to express ourselves briefly, because an unnecessary expansion of language is prohibited. But the division should be made in such a way that it appeals to the intelligence of the common man; and when we expand our idea, it should follow the fundamental pattern that has been laid down.[130] We should, as far as possible, accept this idea of the expansion of numbers; and in case of doubt, understand them in the light of their connection with the pattern.

Words with Defined Meanings

त्रयस्तथेति चेत्॥११॥

न समत्वात्प्रयाजवत्॥१२॥

सर्वपृष्ठे पृष्ठशब्दात्तेषां स्यादेकदेशत्वं पृष्ठस्य कृतदेशत्वात्॥१३॥

विधेस्तु विप्रकर्षः स्यात्॥१४॥

We cannot, however, expand the number three in the same manner, because it can be identified with something that we know, even like the word *prayāja*.[131] Similarly, the meaning of the word *pṛshṭha*[132] is fixed, and it conveys the same idea wherever it occurs in the text: only the difference of its shades of meaning should be understood in the light of the context.

Sāman Hymns

वैरूपसामा क्रतुसंयोगात्त्रिवृद्वदेकसामा स्यात्॥१५॥

पृष्ठार्थे वा प्रकृतिलिङ्गसंयोगात्॥१६॥

त्रिवृद्वदिति चेत्॥१७॥

न प्रकृतावकृत्स्नसंयोगात्॥१८॥

विधित्वान्नेति चेत्॥१९॥

न स्याद्विशये तन्न्यायत्वात्कर्माविभागात्॥२०॥

प्रकृतेश्चाविकारात्॥२१॥

The different *Sāman* hymns, when intelligently grasped, constitute a single whole, like the number three;[133] and the exalted meaning of these hymns is obtained by reducing words to their rudimentary form.[134] But their formation is not simple like that of the number three, because their connection with the rudimentary form is not complete. We cannot say that this is contrary to the rules of interpretation, because it is really in accord-ance with them: only in case of doubt we should not divide into parts words which refer to action,—because they conform to their own pattern.

Tri and Stoma

त्रिवृति सङ्ख्यात्वेन सर्वसङ्ख्याविकारः स्यात्॥२२॥
स्तोमस्य वा ताल्लिङ्गत्वात्॥२३॥

If we make a change in the contents of the number three, we shall have to do so in the case of all numbers (because it is a typical number).[135] The meaning of the word *stoma* is obtained by means of inference in connection with the idea of this number[136].

Bṛhat and Rathantara Sāman Hymns

उभयसाम्नि विश्वजिद्वद्विभागः स्यात्॥२४॥
पृष्ठार्थे वाऽतदर्थत्वात्॥२५॥
लिङ्गदर्शनाच्च॥२६॥

In the case of *Bṛhat-sāman* and *Rathantara-sāman* hymns we should apportion ideas, and understand them in the same manner as we understand the word *viśva-jīt*[137] That would give us the best meaning, because no other meaning can come anywhere near it; and we can understand it by piercing through its "disguise".

Mind, Action, and Enjoyment

पृष्ठे रसभोजनमावृत्तेसंस्थिते त्रयस्त्रिंशेऽहनि स्यात्तदानन्तर्यात् प्रकृतिवत्॥२७॥
अन्ते वा कृतकालत्वात्॥२८॥
अभ्यासे च तदभ्यासः कर्मणः पुनः प्रयोगात्॥२९॥
अन्ते वा कृतकालत्वात्॥३०॥
आवृत्तिस्तु व्यवाये कालभेदात्॥३१॥

When we rise to a height of thought, we realise that there is enjoyment in association with physical objects possessed of shape or form, because of the different actions of the mind and the intellect; and this sequence (of the function of the mind and the intellect, followed by enjoyment) is expressed in accordance with a certain pattern.[138] This enjoyment comes at its appointed time at last; and whenever the function of the mind and the intellect is repeated, enjoyment is repeated too, because it is connected with action every time; and it comes at its appointed time,at last. But the recurrence of enjoyment arises from the passage of time, for a difference (or interval) of time is necessary for the purpose.

Division of Life into Parts

मधु न दीक्षितो ब्रह्मचारित्वात्॥३२॥
प्राश्येतवायज्ञार्थत्वात्॥३३॥
मानसमहरन्तरं स्या[1]द् द्वादशाहे व्यपदेशात्॥३४॥
तेन च संस्तवात्॥३५॥
अहरन्ताच्च परेण चोदना॥३६॥
पक्षे सङ्ख्या सहस्रवत्॥३७॥
अहरङ्गवांशुवच्चोदनाभावात्॥३८॥

Those who are initiated as students, cannot have enjoyment, because they are at a stage of life when enjoyment is not open to them. At this stage even food should be taken in a spirit of sacrifice. The time for enjoyment comes later; and that is so because there is a statement in regard to the division of life into parts, with reference to the functions of the mind,[139] by means of which life itself is praised by all. As when one day ends, another begins, even so there is a rule that there is a higher life (after that of a student). We can give a thousand reasons to explain the theory of the divisions of life; but they are like the functions of the mind,[140] and there is no particular rule against the idea.

Ten and Tenth Part

दशमविसर्गवचनाच्च॥३९॥
दशमेऽहनीति च तद्गुणशास्त्रात्॥४०॥
सङ्ख्यासामञ्जस्यात्॥४१॥

We speak of the tenth part of a thing, because it can easily be given away.[141] Similarly, we speak of the tenth day, because

1. स्याद् भेदेन द्वयेति न्या. मा. पाठः।

there is a direction in regard to it as signifying something special;[142] and the reason for this is that it fits into the context.

Animals

पश्वतिरेके चैकस्य भावात्॥४२॥
स्तुतिव्यपदेशमङ्गेनाविप्रतिषिद्धं व्रतवत्॥४३॥
वचनादतदन्तत्वम्॥४४॥

If there are a number of animals, we can know the nature of all from the nature of one; but there is no prohibition, of the nature of a rule, against praising an object in parts, though that does not make for any definite knowledge (or ascertainment), as we are told[143].

How to Obtain the Meaning of Words

सत्रमेकः प्रकृतिवत्॥४५॥
बहु[1]वचनात्तु बहूनां स्यात्॥४६॥
अपदेशः स्यादिति चेत्॥४७॥
नैकव्यपदेशात्॥४८॥
सन्निवापं च दर्शयति॥४९॥
बहूनामिति चैकस्मिन्विशेषवचने[2] व्यर्थम्॥५०॥
अन्ये स्युर्ऋत्विजः प्रकृतिवत्॥५१॥

The word *satra* is one which can be understood by being reduced to its rudimentary form;[144] and this, as we are expressly told, is true of many other words. It is not necessary to point out each word of this kind, because a single statement should suffice. However, we know that all kinds of words are mixed together in the sacred text;—for there are many words,—and it would serve no useful purpose to make a separate statement in regard to each. But in the case of a number of words we have to get their meaning in the same manner as we get that of the *Ṛtvij* priests,—that is, by reducing them to their rudimentary form.

---

1. बहुवेत्यत्र बहुशब्दरहितः पाठो न्या. मा. संमतः।
2. चनं व्येति न्या. मा. सम्मतः पाठ॥

Institutor of Sacrifice

अपि वा यजमानाः स्युर्ऋत्विजामभिधानसंयोगात्तेषां स्याद्यजमानत्वम्॥५२॥
कर्तृसंस्कारो वचनादाधातृवदिति चेत्॥५३॥
स्याद्विशये तन्न्यायत्वात्प्रकृतिवत्॥५४॥

Even so there should be the institutors of sacrifices[145] too, who get their status as such because of their association with the names of the *Ṛtvij* priests. This should explain the idea of the purification of the doer of the deed,[146] as in the case of one who kindles the sacred fire;[147] but if we have any doubt about the propriety of this method, we should deal with these words according to their pattern[148].

Master of a Sacrifice and Master of a House

स्वाम्याख्याः स्युर्गृहपतिवदिति चेत्॥५५॥
न प्रसिद्धग्रहणत्वादसंयुक्तस्य तद्धर्मेण॥५६॥

We cannot say that the idea of the name *svāmī* is the same as that of *gṛhapati* ("master of the house");[149] because if we understand the character of that which is well known, it does not mean that we can say the same of one that is not so well known, by means of the same characteristics.

Synonyms

बहू[1]नामिति तुल्येषु विशेषवचनं नोपपद्यते॥५७॥

In the case of a number of words which are used as synonyms, there is no special mention of the manner in which their meaning can be obtained.

Contradictory Statements

दीक्षिताऽदीक्षित व्यपदेशश्च नोपपद्यतेऽर्थयोर्नित्यभावित्वात्॥५८॥
अदक्षिणत्वाच्च॥५९॥

We cannot make two contradictory statements at the same time: for instance, we cannot say that something has been

---

1. इदं सूत्रमधिकं वृत्तिकृन्मते।

undertaken as a sacrifice and has not,—for the two things are entirely different; and it is only an awkward person who can make such statements.

Intellect and Mind

द्वादशाहस्य सत्रत्वमासनोपायिचोदनेन यजमानबहुत्वेन च; सत्रशब्दाभिसंयोगात्॥६०॥

The function of the intellect[150] can be like that of the mind, when we take into consideration a certain posture (or approach to a problem), specially where a large number of souls (sacrificers) are concerned; and that is so because of the close connection of the intellect with the mind[151].

Sacrifice

यजतिचोदनादहीनत्वं; स्वामिनां चाऽस्थितपरिमाणत्वात्॥६१॥
अहीने दक्षिणाशास्त्रं गुणत्वात् प्रत्यहं कर्मभेदः स्यात्॥६२॥
सर्वस्य वैककर्म्यात्॥६३॥

Sacrifice makes for wholeness (or freedom from taint);[152] and this happens even where a number of persons engage in an act of sacrifice.[153] In this "wholeness" of action there are a number of parts; and the rule in regard to the payment of *dakṣiṇā*[154] signifies, every time, a difference of action; but the excellence of it arises from the unity of actions of all.

Division of Days

पृषदाज्यवद्वाऽह्नां गुणशास्त्रं स्यात्॥६४॥

The rule regarding the division of days is that they are like curdled butter[155] (together, and yet apart).

Jyotiṣṭoma

ज्यौतिष्टोम्यस्तु दक्षिणाः; सर्वासामेककर्मत्वात्प्रकृतिवत्; तस्मात् तासां विकारः स्यात्॥६५॥

With regard to what relates to *Jyotiṣṭoma* (mass or rays of light), there is a completeness of action (*dakshiṇā*); and that is so of all (rays of light), because, like Nature itself, they are engaged in the same action. Hence there should be a change of form of these names[156] (in order to understand them).

Function of the Intellect

द्वादशाहे तु वचनात्प्रत्यहं दक्षिणाभेदस्तत्प्रकृतित्वात्परेषु; तासां सङ्ख्याविकारः स्यात्॥६६॥

There is an express statement that in an intelligent action (ceremony lasting twelve days), there is a distinct measure of skill (*dakṣiṇā*) in each part (every day); and that is the pattern of expression in other actions too. In order to understand them, the form of all these words should be changed[157].

Need of Change of Form

परिक्रयाविभागाद्वा समस्तस्य विकारः स्यात्॥६७॥

भेदस्तु गुणसंयोगात्॥६८॥

In case we are unable to apportion the share of payment for work done (among the different agents or faculties), we should change the form of all the words used in that context, (when we shall be able to do so); because the distinction between them is expressed by means of the parts of these names.

Function of Different Faculties

प्रत्यहं सर्वसंस्कारः प्रकृतिवत्; सर्वासां सर्वशेषत्वात्॥६९॥

एकार्थत्वान्नेति चेत्॥७०॥

उत्प[1]त्तौ कालभेदात्॥७१॥

विभज्य तु संस्कारवचनाद्द्वादशाहवत्॥७२॥

The proper arrangement of all (the agents of action or faculties) goes on, according to the fundamental nature of each, every day; and we can understand it because we can isolate and consider all of them separately.[158] It is, however, possible to say that we cannot always do so, because their meaning or purpose is not always the same, and they appear to be different

---

1. स्यादुत्पेति न्या. मा. सम्मतः पाठः।

at different times.[159] But we should be able to distinguish between them by understanding their names in their correct formation, just as we interpret the expression "a ceremony lasting twelve days"[160].

How to Decide

लिङ्गेन द्रव्यनिर्देशे सर्वत्र प्रत्ययः स्याल्लिङ्गस्य सर्वगामित्वात्॥७३॥
यावदर्थं वाऽर्थशेषत्वादतोऽर्थेन परिमाणं स्यात्तस्मिंश्च लिङ्गसामर्थ्यम्॥७४॥
आग्नेये कृत्स्नविधिः॥७५॥
ऋजीषस्य प्रधानत्वादहर्गणे सर्वस्य प्रतिपत्तिः स्यात्॥७६॥

When we get a detailed description of an object by means of this "disguised" form of expression[159] we should be convinced in every case that it is correct; because this "disguised" form is of an all-pervading character, like the power of intellect (*Agni*) itself. Its strength or efficacy consists in the fact that the text contains certain words whose meaning remain", as far as possible, unchanged; and that enables us to measure the correctness of the whole. The whole system is purely intellectual; and in this process of thinking, the "residue of thought" (or what is left over) is most important, because it enables us to continue to think and, in due course of time, to understand everything[161].

An Illustration

वाससि मानोपावहरणे प्रकृतौ सोमवस्य वचनात्॥७६॥
तत्राहर्गणेऽर्थाद्वासः प्रकृतिः स्यात्॥७८॥
मानं प्रत्युत्पादयेत्प्रकृतौ तेन दर्शनादुपावहरणस्य॥७९॥
हरणे वा श्रुत्यसंयोगादर्थाद्विकृतौ तेन॥८०॥

If we desire to express the idea of the mind according to this pattern, the direction is that it should be done in terms of wearing clothes;[162] and it is for this reason that the wearing of clothes has for a long time been regarded as the correct thing.

It is in this manner that we can express the idea of the mind: we must think of it in its essential character; and when we understand what it implies, we can bring it down (or express it in terms of the common life of man). If, however, in this process, we are unable to find a rational meaning, we should reduce words to their rudimentary form[163].

PART VII

THE PERFORMANCE AND RENUNCIATION OF ACTION: THE METHOD OF INTERPRETATION

Introduction

When an animal acts, it acts as a whole entity.

Animals are said to be of five kinds; but they may be divided into two classes,—the invertebrate and vertebrate.

There is a reference to cooked and uncooked food: the latter refers to renunciation of action as the goal of life.

Action is performed by the whole man, including his intellect, mind, and the senses. The heart is the seat of satisfaction; but in the end all these are united together, and so, the body is compared to a chariot. But each faculty has its own share of satisfaction too.

We are not able to understand the character of the soul as it is; and so we must think of it in terms of these faculties; and he who uses his intellect gets the largest share of satisfaction.

Those who believe in Nature as the supreme creator of life do not agree that there is joy in action; but such persons deviate from the norm.

It is possible to say that there is joy in some parts of action, but not in others. But, as there is unity in action, there must be unity in satisfaction or joy as well.

He who urges another to action has also his share of satisfaction, though a small one; and even he who says that he has no satisfaction, has it too.

We can understand all this from the text if we understand its language correctly. The words used have two meanings; but there is no contradiction between them.

Where the motives are equally balanced, the intellect appears to get no satisfaction in deciding between them; but even in this case there is satisfaction, whatever it may decide. But in ascertaining whether, as a result of this, a person is happy or not, there might well be a difference of opinion. Except for such cases, a wife should always join her husband in action.

It is not easy to describe an action in words; and if we find that a certain expression is unsuitable, we must not suppose that it is meaningless; and we may have to divide it into parts, as in the case of the word *sruva*.

There can be no great action without the association of the great forces of Nature. This, however, does not apply to subsidiary action.

In order to understand the meaning of the word *ājya*, we must divide it into two parts, in the same manner as we divide the expression *gṛha-medhīya*.

There are some who believe that all desires should be renounced; but the problem involves a number of considerations; and we cannot agree that both the views,—namely, that they should and should not be renounced —can be correct. But, if both these views are to be found in the text, we should admit that we have not understood it aright; and if we do so, we shall find that all desires are not regarded as evil.

When we change the form of a word, all that is required is that its new meaning should be formed out of the meaning of its parts; but we should fix upon one meaning,—such as can appeal to our intellect.

Those who are opposed to this method believe that there is no authority for this division. But no authority is necessary, for we commonly divide words into parts to understand their meaning; and this takes us into the secret of this plan of interpretation.

A Creature acts as a Whole Entity

पशावेकहविष्ट्वं समस्तचोदितत्वात्॥१॥
प्रत्यङ्गं वा ग्रहवदङ्गानां पृथक्कल्पनत्वात्॥२॥
उवदानं स्यात्॥३॥
आज्यभागवद्वा निर्देशात्परिसङ्ख्या स्यात्॥४॥

When we say that an animal performs an intelligent act, it is the whole animal that does so, because it is impelled to it. It acts through every part of its body, just as we do when we lay hold of a thing. The idea of the separate functions of the different parts of the body arises out of our own imagination. A person has to perform a number of different functions again and again; and that is the reason why we ascribe these functions to different parts of the body. But when we examine the character of action and consider it in detail, we find that its divisions are like the divisions of clarified butter[164].

Divisions of Animals

तेषां वा द्व्यवदानत्वं विवक्षन्नभिनिर्दिशेत्पशोः पञ्चावदानत्वात्॥५॥
अंसशिरोनूकसक्थिप्रतिषेधश्च; तदन्यपरिसङ्ख्यानेऽनर्थकः स्यात्
प्रदानत्वात्तेषां निरवदानप्रति षेधः स्यात्॥६॥
अपि वा परिसंख्या स्यादनवदानीयशब्दत्वात्॥७॥
अब्राह्मणे च दर्शनात्॥८॥

Animals are said to be of five kinds;[165] but they have two divisions which should be specially mentioned. There is a class of animals which is without shoulder-blade, skull, back-bone, and thigh-bone; and when we specify another class of animals, we find that it is altogether different; and it would be meaningless to include the one in the other. In the circumstances we cannot assign any common characteristics to them.[166] But though there is nothing in common between them, there should, nevertheless, be a proper enumeration or specification of them; for if we merely see them, we cannot understand them.

Cooked and Uncooked Food

शृताशृतोपदेशाच्चतेषामुत्सर्गवदयज्ञशेषत्वं सर्वेषां न[1] श्रपणं स्यात्॥९॥

There is a reference to cooked and uncooked food in the sacred books; and we may say, as a general rule, that the idea of uncooked food corresponds to that of renunciation of action as the goal of life[167].

How is an Intelligent Action Performed

इज्याशेषात्स्विष्टकृदिज्येत प्रकृतिवत्॥१०॥
त्र्यङ्गैर्वा शरवद्विकारः स्यात्॥११॥

When an action is performed as a sacrifice, we say that it has been performed by *Agni*,—understanding the word in its rudimentary sense (that is, as intellect); but its further development takes place by means of the mind, acting in association with the five senses[168].

The Heart

अधयू[2]धनी होतुरूङ्गवदिडादविकारः स्यात्॥१२॥
शेषे वा समवैति; तस्माद्रथवन्नियमः स्यात्॥१३॥
अशास्त्रत्वात्तु नैवं स्यात्॥१४॥
अपि वा दानमात्रं स्याद्भक्षशब्दानभिसम्बन्धात्॥१५॥

He who acts, wants some satisfaction as its result; and so there is a place above the breast (the heart) which, like the mind, makes for the development of action.[169] In the end, however, all these are united into one; and it is because of this that the body is compared to a chariot.[170] This is not contrary to the teachings of the sacred books. Nevertheless, there should

---

1. न श्रपणं स्यादिति न्या. मालाकृन्मते नास्ति।
2. धनी त्विति तुशब्दोधिको न्या. मालामते।

be a measure of the satisfaction of each faculty, because we do not always find joy in action[171].

The Soul

दातुस्त्वविद्यमानत्वादिडाभक्षविकारः स्याच्छेषं प्रत्यविशिष्टत्वात्॥१६॥
अग्नीधश्च वनिष्ठरधयूधनीवत्॥१७॥

But we do not find that entity (the soul) which can assign these shares of satisfaction to the different faculties; and so there has to be a change in the conception of the "enjoyer" of this satisfaction.[172] As for the rest (the other faculties), we know them, and nothing special need be said about them. But he who uses his intellect, gets the largest share of satisfaction, like the heart itself[173].

Belief in Nature

अप्राकृतत्वान्मैत्रावरुणस्याभक्षत्वम्॥१८॥
स्याद्वा होत्रथवर्म्युविकारत्वात्तयोः कर्माभिसम्बन्धात्॥१९॥

Those who believe in Nature as the supreme creator of things, do not accept this pattern of thought (that there is joy in action); and so, though they are intelligent men, they do not find joy in action.[174] But that is possible only if the mind and the senses, which are closely connected with action, deviate from their normal state[175].

Two Views

द्विभागः स्याद् द्विकर्मत्वात्॥२०॥
एकत्वाद्वैकभागः स्याद् भागस्याश्रुतिभूतत्वात्॥२१॥

It is possible to say that there are two ideas of satisfaction or joy in action; because there are two kinds of action.[176] But, as there is unity of action, there must be unity of satisfaction too; and it would be contrary to reason to divide it[177].

Sharers in Satisfaction

प्रतिप्रस्थातुश्च वपाश्रपणात्॥२२॥
अभक्षो वा कर्मभेदात्तस्याः सर्व प्रदानत्वात्॥२३॥

(There are a number of sharers in this satisfaction; for

instance,) he who urges another to action has his share of satisfaction too, though it is of a limited kind, like the satisfaction derived from the cooking of the marrow of bones. Even he who says that he gets no satisfaction in action, has also his share; and we see that it is so when we understand the secret of action, and look at it in its entirety.

How to Understand This

विकृतौ प्राकृतस्य विधेर्ग्रहणात्पुनः श्रुतिरनर्थकं[1] स्यात्॥२४॥
अपि वाऽऽग्नेयवद्द्विशब्दत्वं स्यात्॥२५॥
न वा शब्दपृथक्त्वात्॥२६॥
अधिकं वाऽर्थवत्त्वात् स्यादर्थवादगुणाभवे वचनादविकारे; तेषु हि तादर्थ्यं स्यादपूर्वत्वात्॥२७॥
प्रतिषेधः स्यादिति चेत्॥२८॥
नाश्रुतत्वात्॥२९॥
अग्रहणादिति चेत्॥३०॥
न तुल्यत्वात्॥३१॥
तथा तद्ग्रहणे स्यात्॥३२॥
अपूर्वतां तु दर्शयेद्ग्रहणस्यार्थवत्त्वात्॥३३॥
ततोऽपि यावदुक्तं स्यात्॥३४॥

All this can be understood from the text if we understand the method of interpretation, and alter the common form of words; and it would be unnecessary to repeat the whole thing again. We should remember that the words have two forms, as in the case of *Agni*;[178] and we cannot get their correct meaning from only one. The additional meaning arises from the fact that it has been given that sense; and (in a number of cases) we can get the explanation of the meaning without dividing words into parts; and there should be no change in the form of a word when the meaning has been defined by special instruction. It will be found in such cases that the words which have this mean-

---

1. नर्थिका स्येति न्या. मालाकृत्सम्मतः पाठः। नर्थकः स्येति वृत्तिपुस्तके मूले पाठः। वृत्त्यनुसारेण नर्थकं स्येति पाठः।

ing have been newly coined for the purpose. But there is no contradiction between the two meanings of these words, for no such instance is known. Nor can such a contradiction arise through want of understanding, because the two sets of meanings are of equal value, as we can see for ourselves, if we understand them correctly. When we do so we shall find that these words are new; and so all that has been stated in the text is true, and should take place[179].

Satisfaction of the Intellect

स्विष्टकृति भक्षप्रतिषेधः स्यात् तुल्यकारणत्वात्॥३५॥
अप्रतिषेधो वा; दर्शनादिडायां स्यात्॥३६॥
प्रतिषेधो वा विधिपूर्वस्य दर्शनात्॥३७॥
शंय्विडान्तत्वे विकल्पः स्यात्; परेषु पत्न्यनुयाजप्रतिषेधेऽनर्थकः स्यात्॥३८॥

Where the motives of an action are equally balanced, the intellect appears to get no satisfaction in deciding which to prefer. But it should not be so; because we find from experience that whatever the intellect may decide, there is some satisfaction in it; and so that cancels the statement previously made.[180] But in ascertaining whether, as a result of this, a person is really happy or not, there might well be a doubt or a difference of opinion.[181] Except for such cases, the wife should always join her husband in acts of sacrifice (good and intelligent actions), and any prohibition against her doing so would be meaningless.

Need of Repetition

नित्यानुवादो वा कर्मणः स्यादशब्दत्वात्॥३९॥
प्रतिषेध[1]वच्चोत्तरस्य परस्तात्प्रतिषेधः स्यात्॥४०॥
प्राप्तेर्वा पूर्वस्य वचनादतिक्रमः स्यात्॥४१॥
प्रतिषेधस्य त्वरायुक्तत्वात्तस्य च नान्यदेशत्वम्॥४२॥
उपसत्सु यावदुक्तमकर्म स्यात्॥४३॥

---

1. षेधार्थवेति न्या. मा. सम्यतः पाठः।

It is not easy to describe an action in words; and so it is necessary to repeat its idea by way of explanation. If in the text a certain expression is not suitable, or does not make sense, what follows should be equally unsuitable too. But if we are able to get the correct meaning of the latter,—such is the language of the text—we find that we can overcome the difficulty of understanding the earlier part. But if we hastily come to the conclusion that the whole thing is meaningless, we cannot make any point or advance any further. Again, if we make a violent "assault" on the language of the text to "grasp" it, we shall not succeed[182].

An Illustration

स्रौवेण वाऽगुणत्वच्छेषप्रतिषेधः स्यात्॥४४॥
अप्रतिषेधो वा प्रतिषिधय प्रतिप्रसव[1]वत्॥४५॥

If, for instance, we take the meaning of the word *sruva* (as a "ladle") and do not divide it into parts, the result will be that it will not make any sense. Even if we do not disallow its meaning (as a "ladle"), we shall find that we have to do so, because there is a direction to that effect in the text[183].

Nature and Action

अनिज्या वा शेषस्य मुख्यदेवतानभीज्यत्वात्॥४६॥
अवभृथे बर्हिषः प्रतिषेधाच्छेषकर्म स्यात्॥४७॥

If the great forces of Nature[184] have no share in it, no great action undertaken by any one can materialise. This, however, does not apply to subsidiary action, which can take place without reference to them.

Meaning of Ajya

आज्यभागयोर्वागुणत्वाच्छेषप्रतिषेधः स्यात्॥४८॥
प्रयाजानां त्वेकदेशप्रतिषेधादवाक्यशेषत्वं तस्मान्नित्यानुवादः स्यात्॥४९॥
आज्यभागयोर्ग्रहणं नित्यानुवादो वा गृहमेधीयवत्स्यात्॥५०॥

---

1. सवादिति न्या. मा. सम्यतः पाठः।

विरोधिनामेकश्रुतौ नियमः स्याद्ग्रहणस्यार्थवत्त्वाच्छरवच्च श्रुतितो विशिष्टत्वात्॥५१॥

In order to understand the meaning of the word *ājya*, we should so arrange as to divide it into two parts and no more[185] (when we shall understand that it refers to the idea of goodness in desire). But because we are told in one place that all desires should be renounced, it does not mean that should be regarded as a rule. Hence it is necessary always to have an explanatory repetition to indicate what exactly is meant. It is thus necessary to have a constant explanatory repetition of the word *ājya*[186]; and to understand how to divide it, we should do as in the case of the expression *gṛha-medhīya*[187], which too requires an explanatory repetition.

Those who oppose this view (regarding desire) find their authority (or fixed rule) in one set of sacred books, according to which what they understand is said to be of excellent meaning, and based on the character of what the senses perceive.

A Number of Questions

उभयप्रदेशा[1]दिति चेत्॥५२॥

शरेष्वपीति चेत्॥५३॥

विरोधयग्रहणात्तथा शरेष्विति चेत्॥५४॥

तथे[2]तरस्मिन्॥५५॥

श्रुत्यानर्थक्यमिति चेत्॥५६॥

(In this connection a number of questions arise:) Can we accept the idea of desire from both sets of sacred books? Is it not true, at least in the light of the evidence of the senses, that all desires should be renounced? Is it possible to understand anything that is opposed to the evidence of the senses[188] and so

---

1. शान्नेतीति न्या. मा. सम्मतः पाठः।
2. तथोत्तरस्मिन्निति न्या. मा. सम्मतः पाठः।

on. But will not the sacred books be rendered useless, if that were so?.

An Answer

ग्रहणस्यार्थवत्त्वादुभयोरप्रतिपत्तिः स्यात्॥५७॥
सर्वासाञ्च गुणानामर्थवत्त्वाद् ग्रहणमप्रवृत्ते स्यात्॥५८॥
अधिकं स्यादिति चेत्॥५९॥
नार्थाभावात्॥६०॥
तथैकार्थविकारे प्राकृतस्याप्रवृत्तिः प्रवृत्तौ हि विकल्पः स्यात्॥६१॥
यावच्छ्रुतीति चेत्॥६२॥
न प्रकृतावशब्दत्वात्॥६३॥

(The answer to these questions is that) if the text is full of meaning and we have understood it, we cannot agree that both views are correct in the same place (namely, that all desires should be renounced, as well as that they should not). But since all parts of the text are full of meaning, we must admit that we have not understood them properly. It would not be correct to say that the other view (regarding desire, namely, that it is not an evil) should be regarded as secondary, because the text would, in that case, become meaningless; and were it really so, we should not be able to change the meaning by changing the form of words; whereas we find that if we do make a change, we get a different meaning (which makes sense). This is not mere hearsay, because it is not based on any oral authority in respect of the rudimentary form of words (and we can test it for ourselves)[189].

Method of Interpretation

विकृतौ त्वनियमः स्यात्पृषदाज्यवद्ग्रहणस्य गुणार्थत्वादुभयोश्च प्रदिष्टत्वाद्गुणशास्त्रं यदेति स्यात्॥६४॥
ऐकार्थ्याद्वा नियम्येत श्रुतितो विशिष्टत्वात्॥६५॥
विरोधित्वाच्च लोकवत्॥६६॥
क्रतोश्च तद्गुणत्वात्॥६७॥

When the form of a word is changed, it does not become

subject to any restrictions. The main condition, however, is that when we interpret it in this manner, its meaning should arise from the meaning of its parts, as in the case of the word *pṛṣad-ājya*[190] In this way both meanings (the common one and that obtained by means of division into parts) arise from a fixed rule; and the rule regarding the meanings of parts is also fixed in the same manner.[191] But we should fix upon a single meaning which, by virtue of its excellence, appeals to our intellect.[192] When, however, the idea of the text appears to be self-contradictory, we should seek some other meaning, as is the common practice of the people[193]; and then we shall find that the plan of the text is that we should get the correct meaning by means of the division of words into parts.

An Objection and its Answer

विरो[1]धिनाञ्च तच्छ्रुतावशब्द त्वाद्विकल्पः स्यात्॥६८॥
पृषदाज्ये समुच्चयाद्ग्रहणस्य गुणार्थत्वम्॥६९॥
यद्यपि[2] चतुरवत्तीति तु नियमे नोपपद्यते॥७०॥
क्रत्वन्तरे वा तन्न्यायत्वात्कर्मभेदात्॥७१॥
यथाश्रुतीति चेत्॥७२॥
न चोदनैकत्वात्॥७३॥

Those who oppose this method of interpretation have a doubt about it on the ground that there is no authority for these sounds (or parts of words) in the sacred text. But if we take the expression *pṛṣadājya* as a whole word, we yet have to divide it into parts in order to understand it. It may be a clever thing to do, but it does not fit into the fixed rule (if there be one, that we should not divide words into parts to understand their meaning). And this takes us into the secret of this plan of interpretation; for if it is appropriate to divide this word into parts, it is equally appropriate to divide other words too,—specially when we get an idea of different actions in this way.[194] It is not necessary that every one should have heard about this method; for

1. इदं सूत्रं वृत्तिकृन्मते नास्ति।
2. इदं सूत्रं वृत्तिकृन्मते नास्ति।

the main point is that it should be based on a uniformity of rules.

PART VIII

THE METHOD OF INTERPRETATION: THE PROBLEM OF DESIRE

Introduction

There are certain rules of interpretation of the text. It is possible to have this system because a number of words are new; but the existing words may also be used if they are equally suitable, and there is no difficulty in using them.

The sacred books have examined the idea of a total renunciation of desire; and it really refers to certain special cases where, because of some dangerous obstacle, action is not advised or allowed; otherwise they enjoin action, and we can understand the meaning by dividing words into parts.

It is a rule that in the *Mantras* or hymns of the Vedas, no words should be left out; and we can understand the meaning of all if, where necessary, we divide words into parts. Thus, if we understand the meaning of the words *Agni* and *mās*, we shall be able to make progress with the text. But it requires some skill to coin a word to have a particular meaning; and when we understand their character, we can interpret them by dividing them into parts, as in the case of *ājya* and the number seventeen.

Good and evil desires can both be associated with an intelligent action; but, though he who uses his mind can combine goodness with intelligence, there is no constant union of the two.

We need to use our intelligence in testing the correctness of our meaning; and in this manner we can understand the idea of the silent perusal of the text as well as of *Prajāpati*. It is not possible to describe adequately the laws of Nature in words, for language is all too weak for the purpose; and so their idea is expressed in accordance with certain rules.

Viṣṇu refers to the function of the mind in association with the intellect and the objects of Nature; and all his actions can be understood in this light. It is this idea that has been expressed in terms of the no-moon and the full-moon night.

Certain expressions have only one meaning, while others have two; and it is necessary to use our intelligence to understand them; otherwise we shall find that we have made a change for the worse. Nor should we give an arbitrary meaning to a word; and a meaning can be regarded as properly fixed only when it yields a proper result; and it must, in any case, arise from the word itself, with all its parts unbroken.

The flow of Time is like one desire following another in an endless chain: hence Time is represented in terms of two successive desires.

Rules of Interpretation

प्रतिषेधः प्रदेशऽनारभ्य विधने[1]प्राप्तप्रतिषिद्धत्वाद्विकल्पः स्यात्॥१॥
अर्थप्राप्तवदिति चेत्॥२॥
न तुल्यहेतुत्वादुभयं शब्दलक्षणम्॥३॥
अपि तु वाक्यशेषः स्यादन्यायत्वाद्विकल्पस्य; विधीनामेकदेशः स्यात्॥४॥

If in the text there is a contradiction in respect of a matter that has been decided, or of a statement that has not been made, we should doubt if there really is such a contradiction. We cannot say that we must accept the meaning as we find it, because it is possible to define the meaning of a word in two ways, if there are equally good reasons for doing so. But if our doubt about the correctness of meaning is misplaced, we shall find that certain parts of the text will not fit into our ideas based

---

1. ने च न्या. मा. सम्मतः पाठः।

on that doubt; and yet, whatever method of interpretation we use, the entire text should be included in it.

New Words and Old

अपूर्वे चार्थवादः स्यात्॥५॥

शिष्ट्वा तु प्रतिषेधः स्यात्॥६॥

न चेदन्यं प्रकल्पयेत्प्रक्लृप्तावर्थवादः स्यादानर्थक्यात्परसामर्थ्यात्[1]॥७॥

पूर्वैश्च तुल्यकालत्वात्॥८॥

उपवादश्च तद्वत्॥९॥

प्रतिषेधादकर्मेति चेत्॥१०॥

न शब्दपूर्वत्वात्॥११॥

It is because the words used in the text are quite new that it is possible to have an explanation of their meaning in this manner. This would not be possible in the case of existing words, used as they are, because they will make for a contradiction. But if a new word is not invented, an existing word may be used if it can explain the idea. But if it does not give the required meaning, or if its meaning remains the same as before, a better word should be used. But it may be done by means of an old word, if it is equally suitable; and a subsidiary statement can easily be made in this manner. It is not correct to say that we cannot succeed, on the ground that the use of old words will involve a contradiction of ideas,—because they would be preceded by a number of other words, and that will enable us to understand the meaning.

Meaning of Total Renunciation

दीक्षितस्य दान-होम-पाक- प्रतिषेधेऽविशेषात्सर्व- दान-होम-पाकप्रतिषेधः स्यात्॥१२॥

अक्रतुयुक्तानां वा धर्मः स्यात्; क्रतोः प्रत्यक्षशिष्टत्वात्॥१३॥

---

1. र्थ्याच्चेति न्या. मा. सम्मतः पाठः।

तस्य वाऽप्यानुमानिकमविशेषात्॥१४॥
अपि तु वाक्यशेषत्वादितरपर्युदासः स्यात्; प्रतिषेधे विकल्पः स्यात्॥१५॥
अविशेषेण यच्छास्त्रमन्यायत्वाद्विकल्पस्य तत्सन्दिग्धमाराद्विशेषशिष्टं स्यात्॥१६॥
अप्रकरणे तु यच्छास्त्रं विशेषे श्रूयमाणमविकृतमाज्यभागवत्; प्राकृतप्रतिषेधार्थम्॥१७॥
विकारे तु[1] तदर्थं स्यात्॥१८॥

If there is a general statement, made by a sensible (or an initiated) person, to the effect that there should be no gifts, oblations, or the cooking of food, we should take it that it applies to all such acts (so that such a person may be said to believe in a total renunciation of action). But this is the law of life according to those who believe in the annihilation of all desires; whereas he who has desires, must accept what has clearly been taught,—(namely, that he must act); and he can come to this conclusion from a general idea of things. If, however, we accept the other view, (namely, that all action should be renounced), we shall find that certain words in the text will have to be omitted; and in that case we should conclude that this view is unwarranted (or is true only in an exceptional case). In case of a total negation of action, we should doubt the correctness of our meaning. Even if there is a statement of a general rule that all actions should be renounced, and we are unable to find an appropriate alternative meaning, it should be construed to refer to some special case where, because of some dangerous obstacle, action is not advised or allowed. But if the statement refers to a subsidiary matter, we should take it that it relates to a particular case; and the words of the text, taken as they are, should be divided into parts in the same manner as we divide the word *ājya*, because their meaning in their common form is not permitted in such a case; and it can be obtained only by changing their form.

1. इदं सूत्रं वृत्तिकृन्मते नास्ति।

Character of the Text

वाक्यशेषो वा क्रतुनाऽग्रहणात् स्यादनारभ्य विधनस्य॥१९॥
मन्त्रेष्ववाक्यशेषत्वं गुणोपदेशात् स्यात्॥२०॥
अनाम्नाते[1] दर्शनात्॥२१॥
प्रतिषेधाच्च॥२२॥

(The character of the text is such that) if, in interpreting it in the light of desire or action, certain words are left out or remain unexplained, we shall find that it is due to the fact that we have not understood some statement of particulars which has yet to be made. In the *Mantras* or hymns of the Vedas (it is a rule that) no words should be left out unexplained, if we understand their meaning in the light of their parts; and even if a particular idea does not appear to have bean mentioned, we shall come to know of it, because there will be some contradictory statement to point it out.

Instances

अग्न्यतिग्राह्यस्य विकृतावुपदेशादप्रवृत्तिः स्यात्॥२३॥
मासि ग्रहणं च तद्वत्॥२४॥
ग्रहणं वा तुल्यत्वात्॥२५॥
लिङ्गदर्शनाच्च॥२६॥
ग्रहणं समानविधानं स्यात्॥२७॥
मासि ग्रहणमभ्यासप्रतिषेधार्थम्॥२८॥

If we know what the offering made to *Agni* means (namely, that it refers to the action of the intellect), we shall be able to make progress with the text; and the same thing applies to the word *mās*, because it is of the same kind, and we can understand it in the same manner, when we see through its "disguise"[195].

When we interpret a word in this manner, its meaning should correspond to the statement of particulars given in the text; and so when we understand the meaning of the word *mās*, we see that it has been used (for the mind) to prevent repetition.

---

2. ते च देति न्या. मा. सम्मतः पाठः।

Exercise of Skill

उत्पत्तितादर्थ्याच्चतुरवत्तं; प्रधानस्य होमसंयोगादधिकमाज्यमतुल्य-त्वाल्लोकवदुत्पत्तेर्गुणभूतत्वात्॥२९॥

तत्संस्कारश्रुतेश्च॥३०॥

ताभ्यां वा सह स्विष्टकृतः सहत्त्वे[1]; द्विर[2]भिघारणेन तदाप्ति-वचनात्॥३१॥

तुल्यवच्चाभिधाय सर्वेषुभक्त्यनुक्रमणात्[3]॥३२॥

साप्तदश्यवन्नियम्येत॥३३॥

हविषो वा गुणभूतत्वात्तथाभूतविवक्षा स्यात्॥३४॥

To produce or coin a word to have a particular meaning is a matter of skill. When the principal idea is characterised by intelligence (*Homa*), it is possible to superimpose on it the idea of goodness (*ājya*) too.[196] But when the two are not balanced, we should do as the people do (that is, balance them); and all this can be effected by means of the parts of words; but it can be accomplished by means of intelligence. For instance, in the case of the word *ājya*, the required effect is produced by means of its two parts; and if we use our intelligence, we can understand its meaning at once.[197] The text tells us that it is sprinkled over the fire twice; and we should be able to understand the meaning of this too from what has been taught.[198] Having equated words in this manner, we should proceed methodically to distribute them; and we shall find that their meaning can be determined in the same manner as that of the number seventeen;[199] for if we wish to describe an intelligent act (*havis*),[200] we shall find that it has to be divided into parts in the same manner.

Two Kinds of Desire: A Simile

पुराडाशाभ्यामित्यधिकृतानां पुरोडाशयोरुपेदशस्तच्छ्रुतित्वा-द्वैश्यस्तोमवत्॥३५॥

न त्वनित्याधिकारोऽस्ति; विधेर्नि-(धौ नि-)त्येन सम्बन्धस्तस्मादवाक्य-

1. सकृत्त्वे इति न्या. मा. सम्मतः पाठः।
2. रवघेति तुशब्दोधिको न्या. मा. सम्मतः।
3. क्रमादिति वृत्तिकृत्सम्मतः पाठः।

शेषत्वम्॥३६॥
सति च[1] नैकदेशेन कर्तुः प्रधान भूतत्वात्॥३७॥
कृत्स्नत्वात्तु तथा स्तोमे॥३८॥
कर्त्तुः स्यादिति चेत्॥३९॥
न गुणार्थत्वात्प्राप्ते न[2] चोपदेशार्थः॥४०॥
कर्मणोस्तु प्रकरणे; तन्यायत्वाद् गुणानां लिङ्गेन कालशास्त्रं स्यात्॥४१॥
यदि तु सान्नाय्यं सोमयाजिनो न ताभ्यां समवायोऽस्ति विभक्त कालत्वात्॥४२॥

There are some who maintain that an intelligent action is performed by means of two kinds of desire[201] (good and bad); and they explain this idea in a manner that appeals to our intelligence, by comparing desires to a collection of peasants or working men (some good, some otherwise). This claim in regard to the character of desire is not unwarranted, because it is in accordance with an eternal law; and so the whole idea is complete and has been properly expressed. This being so, action cannot be performed by means of only one kind of desire, because we have to take into consideration the character of the doer of the deed; for the totality of desire is indeed like the *mass* of people (some good, some otherwise). All desire, however, does not arise from the doer of the deed; and since this can be understood from the meaning of the parts of words used in the text, it is not necessary to point this out separately. This is how we explain action; and because it is a proper method of doing so, the parts of words, in their "disguised" form, should tell us what is appropriate to the occasion. But, though he who uses his mind[202] can combine goodness with intelligence[203], there is no constant union of the two, because at different times they can remain apart.

Need of Intelligence

अपि वा विहितत्वाद्गुणार्थायां पुनः श्रुतौ सन्देहे श्रुतिर्द्विदेवतार्था

1. ति न चैकेति वृत्तिकृत्सम्मतः पाठः।
2. प्ते च नोपेति न्या. मा. पाठः।

स्याद्यथाऽनभिप्रेतस्तथाऽऽग्नेयो दर्शनादेकदेवते।।४३।।
विधिं तु बादरायणः।।४४।।
प्रतिषिद्धविज्ञानाद्वा।।४५।।
तथा चान्यार्थदर्शनम्।।४६।।

(We need to use our intelligence to test the correctness of our meaning: for instance,) if an idea is expressed by means of the parts of a word, and, while so interpreting it, we have a doubt in regard to its real meaning, it would give us two meanings, associated with the character of two great forces of Nature (gods).[204] But it is not possible (to have two such forces), even as it is not possible to speak of two intellects in a man. Indeed, we have been taught that each idea (and so a part of a word) refers only to one great force of Nature; and *Bādarāyaṇa* agrees that is the rule; and we find that it is so when we understand which of the meanings has to be rejected, and know the other (or the correct) one.

Silent Reading of the Text

उपांशुयाजमन्तरा यजतीति हविर्लिङ्गाश्रुतित्वाद्यथाकामी प्रतीयेत।।४७।।
ध्रौवाद्वा सर्वसंयोगात्।।४८।।
तद्वच्च देवतायां स्यात्।।४९।।
तान्त्रीणां प्रकरणात्।।५०।।
धर्माद्वा स्यात्प्रजापतिः।।५१।।
देवतायास्त्वनिर्वचनं; तत्र शब्दस्येह मृदुत्वं; तस्मादिहाधिकारेण।।५२।।

When in the text there is a reference to its silent reading, we may interpret it as we like, if the materials of action (sacrifice) are not known; or if they are fixed, it is so because it is of a universal character; and the same is true of the great forces of Nature.[205] This is the system of those who follow rules in a scientific manner, because they can explain the text properly in this way; and we should be able to understand the real idea of *Prajāpati*[206] by means of the application of this rule. It is not possible to describe the laws of Nature adequately in words,—for language is all too weak for the purpose; and so the whole idea is expressed by means of the governing rule in this system[207].

Viṣṇu

विष्णुर्वा स्याद्धौत्राम्नानादमावास्याहविश्च स्याद्धौत्रस्य तत्र दर्शनात्॥५३॥
अपि वा पौर्णमास्यां स्यात् प्रधानशब्दसंयोगाद्; गुणत्वान्मन्त्रो यथाप्रधानं स्यात्॥५४॥
आनन्तर्यं च सान्नाय्यस्य पुरोडाशेन दर्शयत्यमावास्याविकारे॥५५॥
अग्नीषोमविधानात्तु पौर्णमास्यामुभयत्र विधीयते॥५६॥
प्रतिषिद्ध्य विधानाद्वा विष्णुः समानदेशः स्यात्॥५७॥
तथा चान्यार्थदर्शनम्॥५८॥

If we understand the idea of *Viṣṇu* through a study of the sacred books, we find that he refers to that which refers to the functions of the mind (*hautra*), where the mind is associated with the intellect as well as the objects of Nature. This is signified by the no-moon night,[208] and becomes intelligible when we understand what relates to the functions of the mind (*hautra*).

The same idea can be understood in terms of the night of the full moon; and we can understand this if we know the meaning of the principal words.[209] In the same manner we shall find that if we divide words into parts, the hymns of the Vedas become as easy to follow as the principal words.[210] Then we shall understand how, when the no-moon night changes into the new-moon night, it represents the uninterrupted succession of goodness combined with intelligence,[211] by means of the character of desire[212]; and when we understand the detailed description of *Agni* and *Soma*, we shall see how they can both be fitted into the idea of the full moon.[213] Although the no-moon night is the opposite of the full-moon night, both of them represent, by special arrangement, the same idea[214]; and *Viṣṇu* occupies the same place in both.[215] It is in this manner that we can understand the meaning of other terms used in the text.

Special Cases

न चानङ्गं सकृच्छ्रुतावुभयत्र विधीयेतासम्बन्धत्॥५९॥

गुणानां1 च परार्थत्वात्प्रवृत्तौ विधिलिङ्गानि दर्शयति॥६०॥
विकारे चाश्रुतित्वात्॥६१॥
द्विपुरोडाशायां स्यादन्तरा (लगुणा) र्थत्वात्॥६२॥
अजामिकरणार्थत्वाच्च॥६३॥
तदर्थमिति चेन्न तत्प्रधानत्वात्॥६४॥
अशिष्टेन च सम्बन्धात्॥६५॥
उत्पत्तेस्तु निवेशः स्याद्गुणस्यानुपरोधेनार्थस्य विद्यमानत्वाद्विधनादन्तरार्थस्य; नैमित्तिकत्वात् तदभावेऽश्रुतौ स्यात्॥६६॥
उभयोस्तु विधानात्॥६७॥
गुणाञ्च परार्थत्वादुपवेषवद् यदेति स्यात्॥६८॥
अनपायश्च कालस्य लक्षणं हि पुरोडाशौ॥६९॥
प्रशंसार्थमजामित्वम्॥७०॥

An expression for a formless or abstract idea, uttered at once, should not be arranged in two different ways, as it would lose its connection thereby; and that is due to the fact the parts of words are intended to serve a different purpose; and the use of such words enables us to understand the law of symbols used in the text.[216] But if there is lack of intelligence in the application of this method, we shall find that we have made a change for the worse; for instance, we shall get two meanings of the word *puroḍāśa*,[217] because of the different ways of understanding it; and we must use our intelligence so as not to create (unwarranted) relationships between the meanings of words. We must not agree to an arbitrary meaning of a word, because the words used in the text have a special significance of their own; and they are so inter-connected, that not a single word can be left out. But the meaning should be regarded as properly fixed only when it yields a proper result,—and that should be obtained with all the parts of a word remaining uninjured or whole, when we have discovered a suitable meaning, and there is a proper effect of that meaning on the rest of the text. In the absence of this, we should take it that the method of interpretation has not been intelligently applied. (However we interpret the text,—whether in the common way or by division of words into parts,) the meaning in both cases should arise from the manner in which the words are arranged; and we must remember that the parts of a word exist not for themselves, but for the sake of the meaning of the whole; and they serve this purpose like sticks of green wood used to stir the sacrificial fire whenever required.

As one desire follows another in an endless succession, such is the uninterrupted flow of Time; and so Time is represented in terms of two successive desires. This is done to avoid repetition, and to elicit praise.

NOTES

1. As sacrifice refers to action a preliminary sacrifice is something that may be said to precede action; and, as desire does so too, they may be said to have common characteristics.
2. Desire is intimately connected with the mind, and the two are inseparable; but not so a preliminary sacrifice and the mind. However, we can compare desire and a preliminary sacrifice, as being similar in certain respects,—as both are precursors to a great action.
3. Purpose is always associated with the intellect. In order to have a purpose or aim, it is necessary to come to a decision; and that is the function of the intellect.
4. When we understand the idea of the text, we shall find that the idea of *prayāja* or a preliminary sacrifice fits into that of desire to which it has been compared.

   We are told that we can get this meaning by seeing through the disguised" form of the word, that is, by dividing it into parts *prayāja,-pra,yā,ja* would then mean "*(ja)* peculiar to or connected with *(yā)* attaining *(pro)* very much"; and that which is "very much connected with attaining an object" may easily be said to be desire
5. *Ajya*, as has already been explained, refers to goodness; and we can get its meaning by means of division into parts, in a manner similar to that of *prayāja*.

   Agni refers to the intellect; and so we can connect *ājya* or goodness with it.
6. A god or deity refers to thegreat forces of Nature; and both intellect and goodness can be conceived to be great forces that work through different forms of life in Nature. It is not only man but other creatures too, that are characterised by both goodness and intelli-gence; and so they may be said to be like forces of Nature Hence, both *ājya* and *Agni* can be connected with the idea of a god Indeed" *Agni* is always personified as a god; and the *Mīmāṁsā* tells us that *ājya* too can be conceived of in the same manner.

   Agni refers to the intellect; and so we can connect *ājya* or goodness with it.
7. The word *paśu* means "an animal". The *Mīmāṁsā* says that the word is

self-explanatory, though we can get its meaning by dividing it into parts as well. *Paśu—pa, ś, u*—would then mean "(*u, s*) the senses associated with (*pa*) their objects"; and this would be the rudimentary idea of an animal,—a creature who has senses of knowledge and action, and associates them with their objects. It is said that there are five kinds of *paśus* or animals,—men, horses, cows, goats, and sheep; and of these the cow and the horse symbolise the senses.

8. The common meanings of the word *kapāla* are "a cup, an alms bowl, a skull"; but they are obscure. The word may, however, be divided into *k, pa, ā, la,*—when its meaning would be "(*k*) the intellect (apa) away from (*d*) leading to or association with (*la*) the functions of the ten senses". It signifies, therefore, a decision by the intellect to refrain from all action; and that is symbolised by the "alms-bowl" and "skull",—for a man must believe his end to be near if he renounces action, and seeks to live on charity.

9. We have already explained the meaning of *svāhā,—sva, ā, hā,*—as expressive of the satisfaction of the soul at action, so that action is blessed, and continues without end (VIII, iv, u, 16-21; p. 209, n.).

10. According to the ancients, the planets are seven in number,—the Sun, Moon, Mars, Mercury, Jupiter, Venus, and Saturn; and to these are added *Rāhu* and *Ketu* or the "ascending and descending nodes". These are obviously great forces of Nature, as the *Mīmāṁsā* tells us.

    It may be of interest to point out that these planets were believed to correspond to all that is in Nature: the Sun to the intellect; the Moon to the mind; and the remaining five planets to the five great "elements" —Ether, Air, Fire, Water, and Earth—and their respective properties and the corresponding senses of knowledge and action. All these figure in ancient astronomy as well astrology; and the whole idea has been discussed at some length elsewhere (MM. I, 153-158).

11. The literal meaning of the word *prayāja*, as already explained, is "that which is very much connected with obtaining something" and when we understand this to refer to desire, we are adding some-thing of our own to make the idea intelligible.

12. The word *charu* means "a kind of vessel; an oblation of rice, barley, or pulse, boiled with butter and milk for presentation to the gods or the manes". But if we divide it into parts—*cha, r, u*—the meaning would be "(*cha*) the mind, associated with (*r*) the senses of action, and (u) the senses of knowledge". It refers, therefore, to the function of the mind in association with both the senses of knowledge and action. It is, accordingly, a complete function of the mind, which may be identified with that of the intellect, as we have been told. Now *havis* means a burnt offering; and, as fire refers to the intellect, it signifies the function of the intellect. Hence, charu is a variation of *havis*, when we understand what these words really signify.

13. Similarly, *odana* means "cooked rice", and *anna* means "food"; and the

one is a variation of the other, for rice is said to be the best kind of grain.

14. But in this case, says the *Mīmāṁsā*, the idea is clear enough, and there are no two meanings of these words.
15. The meaning of *kapāla* has already been explained (See p. 248, n.)
16. The relation between *charu* and *havis* or the function of the mind and the intellect has already been explained.
17. Normally the word *odana* does not need to be divided into parts, because its meaning as "boiled rice" is suitable, and it can easily be substituted for *anna* or food, as has already been explained. But in certain circumstances the form of even this word may have to be changed.
18. These are three different ways in which we can understand that a word has a "disguise": we may have a doubt about its real meaning, as in the case of the word *kapāla*; or we may not be able to understand it at all; or the meaning may be contradictory.
19. This means that even the ordinary meaning of a word, believed to be under a "disguise", has some reason for it. It may be called its secondary sense; and this would explain how the meaning of the *Mantras* is as continuous as the philosophic rendering of the hymns. This is equally true of the "stories" of the Epics and the *Purāṇas*, which are as continuous as their more philosophic explanation.
20. We can explained that the real meaning of the word *charu* (*cha*, *r, u*) is that it refers to the function of the mind in association with the senses of knowledge and action. We cannot get this meaning of the word if we associate it with the idea of eating.

    It has, however, been observed, that the word is connected in a secondary sense with the idea of "drinking"; and that is the reason for its meaning as a "vessel or cup"; and the idea of "drinking" is connected in a subsidiary way with that of the mind too. We have explained that *Soma* refers to the mind; but it is also said to be a kind of wine; and we have explained that the "juice" of the plant refers to desire, which is an attribute of the mind. Hence, the idea of "wine" or "drinking" is connected with that of the mind. Hence, the idea of "wine" or "drinking" is connected with that of the mind; and, as the energy of the mind is said to be electric, wine would possess some electric properties too.

    It is in this manner that primary and secondary ideas are connected together in the sacred books; and the two meanings of the text appear to run as if one parallel lines.
21. We can get the real meaning of the word *catur* by dividing it into parts,—*c, t, u, r*—meaning "(*ca*) the mind associated with (*t, u, r*) the senses of knowledge and action"; and so, like *caru*, it represents the complete function of the mind, which may, for practical purposes, be identified with that of the intellect. It is for this reason that it refers to the idea of completeness or skill in action.

There are a number of references in the *Upaniṣads* to the importance of the number four: for instance, the cow is said to stand on four legs, a staȲa on four verses, etc.

It may be of interest to point out that there are four stages in the evolution of things in Nature: for instance, the organic cell passes through four stages to attain to maturity. As this would appear to be the law of life, the number four represents the idea of completeness.

The word *catura* is sometimes distinguished from *catur*,— the one meaning "clever, skilful", and the other "the number four"; but the two may also be used in the same sense alike. Hence, the use of the word *catura* should tell us that the meaning of chatur is also the same,—that is "clever, etc.".

22. As *ājya-bhakṣa* refers to an article of food and drink, it expresses the idea of pleasure clearly enough, and so it is not necessary to change its form.
23. *Hiraṇya* means "gold", which is allied to the sun, as silver is to the moon; and the one refers to the intellect and the other to the mind. As fire or *Agni* also refers to the intellect, *hiraṇya* (gold) is said to be like an offering made to fire. It is accordingly one of those words the meaning of which has been defined.
24. We have explained how the meaning of *ājya* can be obtained by dividing it into parts.

    These three words tell us how the text has to be interpreted: we should take some words as they are; the meanings of some are defined; while others have to be divided into parts.
25. The *Mīmāṁsā* has already referred to the supposed "misconduct" of *Indra*. *Kṛṣṇa* too is similarly accused; but if we examine the language of the *Mahābhārata* and the *Bhāgavat Purāṇa* properly, we shall find that what the *Mīmāṁsā* says here is literally true.
26. We have explained that the *Ṛtvij* priests refer to the four faculties of man,—his intellect, *ahaṅkāra*, mind, and the senses—which take part in action. Each of them is given a "gift" to indicate that it has done its work properly.
27. The idea of satisfaction derived from the action of each of these faculties is expressed in terms of *dakṣiṇā* or gift given to the "priests", because the word means "a gift" and also signifies "skill, cleverness". Hence, it is appropriate.
28. Living on food grown in the forest signifies a life of renunciation of action, as has already been explained. It has merely to be fetched, and is very different from what has to be paid for.

    That is the reason why those who believe in renunciation praise this kind of life, or living on food grown in the forest.
29. Living on remnants of food may also be regarded as a symbol of renunciation, as is signified by the word *kapāla*, which means "a beggar"s bowl",—and beggars live on such remnants.

30. As all remnants may be regarded as alike, remnants of food may also express the idea that all things, however apparently different, are really the same. That is, he who lives on remnants, may be said to believe this.

31. We have already explained that the four *Ṛtvij* priests refer to the four faculties of man; while *Soma* refers to the mind. All these faculties engage in action, which is caused by desire, an attribute of the mind. Hence, the *Ṛtvij* "priests" are associated with a *Soma* sacrifice, or a proper function of the mind.

    The *Mīmāṁsā* tells us clearly that we honour these "priests" because they act for us (or the soul,—the "institutor" of the sacrifice); and they are paid for their task, to indicate that these faculties really act at the bidding of the soul, and in answer to our desire.

32. The *Mīmāṁsā* tells us that the prohibition against action,—or inaction, as it may be called—is really like action, or is another form of action. It is a kind of action at a certain stage of our life, when our intellect tells us that the spark is extinguished, and so it is our duty to renounce all action. It is at this stage that action is prohibited, and it is described in special terms: we have to proceed, as a matter of duty, to that part of the sacrificial enclosure (symbolic of action) where the fire has been extinguished (our intellect tells us that the spark has died out).

    It may be of interest to point out that the *Bhāgāvad Gītā* too tells us that what is called inaction is really a form of action (BhG. IV, 18).

33. The word *dakṣiṇā* signifies skill in action, and not inaction; and so it cannot in any case refer to prohibition against action.

34. This means that action is not only preceded, but also followed by desire, as a result of which a person engages in one action after another. This also implies that we are satisfied that the previous action should come to an end; and, as *dāna* or gift represents this idea of satisfaction, it is a duty to offer it at the end of an action.

35. A double sacrifice means an action that is doubly good and intelligent; and there can be no ambiguity about its idea.

36. The different *Ṛtvij* priests refer to the different faculties of man, each of which has its own special part to play,—though all of them have their share in action. Hence, we must find out which of them has the most important role at any particular moment of time.

    We have already explained that their meanings can be obtained by dividing their names into parts (See Appendix I).

37. The idea of *dāna*, as expressive of the idea of satisfaction, has already been explained. As desire is an attribute of the mind, we have a reference to the mind in this *Sūtra*; and the word for it is *Soma*.

38. *Dakṣiṇā*, as has already been explained, signifies "skill in action"; and so conceives of action as something good. It is therefore said to mean a sacrificial fee. An enemy is one who does evil, and *dakṣiṇā* cannot be offered to an enemy.

39. The four *Ṛtvij* priests or the four faculties of man act at the bidding of the "master of the sacrifice" or the soul; and so they can function only when a person is alive. Hence, they cannot take part in a "bone-sacrifice" which is meant to express the idea of action in connection with the dead.
40. This would explain why the *Bhagvad Gītā gives* the highest place among all sacrifice to *japa* (BhG. X, 25): it symbolises the idea of a purely selfless action.
41. The *Bhāgāvad Gītā* conceives of desires that are not opposed to *Dharma* as worthy of all praise (BhG. VII, II); and we are told that the wise ones are ever intent on doing good to all (BhG. V, 25). The desires of good men should, therefore, not be limited to securing some particular object only: they should be for the benefit of all.
42. The expression in the text is *sarva-svāra*, which is the name of a *Soma* sacrifice lasting for a day only. As *Soma* refers to the mind, and the period of a day is a short one, this has been rendered as referring to "action (sacrifice) involving the function of the mind (*Soma*), however small (lasting a day)"
43. The expression in the text refers to a bone-sacrifice, which is said to be a part of funeral rites, and so refers to them.
44. The word used in the text is *dravya*, which has a number of meanings. But when used in a philosophical sense, it refers to a fundamental substance mentioned in the *Darśanas* or systems of philosophy. The *Vaiśeṣika* mentions nine such *dravyas*,—the five great "elements," space, time, mind and the soul.

    The *Mīmāṁsā* tells us that when words refer to these fundamental substances, it is necessary to divide them into parts to understand their meaning, for they have been framed in that manner. We have already been told that a number of words used in the text are newly coined for the purpose.
45. It would obviously be impossible to get the correct meaning of words by dividing them into parts, unless they are newly coined or specially formed for this purpose; and that is what the *Mīmāṁsā* tells us.
46. The argument of these *Sūtras* is that if there is but one method of interpretation, we should always be able to get the correct meaning, however we interpret the text. Thus, if we are able to get the correct meaning by dividing words into parts, that should also be their common meaning; and if we find that it is so, we shall agree that all words are like principal words, and can be treated alike.

    However, as we find that the common meaning is not the same as that obtained by means of division of words into parts, it is not possible to have a single method of interpretation.

    But there are cases where the common meaning is the same as that obtained by means of division into parts; and the *Mīmāṁsā* goes on to give an illustration of that; and it is only in such cases that we can do what we like,—take the common meaning or divide words into parts.

47. The word *Hiraṇyagarbha* belongs to that class where the common meaning is the same as that obtained by means of its division into parts. The common meaning of the word *hiraṇya* is "gold imperishable matter"; and of *Hiraṇyagarbha*" the "Golden Egg", out of which the great creator *Brahmā* is said to have been born.

Now if we divide the word *hiraṇya* into parts,—and that is the principal word—we get *h, i, ra, ṇ, ya*—and the meaning is "(*ya*) that which is (*ṇ*) the intellect, associated with (*ra*) the senses of action, and (*ṇ*) connected with (*h*) the mind". Thus it signifies in-tellect, associated with the mind and the senses,—that is, in action; and the *Mīmāṁsā* has already explained that the real meaning of the word is intellect, to which the idea of gold is said to correspond; and so the meaning is the same whichever way we interpret the word.

Similarly, *Hiraṇyagarbha* would mean "(*garbha*) containing (*hiraṇya*) imperishable matter" or *Prakṛti*, which is said to be imperishable: hence it refers to Nature, the first manifest form of which is the intellect, which is said to correspond to gold. Thus the parent of *Brahmā* is *Prakṛti* itself; or he may be said to be the first idea of God arising out of an examination of the character of Nature, for that is how we get the idea of God.

48. The meanings of the letters of the alphabet as well as syllables, which constitute the parts of words, are such as may be found in a good dictionary.

49. *Soma* refers to the mind, and it is the sixth in order after the five senses. Hence, the six things required in a *Soma* sacrifice or the function of the mind are the senses and the mind.

50. It is not difficult to understand this: for *Agni* means the intellect, and so kindling the sacred fire refers to the function of the intellect.

Similarly, *dakṣiṇā* or "fee" is skill in action; and "payment" or dāna implies satisfaction. The real meaning would thus be as follows: "It is said that there is sometimes a special cause for the exercise of the intellect (kindling the sacrificial fire); but the action consists of a number of parts; and if it is necessary to make a change in any of these parts, we should see to it that the work is done with proper skill and gives satisfaction (an additional sacrificial fee should be paid)".

51. The two options are that we may take the common meaning of a word or divide it into parts. The *Mīmāṁsā* tells us that both these options are possible in certain cases; and gives instances of the words *vāsa* and *vatsa* to explain the idea.

52. The common meaning of *vāsa* is "clothes"; and of *vatsa* "a young one." These two meanings are apparently very different; but the *Mīmāṁsā* says that, if we divide these words into parts, we shall find that they are closely allied; and then we shall see, by means of inference, the reason for their common meanings too.

Accordingly, the word *vāsa—v, ā, sa*—means "(*sa*) the mind (ā) associated with (*v*) Nature"; while *vatsa—va, t, sa*—means" (*sa*) the mind associated with (*t*) the senses of action, and (*va*) Nature". We see that there is very little difference between the ideas they convey; for both refer to the association of the mind with the objects of Nature: only vatsa implies more of (the senses of) action.

The *Mīmāṁsā* tells us that both the meanings of these words are correct and allied together; and that the idea of "clothes" and "young ones" is connected with the function of the mind and its association with the objects of Nature. Let us see how that can be made good.

If the common and "literal" meanings of these words are connected together, it means that a person should wear clothes, and have children, when his mind functions properly in association with the objects of Nature.

Now, the attribute of the mind is desire; and we know that a man desires to live, and also to propagate his species,—for then he lives through his young ones again. The most elementary desires in connection with existence are food, shelter, and clothes; and a man shares the first two of these with the lower animals; and it is only the third,—wearing clothes—that distinguishes him from them. The art of making and wearing clothes is thus a distinguishing characteristic of a civilized man—though even savages cover their bodies in some sort of way. Wearing clothes may thus be said to symbolise a belief that certain desires,—over and above those for the barest existence —are good, and it is necessary to satisfy them. It implies, therefore, a belief in the necessity of performing good actions, which too is a distinguishing characteristic of a civilized man.

There are a number of references, to the wearing and removal of clothes in the sacred books; and they need all to be interpreted in this light. For instance, the attempt to remove the clothes of *Draupadī* in the story of the *Mahābhārata* is meant to illustrate the point of view of those who believe that it is not necessary to perform good actions,—for sooner or later all things must come to an end. The attempt fails, because this cannot be admitted; for that would mean that we must put an early end to our own life. The idea of *Kṛṣṇa* taking away the clothes of the *Gopīs* in the story of the *Bhāgavat Purāṇa* has a similar significance; and the whole idea would be explained in its proper place.

It may be of interest to observe that this is the real explanation of the difference between the *Digambasa* and *Śvetāmbara* schools ai Jaimini: the one believing that we should not, and the other that we should wear clothes. The real point of the *Digambara* school is that it is not necessary to perform even good actions if one wishes to make himself free from all association with Nature; while the *Śvetāmbara* school holds otherwise.

The idea of having young ones has already been explained; and it is for this reason that the *Mīmāṁsā* tells us that one of the duties of a *Brahmāna* or an intellectual person is to have children.

Thus, we see how both the words *vāsa* and *vatsa* are closely connected with the desires of man or the function of his mind.

53. The *Mīmāṁsā* has already explained that *dāna* or gift signifies satisfaction in action; and that is the reason why it is made. It produces a certain effect,—satisfaction—and so that is what it signifies.

54. It is necessary to cook food; and that is signified by the word *pāka*: that is, it refers to the necessity of performing actions.

55. We have seen that clarified butter refers to goodness; and sprinkling it over the fire is associating goodness with intelligence,—for that is what fire really means.

56. The *Mīmāṁsā* has already told us that this is the way of getting the real meaning of dravyas or fundamental substances like the great "elements," time, space, mind and the soul.

57. The word *paśu* is applied to five kinds of animals,—men, cows, horses, goats, and sheep. They are different, and yet, says the *Mīmāṁsā*, they have certain common characterisics.

58. If we divide the word "*go*" into parts,—*ga, u*—the meaning would be "(*ga*) the senses of knowledge, associated with (*u*) the senses of knowledge". The "*go*" or the "cow" accordingly refers to the senses in general and to those of knowledge in particular. We have already explained that the senses of knowledge are closely allied to those of action, and one of them—the tongue—is both a sense of knowledge and of action. Hence, their ideas can be interchanged; and we can say that the "cow" refers to both the senses of knowledge and action, or to the sense of knowledge alone, as should suit the context.

59. If we divide the word *dāna* into parts,—*d, ā, na*—the meaning would be "(*d*) sacrifice (*ā*) associated with (*no*) the senses of knowledge"; and it would signify "the sacrifice or proper function of the senses of knowledge;" and the idea becomes different from that of a "gift".

60. We are told that if we divide the word *dhenu* in the same manner as the word *iṣṭi*, we can get its correct meaning, and it will be found to be the same as that of the word go; and their common meaning is the same, *viz.*, a cow.

Now, we can divide the word *iṣṭi* into *iṣ*, *ṭ i*, when its meaning would be "(*iṣ*, 'to desire") desire, associated with (*t*) the senses of knowledge and (z) the mind"; and that is the idea of desire it conveys.

We are asked to divide the word *dhenu* in the same manner,—that is into *dhe, n, u,*—when the meaning would be "(*dhe*, 'to nourish") nourishing (ṇ) the senses of knowledge, associated with (ṇ) the senses of knowledge". Thus, we find that the word *dhenu*, when divided into parts, refers to the senses in general, and the senses of knowledge in particular, in the same way as the word go; and their meanings are also the same.

61. Similarly the word *dakṣiṇā*, which is a feminine form of *dakṣiṇā*, has to be divided into, *dakṣ, i, ṇa,*—when its meaning would be "(*dakṣ*, 'to act to the satisfaction of) action performed to the satisfaction of (i) the mind and (*na*) intellect"; and that is why it means skill in action, and is associated with *dāna*, which means satisfaction.

These are instances to explain this method of interpretation, where roots or verbs like *iṣ, dhe, dakṣ,* can be combined with other letters in the division of words into parts. But we are told that roots themselves are not to be subdivided.

62. These examples explain how the common meanings of words are linked up with their real ones.

63. *Dhenu* refers to the senses of knowledge, and these are five such senses. The meaning of the number five is said to be the same: that is, it refers to the senses.

64. *Vatsa* refers to the mind in association with the senses and the objects of Nature, as has already been explained. The *Mīmāṁsā* tells us the idea of tri, or the number three, is the same; and if we divide it into *t, r, i*, the meaning would be "(*i*) the mind associated with (*r, t*) the senses of action"; and we see that the idea of the two is the same. And so the *Mīmāṁsā* tells us that the number three refers to the function of the mind.

65. This *Sūtra* tells us that if we think over the words used in the text, we shall get certain suggestions which would indicate what the correct meaning is. Experience has shown that this is correct.

66. The common meaning of this would be that the gift of a cow or a horse is the same (or there is no difference between them), for both are to be given to a *Brāhmaṇa*.

But we know that the word "*go*" (cow) refers to the senses of knowledge, and a *Brāhmaṇa* to the intellect, while *dakṣiṇā* means skill; and so the real meaning is that the idea of the senses as expressed by the word "go" (cow) is the same as that expressed by the word "*aśva*" (meaning a horse). That means that the horse also refers to the senses in the same manner as the cow, for both are associated with the intellect (*Brāhmaṇa*); and their "skill" in action is the same.

67. The next *Sūtra*, however, tells us that there is also a difference between their idea: for the horse is associated with an actor,—that is. the senses are those of action, as distinguished from those of knowledge, with which the cow is associated; and we are able to make this distinction, because the horse can turn about more freely than a cow. Thus, both the cow and the horse refer to the senses in general; but when we distinguish between them, the one refers to the senses of knowledge, and the other to those of action; and it is by means of this special symbol, says the *Mīmāṁsā*, that we can understand this distinction.

It may be of interest to point out that the *Upaniṣads* too tell us that the horse refers to the senses,—more specially those of action.

68. We are asked to divide the word *aśva* into parts in the same manner as the word *hiraṇya* when, we are told, we shall get its real meaning as referring to the senses of action. We have seen that we have to divide the latter into all the letters composing it; and so we must do the same in case of aśva too (and if we divide it into *as, va*, —as in the case of words like *iṣṭi*, *dākṣiṇā*, etc., we shall not be able to get any sense out of it).

Now if we divide the word *aśva* into *a, ś, va*,—the meaning would be "(*a*) like (ś) the senses of knowledge, associated with (*va*) Nature or *Prakṛti*"; and we know that what is "like" or resembles the senses of knowledge are the senses of action; and that is further indicated by the reference to Nature, the special attribute of which is action. This is how we can get the meaning of the word *aśva* (meaning a horse), as the senses of action.

69. We are asked to divide the word *Soma-chamasa* in the same manner to get its meaning. We have seen that we have to divide the word *Soma* into *sa, u, ma* to get its meaning as "(*sa*) the mind associated with (*u, ma*) the senses"; and now we have to divide chamasa into cha, ma, sa, when the meaning would be "(*sa*) he who is (*ma*) the senses of knowledge, associated with (*cha*) the mind"; and so *chamasa* gives us the same idea as Soma. In this case the last part of the word (*sa*) means "he" in the same manner as "yd" does in *hiraṇya*; and that is why the two have been put in the same class. We can now understand why *chamasa* means "a cup for drinking *Soma*".

70. It is not possible regard animals, so called, as animals, because their actions do not correspond to those of the latter. For instance, they all can speak,—monkeys, cranes, fish,—all. The monkey-chief, *Hanumān* knows the *Sanskṛt* language too. We are told that we must change the form of these words to understand their meaning. Indeed, we shall then find that their idea is very different. This lias been explained in the story of the *Mahābhārata*, and will be found to be true in the *Rāmāyaṇa* and the *Purāṇas* too.

71. When we understand the real idea of a prohibited act and of *dakṣiṇā*, we shall understand why there is no objection to giving *dakṣiṇā* in connection with such an act too.

As the *Mīmāṁsā* tells us in the course of these pages, a prohibited act is one which should not be done because of the obstalces in its way; but there can be no real objection to a man attempting to do even the impossible and showing skill in it too. Hence, as *dakṣiṇā* means skill in action, a person may get recognition for his skill even in an action believed to be impossible.

But if we take the meaning in its ordinary sense, a Brāhmaṇa or a good man is shown to be of a shady character, for doing prohibited things; and he who gives him *dakṣiṇā* on such occasion is equally so. But if we understand the meaning of a *Brāhmaṇa* as an intelligent person, of prohibited action as an action full of obstacles, and of *dakṣiṇā* as skill in action,—the whole idea would be changed, and we shall find everything to be in its proper place.

As *dakṣiṇā* means "skill in action", it is always associated with "excellence of design or plan".

72. We have seen that the *Adhvaryu* "priests" refer to the senses of knowledge and action; and the *Mīmāṁsā* tells us that whenever there is reference to their taking part in a sacrifice or a good and intelligent action, we should assume that they would act with skill, and so they should be paid their *dakshiṇā* in recognition of it; and if we change the form of the word into *daksh, i, ṇā,* we shall know that it refers to skill.

73. All kinds of skill (*dakṣiṇās*) are produced by the intellect; and so the share of the senses can only be of a limited character. Hence, the *Adhvaryu*, who refers to the senses, can get or claim only a small share of *dakṣiṇā*.

74. These symbols are the letters and syllables which compose the original word,—the parts into which it can be divided.

75. The point of this is that when we alter the form of a word by dividing it into its parts, there should be no change in the contents of the word: for instance, when we divide the word *pṛṣtha* into parts, we cannot have it as *Pra-stha* (as is often done), but only as *Pṛ-ṣṭha*. Similarly, *Kṛṣṇa* must remain as *K, r, ṣ, ṇa*, and not as *K, ra, ṣ, ṇa*; and so on.

76. *Prajāpati* means literally "lord of creatures"; and the term is applied to a number of gods,—*Sun, Soma, Agni, Indra*, etc. in the *Vedas*. In later times it is applied to *Viṣṇu, Siva*, Time, etc. It is also used specially in connection with the ten "lords of creatures" created by Brahmā, viz., *Marici, Atri, Angiras, Pulastya, Pulaka, Kratu, Vasiṣtha, Dakṣa or Prachetas, Bhṛgu, and Nārada.* It would obviously be impossible to divide all these names into parts to explain their meaning: for the Mīmāṁsā says that this is what we must do to understand their idea. It would be enough to mention that the *Mīmāṁsā* is dealing with the Vedas; and so would refer to the idea of the *Prajāpatis*, as they are mentioned in the *Vedas*,— *Soma, Agni, Indra*, etc.; and the meanings of all these gods can be obtained by means of dividing these names into parts (*Cf.*MM.I, Chapter IX).

But the meaning of all other names of *Prajāpatis*, even in later times, can be obtained in the same manner; for the same method of interpretation applies to all the sacred books throughout. The meaning of the ten *Prajāpatis* created by *Brahmā* would be explained in connection with the story of that god in due course.

77. The word in the text is *prayāja*, which is said to mean a "presacrifice"; but, as has already been explained, it refers to desire, which precedes action,—for that is the meaning of sacrifice. The *Mīmāṁsā* tells us that the idea of *Prajāpatis* is not identical with that of desire, for they have a

different meaning. As the *Parjāpatis* would refer to the gods of the *Vedas*, their idea is obviously different; for Agni, for instance, refers to the intellect. *Soma* refers to the mind, and is associated with the idea of desire; but not all *Prajāpatis*. The same is the case with their names in later literature: for instance, *Marīci* refers to desire; and *Atri*, (*A-tri*) means "he who is like the mind"; but the idea of others is different.

78. We have been told that, as a general rule, all *Sāman* hymns, which are intended to be sung, contain words the form of which has to be changed. We are now told that certain *Sāman* hymns contain matter of a special kind; and it is not necessary to change the form of words or make any alteration in the language. But even in these hymns, if we are unable to understand the meaning, we can change the form of words. The author then goes on to explain that there is a general rule in connection with the interpretation of these hymns, based on the kind of words used in the text. If they are long and sound pleasing to the ear, no change should be made in their form; in another case, we may make a change.

79. We have observed that *Jyotiṣṭoma* refers to the mass or rays of light; and, as it is a matter of science, the knowledge of which is not stationary, we are permitted, says the *Mīmāṁsā*, to make certain additions and alterations. As we have explained, the number of these was at first only three, and then was increased to four, five, and finally seven. This would show that the knowledge of these rays was changing from time to time in those days; and the ancients came finally to the conclusion that there were seven such rays (See Appendix II).

80. A large number of names which occur in the *Vedas* are repeated in later works; and that is so because they refer to ideas and have the same meaning throughout. The *Mīmāṁsā* tells us how we can understand them.

81. The root *budh* has a large number of meanings; and the *Mīmāṁsā* tells us that we have to use our judgement in selecting that which suits the context; and we have the same latitude in this case as in that of the *Pavamāna* hymns, referred to in the preceding *Sūtras* (21-25).

82. *Agni*, as has already been explained, refers to the intellect; and the *Mīmāṁsā* tells us that wherever we have such definitions of words, we should not depart from them in any case. We have a number of such definitions in the sacred books: for instance, Indra has been defined to mean *Prajñātman* or the self-conscious soul; and that is how he should always be interpreted. We shall of course have to bear in mind the exact idea of the self-conscious soul, to be able to understand all the actions of *Indra* described in the sacred books,—from the *Vedas* downwards.

83. The word in the text is *Rathantara*, which is said to be a form of *Agni*; and *Agni*, as we have seen, refers to the intellect.

84. The *Mīmāṁsā* describes the meaning of *yūpa* (or a sacrificial post) as follows:—

"If no particular object is secured when an action takes place, it should be deemed to have been done for the benefit of all, because it has been done at its own time. This is represented by the *yūpa* (sacrificial post), because it is not fixed at the time of action" (XI, iii, 2-4).

We can now understand how the idea of yūpa can be obtained by means of its "connection with action", as we are told here.

As *yūpa* means selfless action or action meant for the benefit of all, the idea of "being tied to a *yūpa*" is that a person should act in this manner; and it is for this reason that it is said that he who desires heaven (happiness) should "bind" himself to a *yūpa* made of *khadira* (or function of the mind).

85. We have already been told that the gods represent the great powers of Nature. The planets are such powers too,—and so they are described as gods.

The terms of praise used in honour of the planets are said to refer to their actions; but we have to use our intelligence to understand the idea, in the same manner as we understand the nature of curdled butter.

86. The "master of the sacrifice" is the soul, for whose sake the different *Ṛtvij* priests (or the faculties of man) take part in the sacrifice (or action).

All these act for the sake of the soul or the "master"; but the soul acts for its own sake,—its "purification" or perfection through experience. This is explained in the *Sāṅkhya*, and accepted by all systems.

87. The great powers of Nature (or Nature itself) act for the sake of others,—not their own; and so the gods, who represent them, are invoked at a sacrifice to show how the forces of Nature work in the world.

The *Sāṅkhya* tells us that the actions of *Prakṛti* or Nature are all meant for the sake of the soul; and when the latter has had experience of all that is in Nature, the bond between them breaks, and the soul becomes for ever free.

88. The common meaning of *dadhi* is curd, and of *ājya* clarified butter; and when it is said that dadhi is the protector of *ājya*, because it comes both at the beginning and end of *ājya*,—the common meaning is that, as we make clarified butter out of curd, there is curd or *dadhi* at the beginning of clarified butter or *ājya*: then we find that after clarified butter has been made out of curd, some remnants of curd are left still; and so there is curd at the end of clarified butter too; and it is in this metaphorical sense that we can call curd the "protector" of clarified butter, because like a "protector" it is to be found both at its beginning and end.

But we have seen that the real meaning of *ājya* is "goodness"; and so dadhi must have a bearing on this idea. The *Mīmāṁsā* tells us that we can get the real meaning of the word by dividing it into parts.

The word *dadhi*,— *da, dh, i*— would accordingly mean "(*da*) sacrifice associated with (*dh*) the mind, functioning as *(i)* mind"; that is, the action of the mind as pure mind, having desire for its attribute.

Now *ājya* is goodness associated with the function of the mind, and desire and goodness are closely allied; for every desire has an element of goodness in it,—so far at least as the person who has the desire is concerned; for no one can desire anything that will do harm to his own self. Indeed, it is meant to give him some kind of satisfaction, pleasure, or good.

Now, as it is the mind that creates desire, which has this element of goodness in it, dadhi, which means the proper function (sacrifice) of the mind (or desire), comes before *ājya* or goodness.

Again, we have been told that desire is at the root of action; and when one action ends, some desire still remains; and that is the cause of a succeeding action. Thus, we might say that there is an element of *dadhi* (function of the mind or desire) after *ājya* (goodness or a good deed) once more. We may also say that *dadhi* "protects" *ājya* even as a proper function of the mind or a proper desire can protect goodness.

89. It is in this manner that we can understand the real meaning of the text. We have already explained that the meaning of the word *ājya* has to be obtained by dividing it into parts. It has first to be reduced to *aja*, and then divided into *a, ja*, when we shall get its real meaning as goodness.

90. An instance of this is the word *Soma* or *dadhi*. When we divide *Soma* into *sa, u, ma*, both *u* and *ma* refer to the senses of knowledge; and unless one of them may be said to refer to the senses of action too, it has to be omitted. Similarly, in the case of *dadhi,—da, dh, i—* both *dh* and refer to the mind; and, unless we specially emphasise the idea of the mind, the last one has to be omitted.

91. *Rātri* means "night", and is one of the few words in *Sanskṛt* with a small number of meanings, which are clearly defined, and have all a bearing on the idea of night.

92. An action is to be judged more by its motive than its actual result; and a motive cannot be seen.

93. The number sixteen consists of the five great "elements", their five properties, and the five senses of knowledge,—with the mind making sixteen.

94. It does not refer to action, because it does not contain any reference to the senses of action.

95. But the senses of knowledge perform a kind of action too,—only it is of a subsidiary character; and as the number sixteen refers to them, it is associated with a subordinate kind of action.

96. The word in the text is *āgrayaṇa*, which means "the first *Soma* libation at the *Agniṣṭoma* sacrifice". As *Soma* refers to the mind, and *Agni* to the intellect, this has been rendered as "the function of the mind (*Soma* libation) in association with that of the intellect (*Agniṣṭoma* sacrifice)". We have already seen that it is only when the intellect plays its own part that an action can be complete.

97. We have already explained that *Soma* refers to the mind.

98. The literal translation of the *Sūtra* (47) is as follows:—"And because of *āgrayaṇa*, the direction of the word (number three),—because of its signifying a particular point or place,—is like the renewal of the sacred fire". We have explained that *āgrayaṇa* means "the first *Soma* libation at the *Agniṣṭoma* sacrifice", and so refers to the function of the mind (*Soma*) in connection with that of the intellect (*Agniṣṭoma*). Again, as fire refers to the intellect, the "renewal of the sacred fire" would mean the renewal of the function of the intellect. The real meaning of the *Sūtra* would accordingly be as follows:—

"And because the function of the mind is linked up with that of the intellect (*āgrayaṇa*), the direction of the word (the number three, or the mind), when it signifies a particular point or place, is like that of the renewal of the function of the intellect".

99. The number three refers to the mind as being, for practical purposes, identified with the intellect, and so with action; while the number sixteen does not refer to action, as the *Mīmāṁsā* has told us: that is the distinction between them.

100. There are a number of references to the number three in the sacred books, and it should always be understood to refer to the mind as closely allied to the intellect.

101. The word *śastra* means "a sword"; and its syllable "*tra*" is derived from the root "trai" which means "to protect". *Sastra (śas-tra)* accordingly means " *(tra)* a protector of *(śas*, 'to kill") what kills"; that is, something that enables us to slay; and so it means "a knife or sword".

102. "Seeing through a disguise" means dividing the whole word into parts; and so if we divide the word *śastra* into *śa, s, t, ra,*—the meaning would be "(*śa*) the senses of knowledge, associated with (*s*) the mind, and (*t, ra*) the senses of action". The word *śastra* refers, therefore, to the function of the senses of knowledge and action in association with the mind, and so, it is a complete function of both. Thus when we speak of *śastra* as a knife or a sword", it really means an argument relating to the character of this function, which can "cut" like a knife or a sword.

The word *śastra* gives us another instance of a redundant letter (*ra*) which has the same meaning as the preceding one (*t*), and needs to be omitted.

103. The two meanings of "*tra*" have already been explained in connection with the word *śastra*.

104. The *Mīmāṁsā* tells us that the syllable tra in *ati-rātra* has to be taken differently; though even in this case it may have a reference to the mind, in connection with a subject that has not been dealt with in these pages. Let us see what that means.

Ati-rātra is said to be a part of the *Jyotiṣṭoma* sacrifice; but, as we have explained, the latter refers really to the mass of rays of light, of which *ati-rātra* is only one. It means "(ati) beyond (*rātra*) the night"; and so would correspond to the ultraviolet ray (See Appendix II). In the circumstances we have to take the word *rātra* as a whole word, and not divide it into parts; and so the syllable "*tra*" in it would not refer to the mind or (*t, ra*) the function of the senses.

105. But the *Mīmāṁsā* says that even here the "*tra*" of "*rātra*" may be connected with the idea of the mind, in which case the meaning of ati-rātra,—*ati, r, ā, tra*—would be "(*ati*) beyond (*r*) the senses of action (*ā*) associated with (*tra*) the mind"; and so it refers to something that is beyond the character of the functions of the senses and the mind.

As *ati-rātra* is said to refer to a ray of light, we can make sense of its association with the function of the senses and the mind only if the latter refer to certain energies; and we are told that the energy of the mind is electric, while that of the senses magnetic; and so the association of the two gives us electro-magnetic energy (or electric energy in motion or action). The word *ati-rātra* would thus refer to something that is beyond or more powerful than electro-magnetic energy; and, as it refers to ultra-violet light, it implies that that is the character of the latter too. It follows from this that *rātra* or night has electro-magnetic properties.

106. We have already explained that the number four refers to four stages of development in all states of life, beginning with the organic cell. We can think of four stages In eating food too: the materials, which must be prepared as food; then they must come to us as our share, to be finally eaten as food.

107. We have explained the special manner in which the idea of the number four can be obtained. We can understand that it refers to completeness or the different stages of development when we examine it with reference to the development of the organic cell. We find that the cell passes through four stages to become mature; and, as the ancients say that whatever is in the cell is also in the whole universe (*Yathā piṇḍe tathā Brahmāṇḍe*), we may conclude that it is a law of universal application.

This would enable us to understand the idea of the "four arms" of certain gods and goddesses to which there is a reference in the sacred books. As the number four signifies completeness or perfection, and as arm is an instrument of action, "four arms" would express the idea of perfection of action; and when they are associated with a god or goddess who, as we have seen, represents the idea of a great force of Nature working in accordance with a good and intelligent law, they imply perfection in the working out of that law. Thus the four arms of *Kṛṣṇa* would convey the idea of God as a perfect actor, who acts and yet is free from the bondage of action, because all His actions are a sacrifice: and we see that this is what the *Bhāgāvad Gītā* tells us about *Kṛṣṇa*.

108. When we understand all this, we can count the four stages in connection with eating food; and this has already been explained.

109. The importance of the Sāma Veda has been emphasised in the *Bhāgāvad Gītā*, where *Kṛṣṇa* says, "Of Vedas I am *Sāma Veda*" (BhG. X, 22); and we can now understand the reason for it. In this connection we have already referred to the range of all the four *Vedas*: the *Ṛg Veda* deals with the problem of action, conceived in its widest significance and embracing the whole world of Nature. The range of the *Sāma Veda* is more restricted, as it deals with the problem of living creatures; but all that relates to them is to be found in both the Ṛg and *Sāma Vedas*. Then the *Yajur Veda* is said to deal with the problem of Sacrifice, which is a moral and intelligent action. The idea of action in the *Ṛg Veda* is a much wider one, as it includes all kinds of action, and not merely action conceived as a sacrifice. The *Yajur Veda* limits its range to such action alone; and as both man and Nature can be associated with such action, it deals with its chacarter in relation with both; and it is for this reason that it is divided into two parts,—the black and white *Yajur Veda*. Finally, the *Atharva Veda* deals with the moral and intelligent action of living creatures, specially human beings. Thus, we come down by stages from Nature to Man: and this is the subject-matter of all the *Vedas* (VII, ii, I, n.).

110. We have already explained that *Indra* refers to *Prajñātman* or the self-conscious soul.

Vāyu is said to mean Air; and that would obviously refer to the vital breath in connection with Indra or the soul. Indeed, the soul is said to have the vital breath for its vehicle, because it is by means of it that it moves through the body; and we see that when the breath departs from the body, so does the soul, and a creature is said to be dead.

Thus, if we understand the idea of Indra and *Vāyu* as soul and vital breath, we can see that they are inseparable. There are a number of references to them in the Vedas and later works; and they are both described as *Soma* drinkers, and are invoked together as partakers of the juice; and this will explain the connection of the two with the character of the mind and desire, for that is the idea of *Soma* and its juice respectively. They are said to be friendly-minded, and a sovereign pair of heroes,—which is easy to understand. They are associated with horses and cows, (which refer to the senses), and are seated in the same chariot (or the body); while in the *Śatapatha Brāhmaṇa* they are even identified.

111. But the *Mīmāṁsā* tells us that they have different characteristics, and there is a difference in their actions too.

In this connection it would be of interest to observe that the great "element" Air is associated with Action, corresponding to which the Hand or the Arm is the special organ of action associated with it. *Vāyu* would accordingly refer also to *ahaṅkāra* or the I-as-an-actor; and the relation of *Indra* and *Vāyu* corresponds also to that between the soul and *ahaṅkāra* (the I within us that acts). Now all systems of philosophy agree that the attributes and actions of the two are different, and it is necessary to distinguish between them. Indeed, the *Sāṅkhya* tells us,—and it is followed by the other systems, that *ahaṅkāra* is a creation of *Prakṛti*, while the *puruṣa* or the individual soul is altogether different. The *Sāṅkhya* believes that the *puruṣa* is not an actor, but only imagines,—according to it wrongly, of course,—that it is so; and it is only when it comes to have true knowledge of itself as something entirely different from all that is in Nature, and as devoid of all action too,—that it can become happy and free. On this point, however, there is a sharp difference of opinion among the different systems; and the final conclusion of *Vedānta* is that it is the soul that is the real actor within us. All this would be explained in due course.

112. *Indra* refers to the soul and *Vāyu* to its vital breath; and so the *Ṛg Veda* tells that they are seated together in the same chariot (RV. IV, xlviii, 2) which, according to both the *Upaniṣads* and the *Mīmāṁsā*,refers to the body; and so they both abide in the body of living creafures, and cannot be separated.

The chief place of the soul is said to be the heart; and the *Upaniṣads* tell us that it abides in the "ether of the heart". As the chief characteristic of Ether is motion or sound, this means that the soul abides in the motion of the heart, which produces sound as well. The vital breath is also linked up with the heart; for though the lungs regulate the motion of breath in the body, they themselves are controlled by the heart.

113. There can be no action without desire; and so *Vāyu* as *ahaṅkāra* or the I-as-an-actor must be characterised by desire; and if we believe that the soul is an actor too, it also must be associated with desire. It may be of interest to point out that the *Nyāya, Vaiśeṣika* and the *Mīmāṁsā* all agree that the soul is characterised by desire.

114. We have explained how desire is connected with the soul as well as with vital breath, or the instrument of its action, *ahaṅkāra* or the I-as-an-actor. Even if we assume that the soul does not act, we must admit that it is characterised by knowledge; and we have seen that desire begins as knowledge, and ends as action; and the idea of the two is expressed by means of the new and the full moon.

115. We can see for ourselves that the soul and vital breath are connected together from the very beginning. It is they together that make the body live; for they depart together, and when they do so, the body dies. This is made still more clear in the following *Sūtra* (13).

116. Seeing through the "disguise" means understanding the meaning of a word by means of its division into parts; and it is in this way that the meaning of both Indra and *Vāyu* has been explained elsewhere (MM. I, 339-357; 412-419).

117. There are a number of references to this idea in the story of the quarrel of the *prāṇas* or the vital organs of the senses in the *Upaniṣads*. We are told that it was agreed among the senses that he by whose departure the body

seemed worse than the worst, should be deemedto be the best; and it was found that the vital breath had this eminence (Chā. Up. V, i, 1-15).

118. We have seen that the word *tri* (meaning three) should be divided into parts,—*t, r, i*—when it would give us the idea of the mind functioning in association with the senses.

119. This idea of the mind, as signified by the word *tri*, is, for all practical purposes, the same as that of the intellect; and we have seen how when the intellect desires anything, it is called the mind.

120. Nevertheless, the intellect has its own special function too: and that is reasoning, decision, discrimination; and that is said to be higher than its association with desire, when it is transformed into the mind. But the proper function of the intellect as pure intellect, or in its form as mind, means that there is unity of action.

121. We have seen that the number three refers to the mind in association with the senses; and the same idea is even more clearly expressed by the number eleven, which refers to the ten senses of knowledge and action, with the mind as the eleventh.

The words used in the text are *tryaṇikā* and *ekādaśini*,—meaning "three-faced" and "consisting of eleven days" respectively. The *Mīmāṁsā* tells us that both these refer to the character and functions of the mind in association with the senses, when it may even be identified with the intellect; and this is how we should understand their idea when it is not clear otherwise.

122. We have already explained that the number thirty-three, like the number twenty-three, refers to all manifest forms of Nature or *Prakṛti*; and all systems of philosophy agree that all this exists for the sake of *puruṣa* or the soul. Now, the *Mīmāṁsā* tells us that the same idea of the soul, associated with its vital breath, is expressed by *Indra* and *Vāyu*; and so we might say that all that is comprised in the number thirty-three is but a substitute for what belongs to them.

123. The number thirty-three is a multiple of the numbers three and eleven; and if we know what they represent, we shall find that they refer to all that is contained in Nature; for they refer to the function of the mind in various forms,—where the mind may, for practical purposes, be identified with the intellect.

The *Mīmāṁsā* further tells us that if we see through the "disguise" of the words *tri* and *ekādaśa* (three and eleven), we can understand all this. We have seen that *tri*—*t, r, i*—refers to the association of the ten senses with the mind. Now *ekādaśa* may be divided into *a, i, k, ā, daś*"a—meaning "*(daśa)* the ten (*ā*) associated with (*k*) the intellect (*i*) arising from (*a*) the unmanifest". If we understand the "ten" here as referring to the five "elements" and their five properties, —we get almost all that is contained in Nature from these two words, *tri* and *ekādaśa*.

124. We are told that it is necessary to change the form of these words to understand their meaning. But, as we can do so only with reference to the context in which they are used, it would not serve any useful purpose to analyse them here. We have however seen that we can get the real meaning of the word *kapāla* by dividing it into parts, when it gives us the idea of renunciation of action.

125. The *Mīmāṁsā* has told us that there are three ways of reciting the *Vedas*, singing, silent recital, and normal tone. The first indicates that the form of words should be changed; the second that it should not; while the third would leave the matter undecided. We are now told that in a strophe consisting of three verses, we have to divide words into parts.

126. We have already explained that the idea of Time is purely intellectual, and so too of its division into *Yugas*, *Manvantaras* and *Kalpas*. It may be of interest to observe that the ancients measured Time in terms of the motions of the sun and the moon, and their system continues to this day. But the sun and the moon represented, according to them, the energy of the intellect and the mind respectively; and so we might say that they measured time in terms of the latter; and this would show how purely intellectual the whole conception is, for the mind itself may, for practical puiposes, be identified with the intellect.

127. Time is the cause of change in all things in the world, but is not affected by anything itself. Hence, it may be said to exist for the sake of other things, not its own. It is in this respect like Nature or *Prakṛti*, which is said to exist and act for the sake of the soul.

128. The ancients may be said to have understood the nature of Time. We have already stated that they believed that it could be represented in the form of a Serpent-wave. As we can conceive of it only in terms of the intellect and the mind (or the sun and the moon), it may be said to be of the nature of a radiation, emanating from the sun and the moon,—specially the sun; and science tells us that these radiations have the form of waves. One of these radiations or waves is Time, and it has the form of a Serpent, as the ancients conceived it to be.

129. The ancients divided Time also in terms of day and night; and so the sacred books tell us of the day and night of men, of the departed ones, of the gods, and of *Brahmā* himself; and *Yugas*, *Manvantaras*, and *Kalpas* are all associated with this idea: for instance, a day of *Brahmā* is no less than a whole *Kalpa*, consisting of innumerable years. We have a reference to this in the *Bhāgāvad Gītā* too (BhG. VIII, 17-19).

130. We have seen how we can understand the idea of numbers,—5, 6, 10, ii, etc. We have to refer them to the corresponding *dravyas* or fundamental substances of philosophy, like the "elements", mind, senses, etc. For instance, the number eleven is made up of the ten senses and the mind,—making a total of eleven. It is in this way that we expand these numbers.

This division is said to be like the division of Time in the sense that each part, though connected with the other, is yet separate, and has its own story to tell.

131. The number three, as has already been explained, refers to the mind; but that may be said to be its definition, and we cannot get at its idea in the same manner as in the case of the number eleven.
Prayāja means "pre-sacrifice", but really refers to desire, as a precursor to action; and this has already been explained. This too may be said to be a definition or a special explanation of the word.

132. *Pṛṣṭha*, as has already been explained, refers to action (MS. VII, iii, 6, 36).

133. We do not get the idea of the number three in the same manner as of the number eleven. Both of them convey the same idea, but the manner of getting at their meaning is different. Whereas we have to expand the idea of the number eleven into ten senses and the mind, that of the number three may be said to constitute a single whole. The *Sāman* hymns are said to be like that, and need to be interpreted in the same way.
Further, we are told that the *Sāma Veda* refers to all that belongs to the living; and all living creatures are characterised by desire, which is an attribute of the mind. As the number three refers to the mind, it is in this sense too that there is a connection between the *Sāma Veda* and the number three.

134. As the hymns of the *Sāma Veda* are intended to be sung, we can obtain the real meaning of words by reducing them to their rudimentary form. But it cannot be obtained in the same simple way as that of the word *tri*, which by division into *t, r, i*, gives us the idea of the function of the mind in association with the senses. We have to use some intelligence in this case, as the idea of the senses of action is repeated twice (*j, r*); and instead of omitting one, we have to take it that the other refers to the senses of knowledge. But in the case of words used in the *Sāma Veda* we have to use our intelligence on a more extensive scale, when we shall find that the meaning is all in accordance with the rules of interpretation.

135. We have seen that we cannot get the meaning of the number three by expanding in the same way as the number eleven.

136. If we divide the word *stoma* in the same manner as we divide the word tri, we shall get its meaning too; for then *s, ta, u, ma* would mean "(s) the mind associated with (*ta*) the senses of action and (*m, ma*) the senses of knowledge"; and we see that the meaning of *tri* is similar too.
The letters *u* and *ma* in this case refer to the senses of knowledge, and one of them can easily be omitted. This, as the *Mīmāṁsā* has told us, is in accordance with the rules.

137. These hymns would appear to constitute the essence of the *Sāma Veda*; for *Kṛṣṇa* describes himself in terms of. *Bṛhat-sāman* hymns in the *Bhagdvad Gītā* (BhG. X, 35).

Viiva-jīt means "all-conquering"; but it is also a particular name of *Agni* which, as has already been explained, refers to the intellect.

The *Mīmāṁsā* has told us that it refers to action,—action of the intellect —by means of which we can conquer everything.

The *Mīmāṁsā* tells us that we can understand the meaning of these hymns in the same manner as we understand the real meaning of the word *viśvajīt*.

138. The text refers to the number thirty-three which, as we have seen, refers to the function of the mind and the intellect. It is a multiple of three and eleven, and refers to all that they signify. It is said that there are thirty-three gods; and that, as we have explained, refers to all manifest forms and forces of Nature.

139. The stage of life, after that of a student, is that of a house-holder or a family-man; and, as the basis of this life is desire,—conceived in its widest significance—it is associated with the function of the mind, which has desire for its attribute, in a special way. The reason why this life is praised is that it enables a man to realise the idea of sacrifice, for he must act selflessly, intelligently and for the benefit of the whole family to keep it up.

140. The ancients divided life into four stages: of a student, a house-holder, one to whom the whole world is a family, and one who in the end must pass away. All this means different forms of knowledge and action, which are linked together by means of desire, which is an attribute of the mind. Hence, they are said to be like the function of the mind.

141. This would appear to be the basis of the decimal system, which makes for easy division; and it is believed to have originated in India.

142. This would appear to refer to multiplication, the basis of which is the number ten. It may be of interest to point out that the numerals, from one to ten, had their origin in India; and they constitute the basis of all mathematical calculation to this day.

143. Although one animal can give us an idea of the nature of all, there is no objection to describing different or a number of animals. That would not, however, add substantially to our fundamental knowledge, says the *Mīmāṁsā*. This means that there are instances of both kinds in the description of animals in the *Vedas*.

144. *Satra—sa, t, ra*—means "(*sa*) the mind associated with (*t, ra*) the senses of action", and so it refers to the action of the mind. It is accordingly said to be a great *Soma* sacrifice; and *Soma*, as we have seen, refers to the mind, and sacrifice is action.

The letters *t* and *ra* both refer to the senses of action; but the two together would refer to the senses of knowledge and action, as has been pointed out in a number of other cases.

145. "The institutor of the sacrifice" is theYajamāna who, as we have already explained, refers to the soul; for it is the soul that calls upon the *Ṛtvij* priests or the different faculties of man to engage in action.

146. Action of this kind makes for the purification of the soul, even as the *Bhāgāvad Gītā* tells us (BhG. V, 11).

147. Fire refers to the intellect; and so "kindling the sacred fire" means acting intelligently and in a spirit of sacrifice. Such an action is said to purify the soul and make for freedom from the bondage of action (*Cf.* BhG. III, 9; V, 11).
When we get a reference to the institutors of sacrifice, etc., we can understand the idea of the purification of the soul by means of intelligent action performed as a sacrifice: that is what the *Mīmāṁsā* says.
148. But if we do not understand all this, we should deal with words according to pattern,—that is, divide them into parts or not as suits the occasion.
149. The word *svāmī* refers to the soul, as we have explained; and so does *gṛhapati* or "the master of the house"; for the body is the house in which the soul abides. But the idea of the two, says the *Mīmāṁsā*, is not the same. Indeed, broadly speaking, we can conceive of the soul in two ways: as an actor, and as a spectator; and the former would appear to correspond to *gṛhapati*, and the latter to *svāmī*. This is supported by the reference to the "*Gārhapatya* fire" or the "fire of the householder", in connection with the three forms of *Agni*; and that, as we have explained, means intelligent action for the preservation of one"s self and the family. Hence *gṛhapati* is the soul as an actor, and *svāmī* as a spectator. It is easy to understand the idea of the soul as an actor, but not as a mere spectator; and the two cannot be identified.
150. The expression in the text is "sacrifice lasting twelve days"; and the number twelve refers to the intellect, as eleven does to the mind; while sacrifice is action. Hence, it refers to the function of the intellect.
151. The *Mīmāṁsā* has already explained that the mind and the intellect may for practical purposes be identified; and we have pointed out that when the intellect desires anything, it is called the mind.
The word for the mind in the text is *satra*, which refers to a great *Soma* sacrifice, or a function of the mind.
The word for "soul" is *Yajamāna* in the text. The point of the author is that when a number of persons take part in an action, it is difficult to distinguish between the function of their mind and the intellect. In the case of an individual it is more easy; for the special attribute of the intellect is decision, judgement, or discrimination, which is difficult to spot in the case of a group.
152. This is what the *Bhāgāvad Gītā* says too (BhG. III, 9).
153. The word in the text is *svāmī*, which refers to the soul, but more as a spectator than an actor. But even one who believes that his soul is a mere spectator, must act; and so the *svāmī* too engages in action.
154. The idea of *dakṣiṇā* has already been explained: it signifies skill in action; and each "priest" who takes part in a "sacrifice" is given his *dakṣiṇā* because he has done the work specially assigned to him with skill. Hence *dakṣiṇā* signifies skill in the performance of different actions. But with all this difference, there must be unity in all parts of an action.

155. Curdled butter is butter and curd mixed together; and yet the two can be separated. The idea of the division of days or Time is similar. We can divide Time, and yet it is a continuous whole.

156. This *Sūtra* tells us that in order to understand the idea of *Jyotiṣṭoma* we should divide words used in that connection into parts.
It also tells us that these rays of light have a number of common characteristics (See Appendix II).

157. The number twelve refers to the intellect; and a ceremony lasting twelve days, to intelligent action. This has already been explained.
The *Mīmāṁsā* tells us that in order to understand the part played by the different faculties of man in a certain intelligent action, we need to divide words into parts. This is made more explicit in the following *Sūtras* (67-68).

158. It is possible to isolate the different faculties of man,—his intellect, *ahaṅkāra*, mind, and senses,—and say which function has been performed by each.

159. We have seen that the mind and the intellect can function in a similar way; the mind is sometimes spoken of as an organ of sense. The *Mīmāṁsā*, as we shall see in the"course of these pages, also tells us that there is a close connection between *ahaṅkāra* and the. mind, and *ahaṅkāra* and the intellect. It is therefore possible to say that we cannot always distinguish between these faculties of man; but the *Mīmāṁsā* says that we can, if we understand the text aright; for though connected, these faculties are different from one another too.

160. A ceremony lasting twelve days refers to a great function of the intellect, as has already been explained.

161. What the *Mīmāṁsā* says in respect of the *Vedas* is equally applicable to. the Epics and the *Purāṇas*. Their text contains certain words, which can be taken in their common connotation, and they suggest what should follow; and then, if we reduce certain other words to their rudimentary form, we are able to understand the real meaning.

162. The connection between the mind and wearing clothes has already been explained.

163. The *Mīmāṁsā* tells us that there are two ways of getting at the correct idea of the working of the human mind. We should understand its essential character, and find out how a normal mind works; and then express its idea in terms of the common life of man. For instance, the special attribute of the mind is desire; and we see that what distinguishes man from other animals is the desire to wear clothes. Indeed, it is man alone who can make and wear clothes; and the other necessary desires,—to eat food and have shelter—he shares with other animals too. But clothes are a special characteristic of man,—a civilized man; and so we may associate the idea of wearing clothes with the function of the mind.

But if in spite of all this, we are unable to understand the meaning of the text, we should divide words into parts: and this is the second way of understanding the idea.

In the present case the word for clothes is *vāsa,—v, ā, sa*—meaning "(so) the mind *(ā)* associated with (*v*) Nature"; and so we might say that the idea of wearing clothes is in harmony with the character of a natural, normal mind.

164. We cannot divide clarified butter or "*ghee*" into parts, even if we try to do so.

The word in the text is *ājya* which, as we have seen, also refers to goodness, associated with desire. We cannot divide goodness too.

165. The five kinds of animals are said to be men, horses, cows, goats, and sheep.

166. This corresponds exactly to the modern division of animals into invertebrate and vertebrate.

167. If a person believes that he must not eat cooked food, it means that he believes in the renunciation of action as the goal of his life. He must, in that case, live on the produce of the forest,—things that grow without any effort on the part of man; and this, as has already been explained, symbolises the idea of renunciation of action.

168. The word for the mind in the text is *tri* ("three"), and for the senses *śara*. We have seen that the former refers to the mind; while the latter is the name of the number five which, as we have seen, refers to the five senses. We can get the same meaning by dividing it into parts,—*śa, ra*—when it would mean "*(śa)* the senses of knowledge, associated with (*ra*) the senses of action".

169. The heart is said to be the seat of pleasure and pain; and so the soul, abiding in it, partakes of it. The heart is said to make for the development of action, and its energy is like that of the mind (*Cf.* MM. I, 63).

170. The *Upaniṣad* describe the body as a chariot (*Kath*. Up. I, iii,3; *Mail. Br. Up*. II, 6; etc.). We can now understand why it is so: a chariot consists of a number of parts, and yet moves as a whole; the body does the same. This should enable us to understand the real idea of "car-warriors" in the *Mahābhārata*. They are persons who have different ideas about the character of the human body.

171. There are some who do not believe that there is any joy in action; and so it is necessary to examine the problem in detail, when we shall find that each faculty of man gets its share of satisfaction in action.

172. The *Upanishads* speak of the soul as the enjoyer; and the Gītā says so too (*KaihUp*. I, iii, 4; BhG. XIII, 22-23). The *Mīmāṁsā* tells us that we cannot understand the soul as soul; and so we have to grasp its idea in the light of the other faculties: for instance, it may be identified with the intellect.

173. It is the soul that uses all the faculties, including the intellect; and so the highest satisfaction in action belongs to the soul.
174. The text refers to *Maitra-Varuṇa*; and we have explained that the former refers to the intellect, and the latter to Nature as the supreme creator of things. We have also explained the dea of the combination of the two; and it has been rendered here as "an intelligent person who believes in Nature as the supreme creator of things.
175. The *Mīmāṁsā* tells us that no sensible person, in his normal state of mind, can really believe that there is no satisfaction in performing actions.
176. It may be said that some actions give pleasure, but there are others that give pain; and so we have two kinds of actions.
177. But the *Mīmāṁsā* tells us that there is saitsfaction in the performance of all kinds of action, and we cannot divide satisfaction in this way. The result of an action may be pain; but when a person performed it, he expected to derive some satisfaction out of it. Hence, even those actions the result of which is pain, are characterised by satisfaction. We must not mix up the result of action with its performance, for the law of the two is different; and the result may often be unexpected.
178. *Agni*, as we have seen, has two meanings,—fire, and intellect.
179. There are a number of references in the sacred books to things which are apparently impossible: for instance *Hanūmān* leaping over the ocean, or bringing down a portion of the *Himālayas* on the palm of his hand. But if we understand the real meaning of *Hanūmān*, the ocean, and the *Himālayas*, we shall understand that what has been stated in the text is true, and did take place. A number of such events in- the *Mahābhārata* have been explained in another place (MM. III-V); and those in the *Rāmāyaṇa* and the *Bhāgavat Purāṇa* would be explained in due course.
180. The previous statement in *Sūtra* 35 that the intellect gets no satisfaction in certain cases, is cancelled by the following one.
181. The *Mīmāṁsā* distinguishes between satisfaction obtained when an action is performed, and its result. The result of an action may be pain or unhappiness; but when a person engages in action, he gets some satisfaction out of it at the time; and this cannot be disputed.
182. This is found to be true of the *Mahābhārata, Rāmāyaṇa* and the *Bhāgavat Purāṇa*; and so it may be said to be true of all sacred books.
183. If we divide the word *sruva* into parts,—*s, r, u, va*—the meaning would be "(s) the mind, associated with ṛ) the senses of action, and (ṇ) the senses of knowledge, and (va) objects of Nature."
184. The word in the text is *Devatā* which, as has already been explained, refers to the great forces of Nature.
185. We have already explained that we have to reduce the word *ājya* first of all to *aja*, from which it is derived, and then divide *aja* into *a, ja*,—when we can get its correct meaning as signifying goodness, which is inherent in all desire.

186. *Ajya* means goodness associated with desire; and so it is a kind of desire which should not be renounced. In order to understand this clearly, there should be an explanatory repetition of the idea, so that there should be no ambiguity.
187. We have to divide the expression *gṛha-medhīya* into two parts, *gṛha* and *medhīya*—in order to understand its meaning. The *Mīmāṁsā* tells us that the word *ājya* has to be divided into two parts in a similar manner. That is possible only if we reduce it to aja, and then divide it into *a, ja*; and this has already been explained. '*Gṛha-medhīya*" means "relating to domestic sacrifice".
188. The idea of these *Sūtras* is that although we find in some sacred books that all desires should be renounced, we really cannot do so; and since these books contain nothing that is incongruous, we must take it that we have not properly understood them. This is made more clear in the following *Sūtras*. We can renounce all desires only when we die.
189. The point of these *Sūtras* is that, if it be correct that we should renounce all desires, as some sacred books are believed to say., we should not be able to get a different meaning when we divide words into parts. This is not mere hearsay, and we can test it for ourselves. This discussion is continued in (X, viii, 12-18.)
190. *Pṛṣad-ājya* means "curdled butter or ghee mixed with coagulated milk"; and we get this meaning from its parts,—*pṛṣad* and *ājya*. If this is permitted, there can be no objection to our extending the same principle and getting the meaning of a word by dividing it further into its syllables and letters: for the authority in both cases is the same. This is what the *Mīmāṁsā* tells us.
191. All meanings are fixed by means of the application of the rules of grammar. The syllables and letters composing a word have their fixed meanings too, like all other words; and we have to follow a good dictionary.
192. We are, however, required to fix upon one meaning, which we regard as most suitable.
193. But a letter or syllable may have a number of meanings; and we are not bound to give the same meaning to the same part every time and everywhere. This method of interpretation gives us a certain latitude to fix meanings according to the requirements of each case; only we must not invent our own meanings.

    It may be of interest to observe that this is exactly what has been done in *The Mystery of the Mahābhārata*; the meanings of letters and syllables are, as a rule, the same throughout; but a certain variation has been allowed.
194. This, as the *Mīmāṁsā* tells us, is our authority for dividing words into parts, and no other authority is required. If we can divide the word *pṛṣad-ājya* into two parts to get its meaning, we can also further divide it or any

other word into its component syllables or letters or both. The test in each case is the meaning we are able to obtain. This is the secret of this method of interpretation.

195. The word *mās* means "the moon", which, as we have seen, refers to the mind. If we see through its "disguise" or divide it into parts, —*m, ā, s*—the meaning would be "(*s*) the mind, (*ā*) associated with (*m*) the senses of knowledge"; and we notice that its idea is similar to that of *Soma*, which has the same meaning too.
196. The text refers to *Homa* and *ājya*; and the one means intelligence and the other goodness, as has already been explained.
197. We have explained that it is necessary to reduce *ājya* to aja, from which it is derived; and then its meaning can be obtained by reducing *aja* to two parts,—*a, ja*.
198. The common meaning of *ājya* is "clarified butter"; and it is said to be sprinkled over the fire. But it really means "goodness", while "fire" means "intelligence". To sprinkle "clarified butter" twice over the "fire" would, therefore, mean a double measure of goodness added to intelligence, so as to make it extremely good.
199 The number seventeen, as has already been explained, refers to the soul or the intellect.
200. *Havis*, as has already been explained, refers to an intelligent action.
201. The word in the text is *puroḍāśa*, which means " *Soma-juice*". As Soma refers to the mind, its "*juice*" is obviously desire. Hence *puroḍāśa* means "desire arising from the mind".
202. The word in the text is *Soma*, which refers to the mind.
203. The word in the text is *sāmnayya*, which means "any substance mixed with clarified butter and offered as a burnt offering". We have explained that "clarified butter" refers to goodness; while fire (burnt offering) to the intellect; and so the mixture of the two is a combination of goodness with intelligence. The author has already told us that an intelligent action is not always good action or characterised by a good desire; and this is emphasised again.
204. A god refers to the great forces of Nature. As the text deals with the working of the great laws of Nature, it describes the working of the great forces of Nature, which should not be mixed up.
205. We have been told that in case where the text has to be recited silently, there should be no change in the form of words. Here we are told that we may do so if we like in certain cases,—where either we do not know the "materials of action", or they are fixed, because they relate to universal laws, as in the case of the great forces of Nature. In such cases there is no difference in meaning whether we take words as they are or divide them into parts.
206. *Prajāpati* is an instance of a great power of Nature,—something of the character of a universal law; and so the meaning of his name is the same

whether we take the word as it is or divide it into parts. *Prajāpati* means "the lord or creator of all created beings"; and we must agree that there is one, for these creatures have not created themselves. But his idea is not the same as that of God, conceived in a moral sense; and this has already been explained.

207. The governing rule in this system is that if we get a rational meaning without dividing words into parts, we should accept it; otherwise we should divide words into parts.

208. *Hautra* means "relating to *Hotṛ*", who refers to the mind.

It is said that the moon is invisible on the no-moon night, because it dwells with the sun. As the moon refers to the mind, and the sun to the intellect, the idea of the moon dwelling with the sun is the same as that of the union of the mind and the intellect; while the night refers to Nature, as the day to *Puruṣa* or God, as we have explained. Thus, we might say that the no-moon night is symbolic of the association of the mind (moon) with the intellect (sun) as well as the objects of Nature; and it is this that is represented by *Viṣṇu*.

The *Mīmāṁsā* has explained that if we divide words into parts, we should be able to get their real meaning. It has also told us that this should specially be done in the case of the gods referred to in the *Vedas*. As *Viṣṇu* is one of these gods, we should be able to get his exact idea by dividing the name into parts; and that will enable us to see if it fits into the meaning given here.

The word *Viṣṇu*,— *V, i, ṣ, ṇ, u*—would mean "(u, a particle implying assent or emphasis) verily (*n*) the intellect and (*ṣ*) the mind (*i*) associated with (*v*) Nature"; and so we find that the analysis of the parts of the name gives us the same identical meaning.

We are told that *Kṛṣṇa* is a perfect "incarnation" or embodiment of the idea of *Viṣṇu*; and so his name too should give us the same meaning; and we find that it is so: for *Kṛṣṇa—K, ṛ, sh, ṇa*—means "(*ṇa*) the intellect and (sh) the mind (ṛ) associated with (k) Nature". We notice that the idea is exactly the same. (Cf. MM. I, 398-412). It has been said that the no-moon night refers to the union of the moon and the sun, or the mind and the intellect; and that is indicated in the conjunct consonant ***sh-n*** in both *Viṣṇu* and *Kṛṣṇa*.

It may be of interest to observe that the sun and the moon actually travel together during the period covered by the no-moon night. They are together in the east on the morning of that day, and set together in the west in the evening; and so they are said to dwell together.

209. We have already explained that the full moon refers to the full action of the mind, when desire develops into deeds; and the *Mīmāṁsā* tells us that the idea of *Viṣṇu* is represented also by the full moon, —that is, by the full function of the mind, when the latter may, for practical purposes, be identified with the intellect. That is, it re-presents the union of goodness with

intelligence in the working of the great forces of Nature; and that is the idea of *Viṣṇu*, says the *Mīmāṁsā*. It also tells us that we can understand it if we know the idea of the principal words,—that is, the sun and the moon here. If we understand that they refer to the intellect and the mind, we shall know what the exact idea is.

210. We have been told that if we understand the real meaning of words by means of this method, the *Mantras* or hymns would be transformed into *Vidhi* or the laws of Nature.

211. The word used in the text is *sāmnayya* which, as has already been explained, refers to goodness combined with intelligence.

212. The word in the text is *puroḍāśa* which, as has already been explained, refers to desire as an attribute of the mind.

213. We have already explained that *Agni* refers to the intellect, and *Soma* to the mind; while the full moon refers to the full function of the mind, when it may, for practical purposes, be identified with the intellect. Thus the combination of *Soma* and *Agni* is the combination of the mind and the intellect, which is symbolised by the full moon.

214. The no-moon night gives us the idea of the union of the moon and the sun or the mind and the intellect; and the full-moon does the same.

215. *Viṣṇu* refers to the union of the mind with the intellect; and so is associated with both the no-moon and full-moon nights.

216. The *Mīmāṁsā* has already explained that the purpose of the parts of a word is to express the idea of the different parts of an action or an object; that is, to define things exactly and accurately But if the thing itself is formless or indefinite, no useful purpose will be served by dividing the corresponding word into parts.

217. The word *puroḍāśa* has a number of meanings,—sacrifice, prayer, *Soma-juice*, etc., and we have to use our intelligence to fix upon a proper one and to explain it correctly too. Even if we take it to mean *Soma-juice*, we have again to explain it as meaning desire. If we do not use our intelligence, we shall get more than one meaning of the word, and that will cause confusion.

CHAPTER - XI

ACTION, EFFORT AND RESULT : THE METHOD OF INTERPRETATION

PART I

Every action has an aim, and there is unity in all action; but the result of each action is different.

Each part of a word refers to a separate action, or its object or result, as well as the character of the doer of the deed.

We can express the idea of a single action by means of a single note, and that is the best mode of its expression; and this is based on the principle that there is only one exercise of intelligence at a time: it also prevents repetition; but we can do as we like in the concluding parts of a word.

All action implies effort and also an expectation of result; but the result arises out of something more. When, however, the result accompanies action, its idea should be described by means of the common meaning of words; or we may do as we like. But if a whole idea is expressed by means of a single word, it is necessary to divide the latter into parts.

The common people judge an action by its result. The idea of result is important, for an action comes to an end only when its result does so. The result of an action corresponds to its purpose or design; but it is not possible to lay down any fixed rules as to how this purpose should be expressed. If there is no expectation of result, an action may be said to have been performed for its own sake.

We should, as far as possible, avoid repetition, for it can easily cause confusion.

The principle of interpretation is that we should take the common meanings of words; but if they do not make sense, we should divide them into parts. We cannot, however, put in much in the last portions of a word (or the text).

All intelligent action involves a reference to the forces of Nature; and we can understand this if we divide words into parts; and this design of division is indicated by the *Krama* method of reading the text. When, however, the parts of an action are equal, the idea can be expressed by means of a single note.

The parts of a word which have the same meaning should be in close proximity to one another; and this rule commonly applies to all principal words.

We cannot have a single method of interpretation; but whatever method we adopt, it should have a regular plan, and be governed by definite rules.

There is a difference of time even in notes uttered simultaneously. This has a special importance, and is expressed by means of a separate rule.

Unity in Action

प्रयोजनाभिसम्बन्धात्पृथक् सतां ततः स्यादैककर्म्यमेकशब्दाभि-संयोगात्॥१॥

शषवद्वा प्रयोजनं प्रतिकर्म विभज्येत॥२॥

अविधानात्तु नैवं स्यात्॥३॥

शेषस्य हि परार्थत्वाद्विधानात्प्रतिप्रधानभावः स्यात्॥४॥

As each action, taken separately, is connected with a purpose or aim, there is a unity in all actions performed by creatures; and that is expressed by means of the connection of each part of a word with the other. We should thus be able to assign a motive to each action, even as we assign to it an effect or result; and all this is in accordance with a law. So far as effect is concerned, it is for the sake of something other than the action; for that is its law, as we may see in every principal action.

How Described

अङ्गानान्तु शब्दभेदात्क्रतुवत्स्यात् फलान्यत्वम्॥८॥
अर्थभेदस्तु तत्रार्थेहैकार्थ्यादैककर्म्यम्॥६॥
शब्दभेदान्नेति चेत्॥७॥
कर्मार्थत्वात्प्रयोगे ताच्छब्द्यं स्यात्तदर्थत्वात्॥८॥

(All this is described by means of words, which need to be divided into parts to be understood). With regard to the parts of a word,—as they consist of different notes, (each of them represents an action or a part of an action), and they should each, according to this design, have a separate effect. As there is a separate purpose in the case of each action, even so there is a separate meaning in the case of each note of a word; and so we might say that a singleness of purpose makes for a singleness of action. We cannot deny that this is true (of the different notes or parts of a word), for if it is true that every action has a purpose, (and it has to be described by means of words), it follows that this can be done by means of the different notes or parts of words, each with a meaning of its own.

Connection between Actions and Words

कर्तृविधेर्नानार्थत्वाद्गुणप्रधानेषु॥९॥
आरम्भस्य शब्दपूर्वत्वात्॥१०॥

Every person has his own manner of performing action, and each action has a purpose of its own; and it is in order to represent this that the principal words in the text are divided into parts. (This illustrates the connection between actions and words), for the commencement of action is preceded by words.

How Described

एकेनापि समाप्येत कृतार्थत्वाद्; यथा क्रत्वन्तरेषु प्राप्तेषु चोत्तरावत्स्यात्॥११॥

फलाभावादिति चेत्॥१२॥

न कर्मसंयोगात्प्रयोजनमशब्ददोषं स्यात्॥१३॥

ऐकशब्द्यादिति चेत्॥१४॥

नार्थपृथक्त्वात्समत्वादगुणत्वम्॥१५॥

We should be able to describe the idea of an action by means of a single note, and we can succeed in the task, with the result that our aim and achievement would be expressed in the highest form. We cannot say that it is impossible to achieve this result, because each note can refer to an action, so that there would be no lack of proper expression. Nor can we say that a single note cannot represent a single action,—for each object of action is separate, and it can be made equal to a single note; and there would be no need of further sub-division.

A Scientific Method

विधेस्त्वेकश्रुतित्वादप र्यायविधानान्नित्यवच्छ्रुतभूताभिसंयोगादर्थेन युगपत्प्राप्तेर्यथाक्रमं स्वशब्दो[1] निवीतवत्तस्मात्सर्वप्रयोगे प्रवृतिः स्यात्॥१६॥

तथा कर्मोपदेशः स्यात्॥१७॥

क्रत्वन्तरेषु पुनर्वचनम्॥१८॥

This mode of expression is based on the principle that there is a single exercise of intelligence at a time; and the arrangement is such that there is no repetition. That is easily seen, because we can get the meaning if we read the text according to *Krama*.[1] Each principal word is capable of being handled as the author thinks fit; and that is the reason why the whole presentation is so fine. It is in this manner that action should be described, for in any other mode of writing there is bound to be a repetition of words.

---

1. स्वशब्द इति वृत्तिकृन्मते न पठ्यते।

An Exception

उत्तरास्वश्रुतित्वाद्विशेषाणां कृतार्थत्वात्स्वदोहे यथाकामी प्रतीयेत॥१९॥

But if the concluding parts of a word are not distinct, and if we are able otherwise to get a satisfactory meaning of special terms, we may deal with them as we like[2].

Action and Result

कर्मण्यारम्भाव्यत्वात्कृषिवत् प्रत्यारम्भं फलानि स्युः॥२०॥
अधिकारश्च सर्वेषां कार्यत्वादुपपद्यते विशेषः॥२१॥
सकृत्तु स्यात्कृतार्थत्वादङ्गवत्॥२२॥
शब्दार्थश्च तथा लोके॥२३॥
अपि वा संप्रयोगे यथा कामी प्रतीयेताश्रुतित्वाद्विधिषु वचनानि स्युः॥२४॥
ऐकशब्द्यात्तथाङ्गेषु॥२५॥

All action implies effort; and, as we expect a result when we cultivate the soil, there should be result following an effort or the commencement of an action. Those who act, lay claim to the result of action; but it arises only when something special takes place[3]; and that too immediately after an act is done; and we have the same thing in the case of the sub-division of words into parts.[4] Where, however, the result accompanies action, the meaning of a word is its common meaning; or we may, by common consent, take it as we like[5]; and if the mode of expression is such that the idea is not clear, a number of words may be used. But if we wish to express the whole idea by means of a single word, we have to divide it into parts.

Result as a Continuation of Action

लोके कर्माऽर्थलक्षणम्॥२६॥
क्रियाणामर्थशेषत्वात्प्रयक्षम (त्यक्षोऽ) तस्तन्निर्वृत्त्याऽपवर्गः स्यात्॥२७॥
धर्ममात्रे त्वदर्शनाच्छब्दार्थेनापवर्गः स्यात्॥२८॥

So far as the common people are concerned, they understand the idea of action in terms of its result. Its direct perception also arises from that (result); and it is for this reason that it is only when the result of an action comes to an end, that the action itself really comes to an end too. As a matter of common practice, however, we do not understand this; so that we often believe that there is an end to action when we have described its meaning in words.

Connection between Result and Aim

क्रतुवद्वानुमानेनाभ्यासे फलभूमा स्यात्।।२९।।
सकृद्वा कारणै[1]कत्वात्।।३०।।
परिमाणं चानियमेन स्यात्।।३१।।
फलारम्भनिवृत्तेः क्रतुषु स्यात् फलान्यत्वम्।।३२।।

The result of an action corresponds to its design or plan; and if we use our power of inference properly, we should be able to get the idea of the entire result of action from what we expect to happen. But where there is only one action, the result should arise immediately; only in such a case there is, no fixed rule for measuring it. All that we can say is that when a person has done with one result, he plans another.

Difficulty of Measuring Purpose

अर्थवांस्तु नैकत्वादभ्यासः स्यादनर्थको यथा भोजनमेकस्मिन्नर्थस्यापरिमाणत्वात्प्रधाने च क्रियार्थत्वादनियमः स्यात्।।३३।।
पृथक्त्वाद्विधितः परिमाणं स्यात्।।३४।।

If a word does not convey its meaning properly, its repetition would be as useless as the repetition of food. As the meaning of a word cannot be limited to one sense, whereas the purpose of an action is connected with the principal word, it is not possible to lay down any fixed rules as to how this purpose in action can be described in words. Its only measure is that it should be fixed separately in each case.

Action Performed for its Own Sake

अनभ्यासो वा प्रयोगवचनैकत्वात्सर्वस्य युगपच्छास्त्रापदफलत्वाच्च कर्मणः स्यात्क्रियार्थत्वात्।।३५।।

There should be no repetition if, by uttering one word, we are able to express the whole idea, and if a single direction

1. द्वा कारेति न्या. मा. पाठः।

applies to all cases simultaneously. If there is no expectation of the fruit of action, the action should be regarded as having been performed for its own sake.

Cases for Repetition and no Repetition

अभ्यासो वा छेदनसम्मार्गाऽवदानेषु वचनात्सकृत्त्वस्य॥३६॥

अनभ्यासस्तु वाच्यत्वात्॥३७॥

But it would be necessary to have repetition in cases of removal of doubt, purification, and great and glorious deeds, because what has been said about the principle of simultaneity (should apply to such cases). But if a thing has been expressly stated or denned in a particular manner, there should be no repetition at all.

Cases for an Alternative Explanation

बहुवचनेन सर्वप्राप्तेर्विकल्पः स्यात्॥३८॥

दृष्टः प्रयोग इति चेत्॥३९॥

तथेह॥४०॥

भक्त्येति चेत्॥४१॥

तथेतरस्मिन्॥४२॥

If we are able to obtain everything from the text, but it is done by means of too many words, we should believe that there is an alternative to it. Indeed, we shall find that it is so; but it is not so in a number of cases in succession: it is so only in a few scattered places.

Principle of Interpretation

प्रथमं वा नियम्येत; कारणादतिक्रमः स्यात्॥४३॥

श्रुत्यर्थाविशेषात्॥४४॥

तथाचान्यार्थदर्शनम्॥४५॥

प्रकृत्या च पूर्ववत्तदासत्तेः॥४६॥

The principle of interpretation is that we should follow the fixed rules of composition, and they should be varied only for some special reason; but we should see that the meaning of the text is uniform throughout. It is in this manner that we can understand all other meanings of the text; and that, as has already been explained, can be done by reducing words to their rudimentary form because we can get an uninterrupted sequence of meaning of the text in this manner.

What can be Stated at the End

उत्तरासु न यावत्स्वमपूर्वत्वात्॥४७॥

यावत्स्वं वाऽन्यविधानेनानुवादः स्यात्॥४८॥

साकल्यविधानात्॥४९॥

बह्वर्थत्वाच्च॥५०॥

In the last portion of the text it is not possible to put in all that we might like to do, if it has not already been stated before. But if there is an earlier statement of particulars to the same effect, we may put in whatever we like by way of further explanation. This is permitted, because the idea is to make a complete statement of all particulars, and to satisfy the requirements of many other things.

Intelligent Action and Forces of Nature

अग्निहोत्रे चाशेषवद्यवागूनियमः॥५१॥

इति[1] व्याख्यातम्॥ ५१अ.

तथा पयः प्रतिषेधः कुमाराणाम्॥५२॥

The rule in regard to an intelligent action[6] is that it involves a reference to Nature[7] as a whole; and this has already been explained. It is for this reason that the knowledge of Nature[8] is forbidden in the case of children.

Effect of "Disguise" and *Krama*

सर्वप्रापिणापि लिङ्गेन संयुज्य देवताभिसंयोगात्॥५३॥

प्रधानकर्मार्थत्वादङ्गानां तद्भेदात् कर्मभेदः प्रयोगे स्यात्॥५४॥

क्रमकोपश्च यौगपद्ये स्यात्॥५५॥

तुल्यानां तु यौगपद्यमेकशब्दोपदेशात् स्याद्विशेषाग्रहणात्॥५६॥

---

1. वृत्तिकृन्मते इदं सूत्रमधिकम्।

ऐकार्थ्यादव्यवायः स्यात्॥५७॥
तथा चान्यार्थदर्शनं कामुकायनः॥५८॥

Even though we may be satisfied that we have got all that we wanted out of the text, we shall find,—if we refer to its "disguised" form—that it is connected with the great forces of Nature.[9] In this design or form of presentation, each part of a word represents a distinct part of a principal action, and expresses its meaning. This is also indicated by the *Krama* method of reciting the text, for if we pronounce all parts of a word simultaneously, it would be incompatible with *Krama*.[10] Where, however, the parts of an action are equal or the same, we can pronounce all the parts simultaneously; because they can be represented by a single note, and we cannot perceive any difference between them. These parts of a word should, however, be very close to each other, because they have the same meaning. In this manner we can understand other meanings too, says *Kāmukāyana*[11].

A Proper Mode of Expression

तन्न्यायत्वादशक्तेरानुपूर्व्यं स्यात् संस्कारस्य तदर्थत्वात्॥५९॥
असंस्पृष्टोऽपि तादर्थ्यात्॥६०॥
विभवाद्वा प्रदीपवत्॥६१॥

This is a proper mode of expression; and where we are unable to understand the meaning of the text, it should be regarded as the normal mode of expression, because that is what we mean when we speak of the correct formation and use of words.[12] Even a single word, unconnected with any other word, is intended to mean the same thing.[13] (There is no obscurity about it) for it is to be found everywhere, and is clear like a lamp.

A Single Method is not Possible

अर्थात्तु लोके विधिः प्रतिप्रधानं स्यात्॥६२॥
सकृदिज्यां कामुकायनः, परिमाणविरोधात्॥६३॥
विधेस्त्वितरार्थत्वात् सकृदिज्याश्रुतिव्यतिक्रमः स्यात्॥६४॥

विधिवत्प्रकरणाविभागे प्रयोगं बादरायणः॥६४॥
अपि[1] चैकेन सन्निधानमविशेषको हेतुः॥६५॥
क्वचिद्विधानान्नेति चेत्॥६६॥
न विधेश्चोदितत्वात्॥६७॥

(It may be argued that) this rule should commonly apply to every principal word, for it stands separately by itself.[14] According to *Kāmukāyana*, there should be only one way of interpreting the text, for otherwise there would be a conflict in the measure of values. But if this rule does not make for a proper meaning of the text, a single method of dealing with it would be irrational. According to *Bādarāyaṇa*,[15] there should be some method in our plan of interpretation, and there should be no break in the explanation. But there are some who hold that there should be a uniform method of dealing with all words. However, we cannot say that there are no rules in connection with our method of interpretation, for it is all governed by definite rules.

Time Factor in Action: How Described

व्याख्यातं तुल्यानां योगपद्यमगृह्यमाणविशेषाणाम्॥६८॥
भेदस्तु कालभेदाच्चोदनाव्यवायात् स्याद्विशिष्टानां विधिः प्रधानकालत्वात्॥६९॥
तथा चान्यार्थदर्शनम्॥७०॥
विधिरिति चेन्न वर्तमानापदेशात्॥७१॥

As has already been explained, the parts of words expressive of things of equal or the same value, should be uttered simultaneously, because we cannot perceive any difference between them. But there may be a difference even among such things, arising from the difference of time. That, however, should be expressed in a special way; for the Time-factor is important, and so there should be a special rule in connection with it.[16] It is in this manner that we can understand the differ-

१. वृति न्या. पुस्तकयोर्नास्ति।

ent meanings (or implications) of the same thing. But this is not governed by a general rule, and depends on the statement of the facts as they are.

PART II

THE METHOD OF INTERPRETATION

Introduction

If a single note expresses the idea of principal things, they should be found together, and should have the same maker.

All things are connected together in accordance with a law; and even so the meanings of all expressions are connected with the principal word; but not so the meanings of parts of words where the great forces of Nature are concerned. In other cases, however, it should be possible to have this connection; and it is in this manner that we understand the meaning of the text.

Each part of a word is separate, because it has to correspond to each part of an action, and has a bearing on the idea of the principal word; but not so in the case of the great forces of Nature.

There is a theory in connection with the idea of the parts of a word, which enables us to understand the rest of the text. In certain cases we can easily understand the meaning of an expression from that of its parts, for they have been formed in accordance with this theory. In the case of animals, however, this theory needs to be modified, because the nature of their impelling force is different; but we can represent the function of the mind and its relation to desire in this manner. With regard to words formed in accordance with this theory, we can understand their meaning from their parts.

An intelligent action is connected with the great forces of Nature; but the latter may be different at different times.

If the principal word is removed, we cannot understand the meaning of the text.

We can understand the real idea of the gods only if we divide their names into parts; but it requires intelligence to do so, and there should be general agreement about it. No great knowledge is, however, required to understand all this.

There appear to be two intelligent conceptions of life in the sacred books, and according to one of them we are required to renounce all action. But we should understand what all this really means.

A principle or rule means that what applies to one case should apply to all similar cases too; but, as there are different categories of actions, there are also different sets of rules.

A Single Word and Principal Things

एकदेशकालकर्त्तृत्वं मुख्यानामेकशब्दोपदेशात्॥१॥

If a single note is used to describe something in connection with principal things, they should be found in the same place and at the same time, and should have the same maker.

Connection between Objects, Actions and Words

अविधिश्चेत्कर्मणामभिसम्बन्धः प्रतीयेत तल्ल[2]क्षणार्थाभिसंयोगाद् विधि त्वाच्चेतरेषां प्रतिप्रधानं भावः स्यात्॥२॥
अङ्गेषु च तदभावः प्रधानं प्रति निर्देशात्॥३॥
यदि तु कर्मणो विधिसम्बनधः स्यादैकशब्द्यात्प्रधानार्थाभिसंयोगात्॥४॥
तथा चान्यार्थदर्शनम्॥५॥

If there were no prescribed law, we should have to admit that there is no close connection between actions. But since there is a law, and things are closely connected with one an-

२. येत लक्षेति वृति पाठः।

other, the meaning of all expressions should be related to the principal word. But this is not so with the parts of a word in their relation to the principal word, in the case of the great forces of Nature, with reference to their relation to the objects of life.[17] But if each action is governed by a law, it should be possible to express the idea of this connection by means of a single note, because it can be closely connected with the principal object. Thus, all parts of a word can be closely connected with one another; and it is in this manner that we can understand the rest of the meaning of the text.

Parts of a Word and the Principal Word

श्रुतिश्चैषां प्रधानवत्कर्मश्रुतेः परार्थत्वात्कर्मणोऽश्रुति[1]त्वाच्च॥६॥
अङ्गानि तु विधानत्वात्प्रधानेनोपदिश्येरंस्तस्मात्स्यादेकदेशत्वम्॥७॥

There is a reason why each part of a word should be separate, even as we find in the case of the principal word; because it is a law of life that all action is performed for the sake of something else; and it is necessary to remember this, because the idea of action is not always clearly understood. The text is so arranged, that each part of a word has a bearing on the idea of the principal word, and can be explained in its light; and it is in this manner that the whole text has been integrated.

Forces of Nature and Parts of Words

द्रव्यदेवतं तथेति चेत्॥८॥
न चोदनाविधिशेषत्वान्नियमार्थो विशेषः॥९॥

But the idea of the great forces of Nature, in their relation to their objects, does not correspond to that of the parts of words, because the direction in regard to the latter is of a subsidiary character, whereas that in respect of the forces of Nature is a special one.

---

1. श्रुतत्वेति न्या. मा. पाठः।

Theory of Parts of Words

तेषु समवेतानां समवायात्तन्त्रमङ्गानि भेदस्तु; तद्भेदात्कर्मभेदः प्रयोगे स्यात्तेषां प्रधानशब्दत्वात्तथा चान्यार्थदर्शनम्॥१०॥

There is a theory[18] in connection with the parts of words, explaining how and why they are brought together, as well as the distinction between them. When we understand this, we shall understand the distinction between the different kinds of actions that has been made by means of them, as also their connection with the principal word, which will enable us to understand the rest of the text.

Illustrations

इष्टिराजसूयचातुर्मास्येष्वैककर्म्यात् अङ्गानां तन्त्रभावः स्यात्॥११॥
कालभेदान्नेति चेत्॥१२॥
नैकदेशत्वात्पशुवत्॥१३॥
अपि वा कर्मपृथक्त्वात्तेषां तन्त्रविधानात्साङ्गानामुपदेशः स्यात्॥१४॥
तथा चान्यार्थदर्शनम्॥१५॥
तथा तदवयवेषु[1] स्यात्॥१६॥

In words like *iṣṭi, rājasūya*, and *caturmāsya*,—as they are characterised by unity of action—we should find the characteristic features of their parts.[19] We cannot, however, say that the difference in the idea of action, as expressed by them, arises from the difference of Time, because they are conceived as parts of a whole, and we can distinguish between them as we can in the case of animals.[20] They refer to different states of action;[21] and, as they have been formed in accordance with the theory (referred to above), we should know what they mean from the parts of which they are composed. It is in this manner that we can understand other meanings too; and find them in the parts of words.

Case of Animals

पशौ तु चोदनैकत्वात्तन्त्रस्य विप्रकर्षः स्यात्[2]॥१७॥

---

1. तथा तदवयवेत्यस्य स्थाने वृत्तिकृ. तदावयेति पाठः।
2. वृत्तौ स्यादिति नास्ति।

In the case of animals, however, this theory will have to be modified, because the nature of their impelling force is different[22].

The Mind

तथा स्यादध्वरकल्पेष्टौ[1] विशेषस्यैककालत्वात्॥१८॥
इष्टिरिति चैकवच्छ्रुतिः॥१९॥

We can represent the action of the mind in this manner, and fit it into the idea of desire, which is its special attribute, and arises at the same time with it, even as we have understood it.

Iṣṭi

अपि[2] वा कर्मपृथक्त्वात्तेषां च तन्त्रविधानात्साङ्गानामुपदेशः स्यात्॥२०॥
प्रथमस्य वा कालवचनम्॥२१॥
फलैकत्वादिष्टिशब्दो यथान्यत्र॥२२॥

With regard to the different ideas of action signified by these (three) names,—as they have been formed in accordance with this theory—we should be able to get their real meaning from their parts.[23] With regard to the first of these (namely, *iṣṭi* or desire), the idea of Time is specially associated with it.[24] We can take this word *iṣṭi* like any other word, for its result will be the same in whichever way we take it[25].

Intelligent Action, Time, and the Forces of Nature

वसाहोमस्तन्त्रमेकदेवतेषु स्यात् प्रदान[3]स्यैककालत्वात्॥२३॥
काल[4]भेदात्त्वावृत्तिर्देवता भेदे॥२४॥
अन्ते यूपाहुतिस्तद्वत्॥२५॥
इतरप्रतिषेधो वा; अनुवादमात्र मन्तिकस्य॥२६॥
अशास्त्रत्वाच्च देशानाम्॥२७॥

---

2. कल्पेष्टावित्यस्य स्थाने कल्पायामिति पाठो वृत्तौ।
3. न वा कर्मपृथक्त्वात्तेषां चाङ्गेति वृत्तिपाठः।
4. प्रधानेति वृ. पाठः।
5. भेदे त्वावृत्तिरिति वृत्तिग्रन्थे पाठान्तरम्।

If we are dealing with one clear intelligent action (*Homa*), it should refer to only one act of the great forces of Nature (*Devatā*), if it is declared to have been done at one time. If, however, the times are different, the forces of Nature may be different too. In conclusion we might say that all intelligent action is like that,[26] because anything different is not possible; and this is only an explanatory repetition of what has already been said; (only it has been stated more directly) because it would be contrary to rules to think of the intellect as being different at different places[27].

Importance of Principal Word

अवभृथे प्रधानेऽग्निविकारः स्यान्न हि तद्धेतुरग्निसंयोगः॥२८॥

द्रव्यदेवतावत्॥२९॥

साङ्गो वा प्रयोगवचनैकत्वात्॥३०॥

लिङ्गदर्शनाच्च॥३१॥

If the principal word is omitted, we cannot understand the meaning of the text; and it would be incorrect to imagine that we can, in spite of it; for the connection between understanding and the principal word is as close as that between the great forces of Nature and the fundamental substances associated with them.[28] Each word, complete in all its parts, is accordingly made to fit into this plan of composition; and we can understand its meaning if we see through its "disguise".

Meaning of Gods

शब्दविभागाच्च देवतानपनयः॥३२॥

दक्षिणेऽग्नौ वरुणप्रघासेषु देशभेदात्सर्वं विक्रियते॥३३॥

अचोदनेति चेत्॥३४॥

स्यात्पौर्णमासीवत्॥३५॥

प्रयोगचोदनेति चेत्॥३६॥

त (अ) थेह॥३७॥

It is only when we divide words into parts, that we can

eliminate erroneous ideas about the gods of the Vedas.[29] Thus if we understand the meaning of the words *Dakṣiṇa-Agni* and *Varuṇa-praghāsa*, their whole idea would, because of change of place, be altered.[30] There may be no direction to point to this interpretation; but we should understand it in the same manner as we understand the reference to the full-moon.[31] There is at least a direction in regard to the connection, with the idea of the full moon;[32] and it is even so in the present case.

Opinion of Learned Men

आसादनमिति चेत्॥३८॥
नोत्तरेणैकवाक्यत्वात्॥३९॥
अवाच्यत्वात्॥४०॥

All this, however, is not laid down in the text; but it is obtained by something higher still,—the unanimous opinion of learned men; and we invoke their authority, because the idea has not been distinctly expressed.

The Language of the Vedas

आम्नायवचनं तद्वत्॥४१॥
कर्तृभेदस्तथेति चेत्॥४२॥
न समवायात्॥४३॥
लिङ्गदर्शनाच्च॥४४॥

The language of the Vedas is like that; and that is not due to any difference between the authors of the text, but rather to their fullest agreement; and we can understand their real meaning if we see through the "disguise" of words.

How to Understand This

वेदिसंयोगादिति चेत्॥४५॥
न देशमात्रत्वात्॥४६॥
एकाग्नित्वादपरेषु तन्त्रैः स्यात्॥४७॥
नाना वा कर्तृभेदात्॥४८॥

It does not require a great deal of knowledge to understand all this: what is necessary is that we should know the measure of words (or how to divide them into parts and understand their meaning). Thus if we understand the meaning of the word *Agni*,[33] we can get the meaning of other words too by means of the same principles (of interpretation). There is, however, a difference between the mode of composition of different authors of the text.

Two Views regarding Intellect

पर्यग्नि कृतानामुत्सर्गे प्राजापत्यानां कर्मोत्सर्गः; श्रुतिसामान्यादारण्यवत्तस्माद्ब्रह्मसाम्नि चोदनापृथक्त्वं स्यात्॥४९॥
संस्कारप्रतिषेधो वा वाक्यैकत्वे क्रतुसामान्यात्॥५०॥
वपानां[1] चानभिघारणस्य दर्शनात्॥५१॥
पञ्चशारदीयास्तथेति चेत्॥५२॥
न चोदनैकवाक्यत्वात्॥५३॥
संस्काराणां च दर्शनात्॥५४॥

When we think of *Agni* (or intellect) in the light of any general rules, we find that its idea is the same as that of a great creative power.[34] At the same time there is another equally important view (in connection with the function of the intellect), according to which we are required to go and dwell in a forest (or renounce action). Hence in any hymns addressed to *Brahman*, we should have a clear (or separate) direction as to which idea (of the intellect) is meant to be conveyed.[35] But if the statement is the same (in both cases), and there is no attempt at "refinement" (or distinction), it is because there is common ground (in regard to the whole conception of life).[36] Indeed, if we understand the nature of things, we shall realise that there can be no question of associating anything good with what is worthless.[37] But we cannot say that the function of the senses is an evil even in the autumn of our life;[38] and there is unanimity of opinion in the matter. The expressions used in the text in this connection are quite clear, as we can see for ourselves.

---

1. पायां चेति वृत्तौ पाठः।

Meaning of a Principle

दशपेये क्रयप्रतिकर्षात्प्रतिकर्षस्ततः प्राञ्चां; तत्समानं तन्त्रं स्यात्।
समानवचनं तद्वत्॥५६॥
अप्रतिकर्षो वाऽर्थहेतुत्वात्सहत्वं विधीयते॥५७॥
पूर्वस्मिंश्चावभृथस्य दर्शनात्॥५८॥

(A principle or rule means that what applies to one case should apply equally to all similar cases: for instance,) it is a rule that when the mind functions[39] (or desire awakens), we have to pay for it; and if we anticipate this in one case, we should be able to do so in all similar cases too: A principle or theory is like that; and similar statements made in the text are of this kind. But even if there is no express mention of what we should anticipate, we should assume it, if it is warranted by the meaning of the text: for instance, we know from experience that what is true of an initial action is true of a supplementary action too.

Different Kinds of Action

दीक्षाणां चोत्तरस्य॥५९॥
समानः कालसामान्यात्॥६०॥
निष्कासस्यावभृथे तदेकदेशत्वात् पशुवत्प्रदान विप्रकर्षः स्यात्॥६१॥
अपनयो वा प्रसिद्धेनाभिसंयोगात्॥६२॥
प्रतिपत्तिरिति चेन्न कर्मसंयोगात्॥६३॥
उदयनीये[1]च तद्वत्॥५४॥
प्रतिपत्तिर्वाऽकर्मसंयोगात्॥६५॥
अर्थकर्म वा शेषत्वाच्छ्र[2]पणवत्तदर्थेन विधानात्॥६६॥

With regard to serious actions, the rule is that they should be performed after due preparation, and for a higher end. Again, we may have the same kind of actions if the occasion for them is the same. In the case of a supplementary action,—if

---

१. प्रयणीये इति वृत्तौ पठः।

२. च्छ्रयणेति न्या मा पाटः।

it continues in the same place—its withdrawal may be represented in the same manner as an animal "dragged away."[40] But there may still be cases of misconduct, as is well known. This is not a mere supposition, for we know what happens when such acts are done; and we find that the result is like that.[41] It is, however, true that it would be a mere supposition if it had no relation to real action; for an action has a meaning only in the light of its result. This is like a mixture of things, and we have to sort out its purpose from the statement of particulars.

PART III

THE INSTRUMENTS AND OBJECT OF ACTION

Introduction

The meaning of the parts of words should be the same throughout.

When no particular purpose is served by an action, it should be deemed to be for the benefit of all. This is represented by *yūpa* or a "sacrificial post"; and we can understand its meaning by dividing it into parts. The *svaru* (another word for a sacrificial post) completes the whole idea of action. Its time of occurrence may, in certain cases, be compared to a sacrificial seat.

If in a great sacrifice a person casts away the best, it means that there is a doubt about the action itself.

A person does the best he can at a time; and this is represented by the direction that we should follow up the working of the mind early in the morning, for the mind is at its best at the time. The direction to engage in a sacrifice means the same thing.

Animals too have a mind. The union of the mind with the intellect makes for the best action, as well as freedom from its bondage. The parts of a great action are represented by the days for which a sacrifice is said to last.

The main factor of action is the I-as-an-actor. It may be regarded as an aspect of the soul, which is said to be a non-actor, if we wish to distinguish between the performers of action. But it is not like the intellect, though in popular language they may be taken to be so.

We should fix upon the instruments of action in the light of our knowledge; and this enables us to understand the character of the soul. When a person has acquired complete knowledge, he can take these instruments as he likes, because they all serve the same purpose.

A person should do his best, for there is no fixed time for death; and he who dies in the midst of a great and good action is the best. One cannot become the best by a mere study of the sacred books; he does so by acting like a leader, for the leader is really the best.

The difference of opinion regarding action is contained in the sacred books themselves: but their purpose is the same,—the attainment of perfection; and when we understand them properly, we find that they support the idea that all good and intelligent actions should be performed.

No one can tell anything about the time of creation of life,—for the best of minds cannot know it. When it is said that some one knows, it is only an exuberance of language.

Rule regarding Parts of Words

अङ्गानां मुख्यकालत्वाद्वचनादन्यकालत्वम्॥१॥

If the parts of a word are properly used in a certain sense on a principal occasion, they should be used in the same sense on another occasion too,—for that is the rule[42].

Action for the Benefit of All: Illustrated by Yūpa

द्रव्यस्या[1]कर्मकालनिष्पत्तेः प्रयोगः सर्वार्थः स्यात्स्वकालत्वात्॥२॥
यूपश्चाकर्मकालत्वात्॥३॥
एक[2]यूपं च दर्शयति॥४॥

If no particular object is gained when an action takes place, it should be deemed to have been done for the benefit of all, because it has been done at its own time. This is the idea of *yūpa* (or the sacrificial post), because it is not fixed at the time of action; and so only one such post is seen[43].

How to Understand This

संस्कारास्त्वावर्तेरन्नर्थकालत्वात्॥५॥

तत्कालास्तु; यूपकर्मत्वात्तस्य धर्मविधानात्सर्वार्थानां च वचनादन्यकालत्वम्॥६॥

सकृन्मानं च दर्शयति॥७॥

But we should always have a correct formation[44] of words to get their real meaning; and this should be done at once; because if we know what *yūpa* signifies, we can, from an enumeration of particulars and the application of rules, know tnat whenever the word is used on other occasions, it will have the same meaning; and that will enable us to understand the whole design at once.

Svaru

स्वरुस्तन्त्रापवर्गः स्यादस्वकालत्वात्॥८॥

साधारणो वाऽनुनिष्पत्तिस्तस्य साधारणत्वात्॥९॥

सोमान्ते च प्रतिपत्तिदर्शनात्॥१०॥

The word *svaru*[45] should complete the whole theory (of action), because it has no time of its own; and we can easily understand the result, which is caused by means of a common conception, and arises from the experience of our own mind.

Time of Occurrence

तत्कालो वा प्रस्तरवत्॥११॥

न वोत्पत्ति वाक्यत्वात्प्रदेशात् प्रस्तरे तथा॥१२॥

---

1. व्यस्य चाकेति नय. मा. पाठः।
2. इदं सूत्रं वृत्तिकृन्मते नास्ति।

The time of occurrence may be compared to the sacrificial seat; but not always. If, however, there is a statement in respect of it to that effect, it should be taken to be so.

Description of Doubt

अहर्गणे विषाणाप्रसानं धर्मविप्रतिषेधादन्त्ये प्रथमे वाहनि विकल्पः स्यात्॥१३॥

If in an important action, lasting many days, a person casts away the best of what has been achieved, it should,—since it is so unprecedented (or contrary to law)—raise a doubt as to whether something has not gone wrong with the beginning or the end of such action.

Idea of Early Morning Work

पाणेस्त्वश्रुतिभूतत्वाद्विषाणानियमः स्यात्प्रातः सवनमध्यत्वाच्छिष्टे चाभिप्रवृत्तत्वात्॥१४॥

It is possible that the hand may not, sometimes, act in accordance with the direction of the intellect: still the law of action is that a person does the best he can at a time. It is for this reason that we are directed to follow up the working of the mind early in the morning, for it is at its best at the time.

Idea of Breaking Silence

वाग्विसर्गो हविष्कृतो बीजभेदे तथा स्यात्॥१५॥

If a person breaks silence in order to disclose the truth, and bids us engage in a sacrifice (or a good and intelligent act), it should be deemed to be like that (or for the best).

Case of Animals

पशौ च पुरोडाशे समानतन्त्रं भवेत्॥१६॥

We see the same characteristic in the case of animals too, so far as their desire is concerned[46].

Freedom from the Taint of Action

अग्नियोगः सोमकाले तदर्थत्वात् संस्कृतकर्मणः परेषु साङ्गस्य;

तस्मात्सर्वापवर्गे विमोकः स्यात्॥१७॥
प्रधानापवर्गे वा तदर्थत्वात्॥१८॥
अवभृथे च तद्वत्प्रधानार्थस्य प्रतिषेधोऽपवृक्तार्थत्वात्॥१९॥

The object of the union of the function of the intellect with that of the mind[47] is that good actions or actions well performed would become the best in every part. It is only when this happens, that a person can make himself free from the limitations of action[48]; for that is the reason for these limitations.[49] For the same reason, a supplementary or minor action cannot take the place of a major one, so far as the fulfilment of its purpose is concerned[50].

Parts of an Action: How Described

अहर्गणे च प्रत्यहं स्यात्तदर्थत्वात्॥२०॥

In a great sacrifice (or action) lasting many days, each day represents a part of such action, well performed, because that is what it is meant to do.

Importance of Ahaṅkāra or I-as-an-Actor

सुब्रह्मण्या तु तन्त्रं दीक्षावदन्यकालत्वात्॥२१॥
तत्कालत्त्वावर्तेत प्रयोगतोविशेष[1]सम्बन्धात्॥२२॥

But the main thing in action is the I-as-an-actor[51], ever ready to act at all different times. It functions at once, and again and again, because it is connected with what has to be done in a very special way.

Ahaṅkāra and the Soul

अप्रयोगाङ्गमिति चेत्॥२३॥
स्यात्प्रयोगनिर्देशात्कर्तृभेदवत्॥२४॥

It is possible to regard it as a part of a mental organ which does not act (that is, the soul), because it enables us to point

---

1. षसंयोगादिति वृत्तिकृन्मते पाठः।

out its function, in case we wish to distinguish between the performers of action[52].

Ahaṅkāra and the Intellect

तद्भूतस्थानादग्निवदिति चेत्त[1]दपवर्गस्तदर्थत्वात्॥२५॥

अग्निवदिति चेत्॥२६॥

न प्रयोगसाधारण्यात्॥२७॥

लिङ्गदर्शनाच्च॥२८॥

तद्धि तथेति चेत्॥२९॥

नाशिष्टत्वादितरन्यायत्वाच्च[2]॥३०॥

विध्येकत्वादिति चेत्॥३१॥

न कृत्स्नस्य पुनः प्रयोगात् प्रधानवत्॥३२॥

लौकिकेषु यथाकामी संस्का[3]रानर्थलोपात्॥३३॥

We cannot, however, say that it is like the intellect,—on the ground that, so far as the body of a living creature is concerned, it appears to be like the intellect and functions for its sake,—because its action is of a universal character[53]; and we can understand this if we know their characteristics;[54] But we cannot say that their characteristics are the same and so they are alike,— because we have never been taught like that, and we know that they belong to essentially different types. Nor do they arise from the same action or manner of action, because we see that it is so, if we examine with care the origin of a whole action[55]. In popular language, however, they may be taken as we please, because the terms are not always used in an exact sense.

Need of Definition

यज्ञायुधानि धार्येरन्प्रतिपत्तिविधानादृजीषवत्॥३४॥

यजमानसंस्कारो वा तदर्थः श्रूयते तत्र यथाकामी तदर्थत्वात्॥३५॥

1. चेदपेति वृत्तिकृन्मते पाठः।
2. चशब्दो वृत्तिकृन्मते नास्ति।
3. रार्थालोपादिति वृत्तिकृन्मते पाठः।

We should, however, fix upon the instruments of action in the light of our knowledge of what is to be done[56], even as we know the character of the mind together with its desires[57]. The purification of the soul[58] is said to be achieved by this means[59]; and when that is done, a person may do as he likes[60].

The Best

मुख्यस्य[1] धारणं वा मरणस्यानियतत्वात्॥३६॥

यो वा यजनीयेऽहनि म्रियेत[2] सोऽधिकृतः स्यादुपवेषवत्॥३७॥

न शास्त्रलक्षणत्वात्॥३८॥

उत्पत्तिर्वा प्रयोजकत्वादाशिरवत्॥३९॥

शब्दासामञ्जस्यमिति चेत्॥४०॥

तथाऽऽशिरे॥४१॥

But a person should make use of the best instruments of action, for his time is limited, and there is no fixed time for death. But he who dies in the midst of a sacrifice (or a great and good action) should be regarded as the best of men; for he is like a stick of green wood used for stirring the sacrificial fire (which burns itself in the task). A person does not become the best merely by reading the sacred books. He can do so only by acting and causing others to act, as a leader does. This is not an improper use of language (to compare the best of men with a leader), because the leader is really the best in respect of what is expected of him.

Necessity of Action

शास्त्रात्तु विप्रयोगस्तत्रेकद्रव्यचीकीर्षा[3] प्रकृतावथेहापूर्वार्थवद्भूतोपदेशः॥४२॥

प्रकृत्यर्थत्वात्पौर्णमास्याः क्रियेरन्॥४३॥

---

1. ख्यसाधेति न्या. मा. पाठः।
2. म्रियते इति पाठभेदः।
3. कीर्षया कृतेति वृत्ति. पाठः।

अग्न्याधेये वाऽविप्रतिषेधात्तानि धारयेन्मरणस्यानिमित्तत्वात्॥४४॥
प्रतिपत्तिर्वा[1] यथाऽन्येषाम्॥४५॥

But this difference of opinion in regard to action arises from the views expressed in the sacred books themselves[61]. Nevertheless, the object of the whole matter is essentially the same,—the attainment of perfection. There is, however, nothing new in this: only what exists already appears to have an entirely new meaning. When we understand the language of the sacred books in its rudimentary form, we realise that all that is associated with action, performed in the light of the full moon,[62] should be done; and we should perform all actions intelligently, because there is no difference of opinion in the matter when the question of death is not involved[63]; and the pro-cedure is the same in all cases.

Creation

उपरिष्टात्सोमानां प्राजापत्यैश्चरन्तीति सर्वेषामविशेषादवाच्यो हि प्रकृतिकालः॥४५॥
अङ्गविपर्यासो विना वचनादिति चेत्॥४७॥
उत्कर्षः संयोगात्कालमात्रमितरत्र॥४८॥
प्रकृतिकालासत्तेः शस्त्रवतामिति चेत्॥४९॥

It is said of all things, without distinction, that creation follows desire[64]: only the time of creation cannot be told. Can we say that this means a reversal of the function of the mind, for which there is no authority[65]? or that Time alone is the cause of the improvement of things, which are connected with one another[66]? Or can we say that we can know the time of the creation of things,[67] as is the opinion of those who are well versed in the knowledge of the sacred books.

We cannot Know the Origin of Things

न श्रुतिप्रतिषेधात्॥५०॥
विकारस्थान इति चेत्॥५१॥
न चोदनापृथक्त्वात्॥५२॥

---

१. र्वाप्यन्ते इति वृत्तिपाठ

उत्कर्षे सूक्तवाकस्य न सोमदेवतानामुत्कर्षः पश्वनङ्गत्वाद्यथा निष्कर्षेऽनन्वयः।।५३।।

But all this is untenable, as it is contrary to reason. Nor is it a fit case for changing the form of words to understand their meaning, because it arises from a reference to another rule (that is, appeal to reason). Even in the most excellent hymns of the Vedas there is no mention of the powers of the mind which can know the origin of things.[68] We know that animals too have a mind; and the main point in this argument is that we can only compare the mind with the best of its class[69].

An Exuberant Mode of Expression

वाक्यसंयोगाद्वोत्कर्षः समानतन्त्रत्वादर्थलोपादनन्वयः।।५४।।

The reference to knowledge of the origin of things is only an exuberance of language, arising out of a peculiar mode of expression (meant to emphasise things). In the same manner when we are unable to understand the meaning of a thing, we refer it to our idea,—(the highest we can imagine, to see if we can).

PART IV

THE METHOD OF INTERPRETATION : THE FUNCTION OF THE INTELLECT AND THE MIND

Introduction

There are certain cases where it is necessary to divide words into parts to understand their meaning. But this method is subject to certain restrictions, which may be illustrated by means of the word *aveṣṭi*. But all words must have the same meaning throughout, and variations must be specified.

Certain ideas are expressed in special ways: for instance,

certain parts of the text are repeated to explain certain ideas. The parts of a great action can be expressed in terms of the days for which a sacrifice or a great action is said to last; and this can be understood by means of the parts of words. Certain parts of words are combined together to express the idea of the combination of the actor and the result of his action. The idea of Time is expressed by means of a change in the form of words; and so on.

Different objects act in different ways, and their meaning can be obtained by means of the parts of words.

The function of the mind implies a function of *ahaṅkāra* or the I-as-an-actor.

The term "simultaneous" is used only for the sake of illustration.

We can understand objects by means of their characteristics; but there is a difference between brain and brain.

The function of the intellect involves the idea of Time.

There is a difference in the intellectual powers of creatures, though they retain certain common characteristics.

Certain words in the text are repeated once or more frequently to express certain ideas.

Consecration of knowledge means the exercise of intellectual powers in connection with action; and this is described by means of parts of words.

There can be only one action at a time.

Principles are more important than words.

The idea of simultaneity should be understood in its proper light; and so should certain words like *haviṣkṛt*, etc.

Rule of Interpretation

चोदनैकत्वाद्राजसूयेऽनुक्तदेशकालानां समवायात्तन्त्रमङ्गानि॥१॥

प्रतिदक्षिणं वा कर्तृसम्बन्धादिष्टिवदङ्गभूतत्वात्समुदायो हि; तन्निर्वृत्त्या तदेकत्वादेकशब्दोपदेशः स्यात्॥२॥

तथा चान्यार्थदर्शनम्॥३॥

As there is unity or cohesion of ideas in the sacred books, the rule is that, if we find that there is mention of unusual or unheard of things relating to time and place in connection with the function of the mind,[70] we should divide words into parts, when we shall get the correct meaning of the text.

These unusual expressions are due to the cleverness of the author; but, even as one would desire it,—there is a rule, telling us that, in such cases, a whole expression is composed of parts. When we examine the origin or development of such expressions, we should remember that there is a fundamental unity of idea in the text, and that each separate note conveys a meaning of its own. It is in this manner that we can understand all other meanings of words.

Restrictions

अनियमः स्यादिति चेत्॥४॥

नोपदिष्टत्वात्॥५॥

लाघवा[1]तिपत्तिश्च॥६॥

प्रयोजनैकत्वात्॥७॥

विशेषार्था पुनः श्रुतिः॥८॥

We cannot say that this method of interpretation is without restrictions, because there is a specific mention of them; and their object is to prevent hasty conclusions. There is, however, but one purpose underlying this,—namely, to enable us to understand the real meaning of the text; while with regard to special meanings, there is a repetition of names to enable us to do so.

---

1. वापत्तीति वृत्तिकृन्मते पाठः।

An Illustration

अवेष्टौ चैकतन्त्र्यं स्याल्लिङ्गदर्शनात्॥९॥
वचनात्कामसंयोगेन॥१०॥
क्रत्वार्थायामिति चेन्न वर्ण संयोगात्॥११॥

This principle is illustrated by means of the word *aveṣṭi*[71]; and we can undertsand its real meaning by piercing through its "disguise". We can also get it from the word itself by associating it with the idea of desire. It does not refer to sacrifice (as is commonly believed); and we can understand it if we connect it with the letters or syllables of which it is composed.

System of Interpretation

पवमानहविःष्वैकतन्त्र्यं प्रयोग वचनैकत्वात्॥१२॥
लिगङ्गदर्शनाच्च॥१३॥
वचनात्तु तन्त्रभेदः स्यात्॥१४॥

In the case of all intelligent actions which purify, there is but one system, according to which each word has but one meaning throughout; and we can understand it if we pierce through its "disguise". If, however, there is an express mention of a different way of interpretation, the system should be varied accordingly.

Explanatory Repetition

सहत्वे नित्यानुवादः स्यात्॥१५॥

The connection between the different parts of the text should always be represented by means of explanatory repetition to illustrate the idea.

A Great Action: How Described

द्वादशाहे तत्प्रकृतित्वादेकैकमहरपवृज्येत कर्मपृथक्त्वात्॥१६॥
अह्नां वा श्रुतिभूतत्वात्तत्र साङ्गं क्रियेत यथा माध्यन्दिने॥१७॥

In a great intelligent action, lasting twelve days[72], there are a number of different parts, which can be understood separately, because each has special characteristics of its own; and that can be understood by reducing words to their rudimentary form.

Since each part of this action is characterised by intelligence, the idea of all can be completely understood at once in terms of the parts of words referring to such action, as clearly as if it were performed at mid-day.

Action and its Fruit: How Described

अपि वा फलकर्तृसम्बन्धात् सह प्रयोगः स्यादाग्नेयाग्नीषोमीयत्॥१८॥

Since the fruit of action is closely connected with the doer of the deed, certain parts of words should be combined or uttered simultaneously, just as we express the idea of the intellect by means of the word *Agnī*, and of the intellect and mind combined by means of the word *Agnī-ṣomīya*[73].

Parts of Time: How Described. No. Twelve

साङ्गकालश्रुतित्वाद्वा स्वस्थानां विकारः स्यात्॥१९॥

तदपेक्षं च द्वादशत्वम्॥२०॥

When there is mention of Time, with its parts, there should be a change in the form of words which represent this idea (in order to understand their meaning); and this is illustrated by the number twelve[74].

Other Cases

दीक्षोपसदां च सङ्ख्या पृथक् पृथक् प्रत्यक्षसंयोगात्॥२१॥

तथा चान्यार्थदर्शनम्॥२२॥

चोदनापृथक्त्वे त्वैकतन्त्र्यं समवेतानां कालसंयोगात्॥२३॥

भेदस्तु; तद्भेदात्कर्मभेदः; प्रयोगे स्यात्तेषां प्रधानशब्दत्वात्॥२४॥

तथा चान्यार्थदर्शनम्॥२५॥

श्वःसुत्यावचनं[1]तद्वत्॥२६॥

पश्वतिरेकश्च॥२७॥

Words signifying preparation for engagement in a great action should be taken separately, because they have a clear

1. नं च तेति वृत्ति. पाठः।

connection with the text in that way; and it is in this manner that we can understand other meanings too.

Even where things have a separate cause or impelling force,—if they are closely connected together because they occur at the same time—they should be governed by the same system[75].

But there is a difference between such things, as a result of which their actions are different; and the meaning of these words should be found in the parts of their principal words and the connection between these parts. It is in this manner that we can understand all such meanings. The meaning of the expression *śvaḥ-sutyā*[76] is like that; and there are a number of different animals whose meanings have to be understood in the same manner[77].

Mind and Ahaṅkāra

सुत्याविवृद्धो सुब्रह्मण्यायां सर्वेषामुपलक्षणं प्रकृत्यन्वयादावाहनवत्॥२८॥

In the development of the function of the mind there an implication of the function of *ahaṅkāra* or the I-as-an-actor[78]; and we can understand this if we refer the idea to *Prakṛti*, as in the case of the invocation of the deity[79].

Idea of Simultaneity

अपि वेन्द्राभिधानत्वात्सकृत्स्यादुपलक्षणं कालस्य लक्षणार्थत्वाद् विभागगच्च॥२९॥

Again, when *Indra* is described as "one who acts simultaneously", the implication of time (indicated by simultaneity) is for the sake of illustration, and is not intended to convery anything specific[80].

Interpretation by Means of Characteristics

पशुगणे कुम्भीशूलवपाश्रपणीनां प्रभुत्वात्तन्त्रभावः स्यात्॥३०॥
भेदस्तु सन्देहाद्देवतान्तरे स्यात्॥३१॥
अर्थाद्वा लिङ्गकर्म स्यात्॥३२॥

Among the multitude of animals there is one who is supreme by reason of his being able to collect water in a small jar, fight with a weapon or bear a lance, sow seed, and cook food; and we should be able to understand from this that it refers to the characteristic features (of a man). But there may be a difference of opinion in the matter; and, in case of doubt, we should see if the description may not refer to some deity; for it may indeed be the action of *Prakṛti*[81] (or Nature).

Difference Between Brain and Brain

अयाज्यत्वाद्ब्रसानां भेदः स्यात्स्वयाज्याप्रदानत्वात्॥३३॥
अपि वा प्रतिपत्तित्वात्तन्त्रं स्यात् स्वत्वस्याश्रुतिभूतत्वात्॥३४॥

There is a difference between brain and brain (or the intellectual powers of men), because we know that there are some who are unfit to perform good and intelligent deeds (acts of sacrifice); and that is the teaching of the sacred books even in regard to our own people,—relations and friends. Indeed, the main point is that we should understand all things in the light of the intellect, because our own people are different from one another, so far as intellect is concerned.

Intellect and Time

सकृदिति चेत्॥३५॥
न कालभेदात्॥३६॥

The intellect does not act at once or without deliberation, because there is always a difference of time between the function of the intellect and the doing of the deed.

Difference of Intellectual Power

जात्यन्तरे[1]षु भेदः पक्तिवैषम्यात्॥३७॥
वृद्धिदर्शनाच्च॥३८॥
कपालानि च कुम्भीवत्तुल्यसङ्ख्यानाम्॥३९॥
प्रतिप्रधानं वा प्रकृतिवत्॥४०॥
सर्वेषां चाभिप्रथनं स्यात्॥४१॥

---

1. न्तरभेद इति वृत्तिपाठः।

There is a difference of intellectual power among different classes of men, because their development is not the same. We can see for ourselves that it grows (or decreases)[82], so that it cannot be the same in all. Even though the members of a species have the same name, the brain (or the cranium that contains it) of some may be like a small earthen pot (with little substance in it). Nevertheless, each one persists in retaining his original form; and they can all multiply and spread (in different places).

Repetitions

एकद्रव्ये संस्काराणां व्याख्यातमेककर्मत्वम्॥४२॥

तस्मिन्मन्त्रार्थनानात्वादावृतौ; मन्त्रस्यासकृत्प्रयोगः स्यात्तदर्थेन विधानात्॥४२ अ.॥

द्रव्यान्तरे कृतार्थत्वात्तस्य पुनः प्रयोगान्मन्त्रस्य[1] च तद्‌गुणत्वात् पुनः प्रयोगः स्यात्तदर्थेन विधानात्॥४३॥

It has already been explained that a person acts as a whole (or as a single unit) in all that he does in a proper manner[83]. But in such a case there may be a number of meanings of the text, when, in order to understand it, there should be a repetition of the same idea, and we should read the text again.[84] But if the actions in question refer to different persons, this method requires that there should be several repetitions to enable us to understand the meaning,—for that is the peculiarity of the text.

Special Cases

निर्वपणलवन[2] स्तरणाज्यग्रहणेषु च एकद्रव्यवत्प्रयोजनैकत्सात्॥४४॥

द्रव्यान्तरवद्वा स्यात्तत्संस्कारात॥४५॥

In the case of certain expressions which mean "gift", "reaping", "crossing over", and "pouring clarified butter over the sacrificial fire",—there should be only one repetition, as

1. स्थ तेति वृत्तिपाठः।
2. वनास्तेति वृत्तिपाठः।

in cases where only one person is concerned, because there is only one motive of action. But where an action is described in more ornate language, (there may be several repetitions) as in cases where a large number of persons are concerned.

Consecration of Knowledge

वेदिप्रोक्षणे मन्त्राभ्यासः कर्मणः पुनः प्रयोगात्॥४६॥

When we speak of the consecration of knowledge, we mean a repeated exercise of our mental powers arising from a repeated performance of action[85].

Idea of One Repetition

एकस्य वा गुणविधिर्द्रव्यैकत्वात्; तस्मात्सकृत्प्रयोगः स्यात्॥४७॥
कण्डूयने प्रत्यङ्गं कर्मभेदा[1]त् स्यात्॥४८॥

With regard to a case where an action is referred to but one person, there is the method of division of words into parts to explain its meaning; and that is the reason why there is one repetition (or statement) only[86].

Action and Parts of Words—In case of words denoting selection or a process of the intellect, every part of a word should denote a separate action.

One Action at a Time

अपि वा चोदनैककालमेककर्म्यं स्यात्॥५७॥
स्वप्ननदीतरणाभिवर्षणामेध्यप्रतिमन्त्रणेषु चैवम्॥५८॥
प्रयाणे त्वार्थनिर्वृत्तेः॥५९॥

As there is only one urge to action at a time, there can be only one action at a time. This is true in all cases,—in a state of unconsciousness or sleep, in conscious action like crossing a river, in an act of Nature like rain, and in an act of private consultation. It is so even in death, when all things come to an end.

---

१. ज्ञेदः यथेति वृत्तिपाठः।

Ideas are Higher than Sounds

उपरवमन्त्रस्तन्त्रं स्याल्लोकवत् बहु[1]वचनात्॥५२॥

Higher than the sound of the hymns of the sacred text are the principles they teach. We require this in the case of the people too, after they have spoken at length.

Meaning of Simultaneity

न सन्निपातित्वादसन्निपातिकर्मणां; विशेषग्रहणे कालैकत्वात्सकृत् वचनम्॥५३॥

हविष्कृदध्रिगुपुरोऽनुवाक्यामनोतस्यावृत्तिः कालभेदा[2]त्स्यात्॥५४॥

अध्रिगोश्च विपर्यासात्॥५५॥

करिष्यद्वचनात्॥५६॥

There is no conjunction or combination of actions, because they cannot occur at the same time. But if we understand things in a special way, we may use the word "simultaneously".[87] Hence we should utter the words *haviṣkṛt*, *adhṛgu, puronuvākyā*, and *manota*[88] separately, to indicate the difference of time in regard to the occurrence of things. The *adhṛgu* formula signifies that the time fixed is over; and the same idea is expressed by means of the statement,—"It is going to be done".

NOTES

1. The idea of *Krama* has already been explained. It indicates that each part of a word is a separate entity, and conveys an idea of its own. It also ensures that no part of a word is omitted or lost sight of in any case.
2. In certain cases the idea of the last part of a word is not clear. For instance, when we divide the word *Viṣṇu* into parts,— V, i, ṣ, ṇ, u—we get its real meaning from V, i, ṣ, ṇ; and the last *u*, which is interpreted to mean "verily", can easily be omitted; or we may deal with it as we like.
3. The *Bhagavad Gītā* also tells us that we can act, but we cannot claim to get the fruit of its result (BhG. II, 47).
4. We have to do something special to get the meaning of words after dividing them into parts,—that is, use our intelligence. The result of an action requires something similar too: something special following an action.
5. "Doing what we like" means that we may take the common meaning of a word, or divide it into parts, as we like. It would make little difference to

१. वच्च वाणीति वृतिपाठः।

२. पृत्त्किृन्मते स्यादिति नास्ति।

the word, for the meaning would be the same in both cases. We have seen that there are instances of this kind.

6. The word in the text is *Agni-hotra* which, as we have seen, refers to intelligent action.

7. The word in the text is *yuvāgū*, which means "rice gruel, or any weak decoction of other kinds of grain". The *Mīmāṁsā* has already explained that grain,ispecially rice, refers to Nature.

8. The word in the text is *payas*, which means "water;" and that, as the *Mīmāṁsā* has already explained, refers to Nature.

9. The word in the text is *Devatā* which, as has already been explained, refers to the great forces of Nature.
The "disguise" of an expression refers to its formation by means of its parts.

10. This explains clearly the object of reciting the text according to *Krama*. Each part of a word has to be pronounced separately, because it represents a distinct part of a principal action; and so we must not pronounce all the parts of a word simultaneously.

11. *Kāmukāyana* is the name of a teacher or philosopher. The *Mīmāṁsā*, however, does not agree with a number of his views.

12. The "correct formation and use of words" (*Saṁskāra*) refers to their formation by means of parts, for we can get their correct eaning in that way.

13. A single word, unconnected with any other word, is meant to be like a single note or a part of a word; and would serve the same purpose as the latter,—that is, express the idea of a part of an action.

14. There are some who believe that, as the principal word stands by itself, it should be deemed to be like a single word, unconnected with any other word, and so serve the same purpose as the latter; and, as we take this "single word" as a whole word, without dividing it into parts, we should do the same with the principal word. But the *Mīmāṁsā* has told us that we need to divide the principal word into parts to understand its meaning. This is accordingly an opposite view, and is rejected by the *Mīmāṁsā*.

15. *Bādarāyaṇa* is the celebrated author of *Vedānta Sūtras*.

16. There is a reference to Time later in this Chapter (See XI, ii3 21-25; iii, 11-12; iv, 19-20).

17. The expression in the text is *Dravya-Devatā*; and we have explained that *Devatā* refers to the great forces of Nature, and *Dravya* to certain fundamental substances like the great "elements," etc.

18. This theory, as has already been explained, is that a great action is divisible into a number of parts,—each of which is denoted by a part of a word. Ordinarily each part of an action is described by means of one or more words; but in this system each letter or syllable does duty for a whole word or even a number of words. It is, therefore, a simpler and briefer way of describing an action.
Now the question is, what is the connection of the parts of a word with the principal word in the text? It is obvious that the parts of a word must be

connected with one another, because they represent parts of an action, which are connected together in accordance with the law of life. The *Mīmāṁsā* says that the parts of a word are also connected with the principal word, with the exception of cases where we are dealing with the great forces of Nature in their relation to their objects; for these are major ideas, and so the words describing them are complete in themselves, without reference to the principal word in the text.

19. We have explained that the meaning of the word *iṣṭi* can be obtained by dividing it into *iṣ, ṭ, i*,—"(*ish*, to desire) desire, associated with (ṭ) the senses of knowledge and (i) the mind".
Similarly, *rājasūya—r, ā,ja,s, ū,ya*—would mean "(>) the senses of action (*ā*) associated with (*jd*) what is produced by 0) the mind (*u*) woven with (*ya*) the intellect". It refers, therefore, to the func-tion of the intellect and the mind, in association with the senses of action; and that is the idea of *rājasūya* as a sacrifice.
In the same manner *catur-māsya*,—chatur, m, ā, s, ya—would mean (*chatur*) skill associated with (*m*) the senses of knowledge (ā) associated with (s) the mind and (*ya*) the intellect". It means, therefore, skill in action, where the intellect, mind, and the senses play their part.

20. We find that these words represent three different states, to which there is a reference in the following *Sūtra*; and so the difference between them is not due to a mere passage of time,when one thing changes into another. They may rather be distinguished as separate ideas, in the same manner as we distinguish between different kinds of animals,—men, horses, cows, goats, and sheep.

21. The three states represented by these words are as follows:— *Iṣṭi* refers to desire, which comes into being when the mind awakens and is associated with the senses of knowledge at least; *Rājasūya* is the function of the mind and the intellect, when they engage in real action; and *Catur-māsya* refers to skill in such action, by means of which a person canfect and yet be free from the taint of action,—in the same sense in which the *Bhagavad Gītā* calls *Yoga* "skill in action" (BhG. II, 50).

22. The *Mīmāṁsā* has already explained that the idea of animals is so clear that it is not necessary to divide words into parts to understand their meaning.

23. We have seen how we get the meaning of these words by dividing them into parts.

24. We have been told that desire arises at the same time that the mind begins to function: hence the idea of Time is involved in that of desire.

25. The word *iṣṭi*, taken as a whole word, means "desire"; anfl if we divide it into parts we get the same meaning again. This is one of those words which we can take "as we like".

26. The expression in the text is *yūpa-āhuti*; and the *Mīmāṁsā* has already explained that *yūpa* refers to selfless action; while *āhuti* means "offering oblation with fire to the deities"; and, as fire refers to the intellect, and the deities to the forces of Nature,—it means an intelligent action associated

with the great forces of Nature. *Yūpa-āhuti* would accordingly mean such selfless action,—implying that the great forces of Nature act intelligently and selflessly; and it is for this reason that the idea of sacrifice can be associated with them; and the *Bhagavad Gītā* can tell us that "rain arises from sacrifice" (BhG. III, 14); for rain may be regarded as the result of a good, intelligent and selfless action of the great forces of Nature.

27. The intellect of a man is the same, though it may act differently at different times, because of different circumstances.

28. The expression in the text is *Dravya-Devatā*; and *Dravya* refers to great substances like the great "elements," etc.; while *Devatā* signifies a great force of Nature. The two are obviously connected together.

29. The *Mīmāṁsā* has already told us that we can get the real meaning of the gods of the Vedas by dividing their names into parts; and then we shall find that they refer to the great forces of Nature, working intelligently, selflessly, and for the well-being of life itself.

30. The common meaning of *Dakṣiṇa-Agni* is "the southern altar of Agni"; and of *Varuṇa-praghāsa* "a periodical oblation offered at the full moon of the month of *Aṣāḍa*, for obtaining exemption from *Varuṇa's* noose".
But these meanings make little sense. On the other hand, if we understand that the word *Dakṣiṇā* refers to skill, and *Agni* to the intellect,—*Dakṣiṇa-Agni* would mean "a skilful action of the intellect".
Similarly, *Varuṇa* is the god of waters which, as the *Mīmāṁsā* has explained, refer to Nature or *Prakṛti*; while praghāsa means "a devourer". Thus *Varuṇa-praghāsa* would mean "*Varuṇa*, the.de-vourer" or "*Prakṛti*, the devourer". This obviously implies that a certain belief in Prakṛti or Nature makes it into a "devourer"; and that can only refer to Nature being the sole supreme creator of life; for, if we believe this, we must agree that there can be no peace or happiness without renunciation of action,—and that means that we must put an end to our life. Hence this belief makes Nature into a destructive force,—a "devourer".
This is the "snare" or "noose" of *Varuṇa*,—belief in Nature as the supreme creator of life; and we are told that in order to obtain "exemption" or freedom from it, we must make oblation at the full moon of the month of *Aṣāḍa*. Now, we have seen that the full moon refers to the full function of the mind, when the latter may, for practical purposes, be identified with the intellect; while the word *Aṣāḍā* is derived from *A-ṣāḍā*, which means "not to be overcome". "The full moon in the month of *Aṣāḍa*" refers, therefore to the kdetermination of the mind r the intellect not to be overcome bu thisbelief, and to act in a spirit of sacrikfice, by means which we can act and yet be free from the taint of action, and so be free from the "noose of *Varuṇa*".

31. The idea of the full moon has already been explained.

32. There is authority for the association of the Moon with the mind, for the *Ṛg Veda* tells us that the Moon was created out of the Mind of the Supreme (RV.X, xc, 13); and there are repeated references to the association of the two in the sacred books.

The *Mīmāṁsā* tells us that we have to use our intelligence, and understand the meaning of other words in the same manner as we understand the idea of the full moon,—as a full expression of the function of the mind. It is not necessary to have detailed directions or definition of words in every case.

33. *Agni* refers to the intellect, as has already been explained.
Intellect (*Agni*) is a great creative power; and we create things if we act in its light.

34. This is one view of the intellect,—namely, that we should act and create; the other follows.

35. The other important view of life, also in the light of the character of the intellect, is that we should renounce action. As these are two entirely different views of life, there should be a clear indication as to which of the two is really meant.
These two views would appear to correspond to the idea of *Nir-bīja* and *Sa-bīja Samādhi*, to which there is a reference to both in the *Saṇkhya* and *Yoga* systems of philospphy. *Samādhi* meant " intense contemplation of a particular object, as a result of which the contemplator becomes identified with the object contemplated"; and so it is a function of the intellect. *Nirbīja-samādhi* is that act of contemplation which is not followed by any further action; while *Sa-bīja samādhi* is that which is. The one stands for complete renunciation of action, while the other for action; and both are based on the character of the idea of the intellect.
The *Brāhmaṇa* portion of the Veda refers to *Brahman*.

36. Both the ideas are correct,—only at different stages of life. We must act so long as'we live; but when death approaches, we must renounce all action. Hence there is common ground between these two points of view,—time or stages of life.

37. When death draws near, the'body becomes "worthless", and we cannot associate any action or anything good with it. It can only be buried or burnt.
The expressions in the text mean "shavings, shearings", and "act of sprinkling clarified butter or ghee"; and the former has been rendered as "something worthless", and the latter as "something' good". We have seen that "clarified butter" signifies something that is good.

38. A man can cease to act'only when he is actually dying; and he cannot regard action as an evil even in the autumn of his life. Renunciation of action is possible only in the winter of life, not its autumn,—that is, only when the end is near.
The text refers to the number "five" which, as has already been explained, refers to the functions of the senses, for there are five senses of knowledge and five of action.

39. The word in the text is *peya*, which means "to be tasted or drunk"; and that, as in the case of *Soma* or "wine", refers to the function of the mind or its attribute, desire. The idea, is that, if we wish to drink something, or satisfy our desire, we must pay for it. We cannot get something for nothing; and so this may be said to be a principle or a general rule.

40. The idea of an animal being "dragged away" is explained in the next

chapter (XII, ii, 30-37), where it signifies restraint in sex life. The idea here is also the same.

41. Indulgence or excess is a kind of misconduct, and it leads to well known evil results.

42. It would be found on examination that not only words taken as a whole, but also their parts have the same meaning in the text. These parts consist of syllables and letters,—specially the latter; and they have all a number of meanings in *Sanskṛt*. But their range of variation, when used in different word-formations, is strictly limited. This applies to all sacred books, from the Vedas downwards (See *Introduction*, for the meanings of the letters of the alphabet used in the text).

43. *Yūpa* means "a sacrificial post"; but, as it is not fixed at a prescribed time, it represents the idea of action meant for the benefit of all. As only one such post is seen at a time, it means that only one such action can be performed at a time.

44. The "correct formation" of a word means its division into parts; and so the *Mīmāṁsā* tells us that if we divide the word *yūpa* into its parts, we shall know its real meaning; and we shall also find that it is used in the same sense everywhere.

 The word may accordingly be divided into *y, ū, pa*, when its meaning would be "(*y*) the intellect (*ū*) woven with (*pa*) the objects of the senses". *Yūpa*, accordingly represents the idea of a highly intellectual action, requiring the function of the intellect in a special manner; and that, as the Mīmāṁsā tells us, is to be understood as meant for the benefit of all. This may be said to be a definition of the word. There is a reference to such action in the *Bhagavad Gītā* (BhG. V, 25).

45. *Yūpa* means action meant for the benefit of all; and svaru action performed with a purpose; and this completes the whole theory of action. *Yūpa* is fixed at its own time; while svaru has no time of its own,—implying that it may be fixed at all times; and so it refers to a very common idea of action,—that which is performed with a purpose, and is within our own experience. If we divide the word into *s, va, r, u*,—the meaning would be "(*s*) the mind, associated with (*va*) Nature and (*r, u*) the senses of action and knowledge." It is thus an action performed with a desire, an attribute of the mind.

46. What is true of men is also true of all animals: they too regard their desires as being the best for them, for the time being. The word in the text is *puroḍāśa*, which refers to desire, as has already been explained.

47. The words in the text are *Agni* and *Soma*, which refer to the intellect and the mind.

48. We get the highest form of action when the mind is merged in or identified with the intellect; for then desire becomes one with *Dhartna*, and action is transformed into a sacrifice, by means of which, as the *Bhagavad Gītā* tells us, all the taint of action is re-moved. The *Mīmāṁsā* says the same.

49. The reason for the limitations or taint of action is that we should think of a way of escape; and that leads us to the idea of Sacrifice, the highest form of action.

50. A major action is action performed as a sacrifice, while a minor one is different. Thus a minor action cannot take the place of a major one.
51. The word in the text is *Subrahmaṇyā*, which is said to be a particular recitation of certain *Mantras* or hymns by the *Udgātṛ* priests; and it is sometimes used for the *Udgātṛ* priest himself. We have already explained that of the four *Ṛtvij* priests, the *Udgātṛ* refers to *ahaṅkāra* or the I-as-an-actor; and that is the meaning of *Subrahmaṇyā* here: it refers to the Udgātṛ priest or *ahaṅkāra*.
 Ahaṅkāra is usually conceived to be different from the soul,— specially where the latter is regarded as a non-actor. But, if we regard the soul to be an actor, *ahaṅkāra* would be regarded as an aspect of the soul itself: that is when the non-acting soul becomes an actor, we call it *ahaṅkāra* or the I-as-an-actor.
 It may be of interest to point out that different systems have their own ideas of the soul as an actor. The *Sāṅkhya* believes that it is really a non-actor, and so entirely different from *ahaṅkāra*. The *Nyāyā* and the *Vaiśeṣika* would associate the soul with action; the *Mīmāṁsā* gives us both the ideas of the soul; and so does *Yoga*; but *Vedānta* conceives of it purely as an actor,—taking the place of *ahaṅkāra* itself.
 The idea of *ahaṅkāra* has come to be degraded in later times, and it has been described as Egoism even in the *Mahābhārata* and the *Bhagavad Gītā*. It is in this sense identified with *abhimāna*; and its idea is represented in the story of the Epic by *Abhimanyu*, the son of *Arjuna*,—for the latter refers to the soul (Cf. MM. IV-V).
52. If the soul is a non-actor, we must have an actor, and that is *ahaṅkāra*.
53. The function of the intellect is decision, discrimination; while *ahaṅkāra* is a universal actor, ever ready to act at all times. Not so the intellect, which acts only under certain conditions: that is, when there is something to decide.
54. The functions of *ahaṅkāra* and the intellect are not the same, as we have explained. The special characteristic of the intellect is to decide; while that of *ahaṅkāra* is to act. But, as the intellect may decide to act, it becomes closely associated with *ahaṅkāra*; and that is why the latter is said to act for the sake of the intellect. Nevertheless, they belong to two essentially different types, as the *Mīmāṁsā* says.
55. When we examine the origin of action, we find that the decision to act comes first, and then some one within us engages in action. The former is the intellect that decides, and the latter *ahaṅkāra* that acts; and it is for this reason that, in the evolution of life from Nature, *ahaṅkāra* is said to arise from the intellect.
56. There are four instruments of actions (besides the soul),—intel- lect, *ahaṅkāra*, mind and the senses. They all act together, but different actions require more of the one than the other; and it is this idea that is represented by the four *Ṛtvij* priests and the three assistants of each, as has already been explained. The *Mīmāṁsā* tells us that we must find out, in the light of what has to be done, which instrument of action is needed most.

57. The word in the text is jīṣa, which means "the *Soma* plant after its juice has been pressed out"; and we have explained that *Soma* refers to the mind, and its juice to desire.
58. The word in the text is *yajamāna* which, as has already been explained, refers to the soul.
59. The *Bhagavad Gītā* tells us that the *Yogis*, free from all attachment, perform actions with their body, senses, mind, and the intellect for the purification of their soul (BhG. V, 11); and the *Mīmāṁsā* says the same.
60. When we have attained to a state of purification of the soul, we shall find that it is really the soul that acts through all these organs; and so we could take the latter in whichever way we like, for it would make no difference to the idea.
61. The sacred books really enjoin action: at the same time they contain passages which appear to lend support to the idea of its renunciation too. But there is no essential difference between the two statements,—for their object is the same,—perfection of the soul; and that can be achieved at one stage by means of action, and at another by means of its renunciation. The latter refers to the time of death; and, as that is inevitable, there must come a time when a person must renounce all action. This is what the sacred books really mean when they speak of renunciation; and the point is made still more clear in the following *Sūtra* (44).
62. The full moon, as has already been explained, refers to the full function of the mind, when it may, for practical purposes, be identified with the intellect. It refers, therefore, to action which is characterised by desire that is unopposed to Dharma, to which there is a reference in the *Bhagavad Gītā* (BhG. VII, n). The *Mīmāṁsā* tells us that it is laid down in the sacred books that such actions should always be performed (*Cf.* BhG. XVIII, 5-7; 47-49).
63. We have already explained that it is only at the time of death that a person can renounce all action. So long as he lives, or when the question of death is not involved, he must continue to act, and act intelligently: that is what the sacred books say.
64. There are a number of references to the creative power of desire (or the mind) in the sacred books. The *Taittirīyaka Upaniṣad* has the following:- "He wished, may I be many, may I grow forth. He brooded over himself; then sent forth (or created) all,—whatever that is" (II, vi).
    Thus we might say that wish or desire precedes action; and creation is a form of action.
65. The point of this *Sūtra* is, "Is desire first, or the mind first?" If we agree that desire is an attribute of the mind, it follows that the mind must come first. In such a case can we say that desire is the cause of all action or creation?
    In the Hymn of Creation in the *Ṛg Veda* we are told that in the beginning there was but One Thing, and apart from it there was nothing whatsoever. There was nothing but darkness round; and all that then existed was void and formless; and that One was born by the great power of *Tapas*. There-

after rose first of all Desire,— Desire, the primal seed and germ of the Mind (RV. X, cxxix, 1-4).

We gather from this that Desire itself is a creation, and follows *Tapas* or "severe meditation", which is a function of the intellect. It is for this reason that we find in the *Sāṅkhya* that the first creation of Nature or *Prakṛti* is the Intellect, and the Mind comes later.

66. We cannot say that Time is the cause of creation. There is an element of time in all action or creation,—even as the *Bhagavad Gītā* tells us that when an Age of Time comes to an end, all creatures return to *Prakṛti*; and when a new Age begins, another creation takes place; but it is careful to add that it is God who creates (BhG. IX, 7).

67. No one can know the origin of things. The Hymn of Creation in the *Ṛg Veda* has the following:—"Who verily knows, and who can here declare it,—whence it was born, and whence comes this creation? The gods are later than this world's production. Who knows then whence it first came into being? He, the first origin of this creation, whether he formed it all or did not form it,—Whose eye controls this world in highest heaven,—he verily knows it,*—or perhaps he knows not*." If even the great Creator may not know the origin of creation, who else can?

But the point of this is that knowledge, in the sense man understands it, is not possible in this case; for knowledge requires a knower and the object to be known; while in the present case, when the Creator creates, there is no duality: for He is one without a second; and so there can be no knowledge as we understand the term.

68. The *Ṛg Veda* has made it abundantly clear that no one can know the origin of things.

69. It may be argued that since animals too have a mind, perhaps they may know the origin of things, if man cannot. But, says the *Mīmāṁsā*, so far as man is concerned, the highest mind according to him, is the mind of man; and if that cannot understand the origin of things, we are justified in concluding that no one can.

It is indeed true that animals have a mind; but we can compare their mind only with the best of its class,—the mind of man, who is also an animal. Thus we see that no one can know the origin of things; and so the next *Sūtra* tells us that when it is said that some one knows, it is only an exuberant mode of expression, intended to emphasise things.

70. The word in the text is *rāja-sūya* which, as has already been explained, refers to the sacrifice or proper function of the mind in association with the senses and the intellect.

71. The common meaning of the word *aveshṭi* is "appeasing or ex-piation by means of sacrifices"; but the *Mīmāṁsā* tells us that it does not refer to this idea of sacrifice. We are asked to interpret it in two ways,—by piercing through its "disguise" (that is, division into parts), or associating it with the idea of desire; and both would give us the same meaning.

The word *aveshṭi*,*—ava*, *ish*, *ṭ*, *i*—would accordingly mean "(ava) away from (ish, 'to desire') desire, associated with (ṭ) the senses of knowledge and (ṭ) the mind". It accordingly refers to "desire-lessness or absence of desire."

The second method is that we should associate it with the idea of desire: and so we may divide the word into *Ava-iṣṭi*, when the meaning would be "(*ava*) away from (*iṣṭi*) desire"; and we see that the meaning is the same in both cases. We may, therefore, be satisfied that it is correct; and so the word aveshfi illustrates the principle referred to in the previous *Sūtra,*—namely, that it prevents hasty conclusions.

As desirelessness,--in the sense that we may not seek desires—is of the essence of the idea of sacrifice, we can now understand why the word has sacrifice or expiation by means of sacrifice for its meaning. It is in this manner that the real and common meanings of words are linked together.

72. The number twelve refers to the intellect, as eleven does to the mind, and ten to the ten senses of knowledge and action.

73. *Agnī* refers to the intellect, and *Soma* to the mind; and the combination of the two is *Agnī-shomīya*.

74. The number twelve refers to the intellect, which again is identified with the sun, as the mind is with the moon. As Time too refers to the sun, and may be said to be a kind of radiation from it, the number twelve also refers to Time. It will be found on examination that it constitutes the basis of the calculation of the time of day and night, the months of the year, as well as the great ages of Time,—all of which are multiples of the number twelve.

75. These words have to be governed by the same rule that govern Time, to which reference has already been made.

76. *Svaḥ-sutyā* means "tomorrow's preparation for *Soma*"; and, as *Soma* refers to the mind, and morning to time, it refers to the function of the mind in relation to time,—morning, when the mind is said to be at its best. It means, therefore, the best function of the mind.

77. We have to understand the meaning of a number of animals in the same manner. The sacred books refer to a number of animals,—horse, cow, dog, serpent, swan, fish, etc., and they all express special ideas of their own.

78. The words in the text are *sutyā* and *subrahmaṇyā*; and the former refers to the function of the mind, and the latter to *ahaṅkāra* or the I-as-an-actor, as has already been explained.

79. A deity, as has already been explained, refers to the great forces of Nature; and the *Mīmāṁsā* tells us that we can understand the idea of the relation between *ahaṅkāra* and the mnd if we refer them to their origin from, the idea of which is expressed by means of the invocation of the gods. Now the *Sāṅkhya* tells us that *Prakṛti* is at first in a state of rest; and then, when it begins to create, the first thing to arise from it is *Mahat* or the intellect; then from the intellect arises *ahaṅkāra* or the I-as-an-actor; and from *ahaṅkāra* the mind, the ten senses, and their objects. We may conclude from this that the function of the mind implies a function of ahaṅkāra as well, for the mind is said to arise from it.

This may be explained also in a somewhat different manner. We cannot conceive of action without reference to a state of rest; and, as *Prakṛti* implies action, we must think of it in a state of rest at first. Then, before there is action, there must be a decision to act; and as this is a function of the intellect, *Mahat* or intellect is said to arise from *Prakṛti*. But there must be a doer of the deed before an action take place; and that gives us *ahaṅkāra* arising out of the intellect. But the doer of the deed cannot act without desire, or the organs of the senses and their objects; and so we are told that the mind (which has desire for its attribute) and the senses and their objects arise simultaneously out of *ahaṅkāra* or the I-as-an-actor. This would appear to be a simple, rational way of explaining the evolution of life from *Prakṛti*.

80. No one can perform more than one action at a time,—not even *Indra* who, as has already been explained, refers to the self-conscious soul. When, however, it is stated that he can perform a number of acts simultaneously, we are to understand the idea of simultaneity in a relative sense; that is to say, *Indra* or the soul can perform a large number of action, and quickly too. *Indra* is accordingly called *satakratu*, or the performer of a hundred (innumerable) deeds.
81. What is possible for man is even more possible for a great force of Nature or a deity: only in such a case the idea of "cooking food" may be very different,—ripening corn, for instance.
    The word in the text is *liṅga*, which has a number of meanings, including "the image of a god; *Prakṛti*". It has been taken in the latter sense here.
82. The word in the text is *vṛddhi,* which means both "growth" as well as "decrease, cutting off".
83. The *Mimānsā* has told us that it is for this reason that the body has been compared to a chariot, which moves as a whole, though it consists of a number of parts.
84. This *Sūtra* (42a) is a part of the previous one in certain texts; while in others it does not occur at all. It would be advisable to retain it, as it brings out the distinction between an action performed by one person and by several.
85. There is a reference to the "sacrifice of knowledge" in the *Bhagavad Gītā* and we are told that all action is made more complete in knowledge (BhG. IV, 33); and the *Mīmāṁsā* says the same thing.
86. This *Sūtra* (47) would appear to be more appropriate as following No. 45, for it is a continuation of the same idea.
87. There can be no real simultaneity; but when we use this expression, it should be understood in a special sense, as referring to the performance of a number of actions in quick succession.
88. *Haviṣ-kṛt* means "preparing an oblation". *Adhrigu* is the name of a formula concluding with an invocation of *Agni*. *Puronuvākyā* means "an introductory verse".
    Manotā or *Manotā* is a hymn in *Ṛg Veda* (VI, i) containing the word *Manotā*. It also refers to the deity to whom the offering during the recitationn of that hymn is dedicated. It may refer to *Agni*. too.

CHAPTER - XII

SACRIFICE AND INTELLIGENCE : THE INSTINCT OF CREATION

PART- I

Similar theories are governed by similar rules, and dissimilar theories by different ones: the object of action is to find out this. But a theory may change if there is a change in the time or attributes of things. We must, however, accept the best theory.

In the case of theories, the meaning of words, except in special cases, remains unchanged. *Jaimini* says that a person should reject his own theory if he finds a better one.

When *Soma* refers to the new and the full moon, it signifies action characterised by knowledge. Non-action is the opposite of action. All good men act and do good deeds.

Sacrifice arises from an inner urge. Cooking food is not the highest form of action. There are two kinds of intelligent action,—obligatory and optional—and both should be done; and we should understand their meaning in the text by dividing words into parts.

The instinct to have offspring is obvious; but actual creation depends on time and circumstances. It is stronger than reason, and breaks through restraint, which is not always good. We know how it begins and ends; and can understand the meaning of the text. It does not refer to renunciation, the idea of which is different; nor does it imply intelligence, unless it is meant to do some special good.

It is necessary to know the origin and effect of an action. The principle of an action should not be deduced from the manner of its performance. It should make no difference where an action is to be performed, unless it involves considerations of breaking up things.

Theories

तन्त्रिसमवाये चोदनातः समानामेकतन्त्रत्वम्[1] तुल्येषु तु भेदः[2] स्यात् विधिप्रक्रमतादर्थ्यात्तादर्थ्यं श्रुतिकालनिर्देशात्॥१॥

गुणकालविकाराच्च तन्त्रभेदः स्यात्॥२॥

तन्त्रमध्ये विधानाद्वा मुख्यतन्त्रेण सिद्धिः[3] स्यात्तन्त्रार्थस्याविशिष्टत्वात्॥३॥

When a number of theories or principles are connected together by means of a common impelling force, those that are alike should be deemed to be governed by the same rule; while those that are not similar, by a different one. The object of the method of performing an action is to find out this; and we know that it is so at the time when we feel certain that we have understood what things are. But the entire principal idea of a theory may be changed if there is a change in the time or attributes of things. If there are a number of theories and we have a statement of their particulars, we should make use of the best theory, and arrive at our conclusion by its means, because that is the general purpose of a theory.

Language of the Text

विकाराच्च न भेदः स्यादर्थस्याविकृतत्वात्॥४॥

एकेषां चाशक्यत्वात्॥५॥

एकाग्निवच्च दर्शनम्॥६॥

In the case of theories, the language of the text is such that

1. न्त्रमत्त्विति वृत्तिपाठः।
2. भेदो विधिक्रमेति वृत्तिपाठः।
3. सिद्धः स्येति वृत्तिपाठः।

even if we change the form of words by means of their division into parts, it would make no difference, because the meaning would remain the same. This, however, is not possible in certain cases, as, for instance, in the case of the word *Agni*[1].

We must Accept the Best Theory

जैमिनेः परमन्त्र[1]त्वापत्तेः स्वतन्त्रप्रतिषेधः स्यात्॥७॥

Jaimini says that a person should reject his own theory if he finds a better one.

Action and Inaction

नानार्थत्वात्सोमे दर्शपूर्णमासप्रकृतीनां वेदिकर्म स्यात्॥८॥

अकर्म वा कृतदूषा स्यात्॥९॥

पात्रेषु च प्रसंगः स्याद्धोमार्थत्वात्॥१०॥

न्याय्यानि वा प्रयुक्तत्वादप्रयुक्ते प्रसङ्गः स्यात्॥११॥

There are a number of meanings of the word *Soma*; but where it is associated with the new and the full moon, we should take it that it refers to action characterised by knowledge[2]. On the other hand, non-action or negation of action should be regarded as a defilement of the idea of action. Men of worth should be devoted to action, because it serves the purpose of sacrifice.[3] We are directed to perform good actions; but we should be devoted to them even if there be no such rule.

An Inner Urge to Sacrifice

शामित्रे च पशुपुरोडाशो न स्यादितरस्य प्रयुक्तत्वात्॥१२॥

There is an inner urge that makes for the performance of action as a sacrifice, for no animal goes to a place of immolation at the direction of another.

Satisfaction of Hunger is not the Highest End

श्रपणं चाऽग्निहोत्रस्य शालामुखीये न स्यात्प्राजहितस्यविद्यमा

1. तन्त्रापेति वृत्तिपाठः।

नत्वात्॥१३॥
हविर्धाने निर्वपणार्थं साधयेतां प्रयुक्तत्वात्॥१४॥
अप्रसिद्धिर्वाऽन्यदेशत्वात् प्रधानवैगुण्यादवैगुण्ये प्रसङ्गः स्यात्॥१५॥

So far as an intelligent action is concerned, we should not regard cooking food (or the satisfaction of hunger) as the highest end, because there are instances of those who have done this for a time and given it up.[4] There are two kinds of intelligent actions,—obligatory and optional; and both should be performed as directed, because they are meant to do good. But if there is no proof of this, and we are led to a different conclusion,—because we have not divided the principal word into parts, we should retrace our steps, and resort to this method of division into parts.

Instinct to Have Offspring

अनसां च दर्शनात्॥१६॥
तद्युक्तं च कालभेदात्॥१७॥
मन्त्राश्च सन्निपातित्वात्॥१८॥

We see that the instinct to have offspring exists; but how a creature comes to be possessed of it depends on time and circumstances; and the sacred verses are meant to promote it[5].

More Powerful than Reason

धारणार्थत्वात्सोमेऽग्न्यन्वाधानं न विद्यते॥१९॥
तथा व्रत[1]मुपेतत्वात्॥२०॥
विप्रतिषेधाच्च॥२१॥

In this desire (or function of the mind) the function of the intellect is not seen, because it is meant to preserve (the species). In the same manner a solemn vow, actually undertaken, also disappears; and that is so because it means restraint.

Not Always Good: How to Understand It

सत्यवदिति चेत्॥२२॥

---

1. मुपेवत्वेति वृत्तिपाठः।

न संयोगपृथक्त्वात्॥२३॥
ग्रहा[1]र्थं च पूर्वमिष्टेस्तदर्थत्वात्॥२४॥
शेषवदिति चेत्॥२५॥
न वैश्वदेवो हि॥२६॥
स्याद्[2]व्यपदेशात्॥२७॥
न गुणार्थत्वात्॥२८॥
सन्नहनञ्च[3] वृत्तत्वात्॥२९॥

We cannot say that this is always good, because it is different in each case. The first aim is to lay hold of an object,—because that is the purpose of desire; but that is not its end,—for that is what we find everywhere in Nature.[6] But so far as its obvious statement is concerned, we may say that it is so. But we shall not understand this if we divide into parts the words used in the text; because they are closely knitted together to correspond to the state of what has actually happened.

Does not Refer to Renunciation

अन्यविधानादारण्यभोजनं सयादुभयं हि वृत्त्यर्थम्॥३०॥
शेषभक्षास्तथेति चेन्नान्यार्थत्वात्॥३१॥
भृतत्वाच्च परिक्रयः॥३२॥
शेषभक्षास्तथेति चेत्॥३३॥
न कर्मसंयोगात्॥३४॥
प्रवृत्तवरणात्प्रतितन्त्रं वरणं होतुः क्रियेत[4]॥३५॥

Even if there were a different statement of particulars, we would still not be able to conclude that it refers to the renunciation of action[7], because both (action and instinct to have offspring) are meant to serve a common purpose of life. The

1. ग्रहणार्थमिति न्या. मा. पाठान्तरम्।
2. स्याद्वा व्यपेति पाठो वृत्तिकृन्मते।
3. चशब्दरहितः पाठो वृत्तिकृमन्ते।
4. क्रियते इति वृत्ति पाठः।

idea of eating the remnants of food is not the same as that of renunciation of action, because their meaning is different.[8] A hired labourer receives a wage; but the idea of eating the remnants of food is not like that, because the former is connected with labour; while eating the remnants of; food is in every essential part a matter of choice on the part of the doer of the deed.

Not Always a Good or Intelligent Act

ब्रह्मापीति चेत्॥३६॥
न प्राङ्नियमात्तदर्थं हि॥३७॥
निर्दिष्टस्येति चेत्॥३८॥
नाश्रुतत्वात्॥३९॥
होतुस्तथेति चेत्॥४०॥
न कर्मसंयोगात्॥४१॥

We cannot say that it is always an intelligent act;[9] but if it is meant to serve the purpose of a pious or a meritorious deed, it would surely be so. We cannot, however, say that the ; actions of a learned man are always pious, because no one has taught so; nor is it true of the mind,[10] because it is connected with all kinds of actions.

Importance of Knowledge of the Origin and Effect of Action

यज्ञोत्पत्त्युप[1]देशे निष्ठितकर्मप्रयोगभेदात्प्रतितन्त्रं क्रियेत[2]॥४२॥
न वा कृतत्वात्तदुपदेशो हि॥४३॥
देशपृथक्त्वान्मन्त्रो[3]ऽभ्यावर्तेत॥४४॥
सन्नहनहरणे तथेति चेत्॥४५॥
नान्यार्थत्वात्॥४६॥

When we are dealing with a great action or a sacrifice, it

---

1. शेऽनुष्ठीति वृत्ति पाठः।
2. क्रियते इवि वृत्ति पाठः।
3. न्त्रो व्यावेति वृत्ति पाठः

is necessary to have knowledge in regard to its origin and the effect it is likely to produce; for then we shall know the different ways in which such an action can be undertaken, and every essential part of it can be properly done. Indeed, we should not deduce the principle of an action from the manner in which it is performed. If an action has to be performed in a different place or country, the resolution to perform it should not be changed. This, however, does not apply to breaking up things that are held together, because the object of that is different.

PART II

THE LAW OF CREATION

Introduction

The motive of pleasure is powerful enough to lead to the attainment of objects. But it should not cause pain. Pleasure (or joy) should be the motive of the knowers of the Vedas too; and it exists also in deeds of service. But sometimes it is also not there.

Cooking meat for pleasure is forbidden, as it is contrary to the idea of sacrifice; but it may have some other meaning too.

None but living creatures have a desire to procreate, and it serves the purpose of Nature. The female is more active than the male at first; but the male becomes more active later. It is an act of sacrifice, and has no room for vulgarity. It is a creative act, and requires harmony; and involves in particular the function of the mind.

A law or usage is that which is followed by most men; and that is how we should understand the meaning of the text.

Meaning is more important than elegance of expression; but language, like a garment, should have both utility and beauty. But utility or meaning comes first, as in the case of the word *yūpa*; but when we understand its meaning, by dividing it into parts, we find beauty in it too.

We cannot always understand the desires of animals; and they are described in the sacred books in a special form which may appear to be new, but it significant, and would be found to be appropriate too.

Power of Pleasure

विहारो लौकिकानामर्थं साधयेत् प्रभुत्वात्॥१॥
मांसपाकप्रतिषेधश्च तद्वत्॥२॥
निर्देशाद्वा वैदिकानां स्यात्॥३॥
सति चोपासनस्य दर्शनात्॥४॥
अभावदर्शनाच्च॥५॥

In the case of average, ordinary men, it is pleasure that directs them to their object, because it is powerful enough to do so. But it should not cause pain; and it is for this reason that the cooking of meat for pleasure is prohibited. It has specially been mentioned that pleasure (or joy) should be the aim of knowers of the Vedas too.[11] We see that there is pleasure also in deeds of worship or service; but sometimes we also see that it does not exist.

Pleasure and Sacrifice

मांसपाको विहित प्रतिषेधः स्याद् वाहु[1]तिसंयोगात्॥६॥
वाक्यशेषो वा दक्षिणा[2]स्मिन्नारभ्य विधानस्य॥७॥

The prohibition against cooking meat for pleasure is an enjoined or strict prohibition, because of its connection with the idea of sacrifice;[12] or, if it means something else, it should be taken to refer to what is intended to complete an elliptical sense in connection with a description that has just begun.

Desire to Procreate

सवनीये छिद्रापिधानार्थत्वात् पशुपुरोडाशो; न स्यादन्येषामेवमर्थत्वात्॥८॥

---

1. स्यादाह्विति वृत्तिपाठः।
2. दक्षिणेऽस्मिन्नारेति न्या. मा. पाठः।

क्रिया वा देवतार्थत्वात्॥९॥
लिङ्गदर्शनाच्च॥१०॥

There is, in connection with the function of the mind,[13] a desire on the part of an animal to cover an opening in the lower region of the body; but there can be no such desire for such a purpose on the part of anything else. This action takes place to serve the purpose of Nature;[14] and we can see the proof of it ourselves.

An Act of Sacrifice

हविष्कृत्सवनीयेषु न स्यात्; प्रकृतौ यदि सर्वार्था पशुं प्रत्याहूता सा कुर्याद्विद्यमानत्वात्॥११
पशौ तु संस्कृते[1] विधानात्तार्तीयसवन- (नि-) केषु स्यात्सौम्याश्विनयोश्चापवृक्तार्थत्वात्॥१२॥
योगाद्वा यज्ञाय तद्विमोके विसर्गः स्यात्॥१३॥
निशि यज्ञे प्राकृतस्याप्रवृत्तिः स्यात्प्रत्यक्षशिष्टत्वात्॥१४॥
कालवाक्यभेदाच्च तन्त्रभेदः स्यात्॥१५॥
वेद्युद्धननव्रतं विप्रतिषेधात्तदेव स्यात्॥१३॥
तन्त्रमध्ये विधानाद्वा तत्तन्त्रा सवनीयवत्॥१७॥
वैगुण्यादिध्माबर्हिर्न साधयेदग्न्याधानं य यदि देवतार्थम्॥१८॥
आरम्भणीया विकृतौ न स्यात् प्रकृतिकालमध्यत्वात्कृता; पुनस्तदर्थेन॥१९॥
सकृ[2]द्वाऽऽरम्भासंयोगात्॥ १९अ.॥
स्याद्वा कालस्याशेषभूतत्वात्॥२०॥
प्रारम्भविभागाच्च॥२१॥

This desire ceases to be active in those who are devoted to deeds of sacrifice. It is a law of Nature (*Prakṛti*) that, if a suitable female is invited to a male, it is she who should act; and we find that it is so. But the male, while under the influence of desire, becomes more active, because that is how the mind and

1. संशृते इति न्या. मा. पाठः।
2. इदं सूत्रं भाष्ये न्यायमालायां च नास्ति; वृत्तिकृन्मतेऽस्ति।

the senses complete their purpose[15] (or are satisfied). But their union is an act of sacrifice, and they become free when the bond is released. It has clearly been taught that in this sacrifice of the night there is no room for those who are vulgar; and the difference in the means to secure the result is due to the difference in connection with time and speech. It should, however, take place when there is no desire to destroy the vital energy of the mind.[16] In the midst of the process, and while it continues, all the means relating to it correspond to the function of the mind. In case of imperfection, it should not be resorted to; but if it is meant to serve the purpose of Nature, it may yet be done. Those about to begin should not be in a state of agitation or hostility, and should act in the even course of natural time, bearing in mind the object to be achieved. But it may be done at once if a beginning cannot be made, or if there is no time for making a beginning, or if there is a break at the very start.

Conception of a Law

विप्रतिषिद्धधर्माणां समवाये भूयसां स्यात्सधर्मत्वम्॥२२॥

मुख्यं वा पूर्वचोदनाल्लोकवत्॥२३॥

तथा[1] चान्यार्थदर्शनम्॥२४॥

When there is a conflict of opinion in regard to law or usage, that should be deemed to be so which is followed by most men; but the principal law should be that which arises from ancient direction, as is common among the people. It is in this manner that we can understand other meanings of the text.

Utility and Beauty in Language

अङ्गगुणविरोधे च तादर्थ्यात्॥२५॥

परिधिर्द्व्यर्थत्वादुभयधर्मा स्यात्॥२६॥

यौप्यस्तु विरोधे स्यान्मुख्या नन्तर्यात्॥२७॥

---

1. इदं सूत्रं वृत्तिकारमत एव नास्ति।

इतरो वा तस्य तत्र विधानात्॥२८॥
उभयोश्चाङ्गसंयोगः॥२९॥

If there is a conflict between the division of the words of a hymn into parts on the one hand, and elegance of expression on the other, —we should accept that which gives a suitable meaning. A garment is meant for both utility and beauty, and should have both qualities (and the same is true of language). For instance, in the case of the word *yūpa*, a new interpretation becomes necessary, because of the conflict between beauty and utility; and we have to see that there is no break in the continuity of the principal idea (that utility should come first). The word comes to have a different meaning because of the statement of particulars in its place in the text; and then we see that the connection between its parts makes for both utility and beauty[17].

Desires of Animals

पशुसवनीयेषु विकल्पः स्याद्वै कृतश्चेदुभयोरश्रुतिभतत्वात्॥२९॥
पाशुकं वा तस्य वैशेषिकाम्नानात्तदनर्थकं विकल्पे स्यात्॥३०॥
पशोश्च विप्रकर्षस्तन्त्रमध्ये विधानात्॥३१॥
अपूर्वं च प्रकृतौ समानतन्त्रा[1] चेदनित्यत्वादनर्थकं हि स्यात्॥३३॥
अधिकश्च गुणः साधारणेऽविरोधा- त्कांस्यभोजिवदमुख्येऽपि॥३४॥
तत्प्रवृत्त्या तु तन्त्रस्य नियमः स्याद्यथा पाशुकं सूक्तवाकेन॥३५॥
न वाऽविरोधात्॥३६॥
अशास्त्रलक्षणाच्च॥३७॥

In the case of the desires of animals, there can be a doubt as to their exact idea, if they are not natural (or are subject to change), because both (the pair) are not always characterised by reason. As there is a special mention of animals in the sacred books,—and the text makes little sense—it should fill us with doubt as to its exact idea. If we are told that an animal is "dragged away", it implies that it is in the middle of the act, because that is the rule of this mode of expression. It is quite

1. तन्त्र चेदेति वृत्तिपाठः।

new in its basic form, —for were it otherwise, and were its main points similar to other expressions,—since the act is of an occasional character (and so different from others)--the whole idea would be rendered meaningless. In this case if we divide words into parts, it would be an additional point of beauty, because there is no inconsistency in their common meaning; and it is like the case of one who, though he is not the chief, enjoys his drink from a cup of brass or bell-metal. But, as it is necessary to exercise restraint in such matters, the idea, —so far as animals are concerned—has been described in well chosen words. But it may not be necessary to exercise it if it does not cause injury. It is, however, necessary, if its effect is evil or contrary to the teachings of the sacred books.

PART III

THE LAW OF CREATION *(CONTINUED)*

If intelligently performed, the act does not cause injury; but restraint is necessary; and it should be done intelligently and in a state of perfect tranquillity. A great deal, however, depends on one's own disposition.

Conditions of a single act. It is a powerful urge and one should avoid its evil consequences. Resolutions have a value of their own.

The language of the text in this connection is sometimes plain and sometimes ornate as occasion demands.

It is a secret act, and should be preceded by prayer. It is only very intelligent or holy persons who can limit themselves to a single act; and it should result in the birth of a child of special virtue. In general, however, it is meant to secure a variety of objects, and is caused by desire.

Need of Restraint

विश्वजिति वत्सत्वङ्नामधेयादितरथा तन्त्रभूयस्त्वादहतं स्यात्।१॥
अविरोधी वा[1] उपरिवासो हि[2] वत्सत्वक्॥२॥

अनुनिर्वाप्येषु भूयस्त्वेन तन्त्रनियमः स्यात्॥३॥
आगन्तुकत्वाद्वा स्वधर्मा स्याच्छ्रुतिविशेषादितरस्य च मुख्यत्वात्॥४॥
स्वस्थानत्वाच्च॥५॥
स्विष्टकृच्छ्रवणान्नेति चेत्॥६॥
विकारः पवमानवत्॥७॥
अविकारो वा प्रकृतिवच्चोदनां प्रति भावाच्च॥८॥

If the act is performed in an intelligent manner,[18] the skin of the "dear one",—for that is. the name by which it is called—should, in spite of several acts, remain uninjured. There is no incongruity in this, because the skin of the "dear one" remains on the upper side. When it is taken out, there should be a restriction in regard to its subsequent use, for otherwise it would lead to excess. But while the union lasts, one should do one's duty in a specially intelligent manner, if something different has been done at the beginning; and it should be done in a state of perfect tranquillity. After it has been done, it should not be continued; and there should be a change, as in the case of other functions of the mind.[19] But there may be no change, according as one's nature demands, because the urge corresponds to one's own disposition.

A Single Act

एककर्मणि शिष्टत्वाद्गुणानां सर्वकर्म स्यात्॥९॥
एकार्थास्तु विकल्पेरन् समुच्चये ह्यावृत्तिः स्यात्प्रधानस्य[3]॥१०॥
अभ्यस्येतार्थवत्त्वादिति चेत्॥११॥
नाश्रुतित्वात्॥१२॥
सति चाभ्यासशास्त्रत्वात्॥१३॥
विकल्पवच्च दर्शयति॥१४॥
कालान्तरेऽर्थवत्त्वं स्यात्॥१५॥

If a person desires to engage in but a single act,—as it is of a very refined or high character—all his attributes or auxiliary parts should take part in it. But those who desire to

1. धो वोपरिवासो वेति वृत्तिपाठः।
2. वृत्तिकृन्मते हि पदं नास्ति।
3. प्रधानस्येति वृत्तिकृन्मते नास्ति।

engage in but a single act, should hesitate; because when united, there is likely to be a repetition on the part of one who initiates it. We cannot say that he should repeat it if it satisfies his object, because it would be contrary to the sacred books to say so; and if it is done, : it should be in accordance with good counsel or rules; and we see that there are persons who hesitate. There should, however, be a state of satisfaction of desire after the lapse of some time.

A Powerful Urge

प्रायश्चित्तेषु चैकार्थ्यान्निष्पन्नेनाभिसंयोगस्तस्मात्सर्वस्य निर्घातः॥१६॥
समुच्चयस्त्वदोष[1] निर्घातार्थेषु॥१७॥

Those who are dominated by these thoughts, bring it about because that is the one object they seek, and forget everything else; but the union should be such as is not attended with evil consequences.

Importance of Resolutions

मन्त्राणां कर्मसंयोगात्स्वधर्मेण प्रयोगः स्याद्धर्मस्य तन्निमित्तत्वात्॥१८॥
विद्यां प्रति विधानाद्वा सर्वकालं प्रयोगः स्यात्कर्मार्थत्वात् प्रयोगस्य॥१९॥

Resolutions should be characterised by a sense of duty, because they can create such a sense of duty, and lead to action. Since action is performed for the sake of knowledge,[20] it may be undertaken at all times if that is its end.

The Language of the Text

भाषास्वरोपदेशेषु[2] ऐरवत्प्रवचनप्रतिषेधः स्यात्॥१९॥
मन्त्रोपदेशो वा न भाषिकस्य प्रायापत्तेर्भाषिकश्रुतिः॥२१॥
विकारः कारणाग्रहणे[3]॥२२॥

When it is enough to make a plain or common speech, eloquence should be avoided, as in the case of eating or drinking. But we are advised to use learned language and not common speech, when the latter is used freely everywhere; and

---

1. दोषोर्थेष्विति वृत्तिकृन्मते पाठः।
2. देशादैरेति न्या. मा. पाठः।
3. ग्रहे इति वृत्तिपाठः।

the point of changing the form is that others should not understand it.

A Secret Act

तन्न्यायत्वाददृष्टोऽप्येवम्॥२३॥
तदुत्पत्तेर्वा प्रवचनलक्षणत्वात्॥२४॥
मन्त्राणां करणार्थत्वान्मन्त्रान्तेन कर्मादिसन्निपातः स्यात्सर्वस्य वचनार्थत्वात्॥२५॥

The reason why the act is performed unseen by others is that it is proper that it should be so.[21] So far as its origin is concerned, the desire arises from the influence of speech. As the *Mantras* or hymns of the sacred books are meant to serve the purpose of action, the act of union should begin after a prayer or recitation of the *Mantras*, for they are meant to serve all dinds of objects.

The Act

सन्ततवचनाद्धारायामादिसंयोगः॥२६॥
कर्मसन्तानो वा नानाकर्मत्वादितरस्याशक्यत्वात्॥२७॥
आघारे च दीर्घधारत्वात्॥२८॥

In accoudance with eternal teaching, the first union takes place in an opening in the body[22]; and, as a result of a variety of actions, there is a continuity of the act, because anything else would not be possible; and it ends in besprinkling if it holds on for a long enough time.

A Single Act

मन्त्राणां सन्निपातित्वादेकार्थानां विकल्पः स्यात्॥२९॥
सङ्ख्याविहितेषु समुच्चयोऽसन्नि पातित्वात्॥३०॥

Those who think of but a single act should hesitate, because all good counsel in this connection is likely to collapse; but those who are endowed with intelligence engage in it without such collapse.

Its Purpose

ब्राह्मणविहितेषु च सङ्ख्यावत् सर्वेषामुपदिष्टत्वात्॥३१॥

याज्यावषट्कारयोश्च समुच्चय[1]दर्शनं तद्वत्॥३२॥
विकल्पो वा समुच्चयस्याश्रुतित्वात्॥३३॥
गुणार्थत्वादुपदेशस्य॥३४॥
वषट्कारे नानार्थत्वात्समुच्चयः॥३५॥
हौत्रा[2]स्तु विकल्पेरन्नेकार्थत्वात्॥३६॥
समुच्चयो वा क्रियमाणानुवादित्वात्॥३७॥
समुच्चयं च दर्शयति॥३८॥

The act is prescribed in the case of all those who are endowed with divine or holy knowledge, even as it is in the case of those who have intellect; and we see that the union of a good and intelligent woman and a holy and skilful man is in accordance with this. Hesitation in such a case arises from want of understanding of the teachings of the sacred books,—which are meant to secure merit.[23] In the case of a skilful person, however, the union is meant to secure a variety of objects. Those who are full of desire,[24] should hesitate if they wish to engage in but a single act; for the union arises from what one desires to do; and we see that it is a common enough occurrence.

PART IV

CREATION AS A SCRIFICE :

PROOF OF THE EXISTENCE OF THE SOUL

Introduction

We can understand all this by piercing through the "disguise" of words.

Considerations of money play a part, but not the most important one: hence a reference to wealth should be properly weighted.

It is a creative act, meant for great ends; and is different from the making of a cup or the boiling of milk. It is an act with an object, and is not prohibited.

---

1. यस्य देति न्या. मा. पाठः।
2. वृत्तिकृन्मते क्रियमाणानुवादित्वात्समुच्चयो वा होत्राणामित्येवं सूत्रस्य पाठः।

The vulgar ones cause injury, and should be properly instructed. There is harm in indulgence; and indulgence can never be advised.

As a pure act of sacrifice, it is permitted even in a state of dejection.

Perpetual restraint is advised only in the case of one who has lost everything. But there is a general lack of restraint resulting from traditional usage, when a man yield to desire, and does not listen to his soul.

We do not understand the nature of the soul, and believe that its highest funtion is like that of the mind. But the soul is differnt, and we can understand it in various ways: as that which causes all the faclties of man to act we can know its existence because of memory for some one else, is a law that the fruit of action is meant for some one else, —and that some one is the soul it is the fourth to complete the idea of action and it is that for whose sake there is the offering of the monthly *śrāddha* to the deceased.

How to Understand the Text

जपाश्चा[१] कर्मसंयुक्ताः स्तुत्याशीरभिधाना[२]श्च याजमानेजु समुच्चयः स्यादाशीः पृथक्त्वात्॥१॥

समु[३]च्चयं च दर्शयति॥२॥

याज्यानुवाक्यसु तु विकल्पः स्याद्देवतोपलक्षणार्थत्वात्॥३॥

लिङ्गदर्शनाच्च॥४॥

क्रयणेषु तु विकल्पः स्यादेकार्थत्वात्॥५॥

समुच्चयो वा प्रयोगे द्रव्यसमवायात्॥६॥

समुच्चयञ्च दर्शयति॥७॥

संस्कारे च तत्प्रधानत्वात्॥८॥

संख्यासु तु विकल्पः स्याच्छ्रुतिविप्रतिषेधात्॥९॥

---

1. मींस्विति न्या. मा. पाठः।
2. नाच्च येति वृत्तिपाठः।
3. इदं सूत्रं केषुचिद् भाष्यपुस्तकेषु न दृश्यते।

द्रव्यविकारं[1] तु पूर्ववदर्थकर्म स्यात् तथा विकल्पे नियमः प्रध
ानत्वात्॥१०॥

द्रव्यत्वेऽपि समुच्चयो; द्रव्यस्य कर्मनिष्पत्तेः; प्रतिपशु कर्मभेदादेवं सति यथाप्रकृति॥११॥

Silent prayers,—disinterested, because unconnected with any action—and words of blessing and praise, should bring about the union of those who are engaged in sacrifice or good and intelligent deeds,—for there is a separate benediction in respect of them. We see, however, that the act of union is common enough.But in the sacrificial texts and verse recited to invoke the gods, we should hesitate to come to the conclusion that this is their subject-matter, because they deal with all kinds of laws of Nature. We can, however, understand their idea of by piercing through the "disguise" of words.

Reference to Money—In the reference to acts of buying, we should doubt if that is the one meaning ; though the union may at first result from a sum of moneys; and this kind of it can be seen. A pure act, however, arises from the importance of the act itself; and so where calculations of money are involved, we should doubt if the reference is to this, because it would be contrary to the teachings of the sacred books. But wealth can make a change for the worse. As has already been stated, it should be an act performed for its own sake; and so we should refrain from doubting its power, because it is so important. But money too can bring about a union, and is paid in consideration for the completion of the act. But every animal, in spite of its difference of action, acts in accordance with its nature.

A Creative Act

कपालेऽपि तथेति चेत्॥१२॥

न कर्मणः परार्थत्वात्॥१३॥

1. रं च पू इति वृत्तिपाठः।

प्रतिपत्तिस्तु शेषत्वात्॥१४॥
शृतेऽपि पूर्ववत्त्वा[1]त्स्यात्॥१५॥

We cannot say that the making of a cup or a tortoise-shell is of the same kind as this act, for the latter is meant for higher ends; and we know this from actual results. The case with regard to boiled milk is the same as has already been stated (that is, it is not like this act).

An Action with a Purpose

विकल्पे त्वर्थकर्म नियमप्रधानत्वात्[2]। शेषे च कर्मकार्यसमवाया-त्तस्मात्तेनार्थकर्म स्यात्॥१६॥

Even if a person hesitates because there is a purpose in the act, it should still be done because of the importance of the obligation or the law. With regard to the rest (that is, where there is no hesitation), the act is commonly performed because of the result associated with it; and it is because of this that there will always be some act which will be full of purpose.

The Place

उखायां काम्यनित्यसमुच्चयो; नियोगे कामदर्शनात्॥१७॥
असति चासंस्कृतेषु कर्म स्यात्॥१८॥
तस्य च देवतार्थत्वात्॥१९॥
विकारो वा तदुक्तहेतुः॥२०॥
वचनादसंस्कृतेषु कर्म स्यात्॥२१॥
संसर्गे चापि दोषः स्यात्॥२२॥
वचनादिति चेत्॥२३॥
तथेतरस्मिन्॥२४॥

The optional and obligatory union takes place in a particular part of the upper leg; and because of a charming appearance, it results in an intimate bond. In the case of the vulgar or the uninitiated, it may be in a wrong place, and in answer to a natural urge; and then there is an injury, the reason for which has already been explained. In the case of the

1. वत्त्वात्स्येति न्या. कृन्मते पाठः।
2. विकल्पे इत्यादि कर्म न्या. मालाकृत्सम्मतः पाठः।

vulgar or the uninitiated. there; should be proper instruction. There is always harm in indulgence; and we cannot say that indulgence can ever be advised,—for advice can only be in respect of some-thing different.

An Act of Sacrifice

उत्सर्गे अपि[1] परिग्रहः कर्मणः कृतत्वात्॥२५॥
स आहवनीयः स्यादाहुति संयोगात्॥२६॥
अन्यो वोद्धृत्या[2]ऽऽहरणात्॥२७॥
तस्मिन्संस्कारकर्म शिष्टत्वात्॥२८॥
स्थानाद्वा परिलुप्येरन्॥२९॥

Even in a state of dejection, the obligation to act,—if it is necessary—should be accepted; and it should be regarded as an intelligent act because of its connection with a sacrifice;[25] and everything else should be left out of consideration if it conflicts with it. In such a case a pure (or consecrated) act alone is enjoined; and anything different from it should be eliminated.

Perpetual Restraint

नित्यधारणे विकल्पो; न ह्याकस्मात्प्रतिषेधः स्यात्॥३०॥
नित्यधारणाद्वा प्रतिषेधो गतश्रियः॥३१॥

In case of a reference to perpetual restraint, we should doubt its advisability; but there is good reason for self-control. The reference to perpetual restraint is really in respect of one who has lost his all,— wealth, virtue, or grace.

Common Lack of Restraint

परार्थान्येको यजमानगणे॥३२॥
अनियमोऽविशेषात्॥३३॥
मुख्यो वाऽविप्रतिषेधात्॥३४॥
सत्रे गृहपतिरसंयोगाद्धौत्रवत्॥३५॥
आम्नायवचनाच्च॥३६॥
सर्वे वा तदर्थत्वात्॥३७॥

---

1. उत्सर्गेपीति न्या. मा. पाठः।
2. द्धृत्य हेति वृत्तिपाठः।

Among a host of sacrificers or performers of good and intelligent deeds, there is but one whose actions are meant for the benefit of others; and generally speaking, there is an absence of restraint. But the principal act (even in such a case) is not prohibited; though, so far as the great function of the mind is concerned,[26] it is like being full of desires,[27] but without the co-operation of the soul,[28] This happens because of teachings of traditional usage; and is seen in all who have that object in view.

The Soul

गृहपतिरिति च समाख्या सामान्यात्॥३८॥
विप्रतिषेधे परम्॥३९॥
हौत्रे परार्थत्वात्॥४०॥
वचनं परम्॥४१॥

We often use the term "master of the house" or the soul in a general way (without understanding its exact idea); and deny that there is anything higher than that; and associate its highest function with that of the mind;[29] and believe that to be the highest teaching.

Proof of the Existence of the Soul

प्रभुत्वादार्त्विज्यं सर्ववर्णानां स्यात्॥४२॥
स्मृतेर्वा स्याद् ब्राह्मणानाम्॥४३॥
फलचमसविधानाच्चेतरेषाम्॥४४॥
सान्नाय्येऽप्येवं प्रतिषेधः[1] सोमपीथहेतुत्वात्॥४५॥
चतुर्धाकरणे च निर्देशात्॥४६॥
अन्वाहार्ये दर्शनात्॥४७॥

But it is because of the power of the soul that all the other faculties of a man (his intellect, *ahaṅkāra*, mind, and the senses,— called *Ṛtvij* priests) perform their functions.[30] Those who are intelligent, know the existence of the soul because of memory;[31] and also because of the fact that there is a law that the fruit of action is meant for some one else.[32] That is so even where there is a combined function of the mind and intellect or a good and intelligent deed;[33] and we could deny this only if there were no one to experience the function of the mind.[34] We get the same idea from the reference that all things should be made fourfold,[35] as well as from the monthly *śrāddha* in honour of the deceased[36].

NOTES

1. The common meaning of *Agni* is "fire"; but if we divide it into parts, we shall get a very different meaning,—intelligence.
2. *Soma* has a number of meanings,—moon, wine, etc. But its real meaning is the mind, e have explained that the new moon refers to the awakening of the mind in the form of desire or knowledge, and the full moon in connection wwith the new and the full moon, it means action characterised by knowledge.
3. The *Bhagvad Gītā* also tells us that sacrifice is born of action (BhG. II, 14).
4. The word in the text is *prā-jahita*, which is applied to fire that has been abandoned.
5. There are a number of references to desire to have children in the sacred books.
6. The word in the text is *Viśve-devas* which means "all-goods"; and as a god refres to the great forces of Nature, if refers to all Nature.
7. The desire to have offspring cannot in any case refer to renunciation of action
8. The sacred books refer to living ofn remnants of food (*Cf* BhG. IV, 31) but that does not refer to the renunciation of actyion. It sifnifies , as the following *Sūtras* make it clear, a voluntary act of austerity and abasement, which is a form off discipline in action.
9. Sex life is not alwaus governed by reason. The word in the text is Brāhmaṇa which, as has already been explained, referes to the intellect.
10. The mind is characterised by desire, which is not always of the best. The word in the text is *Hotṛ* which, as has already been explained, referes to the mind.
11. Vedas are books of knowledge; and knowledge should give joy. That is the test of highest konledge.
12. Sacrifice in an action meant for the benefit of all, without exception, and it includes animals too; and so slaying animals and cooking meat for pleasure would be contray to the idea of sacrifice. Hence it is strictly prohibited. But if it is permitted,—we are told in the next *Sūtra—the* idea would be very differnt, as we find in the case of the Sacrificof the Horse (*Cf* . MM.V. 782-795 .
13. The word in the text is *Savaanīya* , which meana "*Soma* libation", and we have explained that *Soma* refers to the mind, and liberation or sacrifice to action. *Sacvanīya* referes therefore, to the function of the mind.
14. The word in the text is *Devatā*, which refers to Nature.
15. The words in the text are Soma and the two *Aśvins* and the former refers to the mind and the latter to the two kinds of senses, of knowledge and

action. The two *Aśvins* mean "two horses"; and the "horse" in sacred literature, as has already been explained, refers to the senses. The "two horses" would, therefore, refer to the two kinds of senses,—of motion and action, or knowledge and action.

It may be of interest to observe that in the story of the *Mahābhārata* Nakula and *Sahadeva*, the two twins, are said to be the sons of the two *Asvins*; and, as a son is said to represent his father, the twins of the Epic refer to the senses of motion and action, or the legs and arms of man. Indeed, the five Pāṇḍava brothers would be found to refer to the five parts of a man,—intellect, mind, *prāna* or vital breath as a vehicle of the soul, legs and arms (*Cf.* MM. III—V).

16. The word in the text is vaidyut, which means "arising from lightning"; and lightning or electric energy is the energy of the mind.
17. The common meaning of the word *yūpa* is "a sacrificial post"; but that does not make much sense. It has been defined to mean action meant for the benefit of all (XI, iii, 2-7); and if we divide it into parts, we shall find that it not only makes sense, but makes for beauty too. The whole idea would then appear to be very beautiful. This has already been explained.
18. The word in the text is *viśva-jīt* which, as has already been explained, refers to the intellect.
19. The word in the text is pavamāna, which means "flowing clear as *Soma*"; and *Soma* refers to the mind. It refers, therefore, to the flow or function of the mind.

    Pavamāna is also the name of certain hymns sung at the *Jyotiṣoma* sacrifice which, as has already been explained refers to the action of light and its electric or electro-magnetic energy, which is also the energy of the mind. Thus the word *pavamāna* is always *associated* with the character of the mind; and we get the same idea by dividing it into *pava, māna*, "(*pava*) purification (*māna*) of what relates to the mind."
20. The *Bhagvad Gītā* also tells us that all action is made more complete in knowledge (BhG. IV, 33).
21. There is a reference to the same point in the *Vedānta Sūtras*, where the reason given is that it is a union of souls; and so the two souls withdraw themselves from all other obhects of life in order to be alone with each other.
22. The word in the text is *dhārā,* which means "a hole in a pitcher; a stream or current of water". The reference is obvious.
23. This would appear to refer to children endowed with special merit, as being the object.
24. The word in the text is *Hautra*, which means "relating to *Hotṛ*", who, as has already been explained, refers to the mind, which has desire for its attribute.
25. The words in the text are *āhavanīya* and *āhuti*; and *āhavanīya* refers to one of the three sacred fires, and so signifies an intelligent act of sacrifice, performed for the sake of others. *Āhuti* means "offering oblation with fire to the deities"; and so means an intelligent act of sacrifice performed in the course of nature; and the deities refer to the forces of Nature.
26. The word in the text is *sattra*, which means "a great *Soma* sacrifice"; and,

as *Soma* refers to the mind, it means a function of the mind. The *Mīmāṁsā* has told us that the act is closely connected with the function of the mind, which has desire for its special attribute.

27. The word in the text is *Hautra* which, as has already been explained, refers to *Hotṛ*, the mind, or its attribute, desire.
28. The word in the text is *gṛha-pati* which, as has already been explained, refers to the soul as an actor, and not a mere spectator.
29. It is commonly believed that the highest function of the soul is to procreate. The idea of the "function of the mind" has already been explained.
30. We have already been told that it is the *yajamāna* or the institutor of the sacrifice (or the soul) that engages the *Ṛtvij* priests (intellect, *ahaṅkāra*, mind and the senses) to act; and the latter act because of the power of the soul; for when the soul departs, they too cease to act.
31. Memory lasts even after every part of the human body has under-gone a complete change. It is, therefore, regarded as an attribute of something that is permanent within us,—that is, the soul. The *Nyāyā* system regards memory as an attribute of the soul (III,i, 14; III, ii, 28-32, 40); so does the *Vaiśeṣika*, but it also links it up with the mind (IX, ii, 6).
32. The *Sāṅkhya* and other systems tell us that all action is performed for the sake of some one else; and the Sāṅkhya makes it clear that all that Nature or *Prakṛti* does is meant for the sake of the soul.
33. The word in the text is *sāmnāyya*, which means "a substance mixed with clarified butter and offered as a burnt offering". We have seen that "clarified butter" refers to goodness as an attribute of the mind, while fire is symbolic of the intellect. A mixture of the two is a combination of a good and intelligent act, or a function of the mind and the intellect.
34. The *Bhagavad Gītā* describes the soul as an experiencer or enjoyer of things (BhG. V, 29; IX, 24; XIII, 22-23).
35. We have already been told that all things are completed through four stages, and so the number four signifies completeness. Similarly, there should be four factors of action,—the fourth being the soul.
    The *Bhagavad Gītā* tells us that there are three constituents of action,—the actor, the action, and the instruments of action (BhG. XVIII, 18); but the actor can easily refer to any one of the great faculties of man,—his intellect, *ahaṅkāra*, mind, and the senses (*Riwij* priests), which take part in an action. But these cannot function without the presence of the soul; and so we must bring in the idea of the soul to complete the tale.
36. The idea of a *śrāddha* ceremony, held in honour of the deceased, would be meaningless without a belief in the existence of the soul. We have faith that the soul lives somewhere even after death, and *śrāddha* is offered to remember that; and so the word itself means faith.

APPENDIX - I

ṚTVIJ PRIESTS

There are a number of references to the *Ṛtvij* priests in the *Mīmāṁsā*, and they are said to take part in a sacrifice at the desire of the *Yajamāna* or the institutor of the sacrifice. They are four in number,—*Brāhmaṇa*, *Udgātṛ*, *Hotṛ*, and *Adhvaryu*; and each of them again has three assistants. The assistants of the *Brāhmaṇa* are *Brāhmaṇācchaṁsin*, *Agnīdhra*, and *Potṛ*; of the *Udgātṛ*,—*Prastotṛ*, *Pratihartṛ*, and *Subrahmaṇyā*; of the *Hotṛ*,—*Maitrāvaruna*, *Acchā-vāka*, and *Grāva-stut*; and of the *Adhvaryu*,—*Prati-prasthātṛ, Neṣṭṛ,* and *Un-netṛ*.

With regard to the principal *Ṛtvij* priests, the *Mīmāṁsā* has told us that the *Brāhmaṇa* refers to the intellect, and the *Adhvaryu* to the ten senses of knowledge and action; and it has further been stated that the meaning of all can be obtained by means of the method of interpretation explained in the *Mīmāṁsā*. Indeed, this should apply not only to the principal priests, but to their assistants too.

In this connection we have observed that the four principal priests are really the four principal faculties of man,—his intellect, *ahaṅkāra* or the I-as-an-actor, mind, and the senses; while the *Yajamāna* or the institutor of the sacrifice is the soul, for whose sake all of them act. We have also stated that the three assistants of *Brāhmaṇa* or the intellect are the three remaining faculties of man,—his *ahaṅkāra*, mind, and the senses; of the *Udgātṛ* or *ahaṅkāra*, the three remaining faculties,—intellect, mind, and the senses; of *Hotṛ* or the mind,—the intellect, *ahaṅkāra*, and the senses; and of *Adhvaryu* or the senses,—the intellect, *ahaṅkāra* and the mind. The idea of all this obviously is that, when an action is performed at the bidding of the soul,— that is, a conscious or deliberate action—while the principal role may belong to any one of the four faculties of man, —his intellect, *ahaṅkāra*, mind, or the senses—they cannot act without the assistance of the remaining three. That is to say, all the four faculties of man are required to function in the performance of a deliberate action, though the principal role may belong to any one of them. Thus, when a person sees, while the principal role belongs to a sense of knowledge, the other three faculties also play their part.

We have observed that the *Yajamāna* or the institutor of the sacrifice is the soul, which desires that an action should be performed; and, as it cannot act by itself, it has to make use of these faculties. The *Yajamāna* is accordingly stated to engage these "priests" and to "pay" for what they do; and the *Mīmāṁsā* has explained that this "payment" is meant to show that the work has been properly done, and that the faculties derive their share of satisfaction from it.

As we have been told that it is possible to find out the meaning of all these names, let us see how it can be done.

The word *Ṛtvij* is derived from the root *Ṛ*, which has a number of meanings,—including "to pierce through, go toward, apply" etc., all of which imply action. The word *Ṛta*, derived from the same root, accordingly means "a sacred action". The word *Ṛtvij* is also derived from the root *Yaj*, which means "to sacrifice"; and sacrifice, as the *Bhagavad Gītā* tells us, arises from action. The *Ṛtvij* priests may accordingly be said to be the devotees of action, and refer to the faculties of man that take part in it.

We have observed that the *Mīmāṁsā* has explained that the *Brāhmaṇa* refers to the intellect; and it may be of interest to point out that that is also one of the dictionary meanings of the word.

Similarly, we are told that the *Adhvaryu* priests are ten in number, and this number refers to the ten senses of knowledge and action. In this connection we have explained that the word is really derived from the root *Dhvṛ*, which, when properly analysed, gives us the idea of the senses of knowledge and action (p. 71, n. 1).

The word *Hotṛ* is derived from the root *Hu*, which means "to sacrifice"; but as this does not explain the idea, we need to divide it into parts to understand its meaning. *Hu—h*, u—accordingly means "(the moon, a symbol of the mind) mind associated with (u) the senses of knowledge." *Hotṛ* would accordingly mean the mind associated with the senses of knowledge. We have a reference to the senses, because it is not easy to conceive of the mind entirely by itself; and the "mind associated with the senses of knowledge" gives us as good an idea of the mind as we can imagine. Indeed, the mind itself is sometimes spoken of as an organ of sense,—the sixth sense; and it may be of interest to point out that *Hotṛ* is also a name of *śiva*, who is specially associated with the character of the mind, as has been explained elsewhere.

The word *Udgātṛ* is made up of *ud, gā, tṛ,*—of which the last is a suffix, as in the case of *kartṛ* etc., signifying an actor; and so we have to understand its meaning in the light of *ud* and *gā*. It usually means "a chanter of hymns"; and it would be permissible to infer that this should refer to *ahaṅkāra* or the I-as-an-actor, as being the chief actor or "singer of hymns". The same idea is, however, conveyed by the two parts of the word, *ud* and *ga*. The word *ud* has a number of meanings, and implies "superiority in place, pride, pre-eminence, power, motion upwards," etc.—all of which can be associated with the idea of *ahaṅkāra*. Similarly, *gā* means not only "singing", but also "to obtain, to pursue, to come into a state," etc. *Udgātṛ* would accordingly mean "(*tr,* a suffix denoting an actor) he who (*gā*) pursues (ud) pride"; and that may be said to be a description of *ahaṅkāra*, even as we find in the *Bhagavad Gītā* (BhG. XVI, 18).

Thus, we might say that the four *Ṛtvij* priests,—*Brāhmaṇa*, *Udgātṛ*, *Hotṛ*, and *Adhvaryu*—refer to the four faculties of man,—his intellect, *ahaṅkāra*, mind and the senses respectively.

We have now to understand the meaning of the "assistants" of the *Ṛtvij* priests.

Of the three assistants of a *Brāhmaṇa*, *Brāhmaṇāccaṁsin* is composed of two parts, *Brahmaṇāt-śaṁsin*; and the meaning is "(śansin) announcing, as arising (*Brahmaṇāt*) from *Brāmāna* (or what relates to a *Brāhmaṇa* or the intellect)". Now the *Sāhkhya* system tells us,—and all others agree—that what arises from Mahat or the intellect is *ahaṅkāra* or "the I-as-an-actor"; and so this may be said to be the meaning of the word.

The second assistant of a *Brāhmaṇa* is *Agnīdhra*,—*Agni*, i, *dhra*—which means "(*dhra or dhara*) sustaining (i) the mind, associated with (*Agni*) the intellect". He refers, therefore, to the mind, associated with the intellect. We have already observed that we cannot think of the mind by itself, and so it needs to be associated with something else to be properly understood; and here it is associated with the intellect, as it is with the senses in the case of *Hotṛ*.

The third assistant of a *Brāhmaṇa* is *Potṛ*,—*pa, u, tṛ*—meaning "(*tṛ*, a suffix signifying an actor) he who refers to (*u*) the senses of knowledge, associated with (*pa*) the objects of the senses." As the senses of knowledge refer also to those of action, and one of them, the Tongue, is also a sense of action,—*Potṛ* would refer to the senses of knowledge and action associated with their objects.

Thus we see that the three assistants of the *Brāhmaṇa* or the intellect are *ahaṅkāra*, mind, and the senses of knowledge and action.

Of the three assistants of *Udgātṛ* or *ahaṅkāra* (I-as-an-actor), the first is *Prastotṛ*; and this word is derived from *Prastu*, meaning "to praise before anything else". It would accordingly refer to the first manifest form of life, praised before anything else,—and that can only be *Mahat* or the intellect, the first to arise from *Prakṛti*.

The second assistant is *Prati-hartṛ,*—meaning "(*Prati*) relating to (*hartṛ*) one who seizes or takes away, or one who severs or cuts off"; and that would obviously refer to the senses of knowledge and action whose function it is to do so.

The third assistant is *Subrahmaṇyā,—Su, brahmaṇya—* meaning "(Su, good) goodness, associated with (*brahmaṇya*) what relates to a *Brāhmaṇa* or the intellect." As goodness is an essential element of desire, which is an attribute of the mind, it refers to the mind; and that would be the idea of the word,—mind associated with the intellect. We have already explained that the mind needs to be associated with something else to be properly understood.

Thus, the three assistants of *Udgātṛ* or *ahaṅkāra* (I-as-an-actor) are the intellect, senses, and the mind.

Of the three assistants of *Hotṛ, Maitrāvaruṇa* means "descended or derived from *Mitra* and *Varuṇa*". We have explained that *Mitra* refers to the intellect; while *Varuṇa*, the deity of the waters, refers to Nature or *Prakṛti*. We have already explained that what, according to the systems of Hindu philosophy, is derived from the intellect is *ahaṅkāra*; and that is specially mentioned in the *Sāṅkhya*, the system based on Nature as the supreme creator of the universe—symbolised by the idea of *Varuṇa*. Hence *Maitrā-varuṇa*, or what is derived from *Mitra* and *Varuṇa*, is *ahaṅkāra* or the I-as-an-actor.

The second assistant is *Acchā-vāka,—accā, v, ā, ka* —meaning "(*ka*) the intellect (*ā*) leading to or associated with (v) Nature (*acchā*) clearly." Hence, he refers to the intellect.

The third assistant is *Grāva-stut,—g, r, ā, va*, stut— meaning "(*g*) the senses of knowledge and (*r*) the senses of action (ā) associated with (*va*) Nature, conceived as (*stut*) a hymn of praise." He refers, therefore, to the senses of knowledge and action.

The three assistants of *Hotṛ* or the mind are accordingly *ahaṅkāra*, intellect, and the senses.

Of the three assistants of the *Adhvaryu*, the ftrst is *Pratiprasthāṭṛ*, meaning "*(prati)* concerning *(prasthāṭṛ)* one who urges on"; and that would appear to refer to *ahaṅkāra* or the I-as-an-actor, whose function it is to urge one to action.

The second assistant is *Neṣṭṛ*. The nominative form of this word is *Neṣṭā,—na, iṣṭā*—and its meaning would be "*(iṣṭā*, fem. of *iṣṭā*) what is desired in association with (*na*) the senses of knowledge." As desire is an attribute of the mind, Neṣṭṛ would refer to the mind in association with the senses of knowledge; and we see again that the mind needs to be associated with something else.

The third assistant is *Un-netṛ,* which is derived from *Un-nī*, meaning "to infer, discover by inference". As this is a special function of the intellect, *Un-netṛ* would refer to the intellect.

Thus, the three assistants of the *Adhvaryu* priests or the senses of knowledge and action are *ahaṅkāra* (or the I-as-an-actor), mind, and the intellect.

APPENDIX- II

JYOTIṢṬOMA

A proper study of the different systems of Hindu philosophy would show that the ancients knew a great deal of science in the modern sense of the term. The evolution of Nature or *Prakṛti* from the unmanifest into the manifest, as described in the *Sāṅkhya*, cannot be regarded as anything but scientific; for we are told that it is based on inference derived from the working of the great forces of Nature and Man. The ancient idea of the great "elements,"—Earth, Water, Fire, Air, and Ether—is undoubtedly different from the elements of modern science; but the ancients conceived of them as *Bhutas* or the great forms of life which enter into the constitution of all things in the world; and it is in this sense that they have been conceived to be "elements". Again, their idea of Ether has given rise to a difficulty. But Ether, according to them, is characterised by the attributes of motion and sound, and is something that pervades everything. It may, accordingly, be regarded as a medium in which all motion, vibration or radiation takes place; and sound itself is a form of motion, as we know. There is thus no contradiction between the ancient and modern conception of this medium; and the difference is only in names.

It would be obvious to even the most casual reader of the different systems of philosophy, and of the *Mīmāṁsā* in particular, that the whole approach of the ancients to the problem of life is scientific. The Vedas are said to deal with the laws of action,—embracing all forms of life in the world of Nature and Man; and the great gods are said to be nothing but personifications of the mighty forces that are at work everywhere. Indeed, Man, as a part of Nature, contains within himself the essence of all that Nature has; for without that there can be no knowledge of Nature itself, as the latter is limited to the reactions it can evoke in him. The energy of the senses, mind, and the intellect of Man is accordingly conceived to be a part of the corresponding forces of Nature itself,—the great "elements" (or the planets), and the moon and the sun respectively; while the soul,—even if we regard it as a separate entity—can be understood only in their light. The whole life of Man has accordingly been integrated into the life of Nature in the midst of which he lives.

But there are also certain direct references to the problems of physical science in the different systems of Hindu philosophy: for instance, the *Nyāyā* and the *Vaiśeṣika* have considered the question of the division (or splitting) of the atom. We are told that the atom cannot be divided; and again, that it can,—but, if it is divided, it would cease to be an atom. The origin of sound is traced to the meeting and parting of things, and to other sound or resonance. *Yoga* tells us that if we understand the relation of a body to motion, it can be made as light as cotton; and the *Mīmāṁsā* classifies animals into vertebrate and invertebrate, and examines the nature of Time. It also refers to *Jyotiṣṭoma*, which means literally "a mass of light", and tells us that its idea is based on scientific knowledge, and that we can understand it if we get the meaning of words used in this connection by dividing them into parts.

If, as we might imagine, the ancients knew a great deal of science in the modern sense of the term, it would be of interest to examine the idea of *Jyotiṣṭoma* in the light of the method of interpretation referred to in the *Mīmāṁsā*,—that is, by means of the division of words into parts.

The word *Jyotiṣṭoma* (*Jyotis-stoma*) means literally "(*stoma*) mass of (*jyotis*) light". It is said to be the name of a

Soma ceremony; and we are told that *Soma* should be regarded as most important in this connection.

Now we know that *Soma* refers to the mind which, according to the ancients, is said to be characterised by electric energy; and that is said to be its modern idea too. Thus, if *Soma* should be regarded as the most important thing in *Jyotiṣṭoma*, it really means that the most important part of the mass of light is electric energy or the electric ray.

Again, we are told that *Jyotiṣṭoma*, as a name of a *Soma* ceremony, is typical of a whole class of ceremonies, consisting originally of three, and later on of four, five, or seven subdivisions. The names of the ftrst three are said to be *Agniṣṭoma*, *Ukthya*, and *Ati-rātra*; while the remaining four are *Ṣoḍaśin*, *Atyagniṣṭoma*, *Vāja-peya*, and *Aptoryāma*.

If the word *Jyotiṣṭoma* signifies "a mass or rays of light", these subdivisions would also refer to the great divisions of light; and it would also mean that the ancients knew at first of three such divisions; and then, as their knowledge grew, they came to know of four, five, and seven of them. As the *Mīmāṁsā* claims that these divisions are based on scientific knowledge, and their meaning can be obtained by dividing these words into parts, in accordance with its method of interpretation, we should be able to know what they mean, and whether they have any relation to our present day knowledge of light.

The first division is called *Agnīṣtoma* (*Agni-stoma*) which means "(*stoma*) mass of (*Agni*) *Agni*"; and, as *Agni* refers to the intellect as well as gold and the sun, it would refer to the rays of the sun.

The second is called *Ukthya*, a word which is derived from *Vac*, which means "to speak". But, as it does not convey any clear idea in any of these two forms, it is necessary to divide it into parts in accordance with the method of interpretation explained in the *Mīmāṁsā*. We have to take it in its rudimentary form as *Vac* (*Va,c*), and the meaning would be "(*c*, moon, symbolic of the mind) mind energy, associated with (*va*) Nature or *Prakṛti*." The word *Ukthya* would accordingly refer to the light of the moon, as *Agni-ṣṭoma* does to that of the sun. But as the moon refers to the mind, the energy of which is said to be electric or like lightning, *Ukthya* would also refer to the radiation of lightning or electric energy as part of *Jyotiṣṭoma* or "mass of light."

The third division is called *Ati-rātra*, which means "(*ati*) beyond (*rātra*) the night (or darkness of night)". It may accordingly be said to refer to the ultra-violet rays, which would appear to correspond to this description.

The fourth is called *Ṣoḍaśin*, which means "consisting of sixteen parts"; and this number refers to the mind, with the ten senses, and their five objects, making a total of sixteen. We have pointed out that it is difficult to think of the mind by itself, and so it is often associated with something else, —more specially the senses and their objects; and that is signified by the number sixteen. But we have explained that the energy of the mind is said to be electric; and so it is necessary to find out what the idea of the senses and their objects in terms of energies may be. This has been examined at some length elsewhere (MM. I, 43, *seq*,); and it would be enough to observe here that the five great "elements" and their properties, which constitute the objects of the senses, are said to be characterised by magnetic energy; for they are said to have been created out of the mind; and, as electric energy, the energy of the mind, is transformed into magnetic energy, even so is the mind said to be trans-formed into these "elements" and their properties. *Shoḍaśin*, or the mind associated with the ten senses and their objects, would accordingly give us electro-magnetic energy or the electro-magnetic rays of light.

The fifth is *Atyagniṣṭoma* (*Ati-agni-ṣṭoma*), which means "(*ati*) beyond (*Agni-ṣṭoma*) the rays of the sun". Hence, if *Ati-rātrā* refers to the ultra-violet rays, this would obviously refer to the infra-red rays.

The sixth is *Vāja-peya*, which means "(*vāja*) energy (*peya*) fit to be drunk or absorbed." The word *Vāja* also means food, which, as the *Mīmāṁsā* tells us, refers to Nature; and so *Vāja-peya* would refer to that energy of light which is absorbed by all Nature to make it grow. Again, the word *Vāja* is derived from the root *Vaj*, which also gives us the word *Vajra*, meaning "thunderbolt or lightning", associated with it. As the latter is electric or electro-magnetic energy, the energy signified by the word *Vāja* would be the same; and so we might say that *Vāja-peya* or the energy absorbed by matter is electric or electro-magnetic.

The last division is called *Aptor-yāma*; and *Aptor* is derived from *Aptu*, which again is connected with *Aptur*, meaning "active, busy". *Aptor-yāma* would accordingly mean "(*yāma*) cessation of (*aptor*) activity"; and so it implies that this is a destructive part of light, making for cessation of all activity.

The seven divisions of *Jyotiṣṭoma* are accordingly seven divisions of light or radiations of light,—(i) sun light (*Agniṣṭoma*), (2) moon light or electric energy (*Ukthya*), (3) ultra-violet rays (*Ati-rātra*) (4) electro-magnetic rays (*Ṣoḍaśin*), (5) infra-red rays (*Atyagniṣṭoma*), (6) electro-magnetic rays absorbed by matter (*Vāja-peya*), and (7) rays that make for destruction (*Aptor-yāma*). Of these the electric or the moon light rays are, according to the *Mīmāṁsā*, said to be the most important; and there are a number of references to the power of the moon over all that is on earth in the sacred books. This would appear to be the reason why they are called *Ukthya*, meaning "deserving praise".

As all this is said to be based on scientific knowledge, it would be of interest to compare it with our present day knowledge of the subject.

Modern science tells us that there are seven kinds of radiations of light. Of these the visible ray has a spectrum of seven colours,—the colours of the rainbow,—with the violet at one end, and red at the other; and this visible ray may be said to correspond to *Agniṣṭoma* or the ray of the sun, which has the same spectrum.

We are told that there are a number of radiations on either side of the red and violet ends of the spectrum; and beyond the red is the infra-red, which would obviously correspond to the *Ati-agni-ṣṭoma* (or that which is beyond the rays of the sun, as the word literally means).

Beyond the infra-red we are told there is the electric ray, which gives us the wireless rays; and this may be said to correspond to the *Ukthya*. As this refers also to the moon, the light of the moon would appear to have a special affinity for wireless waves.

At the other end of the spectrum we have the violet ray, and beyond it is the ultra-violet ray; and this would appear to correspond to *Ati-rātra*, or "that which is beyond darkness", as the word literally means. The word *Rātra* may also be analysed into *r, ā, tra*, meaning " (*tra*, which as the *Mīmāṁsā* tells us, refers to the mind) mind (*ā*) associated with (*r*) the senses of action"; and, as the energy of the mind is electric, and of the senses magnetic, *Rātra* would convey the idea of electro-magnetic energy, and imply that this is the energy of darkness or night; and *Ati-rātra* would mean something more powerful ("that which goes beyond") than electro-magnetic rays. Thus, if the ultra-violet rays correspond to the *Ati-rātra*, it would mean that the ancients knew that these rays were more powerful than electro-magnetic rays.

Beyond the ultra-violet we get the X-rays, and their property is that they are absorbed by matter in proportion to its density. They may accordingly be said to correspond to *Vāja-peya*, which means the same thing.

Beyond the X-rays we have the *gamma* rays, which are said to have electro-magnetic properties; and they would appear to correspond to the *Ṣoḍaśin*.

Finally, beyond the *gamma* rays there are the cosmic rays, which are said to have great disintegrating properties; and they would appear to correspond to *Aptor-yāma*, which means the same thing.

APPENDIX - III

THE FOUR CASTES

There are a number of references to the four castes in the sacred books, but their exact idea has not been properly understood. We have their ftrst mention in the *Ṛg Veda*, where they are said to have risen from the body of the Supreme *Puruṣa* himself. We are told that they divided Him into parts; and out of his mouth rose the *Brāhmaṇa*; from both his arms came the *Rājanya*; his thighs became the *Vaiśya*; while the śūdra was created from his feet (RV. X, xc, 11-12). These are the four "castes": and of these the *Brāhmaṇa* is said to be the priest or the man of knowledge; the *Rājanya* or the *Kṣatriya* is the warrior or king; the *Vaiśya* is the producer of wealth; while the *Śūdra* is believed to be the servant of all the three.

If we examine the idea of the "castes" as emerging from the "body" of the *Puruṣa*, we shall find that they embrace all that is in him,—from his head to his feet; and, as the word also signifies "a man", they may be said to include all that is in a man: and this should enable us to understand what they really mean.

But the *Mīmāṁsā* has explained that the *Brāhmaṇa* refers to the intellect, and the *Śūdra* to the objects of Nature; and that must put an enttrely different construction on the whole idea. Indeed, if we follow this line of thought, we shall find that the two remaining "castes" also refer to the faculties of man, like the *Brāhmaṇa* himself.

The *Bhagavad Gītā* tells us that the four castes have been

created by God by means of the division of actions and *Guṇas* or the attributes of Nature (BhG. IV, 13): that is to say, a person is a *Brāhmaṇa*, *Kṣatriya,* or a *Vaiśya*, according to his innate qualities and the actions he performs. We are accordingly told in the *Mahābhārata* that a person conforms to all these "castes" at different times.

In order to understand this idea more clearly, it is necessary to understand the idea of *Guṇas* or the attributes of Nature. They are said to be three in number,—*Sattva*, *Rajas*, and *Tamas*—and to embrace all forms of life, except the soul. They should accordingly refer to the four principal faculties of man,—his intellect, *ahaṅkāra* or the I-as-an-actor, mind, and the senses. But, as there are three *Guṇas* and four faculties, we have to find out how they can be made to agree.

The *Bhagavad Gītā* tells us that each object of life contains all the three *Guṇas*,—though some may have more of Sattva than *Rajas* and *Tamas*, while others more of *Rajas* than *Sattva* and Tamas, and yet others more of *Tamas* than *Sattva* and *Rajas* (BhG. XIV, 10); and this would appear to correspond to the idea explained in the *Mīmāṁsā* that all the four faculties of man play their part in an action, though the principal role may belong to any one of them. This, as has already been explained, is the idea of the three "assistants" of each of the four principal *Ṛtvij* "priests".

The *Bhagavad Gītā* tells us of the characteristics of these *Guṇas: Sattva* is characterised by knowledge and joy; *Rajas* by desire and action; and *Tamas* by heedlessness and sleep (BhG. XIV, 6-9). It is obvious from this that *Sattva* corresponds to *Buddhi* or intellect, which has knowledge for its attribute; while Rajas corresponds to *ahaṅkāra* and mind combined,—for the attribute of the one is action and of the other passion or desire; while *Tamas* refers to the senses as well as their objects, which are devoid of consciousness by themselves.

Now, if we associate the four castes with the three *Guṇas*, we shall find that the *Brāhmaṇa*, who signifies intellect, refers to *Sattva*; and the *Śūdra*, who signifies the objects of the senses, to *Tamas*. Between them are the *Kṣatriya* and the *Vaiśya*; and we can understand their relation to the *Guṇas* when we know what they really mean.

The word used in the *Ṛg Veda* is Rājanya, and it is easy to see its connection with *Rajas*. We are further told that he arises from the two arms of the Supreme; and we can easily understand that an arm is an instrument of action. But the text refers to two arms; and so we have to understand that there is something more to complete the idea of action; and that can only be desire, without which no action can be performed. We may gather from this that the *Rājanya* refers to *Rajas Guṇa*, or the idea of action and desire, or *ahaṅkāra* and the mind combined.

And now only the *Vaiśya* remains; and we may conclude that he would refer to the senses,—for they alone have been left unaccounted for; and so would correspond to *Tamas* in terms of the *Guṇas*.

Thus, we would say that the *Brāhmaṇa* refers to the intellect and *Sattva*; the *Rājanya* or thev *Kṣatriya* to *ahaṅkāra* and the mind as well as *Rajas*; and the *Vaiśya* to the senses or *Tamas*; while the *Śūdra* signifies the objects of the senses, and can refer only to *Tamas*.

But we have been told that we can get the exact meaning of these "castes" from the words used in the text itself; and that is possible if we follow the method of interpretation explained in the *Mīmāṁsā*.

Now we are told that the *Brāhmaṇa* has risen from the "mouth" of the Supreme; and the word used in the text is *Mukha*, which means "head, chief, the best"; and this, as we can easily see, corresponds to his idea as intellect, which is obviously the best.

We have explained that the word *Rājanya* is associated with *Rajas*; and the two arms of the Supreme refer to the two parts of action,—desire and action. Hence, *Rājanya* or the warrior caste refers to the mind and *ahaṅkāra* as well as to

Rajas. The idea of *Kṣatriya* (*Kṣa, tri, ya*) is the same,—for the meaning of the word is "(*ya*) he who is (*tri*, three, which, as the *Mīmāṁsā* tells us, refers to the mind) mind, associated with (*ksha*, lightning or electric energy, a characteristic of the mind) the mind". The word *Kṣatriya* gives us, therefore, the idea of the mind, conceived as pure mind,—as characterised by desire and having in it the germ of action.

The word *Vaiśya* is an elongated form of *Viśya* (*V, i, ś, ya*), which means "(ya) he who refers to (ś) the senses of knowledge (*i*) associated with (*v*) Nature or *Prakṛti*". As the senses of knowledge may include those of action too,—and one of them, the Tongue, is both a sense of knowledge and action, the *Vaiśya* would refer to the senses of knowledge and action; and the idea of the latter is also implied by the reference to Nature or *Prakṛti*, which is characterised by action.

The *Vaiśya* is said to arise from the "thighs" of the Supreme; and the word in the text is *ūru* (*ū, r, u*), meaning "(u) the senses of knowledge and (*r*) the senses of action (*m*) woven together". Thus, we see clearly that the *Vaiśya* refers to both the senses of knowledge and action.

The *Śūdra*, as the *Mīmāṁsā* has explained, refers to the objects of Nature; and the idea of Nature is contained in the word itself.1 He is said to arise from the "feet" of the Supreme, and the word used in the text is *Pad* (*Pa, d*) meaning "(*d*) giving (pa) the objects of the senses." Thus we see how the *Śūdra* refers to the objects of Nature.

It is in this manner that we can get the real idea of the Caste System, as originally conceived by the ancients. The *Brāhmaṇa* refers to the intellect and *Sattva*; the *Kṣatriya* to *ahaṅkāra* and the mind, as well as *Rajas*; while the *Vaiśya* refers to the senses of knowledge and action as well as *Tamas*. These refer to the four faculties of man, which take part in action and partake of its results. The *Śūdra*, on the other hand, refers to the objects of Nature which, being inanimate, cannot have knowledge or possessions; and, as they are meant to serve the purpose of the living, the *śūdra* has been degraded into a "servant" whose only purpose in life is to serve the three higher "castes". It is not necessary to point out how far the original idea of the Caste System has been lost in later times, and with what tragic results.

GLOSSARY

A

Abhighāraṇa	Sprinkling clarified butter on the fire Association of goodness with intelligence.
Abhimanyu	Name of a son of *Arjuna*, the hero of the *Mahābhārata*. Personification of *abhimāna* or egoism.
Abhimāna	Egoism
Achchhāvāka	One of the three assistants of the *Hotṛ* priest. the intellect.
Adhrigu	Name of a formula concluding with an invocation of *Agni*. A function of the intellect.
Adhvaryu	Name of one of the four *Ṛtvij* priests. The senses of knowledge and action.
Agni	The god of Fire. Intellect.
Agnihotra	An oblation to *Agni* or the god of Fire. An intelligent act.
Agniṣṭoma	Praise of *Agni*; name of a sacrifice. An intelligent act or a function of the intellect.
Agnīdhra	One of the three assistants of a *Brāhmana*. The mind functioning in association with the intellect.
Agnīṣomīya	Relating to *Agni* and *Soma*. A combination of intellect and the mind.
Ahaṅkāra	Egoism. The I-as-an-actor; an aspect of the soul when action takes place, but the soul is conceived to be a non-actor.

Aitiśāyana	Name of a philosopher.
Alekhana	Name of a philosopher.
Anagni	Without fire. Without intelligence.
Aṅga	A limb, part; a sub-division of the Mantras of the Vedas; an auxiliary part of the Vedas.
Anna	Food. A symbol of Nature or *Prakṛti*.
Anushṭup	Name of a metre in *Sanskṛt*.
Anuyāja	A secondary or final sacrifice. A good and intelligent action.
Anya	Inexhaustibleness; this world.
Apanaya	Taking away; a bad policy. Certain desires that should be taken away or shunned.
Aptor-vāda	A division of *Jyotiṣṭoma*. Cessation of activity; a destructive ray of light.
Arjuna	The hero of the *Mahābhārata*. The soul of man.
Artha-vāda	A division of the *Brāhmaṇa* part of the *Vedas*. An explanation of *Vidhi* or the laws of Nature.
Asura	A demon. A personification of the forces of Nature, making for evil, pain, or death.
Aśva	A horse. A symbol of the senses, specially those or action.
Aśvattha	The sacred Fig-tree. A symbol of Nature or *Prakṛti*.
Aśvins	Horses. The senses of knowledge and action.
Atha	Inexhaustibleness.
Ati-rātra	A part of the *Jyotiṣoma* sacrifice. Beyond the night; ultra-violet rays of light.
Atyagniṣṭoma	Beyond the rays of the sun; infra-red rays of light.

Auṣadha	Consisting of medicinal plants. A symbol of the healing powers of Nature.
Avabṛtha	The purification of the sacrificer and sacrificial vessels after a sacrifice. A supplementary sacrifice, or good, intelligent and joyous action.
Aveṣṭi	Expiation by means of sacrifice. Absence of desire.

Ā

Āditya	The sun. Intellect.
Āgrāyaṇa	The first *Soma* libation at the *Agniṣṭoma* sacrifice. The function of the mind in association with the intellect.
Āhavanīya	Name of one of the three sacrificial fires; the consecrated fire taken from the householder'perpetual fire and prepared for receiving oblations. The function of the intellect in association with the soul, and referring to the whole world.
Āhuti	Offering oblation with fire to the deities. An intelligent act performed in the course of nature, or associated with the forces of Nature.
Ājya	Clarified butter. Goodness, as an esinteal element of desire.
Ājya-bhaksha	Drinking clarified butter. A symbol of an element of pleasure in life.
Āsmarthya	Name of a philosopher.
Ātreya	Name of a great *Ṛṣi*, an author of a number of Vedic hymns.

B

Bādarāyaṇa	Name of the author of *Vedānta Sūtras*.
Bādari	Name of a philosopher.

Bhīma	One of the five *Pāṇḍava* brothers in the story of the *Mahābhārata*. The mind of man.
Bhṛgu	Name of one of the ten *Maharṣhis* created by the first *Manu*. The senses of knowledge and action associated with Nature.
Bṛhatī	Name of a metre in *Sanskṛt*.
Bṛhat-sāman	Name of a verse intended to be chanted.
Brahmā	One of the three Gods of the Hindu *Trimūrti*, conceived to be the Supreme Creator.
Brāhmaṇa	The first of the four "castes", consisting of priests. The intellect.
Brāhmaṇacch	One of the three assistants of the *Brāhmaṇa*. *Ahaṅkāra* of the I-as-an-actor.
Brāhmaṇavatī	Name of a particular brick used in building the sacrificial altar. Neutrality or disinterestedness in action.
Buddha	The ninth incarnation of *Viṣṇu*. Perfection in the path of death.

C

Caitra	The first month of the Hindu lunar year.
Chamasa	A vessel for drinking *Soma*; sweetmeat. Satisfaction in action.
Cariot	A symbol to represent the body, which acts as a single unit.
Caru	A cloud. A symbol to represent Nature.
Catur	The number four. The mind associated with the senses of knowledge and action.
Chanda	Desire, conceived to be an obstacle
Cow	A symbol to represent the senses of knowledge.

D

Dadhi	Curd. A symbol to represent Nature.
Dakṣiṇa	The south. Skill.
Dakṣiṇā	A gift given to the priests. Skill.
Dakshiṇāgni	The southern altar of *Agni* or the god or Fire. A skilful act of the intellect.
Darvi-homa	An oblation made with a ladle. A good and intelligent action or An act of sacrifice.
Dāna	An act of charity or gift. An act of renunciation; satisfaction in action.
Deva	A god. A great force of Nature, governed by the law of Sacrifice.
Dharma	The law of good and intelligent action.
Dhāraṇa	Holding, restraining. Immovable concentration of the mind.
Dhenu	A cow. A symbol of the senses of knowledge.
Digambara	A school of Jainism, according to which it is believed that a person should not wear any clothes. A school of thought advocating a total renunciation of action.
Dravya	An elementary substance in philosophy, e.g. the five "Elements", Time, Space, Mind, and the Soul.

E

Ekāṣṭakā	The eighth day after the full moon. Nature or *Prakṛti*.
Etad	This world.

G

Gārhapatya	The house-holder's fire, received from his father and transmitted to his descendants. The function of the intellect in association with the soul.

Gāyatrī	Name of a *Sanskṛt* metre.
Go	A cow. A symbol or the senses of knowledge.
Go-sava	Name of a *Soma* sacrifice. A function of the mind.
Grāva-stut	One of the three assistants of the *Hotṛ* priest. The senses of knowledge and action.
Guṇa	An attribute of an object of Nature. There are three such attribute,—*Sattva*, *Rajas,* and *Tamas*.

H

Haraṇa	A hand, arm.
Havis	A sacrifice. The function of the intellect, as distinguished from that of the mind.
Hiraṇya	Gold. Imperishable matter, symbolic of Nature.
Hiraṇyagarbha	The Golden Egg. A symbol to represent Nature.
Homa	An oblation offered to the gods by pouring clarified butter into the fire. Goodness added to intelligence in action.
Horse	A symbol of the senses of action.
Hotṛ	Name of a priest. The mind.

I

Iḍānta	A word without a meaning.
Indra	Name of a god. The self-conscious soul.
Iṣṭi	Desire.

J

Jaimini	The author of *Mīmāṁsā Sūtras*.
Japa	Silent repetition of a sacred name. A pure act of sacrifice.
Jauhava	Relating to *Juhū* or a sacrificial ladle. Nature as seen in the light of the senses of knowledge and action.

Juhoti	A technical term for certain sacrificial ceremonies. The role of the great forces of Nature in an act of sacrifice.
Jyotiṣoma	Name of a Soma cermony. The rays of light.

K

Kakubha	Name of a *Sanskṛt* metre.
Kalki	The tenth incarnation of *Viṣṇu*. A universal conception of God.
Kalpa	A period of a thousand *Yugas* of Time.
Kapāla	The alms-bowl of a beggar: a symbol to represent a life of renunciation.
Karṇa	A character in the story of the *Mahābhārata*. Grain or Seed, as symbolic of *Prakṛti*.
Kaśyapa	Name of a *Ṛshi* or a divine being. A personification of the withdrawal of the senses from their objects.
Kavaṣa	A shield. Protection rom the evil effects of desire.
Kāla	Time; a serpent. A personification of Time in the form of a Serpent.
Kāma-deva	The god of Love or Desire. Desire personified as a god.
Kāmukāyana	Name of a teacher or philosopher.
Kārṣṇājini	Name of a philosopher.
Khādira	Made of the *Khadira* tree. A symbol of the mind.
Kṛṣṇa	The highest incarnation or embdiment of the idea of *Viṣṇu* or God. The idea of goodness intelligence and joy associated with Nature, transforming it into God.
Krama	A peculiar manner of reading the text of the Vedas.

Kṣatriya — The warrior or kingly "caste"..A personification of the mind and *ahaṅkāra* or the I-as-an-actor.

Kumbha-karṇa — A character in the story of the *Rāmāyaṇa*. A personification of the Vegetable Kingdom, as symbolic of Nature or *Prakṛti*.

Kuntī — The mother of the *Pāṇḍava* brothers in the *Mahābhārata*. the planet Earth.

Kūrma — Tortoise. An incarnation of *Viṣnu*. A symbol to represent the withdrawal of the senses from their objects.

L

Lāvukāyana — Name of a philosopher.

Lokam-pṛṇā — Name of a kind of bricks used in constructing the sacrificial altar. A symbol to represent the idea of penetrating everything.

M

Mahat — The great. Intellect.

Mahādeva — A name of *Siva*.

Maitrā-varuṇa — Descended from *Mitra* and *Varuṇa*. *Ahaṅkāra* or the I-as-an-actor.

Man-Lion — The fourth incarnation of *Viṣṇu*. The essence of joy in Nature.

Manotā — A hymn in the *Ṛg Veda* containing the word *Manota*.

Matsya — The Fish. The first incarnation of *Viṣṇu*. The individual soul.

Medha-pati — The lord of sacrifice. The soul.

Mitra — Name of a sun-god. The function of the intellect and the mind.

Mīmāṁsā — Name of a system of philosophy.

N

Nakula	One of the five *Pāṇḍava* brothers in the story of the *Mahābhārata*. The arms of a man.
Nara-siṁha	Man-lion; the fourth incarnation of *Viṣṇu*. The essence of joy in Nature.
Nirmanthya	To be churned. To be understood.
Niṣāda	Name or a wild non-āryan tribe. One who, leading a life or the senses , rises to a conception or the mind and the idea of sacrifice .
Nyāya	Name of a system of philosophy.

O

Odana	Cooked rice. The best kind of food, symbolic of Nature or *Prakṛti*.

P

Paraśurāma	Name of the sixt incarnation of *Viṣṇu*. A perfect student or seeker after knowledge.
Paśu	An animal. The senses associated with their objects.
Paśu-Soma	The mind of an animal.
Pavamāna	Name of certain hymns. Purification of the mind.
Payas	Water, symbolic of Nature.
Pāka	Cooking. Necessity of performing actions.
Pāṇḍavas	The sons of *Pāṇḍu*, and princupal characters in the story of the *Mahābhārata*. Five parts of a man,—his intellect, mind, sense-organs through which the soul acts, and arms and legs.
Potṛ	Name or one of the three assistants of a *Brāhmaṇa*. The senses of knowledge and action associated with their objects.
Ṛṣhṭha	Standing forth prominently. Action.

Pṛthā — Name of the mother of the *Pāṇḍavas*. The Earth.

Prahlāda — Naıne of a demon child devotee of *Viṣṇu*. A personfication of joy.

Prajāpati — The lord of creatures.

Prakṛti — Name, characterised by inherent action.

Prastotṛ — Name of one of the three assistants of the Udgātṛ priest. The intellect.

Prati-hartṛ — Name of an assistants of the *Udgātṛ* priest. The senses of knowledge and action.

Prati-prasthātṛ — Name of one or the assistants ofthe *Adhvaryu* priest. *Ahaṅkāra* or the I-as-an-actor.

Prayāja — A preliminary sacrifice. Desire, which precedes action.

Purāṇa — Name of certain sacred books of the Hindus, said to be eighteen in number.

Puroḍāśa — A mass of ground rice rounded into a kind of cake, and offered as an oblation. *Prakṛti* associated with the imnd, the senses and their objects.

Puruṣa — A person. The individual soul.

R

Rajas — Name of one of the three *Guṇas* or attributes of the objects of Nature, referring to action and desire.

Rathantara-sāman — Name of certain hymns in the *Ṛg Veda*.

Rādhā — Name of a milk-maid, beloved of *Kṛṣṇa*. The creative energy of the mind.

Rājasūya — Name of a sacrifice. The function of the intellect and the mind in association with the senses of action.

Rāmacandra	Name of the seventh incarnation of *Viṣṇu*. A peufect family-man, with a perfectly developed mind.
Rāvaṇa	Name of the ten-headed king of *Laṅkā*. The ten senses of knowledge and action personified.
Rice	The best kind of grain, symbolic of *Prakṛti*.
Rudra	Name of certain gods,—specially associated with *Siva*. Eleven *Rudras* are spoken of; and they refer to the ten senses, with the mind as eleventh.

S

Sahadeva	Name of one of the five *Pāṇḍava* brothers. Personification of the legs of a man.
Sarasvatī	Name of a river. A personification of Nature of *Prakṛti*.
Sarva-pṛṣṭha	Action that conquers everything.
Sarva-svāra	Name of a *Soma* sacrifice lasting only for a day. Action involving a limited function of the mind.
Sattra	A great *Soma* sacrifice. A great function of the mind.
Sattva	The highest *Guṇa* or attribute, making for knowledge and peace.
Saudhanvana	The son of *Sudhanvan*. A *Śūdra*.
Savanīya	Relating to Soma libation. The function of the mind.
Sāmidhenī	Verses recited when the sacrificial fire is kindled. A description of an intelligent act.
Sāmnāyya	A substance mixed with clarified butter and offered as a burnt offering. A good and intelligent action.

Sāṅkhya	Name of a system of philosophy.
Siddhārtha	Name of *Buddha*. One all whose objects are satisfied.
Sītā	Name of the wife of *Rāma* in the story of the *Rāmāyaṇa*. A personification of Sacrifice.
Smṛti	Post-Vedic sacred literature.
Soma	The moon; wine. The mind.
Sreka-parṇa	The relation of the universe to one creator.
Sruc	A wooden ladle for pouring clarified butter on the sacrificial fire. Means of stirring the mind or producing an intelligent desire.
Sruvạ	A ladle. The mind associated with the senses and their objects.
Stha-pati	A chief; king. One who has raised himself from a lower to a higher station by means of a proper exercise of the mind.
Stoma	A hymn; praise. The mind associated with the senses.
Subrahmaṇya	One of the three assistants of the *Udgātṛ* priest. The mind.
Sudarśana-cakra	Name of a weapon of *Kṛshṇa*. A good action.
Sūkara	A name of the *Boar*, the third incarnation of *Viṣṇu*. A personification of goodness in Nature.
Svaru	A sacrificial post. Action performed with a purpose or desire.
Svāhā	Hail! hail! a blessing on action, calling for its repetition.
Svāmin	Master, lord. The soul.
Sviṣṭa-kṛt	Properly done. An intelligent action properly performed.

Ś

Śabda	Oral testimony of true and trustworthy persons.
Śamitṛ	One who keeps the mind calm. Detachment in action.
Śara	A name of the number five. The five senses.
Śastra	A sword. The senses of knowledge and action associated with the mind.
Śata-kratu	A name of *Indra*. Performer of a hundred deeds.
Śikhaṇḍin	A character in the *Mahābhārata*, who was born as a woman, and was transformed into a man by means of penance and sacrifice. A personification of the idea of Sacrifice transforming *Prakṛti* into *Puruṣa* or God.
Śiva	One or the three principal gods of the Hindus.
Śruti	Vedic literature.
Śunaka	Name of a *Ṛshi*. The senses of knowledge associated with Nature.
Śūdra	A member of the lowest or fourth "caste" of the Hindus. A personification of the inanimate world of Nature which supports the animate.
Śvaḥ-sutyā	Tomorrow's preparation for *Soma*. The best function of the mind.
Śvetāmbara	A school of Jainism.
Śyena	A falcon; hawk. Nature characterised by desire.

Ṣ

Ṣoḍaśin	Consisting of sixteen parts; name of a subdivision of *Jyotiṣoma*. An electro-magnetic ray of light.

T

Tad	That; a name of *Brahma*. Sacrifice.
Tamas	The lowest of the three *Guṇas* or attributes of Nature.
Tapas	Meditation.
Tra	Three. The senses of action.
Tri	Three. The mind associated with the senses of action.
Tryanīkā	Three-faced. The character and functions of mind in association with the senses, when it may be identified with the intellect.
Tvaṣṭṛ	Name of a god,—the heavenlhy builder and creator of living beings. The Ṣupreme Mind which creates things.

U

Udgātṛ	One or the four *Ṛtvij* priests who take part in a sacrifice. *Ahaṇkāra* or the I-as-an-actor.
Ukthya	One of the seven sub-divisions of *Jyotiṣoma*. An electric ray of light.
Un-netṛ	One of the three assistants of the *Adhvaryu* priest. The intellect.
Upaveṣa	A stick of green wood used for stirring the sacrificial fire. Effectiveness in action or sacrifice.
Upāṁśu-yāja	The full moon. A complete function of the mind.
Ushṇik	Name of a Sanskṛt metre.
Uttara-vedi	The northern altar for the sacrificial fire. Higher knowlege.

V

Varāha	The Boar; the third incarnation of *Viṣṇu*. Goodness in Nature.

Varuṇa	The god of waters. An idea of God associated with Nature..
Vaṣaṭ	A special kind of exclamation. An indication that a particular action may be performed.
Vasiṣṭha	Name of a Vedic sage. Intellect, as associated with Nature.
Vasu	Name of a god. The *Vasus* are said to be eight in number. A division or creation of *Prakṛti* .
Vasu-deva	Name of the father of *Kṛṣṇa*. An idea of God in association with Nature.

INDEX

✦✦✦✦